KT-481-191

The Lyle official **BOOKS** *review*

While every care has been taken in the compiling of this volume, the publishers cannot accept any liability for loss, financial or otherwise, incurred by reliance placed on any information herein.

The Dollar conversions have been made at the rate of exchange prevailing at the date of the sale.

SBN 0-86248-033-7

Copyright © Lyle Publications MCMLXXXI
Glenmayne, Galashiels, Scotland.

Printed by Apollo Press, Dominion Way, Worthing, Sussex, England.
Bound by R.J. Acford, Chichester, Sussex, England.

Copyright © 1981 by Voor Hoede Publicaties B. V.

All rights reserved. This book, or parts thereof, may not be reproduced in any form without permission in writing from the publisher. Published on the same day in Canada by Academic Press Canada, Limited, Toronto.

Library of Congress Catalog Card Number: 80-648146

ISBN 0-698-11115-X

Distributed in the United States by Coward, McCann & Geoghegan, Inc., 200 Madison Avenue, New York, N.Y. 10016.

The Lyle official BOOKS review 1982

Compiled and Edited by

LIZ TAYLOR

The publishers wish to express their sincere thanks to the following for their kind help and assistance in the production of this volume:

TONY CURTIS
JANICE MONCRIEFF
SHONA BROWN
JENNIFER KNOX
MAY MUTCH
KAREN KILGOUR
CHRISTINE O'BRIEN
ELAINE HARLAND
CARMEN MILEVOYEVICH
NICKY PARK
MARGOT RUTHERFORD

Introduction

This is the third edition of the Lyle Official Books Review.

Our subject is books sold in auction or by dealers to other book enthusiasts and we have covered the market by using as sources catalogues from all the major salerooms across Britain and by taking a selection from the catalogues of the most prestigious European and American dealers available.

The list includes not only the very expensive and rare books but also those cheap 'little bargains' which collectors often find on the shelves of second-hand bookshops or even in local sales. The date range runs from some of the earliest books ever printed to modern comics and books by living authors.

Book collecting is a passion which grows more popular every year and anyone interested in the subject will find our book invaluable.

They will notice that we have included fully detailed descriptions for every entry with particulars of the state of the book and its bindings, numbers and type of illustrations and any other relevant information such as date and place of printing or who owned the book in the past.

Where we have given two different prices for the same book this is to show variations in price which can be caused by different auctions or disparate condition of the books themselves.

The Lyle Official Books Review is published on the 1st November enabling Dealers and Collectors to begin each new year with an up-to-date knowledge of the current trends, together with the verified values of books of all descriptions.

Acknowledgements

Allen & May, *18 Bridge Street, Andover, Hamps.*
J. Ash, *25 Royal Exchange, London E.C.3.*
Baitson, *194 Anlaby Road, Hull.*
Richard Baker & Thomson, *9 Hamilton Street, Birkenhead.*
Bennett Book Auctions, *72 Radcliffe Terrace, Edinburgh.*
Bonham's, *Montpelier Galleries, Knightsbridge, London.*
Christie's, *8 King Street, St. James, London.*
Christie's New York, *502 Park Avenue, New York.*
Christie's S. Kensington, *85 Old Brompton Road, London.*
Dacre, Son & Hartley, *1-5 The Grove, Ilkley, W. Yorks.*
Graves, Son & Pilcher, *38 Holland Road, Hove, Sussex.*
Irelands, *2 Upper King Street, Norwich, Norfolk.*
W. H. Lane & Son, *Morrab Road, Penzance, Cornwall.*
Laurence & Martin Taylor, *63 High Street, Honiton, Devon.*
Lawrence Fine Art, *19b Market Street, Crewkerne, Somerset.*
May, Whetter & Grose, *Cornubia Hall, Par, Cornwall.*
Moore Allen & Innocent, *33 Castle Street, Cirencester, Glos.*
Phillips, *7 Blenheim Street, New Bond Street, London.*
Phillips, *New York Gallery.*
Robert W. Skinner Inc., *Bolton Gallery, Massachusetts, U.S.A.*
Sotheby Bearne, *3 Warren Road, Torquay, Devon.*
Sotheby Beresford Adams, *The Cross, Chester.*
Sotheby, King & Chasemore, *Station Road, Pulborough, W. Sussex.*
Sotheby's, *Sporting d'Hiver, Monte Carlo, Monaco.*
Sotheby's, *115 Chancery Lane, London.*
Sotheby's, *New York, U.S.A.*
Sotheby's Belgravia, *19 Motcomb Street, London.*
Tooleys, *33 Museum Street, Bloomsbury, London W.C.1.*
Thomas Watson, *27 North Street, Bishops Stortford.*

BOOKS *review*

To give full significance to events in the book world this year it would be necessary to include a graph or a series of graphs in the 1982 Review.

In the first place there would be a graph of prices – all in a descending level for there is no doubt that the prices of most books are down, some of them significantly. Note that the word however is 'most' – not 'all'.

Secondly there would be a graph of unsold lots. At times throughout the year, especially towards the end of 1980, unsold lots were running as high as 25%.

Both graphs however would take an upward turn from mid 1981 onwards because that was when the gloom began to clear and an upturn came. This more optimistic situation is still fairly delicate but it does seem as if the worst of the severe shaking that the trade received during the last twelve months is over.

It is significant that during the worst recessionary months books which were either withdrawn or unsold were those which only a year ago would have been considered sure fire sellers. The top priced market suffered worst. This could have been due to auction houses not taking full recognition of the setback in trade while doing their estimates. Buyers, more conscious of the lack of money in their pockets, refused to bid up to the higher estimates. 'Hardy Annual' books like natural history, travel and maps, slumped and a comparison between prices paid in the past few years and prices paid now show that they have settled at a new and often significantly lower level. This is, of course, no bad thing as far as the book buyer is concerned and perhaps the message for future months should be 'buy while there are still bargains to be had.'

For bargains there have been, and some of them are still around, especially for more expensive books where prices have taken a nose dive. For example Phillips in London sold 28 coloured plate volumes of Curtis' 'Botanical Magazine' (1787-1808) in good condition for £2,500. At the same sale an 1822 set of the works of Hogarth by Nichols which had been removed unsold from a previous sale, went for £460.

Even more notable was the low price of £850 which Sothebys in Chancery Lane received for an 1849 copy of Joseph Dalton Hooker's classic 'The Rhododendrons of Sikkim Himalaya' with 30 hand coloured plates. Book specialists will not have to be told how attractive that price is! Among other notable buys were 'Coloured Plates of the Birds of Ceylon' (1927-35) sold at Phillips Knowle for £210 and a copy of 'The Birds of Burma' published by the American Mission Baptist Press in 1941, sold at the same sale for £130. Christies sold Saxton's 1579 'Glamorgan Comitatus' for £1,300 and Phillips of Edinburgh sold an admittedly stained and worn 1816 set of three volumes of Jane Austen's 'Emma' for only £240. Also cheap was the £28,000 paid at Christie's for Audubon and Bachman's 'Viviparous Quadrupeds of North America' in three volumes and published between 1845 and 1868.

Other book sale 'stars' repriced this year included a proof copy of David Roberts' 'The Holy Land' which Sotheby Beresford Adams sold at Chester for £13,000; a herbal with woodcuts by John Parkinson called 'Theatrum Botanicum' and published in 1640 which made £460 at Christies; Irby's 'Ornithology of the Straits of Gibraltar' for £240 and Guarini's 'Il Pastor Fido' in a magnificent binding with the cyphers of King Charles I which Moore Allen and Innocent sold for £4,800 last autumn.

Of course no picture is all black. Some remarkable prices were also notched up from time to time for better known books. Occasionally these prices surprised even the auctioneers who had estimated them at a lower level, perhaps forced into that position by the prevailing gloom.

For example, Christies sold Edward Lear's 1863 'Views of the Ionian Islands' for £950 though it was a spotted copy with detached covers. Sotheby's were surprised when a Bartolozzi's 'Seventy Three Prints from the Original Drawings and Paintings in the Collection of His Majesty' sold for £850 to an Italian dealer when they had estimated it at between £100 and £200.

A record price was made at Messenger May and Baverstock by Abbe Jean Chappe D'Autreroche's 'Voyage en Siberie' when it sold for £1,100, double any previous price for this book. Sotheby Beresford Adams found their estimating low too when ten volumes of the 1778-83 second edition of the Encyclopaedia Britannica made £1,100. Their estimate was between £200 and £400. At the same sale 'The Gentleman's Magazine' for 1731-1876 made £1,800 over a £100-£200 estimate and 212 volumes of 'The Sporting Magazine' and the 'New Sporting Magazine' (1795-1857) made £2,800 over a £600-£800 estimate. Another record price was for John Gould's 'Birds of Australia' in eight volumes and dated 1840-69 which sold for a very gratifying £46,000 at Christies in the spring when the market was beginning to pick up. At this sale which notched up £517,000 for only 187 lots five volumes of Gould's 'Birds of Europe' sold for £13,000. Also George Walker's 'Costumes of Yorkshire' 1814 made £3,200; John Nash's 'The Royal Pavilion at Brighton' 1826 made £2,000 and eight volumes of Daniel Ayton's 'Voyage Round Great Britain' made £7,500. Later the same auction house saw buoyancy continue when John Hawkesworth's three volume account of 'The Voyages of Captain Cook' sold for £580.

Of course throughout the year some books of such rarity and value appeared that they made remarkable prices in spite of the prevailing downturn but on the whole these events were more rare than in the past. Many of the high priced books were sold in America and at the Swann Galleries in New York, 'Travels in the Interior of North America by Maximilian, Prince of Wied' dated 1843 in two volumes with 81 aquatints made $43,000 or £14,108. At the same sale Audubon's 'Birds of America' with 500 lithograph plates made $14,000 or £5,809; Gould's 'Monograph on the Trochilidae or Humming Birds' 1849-61 made $30,000 or £12,448 and Proust's 'La Recherche du Temps Perdu' in 13 volumes, all first editions, made $5,000 or £2,075.

Another successful New York sale was conducted by Sothebys when they had a sale of important botanical books which included 'Gart de Gesundheit' by Pieter Schoeffer which was dated 1485 and had 400 hand coloured woodcuts. It cost the buyer $72,000 or £30,126. Also sold for $120,000 or £50,209 was 'Flora Graeca' by Sibthorp Smith and Lindley (1806-40).

Back in London Christies had a successful sale of Natural History and Topographical books during the worst slump months and prices included £8,500 paid for George Brookshaw's 'Pomona Britannica' of 1812. Also £1,900 was paid for John Edward Gray's 'Gleanings from the Menagerie and Aviary at Knowsley Hall 1846-50'. About the same time Sothebys sold the sixth and last part of the magnificent Honeyman Collection of Scientific Books and successful lots included the first statement of the Copernican theory in 'De Libris Revolutionum' by Georg Joachim Rheticus dated 1540 which dealers Quaritch bought for £75,000. Among other rare books were Sir Isaac Newton's 'Philosophiae Naturalis Principia Mathematica' 1687 which fetched £12,500; Robert Recorde's 'The Whetstone of Witte' (1557) sold for £1,700 which seems a low price and another equally modest bid of £2,900 secured Wilhelm Conrad Rontgen's 'Eine Neue Art von Stahlen' which contained the first announcement of X-rays in 1895-96.

One of the most unusual lots to appear on the market was the Baskerville Bible in a magnificent red morocco and gilt binding. This lovely book was the property of the Hon. Colin Tennant and it came from a collection built up by his 19th century ancestor Sir Charles Tennant. When the collection appeared at Sothebys fifteen percent of the lots were bought in but the total for the sale was still over £172,000. The Baskerville Bible was one of the more successful lots and it made £23,000. It was notable for its intricate Irish binding of a type now almost unique because others were almost all destroyed when the Irish Public Records Office was wrecked during the seige of the Four Courts in Dublin in 1922.

The price paid for the Tennant Bible astonished Sothebys who had estimated it at around £6,000.

Another single lot not to be omitted from a review of the year was a first edition copy of Edmind Spenser's 'The Shephearde's Calender' of which only five copies were thought to exist before this one appeared in a rather dilapidated condition at Christies. It sold for an astonishing £38,000 and the delighted vendor said that he had bought it in a bundle of books in a 1978 house sale for £25.

If high prices were difficult to reach for the more important books in the saleroom this year however buyers were still out in force looking for unusual items.

There seems to have been something of a Winston Churchill cult and his prices show a fair increase on last year's level. Christies sold four volumes of Churchill's 'History of the English Speaking Peoples' for £100 – a price that was presumably secured because the books were inscribed. Also inscribed were three volumes of his 'War Speeches' published in 1951-52 which sold for £140 at the same sale.

Messenger May and Baverstock sold a pamphlet 'For Free Trade' published in 1906 and very rare for £800. Churchill's arch enemy Adolph Hitler also appeared in the saleroom and Sothebys in Chancery Lane sold a copy of his 'Mein Kampf' for £500 – a high price for this book.

A survey of the year's auction returns makes entertaining reading because of the number of curiosities that crop up. There seems, firstly, to have been a good trade for autograph letters and manuscripts and among those singled out for notice is an autograph poem by Arthur Conan Doyle written in 1922. This uninspired offering of only 22 words sold at Phillips for £55. A document signed by Henry VIII fetched £1,300 and a letter penned from the Victory by Nelson just before his death sold at Phillips for £440.

When Marc Chagall used a felt tipped pen to scrawl a drawing on the title page of his 'poems' published in 1975 he made the book worth £420 to a buyer in Sotheby's. Thomas Chippendale's marriage certificate of 1748 sold for £620 to the Chippendale Society at Phillips and Bernard Shaw signed a cheque in 1940 that was sold in 1981 by Stanley Gibbons for £160. Lord Byron dashed off a satirical poem about Angerstein, the man whose picture collection formed the basis of the National Gallery, and Sothebys sold the 14 line effort for

£3,500. Other manuscript curiosities included a collection of coal merchant's bills for the years 1766 to 1768 which were sold by Phillips in Edinburgh for £120 and Beethoven's handwritten outline of the 'Moonlight' sonata made $43,000 at Sothebys in New York.

The manuscript craze was reflected on the other side of the Atlantic as well where Skinners of Bolton, Mass., sold a letter from George Washington to the Governor of Rhode Island and dated 1777 for $4,250 or £1,735. A manuscript written by Albert Einstein and rediscovered in an old safe sold at Phillips in New York for $31,000 or £12,971 while at the same sale the earliest American ship's journal for the 18th century sloop 'Success' made $5,000 or £2,092.

Less pricey but as much in vogue were ephemera. This is the new development of the past few years and it still seems to be building up a considerable head of steam among collectors. Ephemera can be almost enything from old menu cards to used bus tickets and collectors had a field day when Sothebys held their first ever sale devoted entirely to ephemera at the end of 1980. It raised £21,694 and covered lots dating from the 16th century to the present day though it was noticeable that 19th century lots made the best prices.

The sort of thing that went under the hammer at the sale were nine World War One posters for £170; 8,000 printed cigar labels for £380; 28 albums of cheese labels for £300 and sets of decorated French writing paper dating from around 1880 for £240. The present day was represented by seven Pirelli calendars dated 1966, 1969 to 1974 which made the astonishing price of £170. Ephemera usually sells to private collectors and the scope seems endless.

Although postcards are not strictly ephemera and belong in a class by themselves it is worth noting that Phillips in Edinburgh sold a set of 26 albums of modern postcards of Scotland for a very creditable £700. Other lots only loosely described as ephemera were newspapers which appeared on the market. Sothebys sold 73 issues of the Palestine News published between 1918 and 1919 for £550 and a collection of English newspapers dating from the early 17th century for £8,195. In Toronto Phillips sold only one copy of the rare Vicksburg Daily Citizen for 1863 for C$660 or £253. This price was achieved because the paper was issued during the eight month seigè of Vicksburg during the American Civil War and it was printed on the reverse side of a roll of wallpaper. Back home a collection of 900 photographs of film actors was sold by Sothebys for £1,400.

Specialist tastes were also much to the fore during the year and these covered every spectrum from railways to erotica.

First of all there were the nationalist and local collectors and it is invariably true that books about a certain district, city or town will always sell better on their home ground. This year has been marked by a strong appearance in book salerooms of Canadian collectors and auction houses who have taken note of this and have been sending Canadian books over for sale in their native country.

In their Toronto saleroom Phillips sold an 1842 copy of Willis and Bartlett's 'Canadian Scenery' for C$1,150 or £404 and at Canadian Book Auctions in Toronto William Hunter's 'Ottawa Scenery' of 1855 made C$1,000 or £377. Canadian buyers also appeared in London where Christie's sold Anthony Lockwood's 'Brief Description of Nova Scotia' for £190 and Aldridge's got a bid of £130 for a four volume set of an obscure novel called 'The History of Emily Montague' written in 1784 only because the novel was set in Canada.

National interest came to the fore too when an Australian dealer paid £14,000 for a set of 15 drawings of animals and flowers called 'The First Fleet Drawings' which were found bound into a 1793 copy of Sir James Edward Smith's 'Botany of New Holland'. Also an Icelandic collector paid £7,500 for a copy of the first Icelandic Bible printed in 1584 at Sothebys early in the season while at the company's New York saleroom a bid of $15,000 was paid for a 1643 copy of 'A Key to the Language of America and the Indians'.

Travel books always have a faithful following and it can be noted that Christies sold 'The Modern Universal British Traveller' by Charles Burlington for £320; Thomas Salmon's 'The Universal Traveller' of 1752 for £550 and Thomas Gardiner's 'Pocket Guide to the English Traveller' of 1719 which included a series of uncoloured strip road maps sold at Taviners in Bristol for £825.

Other travel books included Christie's sale of Captain Beresford's 'Twelve Sketches of Southern Albania' of 1855 for £270 though it was dampstained and Sotheby Beresford Adams sale of 110 guidebooks dating from 1836 to 1930. At least one third of the lot were Baedekkers and they all went for £350. Also associated with travel was a manuscript journal of a tour through France, Germany, Switzerland and Italy kept by Thomas Mill in 1820 and illustrated by him. It sold for £1,900 at Phillips.

Railway enthusiasts were also out in force this year paying £55 for Bradshaw's Railway Time Tables for 1839 and £1,000 for volumes 1 to 32 of 'Railways' covering the years 1939 to 1979.

In the category of sport, cricket was very popular and volumes 1 to 116 with only one missing of Wisden for 1879 to 1979 made £1,100 when sold at Sothebys in Chancery Lane. Car enthusiasts appeared at Clarke Gammon of Guildford when copies of 'Autocar' for 1893 to 1898 sold for £240 and 'A Souvenir of the Automobile Club's 1,000 Mile Trial of 1900' made £205. Racing was represented by Pierce Egan's 'Anecdotes of the Turf' – £220 at Phillips – and the more sedentary film going by 'Picture Show Annuals' for 1926-34 which made £80 at Barnard and Learmount at Iver. Just to show that all tastes can be catered for in book sales, Bonhams sold Aleister Crowley's 'The Book of Goetia of Salomon the King' with manuscript notes by the man of Black Magic himself for £280. A sale of erotic books at Phillips in the spring of 1981 saw De Sade's 'La Nouvelle Justine' selling for £880 and 'Old Man Young Again' making £40.

Periodicals continued to be popular and Christies sold a run of 'The Gentleman's Magazine' for 1731-1845 for £1,200. Phillips Knowle sold 29 volumes of 'The Boy's Own Paper' covering 1884 to 1917 for £94. Messenger May and Baverstock got a bid of £200 for volumes of 'Punch' for 1882 to 1938 and 13 volumes of Beardsley's 'Yellow Book' for 1894-97 made £270. 'Greyfriars Holiday Annuals' for 1927-32 made £34 at Christies and an incomplete run of 'Oz' covering 1972-78 made £90 at Sothebys in Chancery Lane.

Cookery books are always popular and John Milne in Aberdeen sold two reasonably priced copies – 'The Cook's Oracle' by the appropriately named W. Kitchen for £24 and a 1777 copy of 'The Housekeeper's Pocket Book' by S. Harrison for £34.

Children's books too never lose their faithful following in the collecting world and this year, though there were few spectacular prices the market help up very well compared to that of maps, natural history and topographical books. A Rackham illustrated edition of 'The Wind in the Willows' published in 1951 sold for £220 and a Dulac illustrated 'Rubaiyat' made £250. Dulac also did the illustrations for Hans Christian Andersen's 'Fairy Tales' which this year reached its peak price of £400. Sothebys sold a first edition of 'Alice in Wonderland' for £250 and a fine copy of Kate Greenaway's 'Mother Goose' with its pictorial dust jacket made £105. Previous prices for this book had never gone above £35. For older children a copy of Henty's 'St. George for England' reached £55. Phillips sold a Kay Neilsen version of Andersen's 'Fairy Tales' for £350 and a Detmold illustrated and signed edition of 'Arabian Nights' for £210. Sotheby, King & Chasemore found a buyer for Louis Wain's 'Days in Catland' at £55 and Christina Rossetti's 'Goblin Market' made £140 in Sothebys Chancery Lane. Also in the children category were sets of educational cards including an 1680 set that sold for £1,200 and a set of Russian alphabet cards that made £1,050 when they were up for sale at Christies. In America too record prices were notched up for children's books and A. A. Milne's 'When We Were Very Young'; 'Winnie the Pooh'; 'Now We Are Six' and 'The House at Pooh Corner' made $1,600 or £773 at Swann's Galleries in New York for the set, all first editions.

Perhaps the strongest area of the market this year has been books by modern authors. Some interesting lots have appeared on the market and it is noticeable that certain writers make increased prices every time their books appear. These include Richard Adams whose 'Watership Down' in first edition made £90 at Christies. Tolkein too has a strong following and a 1937 copy of his 'The Hobbit' with original dust jacket made £520 while a black morocco bound copy of 'The Lord of the Rings' dated 1954 made £2,700.

Another good price was recorded at Sothebys in New York for a 1916 copy of Vladimir Nabokov's 'Stikhi' which made $6,400 or £2,667. Few copies of this book survive because the Russian government destroyed most of them. At the same sale Henry Miller's 'Tropic of Cancer' printed in Paris in 1934 made $4,100 or £1,708. Sothebys in Chancery Lane sold a proof copy of T. S. Eliot's 'Poems 1909-25' for £480 and also the rare first book of Laurence Durrell, 'Ten Poems 1932' for £920. These last books were all in the De La Mare collection and most were inscribed. The collection also included such gems as Sassoon's 'Memoirs of a Fox Hunting Man' for £880; Evelyn Waugh's 'The Ordeal of Gilbert Penfold' for £370 and a proof copy of Ian Fleming's 'Dr No' for £1,100.

A 1922 copy of James Joyce's 'Ulysses' in its original wrappers fetched £240; Samuel Becket's first published work, his poem on Descartes, written in 1933 sold for £290; a first edition of Dylan Thomas' '18 Poems' made £85 and Aldous Huxley's 'Point Counter Point' another signed first edition sold for £48. Sotheby, King and Chasemore had Mervyn Peake's 1944 'Rhymes Without Reason' at £40 while Sothebys sold Joseph Conrad's 'Youth' for £300 and John Galsworthy's first book, written under a pseudonym of John Sinjohn for £75. A scandal of its day, lesbian Radclyffe Hall's 'The Well of Loneliness' sold for £30.

Readers of Evelyn Waugh's diaries would also be interested in a book of 34 decorative designs by Francis Crease who taught Waugh calligraphy which was sold for £300 at Sothebys. Arthur Waugh's 'Oxford' published in 1905 was also sold at Sothebys for £520. Other moderns like Gertrude Stein were represented in the sales returns when her 'Plays and Operas' of 1932 sold for £90. An early J. B. Priestley, 'The Chapman of Rhymes' made £260 and William Faulkner's 'Dr Martino and Other Stories' sold for £80.

Also the name of P. G. Wodehouse cropped up in lists this year when a collection of his early works – 'A Prefect's Uncle' (1903); 'A Gentleman of Leisure' (1910) and 'William Tell Told Again' (1904) sold for £200, £180 and £65 respectively. Another Wodehouse, 'The Pothunters' made £280 at Sothebys.

Looking back over the year it appears that buyers have begun looking in new fields for their bargains and the emphasis has shifted from the regular favourites to more unusual books. Perhaps that is where hunters after bargains should be searching in the future.

LIZ TAYLOR

ABBATE, G.
'Raccolta de Piu e Interessant Dipinti ..... di Ercolano, di Pompei e di Stabia' – 150 engraved plates – mss index at end – some spotting – contem. half calf, worn – 4to – Naples 1859.
(Sotheby's) $25 £12

ABBOT, EVELYN
'The History of Antiquity from the German of Professor Max Duncker' – 6 vol. – 1877-82 – contemp – calf, rebacked and recornered, with old spine laid down.
(Christie's S. Kensington) $65 £30

A'BECKETT, GILBERT A.
'The Comic History of Rome' – illus. by John Leech with 10 plates in colour.
(Baitson, Hull) $35 £17

ABELA, GIOVANNI FRANCESCO
'Malta Illustrata' – 2 vol. – engraved frontis – 21 plates – wormed – 19th cent half calf, wormed and defective – folio – Malta 1772-80.
(Sotheby's) $275 £130

ABERCROMBIE, JOHN
'Pathological and Practical Researches on Diseases of the Stomach' – some soiling, later half-morocco, joints rubbed – Philadelphia 1830.
(Christie's S. Kensington) $30 £15

ABRACADABRA, Goodliffe (editor C. G. Neale)
vol. 1-68 and Summer and Christmas special issues for 1946 and '47 – illus. – first 7 vols. in cloth and the remainder orig. wrappers as issued – 8vo. – Birmingham 1946-47.
(Sotheby's) $150 £70

ABRAHAM LINCOLN
DS as President – orders to affix patent – framed – 1861.
(Robert W. Skinner Inc) $950 £450

ACADEMIE ROYALE DES SCIENCES
'Memoires de Mathematique et de Physique' – vol. 1 and 11 – 44 folding engraved plates – slight browning, contem. sprinkled calf, joints split, rubbed – 4to – Paris 1750-55.
(Sotheby's) $65 £30

ACADEMIE UNIVERSELLE DES JEUX
old calf, worn – Paris 1739.
(Phillips) $45 £22

ACCUM, FRIEDRICH
'A System of Theoretical and Practical Chemistry' – 2 vol. – 1st Edn. – 5 plates – half titles – orig. pink boards, rebacked, uncut – 8vo – for the author by G. Kearsley, 1803.
(Sotheby's) $125 £60

ACHDJIAN, A.
'Un Art Fondamental de Tapis' ..... text in French and English – coloured and other plates – wrappers over boards – Editions Self – Paris 1949.
(Bennett Book Auction) $20 £10

ACKERMANN, RUDOLPH
'The Microcosm of London' – half title and engraved title to vol. 3 – engraved dedication – 22 hand-coloured aquatints – 66 leaves of text only, disbound.
(Christie's S. Kensington) $315 £150

ACKERMANN'S
'World in Miniature: Austria' – 32 coloured plates – 2 vols. – 12mo. hf. cf. – 1823.
(Bonhams) $85 £40

ACLAND, JAMES
'The Hull Portfolio' – 1st vol. only – Aug.-Dec. 1831.
(Baitson, Hull) $85 £41

ACTS
Anno Regni Willielmi et Mariae – 66 acts bound in one vol. – calf worn – small folio – all c. 1690.
(Phillips) $105 £50

ADAM, MADAME JULIETTE LAMBER
'La Chanson des Nouveaux Epoux' – no. 10 of 100 copies on Papier du Japon – portrait of author and 10 plates – green morocco – gilt – Paris 1882.
(Sotheby Parke Bernet) $2,045 £975

ADAMS, DAVENPORT
'The White King or Charles the First' – 2 vol. – extra illustrated with about 160 plates – mainly portraits – morocco gilt. rubbed, g.e. inlaid to folio – 1889.
(Christie's S. Kensington) $190 £90

ADAMS, GEORGE
'An Essay on Electricity' – 3rd Edn. – engraved folding frontis – 8 plates – engraved title – some stains, calf rebacked – 8vo. – R. Hindmarsh for author – 1787.
(Sotheby's) $75 £35
'Essays on the Microscope' – frontis – 32 double page plates – old calf – 4to. – 1798.
(Philips) $230 £110

ADAM'S ILLUSTRATED PANORAMA OF HISTORY
folding col. panorama 27 x 264 inches – orig. half morocco, rubbed – n.d.
(Christie's) $65 £30

ADAMS, J.
'Sketches Taken During Ten Voyages to Africa' – 2 maps – 1 folding – library stamps – title trimmed – modern cloth, faded – 4to. – n.d.
(Sotheby's) $90 £42

ADAMS, JOSEPH
'Observations on Morbid Poisons' – 2nd Edn. – 4 coloured plates – some browning – modern cloth – 4to. – 1807
(Sotheby's) $20 £10

ADAMS, R.
'The Thames in the Year of the Spanish Armada' – from the original parchment – uncoloured – repaired – 405mm x 680mm. – J. Pine, London 1740.
(Tooleys) $380 £180

ADAMS, R.
'The Narrative of a Sailor who was Wrecked on the Western Coast of Africa' – folding engraved map – spotted – contem. half morocco, rubbed – 4to. – 1816.
(Sotheby's) $150 £72

ADAMS, RICHARD
'Watership Down' – 1st Edn. – folding map – orig. cloth – dust jacket – 8vo. –1972.
(Sotheby's) $190 £90

ADAMS, W. H. D.
'The White King or Charles 1' – 2 vol. – text mounted in folio and extra illus. – 250 plates – engraved portraits – some views – some col. – contem. morocco – gilt – rubbed – folio – 1889.
(Sotheby's) $390 £180

ADDINGTON, A. G.
'The Royal House of Stuart' – 3 vols. – plates – orig. cloth – gilt – 4to. – 1969-76.
(Sotheby's) $20 £10

ADRICHOMIUS, C. AND HORN, G.
'Dimidiam Tribum Manasse Ultra Jordanem' – uncol. map – worn – 251mm x 503mm. – Luneberg 1665.
(Phillips) $60 £28

ADVENTURES OF A BEE, THE
1st Edn. – 12 wood engraved illus. some col. by former owner – 3 pp adverts – orig. Dutch floral boards – F. Power 1790.
(Sotheby's) $400 £190

ADVENTURES OF LITTLE DOG TRIM AND HIS FUNNY COMPANIONS – 16 pp each with verse and illus. col. by hand – orig. wrappers – pictorial label on upper cover – defective – rubbed – roan backed case – 8vo. – G. Martin 1818.
(Sotheby's) $75 £35

ADVERTISEMENTS
A collection of 30 various 18th cent single sheet trade advertisements or cards for commodities including perfumes, powders for destroying insects, musical instruments, liqueurs and sedan chairs – some engraved – others with woodcut devices – minor defects.
(Sotheby Beresford Adams) $200 £95

AEROPLANE SUPPLY COMPANY
The First Aviation Catalogue – compiled by Bernard Isaac with descriptive sketches – prices and plates – orig. cover – October 1909.
(Phillips) $105 £50

AESOP
'Fables of Aesop and other Eminent Mythologists by Sir Roger L'Estrange' – engraved portrait and one plate – 134 plates by William Hollar and others – one bound as frontispiece with an engr. portrait of John Ogilvy mounted on verso – some shaved – old calf, worn – folio – 1692.
(Christie's S. Kensington) $315 £150

AFLALO, F. G.
'Sports of the World' – 2 vols.
(Laurence and Taylor) $10 £4

AGRICULTURE AND INCLOSURE
Collection of approx 75 Parliamentary Blue Books – a few folding maps – mostly disbound – folio – c. 1800-60.
(Sotheby's) £505 £240

AGRIPPA, A. C.
'Three Books of Occult Philosophy' – engr. portrait – one folding table – contemp. calf backed boards – joints cracked 1651.
(Christie's S. Kensington) $230 £110

AIKIN, ARTHUR AND CHARLES ROCHMONT
'A Dictionary of Chemistry and Mineralogy' – 2 vols. – 15 numbered plates – 1 unnumbered – half calf – spines repaired – 4to. – J. and A. Arch 1807-14.
(Sotheby's) $90 £42

AIKIN, J.
'Essay on Song Writing' – calf gilt – 1774.
(Phillips) $35 £16

AKBAR'S SONS
Inscribed 'The Work of Manohar', the princes identified by inscriptions on the pillars – minor staining and rubbing – laid arabesques outlined in gold – Mughal c. 1600-1605.
(Christie's) $11,550 £5,500

AKEN, CONRAD
'Thee' – 1st Eng. Edn. – one of 100 – signed by author – illus. by Gillian Ruff orig. quarter morocco – fine.
(J. Ash) $35 £16

ALBERTI, L. B.
'Della Architectura Della Pittura Della Statua' – Trans. G. Bartoli – engraved title – 69 plates – vellum gilt – folio – Bologna 1782.
(Phillips) $400 £190

ALBIN, ELEAZER
'A Natural History of Birds' – 3 vols. – 306 hand col. engraved plates – some shaved and offset – list of subscribers – half morocco – 4to – 1738.
(Christie's) $5,460 £2,600

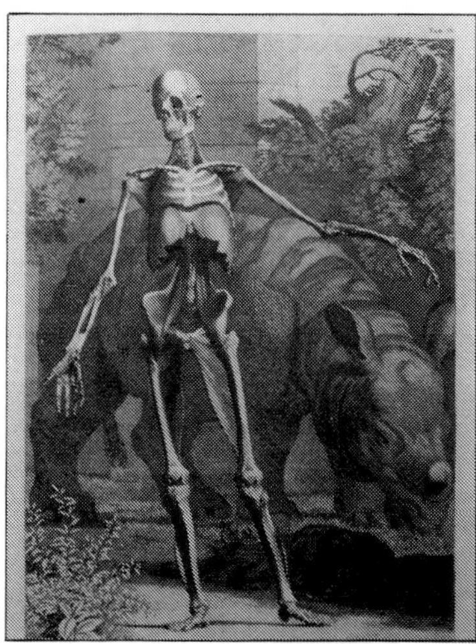

ALBINUS, BERNARD SIGFRIED
'Tabulae Sceleti et Musculorum Corporis Humani' – engraved illus. on titles – 51 engraved plates after Grignion, Scotin, Ravenet, Muller and others – half morocco, spine rubbed – elephant folio – John and Paul Knapton 1749-50.
(Christie's) $1,260 £600

ALBUM
Compiled by the family of General Sir James Carmichael Smythe – engravings – colour plates – incl. military costumes – 7 pencil drawings of scenes in Barbados 1836-6 – engraved views of railway stations – c. 1840.
(Phillips) $295 £140

ALBUM
of watercolours – pencil sketches – 50 small aqua views of Switzerland.
(Phillips) $1,092 £520

THE ALBUM AMICORUM OF JACOBUS VAN BRONCKHORST DE BATENBURG
In Latin, some words in Greek – illum mss on paper – 62 full page armorial achievements – 3 full page pictures of women in colour – 13 finely painted full page portraits – contem. Parisian brown morocco gilt – binding slightly worn – g.e. – 140mm x 95mm. – Paris 1570-72.
(Sotheby's) $14,700 £7,000

ALBUM OFFICIAL DE LA FETE DES VIGNERONS, VEVEY 1889
folding hand col. panorama – spotted – torn – orig. cloth backed boards – soiled – oblong 8vo. – Lausanne and Vevey 1889.
(Sotheby's) $115 £55

ALBUM PITTORESQUE DE STOCKHOLM
10 litho views – orig. boards broken – library stamp – Copenhagen 1870.
(Bonhams) $315 £150

ALBUQUERQUE, L. S. M. DE
'Curso Elementor de Physica e de Chymica' – 5 vols. – 28 folding plates – tables – library stamp on titles – green cloth – roan spine gilt – sm 4to – Lisbon 1824.
(Sotheby's) $55 £25

ALCOCK, R.
'The Capital of the Tycoon' – 2 vol. – 16 col. plates – 2 folding maps – 1 mounted on linen – illus. – modern calf backed cloth – rubbed – 8vo. – 1863.
(Sotheby's) $230 £110

ALDIN, CECIL (illustrator)
'The Snob' – 1904
(Laurence and Martin Taylor) $10 £4

ALDINGTON, RICHARD
'Portrait of a Genius But' ..... Life of D. H. Lawrence – plates – shaken and used – 1950.
(J. Ash) $6 £3

ALECHINSKY, PIERRE
'Hayterophiles (Atelier 17, Paris 1952-53)' – 11 etched plates – each signed and numbered – 5 coloured – unsewn in orig. cloth portfolio with tie – oblong folio – Paris, La Hune 1968.
(Sotheby's) $200 $95

ALEXANDER, WILLIAM
'The Costume of China' – 47 hand aquatint plates, few tears – soiled – later half calf – rubbed – 4to. – 1805.
(Christie's S. Kensington) $160 £75
'Picturesque Representations of the Dress and Manners of the Russians' – 64 coloured aquatint plates – half morocco – 1814.
(Bonhams) $230 £110

ALEXANDER, SIR WILLIAM, EARL OF STIRLING
'Recreations with the Muses' – 1st Edn. – engraved port frontis – woodcut title – contem. calf – rubbed – contem. ownership inscription – folio – 1637.
(Christie's) $880 £420

ALEXANDRA, QUEEN OF EDWARD VII
ALs 3 pages – 8vo. – Marlborough House, Dec. 1885 to 'My Dear Maharajah' thanking him for 'the lovely flowers'.
(Phillips) $40 £20

ALEXANDRO, NATALI
'Dissertatio de Confessione' – Contem red morocco gilt – dentelle borders – gilt edges – 8vo. – Paris 1678.
(Moore Allen and Innocent) $250 £120

ALEXIS OF PIEDMONT
'The Third and Last Part of the Secretes' ..... – black letter – printer's device on title – a few stains – half morocco – sm 4to – Henry Denham for John Wyght 1566.
(Sotheby's) $160 £70

ALFORD, M.
'Needlework as Art' – 1st Edn. – plates – orig. cloth – polythene wrapper – 8vo. – 1886.
(Sotheby's) $90 £42

ALGREN, NELSON
'Notes from a Sea Diary' – 1st Eng. Edn. – very good – in dust wrapper – 1966.
(J. Ash) $10 £4

ALI BEY
'Travel in Morocco, Tripoli, Cyprus, Egypt, Arabia, Syria and Turkey' – 2 vol. – 1st Edn. – 4 folding engraved maps – 87 engraved plates and plans – 19th cent. half morocco – rebacked – 4to. – 1816.
(Sotheby's) $715 £340

ALI, CHEREFEDDIN
'The History of Timur Bec' – 2 vols. – 5 folding maps – old calf – 1723.
(Phillips) $85 £40

ALISON, A.
'History of Europe' – 23 vols. – 2 series – calf gilt – a T.C.D. prize binding – 8vo. – 1849-59.
(Sotheby's) $275 £130

ALKEN, HENRY
'The National Sports of Great Britain' – Eng. and French text – 50 hand col. aquatint plates by Clark after Alken – slight browning – contem. purple morocco – gilt – spine tooled – rubbed – g.e. – large folio – 1821.
(Sotheby's) $7,350 £3,500

ALL ENGLAND LAW REPORTS
81 vol. only – orig. blue and fawn cloth – rubbed – 8vo – 1948-78.
(Sotheby's) $630 £300

ALLAN, REV. G. L.
'The Views and Flowers from Guzerat and Rajpootana' – 13 hand col. plates – loose – orig. cloth gilt – P. Jerrard n.d.
(Phillips) $100 £48

ALLARD, H.
'Nova Tabula India Orientalis' – engraved map – hand col. in ouline – scene of elephants with traders – cartouche – 445 mm x 562mm. – Amsterdam c. 1640.
(Sotheby's) $505 £240

ALLEN, JOHN
'History of the Borough of Liskeard' – 1st Edn. – orig. cloth – 1856.
(Lane) $115 £55

ALLEN, THOMAS
'History of the County of York' – 5 vols out of 6 – small paper edit. – 65 steel engravings by Nathaniel Whittock – London 1839.
(Baitson) $100 £48

ALLEN, W. AND OTHERS
'A Narrative of the Expedition to the River Nile' – 2 vol. – 18 plates and maps – some folding – illus. – modern half calf – 8vo. – 1848.
(Sotheby's) $210 £100
'Picturesque Views in the Island of Ascension' – 10 litho plates – 2 folding – vignette on title – spotted – repaired – contem. limp cloth – rubbed – oblong folio – 1835.
(Sotheby's) $505 £240

ALLOM, THOMAS
'Views in the Tyrol' – engraved title, one folding map – 45 plates – spotted – dampstains – contemporary half-calf, worn – 4to. – 1836.
(Christie's S. Kensington) $150 £70
'Constantinople and the Scenery of the Seven Churches of Asia Minor' – 2 vol. – Fisher Son & Co. – two engraved additional titles – two maps – one double page and 94 plates after Allom – including additional unlisted plate – vol. 1 slightly damp – stained – contemp. – red morocco – gilt – slightly rubbed – g.e. – 4to. – n.d.
(Christie's S. Kensington) $150 £70

ALMAIN
'An Armourer's Album' editor Viscount Dillon – col. plates – orig. parchment boards – soiled – folio – 1905.
(Sotheby's) $140 £65

AL-MAMALIK WA-L-MASALIK; AL-MAQALAH ATH-THANIYAH
Geographical treatise with historical comments – arabic mss on buff paper – folio 10 inch x 6 inch – part of a historical work on Cairo – 18th cent.
(Christie's) $525 £250

ALMANACH DE GOTHA
1769, 1771, 1777, 1779-86, 1788-91, 1793-1801, 1803-06, 1808-41, 1843-1939, 1940-42 – Supplements for 1882-84 and duplicates for 1794, 1829, 1853 – 167 vols. in all – plates – some engraved – orig. boards and cloth – some rebacked – rubbed – some slipcases – 12mo and 8vo. – Gotha 1769-1942.
(Sotheby's) $2,520 £1,200

ALMANACH ROYAL
8 vols. – pale green contem. morocco gilt – arms of Cherville onlaid in white and brown on each cover – 1762.
(Moore Allen and Innocent) $590 £280

ALMANACKS
a collection of 23 – mostly the London Kalendar or the Royal Kalendar – browning or soiling – contem calf – rubbed or worn – 12 mp. – 1774 - 1853.
(Sotheby's) $125 £60

ALMA-TADEMA, SIR LAURENCE (painter)
series of A.L.s. – 50 pages – 8vo. – 10 auto cards and 7 envelopes – Townshend House, North Gate, Regent's Park – and other plates – 1881-1910.
(Phillips) $630 £300

ALPHAND, A.
'Les Promenades de Paris' – 2 vol. – plates – spotting – loose in orig. morocco backed cloth – rubbed – folio – Paris 1867-73.
(Sotheby's) $525 £250

THE ALPINE JOURNAL
vol. 1 - part 1 vol. 65 (vol. 63-65 in original parts) and 3 vol. Index (to vol. 58) – plates maps, most uniform cloth – gilt some slightly rubbed – some soiled – together with seven other Alpine Club publications 1864-1960.
(Christie's S. Kensington) $335 £160

ALSTON, J. W.
'Hints to Young Practitioners in the Study of Landscape Painting' – 3rd Edn. – engraved title with vignette – 5 plates – soiling – orig. boards – worn and stained – uncut – 8vo – 1820.
(Sotheby's) $65 £30

ALTAMIRANO
'El Zarco The Bandit' – (Folio Society) – full page wood engravings by Zelma Blakely – spine slightly dulled – 1957.
(J. Ash) $15 £6

ALTMANN, J. G.
'L'Etat et Delices de la Suisse' – 4 vols. – new Edn. – engraved folding map – plates – directions to binder bound in – slight off-setting – contem. mottled calf – gilt – worn – 12 mo – Basle 1776.
(Sotheby Beresford Adams) $3,360 £1,600

AMBLER, ERIC
'Passage of Arms' – very good – slightly rubbed dust wrapper – 1959.
(J. Ash) $10 £4

AMEDEO, LUIGI OF SAVOY – 'On the 'Polar Star'' – Trans by W. le Queux – 2 vols. – port – plates – maps – orig. cloth gilt – t.e.g. – sm 4to. – 1903.
(Phillips) $90 £42

AMELOT,SIEUR, DE LA HOUSSAIE
'Histoire du Gouvernement de Venise' – engraved additional title – later vellum – slightly soiled – 1677.
(Christie's S. Kensington) $80 £38

AMERICA
A collection of approx. 177 books and pamphlets – mostly in Spanish on South America – some with plates – some worn – some defective – various sizes.
(Sotheby's) $610 £290

AMERICA-ANVILLE, J. B. B.
'A New Map of the Whole Continent of America' – engraved map – including inset maps of Labrador, Greenland and Iceland, etc. – large pictorial title vignette fully col. – some tears – some offsetting – each sheet approx. 515mm x 1180mm. – Laurie and Whittle 1794.
(Sotheby's) $230 £110

AMERICAN REVOLUTION
'The Pictorial History of the American Revolution' – Robert Seears, New York, 1845.
(Baitson) $40 £20

AMERICAN SHEET MUSIC
Approx. 50 pieces of engraved music bound in one vol. – piano arrangements for cotillons, quadrilles and ballads etc. – 8 litho pictorial titles – presentation inscription for 1837 – contem. olive morocco gilt and blindstamped borders – rebacked – worn – folio – New York, Philiadelphia, Baltimore – circa 1830.
(Sotheby's) $65 £30

AMES, JOSEPH AND WILLIAM HERBERT
'Typographical Antiquities' – 3 vol. – frontis – 8 engraved plates – woodcut illus. in text – 19th cent. half calf – rubbed – 4to. – 1785-90.
(Sotheby's) $250 £120

AMICI, DOMENICO
'Raccolta Delle Principal Vedute di Roma' – 3 engraved titles and 41 plates after Amici – contem. half morocco – rubbed – oblong folio – Rome 1835-47.
(Christie's) $125 £60

AMIS, MARTIN
'Success' – very good in dust wrapper – 1978.
(J. Ash) $6 £3

AMUNDSEN, R.
'The South Pole' – 2 vol. – plates – folding maps – orig. cloth – 8vo – 1913.
(Sotheby's) $210 £100

AMUSING INSTRUCTOR,THE
engraved frontis – 8 of 11 plates – 2 woodcut illus. – inkmarks – contem. calf – worn – 12 mo – W. Harris 1769.
(Sotheby's) $17 £8

ANAESTHESIA
'An examination of the question of anaesthesia on the memorial of Charles Thomas Wells to a select committee of the Senate of the United States' – 103pp half cloth – front wrapper bound in – 8vo – Washington 1853.
(Sotheby's) $100 £48

ANARCHARSIS
'Atlas only for the Voyages' – 31 maps and plates – contem. calf – 4to. – Paris 1790.
(Phillips) $85 £40

ANCIENT COINS
A collection of 41 off prints and pamphlets some with plates – wrappers and unbound – 4to. and 8vo.
(Sotheby's) $105 £50

ANDERSEN, HANS CHRISTIAN
'Later Tales published during 1867 and 1868' – 1st Eng. Edn. – 8 wood engraved plates and 5 headpieces – spotted – orig. green cloth gilt – worn – 8vo – Bell and Daley 1869.
(Sotheby's) $20 £10

ANDERSON, ADAM
'An Historical and Chronological Deduction of the Origin of Commerce' – 4 vols. – engraved frontis – 2 folding maps – half titles – contem. speckled calf – gilt – joints split – slight wear – 4to. – 1787-89.
(Sotheby's) $170 £80

ANDERSON, AENEAS
'A Narrative of the British Embassy to China' – 1st Edn. – half title – title and half title soiled – occas. spotting – 19th cent roan backed boards – spine defective – worn – 4to. – 1795.
(Sotheby's) $65 £30

ANDERSON, J.
'Observations on the Means of Exciting the Spirit of National Industry ..... Agriculture, Commerce .. of Scotland' – contemp. calf gilt by Scott of Edinburgh – sp. a little rubbed f. cover detached – thick 4to. – 1st Edn. – Edinburgh 1777.
(Bennett Book Auctions) $400 £190

ANDERSON, J.C.
'Shropshire. Its Early History and Antiquities' – wood engraved plates and illus. – soiled – orig. cloth – spine faded – 1864.
(Christie's) $40 £20

ANDERSON, JAMES
'Selectus Diplomatum & Numismatum Scotiae Thesaurus' – 1st Edn. – title in red and black – 180 engraved plates – foxing – 19th cent russia – upper cover detached some wear – g.e. – folio - Edinburgh 1739.
(Sotheby's) $40 £20
'An Account of the Present State of the Hebrides and the Western Coasts of Scotland' – large folding map – contem. tree calf – worn – rare – 8vo – Dublin 1786.
(Sotheby's) $295 £140

ANDERSON, JOHN
'The Pursuit of Diarmuid and Graunia' – Poem – very good copy – 1950.
(J. Ash) $6 £3

ANDERSON, W.
'The Pictorial Arts of Japan' – plates – orig. morocco backed cloth – rebacked – rubbed folio – 1886.
(Sotheby's) $135 £65

ANDRAE, W.
'Coloured Ceramics from Ashur' – 36 plates mostly colour – cloth – folio – 1925.
(Phillips) $65 £30

ANDRELINUS, P. FAUSTAS
'Epistole Puerbiales, Morales, Strassburg, ex aedibus Matthias Schurer' – some marginal soiling – a few manuscript marginal annotations – modern boards – 1510.
(Christie's S. Kensington) $65 £30

ANDREW, W. J.
'A Numismatic History of the Reign of Henry 1' – plates – soiled – contem. half morocco – 8 vo – 1901.
(Sotheby's) $105 £50

ANDREWS, JAMES
'Choice Garden Flowers' – 12 hand-coloured lithographed plates – orig. cloth g.e. – 1860.
(Christie's S. Kensington) $85 £40
'Flower Painting' – 24 plates incl. 12 hand-coloured – half calf – oblong 4to. – 1835.
(Phillips) $230 £110

ANDREWS, J.
'A New and Accurate Map of the Country twenty-five Miles Round London' –coloured – on 36 sheets backed with linen – 1777.
(Bonhams) $80 £38

ANDRICHOM, C.
'Situs Terrae Promissionis' – uncol map of the Holy Land – J. Janson Amsterdam circa 1650.
(Phillips) $200 £95

ANDRIVEAU-COUJON, J.
'Atlas Classique et Universal de Geographie Ancienne et Moderne' – 32 engraved maps – coloured in outline – some foxed – red quarter morocco – worn – large folio – Paris 1835
(Sotheby's) $55 £25

ANGAS, GEORGE FRENCH
'The New Zealanders Illustrated' – limited facsimile Edn. – col. title and plates – orig. half morocco – gilt – folio – Wellington 1966.
(Sotheby's) $150 £70

ANGELO, DOMENICO
'The School of Fencing' – 1st Edn. – text in Eng. and French – 44 engraved plates of 47 – English title repaired – some soiling and staining – modern half cloth – oblong folio – 1765.
(Sotheby's) $675 £320

ANGHIERA, PIETRA MARTIRE D'
'De Orbe Nuou Decades' – 1st complete Edn. of first Three Decades – Spanish calf rebacked – covers scuffed – g.e. – folio – Alcala 1516.
(Christie's) $3,780 £1,800
'Angliae,Scotia et Hibernia' – hand-col. map – vig. sailing ships – in mount – Mercator? – circa 1600.
(Phillips) $150 £70

ANGLO-SAXON REVIEW
Editor Lady Spencer Churchill – 10 vol. – orig. morocco – gilt – rubbed – 4to. – 1899-1901.
(Sotheby's) $115 £55

ANGUS, W.
'Seats of the Nobility in Great Britain and Wales' – 62 of 63 plates – some repaired – cloth backed boards – oblong 4to. – 1787.
(Phillips) $190 £90

'L'ANNEE DES DAMES NATIONALES
ou Histoire jour-par-jour d'une Femme de France' – 12 vol. – engraved frontis and plates – soiling – contem. wrappers – 12 mo – Geneva 1794.
(Christie's) $40 £20

ANNUAL REGISTER OR A VIEW OF THE HISTORY, POLITICS AND LITERATURE
42 vols. including index – contem. calf gilt – 1758-99
(Phillips) $250 £120

ANONYMOUS
'Curiesur Nachrichten Aus dem Reich der Beschnittenen' – 4 parts in one – 1st Edn. – double page woodcut – slight tear – modern leather – rare – 4to. – Frankfurt am Main 1737.
(Sotheby's) $2,730 £1,300

ANSON, G.
'A Voyage Round the World by R. Walter' – 42 maps and plates – some folding – 5th Edn. – old calf worn – 4to. – 1749.
(Bonhams) $180 £85

ANSTEY, F.
'The Giant's Robe' – Author's second book – spine creased – lacks endpapers – shaken – 1884.
(J. Ash) $10 £5

ANTHOLOGY
'The Best Poems of 1924' – Poems by Sackville-West, Aiken, Sitwell, Muir, Davies, Coppard, Graves etc. orig. boards – bumped –dust wrapper – 1925.
(J. Ash) $8 £4

ANTHONY, GORDON
'Russian Ballet' – mounted – plates – original cloth – slightly soiled – 1939.
(Christie's S. Kensington) $40 £18

ANTIGUA
Auto letter signed by L. L. Hodge – 4 pages – folio – to Christopher Codrington reporting on Bolans estate bearing a superb strike of the large Antigua fleuron datestamp for Sep. 17, year omitted – Sept. 1815.
(Sotheby's) $2,310 £1,100

ANTIGUA - BELLIN J. N.
Engraved map, hand col. in outline – title cartouche fully col. – compass lines etc. – 565 mm x 414 mm. – Paris 1758.
(Sotheby's) $135 £65

ANTIQUE COSTUMES
45 hand coloured fashion plates and uncoloured plates from Lady Magazine – half morocco gilt – 8vo. – circa 1834.
(Phillips) $210 £100

ANTIQUITY
Vol. 1-46 in 164 – plates – contem cloth and orig wrappers – rubbed – 8vo – 1927-72.
(Sotheby's) $420 £200

APIANUS, PETRUS
'Astronicum Caesarium' – 1st Edn. – woodcuts on title – arms of Apianius at end – woodcut illus. – 36 full page woodcuts – col. throughout by contem. hand – contem. German calf – covers with blind stamped historiated and crested rolls – rubbed and rebacked – large folio – Ingoldstadt May 1540.
(Christie's) $16,800 £8,000

APOLLINARIS
'Opera' – 17th cent French binding of brown calf gilt – gilt edges – back decorated in compartments – restored – 4to. – Paris 1599.
(Moore Allen & Innocent) $360 £170

APOTHEGMATA GRAECA REGUM & DUCUM
16th cent French binding of light brown morocco gilt – back decorated with strapwok and arabesques – head and tail bands restored – 16 mo. – Paris 1568.
(Moore Allen & Innocent) $230 £110

APPELL, J. W.
'Le Rhin et Ses Bords' – 148 engraved views –orig. half roan – slightly worn – joint split – 8vo. – Darmstadt and Paris 1854.
(Sotheby's) $3,360 £1,600

APPERLEY, C. J. (NIMROD)
'Nimrod Abroad' – 2vols. – orig. cloth – spines faded – otherwise good – 1842.
(J. Ash) $75 £36
'The Horse and the Hound' ..... 3rd Edn. – plates – illustrations – occasional spotting – original morocco – rubbed – front inner hinge broken – g.e. – 1858.
(Christie's S. Kensington) $55 £25

APPIANI, ALEXANDRINI
'Romanarum Historiarum' – contem. full calf – gold tooled with centre medallion of arms of Pierre Louis Farnese, sm folio – 1554.
(Phillips) $275 £130
'Appianus of Alexandria Rom. Historiarum, Punica, sive Carthiginiensis' ..... title detached – spotted first few leaves with slight marginal worming – slight spotting – old calf – rebacked – worn folio – Geneva excudebat Henricis Stephanus, 1591.
(Christie's S. Kensington) $55 £25

APPLICATION OF IRON TO RAILWAY AGE STRUCTURES, REPORT OF THE COMMISSIONERS
2 vols. – 77 plates – folding – some soiling – modern half calf – folio 1849.
(Sotheby's) $545 £260

ARBER, EDWARD
'The Term Catalogues' – 3 vol. – 1st Edn. – orig. cloth – slightly worn – 4to. 1903-06.
(Sotheby's) $210 £100

ARBUTHNOT, JOHN
'Tables of Ancient Coins' – 18 engraved tables – last folding – title in red and black – errata slip – title strengthened – contem calf – spine and hinges worn – 4to. – J. Tonson, 1727.
(Sotheby's) $20 £10

ARCHAEOLOGIA
Vol. 56-98 in 50 – orig. cloth – rubbed – 4to. 1898-1961.
(Sotheby's) $335 £160

ARCHER, J. W.
'Vestiges of Old London' – 1st Edn. – 37 etched plates – india paper – contem. brown morocco – worn – covers detached – folio – 1851.
(Sotheby's) $85 £40

ARCHITECTURAL REVIEW
Vol 69-147 with duplicates for 113-114 – 86 vols altog. – orig. wrappers – some publisher's cloth – 4to. – 1931.
(Sotheby's) $1,325 £630

ARCTIC CIRCLE
Engraved circular hydrographic chart of the Artic regions of Europe, Asia and America – with mss additions in ink – approx. diameter 606 mm. – February 1818.
(Christie's) $275 £130

ARFWEDSON, C. D.
'The United States and Canada' – 2 vol. – frontis – browned – modern calf backed cloth – 8vo. – 1834.
(Sotheby's) $100 £48

ARIEL POEMS (no. 1-8)
Hardy, Thomas; Newbolt, Sir Henry; Binyon, Laurence; De La Mare, Walter; Chesterton, G. K.; Gibson, Wilfrid; Sassoon, Seigfried; Eliot, T. S. 'Journey of the Magi' – 1st American Edn. – limited to 27 copies – printed to secure copywright in USA – orig. wrappers – uncut – 8vo. – New York, 1927.
(Sotheby's) $545 £260

ARIOSTO, LUDOVICO
'Orlando Furioso' – full page illus. and decorations – margins shaved – contem. vellum – soiled – 4to. – Venice.
(Christie's) $210 £100

ARLAND, MARCEL - CHAGALL, MARC.
'Maternite' – 5 etched plates by Chagall – orig. wrapper – faded – uncut – 4to. – Paris, Au Sans Pareil, 1926.
(Sotheby's) $545 £260

ARLEN, MICHAEL
'The Green Hat' – 1st American Edn. – some damage – foxed – otherwise nice – New York 1924.
(J. Ash) $17 £8

ARMOUR, G. D.
'Humour in the Hunting Field' – mounted coloured plates by Armour – orig. cloth – rubbed and soiled – lge 4to. – 1928.
(Christie's S. Kensington) $65 £30

ARMSTRONG, JOHN
'The Art of Preserving Health' – 1st Edn. – browning – contem. mottled calf – label – rubbed – 4to. – 1744.
(Sotheby's) $160 £75

ARMSTRONG, JOHN
'The History of the Navigation of the Port of King's Lyn and Cambridge' – 6 engraved maps – 2 hand col. – 1 plan – waterstains – modern half calf – folio – 1725.
(Sotheby's) $315 £150

ARMSTRONG, WALTER
'The Thames' – 2 vol. – addit. titles – 13 plates – 2 maps – illus. – contem. half calf – rubbed – 4to. – n.d.
(Christie's) $75 £35
'Industrial Resources of the Tyne' – illus. half morocco gilt – teg. – 1864.
(Phillips) $105 £50

ARMY AND NAVY
Collection of approx. 700 Parliamentary Blue Books and Papers on the Army, Navy Ordnance, Pay etc. – various bindings – worn – some disbound – folio – circa 1800-1860.
(Sotheby's) $2,205 £1,050

ARMY MEDICAL LIBRARY: INDEX CATALOGUE OF THE LIBRARY OF THE SURGEON-GENERAL'S OFFICE, UNITED STATES ARMY
First series, 16 vol., Washington; fourth series, 11 vol. 1936-55; fifth series, 3 vol., 1959-61 – all orig. cloth – rubbed or marked – 4to. – 1880-95.
(Sotheby's) $460 £220

ARNOLD, DR.
'Zorniski, As Performed ... At The Theatre Royal Haymarket ... For The German Flute' – wrappers – nd.
(Bennett Book Auctions) $4 £2

ARNOLD, E. C.
'British Waders' – col. plates – orig. cloth gilt – spine bleached – 4to. – 1924.
(Phillips) $85 £40

ARNOLD, MATTHEW
'Merope' – bookplate and inscription of A. A. Jackson – variant blue cloth – 1858.
(J. Ash) $30 £14

ARNOTT, NEIL
'Elements of Physics or Natural Philosophy' – 1st Edn. – 1 plate in supplement – 2pp auto letter by author – dated October 1824 – half calf – 8vo – Th. and G. Underwood, 1827.
(Sotheby's) $85 £40

ARNOULD, E. J.
'La Genese du Barbier de Seville' – 543 copies – orig. cloth – 4to. – Dublin and Paris, 1965.
(Sotheby's) $485 £230

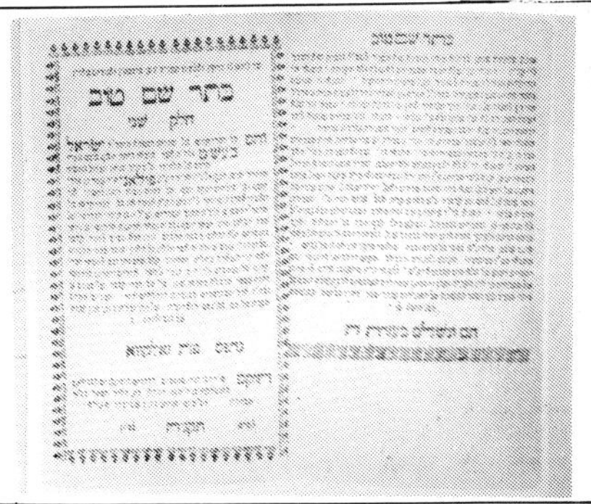

ARON COHEN OF APTA
'Keter Shem Tov' – 1st Edn. – 2 parts in one vol. – some missing leaves – stained – shaved – half leather – 8vo. – 1795.
(Sotheby's) $335 £160

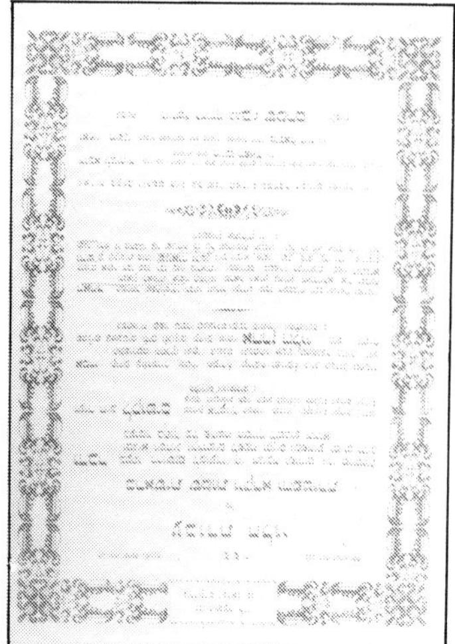

ARON HA'LEVI OF STAROSELYE
'Avodat Ha'levi; Likutim; She'eilot U.teshurog' – 5 parts in one – 1st. Edn. – titles with typo borders – boards – 4to. – Johannesburg 1842.
(Sotheby's) $250 £120

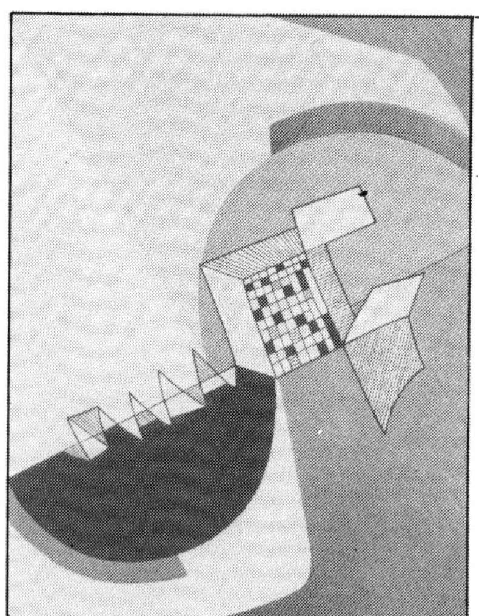

ARP, JEAN
10 lithographs including works by Sonia Delauney, Alberto Magnelli, Sophie Taeuber-Arp – limitation statement – unsewn – uncut – orig. folder and slipcase – 4to. – Paris, Aux Nourritures Terrestres, 1950.
(Sotheby's) $800 £380

ARROWSMITH, A.
'A Map of the Environs of Constantinople' – col. by hand – 2 sheets of 2 sections joined – each sheet approx. 630 mm x 1,580 mm. – 1804.
(Sotheby's) $105 £50

ART OF ANCIENT EGYPT, THE
A series of photographic plates – 27 mounted photographs slightly faded – original cloth – rubbed and soiled – 4to. – privately printed – 1895.
(Christie's S. Kensington) $115 £55

ART AT AUCTION
3 vols. – various – orig. cloth – dust jackets 1967-72.
(Christie's S. Kensington) $30 £15

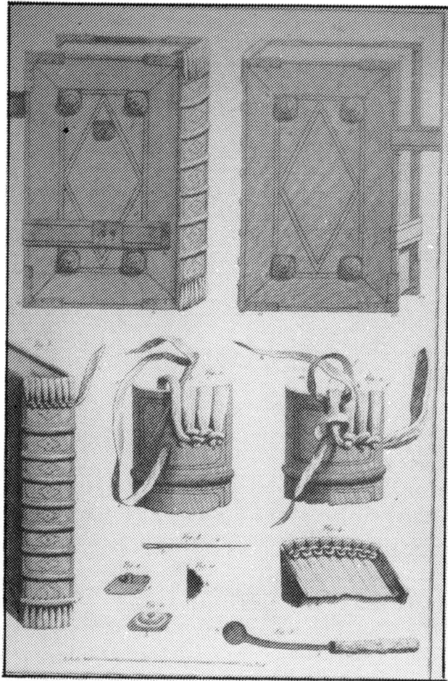

ART DE FAIRE LE PAPIER
14 engr. plates – one folding – Art Du Cartonnier; Art du Cartier; L'Art du Relieur d'Oreur de Livres; L. Art de L'Indigothier. L'Art du Plombier et Fontainier' – all with engraved plates – 6 parts in one vol. – 1762-73.
(Christie's) $4,830 £2,300

ART JOURNAL, THE
Plates and illus. – 8 vols. – half calf worn – 4to. – 1849, 1852, 1854, 1857-59, 1862.
(Bonhams) $460 £220

L'ART DE LA MODE
2 vol – plates – hand col. – orig. cloth – soiled – folio – Paris 1881.
(Sotheby's) $125 £60

ART PRICES CURRENT
Vol. 1-4 series, vol 16, 24-28, 30-40, 42, 44, 45, together 24 vols. only – orig. cloth – rubbed – 8vo – 1908-69
(Sotheby's) $65 £30

L'ART DE VOYAGER DANS LES AIRS OU LES BALLONS
lacks plates – orig. wrappers – rebacked – uncut – 8vo. – Paris 1784.
(Sotheby's) $115 £55

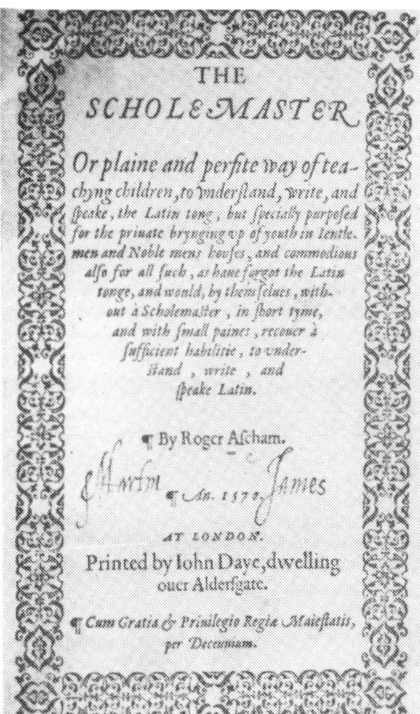

THE
SCHOLEMASTER.
Or plaine and perfite way of teachyng children, to vnderstand, write, and speake, the Latin tong, but specially purposed for the priuate brynging vp of youth in Ientlemen and Noble mens houses, and commodious also for all such, as haue forgot the Latin tonge, and would, by themselues, without a Scholemaster, in short tyme, and with small paines, recouer a sufficient habilitie, to vnderstand, write, and speake Latin.
By Roger Ascham.
An. 1570.
AT LONDON.
Printed by Iohn Daye, dwelling ouer Aldersgate.
Cum Gratia & Priuilegio Regiæ Maiestatis, per Decennium.

ASCHAM, ROGER
'The Scholemaster' – 1st Edn., 1570; 'Report and Discourse' 1st Edn.; 'Demosthenes' 1st Edn. 1570 – three works in one vol. – contem. calf rebacked, sm 4to.
(Christie's) $4,200 £2,00

ASHBEE, C. R.
'The Masque of the Edwards of England' – one of 300 copies – 18 coloured plates – orig. cloth – soiled – oblong folio – Essex House Press, 1902.
(Sotheby's) $40 £20

ASHENDENE PRESS – CERVANTES
'The History of the Valourous and Wittie Knight Errant Don Quixote de la Mancha' – 2 vols. – one of 225 copies on paper – translated from Spanish by Thomas Shelton – text in red and black – woodcut borders and initials after Louise Power – orig. white vellum – uncut – folio – Ashendene Press, 1927.
(Sotheby Beresford Adams) $800 £380

ASHENDENE PRESS ..... DESCRIPTIVE BIBLIOGRAPHY OF BOOKS PRINTED AT THE, 1895-1935
No. 278 of 390 copies signed by C. H. ST J. Hornby – presentation copy for Eric Millar – orig. calf – upper cover with gilt device – spine faded – rubbed – t.e.g. – A.L.s. from Hornby to Millar inserted – folio – 1935.
(Sotheby's) $1,090 £520

ASHLEY, KENNETH
'Up Hill and Down Dale' – Poems – very good partially unopened copy in dust jacket – 1924.
(J. Ash) $6 £3

ASHTON, SIR LEIGH
'The Art of India and Pakistan' – plates – some col. and mounted – orig. cloth – dust jacket – 4to. – 1950.
(Sotheby's) $30 £15

ASPIN, J.
'Cosmorama, a View of the Costumes and Peculiarities of all Nations' – 1st Edn. 18 engraved plates – later roan gilt – g.e. – 12 mo – J. Harris 1827.
(Sotheby's) $180 £85

ASSIETTE DU BEURRE, L'
Nos. 1 to 40 bound in one vol. – illus. – quarter morocco – 4to. – April 1901 – January 1902.
(Phillips) $755 £360

ASSOCIATION FOR PROMOTING THE DISCOVERY OF THE INTERIOR PARTS OF AFRICA
Proceedings – folding engraved map – orig. boards – rebacked – worn – uncut – 4to. – 1790.
(Sotheby's) $85 £40

ASTELL, M.
'Essay in Defence of the Female Sex' – frontis – bound in calf – 1696.
(Phillips) $190 £90

ASTLE, T.
'The Origin and Progress of Writing' – large paper copy – plates – contem. half morocco, rubbed – folio 1876.
(Sotheby's) $100 £48

ASTLEY, THOMAS
'A New General Collection of Voyages and Travels' – vol. 1-3 only – engraved plates and maps – contemporary calf, rubbed, joints cracked – 4to. – 1745-6.
(Christie's S. Kensington) $210 £100

ATKINSON, JAMES
'Epitome of the Art of Navigation' – editor William Mountaine – 10 folding engraved plates, wormed – contem. sheep, slightly worn, joints weak – 8vo. – 1744.
(Sotheby's) $95 £45

ATKINSON, JAMES
'Sketches In Afghaunistan' – uncoloured lithographed title and 25 plates – soiling and staining, a few marginal tears – one leaf of letterpress – orig. morocco backed cloth, worn and disbound – folio – 1842.
(Christie's S. Kensington) $150 £70

ATKYNS, ROBERT
'The Ancient and Present State of Gloustershire' – 2nd Edn. – folding engraved map – 72 engraved plates, mostly folding – contem. calf – gilt arms – folio – 1768.
(Christie's) $800 £380

ATLAS DE LA MONARCHIE PRUSSIENNE
10 engraved double page maps by Tardieu – 93 engraved plates – 5 double page – some folding tables – half title – contem. half calf – folio – A Londres 1788.
(Sotheby's) $400 £190

ATMOSPHERIC RAILWAYS
Report from the Select Committee – disbound – folio 1845.
(Sotheby's) $275 £130

AUDEBERT, JEAN BAPTISTE
'Histoire Naturelle des Singes et Des Makis' – 1st Edn. – 62 of 63 plates, includ. 60 in colour finished by hand – cont. diced russia – gilt borders on sides, rubbed, joints cracked – folio – Paris, 1798-99.
(Christie's) $2,520 £1,200

AUDEN, W. H.
'Another Time' – 1st Eng. Edn. – dust wrapper with small hole – 1940.
(J. Ash) $40 £20

George Washington Hotel
Twenty-Third Street and Lexington Avenue
New York City, N. Y.

Ode

In this epoch of high-pressure selling
When the salesmen give us no rest,
And even Governments are yelling
'Our Brand is Better than Best.'
When the hoardings announce a new diet
To take all our odor away,
Or a medicine to keep the kids quiet,
Or a belt that will give us S.A.,
Or a soap to wash shirts in a minute,
One wonders at times, I'm afraid
If there is one word of truth in it,
And how much the writers were paid

Auto mss of his 'Ode to the George Washington Hotel' comprising 60 lines with 2 revisions signed and inscribed to the Manager and all staff – written on headed notepaper – 5 pages – octavo and small quarto.
(Sotheby's) $1,155 £550

Cecil Beaton
with best wishes
from
Wystan Auden

AUDEN, W. H. AND GARRETT, JOHN (Editors)
'The Poet's Tongue' – 2 vol. in one – trade issue – press copy – inscribed to Cecil Beaton – orig. cloth – 8vo. – 1935.
(Sotheby's) $135 £65

Auden's The Dance of Death 10

D. Honestly, Sir Edward, I couldn't. He's in a most critical condition. Any exertion now might be fatal.

Sir E. Couldn't you give him an injection or something? I've a friend with me who would be most annoyed if the performance were to come to an end now. I don't know what I shall say to him. You must do something. I know that he'd see that your position was secure if anything unfortunate happens.

D. Who is he?

Sir E. 'Sh not so loud. (*Whispers in doctor's ear.*) As a matter of fact he is very anxious to meet you. Come and have supper with us when the show's over.

D. Very well, but I don't like it. I'll give him an injection [*Turning to actors.*] Listen. I've decided to let him go on

Chorus. O thank you, doctor.

D. But mind. There's to be no excitement of any kind—no politics, for instance, something quite peaceful, something, shall we say, about the country or home life?

Chorus. We understand.

D. After you, Sir Edward.

Sir E. After *you* doctor.

[*Exeunt to audience.*]

A. Very well, fellows, what shall we do?

x. Oh, go and drown yourselves.

B. Be true
To the inner self. Retire to a wood
The will of the blood is the only good
We must learn to know it.

A. I see what you mean
We must keep our primal integrity clean.

B. Exactly.

C. That's clear.
What a good idea.

AUDEN, W. H.
'The Dance of Death' – Galley proofs for 1st Edn. – number of auto corrections – revisions in pencil by author – other markings – unbound – 1933.
(Sotheby's) $715 £340

AUDSLEY, GEORGE ASHDOWN
'The Ornamental Arts of Japan' – 2vols. – col plates – illus – contem. half morocco – gilt spines, rubbed – g.e. – folio – 1882.
(Sotheby's) $440 £210

AUDSLEY, G. A. AND M. A.
'The Practical Decorator and Ornamentist' – col plates – parts 1-15 – origl. wrappers – n.d.
(Bonhams) $115 £55

AUDSLEY, GEORGE ASHDOWN AND JAMES, LORD BOWES
'Keramic Art of Japan' – 2 vols. – chromo-lithographed plates – contem. morocco – gilt, rubbed, joints weak – folio – 1875.
(Sotheby's) $400 £190

AUDUBON JOHN JAMES
'Ornithological Biography or an account of the Habits of the Birds of the United States' – vol. 1 to 111 only of five – calf gilt – bookplate of Thomas Carnegie of Craigo – 8vo. – Edinburgh 1831-35.
(Sotheby's) $25 £12

AULT, LENA
A collection of 22 watercolour drawings for Christmas cards including 2 of a lady in a sedan chair and 10 printed cards from similar designs by Lena Ault – various sizes.
(Sotheby's) $285 £135

AUNT LOUISA'S KEEPSAKE
4 separately published works in one vol, each with 6 col. plates – orig. cloth gilt – 4to – Warne circa 1870.
(Sotheby's) $20 £10

AUSTEN, JANE
'The Novels' – 5 vols. with 'Lady Susan'; 'Fragment of a Novel'; two chapters of 'Persuasion'; 'Letters', together 13 vols. – original cloth backed boards – 8vo. – 1923-51.
(Sotheby's) $505 £240

THE INQUIRER,
A WESTERN AUSTRALIAN JOURNAL
OF POLITICS AND LITERATURE.

AUSTRALIA
Copy of 'The Inquirer' A Western Australian journal of politics and literature – number 19 – 9 Dec. 1840 – 4 pages – folio.
(Sotheby's) $170 £80

AYERS, JOHN
'The Baur Collection; Chinese Ceramics' – 4 vols – limited Edn. – plates – some col. – orig. cloth – dust jackets – slip cases – 4to. – Geneva 1968-74.
(Sotheby's) $1,575 £750

AYLOFFE, SIR JOSEPH
'Calendars of the Ancient Charters' – four plates, one torn, some spotting – later half morocco, rubbed – t.e.g. – 1774.
(Christie's) $30 £15

AYME, J. J.
'Deportation et Naufrage ....' – calf, worn – 8vo. – Paris 1800.
(Phillips) $40 £20

AYRE, W.
'Memoire of the Life and Writings of A. Pope' 1st Edn. – 2 vols. – 14 ports. – calf gilt – 1745.
(Phillips) $100 £48

AYROUARD, J.
'Plan de la Baye de Ville Franche' – uncol. sea-chart – circa 1732.
(Phillips) $90 £42
Sea Charts Toulon and Antibes – 2 uncoloured – circa 1740.
(Phillips) $85 £40

AZAREVICH, VALENTIN
'Serdtse Zaplate' (Heart in Patches) – duplicated typescript – orig. wrappers, frayed, loose – 8vo. – St. Petersburg 1920.
(Sotheby's) $275 £130

BABBAGE, CHARLES
'The Ninth Bridgewater Treatise' – 1st Edn. – cloth – tear in spine – 1837.
(Phillips) $55 £25
'A Comparative View of the Various Institutions for the Assurance of Lives' – 1st Edn. – folding table – cont. calf – rubbed – 8vo – 1826.
(Sotheby's) $295 £140

BABELON, J. AND LAFAURIE, J.
'Congres International de Numismatique 1953' – 2 vols. – plates – orig. wrappers – 8vo – Paris 1953-57.
(Sotheby's) $180 £85

BABES IN THE WOOD
A series of five watercolour drawings including some of the robbers portrayed as dogs – 75 x 75mm. and 123 x 95mm. – circa 1880.
(Sotheby's) $125 $60

BACH, CARL PHILIPP EMANUEL
Fine auto letter signed about the publication of his vocal works – 1 page quarto to his friend and publisher Breitkopf – Hamburg July 1788.
(Sotheby's) $15,120 £7,200

BACK, GEORGE
'Narrative of the Arctic Land Expedition' – engraved folding map – 16 engraved plates by E. Finden – cont. embossed cloth – 4to – 1836.
(Christie's) $525 £250

BACON, SIR FRANCIS
'Sylva Sylvarum of a Naturall Historie' – 1st Edn. – 2nd issue – woodcut initials and ornaments – cont. calf – spine torn – folio – J. H. for William Lee 1627.
(Sotheby's) $105 £50

BADESLADE, THOMAS
'The History of the Ancient and Present State of the Navigation of the Port of King's Lyn and of Cambridge' – 1st Edn. – engraved maps and plans, some folding and coloured – cont. calf – worn – folio – 1725.
(Sotheby's) $420 £200
'Chorographia Britanniae' – engraved title – dedication and 51 maps and tables, slightly browned, one spotted – calf – worn – joints cracked – boards almost detached – 1742.
(Christie's S. Kensington) $630 £300

BAGLIVUS, G.
'Opera Omnia' – port – plates – old calf gilt – sm. 4to – Lugdun 1714.
(Phillips) $75 £35

BAILEY, T.
'Annals of Nottinghamshire' – 3 vols. – folding map – illus. – half calf gilt – 1853.
(Phillips) $75 £35

BAINES, EDWARD
'Yorkshire Past and Present' – 2 vols. only – divs. I and IV.
(Baitson, Hull) $10 £5
'History of the County Palatine and Duchy of Lancaster' – 4 vols. – engraved double page map, hand coloured in outline – engraved plates and plans – minor defects – later half morocco – rubbed – 4to – 1836.
(Sotheby Beresford Adams) $335 £160

BAINES, THOMAS
'The Gold Regions of South Eastern Africa' – 1st Edn. – 4 photographic plates, including portrait – illus. in text – map in pocket – orig. pictorial cloth – 8vo – 1877.
(Sotheby's) $160 £70
'Yorkshire Past and Present' – 4 vols. – engraved plates – orig. cloth – gilt – spines faded and frayed – g.e. – 4to – n.d.
(Christie's S. Kensington) $60 £28
'History of Liverpool' – 3 folding maps and engraved plate – morocco gilt – 1852.
(Richard Baker & Thomson) $95 £45

BAINES, THOMAS AND FAIRBAIRN, WM.
'Lancashire and Cheshire Past and Present' – 2 vols. in 4 – 2 engraved titles – numerous engraved portraits and plates – a few leaves spotted – orig. cloth gilt – 4to – n.d.
(Sotheby Beresford Adams) $30 £14

BAKER, D. E.
'The Companion to the Play-House' – 2 vols. – 12 mo. – cont. half calf – rebacked – 1764.
(Christie's S. Kensington) $105 £50

BAKER, E. C. STUART
'Indian Ducks and Their Allies' – coloured plates – half morocco gilt – t.e.g. – 1908.
(Phillips) $295 £140
'The Game Birds of India, Burma and Ceylon' – vol. 1 only – 2nd Edn. – addit. title and 33 plates – later half morocco – slightly soiled – t.e.g. – 1921.
(Phillips) $45 £22

BAKER, EZEKIEL
'Remarks on Rifle Guns' – 9th Edn. – 11 engraved plates and tables – 6 hand coloured – spotted – cont. half morocco – rubbed – soiled – 1825.
(Christie's S. Kensington) $135 £65

BAKER, GEORGE
'The History and Antiquities of the County of Northampton' – 5 parts in 2 vols. – 2 engraved frontis plates – 1 hand coloured – 1 hand col. litho plate and 36 engraved plates after Edward Blore – cont. blue morocco – gilt spines – t.e.g. by Zaehnsdorf – folio – 1822-30.
(Christie's) $630 £300

BAKER, HENRY
'An Attempt towards a Natural History of the Polype in a Letter to Martin Folkes' – 1 plate – illus. in text. – cont. calf – upper cover loose – bookplate of Earl Stanhope – 8vo – R. Dodsley 1743.
(Sotheby's) $75 £35

BAKER, OLIVER
'Black Jacks and Leather Bottles' – numbered 421 – signed by author – presentation inscription – col. frontis – plates – illus. – orig. buckram – rubbed – large 4to – n.d.
(Christie's) $55 £25

BAKER, SIR RICHARD
'A Chronicle of the Kings of England' – addit. engraved title – browning and soiling – cont. calf – worn – folio – 1670.
(Sotheby's) $85 £40

BAKER, S.
'Ismailia, A Narrative of the Expedition to Central Africa . . .' – 2 vols. – 2 maps and 53 woodcut illustrations – cloth gilt – 1st Edn. – head and tail vol. 2 snagged, shaken – 1874.
(Bennett Book Auctions) $75 £35

BAKEWELL, R.
'Travels in the Tarentaise and Various Parts of the Grecian and Pennine Alps' – 2 vols. in one – 4 hand col. plates – cont. calf, worn – 8vo – 1823.
(Sotheby's) $200 £95

BALANY, JAMES COCKBURN
'A Treatise upon Falconry' – lacks frontis – some spotting – orig. cloth – spine faded – uncut – 8vo – Berwick upon Tweed 1841.
(Sotheby's) $85 £40

BALESE, W. C.
'Naemia Cornubiae' – 1st Edn. – orig. cloth binding – 1872.
(Lane) $74 £35

BALLON, VIEW OF LONDON
Folding lithographed map – slightly soiled – some tears – orig. board wrappers – rubbed – 62 x 106cm. – 1851.
(Sotheby's) $295 £140

BALOG, P.
'The Coinage of the Mamluk Sultans of Egypt and Syria' – plates – orig. wrappers – 8vo – New York 1964.
(Sotheby's) $360 £170

BALNEIL, LORD AND CLARK, K.
'Commemorative Catalogue of the Exhibition of Italian Art . . . Royal Academy . . . 1930' – 2 vols. including one of plates – cloth – folio – 1931.
(Phillips) $40 £18

BANK OF ENGLAND AND THE SOUTH SEA COMPANY
A collection of 59 Acts of Parliament – some browned or soiled – all disbound – folio – 1697-1820.
(Sotheby's) $420 £200

BANKES, THOMAS
'A New, Royal Authentic and Complete System of Universal Geography' – 2 vols. – 109 engraved plates – morocco gilt – rubbed – folio – 1790.
(Phillips) $860 £410

BANKS – G. LINNAEUS (Editor)
'Blondin: His Life and Performances' – wood engraved portrait and 15 plates – cont. calf – spine worn – 1862.
(Christie's S.
Kensington) $80 £38

BANNERMAN, D. A.
'Birds of West and Equatorial Africa' – 2 vols. illus. – cloth – d.w. ex libris – 1953.
(Phillips) $100 £50

BANNERMAN, HELEN
'Sambo and the Twins' – 1st Edn. – presentation copy, inscribed by author – col. illus. – orig. cloth – dust jacket – 16 mo – New York 1936.
(Sotheby's) $285 £135

BANNET, IVOR
'The Amazons' – limited to 500 copies – this number 31 of 80 signed by author and artist – spec. bound by Sangorski and Sutcliffe – sm. folio – 1948.
(Christie's) $230 £110

BANNISTER, JOHN
'A Glossary of Cornish Names' – 1st Edn. – newly rebound in half morocco – 1871.
(Lane) $50 £25

BANVILLE, THEODORE DE
'Les Princesses' – number 18 of the first 130 copies sur papier du Japon – engravings by Decisy in 3 states with an original watercolour drawing by Rochegrosse at the beginning – brown morocco by Flammarion – silk doublures – orig. wrappers – slipcase – 4to – Paris, Ferroud, 1904.
(Sotheby Parke Bernet
Monaco) $1,115 £530

BAR, JACQUES CHARLES
'Receuil des Tous les Costumes des Ordres Reliqieux et Militaires' – 5 vols. – engraved titles – hand col. engraved frontis – 450 hand col. engraved plates by Bar – cont. calf – sides gilt and tooled – uncut and rubbed – folio – Paris chez l'auteur 1778-85.
(Christie's) $1,785 £850

BARBA, ALBARO ALONSO AND OTHERS
'A Collection of Scarce and Valuable Treatises upon Metals, Mines and Minerals' – 2nd Edn. – frontis – new quarter morocco – 12 mo – J. Hodges 1740.
(Sotheby's) $126 £60

BARBER, JOHN W. AND HOWE, HENRY
'Historical Collections of the State of New York' – engraved frontis and 17 plates – illus. – soiling – a few leaves torn without loss – cont. calf – rubbed – spine chipped – ex-library copy – New York 1842.
(Christie's S. Kensington) $40 £20

BARBER, THOMAS
'Picturesque Illustrations of the Isle of Wight' – engraved vignette title – 40 plates – cloth – spine missing – covers detached – 8vo – 1845.
(Sotheby's) $55 £25

BARBIER, GEORGE
'Almanach des Modes Presentes, Passes et Futures pour 1925' – vignette on title – 12 plates and cover design by Barbier – coloured through stencils – unsewn in orig. wrappers – uncut – 8vo – Paris, Jules Meynial 1924.
(Sotheby's) $115 £55

BARBIER, GEORGE – GAUTIER, THEOPHILE
'Le Roman de Momie' – coloured woodcut frontis – title – 31 illus. – 2 ornamental letters – wrappers by Gasparini after Barbier – 2 plates loose – cont. red half morocco – t.e.g. – orig. wrappers bound in – 4to – Paris, A. and G. Mornay, 1929.
(Sotheby's) $7,350 £3,500

BARBIER, GEORGE – REGNIER, HENRI DE
'Les Rencontres de Monsieur de Breot' – 34 illus. – 10 pictorial initials and cover design by Barbier – all coloured through stencils – orig. wrappers bound in – t.e.g. – sm. 4to – A. and G. Mornay, Paris, 1930.
(Sotheby's) $105 £50

BARBOZA DU BOCAGE, J. V.
'Ornithologie d'Angola' – 10 col. litho plates – half calf gilt – orig. wrappers bound in – Lisbonne 1881.
(Phillips) $420 £200

BARBUT, JAMES
'Genera Vermium Exemplified by Various Specimens of Animals' – engraved title – 11 hand col. plates – mottled calf – gilt – 4to – 1783.
(Phillips) $275 £130

BARETTI, J.
'Journey from London to Genoa' – 4 vols. – calf – gilt – 1770.
(Phillips) $100 £50

BARHAM, R. H.
'Ingoldsby Legends' – illus. by Rackham – orig. cloth – gilt – 4to – 1907.
(Phillips) $65 £30

NO FEEBLE DREAM

No feeble dream is as good as to act
Vigorously across pellucid air:
Elude the illusion of the aspiration
But violently keep on the move, your direction
Directs the deviation, Bethlehem star.

Saps away courage the dream
Like semen, breeding nought but fear;
How frail dreams are, how liable
Of callous destruction, proceed carefully
Tread with caution, anaemic feeble people.

But your hind legs support a bare trunk
Born to own its area of earth:
The flickering limbs perform actual breathless tricks;
Their fever to act than dreams
Desires, aspirations, is more worth.

Lines 9&10:

Of callous destruction, travel towards with care,
Tread cautiously, the anaemic feeble regions

BARKER, GEORGE
'Poems' – page proofs for 1st Edn. – extensive auto corrections and revisions by author, including rewritten acknowledgements, many revised and rewritten lines, with a set of revised proofs with new corrections – unbound – 8vo – 1935.
(Sotheby's) $360 £170

BARLOW, T.
'The Gunpowder Treason' – spotting – cont. calf – worn – 8vo – by Thos. Newcomb and Hills 1679.
(Sotheby's) $115 £55

BARNES, JOSHUA
'The History of Edward III' – 1st Edn. – title in red and black – 3 ports. – browning and soiling – cont. calf – worn – folio – Cambridge 1688.
(Sotheby's) $40 £20

BARNUM, PHINEAS T.
'Struggles and Triumphs or Sixty Years Recollections' – signed – plates – morocco gilt with author's name in gilt on upper cover. Included in the lot were 4 als with original envelopes, 2 signed photos and a pass to the Royal Box, Olympia.
(Phillips) $250 £120

BARON, R. A.
'Fruits from the Garden and Field' – illuminated by Owen Jones – orig. stamped calf – back stained – 1850.
(Bonhams) $65 £30

BAROZZIO DA VIGNOLA, GIACOMO
'Riegle des Cing Orders d'Architecture' – engraved title and 42 engraved plates – explanations in French – damp stained – soiled – ownership inscription dated 1727 – cont. calf – worn – folio – Amsterdam circa 1690.
(Sotheby's) $230 £110

BARRATT, THOMAS J.
'The Annals of Hampstead' – 3 vols. – limited to 550 copies signed by author, 1912 – 66 plates, some coloured, some mounted – six folding maps, some coloured – illustrations – orig. cloth – soiled – g.e.
(Christie's S. Kensington) $135 £65

BARRAUD, C. D. AND TRAVERS, W. T. L.
'New Zealand, Graphic and Descriptive' – limited facsimile edn. – col. title and plates – prospectus loosely inserted – orig. half morocco – gilt – folio – Christchurch, New Zealand 1973.
(Sotheby's) $80 £40

BARRIE, J. M.
'Novels, Tales and Sketches' – 8 vols. – half parchment – limited edition – 76/159 copies – author signed – New York and London – 1896.
(Bennett Book Auctions) $115 £55

BARRINGTON, GEORGE
'A Voyage to New South Wales' – modern quarter calf – gilt – London 1795.
(Phillips) $295 £140

BARRON, A.
'Shires and Provinces' – coloured plates and illus. by L. Edwards – orig. cloth – rubbed – folio – 1926.
(Sotheby's) $180 £85

BARROW, J.
'Account of Travels into the Interior of Southern Africa' – folding map – calf – gilt – rebacked 4to – 1801.
(Phillips) $230 £110

BARROW, JOHN
'A Visit to Ireland by Way of Tronyen' – engraved title and plates – slight spotting – orig. cloth – spine faded and slightly torn – 1835.
(Christie's S. Kensington) $75 £35

BARRY, MARTIN
'Ascent to the Summit of Mont Blanc' – 2 litho plates on india paper – inscribed by author – orig. boards – soiled – 8vo – 1823.
(Sotheby's) $275 £130

BARSTOW, STAN
'A Kind of Loving' – slight marks – otherwise good in dust wrapper – 1960.
(J. Ash) $20 £10

BARTH, HENRY
'Travels and Discoveries in North and Central Africa' – 5 vols. – 60 litho plates – 2 loose – 15 folding maps – illus. – browning – orig. cloth – rubbed – 8vo – 1857-58.
(Sotheby's) $525 £250

BARTHOLINUS, THOMAS
'Anatome' – engraved addit. title – portrait – folding plates and illus. – few with tears – one repaired – some marginal soiling – cont. calf – rubbed – joints cracked – Leiden ex Officana Hackiana, 1673.
(Christie's S. Kensington) $210 £100

BARTLETT, W. H. – BEATTIE, WILLIAM
'Switzerland' – 2 vols. – 4to. – George Virtue, 1836 – engraved addit. titles – 106 plates after Bartlett – 1 folding map – some spotting – cont. morocco backed roan – rubbed spines worn and torn with loss – g.e.
(Christie's S. Kensington) $545 £260

BARTOLOZZI, FRANCESCO
'Seventy Three Prints from the Original Pictures and Drawings in the Collection of His Majesty' – 72 engraved plates, portraits and views, majority in sepia by Bartolozzi, Gandolfi, Du Bosc and others – occasional spotting – title and some leaves detached – cont. half russia – upper cover detached – very worn – folio – J. and J. Boydell, circa 1800.
(Sotheby's) $1,785 £850

BARTSCH, A.
'Le Peintre Graveur' – 23 vols. including Supplement and Atlas of plates – engraved plates – spotted – cont. vellum – atlas in half vellum soiled – 8vo and 4to – Vienna, 1803-43.
(Sotheby's) $735 £350

BASAN, P. F.
'Recueil d'Estampes Gravees d'apres les tableaux du cabinet de Monseigneur le Duc de Choiseul' – engraved title – dedication – portrait – table on contents and 124 plates only – margins shaved – browning, spotting, mainly marginal – half morocco – rubbed – 4to – Paris, 1771.
(Christie's S. Kensington) $800 £380

BASNAGE, JACQUES
'Histoire des Juifs' – 15 vols. – titles in red and black – cont. vellum – 1716.
(Phillips) $145 £70

BASS, SABTAI
'Siftei Yesheinim' – First Hebrew Bibliography title within engraved columns – some titles underlined in red – signed – browned – Amsterdam 1680.
(Sotheby's) $545 £260

BASTELAER, RENE VAN
'Les Estampes de Peter Breugel L'Ancien' – plates – later half cloth – rubbed – 4to – Brussels, 1908.
(Sotheby's) $145 £70

BASTILLE, ORDER OF RELEASE BY LOUIS XV, 29 August 1722
(Contemporary note in corner records paper taken from Bastille when it was captured by revolutionaries c1789) – some notes and 5 prints all relating to the Bastille.
(Bennett Book Auctions) $45 £22

BATE, PERCY
'English Table Glass' – plates – orig. cloth – 1913.
(Christie's) $25 £12

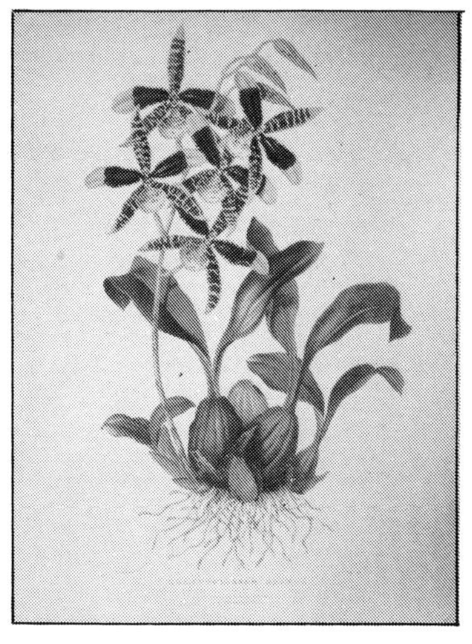

BATEMAN, JAMES
'The Orchidaceae of Mexico and Guatemala' – litho title – soiled and frayed – 40 hand col. plates after Miss Drake, Miss Jane Edwards and others – vignettes in text by Lady Jane Walsh, Lady Grey of Groby and others – half morocco – very worn – covers detached – elephant folio – Printed for the author 1837.
(Christie's) $10,920 £5,200

BATES, H. E.
'A Love of Flowers' – illus. by Pauline Ellison – very good in slightly rubbed dust jacket – 1971.
(J. Ash) $8 £4
'The Last Bread' – the author's first book orig. wrappers – very good – 1926.
(J. Ash) $60 $28

BATES, RALPH
'Sierra' – the author's first book – very good in slightly rubbed and browned dust wrapper – 1933.
(J. Ash) $17 £8

BATESON, F. W. (editor)
'The Cambridge Bibliography of English Literature. Vol. III' – large 8vo – Cambridge 1940.
(J. Ash) $30 £15

BATTERSBY, MARTIN
'The Decorative Thirties' – illus. – 1971.
(Baitson) $4 £2

BATTLE'S HULL DIRECTORY
to which is added a Directory for Beverley.
(Baitson) $55 £25

BAWDEN, EDWARD (illustrator)
'Review of Reviews and Other Matters' – other illustrators include William Nicholson – nice copy – 1930.
(J. Ash) $8 £4

BAXTER, G.
'The Pictorial Album or Cabinet of Paintings' – 3 copies – col. title and 10 plates – some spotted and loose – orig. morocco – rubbed – 8vo – 1837.
(Sotheby's) $440 £210

BAXTER, W.
'British Phaenogamous Plants' – vols. 1, 2, 3 and 6, 4 vols. – 336 hand col. plates – half morocco, worn – 1834-37.
(Phillips) $485 £230

BAYEUX TAPESTRY
17 hand col. plates by J. Basire from Society of Antiquaries of London – vol. VI – modern cloth – gilt – large oblong folio – plates dated 1819-23.
(Phillips) $95 £45

BAYLE, P. AND BARRIN, J.
'Nouvelles de la Republique des Lettres' – 40 vols. – engravings – some folding – cont. calf – Amsterdam 1684-1718.
(Phillips) $200 £95

BAYLY
'Collection of Anthems' – cont. English binding of red morocco, gilt with crowned cipher of Chapel Royal at St. James – 8vo – 1769.
(Moore Allen & Innocent) $250 £120

BAYLY, T. H.
'Flowers of Loveliness' – 12 plates – cloth gilt – 4to – Ackermann 1837.
(Phillips) $40 £18

BEACONSFIELD, EARL OF
'An Appreciative Life Of The Earl Of Beaconsfield' – 7 vols. – 27 actual photographs laid in – 1881.
(Baitson) $8 £4

BEAMISH, N. LUDLOW
'History of the German Legion' – 10 maps and plans, 9 hand coloured plates of military uniforms – half calf – 1832-37.
(Phillips) $230 £110

BEARD, C. R.
'Catalogue of the Collection of Martinware formed by Mr. Frederick John Nettlefold' – some plates coloured – cloth – gilt – s.c. – folio – 1936.
(Phillips) $420 £200

BEARDSLEY, AUBREY AND HICKES, FRANCIS (translator)
'Lucian's True History' – number 50 of 500 copies – plates by Beardsley and others – cont. blue half calf – by Sangorski and Sutcliffe – spine faded – t.e.g. – sm. 4to – 1902.
(Christie's S. Kensington) $40 £20

BEATLES, THE
Als. by Paul McCartney, 4 pages, 4 to Virgin Islands n.d. to 'Dad and Mike' about his and Jane Asher's holiday etc. – Virgin Islands.
(Sotheby's) $180 £85

Fine photograph signed by all four – 10 x 8in.
(Sotheby's) $335 £160

BEATON, CECIL
Project for the design of Nureyev's costume as Armand – brown wash heightened with white gouache – signed – 28.5 x 21.2cm.
(Sotheby's) $1,050 £500

BEATTIE, WILLIAM
'The Ports, Harbours, Watering-Places And Coast Scenery of Great Britain' – 2 vols. – two steel-engraved additional titles and 123 plates after W. H. Bartlett, only (of 124) spotting – cont. half calf – worn – 4to – George Virtue – 1842.
(Christie's S. Kensington) $505 £240

'The Bosphorous and the Danube' – 3 parts only – engraved title-vignette – slightly soiled – about 60 plates after W. H. Bartlett – two maps – orig. cloth – slightly faded – g.e. – 4to – n.d.
(Christie's S. Kensington) $115 £55

'Scotland' – 118 plates and folding map – morocco gilt – 4to – 1838.
(Laurence & Martin Taylor) $135 £65

BEAUCLERK, CAPTAIN G.
'A Journey to Morocco in 1826' – 8 litho plates on india paper – wanting 2 plates – cont. half calf – morocco label – joints rubbed – 8vo – 1828.
(Sotheby's) $25 £12

BEAUMONT, CYRIL (translator and printer)
'Orchesography', by Thoinot Arbeau – cont. levant by Fox – g.e. – boxed.
(Christie's S. Kensington) $60 £30
'Ballet Design Past and Present' – illus. – some coloured – orig. cloth – dust jacket – 4to – 1940.
(Christie's S. Kensington) $30 £15

BEAUMONT, CYRIL W. AND SITWELL, SACHEVERELL
'The Romantic Ballet' – plates, some coloured – orig. cloth – dust jacket – 8vo – 1938.
(Sotheby's) $250 £120

BEAUMONT, FRANCIS AND FLETCHER, JOHN
'Comedies and Tragedies' – 1st collected Edn. – double columns – browned and soiled – lacks portrait – some leaves repaired – 19th century red half morocco, worn – upper cover and title detached – folio – For Humphrey Robinson and Humphrey Moseley 1647.
(Sotheby's) $105 £50

BEAUTIES OF THE BRITISH SENATE
2 vols. – calf backed boards – 1786.
(Phillips) $40 £20

BEAUTIES OF NATURE AND ART DISPLAYED – 14 vols. – plates and maps – calf – gilt – 12 mo – 1763-4.
(Phillips) $135 £65

BEAUTIFUL BIRDS
3 vols. – 36 hand coloured lithographed plates – a few detached – orig. cloth – slightly dampstained – g.e.
(Christie's) $135 £65

BEAUVILLIERS, A.
'L'Art du Cuisinier' – 2 vols. in one – 1st Edn. signed by author – 9 folding plates – some spotted – half sheep – 8vo – Paris 1814.
(Phillips) $335 £160

BECHSTEIN, J. M.
'Cage and Chamber Birds' – 31 hand coloured plates – illus. – orig. cloth – spine slightly chipped – 1853.
(Christie's) $160 £75

BECKFORD LIBRARY – Fonthill Abbey Sale catalogue – cont. half morocco – rebacked – 8vo – 1823.
(Sotheby's) $210 £100

BECKFORD, W.
'A Descriptive Account of the Island of Jamaica' – 2 vols. – lacks half title – cont. calf – rubbed – 8vo – 1790.
(Sotheby's) $400 £190
'Italy, with Sketches of Spain and Portugal' – 2 vols. – 1st Edn. – engraved plate tipped in – offset – cont. half calf – rubbed – one label missing – 8vo – 1834.
(Sotheby's) $115 £55

BECKMAN, J.
'History of Inventions and Discoveries' – 3rd Edn. – 4 vols. – half calf – 8vo – 1817.
(Irelands) $105 £50

BECON, THOMAS
'The Works' – 2 vols. in one – black letter – title in fine woodcut border – woodcut of author – cont. calf – very worn – folio – 1564-60.
(Sotheby's) $160 £75

BEDDOES, THOMAS
'Essay on the Causes, Early Signs and Prevention of Pulmonary Consumption' – 2nd Edn. – boards – calf spine – 8vo – Longman 1799.
(Sotheby's) $25 £12

BEDFORD, F. AND WARING, J. B. (editor)
'Art Treasures of the United Kingdom' – chromolith title – 100 plates by Bedford – some torn – spotting – cont. brown calf – rubbed – disbound – g.e. – folio – 1858.
(Christie's) $65 £30

BEDOUKIAN, P. Z.
'Coinage of Cilician Armenia' – plates – orig. wrappers – 8vo – New York 1962.
(Sotheby's) $115 £55

BEEBE, W.
'Pheasants, their Lives and Homes' – 2 vols. – signed Limited Edn. – plates many colour – uncut boards – gilt – t.e.g. – 1926.
(Phillips) $170 £80

BEERBOHM, MAX
'Observations' – 1st Edn. – col. plates – blue cloth – 4to – 1925.
(Phillips) $45 £22

BEETHOVEN, LUDWIG VAN
Example of his handwriting removed from a letter, 29 words, on a slip of paper 1 x 4½in.
(Sotheby's) $670 £320

BEETON, MRS. ISABELLA
'Household Management' and 'Everyday Cookery' – 1923.
(Laurence & Martin Taylor) $10 £5
'Book of Household Management' – 24 in 23 orig. parts. – col. title and 12 plates of 13 – illus. – spotting – orig. wrappers – torn and soiled – some loose – 8vo – 1859-61.
(Sotheby's) $190 £90

BEEVERELL, JAMES
'Les Delices de la Grande Bretagne et de L'Irelande' – 8 vols. in 9 – addit. double page engraved titles, titles in red and black – numerous double page engraved maps – plates by J. Foeree and others – some folding – cont. sprinkled calf – spines gilt – 8vo – Leiden 1707.
(Christie's) $840 £400

BEGGAR'S DAUGHTER OF BEDNALL GREEN, THE
Wood engraved frontis – 5 plates and tail-piece – printed throughout on india paper – dark green morocco – joints rubbed – t.e.g. – 8vo – Jennings and Chaplin 1832.
(Sotheby's) $40 £20

BELIDOR, B. F.
'Architecture Hydraulique' – vol. 2 only – engraved title – 55 plates – calf gilt – upper cover detached – Paris 1739.
(Phillips) $75 £35
'Architecture Hydraulique' –22 parts in 4 vols. – various edns. – 2 engraved frontis – 217 folding plates – cont. mottled calf – rubbed – joints split – 4to – Paris 1750-82.
(Sotheby's) $360 £170

BELL, MRS. A.
'Thomas Gainsborough' – plates – blue levant morocco by Bayntum – gilt – with miniature by F. Gassiez inlaid – 8 semi-precious stones inset – 1 loose – cloth box – 8vo – 1897.
(Sotheby's) $200 £95

BELL, SIR CHARLES
'Essays on the Anatomy of Expression in Painting' – 1st Edn. – large paper copy – 7 engraved plates – 25 engraved illus. – worn – contents loose or detached – uncut – 4to – 1806.
(Sotheby's) $125 £60

BELL, CLIVE
'An Account of French Painting' – 32 plates – front endpaper split, otherwise good – 1931.
(J. Ash) $8 £4

BELL, H. I. AND ROBERTS, C. H.
'Descriptive Catalogue of the Greek Papyri in the Collection of W. Merton' – 2 vols. – illus. – cloth – gilt – 4to – 1948.
(Phillips) $125 £60

BELL, J. (publisher)
'La Belle Assemblee or Bell's Court and Fashionable Magazine' – 4 vols. – various plates – some hand coloured fashion plates – some folding – spotting – cont. half calf – worn – 1809-13.
(Christie's S. Kensington) $190 £90

BELL, J.
'Travels from St. Petersburg in Russia to Various Parts of Asia' – 2 vols. – 2 folding maps – calf, gilt – 1788.
(Phillips) $135 £65

BELL, JOHN
'A Collection of Illustrations from Bell's Editions of British Theatre' – 4 vols. – 201 engraved plates – slight browning – late 18th century English red straight grained morocco – gilt – spines tooled – slightly rubbed – g.e. – bookplate of Wm. Douglas – 4to and 8vo – 1773-76.
(Sotheby's) $7,350 £3,500

BELL, T.
'The Ruins of Livenden' – Historical notes on the family of Trensham – 1848.
(Laurence & Martin Taylor) $10 £5

BELLASIS, GEORGE HUTCHINS
'Views of St. Helena' – 6 hand coloured aquatint plates – list of subscribers – buckram-backed wrappers – orig. printed label – folding half morocco case – oblong folio – 1815.
(Sotheby's) $735 £350

BELLE ASSEMBLEE, LA
New Series – vols. 1-12 – wood engraved titles by Austin, portraits– over 100 hand coloured fashion plates – minor defects – cont. tree calf – gilt – slightly rubbed – some covers detached – 8vo – 1810-15.
(Sotheby Beresford Adams) $335 £160
Vol. 10 only – 13 hand coloured fashion plates – half calf gilt – 1829.
(Phillips) $65 £30

BELLIN, N.
'New Chart of the Coast of New England, Nova Scotia etc.'– framed map hand coloured in outline – 2 framed road maps, 2 framed prints of bridges – Hampton Court & New Bridge, Sunderland, and another framed map.
(Bennett Book Auctions) $65 £30

BELLOC, HILAIRE
'Short Talks With The Dead' – 1st Edn. – 1926.
(Lane) $6 £3

BELOE, WILLIAM
'Anecdotes of Literature and Scarce Books' – 6 vols. – boxed edns. – spotting – cont. calf – worn and stained – bookplate of Holland House – 8vo – 1808-14.
(Sotheby's) $105 £50

BELSHAM, W.
'Memoirs of the Reign of George III' – 6 vols. bound in half calf – 1795.
(Lane) $34 £16

BELVEDERE
'A Journal for Collectors' – 1924-31 – 14 vols. only, in 12 – plates – cont. half cloth – rubbed – 4to.
(Sotheby's) $75 £35

BENDIRE, CHARLES
'Life Histories of North American Birds' – 2 vols. – col. litho plates of eggs – half calf gilt – 4to – Washington 1892-95.
(Phillips) $105 £50

BENEDICTUS, DAVID
'The Fourth of June' – Nice, in jacket – 1962.
(J. Ash) $13 £6

BENEDICTUS, EDOUARD
'Relais 1930' – 15 plates and cover design by Benedictus – coloured through stencils – loose – orig. cloth backed portfolio – ties – folio – Paris, Albert Levy.
(Sotheby's) $2,205 £1,050

BENEZET, A.
'Some Account of Guinea' – half title – cont. calf rubbed – upper cover detached – 8vo – 1772.
(Sotheby's) $90 £40

BENEZIT, E.
'Dictionnaire des Peintres, Sculpteurs, Dessinateurs et Graveurs' – 8 vols. – plates – orig. cloth – worn – 8vo – Paris, 1956-61.
(Sotheby's) $160 £75

BENNETT, A. M.
'The Beggar Girl' – 1st Edn. – 7 vols. – calf gilt – 12 mo – Minerva Press 1797.
(Phillips) $460 £220

BENNETT, CHARLES H. AND BROUGH, ROBERT B.
'Shadow and Substance' – 30 engraved plates coloured by hand – cont. red straight grained morocco – gilt – g.e. – 8vo – W. Kent, 1860.
(Sotheby's) $160 £75

BENNETT, GEOFFREY D. S.
'Famous Harness Horses' – 3 vols. – number 592 of 600 signed by author – plates – orig. cloth – soiled – t.e.g. – 4to – 1926-32.
(Sotheby's) $200 £95

BENOIS, ALEXANDRE
Costume design for four young girls with toys – pencil, pen and indian ink and watercolour – signed with initials and inscribed in Russian – 28 x 20cm. – 1919.
(Sotheby's) $1,365 £650

BENSLEY, HENRY
'The South of Devon and Dartmoor' – maps and engravings – orig. cloth bindings – circa 1860.
(Lane) $40 £20

BENSON, A. C.
'Everybody's Book of the Queen's Dolls House' – together with a letter written by Queen Mary and dated 1924.
(Lane) $20 £10

BENSON, E. F.
'Make Way For Lucia' – complete set of Lucia books in one vol. – Crowell, New York 1971.
(Laurence & Martin Taylor) $5 £2.50
'Daisy's Aunt' – title label flaking, otherwise good – 1910.
(J. Ash) $6 £3

BENSON, R. H.
'Poems' – slight bump, otherwise nice – n.d.
(J. Ash) $6 £3

BENTHAM, JEREMY
'Chrewtomathia; Being a Collection of Papers explanatory of the Design of an Institution' – 1st Edn. – 5 folding printed tables – half title – browned – cont. half calf – lacks spine – cover detached – 8vo – 1816.
(Sotheby's) $180 £85

BENTLEY, RICHARD
'A Dissertation upon the Epistles of Phalaris' – 2nd Edn. – latter half calf – worn – 8vo – H. Mortlock and J. Hartley, 1699.
(Sotheby's) $10 £5

BERAIN, JEAN
'Ornemens de Peinture et de Sculpture . . du Chateau de Louvre' – 33 engraved plates – 6 folding – some torn and creased – loose – Paris 1676-1710.
(Sotheby's) $200 £95

BERARD, A.
Portrait of Sarah Bernhardt in the title role of 'Gismonda' – charcoal heightened with white chalk – signed and inscribed – 56 x 44cm.
(Sotheby's) $3,150 £1,500

BERENSON, B.
'The Drawings of Florentine Painters' – 3 vols. – plates – orig. cloth – 4to – Chicago 1938.
(Sotheby's) $125 £60
'Italian Pictures of the Renaissance . . . Florentine School' – 2 vols. – plates – cloth – d.w.s. – s.c. – 4to – 1963.
(Phillips) $45 £22

BERESFORD, CAPTAIN G. DE LA POER
'Twelve Sketches in double tinted lithography of Scenes in Southern Albania' – dampstain throughout – marginal tear, fraying and soiling – unbound – folio Day & Son 1855.
(Christie's S. Kensington) $565 £270

BERINGTON, JOSEPH
'The History of the Lives of Abelard and Heloisa' – 2nd Edn. – cont. tree calf – gilt – rubbed – 4to – Birmingham 1788.
(Sotheby's) $75 £35

BERKELEY, G.
'A Treatise Concerning the Principles of Human Knowledge' – modern half calf – 8vo – 1734.
(Sotheby's) $125 £60

BERKSHIRE SERIES, THE
Vols. 1-3 all limited to 550 copies – orig. cloth-backed boards – rubbed – dust jackets – spotted and torn – 1926.
(Christie's) $25 £12

BERNIER, F.
'Voyages' – 18th century French binding of red morocco gilt with arms of Marie Therese of Savoy – 12 mo – Amsterdam 1710.
(Moore Allen & Innocent) $800 £380

BERNINI, DOMENICO
'Historia di Tutte Heresie' – 4 vols. – half title in vol. 1 – slight browning – cont. mottled calf – spine gilt – joints split, rubbed – 4to – Venice 1724.
(Sotheby's) $30 £15

BEROALDUS, PHILIPPE
'Carmen Lugubre' – some marginal soiling – a few manuscript marginal annotations – modern boards – Paris, pro Johanne Petet 1509.
(Christie's S. Kensington) $65 £30

BERRY, WILLIAM
'The History of the Island of Guernsey' – 1st Edn. – 29 plates – 1 folding map – spotting – cont. calf – worn – spine loose – 4to – 1815.
(Sotheby's) $250 £120

BERRYMAN, JOHN
'Delusions etc.' – 1st English Edn. – poems – dust wrapper – 1972.
(J. Ash) $10 £5

BERTALL – BALZAC, HONORE DE
'Petites Miseres de la Vie Conjugale' – 1st Edn. bound from 30 parts – 50 wood engraved plates – illus. in text after Bertall – slightly spotted – cont. half morocco – slightly rubbed – 4to – Paris, Chlendowski, 1845.
(Sotheby's) $2,100 £1,000

BERTHOLLET, CLAUDE LOUIS
'Researches into the Laws of Chemical Affinity' – translated from French by M. Farrell – lacks half title – library stamps – cloth – 8vo – 1804.
(Sotheby's) $125 £60

BERTRAM, CHARLES
'Isn't it Wonderful ?' 1896, 'A Magician in Many Lands' – col. frontis 1911 – illus. – orig. cloth – slightly rubbed – 4to and 8vo.
(Sotheby's) $200 £95
'Isn't it Wonderful?' – presentation copy inscribed and signed by the author – frontispiece – orig. cloth – inner hinge cracked – bookplate of J. B. Findlay – 1896.
(Christie's S. Kensington) $55 £25

BERZELIUS, J.
'An Attempt to Establish a Pure Scientific System of Mineralogy' – translated by J. Black – modern calf-backed cloth – 8vo – 1814.
(Sotheby's) $180 £85

BESANT, SIR WALTER
'The Survey of London' – 10 vols. – plates – orig. cloth gilt – 4to – 1903-25.
(Phillips) $190 £90

BESLEY, HENRY
'The Route Book of Cornwall' – complete with folding map and adverts – circa 1850.
(Lane) $85 £40

BETJEMAN, JOHN
'Ghastly Good Taste' – First issue, author's second book – folding prospectus at rear – orig. quarter cloth – nice copy – 1933.
(J. Ash) $90 £40

'BEWICK'S GLEANING'
being impressions from copperplates and wood blocks engraved in the Bewick Workshops . . . edited by Julia Boyd – small paper copy – signed by the editor – half morocco – rubbed – front inner hinge cracked – t.e.g.
(Christie's S. Kensington) $135 £65

BEWICK, T.
'History of British Birds' – wood engravings – 2 vols. in one – boards broken, one leaf defective and several leaves stained – 1797-1804.
(Bonhams) $75 £35

'Natural History' – 7 parts in one – frontispiece and illustrations after Bewick – some browning – cont. calf – with orig. wrappers bound in – rubbed – covers detached – Alnwick 1809.
(Christie's S. Kensington) $135 £65

BIBLE, ENGLISH
The Holy Bible – 2 vols. in one, continuous signatures – 10 engraved plates – browning and soiling – cont. Irish red morocco – gilt – spine tooled, decorated with floral border – slightly worn – g.e. – large folio – Birmingham Baskerville, 1769-71.
(Sotheby's) $48,300 £23,000

BIBLE, THE HOLY
Printed by Robert Barker . . . and by the Assignes of John Bill – double page map – slightly soiled – old morocco, rebacked – old spine laid down – joints worn – folio – 1632 date altered in ink to 1633.
(Christie's S. Kensington) $105 £50

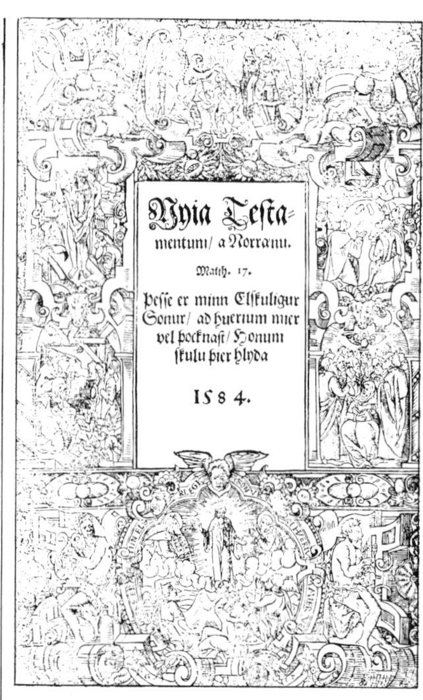

BIBLE
'Biblia Pad Er Oll Heilog Ritning Vilgod a Nooraenu Med Formalum Doct Martin Lutheri' – 1st Edn. – title in red and black in elaborate border – repairs – tears – stains and pencil marks but generally a good copy – raised brass centrepieces and centre box but traces of clasps – worn – folio – Holum, 1584.
(Sotheby's) $15,750 £7,500

BIBLIOGRAPHICA
12 parts – plates – orig. wrappers – torn – 4to – 1895-97.
(Sotheby's) $135 £65

BIBLIOTHECA PHILIPPICA
Collection of approx. 300 sale catalogues, many duplicates – orig. wrappers – worn – 8vo.
(Sotheby's) $95 £45

BICKHAM, G.
'British Monarchy' – engraved title and dedication – 1 folding map – 157 plates – lacks some pages – half calf – rubbed – folio – 1743.
(Phillips) $145 £70

'The Universal Penman' – title, dedication, contents, plates, engraved throughout – some leaves lacking – some minor defects – cont. half calf – slightly worn – folio – Printed for author 1741.
(Sotheby Beresford Adams) $265 £125

BICKLEY, FRANCIS B.
'The Little Red Book of Bristol' – 2 vols. – plates – some folding – orig. buckram – rubbed – 4to – 1900.
(Sotheby's) $40 £20

BICKNELL, W. I.
'Illustrated London' – engraved title – plates by A. H. Payne – text and plates loose – 8vo – circa 1840.
(Phillips) $90 £40

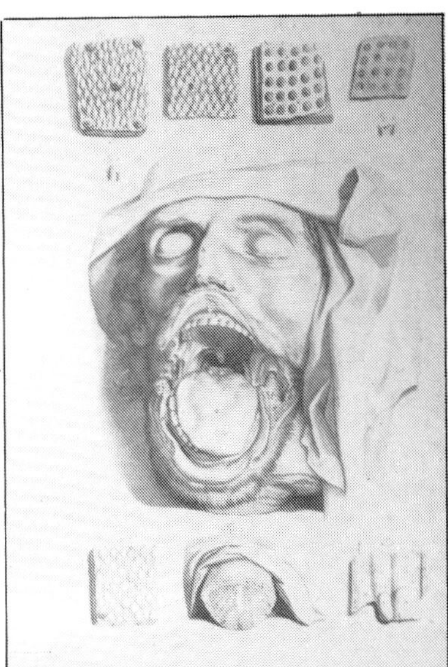

BIDLOO, GOVARD
'Anatomia Humani Corporis' – woodcut printer's device on title – engraved title – frontis portrait and 105 engraved plates – torn, some offset – half morocco – folio – Amsterdam 1685.
(Christie's) $1,575 £750

BIGGAR COURSING CLUB
frontis and plates – ¾ morocco – 4to – 1922.
(Bennett Book Auctions) $8 £4

'BIGGAR COURSING CLUB INSTITUTED 1821'
frontispiece and plates – club button set into front cover – half morocco – Edinburgh 1922 , and
'Historical Sketch of Coursing' – 54pp. pamphlet – bound with 4 portraits – list of members of the Biggar . . . or Upper Ward of Lanarkshire Coursing Club, 1833 and Autumn Meeting of Biggar . . . Coursing Club, 1856 – all bound together – cloth.
(Bennett Book Auctions) $135 £65

BILBO, JACK
'Jack Bilbo, An Autobiography' – presentation copy, inscribed by the author – plates – an exhibition catalogue of the artist's work loosely inserted – orig. cloth – dust jacket torn – 4to – 1948.
(Christie's S. Kensington) $40 £20

BILINSKY, BORIS
'Symphonie Fantastique' – costume design – pencil and gouache – inscribed Symphonie Fantastique, ballet 1933 on reverse – 58.2 x 31.7cm.
(Sotheby's) $420 £200

BILLING, M.
'Director and Gazeteer of the County of Devon' – 1857.
(Lane) $30 £15

BILLINGS, R. W.
'Illustrations of the Architectural Antiquities of the County of Durham' – 60 plates – foxing – half calf gilt – 4to – 1846.
(Phillips) $60 £30

'The Baronial Ecclesiastical Antiquities of Scotland' – 4 vols. – 240 engraved plates after Billings – some spotting and soiling – cont. panelled calf – rubbed – g.e. – 4to – n.d.
(Christie's S. Kensington) $100 £50

BINDING
'The Whole Book of Psalmes'
Cont. embroidered cloth – a heart surrounded by stylised foliage on the covers, flowers on the spine, worked in silk and metal thread – rubbed – g.e. – 12 mo – Imprinted for the Company of Stationers, 1636.
(Christie's S. Kensington) $250 £120

BING, S.
'Artistic Japan' – 6 vols. in three – some col. – cont. half calf – rubbed – orig. wrappers preserved – folio – 1888-91.
(Sotheby's) $305 £145

BINGHAM, H.
'A Residence of Twenty One Years in the Sandwich Islands' – portrait – 5 plates of 6 – lacks map – dampstained – cont. sheep – rubbed – 8vo – Hartford and New York, 1847.
(Sotheby's) $20 £10

BINGLEY, J.
'The Official Travelling Map of England and Wales' – folding engraved map – hand col. outline – on linen – slipcase – 57 x 45cm. – 1829.
(Sotheby's) $65 £30

BINGLEY, WILLIAM
'Animal Biography' – 3 vols. – occasional spotting – cont. calf – rubbed – joints cracked – 1803.
(Christie's S. Kensington) $25 £12

BINNS, W. M.
'The First Century of English Porcelain' – plates – some spotting – orig. cloth – soiled and rubbed – 4to – n.d.
(Christie's) $40 £18

BINYON, L. AND SEXTON, J. J. O'BRIEN
'Japanese Colour Prints' – limited edn. – signed by authors – plates – orig. pigskin – 4to – 1923.
(Sotheby's) $250 £120

BINYON, LAURENCE
'The Poems of Nizami' – 16 col. plates – orig. cloth – dust jacket – folio – The Studio 1928.
(Christie's) $60 £30

BION, NICOLAS
'The Construction and Principal Uses of Mathematical Instruments' – 1st English Edn. – title in red and black – 26 folding engraved plates – soiled – minor discolouration in plates – some foxing – cont. panelled calf – folio – 1723.
(Christie's) $505 £240

BIRCH, SAMUEL
'History of Ancient Pottery' – 2 vols. – plates – orig. cloth – gilt – 8vo – 1858.
(Sotheby's) $40 £20

BIRCH, THOMAS
'The Heads of Illustrious Persons of Great Britain' – titled with engraved vignette – 108 plates – title repaired – large copy in 19th century russia – rebacked – slightly worn – folio – 1756.
(Sotheby's) $190 £90

BIRD, JOHN
'Grounds of Grammer Penned and Published' – 2nd Edn. – title in red and black – cont. sheep – worn – sm. 8vo – Oxford 1641.
(Christie's) $315 £150

BISSET, R.
'Modern Literature' – 3 vols. – calf gilt – 1804.
(Phillips) $170 £80

B.J.L.
'The Butterfly's Funeral' – 1st Edn. – engraved frontis and 11 illus. 'by a lady' – letterpress title – orig. printed wrappers – cloth case – 16 mo – John Wallis Jnr., 1808.
(Sotheby's) $460 £220

BLACKBURN, HENRY AND CALDECOTT, RANDOLPH
'A Personal Memoir of his early Art Career' – mounted portrait photograph, detached – illustrations – first two leaves slightly spotted – orig. cloth – g.e. – 1886.
(Christie's S. Kensington) $17 £8

BLACKBURN, MRS. HUGH
'Birds from Moidart and Elsewhere' – 1st Edn. – litho title and 87 litho plates – orig. red cloth – spine faded – t.e.g. – 8vo – Edinburgh 1896.
(Sotheby's) $55 £25

BLACKER, J. F.
'The A.B.C. of English Salt Glaze Stone Ware' – plates – illus. – orig. cloth – dust jacket – 8vo – 1922.
(Sotheby's) $55 £25

BLACKSTONE
A Collection of 34 programmes, prospectuses and brochures for performances by Blackstone in Great Britain, Canada and the U.S.A. – various sizes – circa 1945-50.
(Sotheby's) $145 £70

BLACKWOOD, ALGERNON
'The Lost Valley' – Second Impression – 8 plates – by Graham Robertson – stains – one plate loose – otherwise very good – 1910.
(J. Ash) $6 £3

BLACKWOOD, LADY ALICIA
'Scutari, Bosphorous, Crimea' – 2 vols. – folio – litho titles and 19 plates all uncoloured, one torn – dampstain throughout – some marginal soiling – orig. wrappers – soiled.
(Christie's S. Kensington) $180 £85

BLADES, WILLIAM
'The Enemies of Books' – 2nd Edn., with related Als. from the author discussing bookworks – plates – slight spotting – orig. wrappers – 1880.
(Christie's S. Kensington) $40 £20

BLAEU, JOHANNES
'Le Grand Atlas ou Cosmographie Blaviane' – 12 vols., complete set – text in French – vols. VI and LX 1st Edns., others 2nd – 598 engraved maps, plans and plates, coloured – some soiling – uniformly bound in cont. vellum – panelled in gilt – spines gilt – g.e. – folio – Amsterdam Chez Jean Blaeu, 1667.
(Christie's) $113,400 £54,000

BLAEU, W. J.
'Comitatus Northantonensis' – engraved map, hand coloured in outline – 19 x 16in. – stained – framed and glazed – 1645 or later.
(Christie's S. Kensington) $115 £55

Map of Saxon Britain – hand coloured – double glazed frame with text to reverse – 19¼ x 23½in.
(Richard Baker & Thomson) $380 £180

'Polonia Regnum et Silesia Ducatus' – engraved map, hand coloured in outline – 17 x 20 in. – framed and glazed – 1634 or later.
(Christie's S. Kensington) $85 £40

BLAIR, H.
'Lectures on Rhetoric and Belles Lettres' – 2 vols. – frontis – cont. calf – 1st. Edn. London 1783 – joints weak – spine rubbed.
(Bennett Book Auctions) $105 £50

BLAIR, REV. JOHN
'A Map of the East Indies' – engraved map, hand coloured in outline, inset map of the Phillipine Islands – 421 x 557mm. – 1773.
(Sotheby's) $10 £5

BLAKE, W.
'The Book of Urizen' – no. 50 of 526 copies – coloured title and 26 plates – orig. morocco backed boards – slipcase – 4to – Trianon Press 1958.
(Sotheby's) $370 £175

BLAKE, WILLIAM
'An Introduction to the Study of Blake' by Max Plowman – 1st English Edn. – plates – 1927.
(J. Ash) $8 £4
'Works' – Edited by W. B. Yeats – orig. publisher's cloth – 3 vols. – London 1893.
(Robert Skinner) £310

BLAKEY, D.
'The Minerva Press' – plates – Als. from author inserted – orig. buckram-backed boards – sm. 4to – Bibliographical Socy. 1939.
(Sotheby's) $95 £45

BLAKSTON, W. A., SWAYSLAND, W. AND WIENER, A. F.
'Illustrated Book of Canaries and Cage Birds' – coloured plates – half morocco gilt – 4to – Cassell, n.d.
(Phillips) $85 £40

BLANDFORD, MARQUESS OF
'Twelve Glees, Ten for Three Voices and Two for Four Voices' – title and 44 pp. of musical arrangements – engraved throughout – cont. half morocco gilt – arms of Duke of Marlborough in gilt – rubbed – oblong folio – Privately printed 1798.
(Sotheby Beresford Adams) $40 £20

BLANDFORD, W. T.
'Observations on the Geology and Zoology of Abyssinia' – col. folding frontis – col. map – plates including 8 of birds – orig. cloth – 1870.
(Phillips) $180 £85

BLASHILL, THOMAS
'Sutton in Holderness' – large paper Edn. – illus. – 1896.
(Baitson) $65 £30

BLATCHFORD, ROBERT
'A Bohemian Girl' – 3rd Impression, signed by the author – orig. decorative cloth, gilt – good copy – 1901.
(J. Ash) $12 £6

BLES, J. R.
'Rare English Glasses of the XVII and XVIII Centuries' – plates – orig. cloth worn – t.e.g. – 4to – G. Bles 1925.
(Phillips) $160 £75

BLESSINGTON, COUNTESS OF
'Rambles in Waltham Forest' – frontis – litho plates – orig. boards – small 4to – 1827.
(Phillips) $100 £50

BLEWITT, O.
'Panorama of Torquay' – coloured map – litho title and plates – orig. cloth – 1832.
(Bennett Book Auctions) $40 £20

BLIGHT, J. T.
'Churches of West Cornwall' – cloth binding marked – 1884.
(Lane) $30 £15

BLISS, D. P.
'History of Wood-Engraving' – frontispiece – plates – illus. – orig. cloth – dust jacket – 1928.
(Christie's S. Kensington) $80 £40

BLOCH, MARCUS ELIESER
'Zichthyologie ou Histoire Naturelle, Generale et Particuliere des Poissons' – 12 vols. – titles with engraved illus. by Berger and 432 hand col. engraved plates – heightened with silver – foxing – cont. half russia – rubbed – some covers detached – folio – Berlin 1785-97.
(Christie's) $17,850 £8,500

BLOME, R.
'Canaan' – uncoloured map – 1687.
(Phillips) $75 £35

BLOMEFIELD, F.
'The History of Norfolk' – vol. 1 only – sheep – folio – 1739.
(Ireland) $115 £55

BLOMFIELD, REV. E.
'A General View of the World' – vol. 2 only – engravings and maps – leather bound – 1807.
(Baitson) $30 £15

BLOOMFIELD, ROBERT
'The Farmer's Boy' – 1st Edn. – wood engraved vignette on title – inscribed to Walter de la Mare – red half morocco – 4to – 1800.
(Sotheby's) $145 £70

BLOSSOMING PASSION FLOWER, A
Red tipped white blooms – gouache on cotton – slightly stained – laid down on album leaf – panels of nasta'liq applied – polychrome border on cream leaf, three floral border designs on a single strip of cotton – laid down on similar album leaf – 16.5 x 8cm. – Mughal, circa 1700-1750.
(Christie's) $945 £450

BLOSSOMS OF MORALITY, THE
First illus. Edn. – 47 wood engraved illus. by John Bewick – orig. sheep – joints split – rubbed – 12 mo – E. Newbery 1796.
(Sotheby's) $65 £30

BLUETT, EDGAR E.
'Chinese Pottery and Porcelain in the Collection of Mr. and Mrs. Alfred Clark' – 4 col. plates – illus. – orig. cloth – soiled – t.e.g. – 4to – n.d.
(Christie's) $80 £40

BLUNDEN, EDMUND
'English Poems' – some foxing – title label faded – nice copy – 1925.
(J. Ash) $12 £6
'Masks of Time' – limited edn. – uncut – orig. cloth-backed boards – Beaumont Press 1926.
(Phillips) $40 £20
'A Summer's Fancy' – limited edn., signed by author and artist – quarter vellum gilt – Beaumont Press, 1930.
(Phillips) $75 £35

BOADEN, JAMES
'Memoirs of Mrs. Siddons' – 2 vols. – later half calf gilt, by Bayntum – rubbed, chipped – bookplates of Baron Northcliffe – 1827.
(J. Ash) $125 £60

BOAR'S HEAD PRESS
'Sappho' – number 196 of 250 copies – text arranged with translations by E. M. Cox – woodcut illus. by Lettice Blandford – orig. morocco backed boards – 8vo – Boar's Head Press 1932.
(Sotheby Beresford Adams) $65 £30

BOCCALINI
'De Ragguagli di Parnaso' – 2 vols. – early 19th century bindings of dark blue straight morocco gilt – arms of Duchesse de Berry on covers by Simier and signed – 12 mo – Amsterdam 1669.
(Moore Allen & Innocent) $670 £320

BOCKLERI, GEORG ANDREA
'Theatrum Machinarum Novum' – without engraved title – 153 engraved plates only, lacking plate 154, plate 153 torn – margins browned – title soiled, joints slightly cracked – folio – Cologne, Pauli Principis, 1662.
(Christie's S. Kensington) $485 £230

BODLEY, SIR THOMAS
'Pietas Oxoniensis, In Memory of . . . and the Foundation of the Bodleian Library' – frontis and plates – cloth gilt – 4to – Letters of Sir Thomas Bodley to the University of Oxford, for private circulation, 1927 (editor's letter tipped in) and 3 pamphlets all relating to the Bodleian Library – 1902-1907.
(Bennet Book Auctions) $20 £10

BODMER, H.
'Leonardo' – plates – cloth gilt – 8vo – 1931.
(Phillips) $85 £40

BODONI, GIAMBATTISTA
'Manuale Tipografico' – 2 vols. – limited to 500 copies – portrait – orig. boards – slipcase – sm. folio – Holland Press 1960.
(Christie's S. Kensington) $60 £30

BODWELL, W. AND T.
'Mesolabium Architectionicum' – unbound – 1639.
(Phillips) $75 £35

BOEMUS, JOHANNES
'Omnium Gentium Mores, Leges et Ritus' – early library stamp on title – cont. calf, gilt – ornaments on covers – rebacked – rubbed – mid 16th century black stamp and signature of Frater Desiderius Buffet on title – 8vo – Paris, Jean Petit 1538.
(Sotheby's) $75 £35

BOERHAAVE, HERMANN
'Institutiones et Experimenta Chemicae' – 2 vols. in one – unauthorised Edn. – folding plate at end – engraving – worming – cont. calf – 8vo – Paris 1724.
(Sotheby's) $230 £110

BOETHIUS, A. M. T.
'Summum Bonum or an Explication of the Divine Goodness' – device on title – cont. calf – joints split – worn – 8vo – Oxford 1674.
(Sotheby's) $40 £20

BOGG, EDMUND
'A Thousand Miles in Wharfedale' – illus. – 1892.
(Dacre, Son & Hartley) $65 £30

BOHN, H. G. (publisher)
'Italian School of Design' – 91 plates engraved by Bartolozzi and others – half morocco gilt – 4to – 1842.
(Phillips) $115 £55

BOHUN, E.
'Geographical Dictionary' – engraved title – title in red and black – 5 maps – stained – modern calf gilt – 8vo – 1691.
(Phillips) $100 £50

BOHUN, RALPH
'A Discourse Concerning the Origin and Properties of Wind' – 1st Edn. – 3 engravings – half calf – upper cover loose – 8vo – Oxford 1671.
(Sotheby's) $90 £40

BOILLEREE, S.
'Nieder-rhein' – twelve lithographed plates – marginal tears and soiling – unbound – original wrappers – soiled – Munich 1842.
(Christie's S. Kensington) $440 £210

BOISGELIN, LOUIS DE
'Travels Through Denmark and Sweden to which is prefixed a Journal of a Voyage Down the Elbe' – 2 vols in one – 13 hand col. aquatint plates – cont. diced calf – gilt – rebacked – 4to – 1810.
(Sotheby's) $250 £120

BOIZARD, JEAN
'Traite des Monoyes, de leur circonstances et dependances' – 1st Edn. – 3 engraved plates – some browning – cont. calf – worn – 12 mo – Paris 1692.
(Sotheby's) $250 £120

BOLAFFI, G.
'Catalogo Bolaffi della Graffica Italiana' – vols. 1-8 each with orig. etching inserted – orig. cloth – 4to – Turin 1970-78.
(Sotheby's) $145 £70

BOLDEWOOD, ROLF
'A Modern Buccaneer' – 3 vols. – orig. cloth – blemishes – scarce – 1894.
(J. Ash) $250 £120

BOLINGBROKE, VISCOUNT ST. JOHN
'A Collection of Political Tracts' – calf gilt – 1748.
(Phillips) $55 £25

BOLTON, A. T.
'The Architecture of Robert and James Adam' – illus. – 2 vols. – cloth slightly worn – folio – 1922.
(Bonhams) $145 £70

BOLTON, JAMES
'Harmonia Ruralis' – 2 vols. – 81 hand col. plates – spotting – recent half calf – 4to – 1824.
(Sotheby's) $630 £300

BONAPARTE, LUCIEN
'Choix des Graveurs a L'Eaux Forte' – 141 engraved plates of 142 – soiling – cont. calf – rebacked – worn – 4to – Londres – n.d.
(Sotheby's) $95 £45

BONAVIA, E.
'Cultivated Oranges and Lemons etc., of India and Ceylon' – 2 vols. including one of plates – orig. cloth – soiled – 8vo and oblong 4to – 1888-90.
(Phillips) $60 £30

BONELLI, GEORGIO AND MARTELLI, NICCOLA
'Hortus Romanus' – 6 vols. of 8 – half titles – titles in red and black – hand col. vignettes – 5 portraits – 600 hand col. plates engraved by Maddalena Bouchard – cont. half vellum rubbed and soiled – folio – Rome 1772-80.
(Christie's) $16,380 £7,800

BONNE, RIGOBERT
'Atlas de Toutes les Parties Connues du Globe Terrestre' – 47 engraved double page maps – 23 tables at end – 10 folding – spotting and staining – cont. calf backed boards – 4to – Geneva circa 1780.
(Sotheby's) $295 £140

BONNEMAISON, FEREOL
'Galerie de Son Altesse Royale Madame la Duchess de Berry' – 2 vols. – 1st Edn. – 20 litho plates – india paper – with 50 scenes and views – cont. half roan – covers detached, worn – folio – Paris 1822.
(Sotheby's) $105 £50

BONNEY, REV. H. K.
'Historic Notices in References to Fotheringhay' – nine engraved plates – slight offsetting – orig. boards – backstrip worn and slightly torn – Oundle 1821.
(Christie's S. Kensington) $40 £20

BOODT, A. B. DE
'Gemmarum et Lapidum Historia' – 1st Edn. – woodcut illus. – folding tables – library stamp on a title – later boards – rubbed – sm. 4to – Hanover 1609.
(Sotheby's) $105 £50

BOOK AUCTION RECORDS
Vols. 1-62 and a duplicate of 36; 64 vols., orig. cloth – rubbed or worn – 8vo – 1903-66.
(Sotheby's) $715 £340
Index Vol. 66-69 (1968-72) – orig. cloth – 4to – Folkestone 1977.
(Christie's S. Kensington) $105 £50

BOOK OF KELLS, THE
Described by Sir Edward Sullivan – no. 8 of 100 copies – mounted col. plates – slight spotting – orig. vellum-backed boards – slipcase – t.e.g. – The Studio Ltd. 1920.
(Christie's S. Kensington) $65 £30

BOOKPLATES
Collection of 13 bookplates designed by James Guthrie of Pear Tree Press, Flansham, Bognor, with associated proofs, sketches and designs including prospectus for 'Bookplates' – circa 1920-30.
(Phillips) $200 £95

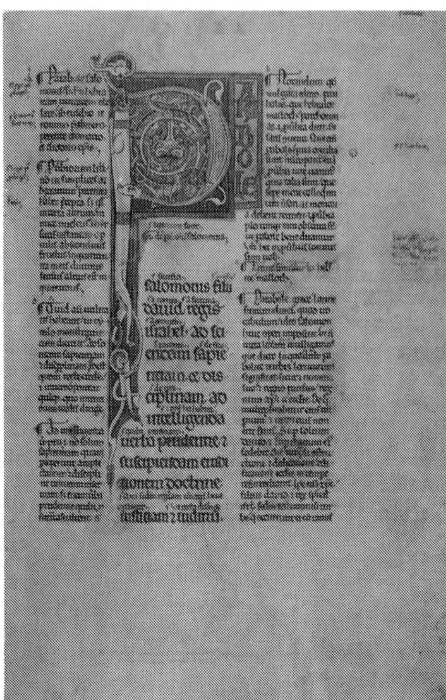

BOOKS OF SOLOMON, THE (GLOSSED)
Illum. mss on vellum – 565 painted initials – large illum. initials – one historiated, five with dragons and lions, in good condition with wide margins, blind stamped dark brown morocco – panelled and ruled in lozenge design – 343 x 240mm. – Paris (probably St. Victor Abbey) circa 1170.
(Sotheby's) $50,400 £24,000

BOON, K. G.
'Netherlandish Drawings of the Fifteenth and Sixteenth Centuries' – 2 vols. including one of plates – cloth, gilt – 4to – 1978.
(Phillips) $55 £25

BOOTH, E. C.
'Australia' – engraved title – 8 maps and 111 plates – 8 orig. parts – orig. cloth – worn – 4to – 1873-76.
(Bonhams) $965 £460

BOOTH, WILLIAM
'In Darkest England' and 'The Way Out' – folding col. frontis – pledge form – clean – 1890.
(J. Ash) $45 £20

BOOTHBY, MRS. FRANCES
'Marcelia' – 1st Edn. – worming – recent morocco – sm. 4to – 1670.
(Christie's) $295 £140

BORELLI, J. A.
'De VI Percussionis' – six folding engraved plates – slightly browned throughout – cont. calf – rubbed – rebacked – 4to – Lieden 1686.
(Christie's S. Kensington) $55 £25

BORGES, JORGE LUIS
'A Universal History of Infamy' – First English Edn. – good in slightly rubbed dust jacket – 1973.
(J. Ash) $10 £5

BORLASE, WILLIAM
'A Natural History of Cornwall' – 1st Edn. – complete with all maps and plates – bound in full calf – folio – 1758.
(Lane) $315 £150

BORN, IGNAZ VON
'Testacea Musei Caesarei Vindobonensis' – 44 engraved illus. and 18 hand col. plates – cont. red straight grained morocco – gilt fillet borders – gilt spine – g.e. – rubbed and cracked – folio – Vienna 1780.
(Christie's) $965 £460

BOROWSKI, G. H. AND HERBEST, J. F. W.
'Gemmeinnuzzige Naturgeschichte Des Thierreichs' – 8 vols. only – 357 hand col. engraved plates only – some occasional spotting – cont. half-roan – spines worn – Berlin 1780-9.
(Christie's S. Kensington) $1,155 £550

BORROW, GEORGE
'Lavengro' – 3 vols. – ownership inscription – dark blue cloth and cream endpapers – slightly rubbed – a little worn – 1851.
(J. Ash) $90 £40

BORTHWICK, J. D.
'Three Years in California' – 8 litho plates – half calf gilt – 1857.
(Phillips) $115 £55

BOSMAN, W.
'New and Accurate Description of the Coast of Guinea' – 2nd Edn. – folding map – 7 plates – calf gilt – 1721.
(Phillips) $250 £120

BOSSERT, H. T.
'Peasant Art In Europe' – col. plates – cloth gilt – 4to – 1926.
(Phillips) $105 £50

BOSWELL, HENRY
'Historical Descriptions of New and Elegant Picturesque Views of the Antiquities of England, Wales' – 49 engraved maps, 190 plans and views extra illustrated with 12 plates – some leaves detached – soiled – cont. calf, worn – n.d. folio.
(Christie's S. Kensington) $880 £420

BOTTRELL, WILLIAM
'Traditions and Hearthside Stories of West Cornwall' – 1st Edn. – orig. cloth – 1870.
(Lane) $30 £14

BOURGOING, J. FR.
'Atlas to the Modern State of Spain' – one engraved map – 28 plates – marginal tears – original wrappers – soiled – 4to – 1808.
(Christie's S. Kensington) $75 £35

BOURNE, HENRY
'The History of Newcastle upon Tyne' – folding map – torn – laid down – browned, soiled – old russia backed boards – worn – folio Newcastle – Printed and sold by John White 1736.
(Christie's S. Kensington) $55 £25

BOURNE, JOHN C.
'The History and Description of the Great Western Railway' – 1st Edn. – 39 tinted litho plates – 2 maps – 1 chart – spotting, tears – cont. boards – spine defective – contents disbound – loose – folio – 1846.
(Sotheby's) $1,090 £520

BOUTET DE MONVEL, MAURICE
'Jeanne d'Arc' – large col. illus. – orig. decorated cloth gilt – oblong 4to – Paris 1896.
(Sotheby's) $65 £30

BOWEN, ELIZABETH
'Collected Impressions' – in slightly nicked dust jacket – very good – 1964.
(J. Ash) $10 £5

BOWES, JAMES L.
'Japanese Pottery' – inscribed by author – plates, some col. – cont. half morocco – rubbed – 8vo – Liverpool 1890.
(Sotheby's) $125 £60

BOWYER, R.
'An Illustrated Record of Important Events in the Annals of Europe during the Years 1812 . . . 1815 . . . with the Campaign of Waterloo' – 2 works in one vol., together with 23 fine full page hand col. aquatints (mainly Continental town views), 5 folding, 4 black and white engraved plates, map and plan and 2 text wood engravings – cont. half morocco – folio 1815-16.
(Bennett Book Auctions) $1,490 £710

BOYDELL, JOHN AND JOSIAH
'Graphic Illustrations of the Dramatic Works of Shakespeare' – engraved title – 99 plates of 100 – lacks frontis – some spotting – cont. calf, worn – covers detached – folio – 1802.
(Sotheby's) $460 £220

BOYER, A.
'Le Dictionnaire Royal Francois Anglais' – portrait – calf – 4to – 1783.
(Phillips) $30 £14

BOYLE, J. R.
'The Early History of the Town and Port of Hedon' – illus. with plates – 1895.
(Baitson) $75 £35

BOYLE, LAURENCE
'Celebrities of the Stage' – 12 orig. parts – col. plates.
(Baitson) $8 £4

BOYLE, HON. ROBERT
'New Experiments and Observations Touching Cold' – 2 parts in one vol. – 2nd Edn. – 2 engraved plates, 1 folding – bookplate of John Rutherford of Edgerston – cont. calf – spine gilt – rubbed – sm. 4to – 1683.
(Sotheby's) $230 £110
'Tentamina Quaedam Physiologica' – 12 mo – title soiled – later boards – joints cracked – Amsterdam, Apud Danielem Elzevirium, 1667.
(Christie's S. Kensington) $55 £25
'Experiment and Considerations about the Porosity of Bodies' – cont. calf – ribbed – upper cover detached – 1684.
(Christie's) $115 £55

BOY'S OWN ANNUAL, THE
15 vols. all but 2 in orig. pictorial cloth – 1901.
(Lane) $80 £40

BOY'S OWN BOOK, THE
'A Complete Encyclopaedia of All the Diversions' – 3rd Edn. – wood engraved illus. – leaves spotted – modern cloth – 8vo – David Bogue 1829.
(Sotheby's) $85 £40

BOYS, WILLIAM
'Collections for a History of Sandwich in Kent' – 1st Edn. – 2 vols. – 52 engraved plates – illus. – some folding – cont. tree calf – 4to – 1892 i.e. 1792.
(Christie's) $295 £140

BRAAKENSIEK, J. AND VAN GELDORP
'A Collection of 58 cartoons issued with the 'Bijvoegsel' or 'Amsterdamsche Courant' all relating to the Boer War – a few slightly frayed – oblong folio – 1896-1902.
(Sotheby's) $125 £60

BRABAZON, WALLOP
'The Deep Sea And Coast Fisheries of Ireland' – 21 lithographed plates – some folding, after William Cooper – browning orig. cloth – spine torn – Dublin 1848.
(Christie's S. Kensington) $80 £40

BRACKEN, C. W.
'A History of Plymouth and Her Neighbours' – 1934.
(Lane) $20 £10

BRACKENBURY, H.
'The Nearest Guard: A History of Her Majesty's Body Guard' – one of 200 copies – plates, 2 coloured – some folding – orig. cloth – rubbed – 4to – 1892.
(Sotheby's) $65 £30

BRADFORD, W.
'Sketches of the Country, Character and Costume of Portugal and Spain' – 54 col. aquatint plates – title and text in English and French – half morocco – slightly worn – folio – 1814.
(Bonhams) $670 £320

BRADLEY, E. 'Cuthbert Bede'
'Glencreggan' – 2 vols. – col. plates – orig. cloth – 8vo – 1861..
(Sotheby's) $40 £20

BRADLEY, R.
'The Gentleman and Farmer's Guide for the Increase and Improvement of Cattle and the Best Manner of Breeding and Breaking Horses' – 4 engraved plates – cont. calf – worn – 8vo – 1729.
(Sotheby's) $360 £170

BRADSHAW, GEORGE
'Map of Canals, Navigable Rivers, Railroads etc. in the Midland Counties of England' – large linen-backed folding engraved map extending to five feet square – border and key – col. in outline – edges strengthened with cloth – Manchester 1830.
(Sotheby's) $80 £40

BRADSHAW'S RAILWAY GUIDE
June/July 1938 and another early Bradshaw's Guide.
(Baitson) $25 £12

BRADY, DR. ROBERT
'An Historical Treatise of Cities and Burghs and Boroughs' – with addenda, supplement and appendix – 2nd Edn. – new cloth – folio – 1704.
(Sotheby's) $55 £25
'An Introduction to the Old English History in Three Tracts' – stained – cont. calf – worn – folio – 1684.
(Christie's) $30 £15

BRAINE, JOHN
'The Vodi' – author's second book – rubbed dust jacket – very good – 1959.
(J. Ash) $17 £8

BRAMHAM PARK, NEAR LEEDS . . .
Views of . . . – 14 etched plates – soiling – cont. wrappers – oblong 4to – n.d.
(Christie's) $190 £90

BRANDE, WILLIAM THOMAS
'A Manual of Chemistry' – 1st Edn. – 3 folding plates showing a laboratory – calf – covers loose – 8vo – John Murray 1819.
(Sotheby's) $40 £20

BRANNER, R.
'Manuscript Painting in Paris during the Reign of St. Louis' – plates – cloth – 1977.
(Phillips) $40 £20

BRANNON, GEORGE
'Graphic Delineations of the Isle of Wight' – 30 engraved plates – soiling – orig. cloth – soiled – rebacked – 8vo – n.d.
(Christie's) $65 £30
'Vectis Scenery' – engraved title – folding map and plans – spotted – orig. cloth – rebacked – rubbed – 4to – 1855.
(Sotheby's) $200 £95

BRANTOME, PIERRE DE BOURDEILLE
'Les Sept Discours Touchant les Dames Galantes' – 3 vols. – one of 20 copies on papier de Chine – portrait and plates by Edward de Beaumont – brown morocco gilt – Paris Jouaust 1882.
(Sotheby Parke Bernet Monaco) $3,715 £1,770

BRAQUE, GEORGES – PERSE, SAINT-JOHN
'L'Ordre des Oiseaux' – 12 col. etchings by Braque – orig. morocco backed and edged silk cut paper bird mounted on cover – uncut – slipcase – worn – folio – Paris, Au Vent D'Arles, 1962.
(Sotheby's) $210 £100

BRASHER, REX
'Birds and Trees of North America' – 2 vols. – col. plates – cloth – oblong folio – N.Y. 1961-62.
(Phillips) $40 £20

BRASSEY, T. A. (editor)
'The Naval Annual' – plates – some folding – orig. cloth – spine faded – 8vo – Portsmouth 1899.
(Sotheby's) $55 £25

BRAUN AND HOGENBURG
'Croneburg' – uncoloured plan – some dampstains – and 8 others including a town plan of Brussels – circa 1600.
(Phillips) $105 £50

BRAY, MRS. A. E.
'Life of Thomas Stothard' – extra-illustrated with portraits, views, many after Stothard – slight spotting – cont. morocco by Hambound – gilt – joints rubbed – 4to – 1851.
(Christie's S. Kensington) $65 £30

BRAY, WILLIAM
'Sketch of a Tour into Derbyshire and Yorkshire' – 2nd Edn. – 9 engraved plates – one folding – spotting – cont. calf – worn – 1783.
(Christie's) $40 £20

BRAYLEY, E. W.
'Delineations, Historical and Topographical of the Isle of Thanet and the Cinque Ports' – 2 vols. in one – large paper copy – one engraved map – two engraved titles and 107 plates – one hand coloured – cont. diced calf – joints rubbed – 1817-18.
(Christie's S. Kensington) $190 £90
'Londoniana or Reminiscences of the British Metropolis' – 4 vols. – engraved maps and plates – some folding – cont. half vellum – rubbed and soiled – 8vo – 1829.
(Sotheby's) $230 £110

BRAZIL, ANGELA
'A Pair of Schoolgirls' 1912; 'Leader of the Lower School' 1913; 'The Youngest Girl in the Fifth' 1914; 'The Girls of St. Cyprians' 1914; 'The Madcap of the School' 1922 – 1st Edns. – plates – one coloured – spotting – orig. pictorial cloth – 8vo.
(Sotheby's) $95 £45

BREE, C. R.
'A History of the Birds of Europe' – 4 vols. – hand col. plates – some spotting – orig. cloth – gilt spines – worn – 8vo – 1866-67.
(Sotheby's) $360 £170

BREES, S. C.
'Railway Practice' – 2 vols. – including atlas of plates – many folding – spotting – cont. cloth – atlas loose and worn – 4to and folio – 1837 and n.d.
(Sotheby's) $85 £40
'Pictorial Illustrations of New Zealand' – limited facsimile Edn. – col. plates – orig. cloth – gilt – 4to – Christchurch 1968.
(Sotheby's) $40 £20

BREHM, ALFRED E.
'Cassel's Book of Birds' – 4 vols. in two – numerous col. plates – illus. in text – dampstains – cont. half calf – rubbed – 4to – 1869-73.
(Sotheby Beresford Adams) $65 £30

BREMER, FREDERIKA
'The H. . . Family' – 2 vols. – 1st English Edn. – trans. by Mary Howitt – frontis portrait – Victorian half calf – lacks labels – slightly loose – some tears – 1844.
(J. Ash) $25 £12

BRETT, W. H.
'The Indian Tribes of Guiana' – plates – 8 hand col. – folding map, creased and cleanly torn – cont. calf – rubbed – 1868.
(Christie's S. Kensington) $95 £45

BREUIL, HENRI
'Les Peintres Rupestres' – 2 vols. – plates, some col. – orig. wrappers – 4to – 1933.
(Phillips) $55 £25

BREVET DE PERFECTIONNEMENT B. & D. Z.
Litho poster depicting a wide variety of court cards, coloured by hand, frayed at edges, mounted on card – 640 x 485mm. – late 19th century.
(Sotheby's) $135 £65

BREVIARIUM
Pars aestiva only – 18th century olive morocco gilt – 8vo – Paris 1714.
(Moore Allen & Innocent) $190 £90

BREVIARIUM ABERDONENSE
2 vols. – a few leaves spotted – cont. half morocco – rubbed – unopened – 4to – 1854.
(Sotheby's) $12 £6

BREWER, J. N.
'A Descriptive and Historical Account of Various Palaces and Public Buildings' – 25 plates – one cleanly torn – some slight spotting and soiling – cont. diced calf – spine worn – 4to – 1821.
(Christie's S. Kensington) $55 £25

BREWSTER, SIR DAVID
'Letters on Natural Magic Addressed to Sir Walter Scott' – wood engraved illus. – orig. boards – rebacked – soiled and worn – 8vo – 1834.
(Sotheby's) $45 £22

BREWSTER, JOHN
'The Parochial History and Antiquities of Stockton upon Tees' – folding monochrome aquatint frontis – 7 engraved plates – list of subscribers, adverts and errata – waterstains – modern half calf – fine copy – 4to – Stockton 1796.
(Thomas Watson) $105 £50

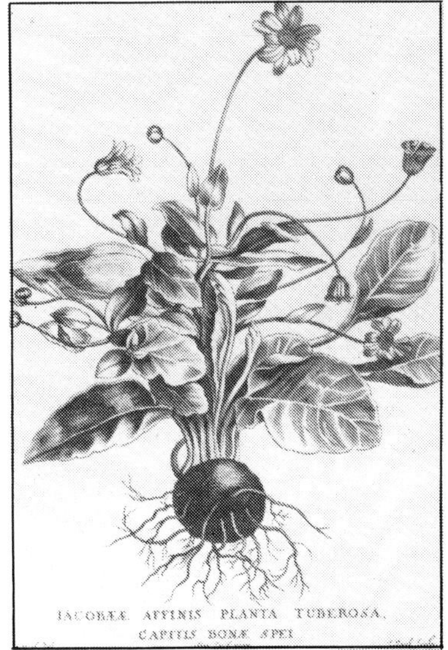

BREYN, JACOB AND RHYNE, W. TEM
'Exoticarum Plantarum Centuria Prima' – 1st Edn. – engraved frontis – 101 numbered engraved plates – plates mostly by Isaac Saal after Andreas Stech – minor spotting and staining – half morocco – folio – Danzig 1678.
(Christie's) $1,575 £750

BRIDGES, ROBERT
'Eros and Psyche' – limited to 300 copies – printed in red and black – 24 wood engraved illus. after Edward Burne-Jones, initials by Graily Hewitt and printed in green – orig. white pigskin gilt – soiled – t.e.g. – 4to – Gregynog Press 1935.
(Sotheby's) $315 £150

BRIDGENS, R.
'Costumes of Italy, Switzerland and France' – hand col. title – 49 hand col. plates – half morocco gilt – 4to – 1821.
(Phillips) $440 £210

BRIGGS, R.
'English Art of Cookery' – 12 plates – calf gilt – 8vo – 1788.
(Phillips) $295 £140

BRIGHT, R.
'Travels from Vienna through Lower Hungary' – 10 plates – 2 maps – folding table – calf gilt – 4to – 1818.
(Phillips) $200 £95

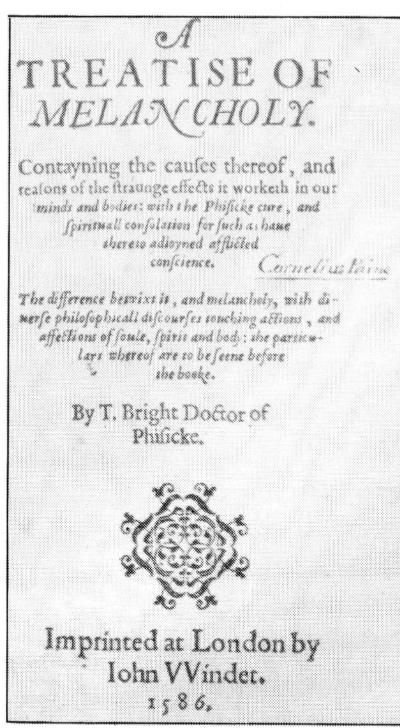

A TREATISE OF MELANCHOLY.

Contayning the cauſes thereof, and reaſons of the ſtraunge effects it worketh in our minds and bodies: with the Phiſicke cure, and ſpirituall conſolation for ſuch as haue thereto adioyned afflicted conſcience.

The difference betwixt it, and melancholy, with diuerſe philoſophicall diſcourſes touching actions, and affections of ſoule, ſpirit and body: the particulars whereof are to be ſeene before the booke.

By T. Bright Doctor of Phiſicke.

Imprinted at London by Iohn VVindet. 1586.

BRIGHT, TIMOTHY
'A Treatise of Melancholy' – minor stains – minor repairs – 19th century half morocco gilt – t.e.g. – sm. 8vo – 1586.
(Christie's) $1,010 £480

BRILLAT-SAVARIN, J. A.
'The Physiology of Taste or Meditations on Transcendental Gastronomy' – designs by A. Johnson – quarter vellum marbled boards – limited edn. 138/750 copies – Cresset Press 1928.
(Bennett Book Auctions) $20 £10

BRITISH MEDICAL JOURNAL, THE
A collection of 8 uncut broadsheets issued in 1874.
(Baitson) $2 £1

BRITISH MUSEUM
'The Book of the Dead' – facsimile of the Papyrus of Ani – coloured plates – cont. half morocco – rubbed – folio – 1890.
(Sotheby's) $220 £105

Catalogue of the Harleian Collection of Manuscripts – 2 vols. – 2 portraits – slightly browned – later calf – rubbed – folio – 1769.
(Sotheby's) $125 £60

'Select Bronzes' by H. W. Walters – 73 plates – cloth – 4to – 1915.
(Bonhams) $80 £40

BRITISH RACEHORSE MAGAZINE, THE
Some in binders, large quantity.
(Laurence & Martin Taylor) $4 £2

BRITTEN, F. J.
'Old Clocks and Watches and Their Makers' – 6th Edn. – frontispiece – illus. – orig. cloth – n.d.
(Christie's S. Kensington) $45 £20

BRITTON
'Laws' – modern half morocco – 2nd Edn. – London 1640 (title mounted).
(Bennett Book Auctions) $85 £40

BRITTON, J. AND BRAYLEY, E. W.
'Devonshire Illustrated' – map – vignette title – 94 engraved views bound with 'Cornwall Illustrated' map – vignette title – 44 engraved views – half morocco gilt – worn – 4to – 1833.
(Phillips) $335 £160

BRITTON, JOHN
'The History and Antiquities of the See and Cathedral Church of Norwich' – engraved addit. title and 24 plates – spotting – cont. half morocco – 4to – 1816.
(Christie's) $60 £30

'Picturesque Antiquities of English Cities' – 60 engraved plates – spotting – orig. cloth – worn – 4to – 1830.
(Christie's) $315 £150

'The Architectural Antiquities of Great Britain' – 4 vols. – five engraved titles and 212 plates and plans only – dampstaining – cont. half morocco – rubbed – 4to – 1807-14.
(Christie's S. Kensington) $125 £60

BROADSHEET
'The Lords Protest, (an account of Parliament's dissatisfaction with George the Second's demands for money to finance the war in Flanders against the French)' – 20½ x 15½in. – printed in red and black – cleanly torn – 1746.
(Christie's S. Kensington) $55 £25

BROADSHEETS
A collection of 16 German religious broadsheets – 14 double page, all versos blank, 15 within typographical borders – 2 with woodcut, many woodcut initials – some cropped, some loose, disbound – folio – Regensburg, Nuremberg and Linz, 1608-44.
(Sotheby's) $170 £80

BROCKEDON, WILLIAM
'Illustrations of the Passes of the Alps' – vol. 1 only – steel engraved plates and maps – spotting – cont. calf – upper cover detached – spine lacking – 4to – 1828.
(Christie's S. Kensington) $250 £120

'Italy' – mounted engraved title – frontispiece and 36 plates, one detached – a few spotted – margins soiled – cont. half morocco – rubbed – g.e. – folio – n.d.
(Christie's S. Kensington) $230 £110

'Road Book from London to Naples' – 1st Edn. – addit. engraved vignette – 29 engraved plates and maps – india paper – cont. half roan – lacking spine – covers detached – bookplate of J. H. Gladstone – 8vo – 1835.
(Sotheby's) $115 £55

BROCKHAUS, A.
'Netsuke' – coloured plates – orig. calf – worn – 4to.
(Sotheby's) $630 £300

BROCKLEHURST, CAPTAIN H. C.
'Game Animals of the Sudan' – illus. – cloth gilt – t.e.g. – 1931.
(Phillips) $85 £40

BRODRICK, T.
'History of the Great War' – 2 vols. – plates – half calf – 8vo – Netherlands 1713.
(Irelands) $250 £120

BROINOWSKI, G. J.
'Cockatoos and Nestors of Australia and New Zealand' – vol. 3 'Parrots – 13 col. litho plates – morocco gilt – g.e. – 4to – 1888.
(Phillips) $1,050 £500

BROMLEY, HENRY
'A Catalogue of Engraved British Portraits' – slight soiling – modern half calf – 4to – 1793.
(Christie's) $275 £130

BRONTE, ANNE
'Self Communion' – 1st Edn. – limited to 30 copies – 2 facsimiles – orig. boards – soiled – 8vo – Privately printed, 1900.
(Sotheby's) $65 £30

BRONTE, CHARLOTTE AND ANNE
Remarkable drawing by Charlotte of Anne inscribed by their father with additional study of Anne's face in the margin. A few fox marks otherwise in good condition – April 1833.
(Sotheby's) $12,600 £6,000

BRONTE, PATRICK BRANWELL
Pencil drawing executed when 11 years of age after Thomas Bewick showing a dog snarling at a cock inscribed and signed by him – laid down and browned – 4¼ x 5in.
(Sotheby's) $1,385 £660

BROOK, RICHARD
'New Cyclopaedia of Botany and Complete Book of Herbs' – 2 vols. in one – hand col. lithographed plates and one additional title – some leaves browned – cont. half morocco – worn – n.d.
(Christie's S. Kensington) $90 £40

BROOKE, H.
'Fool of Quality' – 4 vols. – 4 frontis – cont. calf gilt – 1776.
(Phillips) $80 £40

BROOKE, RUPERT
'1914, five sonnets' – orig. wrappers – a little split – stitching loose – 1915.
(J. Ash) $17 £8

BROUGHAM, HENRY LORD
'Lives of Men of Letters and Science' – 2 vols. – portraits – calf – 8vo – 1846-45.
(Sotheby's) $55 £25

BROUGHTON , U. H. R.
'The Dress of the First Regiment of Life Guards in Three Centuries' – no. 180 of 300 copies – plates, some coloured – orig. pigskin – 4to.
(Sotheby's) $190 £90

BROWN, C. BARRINGTON
'Canoe and Camp Life in British Guiana' – folding map and 10 coloured plates – 1st Edn. – cloth – 1876.
(Bonhams) $65 £30

BROWN, FRANK
'Frost's Drawings of Ipswich and Sketches in Suffolk' – no. 6 of 105 copies signed by author – plates – spotted – orig. cloth – rubbed – folio – 1895.
(Sotheby's) $105 £50

BROWN, J.
'Quakerisme, The Path-Way To Paganisme.' – cont. calf rebacked – 4to – Edinburgh for J. Cairns, 1678.
(Bennett Book Auctions) $45 £20

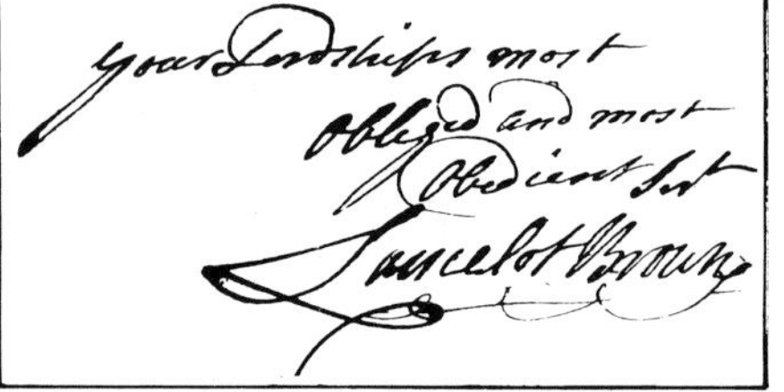
Your Lordships most
Obliged and most
Obedient Servt
Lancelot Brown

BROWN, LANCELOT, ('Capability')
Auto letter signed one page quarto to an unnamed peer asking him to repay a bond – soiled, with engraving after Dance – 16 Dec. 1779.
(Sotheby's) $230 £110

BROWN, R.
'History of Accounting and Accountants' – plates – cloth – Edinburgh 1905.
(Bennett Book Auctions) $40 £18

BROWN, R. N. RUDMOSE AND OTHERS
'The Voyage of the Scotia' – 1st Edn. – plates – 3 maps – spotting – orig. cloth – t.e.g. – Edinburgh and London 1906.
(Christie's) $145 £70

BROWN, ROBERT
'Science for All' – 5 vols. – coloured frontispieces – illustrations – cont. half calf – very slightly rubbed – spines gilt – t.e.g. – 4to – n.d.
(Christie's S. Kensington) $40 £20

BROWN, THOMAS OF MUSSELBURGH
'An Inquiry into the Antivariolus Power of Vaccination' – 1st Edn. – library inscription on title – orig. paper – joints split – uncut – 8vo – Edinburgh 1809.
(Sotheby's) $115 £55

BROWNE, ALEXANDER
'Arts Pictoria' – engraved plates – lacks 25-28 – half russia – worn – folio – 1669.
(Sotheby's) $20 £10

BROWNE, CHRISTOPHER
'Geographica Classica' – 29 double page engraved maps one folding – slight soiling – cont. calf-backed boards – rubbed – joints cracked – 1712.
(Christie's S. Kensington) $160 £75

BROWNE, JOHN
'A Compleat Treatise of the Muscles as they Appear in the Humane Body' –.1st Edn. – portrait frontis – 36 engraved anatomical plates – cont. mottled calf – folio – 1681.
(Christie's) $630 £300

BROWNE, SIR THOMAS
'Certain Miscellany Tracts' – 2nd Edn. – slight browning – lacking portrait and final blank – cont. sheep – worn – sm. 8vo – 1684.
(Sotheby's) $60 £30

BROWNE, W. G.
'Travels in Africa' – plates – tree calf – 4to – 1799.
(Irelands) $190 £90

BROWNE, WILLIAM
'Circe and Ulysses' – no. 156 of 300 copies – plates and full page illus. – orig. cloth backed boards – 1954.
(Christie's) $75 £35

BROWNING, ELIZABETH BARRETT
'The Seraphim' – 1st Edn. – half title – some ms. notes in pencil – orig. cloth – worn – one cover detached – 8vo – 1838.
(Sotheby's) $55 £25

BROWNING, ROBERT
'The Ring and the Book' – 4 vols. – 1st Edn. – orig. cloth – 8vo – 1868.
(Sotheby's) $90 £40
'Paracelsus' – author's second book – orig. boards – expertly rebacked – slight foxing – bookplate – 1835.
(J. Ash) $460 £220

BRUCE, J.
'Travels to Discover the Source of the Nile' – 8 vols., including Atlas, port., 79 plates – calf gilt – 4to – 1804-5.
(Phillips) $380 £180

BRUGIOTTI, D. A.
'Epitome Juris Viarum' – cont. Italian binding of limp vellum with arms of Pope Clement IX with corner ornaments – folio – Rome 1669.
(Moore Allen & Innocent) $315 £150

BRUNET, J. C.
'Manuel du Libraire' – 9 vols. – reprint – orig. cloth – 8vo – Copenhagen 1966-68.
(Sotheby's) $250 £120

BRUNHOF, JEAN DE
'Histoire de Babar le Petit Elephant' – 1st Edn.; 'Babar at Home'; 'Babar's Travels' – col. illus. by author – orig. cloth backed boards – worn – 1931, 1938, 1945.
(Sotheby's) $85 £40

BRUNUS ARETINUS, LEONARDO
'Historiae Florentini Populi' with Poggius Florentinus, 'Historia Fiorentia' – 2 works in one – later half morocco – slipcase – 1st Edn. of both works – folio – Venice Jacob Rubens 12th Feb. and 8th March 1476 (containing earliest printed references to the Life of Dante).
(Bennett Book Auctions) $1,155 £550

BRUZELIUS, A. J.
'Svensk Lakare-Matrikel' – 4 vols. – stains – cont. brown half morocco – rubbed – 8vo – Stockholm, 1886-1901.
(Sotheby's) $30 £15

BRUZEN DE LA MARTINIERE
'Introduction a l'Histoire de l'Asie, de l'Afrique et de l'Amerique' – 2 vols. – titles in red and black – engraved frontis – 3 folding maps – cont. calf, rubbed – 12 mo – Amsterdam 1735.
(Sotheby's) $55 £25

BRY, J. T. AND J. L. DE
'Historia Orientalis Indiae Tomus XII' – map and 13 woodcuts in text – old vellum – some waterstains – folio – 1628.
(Bonhams) $190 £90

BRYAN'S DICTIONARY OF PAINTERS AND ENGRAVERS
New Edn. under the supervision of George C. Williamson – 5 vols. – plates – orig. cloth – soiled and rubbed – t.e.g. – 1909-10.
(Christie's S. Kensington) $145 £70

BRYAN, MICHAEL
'A Biographical and Critical Dictionary of Painters and Engravers' – 2 vols. bound in calf – 1816.
(Baitson) $40 £20

BRYANT, ARTHUR
'The Age of Elegance' – 4th Impression, inscribed by the author – cont. morocco by Sangorski and Sutcliffe – g.e. – 1955.
(Christie's S. Kensington) $25 £12

BRYANT, G. E.
'Chelsea Porcelain Toys' – limited edition signed by author – colour plates – cloth – 4to – 1925.
(Phillips) $190 £90

BRYANT, THOMAS
'The Practice of Surgery' – 2 vols. – 559 illus. – 1876.
(Baitson) $4 £2

BRYANT, W. C.
'Picturesque America' – 4 vols. – engraved titles and plates – cont. half morocco – gilt – rubbed – 4to – n.d.
(Sotheby's) $160 £75

BRYDGES, SIR EDGERTON
'Bertram, A Poetical Tale' – limited to 100 copies – printed on india paper – wood engraved frontispiece and vignettes – slight spotting – cont. white morocco by Reeve – stamped and ruled in gilt – slightly rubbed and soiled – g.e. – Kent, Printed at the private press of Lee Priory by Johnston and Warwick, 1814.
(Christie's S. Kensington) $250 £120

BRYDONE, P.
'Tour Through Sicily and Malta' – 2 vols. – last page damaged – calf gilt – 1773.
(Phillips) $45 £20

BRYNER-JONES
'Live Stock on the Farm' – 6 vols. – 1916.
(Laurence & Martin Taylor) $2 £1

BUCHAN, JOHN
'The Power House' – covers marked – browned – wartime publication – 1916.
(J. Ash) $45 £20
'These for Remembrance' – orig. bindings – privately printed – presentation copy – author signed 1919, idem 'Andrew Jameson Lord Ardwall' – cloth – presentation copy author signed – 1913.
(Bennett Book Auctions) $145 £70

BUCHAN, WILLIAM
'Observations concerning the Prevention and Cure of the Venereal Disease, intended for the ignorant and unwary' – some browning and spotting – cont. calf – rubbed – joints and spines cracked – 1796.
(Christie's S. Kensington) $60 £30

BUCHANAN, G.
'Rerum Scoticarum Historia' – port. frontis – calf – Edinburgh 1727.
(Bennett Book Auctions) $4 £2

BUCK, G. H. & Co. (publishers)
'Botanical Fine Art Weekly Wild Flowers of America' – 288 col. plates on 144 leaves – title worn and repaired – browning – cont. half calf – worn – oblong 4to – New York 1894.
(Christie's) $75 £35

BUCK, SAMUEL AND NATHANIEL
'Views of Ruined Abbeys and Castles in England and Wales' – 83 engraved views of Wales only – later half morocco – oblong folio – 1740-42.
(Sotheby's) $880 £420

BUCKINGHAM, GEORGE VILLIERS
Autograph memoranda signed – one page – folio concerning the jointure of his niece Elizabeth Villiers – lightly mounted – April 1627.
(Sotheby's) $170 £80

BUCKINGHAM, J. S.
'Travels in Palestine' – engraved portrait – – 7 plans and map – spotting – illus. – soiling – modern half morocco – 4to – 1821.
(Christie's) $230 £110
'Travels in Assyria, Media and Persia' – 2 vols. – 2nd Edn. – plates – folding map – some dampstains – cont. calf gilt – rubbed – 8vo – 1830.
(Sotheby's) $180 £85
'Canada' – 7 folding plates and map – cont. half calf – rubbed – 8vo – n.d.
(Sotheby's) $40 £20

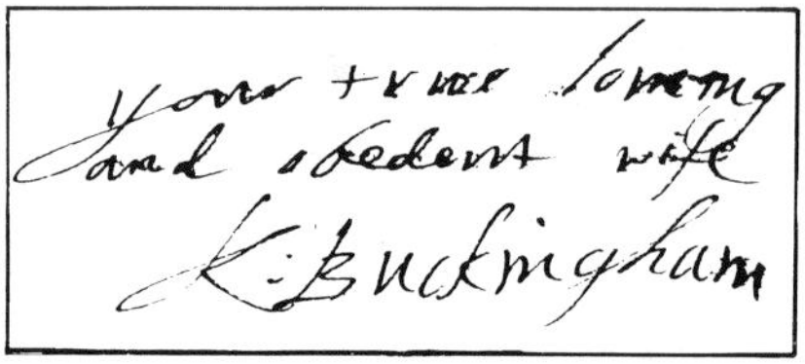

BUCKINGHAM, KATHERINE MANNERS, DUCHESS OF
Autograph letter to her husband George Villiers asking leave to go 'with the wenches' to Oatlands – one page – folio – n.d.
(Sotheby's) $125 £60

BUCKINGHAMSHIRE PARISH REGISTERS
Marriages, vols. 1-9 – limited Edn. – orig. cloth – soiled – 8vo and 4to – 1902-23.
(Sotheby's) $115 £55

BUCKLER, JOHN AND J. C.
'Views of Eaton Hall in Cheshire' – large paper copy – 20 engraved plates on india proof paper – spotting – orig. half morocco – very worn – folio – 1826.
(Sotheby Beresford Adams) $130 £60

BUCKLEY, FRANCIS
'A History of Old English Glass' – 1 of 100 signed copies – plates – pigskin – 4to – 1925.
(Phillips) $90 £40

BUCKMAN, PROFESSOR JAMES AND NEWMARCH, C. H.
'Illustrations of the Remains of Roman Art in Cirencester, The Site of Antient Corinium' – 13 hand engraved plates, 8 hand col. – one map, hand coloured in outline – slightly soiled – orig. cloth, soiled – stitching broken – t.e.g. – 4to – London and Cirencester, George Bell, Baily and Jones, 1850.
(Christie's S. Kensington) $30 £15

BUCKTON, A.
'Through Human Eyes' – no. 56 of 130 copies – orig. wrappers – frayed – Oxford, the Daniel Press 1901.
(Christie's) $85 £40

BUDAY, GYORGY – ORTUTAY, GYULA
'Nyiri es Retkozi Parasztmesek' – presentation copy – inscribed by artist – 45 full page illus. – orig. cloth backed boards – worn and soiled – 8vo – Gyoma, Izidor Kner, 1935.
(Sotheby's) $1,155 £550

BUDGE, E. A. WALLIS
'Syrian Anatomy, Pathology and Therapeutics or the Book of Medicines' – 2 vols. – 1st Edn. – text in Syriac and English – spotting – orig. cloth – faded – 8vo – 1913.
(Sotheby's) $40 £20

BUDGEN, L. M.
'Live Coals, or Faces from the Fire' – mounted additional title and plates – printed in colours – orig. cloth – soiled – g.e. – large 4to – 1867.
(Christie's S. Kensington) $30 £15

BUDGETT, H. M.
'Hunting by Scent' – no. 21 of 50 – signed by author and artist – plates by L. Edwards – orig. vellum backed cloth – t.e.g. – 8vo – n.d.
(Sotheby's) $145 £70

BUFFON
'Histoire Naturelle' – 2 vols. only – cont. French binding of green morocco, gilt with red silk endleaves – worn – 4to – 1788.
(Moore Allen & Innocent) $105 £50

BULL, RENE – JOHNSON, A. E.
'The Russian Ballet' – coloured plates by Bull – slight browning and spotting – orig. cloth – soiled – t.e.g. – 4to – Boston and New York, 1913.
(Christie's S. Kensington) $45 £20

BULLOCK, MRS. H. A.
'A History of the Isle of Man' – engraved frontispiece and folding map – some slight spotting – cont. calf – worn – 1816.
(Christie's S. Kensington) $40 £20

BULMER
'History and Directory of North Yorkshire' – 1892.
(Baitson) $65 £30

BUNBURY, W. H. 'Geoffrey Gambade'
'An Academy for Grown Horsemen' – 12 coloured plates – half leather – rubbed – 4to – 1812.
(Sotheby's) $115 £55

BUNDETO, CARLOS
'El Espejo de la Muerte' – engraved frontis – 4 x 1 engraved full page illus. in text at Romain de Hooghe – some leaves browned and stained – later blue panelled morocco gilt by Winstanley – slightly rubbed – g.e. – 4to – Antwerp 1700.
(Sotheby Beresford Adams) $505 £240

BUNSEN, ROBERT
'Gasometry' – 1st Edn. in English – illus. half title – errata leaf – 8pp. adverts – orig. cloth – 8vo – Walton and Maberly, 1857.
(Sotheby's) $100 £50

BUNYAN, JOHN
'The Life and Death of Mr. Badman' – some browning and soiling – inscription on title – 19th century wrappers – rubbed – 12 mo – 1774.
(Sotheby's) $30 £15

BUONAITI, B. S.
'Italian Scenery – 1st Edn. – 32 engraved hand coloured plates – cont. calf backed boards – repaired – folio – 1806.
(Sotheby's) $545 £260

BUONAPARTE
'Sa Famille et sa Cour' – 2 vols. – no. 104 of an unspecified no. of copies initialled by the publishers – occasional slight spotting – later half calf – slightly rubbed – Paris, 1816.
(Christie's S. Kensington) $90 £40

BURCHELL, W. J.
'Travels in the Interior of Southern Africa' – limited edn. – 2 vols. – plates – cloth – 4to – Capetown 1967.
(Phillips) $85 £40

BURCKHARDT, J. L.
'Travels in Nubia' – 3 maps – half gilt – 4to – 1819.
(Phillips) $190 £90

BURGESS TICKET OF THE BURGH OF CANONGATE
Framed, 1787.
(Bennett Book Auctions) $17 £8

BURKE, SIR BERNARD
'Family Romance or Episodes in the Domestic Annals of the Aristocracy' – 2 vols. – 2nd Edn. – orig. cloth – 1854.
(J. Ash) $35 £16

BURKE, H. F.
'Historical Record of the Coronations of Their Majesties King George the Fifth and Queen Mary' – silk endpapers – morocco gilt – g.e. – 1911.
(Phillips) $40 £18

BURKILL, I.
'Dictionary of the Economic Products of the Malay Peninsula' – 2 vols. – orig. cloth – 8vo – 1935.
(Sotheby's) $145 £70

BURLEIGH, LORD WILLIAM
'A Book of Precepts' – 1936.
(Richard Baker & Thomson) $65 £30

BURLINGAME, H. J.
'Leaves from a Conjurer's Scrap Book' – 1st Edn. – illus. – orig. cloth – slightly worn – 8vo – Chicago 1891.
(Sotheby's) $30 £15

BURLINGTON FINE ARTS CLUB
'Exhibition of Illuminated Manuscripts' – plates – orig. cloth – rubbed – folio – 1908.
(Sotheby's) $135 £65

BURLINGTON MAGAZINE FOR CONNOISSEURS
Vols. I-IV plus Supplements in 5 – limited edns. – plates – illus. – cont. half levant morocco by Root – gilt – 4to – 1903-04.
(Sotheby's) $135 £65

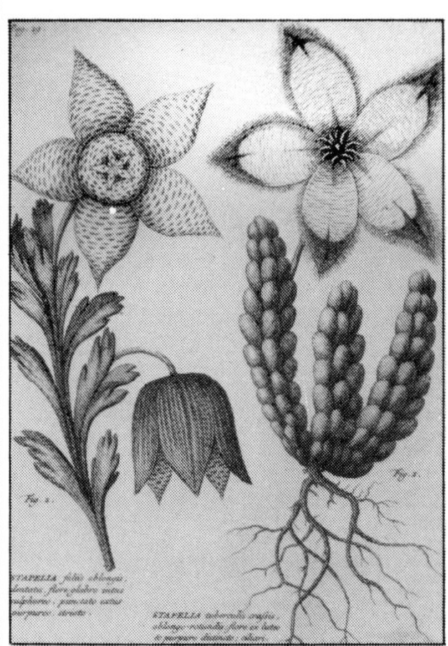

BURMANN, JOHANNES
'Thesaurus Zeylandicus' – title in red and black with large vignette – mezzo portrait – 111 engraved plates – addit. plate – upper cover detached – 4to – Amsterdam 1737.
(Christie's) $1,050 £500

BURMESE
Pali Buddhist text in Burmese square script, on 14 palm leaves with gilded and lacquered decoration, some flaking and splitting, lacking binding boards – 2 framed and glazed – 18th-19th century.
(Phillips) $60 £30

BURNABY, CAPTAIN FRED
'On Horseback Through Asia Minor' – 2 vols. – vol. 2 2nd Edn., 1877 – mounted portrait photograph – two folding coloured maps, one torn – orig. cloth – soiled – stitching weak.
(Christie's S. Kensington) $40 £20

BURNE-JONES, EDWARD
'The Beginning of the World' – 25 illus. by Burne-Jones – slightly soiled – orig. cloth-backed boards – slightly soiled and faded – folio – 1902.
(Christie's S. Kensington) $80 £40

BURNES, A.
'Cabool' – 1st Edn. – plates – some folding – orig. cloth – rubbed – 8vo – 1842.
(Sotheby's) $220 £105

BURNET, BISHOP GILBERT
'The History of the Rights of Princes in the Disposing of Ecclesiastical Benefits and Church Lands' – 2nd Edn. – 4 leafs of adverts at end – browning – cont. red morocco – gilt – rubbed – g.e. – 8vo – 1682.
(Sotheby's) $75 £35

BURNEY, CHARLES
'The Present State of Music in France and Italy' – 2nd Edn. – corrected – a few margins torn – slightly spotted – cont. calf gilt – very worn – 8vo – 1773.
(Sotheby Beresford Adams) $60 £30

BURNS, EDWARD
'The Coinage of Scotland' – 3 vols. – limited edn. – plates – cont. half morocco – rubbed – 4to – 1887.
(Sotheby's) $420 £200

BURROUGHS, EDGAR RICE
'Jungle Girl' – 1st English Edn. – spine faded – edges spotted – nice – 1933.
(J. Ash) $6 £3

BURTON, J. H.
'The Book Hunter' – illus. – posthumous limited edn. of 1,000 – 1882.
(Dacre, Son & Hartley) $40 £20

BURTON, RICHARD
'Winter Evening Entertainments – containing (i) Ten Pleasant and Delightful Relations and (ii) Fifty Ingenious Riddles' – 6th and 5th edns. – woodcut illus. – cont. calf – slightly rubbed – 12 mo – 1737.
(Sotheby's) $10 £5

BURTON, SIR RICHARD
'Falconry in the Valley of the Indus' – 4 tinted litho plates – 1st Edn. – orig. cloth – worn – 1852.
(Bonhams) $210 £100

BURTON, ROBERT
'The Anatomy of Melancholy' – 2nd Edn. – cont. half calf – covers loose – rubbed – 4to – J. Lichfield and J. Short for Henry Cripps, Oxford 1624.
(Sotheby's) $335 £160

BURTON, W.
'A History and Description of English Earthenware and Stoneware' – limited edn. 1904. 'Stoneware' 1906. Both with plates – orig. cloth – rubbed – 8vo.
(Sotheby's) $65 £30

BURY, LADY CHARLOTTE
'The Three Great Sanctuaries of Tuscany, Valambrosa, Camaldoli, Laverna' – mounted engraved portrait – etched addit. title detached – six mezzotint plates after Edward Bury – some spotting, mostly marginal – original cloth – spine chipped – inner hinges cracked – oblong folio – 1833.
(Christie's S. Kensington) $125 £60

BURY, T. T.
'Six Coloured Views of London and Birmingham Railway' – part 1, 6 hand col. aquatint plates – 19th century marbled boards – orig. wrappers – 4to – 1837.
(Sotheby's) $6,300 £3,000

BUSCH, WILHELM
'Buzz a Buzz or the Bees' – wood engraved illus. by Busch – col. by hand – torn – spotted – orig. pictorial boards – worn – rebacked – 8vo – Griffith and Farran 1872.
(Sotheby's) $55 £25

BUSK, G.
'On the Caves of Gibralter in which Human Remains and Works of Art have been Found' – offprint – plates – some folding – 6 cont. Als. inserted – cont. roan – rubbed – 8vo – n.d.
(Sotheby's) $75 £35

BUTCHER, REV. ED.
'Beauties of Sidmouth' – 3rd Edn. – n.d.
(Laurence & Martin Taylor) $20 £10

BUTLER, A. G. AND OTHERS
'British Birds with their Nests and Eggs' – 6 vols. – plates by F. W. Frohawk, those of eggs coloured – margins of one worn – another torn cleanly – some stains – orig. cloth – worn – 4to – Frederick Warne, 1899.
(Christie's S. Kensington) $40 £20

BUTLER, SAMUEL
'Erewhon' – one of 750 copies, published by author – little used – 1872.
(J. Ash) $125 £60

II. Capitul. 117

gen an, wann die Sonn anfahet zuſcheinen, biß zur Nacht, aber gemeiniglich wird es am Morgen, weil es noch nüchtern iſt, beſchnitten, dann es blutet nicht ſo viel, als wann es geeſſen hat.

BUXTORF, JOHANNES, The Elder
'Syngoga Judaica, Oder Juden Schul' – folding title printed in red – engravings – some repairs – without loss of text – staining – boards – 8vo – Frankfurt am Main-Leipzig, 1728.
(Sotheby's) $505 £240

BYNG, ADMIRAL JOHN
'The Trial at a Court Martial' – 2 parts in one – spotted – orig. calf backed boards – worn – folio – 1757.
(Sotheby's) $55 £25

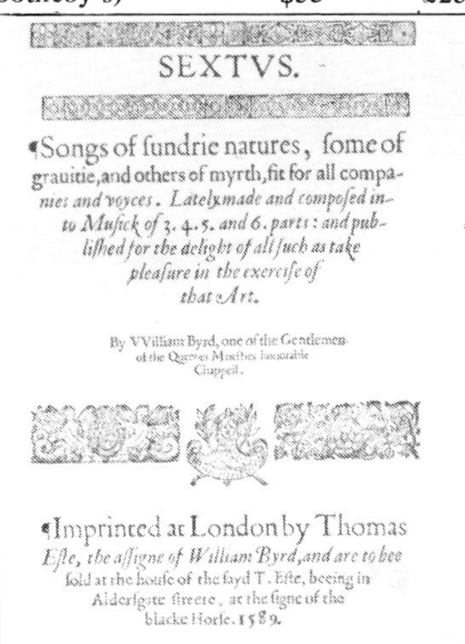
SEXTVS.

¶Songs of ſundrie natures, ſome of grauitie, and others of myrth, fit for all companies and voyces. Lately made and compoſed into Muſicke of 3. 4. 5. and 6. parts: and publiſhed for the delight of all ſuch as take pleaſure in the exercise of that Art.

By William Byrd, one of the Gentlemen of the Queenes Maieſties honorable Chappell.

¶Imprinted at London by Thomas Eſte, the aſſigne of William Byrd, and are to bee ſold at the houſe of the ſayd T. Eſte, beeing in Alderſgate ſtreete, at the ſigne of the blacke Horſe. 1589.

Cum priuilegio Regiæ Maieſtatis.

BYRD, WILLIAM
'Songs of Sundrie Natures' – printed music throughout, with 'Liber Secundus Sacrarum Cantionym' – 2 works in one vol. – water-staining – cont. limp vellum – sm. 4to – 1589.
(Christie's) $800 £380

BYRNE, J. C.
'Twelve Years' Wanderings in the British Colonies' – 2 vols. – folding lithographed map – mounted on cloth – in wallet at back of vol. 2 – modern calf backed cloth – 1848.
(Christie's S. Kensington) $170 £80

BYRON, LORD GEORGE GORDON
Autograph working mss. of an unpublished poem – 14 line satire on Angerstein, founder of the National Gallery – one leaf folio – minor wear and tear.
(Sotheby's) $7,140 £3,400
'Marino Faliero' – First issue modern boards – lacks half title – 1821.
(J. Ash) $55 £25

BYSTANDER, THE
Vols. 20-40 only – illus. cont. cloth – slightly rubbed – 4to – 1908-13.
(Sotheby's) $220 £105

CABELL, J. B.
'Jurgen' – no. 324 of 500 copies – illus. by John Buckland Wright – orig. morocco backed cloth – spine faded – t.e.g. – Golden Cockerel Press 1949.
(Christie's) $65 $32

CADDICK, ARTHUR
'Lyrics from Nancledra' – signed by author and including corres. with Sir G. Nott Bower.
(Laurence & Martin Taylor) $6 £3

CAESAR, C. J.
'Commentariorum' – 2 vols. contem. French binding of citron morocco gilt with arms of Madame Sophie de France, daughter of Louis XV slightly restored – 12 mo. – 1755.
(Moore Allen & Innocent) $360 £170

CAILLIE, R.
'Travels Through Central Africa to Timbuctoo' – 2 vol. – 6 plates – 2 folding maps – torn, soiled – orig. cloth backed boards, worn – 1830.
(Sotheby's) $40 £18

CAIN, GEORGES
'La Place Vendome' – number 91 0f 265 copies on grand velin a la cuve de Rives – foreword by Frederic Masson – plates, some hand col. – illus in text – russet morocco gilt by de Coverley – orig. wrapper bound in – t.e.g. – 4to. – Paris 1908.
(Sotheby Beresford Adams) $90 £42

CAINE, HALL
'The Manxman' – cloth slightly rubbed and marked – 1894.
(J. Ash) $17 £8

CALDECOTT, RANDOLPH
'Last Graphic Pictures' 1888 – 'Graphic Pictures' – 3 parts in one vol. – new Edn. – n.d. – orig. cloth backed boards or cloth – oblong folio.
(Sotheby Beresford Adams) $45 £22

CALDECOTT, RANDOLPH – CARR, MRS COMYNS
'North Italian Folk' – 1st Edn. – no. 150 of 400 copies – illus. col. by hand – orig. linen backed boards, soiled, worn – 8vo. – Chatto and Windus 1878.
(Sotheby's) $45 $22

CALDER-MARSHALL, ARTHUR
'A Crime Against Cania' – number 227 of 250 copies – signed by author – illus. by Blair Hughes-Stanton – orig. morocco backed cloth – t.e.g. 1934.
(Christie's) $40 £18

CALDERWOOD, W.L.
'The Salmon Rivers and Lochs of Scotland' – coloured frontis – plates and maps – buckram backed cloth – limited Edn. 9/250 copies – 1909.
(Bennett Book Auctions) $90 £44

CALDICOTT, J. W.
'The Values of Old English Silver and Sheffield Plate' – plates – cloth, some wear – 4to. – 1906.
(Phillips) $60 £28

CALLENDER, GEOFFREY (editor)
'Realms of Melody' – pictorial title – lower endleaf torn – orig. cloth, slightly worn and soiled – 8vo. – 1916.
(Sotheby's) $90 £45

CALLIGRAPHIC LION
The lion, symbol of Ali – drawn in black with grey wash – calligraphy pricked gold outlined in black – paper browned and defective in places – pale blue borders – black motifs – framed – 23 cm x 33.5cm. – Ottoman, 19th cent.
(Christie's) $1,785 £850

CALLIGRAPHIC PANEL, ARABIC PRAYERS
One line of monumental black naskh with decorative gold rosette – gold rosettes between verses – gold and black rules – inscribed by 'Osman known as Hafiz' – slightly stained – laid down on album leaf – framed – Ottoman 17th cent.
(Christie's) $2,310 £1,100

CALLIGRAPHIC PANEL
One line of monumental black naskh – florette illum. in pink and gold, with two lines of smaller black naskh with similar florettes on pink and beige ground – inscribed 'Sayyid Mustafa Izzet' – illum. panels – central gold medallions – gold corner cartouches – laid down on card – Ottoman circa 1216-1293.
(Christie's) $630 £300

CALLIMACHI, C.
'Hymni, Epigrammata et Fragmenta' – vellum – 12 mo – Antwerp 1524.
(Phillips) $17 £8

CALLIOPE OR ENGLISH HARMONY
Engraved music with engraved headings – vol. 1 – calf frontis – 1739.
(Bonhams) $230 £110

CALVERT, ALBERT F.
'The Exploration of Australia' – 2 vols. – 2 folding col. maps, cleanly torn – orig. vellum backed cloth – 4to. – 1895-6.
(Christie's) $45 £22
'Moorish Remains in Spain; The Alhambra' – 2 vols. – plates, some col. – orig. cloth – 8vo. – 1906.
(Sotheby's) $115 £55

CAMBRIDGE BIBLIOGRAPHY OF ENGLISH LITERATURE, THE
Editor F. Bateson – 4 vol. including index – without supplement – orig. cloth – large 8vo. – Cambridge 1940.
(Sotheby's) $85 £40

CAMBRIDGESHIRE PARISH REGISTERS
Marriages vol. 1-8 and index to vol. 1-6, altogether 9 vols. – limited Edn. – orig. cloth, soiled – 8vo. – 1907-27.
(Sotheby's) $115 £55

CAMDEN SOCIETY
'Publications' – 92 vols. only – orig. cloth, some rubbed – 8vo. – 1838-1975.
(Sotheby's) $715 £340

CAMDEN, WILLIAM
'The Historie of the most Renowed and Victorious Princess Elizabeth' – folio – engr. portrait – heavy dampstaining – some marginal tears – old calf – rebacked – printed for Benjamin Fisher – 1630.
(Christie's S. Kensington) $65 £32
'Remaindes Concerning Britaine' – portrait decorations – crudely hand coloured – dampstaining – later half calf – rebacked – sm 4to – Thomas Harper for John Waterson, 1637.
(Christie's S. Kensington) $40 £18

CAMPBELL, COLEN
'Vitruvius Britannicus' – vol. 1-3 engr. plates – many double page – bookplate of Lord Willoughby de Broke – contemp. blind and gilt-stamped calf, rubbed.
(Sotheby's) $650 £310

CAMPBELL, DONALD
'A Journey Overland to India' – 1st Edn. – spotting – tree calf – upper cover loose – 4to. 1796.
(Sotheby's) $30 £15

CAMPBELL, JOHN
'Candid and Impartial Observations on the Nature of the Sugar Trade ... in the West Indies' – 3 coloured folding maps – half title – red morocco gilt – spine gilt – g.e. – 8vo. – R. Baldwin 1763.
(Sotheby's) $250 £120

CAMPBELL, JOHN
'A Political Survey of Britain' – 2 vol. – 1st Edn. – half titles – browning – contem. sprinkled calf, rubbed – 4to. – 1774.
(Sotheby's) $55 £25

CAMPBELL, MRS. R.
'Scottish Scenery, Sketches from Nature' – 48 plates – cloth f. cover detached – small oblong 4to. – nd.
(Bennett Book Auction) $34 £16

CAMPBELL, T.
'Gertrude of Wyoming' – orig. boards – uncut – 4to. – 1st Edn. 1809.
(Bennett Book Auction) $34 £16

CAMPEN, JACOB VAN
'Afbeelding Van't Stadt Huys Amsterdam' – 1st Edn. – engraved title – portrait and 29 plates – discoloured – contem. vellum – folio – Amsterdam 1661.
(Christie's) $630 £300

CAMPER, P.
'Works' – portrait and plates – 4to. – old mottled calf – 1794.
(Bonhams) $20 £10

CAMUS, ALBERT
'The Plague' – 1st Eng. Edn. – trans. by Stuart Gilbert – 1948.
(J. Ash) $8 £4

CANALS
A collection of 18 Acts of Parliament – all disbound – folio – 1783-97.
(Sotheby's) $200 £95

CANNING, VICTOR
'The House of the Seven Flies' – cloth slightly marked – spine faded – chipped jacket – 1952.
(J. Ash) $6 £3

CANNON MISSAE AD USUM EPISCOPORUM ACPRAELATORUM
Engraved additional title – title vignettes and illustrations – most full page – printed in black and red – musical scores – a few pages torn and repaired without loss of letters, soiling – contemp. morocco – gilt –with cardinal's arms on covers, rubbed – g.e. folio – Rome ex Typographici Vaticana 1725.
(Christie's S. Kensington) $115 £55

CANTELLI, DA VIGNOLA, GIACOMO
'La Gran Tartaria' – engraved map – hand col. in outline – large cartouche with human figures – fully coloured – 430 mm x 540mm. – Rome, G. G. De Rossi, 1693.
(Sotheby's) $40 £20

CANTERBURY MARRIAGE LICENCES
First to sixth series – 6 vols. – contem. morocco, rubbed – t.e.g. – 4to. – 1892-1906.
(Sotheby's) $115 £55

CANTON, FRANCISCO
'Goya and the Black Paintings' – col. plates – some folding – illus. – some coloured and mounted – orig. cloth – dust jacket – slip cover – folio – 1964.
(Sotheby's) $60 £28

CAPE OF GOOD HOPE
Papers relevant to the Condition and Treatment of the Native Inhabitants – part 1 only – spotted – contem. cloth, rubbed – folio – 1835.
(Sotheby's) $30 £14

CAPOTE, TRUMAN
'Other Voices, Other Rooms' – 1st Eng. Edn. – author's first book – wrinkled in spine, otherwise a nice copy – 1948.
(J. Ash) $20 £10

CAPPER, B. P.
'A Topographical Dictionary of the United Kingdom' – 46 uncoloured engr. maps – a few folding – occasional light dampstains – contemp. russsian – joints and spine split – 1808.
(Christie's S. Kensington) $115 £55

CARADOC PRESS
Kalendar MDCCCC – orig. wrappers, soiled – oblong 12 mo. – December 1899.
(Christie's) $45 £22

CARD CASTLE, THE
Pack of attached cards – wooden tray with trick baize lining – instructions – 500 mm x 315 mm.
(Sotheby's) $20 £10

CARDS, COLLECTION OF
Signed and inscribed by Caruso, McCormack, Tetrazzini, Melba and Chaliapine with signed photos of Tetrazzini, Del Monte, Destinn and others – a programme for the first performance of the Royal Opera House of Wozzeck, signed by Kleiber and other performers and a letter by Palmerston.
(Sotheby's) $105 £50

CARIBBEAN ISLANDS
Engraved maps and plans – most hand col. – various sizes – five in all – Paris circa 1764.
(Sotheby's) $30 £15

CARLETON, CAPT. G.
'Memoirs of ...' – calf - gilt – 1743.
(Phillips) $60 £28

CARLEVARIS, LUCA
'Le Fabriche e Vedute di Venezia' – engraved title and 49 plates only of 103 – contem. half calf, rubbed – oblong folio – Venice 1705
(Sotheby's) $3,990 £1,900

CARLYON-BRITTON
'Collection of Coins' – 3 vol. in 1 – plates– modern cloth – 4to. – 1913-18.
(Sotheby's) $250 £120

James Ellis

What is Heaven? and what are ye
Who its brief expanse inherit?
What are suns & spheres which flee
With the instinct of that spirit
Of which ye are but a part?
Drops which natures mighty heart
Drives thro thinnest veins —
What is Heaven? a globe of dew,
Filling in the morning new
Some eyed flower whose young leaves waken
On an unimagined world:
Constellated suns unshaken,
Orbits measureless, are furled
In that frail & fading sphere
With ten millions gathered there,
To tremble, gleam, & disappear

T. Carlyle

CARLYLE, THOMAS
'Sartor Resartus' – front free endpaper with apparently unpublished poem in mss. cloth backed boards – soiled – 1838.
(Christie's) $135 £65

CARMICHAEL, J. W. AND WELFORD, RICHARD
'Pictures of Tyneside or Life and Scenery on the River Tyne Sixty Years Ago' – 33 mounted engraved plates after Carmichael – staining – contem. half morocco, worn – t.e.g. – folio – Newcastle 1881.
(Christie's) $55 £25

CARNE, JOHN
'Syria, the Holy Land and Asia Minor' – 3 vols. – 3 engraved titles – 2 maps – 117 engravings – half calf – 4to. – n.d.
(Phillips) $200 £95

CAROLINA – LE ROUGE, G. L.
'Nouvelle Carte des Cotes des Carolines' – engraved chart of the coast of Carolina from Cape Fear to South Edisto – col. by hand in outline – compass rose – series of coastal contours full col. – compass lines and soundings – 395 mm x 533mm. – Paris 1777.
(Sotheby's) $250 $120

CAROLSFIELD, L. S. VON AND HUTH, H.
'Die Sammlung Erich von Goldschmidt – Rothschild' – plates original wrappers – backstrip slightly soiled and frayed – 4to. – Berlin 1931.
(Christie's S. Kensington) $65 £30

CARR, J.
'The Stranger in France or a Tour from Devonshire to Paris' – 12 plates – calf, gilt - 4to. – 1803.
(Phillips) $100 £48

CARR, J. COMYNS
'Example of Contemporary Art' – plates – orig. cloth, slightly soiled and torn – t.e.g. – folio – 1878.
(Christie's) $30 £15

CARRINGTON, HENRY
'The Plymouth and Devonport Guide' – 1st Edn. – in an envelope – 1828.
(Lane) $75 £35

CARTER, FREDERICK
'D. H. Lawrence and the Body Mystical' – limited Edn. of 250 copies – some pencil underlining – large 8vo. – 1932.
(J. Ash) $55 £26

CARTER, H. AND MACE, A. C.
'The Tomb of Tut-an-Kamen' – 3 vols., vols 2 and 3 1st Edn. – plates – cloth gilt – d.w.s. 1930-33.
(Phillips) $125 £60

CARTER, J. AND MUIR, P. H.
'Printing and the Mind of Man' – orig. cloth – 4to. – 1967.
(Sotheby's) $190 £90

CARTER, JIMMY, 39th President of U.S.A.
Autograph cheque signed J. E. Carter Jr for $14.08 and stamped Carters Warehouse/ Plains Georgia, with autograph cheque signed by Rosalynn Carter when head book-keeper of the warehouse – printed with mss insertions – stamps and endorsements – Oct. and Nov. 1960.
(Sotheby's) $945 £450

CARTER, JOHN
'The Ancient Architecture of England ... with notes and copious index by John Britton' – two engr. add. titles and 107 plates, some staining – contemp. half morocco, rubbed, joints worn – folio – Henry G. Bohn 1837.
(Christie's S. Kensington) $60 £28

'Specimens of the Ancient Sculpture and Painting now remaining in England' – new Edn. – folio – two engraved add. titles and 118 plates – some hand coloured – two folding one double page – some leaves detached – some spotting – contemp. half morocco worn – 1838.
(Christie's S. Kensington) $65 £32

CARTOONS
A collection of approx. 360 vols. including work of Osbert Lancaster, Searle, Jak, Giles etc. – original bindings – many paper-backs – various sizes.
(Sotheby's) $485 £230

CARVER, JOHN
'New Universal Traveller' – frontis – plates – maps by T. B. Owen – folio – 1779.
(Phillips) $170 £80

CARY, JOHN
'New and Correct English Atlas' – engraved title – 46 maps – hand coloured in outline – half calf – worn – 4to. – 1787.
(Christie's S. Kensington) $420 £200

'New Map of England and Wales with part of Scotland' – 4to. – engraved map on 81 sheets – hand coloured in outline – advertisement at end dated 1804 – contemp. limp calf – new endpapers – 1794.
(Christie's S. Kensington) $115 £55

'New Itinerary ... throughout England and Wales etc.' – large folding and 6 other maps – 7th edition with improvements – uncut – 1817.
(Bennett Book Auctions) $40 £18

CARY, JOYCE
'The African Witch' – dull and rubbed – 1936.
(J. Ash) $10 £5

CASATI, MAJOR G.
'Ten Years in Equatoria' – 2 vols. – maps – plates – orig. pictorial cloth – 1891.
(Phillips) $115 £55

CASSINI, J. D., P. F. A. MECHAIN AND A. M. LE GENDRE
'Expose des Operations Faites en France en 1787 pour la Jonction des Observatories de Paris et de Greenwich' – 5 folding engraved plates – repairs – contem. mottled calf – arms of Baron Stuart de Rothesay – worn – 4to. – Paris n.d.
(Sotheby's) $380 £180

CASTIGLIONE, COUNT BALTHAZAR
'Le Parfait Courtisan' – Last imprint leaf – some leaves soiled – 19th cent half calf – rebacked and repaired – 8vo. – Lyons pour Loys Cloquemin 1580.
(Sotheby's) $105 £50

CATALOGUE OF THE CELEBRATED COLLECTION OF ANCIENT MARBLES IN THE POSSESSION OF THE MOST HONOURABLE THE MARQUIS OF LANSDOWNE
plates – orig. board – spines chipped – 1930.
(Christie's) $45 £22

CATLIN, GEORGE
'Catlin's North American Indian Portfolio – Hunting Scenes and Amusements of the Rocky Mountains and Prairies of America' – 1st Edn. – 25 tinted litho plates, orig. half roan – rubbed – large folio – 1844.
(Christie's) $5,670 £2,700

'The Manners, Customs and Conditions of the North American Indians' – 2 vol. – 1st Edn. – 200 col. plates and maps – some loose – orig. cloth – slightly soiled – 8vo. – 1841.
(Sotheby.s) $285 £135

CATTON, C.
'Animals Drawn from Nature' – 7 aquatint plates of 36 – framed and glazed – 1788.
(Sotheby's) $30 £15

CAULFIELD, JAMES
'Cromwelliana' – Chronological detail of events – illus. morocco gilt – g.e. – 1810.
(Phillips) $105 £50

'Portraits and Memoirs of Remarkable Persons from 1688 to the End of the Reign of George 11' – 4 vol. – portraits – spotting – contem. morocco tooled in gilt and blind – spines cracked – g.e. – 1819-20.
(Christie's) $100 £48

CAUNTER, HOBART
'The Oriental Annual or Scenes in India' – engraved frontis – addit. title and 22 plates after William Daniell – some spotting – some leaves detached – contem morocco – rubbed – g.e. – 1836.
(Christie's) $25 £12

CAW, J. L.
'Scottish Painting Past and Present 1620-1908' – plates – buckram – Edinburgh 1908.
(Bennett Book Auctions) $34 £16

'Scottish Portraits' – 5 vol. – 13 of 250 copies – plates – unbound as issued in orig folio – Edinburgh 1902-03.
(Christie's) $25 £12

CAXTON, MASTER WILLIAM
'The Golden Legend of ....' – 3 vols. – 500 copies printed – 2 full page woodcut illus. by Burne Jones – woodcut – orig. limp vellum silk ties – 4to. – The Kelmscott Press 1892.
(Christie's) $630 £300

One leaf from the Higden 'Polychronicon' rubricated – wide margins – good condition – After July 1482.
(Phillips) $275 £130

THE
CERTAINTY
OF
SALVATION
To Them who Dye in the LORD.
A
SERMON,
PREACHED
At the FUNERAL of the Right Honourable,
GEORGE Lord DELAMER;
AT
BODEN,
In the County-Palatine of CHESTER:
September the 9th. 1684.

By ZACHARY CAWDREY;
Rector of BARTHOMLY, in the said County-Palatine of CHESTER.

LONDON, Printed for Peter Gillworth, Book-seller in New-Castle, in Staffordshire; and James Thurston, Book-seller in Nantwich. 1684.

CAWDREY, ZACHARY
'The Certainty of Salvation to them who dye in the Lord' – disbound with 8 others all published in Staffordshire – 1684.
(Sotheby Beresford Adams) $230 £110

DVE
TRATTATI
VNO INTORNO ALLE OTTO
PRINCIPALI ARTI
DELL'OREFICERIA.
L'altro in materia dell'Arte della Scultura; doue si veggono infiniti segreti nel lauorar le Figure di Marmo, & nel gettarle di Bronzo.
COMPOSTI DA M. BENVENVTO CELLINI
SCVLTORE FIORENTINO.

CELLINI, BENEVENUTO
'Due Trattati' – 1st Edn. – Medici arms on title – fine woodcut initials – 18th cent calf – rubbed rebacked – sm. 4to. – 1568.
(Christie's) $1,090 £520

'The Life' ... Translated by John Addington Symonds – 2 vol. – limited to 750 copies – plates – orig. calf backed boards – t.e.g. – 1888.
(Christie's S. Kensington) $65 £30

CENOTAPHIUM
'Leonardi Antonelli Cardinalis & Pisauri' – 8 vol. – contem. brown Spanish calf gilt – arms of Ferdinand, King of Spain 1819-33 on each cover – 1825.
(Moore Allen & Innocent) $360 £170

CENTENO, AMARO
'Historia de Cosas del Oriente Primera y Segunda parte' – 1st Edn. – badly stained – title defective – restored – 19th cent. calf gilt – sm 4to – Cordoba, 1595.
(Sotheby's) $295 £140

CENTORIO DEGLI HOTENSII (ASCANIO)
'Discorsi Di Guerra' – four parts only in one vol. – title and first few leaves slightly soiled and torn – contemp. vellum – worn – 4to. – 1568-59.
(Christie's S. Kensington) $40 £18

CENTURY ILLUSTRATED MONTHLY MAGAZINE, NEW SERIES
Vol. 1-53 (lacking vol. 10 and 53) plates – contemp. – half morocco – rubbed – 8vo. – 1881-1908.
(Sotheby's) $115 £55

CERIO, EDWIN
'That Capri Air' – 1st Eng. Edn. – trans by Norman Douglas, Louis Golding and Francis Brett Yound – very good in chipped dust wrapper – 1929.
(J. Ash) $17 £8

CESCINSKY, H. AND WEBSTER, M. R.
'English Domestic Clocks' – col. frontis – half morocco – rubbed – 4to. – 1914.
(Phillips) $160 £75

CESCINSKY, HERBERT
'The Old English Clockmakers' – illus. – orig. cloth – slightly rubbed – 8vo. – 1906.
(Sotheby's) $125 £60
'English Furniture from Gothic to Sheraton' – plates – orig. cloth – slightly soiled – lge 4to. – Grand Rapids – 1929.
(Christie's S. Kensington) $55 £25

CESCINSKY, HERBERT AND GRIBBLE, ERNEST R.
'Early English Furniture and Woodwork' – 2 vol. – 4to. – coloured frontispiece – illustrations – orig. cloth – slightly rubbed – t.e.g. – 1922.
(Christie's S. Kensington) $135 £65

CEYLON, SRI LANKA – ARROWSMITH, A.
'Map of the Island of Ceylon' – large engraved map – col. by hand – slight offsetting – 932 mm x 590 mm. – 1805.
(Sotheby's) $85 £40

CEZANNE, PAUL – MIRBEAU, OCTAVE
'Cezanne' – etched frontis by Cezanne – 6 lithos – 2 other designs – 30 repros – spotted – contem. morocco backed buckram – rubbed – inscribed on flyleaf – folio – Paris, Bernheim-Jeune, 1914.
(Sotheby's) $1,050 £500

CHABERT, M.
'Galerie des Peintres ou Collection de Portraits' – 2 vol. – litho plates – contem. morocco – folio – Paris n.d.
(Sotheby's) $210 £100

CHAFFERS, W.
'The Keramic Gallery' – 2 vols. – plates – spotted – contem. half morocco – 8vo. – 1872.
(Sotheby's) $60 £29

'Marks and Monograms on Pottery and Porcelain' – 4th Edn. – Facimiles – orig. cloth – rubbed – 8vo. – 1874.
(Sotheby's) $25 £12

'Hall-marks on Gold and Silver Plate' – illus. cloth gilt – 1905.
(Bonhams) $40 £20

CHAGALL, MARC
'Chagall Lithographie 1962-68 Catalogue et Notices Ferdinand Mourlot Charles Sortier' – 4to. – coloured frontis – illustrations – some full page – most coloured – orig. cloth – dust jacket – 1969.
(Christie's S. Kensington) $100 £48

CHAGALL, MARC – MOURLOT, FERNAND
'The Lithographs of Chagall' – 12 lithographs by Chagall – including dust jacket – numerous plain and coloured reproductions – orig. cloth – dust jacket and cellophane wrappers – slipcase – 4to. – Monte Carlo, Andre Sauret – 1960.
(Sotheby's) $5,250 £2,500

CHALDEAE
'Seu Authiopicae Linguae Institutiones' – some browning – later boards – backstrip worn – Rome 1630.
(Christie's S. Kensington) $55 £25

CHALMERS, A.
'A History of the College, Halls and Public Buildings attached to the University of Oxford' – 2 vols. – engraved addit. title – 31 plates – spotting – contem. straight grained calf – spine rubbed – Oxford 1810.
(Christie's) $145 £70

CHALMERS, GEORGE
'Caledonia' – 3 vol. – folding map – tables and plates – contem. polished calf – joints weak – large 4to. – 1801-24.
(Sotheby's) $20 £10

CHALON, A. E. AND LANE, R. J.
One leather bound album of autographed photos and postcards of actors and actresses including a signed self portrait by Caruso, dated 1907 – signatures of Ellen Terry, Gerald du Maurier, Nellie Melba and Marie Lloyd.
(Sotheby's) $460 £220

CHAMBERLAIN, H.
'New and Complete History and Survey of London and Westminster' – engravings – some repairs – half calf – folio – 1770.
(Phillips) $95 £45

CHAMBERLAINE, JOHN
'Original Designs of the Most Celebrated Masters of the Bolognese, Roman, Florentine and Venetian Schools' – 3 titles – hand col. engraved frontis – 72 plates on 67 leaves – contem. half maroon morocco – spine gilt and faded – folio 1812.
(Sotheby's) $880 £420

CHAMBERS' BOOK OF DAYS
Illus. 2 vols. – 1863/4 and 'Survey of English Dialects'; Southern Counties' – Part 1-3 etc. – 4 vols. – 1962-67.
(Bonhams) $20 £10

CHAMBERS, DAVID
'Le Recherche des Singulaitez plus Remarquables Concernant L'Estat d'Ecosse ....' – 2 works in one vol. – woodcut device on titles – dampstains – 19th cent. calf – arms of Duke of Sutherland on upper cover – sm. 8vo. – Paris 1579.
(Sotheby's) $135 £65

CHAMBERS, E.
'Cyclopaedia; or, an Universal Dictionary of Arts and Sciences' – 4 vol. only – folio – title to vol. 4 lacking – some leaves detached – some worming – contemp. calf – worn – circa 1786.
(Christie's S. Kensington) $40 £20

CHAMBER'S ENCYCLOPAEDIA
10 vol. new Edn. – folding coloured maps – contemp. – half morocco – very slightly rubbed – 1895.
(Christie's S. Kensington) $85 £40

CHAMBERS, R.
'Biographical Dictionary of Eminent Scotsmen' – 4 volumes – engraved plates – cloth – Glasgow 1835.
(Bennett Book Auctions) $17 £8

CHAMBERS, SIR WILLIAM
'Designs of Chinese Buildings' – 1st Edn. – 21 engraved plates – title and 3 pages foxed – contem. half calf – very worn – bookplate of the Baptist College Library, Bristol – folio – 1757.
(Sotheby's) $380 £180
'Elevations, Sections and Perspective Views of the Gardens and Buildings at Kew in Surrey' – 43 plates by Rooker and others – 2 double-page – 1st Edn. – folio – orig. half calf – worn – 1763.
(Bonhams) $1,010 £480

CHAMFORT, S.R.N. DE
'Maxims and Considerations' – 2 vol. – number 91 of 550 copies – orig. boards – dust jackets – spotted and torn – vol. 1 unopened – 1926.
(Christie's) $17 £8

CHAMOUIN
'Collection de 28 Vues de Paris' – 28 engraved plates – some stained – orig. calf backed cloth – rubbed – oblong folio – Paris n.d.
(Sotheby's) $170 £80

CHANCELLOR, E. BERESFORD
'The History and Antiquities of Richmond, Kew, Petersham, Ham etc.' – folding frontis – plates – illus. – orig. cloth – t.e.g. – 1894.
(Christie's) $40 £20

CHANDLER, RICHARD
'Travels in Asia Minor and Greece' – 2 vols. – 3rd Edn. – 7 engraved plans and maps – many folding – some defects – bookplates of Earl of Wicklow – contem. sprinkled calf – slightly rubbed – 4to. – 1817.
(Sotheby Beresford Adams) $125 £60

CHANLAIRE, P. G.
'Atlas National de la France' – 111 double page engraved maps – col. in outline – spotting and soiling – 19th cent. half calf – worn – front cover detached – folio – Paris 1806.
(Sotheby's) $630 £300

CHANTREAU, P. N.
'Philosophical, Political and Literary Travels in Russia' – 2 vols. – folding map – 3 plates – calf gilt – Perth 1794.
(Phillips) $180 £85

CHAPBOOKS
'The Banjo Songster'; 'Watty and Meg'; 'Peep at the Fair' and 12 others – 15 works in one vol. – contem. half morocco – slightly rubbed – wood engraved titles and illus. in text.
(Sotheby Beresford Adams) $180 £85

CHAPELLE ET BACHAUMONT
'Voyage en France' – 4 vols. – 1796.
(Moore Allen & Innocent) $105 £50

CHAPLIN, CHARLES
Good photgraph in black and white signed in black ink, 10 x 8 inches
(Sotheby's) $295 £140

CHAPMAN, A.
'The Borders and Beyond Arctic, Cheviot, Tropic' – col plates – maps – diagrams – cloth – 1924 – idem. 'Memories' coloured and other plates – 1930.
(Bennett Book Auction) $80 £38

CHAPMAN, A.
'Savage Sudan' – illus. – cloth gilt – t.e.g. – 1921.
(Phillips) $105 £50

CHAPMAN, G. AND HODGKIN, J.
'A Bibliography of William Beckford' – one of 500 copies – plates – orig. vellum backed boards – 8vo. – 1930.
(Sotheby's) $210 £100

CHAPTAL, JEAN ANTOINE
'Chemistry Applied in Arts and Manufactures' – 4 vol. 1st. Edn. in English – trans by William Nicholson – 12 folding plates – contem. diced calf – rubbed – spine defective – 8vo. – Richard Phillips 1807.
(Sotheby's) $170 £80

CHARACTERS IN THE GRAND FANCY DRESS BALL GIVEN BY THE BRITISH AMBASSADOR, SIR HENRY WELLESLEY AT VIENNA
13 hand col. plates – slightly spotted contem. half calf – few defects – 4to – for R. Ackermann 1828.
(Sotheby Beresford Adams) $160 £76

CHARCOT, DR. JEAN
'The Voyage of the 'WhyNot' in the Antarctic' – folding frontis – orig. cloth gilt – 1911.
(Phillips) $105 £50

CHARCOT, JEAN MARTIN
'Lectures on Bright's Diseases of the Kidneys' – 2 col. plates – orig. cloth – spine faded – stamp of Aberdeen Medico Chirurgical Society on title – 8vo. – 1879.
(Sotheby's) $65 £30

CHARDIN, SIR JOHN
'Persian und Ost-Indische Reise Beschreibung' – 1st German Edn. – engraved frontis and title – title in red and black – folding engraved map – 15 engraved plates – 9 folding – some torn – browned – contem. calf – worn – 4to. – Leipzig 1687.
(Sotheby's) $230 £110

CHARLES I, KING OF ENGLAND
'Eikon Basilike' – 1st Edn. – third issue – folding engraved frontis – soiling – modern half calf – g.e. – 8vo. – 1648.
(Sotheby's) $40 £20

A. L. s. to Prince Rupert – 1 page – folio – urging him to 'prosecute the desyne of reliving Yorke and beating the Scots' – some wearing at folds – one reinforced – contem. endorsement – Burford, 17 June 1644.
(Sotheby's) $1,220 £580

A large declaration 'concerning the late tumult in Scotland' – engraved portrait – colophon leaf at end – woodcut initial letters – rust hole – contem. panelled calf – worn – rebacked – folio – Robert Young 1639.
(Sotheby's) $65 £30

CHARLES II
Coloured initial letter portrait of the King in the first letter of a Royal Letters Patent advancing Francis Baron Augier de Longford in the Irish peerage to the rank and dignity of Viscount Longford – document on vellum – margins decorated with coats of arms and devices – wanting seal – dust marked – framed and glazed – Westminster November 1675.
(Sotheby's) $1,510 £720

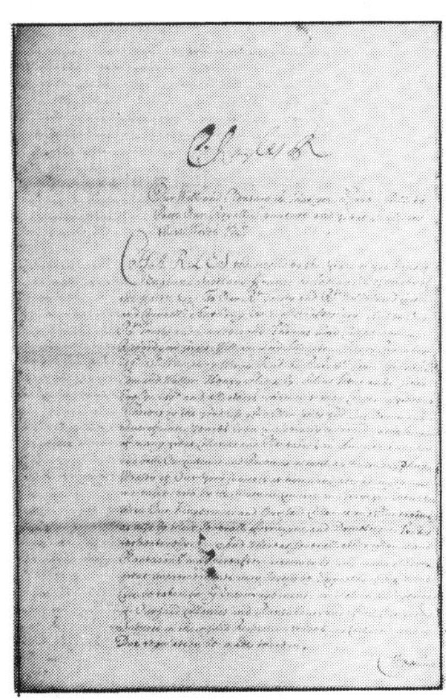

CHARLES II, KING OF ENGLAND
Letter relating to plantations in America – counter signed by Earl of Arlington – 1672.
(Robert Skinner Inc.) $2,100 £1,000

CHARLES V, EMPEROR
'Correspondence 1513-1556' – 3 vol. – 5 folding facsimiles – spotting – contem half calf – 8vo. – Liepzig 1844-46.
(Sotheby's) $25 £12

CHARTARIUS (or CARTARI, VINCENTIUS)
'Images Deorum' editor Paul Hachenburg – engraved title – slightly damaged – printed title in red and black – 88 engraved plates – 18th cent. marbled boards – rubbed – 4to. – Frankfurt 1687.
(Sotheby's) $115 £55

CHARTER OF THE ROYAL HOSPITAL NEAR DUBLIN FOR THE RELIEF OF ANTIENT AND MAIMED OFFICERS AND SOLDIERS
browning – contem. calf – rubbed – Dublin 1760.
(Christie's) $65 £32

CHARTERS,
'List of copies of .... for Trade and Plantations .... American Colonies, Maryland, Connecticut – Rhode Island, Pennsylvania, Massachusetts, Georgia – nf. calf – folio – London 1741.
(Phillips) $180 £85

CHARTON, EDOUARD (Editor)
'Le Tour de Monde Nouveau, Journal des Voyages' – 10 vol. – lge 4to. – wood engraved maps and illustrations – some full page – contemp. morocco backed boards – rubbed – some spines torn – Paris 1860-69.
(Christie's S. Kensington) $125 £60

CHASE, OWEN AND OTHERS
'Narratives of the Wreck of the Whale Ship Essex' – no. 79 of 275 copies – wood engraved pictorial title – 15 illus. by Robert Gibbings – orig. cloth – slightly soiled – t.e.g. – sm. folio – 1935.
(Sotheby's) $360 £170

CHASEMORE, A.
Large sheet with 9 captioned watercolour illus. entitled 'Aunt Sophia's Valentine' with a similar sheet sketched at the Boat Race 'by Uncle Peter, June 17 1836' and five other sheets with pen and ink illus. of pantomimes etc. each signed by artist in card mounts – various sizes.
(Sotheby's) $220 £105

CHATEAUBRIAND, F. A. DE
'Travels in Greece, Palestine, Egypt and Barbary' – 2 vols. – folding map – calf – 1812.
(Phillips) $85 £40

CHATELET, DUKE DE
'Travels' – 2 vols. ed. J. F. Bourgoing – trans. J. J. Stockdale – folding map – calf – 1809.
(Phillips) $95 £45

CHATTERBOX
6 annuals for years 1907/10/16/21 illus. with coloured plates.
(Baitson) $14 £7

CHATTERTON, E. KEBLE
'Old Sea Paintings' – plates – orig. cloth – rubbed – 4to. – 1928.
(Sotheby's) $135 £65

CHATTO, WILLIAM ANDREW
'A Treatise on Wood Engraving' – 1st. Edn. – numerous wood engraved illus. in text by John Jackson – errata leaf at end – soiling – 19th cent. half roan – rubbed – t.e.g. – 4to. – 1839.
(Sotheby's) $45 £22

CHAUCER, GEOFFREY
'The Works' – 7th Edn. – black letter – title in woodcut border – 1 woodcut illus. in text – browning and soiling – lacking portrait – 17th cent. calf – rebacked – label – slightly worn – folio – A. Islip 1602.
(Sotheby's) $170 £80

CHAVANCE, M.
'Emblems ou Devises Chretiennes' – engr. title and 100 emblematic plates – 8vo. – old calf gilt – worn – Lyon 1720.
(Bonhams) $100 £48

CHEAP REPOSITORY TRACTS
Editor Hannah More – woodcuts in text by Lee – title slightly soiled – later calf backed boards – 12 mo. – S. Hazard, Bath 1799.
(Sotheby Beresford Adams) $30 £15

CHERRY - GARRARD, A.
'The Worst Journey in the World' – 2 vol. only lacks supplement – 1st Edn. – later issue – plates – some folding – orig. blue cloth – 8vo. – 1922.
(Sotheby's) $130 £62

CHESEELDEN, WILLIAM
'Osteographia or the Anatomy of the Bones' – engraved frontis – 119 eng. plates – including double suite of 56 plates – contem. diced calf – gilt tooled cornerpieces – large folio – 1733.
(Christie's) $1,365 £650

CHESNAU
'Orpheus Eucharisticus' – engravings – contem. French prize binding of brown calf with arms of Louis XIV surrounded by fleur de lys – gilt edges – restored – 8vo. – 1657.
(Moore Allen & Innocent) $880 £420

CHESNAU, ERNEST
'Ecole Francais, Les Estampes en Couleurs du XVIIIe Siecle' – edition limited to 100 numbered copies – 2 vols. – title with engraved vignette – 50 plates – 10 vignettes and 5 decorated initials – each in 2 states – red morocco – gilt – g.e. by Zaehnsdorf – scuffed – large folio – Paris 1885-90.
(Christie's) $2,520 £1,200

CHESNEY, F. R.
'Reports on the Navigation of the Euphrates' – 2 folding plates – dampstains – contem. morocco – gilt – rubbed – folio 1833.
(Sotheby's) $200 £95

CHESS PLAYER'S CHRONICLE, THE
Vol. 1
Illus. – no title – modern half calf and four others by same – 8vo.
(Sotheby's) $210 £100

CHESTERTON, GILBERT KEITH
'Ubi Ecclesia' – 1st Edn. – limited to 400 copies – this unnumbered with self caricature of author 'hurled from the office for making a blot' – illus. by Diana Murphy – orig, boards – uncut – 8vo. – Ariel Press no. 21-1929.
(Sotheby's) $265 £125

CHEYNEY, PETER
'Lady Behave' – Nice in chipped dust wrapper – 1950.
(J. Ash) $6 £3

CHILD, SIR JOSIAH
'A New Discourse of Trade' – 3rd Edn. – contem. sheep – worn – 12 mo. – 1698.
(Christie's) $125 £60

CHILDREN'S CIRCUS AND MENAGERY BOOK
Pictorial title and 47 illus. – 20 col., remainder tinted – 7 double page – loose in orig. cloth backed pictorial boards – rubbed – large 4to. – Routledge circa 1882.
(Sotheby's) $110 £52

CHILE – BLAEU, W. AND J.
Engraved map – hand col. in outline – cartouches – compass rose – sea monster etc. – full col. – Latin text on verso – repairs – discoloured – 356 mm x 480 mm – Amsterdam circa 1640.
(Sotheby's) $40 £20

CHIMOT, EDOUARD - LOUYS, PIERRE
'Les Poesies de Meleagre' – 15 coloured etched plates by Chimot – unsewn in orig. wrappers – folder – slipcase – slightly damaged – Paris, Editions D'Art Devambez, 1926.
(Sotheby's) $275 £130

CHINESE EXHIBITION
A Commemmorative Catalogue of the International Exhibition of Chinese Art – Royal Academy, 1935-36 – plates and orig. cloth – 4to. – 1936.
(Sotheby's) $170 £80

CHIODI, PASQUALE
'Torantello Bello Napolitano' – title – 20 hand col. plates – disbound – 1834.
(Phillips) $545 £260

CHITTENDEN, FRED. J. (Editor)
'The Royal Horticultural Society Dictionary of Gardening' – 4 vol. – orig. cloth – 4to. – Oxford – 1951.
(Christie's S. Kensington) $30 £15

CHOICE COLLECTION OF RIDDLES, CHARADES, REBUSSES ETC.
Engraved frontis – orig. boards – printed label – worn – rebacked – 12 mo. – E. Newbury 1800.
(Sotheby's) $110 £52

CHOISEUL-GOUFFIER, M. G. F. A. COMTE DE
'Voyage Pittoresque de la Grece' – 2 vols. bound in 3 – engraved titles – portrait engraved titles – portrait and 285 maps and plates on 170 sheets by Choffard, Le Mire and others after the author – some maps – a few plates double page – engraved illustrations – major foxing – vol. 1 green morocco gilt by Derome – vols. 11 and 111 in green morocco tooled – folio – Paris 1782-1809 - 1822.
(Sotheby Parke Bernet) $13,010 £6,195

CHORIER, NICOLAS
'The Dialogues of Luisa Siega' – 6 parts in one – orig. parchment gilt – t.e.g. – Paris 1890.
(Phillips) $115 £55

CHRISTIE'S
'Review of the Year 1964-68' – 5 vols. – various – plates – illus. – orig cloth – dust jackets – 4to.
(Christie's) $40 £18

CHRISTIE CATALOGUES
Collection of 53 mostly on pictures – some priced – circa 1890-1936.
(Phillips) $180 £85

Then the visitation pass'd.
Once more I saw the distant hills:
Where yet receding faint and fast
A fiery rainbow cloud distils.

So I must travel on in haste
Thro' many a wild and thorny waste,
Ere yet my destiny fulfils
And I attain the holy hills.

7

CHUBB, RALPH
'Songs Pastoral and Paradisal' – no. 16 of 100 copies – signed by author – pres inscriptn. from Vincent Stuart – half title – title – orig. half morocco – uncut – 4to. – 1935.
(Sotheby's) $315 £150

CHURCH, RICHARD
'The Solitary Man and other Poems' – limited to 900 copies – very good – marked dust wrapper – 1941.
(J. Ash) $12 £6

CHURCHILL, SIR WINSTON
Fine photograph of the young Churchill – signed on mount – 9 x 7½ inches.
(Sotheby's) $525 £250

Early postcard photograph signed in black ink.
(Sotheby's) $460 £220

CHURCHILL, SIR W. S.
'Liberalism and the Social Problem' – 1st Edn. – cloth gilt – 1909.
(Phillips) $55 £25
'The River War' – 2 vol. – second impression – plates – folding maps – cont. half calf by Sotheran – spines gilt – t.e.g. – 1900.
(Christie's S. Kensington) $115 £55

CIAMPINI, JOANNIS
'Vetera Monumenta' – 2 vol. – folio – two engr. additional titles – slightly shaved – 134 plates – 43 folding – some browned – contemp. vellum – soiled – bookplate of 'Marchionis Salsae' – Rome 1690-99.
(Christie's S. Kensington) $315 £150

CICERO
'Epistolarum ad Atticum' – Old English brown calf with Queen Elizabeth's badge of a crowned falcon – traces of ties – in red morocco slipcase – 8vo. – Paris 1573.
(Moore Allen & Innocent) $545 £260

CIGARETTE CARDS
Adolf Hitler – an album of photographic cards laid within text – 4to. – cloth – 1936.
(Bennett Book Auction) $30 £15

CILLE, F. AND A. ROCKSTUHL
'Musee de Tzarskoe Selo ou Collection d'Armes de Sa Majeste L'Empereur de Toutes les Russies' – 3 vol. 186 plates – some on india paper – loose as issued – orig. folders – spines missing – folio – St. Petersburg and Carlsruhe 1835-53.
(Sotheby's) $190 £90

CLAIRIN, GEORGES
Designs – sketches of female headdresses and costumes – pencil – 28 cm. x 45.2cm.
(Sotheby's) $105 £50

CLAN TARTANS
A book of 24 samples – 54 inch super Saxony' – each sample measuring 6 x 5 inches – circa 1890 – and book on Scottish District Checks 1968.
(Bennett Book Auction) $30 £14

CLARE, JOHN
'Green Shadows, the Life of John Clare' – plates – nice copy in worn dust wrapper – 1951.
(J. Ash) $8 £4

CLARE, M.
'The Motion of Fluids, Natural and Artificial' – nine engraved plates – occasional slight spotting – contemporary calf – rebacked – 1735.
(Christie's S. Kensington) $65 £30

CLARK, D. K. AND COLBURN, Z.
'Railway Machinery' – 3 vol. – including supplement – 91 plates – some fldg. – dampstaining – contemp. half morocco rubbed – hinges split folio – 1860-62.
(Sotheby's) $170 £80

CLARKE, E. D.
'Travels in the Various Countries of Europe, Asia and Africa' – 3 parts in 6 vols. – 'Life and Remains' – together 7 vols. – engraved plates and maps – folding – spotting – contem. calf – rebacked – rubbed – 4to. – 1810-24.
(Sotheby's) $315 £150

CLARKE, HARRY
'Fairy Tales' by Hans Christian Andersen – 40 plates – 16 col. and illus. in text by Clarke – orig. pictorial cloth – pictorial label – t. e. g. – 4to. – 1916.
(Sotheby's) $265 £125
'The Centenary Baxter Book' – plates – some folding – one of 125 copies – 4to. – boards – buckram back. in d.w. – 1906.
(Bonhams) $100 £48

CLARKE, J.
'An Essay upon Study' – contemp. calf – London 1731.
(Bennett Book Auction) $40 £20

CLARKE, J.
'Practical Essay on the Management of Pregnancy and Labour' – 1st Edn. – half calf – 1793.
(Bonhams) $80 £35

CLARKE, SAMUEL of St. Bennet Fink
'The Lives of Sundry Eminent Persons in this Later Age' – 1st Edn. – title in red and black – engraved frontis – contem. calf – rubbed – folio – 1683.
(Sotheby's) $40 £20

CLARKSON, THOMAS
'Essay on the Slavery and Commerce of the Human Species' – 1st Edn. in English – spotted – title mounted – contem. calf – rebacked – 8vo. – 1786.
(Sotheby's) $170 £80

'The History of the Rise, Progress and Accomplishment of the Abolition of the African Slave Trade' – 2 vol. – 1st Edn. –folding engraved chart and 2 plates – some spotting and foxing – contem. tree calf – rebacked – spines rubbed – 8vo. – 1808.
(Sotheby's) $295 £140

CLAY, E.
'Sonnets and Verses' – wood engraving by Eric Gill – limited Edn. – cloth backed boards – Golden Cockerel Press 1925.
(Phillips) $85 £40

CLEAVELAND, P.
'Elementary Treatise on Mineralogy and Geology' – map and 5 plates – 2 vols. – orig. boards (backs defective) – Boston 1822.
(Bonhams) $105 £50

CLERK, REV. A.
'Memoir of Colonel John Cameron .. Lieutenant Colonel of the Gordon Highlanders' – cloth – 4to. – Glasgow 1859.
(Bennett Book Auctions) $25 £12

CLERK, J.
'An Essay on Naval Tactics Systematical and Historical' – 4 parts – 52 folding hand coloured plates – cont. speckled calf – 4to – 2nd Edn. – Edinburgh, 1804.
(Bennett Book Auction) $170 £80

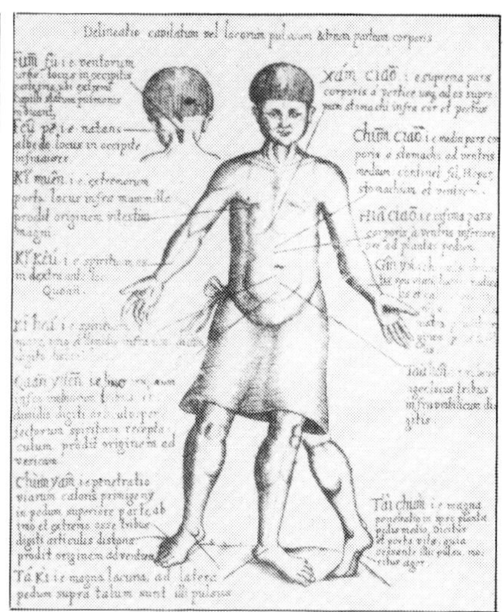

CLEYER, ANDREAS
'Specimen Medecinae Sinicae' – 1st Edn. – title – 30 engraved anatomical and medical plates – woodcut illus. in text – 18th century – paper boards – sm 4to – Frankfurt 1682.
(Christie's) $2,058 £980

CLICHTOVEUS, JADOCUS
'Homilia' – cont. stamped calf by John Reynes – clasps – box – 1535.
(Phillips) $170 £80

CLOQUET, JULES
'Manuel D'Anatomie Descriptive du Corps Humain' – 2 vols. – 4to – Paris – litho. title – 329 plates only – some spotting – a few browned – vol. 1 cont. russia – vol. 2 half calf – crudely repaired – both rubbed – 1825-31.
(Christie's S. Kensington) $135 £65

CLOWES, W. L.
'The Royal Navy' – 7 vol. – plates – orig. cloth – 4to. – 1897-1903.
(Sotheby's) $715 £340

CLUTTERBUCK, R.
'History and Antiquities of the County of Hereford' – 3 vols. map – plates – half morocco gilt – folio – 1815-27.
(Phillips) $250 £120

CLUVERIUS, PHILIP
'Introductionis in Universam Geographiam' – 2 engraved plates and 41 of 43 engraved maps – most double page – all hand col. and on guards – ms index – later panelled calf – rubbed – 4to. – Amsterdam 1682 or later.
(Sotheby Beresford Adams) $630 £300

COATES, CHARLES
'The History and Antiquities of Reading' – folding town plan – 7 plates – half calf – 4to. – 1802.
(Phillips) $145 £70

COBDEN, R.
'Speeches' – 2 vols. – calf gilt – 1870.
(Bonhams) $60 £28

COBDEN-SANDERSON, T. J.
Paper read at a meeting of the Art Workers' Guild – dark blue morocco tooled in gilt with interlocking panels – g.e. – Doves Bindery 1906.
(Phillips) $400 £190

COCHRAN-PATRICK, R. W.
'Records of the Coinage of Scotland' – 2 vol. – plates – contemp. half morocco,
(Sotheby's) $160 £75

COCKBURN, JAMES
'Swiss Scenery' – engraved title and 59 plates – two lacking – marginal dampstains – slight spotting – half calf – rubbed – 4to. – 1820.
(Christie's S. Kensington) $715 £340

COCK ROBIN, A PRETTY GILDED TOY FOR BOY OR GIRL
Chapbook – folded sheet of 16 pp including title and 15 woodcut illus. with verses – 32 mo. – John Evans circa 1800.
(Sotheby's) $60 £28

COCKTON, HENRY
'The Life and Adventures of Valentine Vox' – 1st Edn. – etched frontis – title and 58 plates after T. Onwhyn – few spotted – modern half calf – slightly rubbed – 8vo. – Robert Tyas 1840.
(Sotheby's) $75 £35

CODRINGTON, K. De B.
'L'Inde Ancienne ... traduit de L'Anglais par Mme Jean Locquin' – folio – Paris – Dorbon Aine – plates – orig. cloth – n.d.
(Christie's S. Kensington) $40 £20

COHEN, TUVIA
'Maase Tuvia' – 3 parts in one vol. – 1st Edn. – title in ornate archit frame – portrait of author – diagrams and plates – last page in Italian – staining – worming – modern cloth – rare – 4to. – Venice 1707-8.
(Sotheby's) $1,575 £750

COLBURN, ZERAH
'Locomotive Engineering' – 2 vols. – 63 folding plates – some spotting – illus. – contem. half morocco – rubbed – folio – 1871.
(Sotheby's) $85 £40

COLCHESTER: SPARROW, THOMAS
'Survey of the Ancient Town and Borough of Colchester' – large engraved plan – pictorial title vignette – 4 inset engravings – uncut – a few marginal tears – 505 mm x 700 mm. – 1767.
(Sotheby's) $200 £95

COLDSTREAM, J. N. AND HUXLEY, G. L.
'Kythera' – plates and maps – some folding – orig. cloth – dust jacket – 1972.
(Sotheby's) $10 £5

COLEMAN, W. S. AND OTHERS
'The Book of the Thames' – numerous wood engraved illus. – adverts at end – orig. cloth gilt – g.e. – 8vo. – 1859.
(Sotheby Beresford Adams) $25 £12

COLERIDGE, S. T.
'Christabel; Kubla Khan; The Pains of Sleep' – later quarter calf – rubbed – browning – 1816.
(J. Ash) $630 £300
'Aids to Reflection' – 1st Edn. – 2 pp of publisher's ads. at back – half title lacking – slight browning – later half morocco – slightly affected by damp.
(Christie's S. Kensington) $45 £22

COLERIDGE, S. T., P. B. SHELLEY AND J. KEATS
'The Poetical Works' – frontis – spotted – contem. calf – rebacked – 8vo. – Paris 1829.
(Sotheby's) $75 £35

COLETTE, SIDONIE GABRIELLE – DIGNEMONT
'L'Ingenue Libertine' – 15 etched plates by Dignemont – unsewn in orig. wrappers – uncut – unopened – folder – slipcase – 4to. – Paris, Cite des Livres, 1928.
(Sotheby's) $440 £210

COLLECTING
20 vols. including 10 of the 'Chats' series – china – pewter – furniture – glass etc. – all illustrated – circa 1915.
(Phillips) $200 £95

COLLIER, JEREMY
'Essays' – contem calf – 1698.
(Phillips) $75 £35

COLLIN
'Vie de Marie Lumagne' – in contem. French binding of red morocco gilt and large arms of Madame de Pompadour in quarter orange morocco gilt slip case – 8vo. – 1744.
(Moore Allen & Innocent) $1,365 £650

COLLIN, RAPHAEL – LONGUS
'Daphnis et Chloe' – frontis – vignette – 12 plates and 28 illus. by Champollion after Collin – violet morocco spine and covers with decorations – watered silk doublures and endleaves – g.e. – morocco backed folder and slipcase – Paris, H. Launette, 1890.
(Sotheby's) $250 £120

COLLING, JAMES K.
'Suggestions in Design' – 4to. – frontispiece and 101 plates after John Leighton – occasional slight spotting – original (?) – morocco – slightly rubbed – gilt inner dentelles – g.e. – 1880.
(Christie's S. Kensington) $85 £40

COLLING, J. R.
'Gothic Ornament' – 2 vol. – prospectus bound in at front of vol 1 – coloured lithographed add. titles – plates – some coloured – spotting – staining – margins of a few leaves repaired – contemp. half calf – worn – lge. 4to.
(Christie's S. Kensington) $65 £32

COLLINGWOOD, FRANCIS AND WOOLAMS, JOHN
'The Universal Cook' – frontis lacking – 11 bill of fare plates – some leaves lacking – dampstains – modern cloth – 1792.
(Christie's) $30 £15

COLLINS, DAVID
'An Account of the English Colony in New South Wales' – vol. 1 only – 1st Edn. – engraved map – large folding chart – 18 plates – 4 engravings in text – browning – contem. diced calf – gilt spine and hinges rubbed – 4to. – 1798.
(Sotheby's) $735 £350

COLLINS, CAPT. GRENVILLE
'Great Britain's Coasting Pilot' – being an exact survey of the sea coast of England and Scotland – engraved frontispiece – 49 charts and coastal profiles – some folding – mounted on guards throughout – chart of Carlingford torn with loss – two charts soiled – frontispiece and title creased and a little soiled – original calf – worn – hinges cracked – spine worn – large folio – J. Mount and T. Page, 1763.
(Christie's S. Kensington) $3,780 £1,800
Sea Chart of the East Coast of Scotland – hand col. – circa 1750.
(Phillips) $100 £48

COLLINS, W. WILKIE
'Rambles Beyond Railways' – 1st Edn. – bound in half morocco – 1851.
(Lane) $55 £25

COLLINSON, J.
'History of Somersetshire' – vol of plates only 38 plates – calf gilt – 4to. – 1766.
(Phillips) $125 £60
'The History and Antiquities of the County of Somerset' – 3 vols. – folding engraved map – numerous engraved plates – contem. polished calf – gilt – 4to. – Bath 1791.
(Christie's) $335 £160

COLMAN, GEORGE
'The Dramatic Works' – 4 vols. – tree calf gilt – 1777.
(Phillips) $75 £35
'Poetical Vagaries' – 4to. – printed for the author – spotted – contemp. – half calf – rubbed – 1812.
(Christie's S. Kensington) $25 £12
'Broad Grins'.
(Laurence & Martin, Taylor) $25 £12

COLOPHON, THE
Part 1, 3-16; New Series Vol. 1-3 in 12 – new graphic series no. 1-4 – together 31 vol. – orig. boards and cloth – some rubbed – 4to. and 8vo. – New York 1930-40.
(Sotheby's) $360 £170

COLQUHOUN, P.
'A Treatise on the Commerce and Police of the River Thames' – folding map – 2 tables – contem. calf gilt. – 1800.
(Phillips) $190 £90

COLTON, G. WOOLWORTH
'Atlas of the World' – 2 vols. engraved frontis – 92 maps and 8 plans – mostly coloured – some double page – orig. quarter roan – gilt – worn – disbound – folio – New York 1856.
(Sotheby's) $190 £90

COLTON, H. E.
'Mountain Scenery; The Scenery .. of Western North Carolina, and Northwestern South Carolina' – 4 lithographed plates – 1 folding map – slightly torn – some spotting – original cloth – Raleigh, 1859.
(Christie's S. Kensington) $40 £18

COLUMBUS, CHRISTOPHER
'Christopher Columbus his Own Book of Privileges' – col. frontis – 3 plates – contem. half roan – rubbed – t.e.g. folio – 1893.
(Christie's) $40 £20

COMBE, WILLIAM
'The Tour of Doctor Syntax in Search of the Picturesque'; 'The Second Tour of Doctor Syntax in Search of Consolation' – 9th Edn. and 3rd Edn. – plates – soiled – modern half morocco – 8vo. – n.d. and 18 1820.
(Sotheby's) $190 £90

COME, GEORGE
'A System of Phrenology' – 2nd Edn. – folding frontispiece – soiled throughout – modern calf backed boards – Edinburgh 1825.
(Christie's S. Kensington) $20 £10

COMMINES
'Histoire' – contem. English binding of brown calf gilt with arms of Queen Elizabeth – end papers renewed traces of ties – cloth slip case – joint and ends repaired – folio – 1596.
(Moore Allen & Innocent) $800 £380

COMPANY 4th SCOTTISH BORDER BATTALION HOME GUARD
Index book containing several pages mss lists of members and their occupations (mainly shepherds) and some results and details of proficiency tests taken – circa 1940-1944.
(Bennett Book Auctions) $55 £26

COMPTON, THOMAS
'The Northern Cambrian Mountains or a Tour Through North Wales' – original 10 parts – 1st Edn. – 30 hand col. aquatint plates – orig. wrappers – frayed – reserved in cloth box – oblong folio – 1817.
(Sotheby's) $1,300 £620

COMPTON-BURNET, IVY
'Men and Wives' – rubbed and slightly torn – Mudie label – otherwise acceptable copy of scarce title – 1931 .
(J. Ash) $20 £10

CONDY, NICHOLAS AND ARUNDELL, FRANCIS J.
'Cothele on the Banks of the Tamar' – col. litho title – plan – 16 plates – foxing – conte – maroon morocco backed boards – Edgcumbe arms – folio – circa 1850.
(Sotheby's) $230 £110

CONEY, JOHN
'Ecclesiastical Edifices of the Olden Time' – 2 vols. – engraved plates – some folding – contem. half morocco – rubbed – t.e.g. – folio – 1842.
(Sotheby's) $125 £60

CONGREVE, COL. W.
'The Details of the Rocket System' – 12 hand coloured plates only – lacks plain plate – soiled – title torn – contemp. calf – lacks spine – worn – oblong folio – 1814.
(Sotheby's) $1,260 £600

CONNAISSANCE DES ARTS
No. 33-190 in 12 vols. – illus. – lacks adverts – modern half morocco – gilt ornaments on spines – 4to. – Paris, 1954-67.
(Sotheby's) $190 £90

CONNOISSEUR, THE
12 bound vols. – collector's magazine with coloured plates.
(Baitson) $30 £14

CONNOLLY, A.
'Journey to the North of India' – 2 vol. – engraved frontis – folding map on linen – modern calf backed cloth – slightly rubbed – 8vo. – 1834.
(Sotheby's) $105 £50

Les Pavillons

inscribed for my
old – or why should
I not admit –
my OLDEST friend
Cecil
who would have done it
so much better.
1916 – 1962.
from
Cyril Connolly

CONNOLY, CYRIL AND ZERBE, JEROME
'Les Pavillons' – 1st Edn. – pres copy – inscribed by Connolly to Cecil Beaton – coloured frontis – illus. – a few mss corrections in text, orig. cloth, 4to. – New York 1962.
(Sotheby's) $170 £80

CONRAD, JOSEPH
'The Secret Agent' – number 579 of 1000 copies signed by the author – portrait – original parchment backed cloth soiled – 1923.
(Christie's S. Kensington) $90 £42
'The Arrow of Gold' – 1st Edn. – cloth – and others by the same – 1919.
(Bonhams) $75 £35
'A Set of Six' – secondary issue in bluecloth – some marks – 1908.
(J. Ash) $20 £10

CONSEILLER DES DAMES, LE
Tome troiseme – 10 engr. fashion plates only – hand coloured – contemp. cloth – worn.
(Sotheby's) $40 £18

CONSTABLE, JOHN
'English Landscape Scenery' – mezzo tint plates by David Lucas – contem. half morocco – folio – 1855.
(Sotheby's) $440 £210

CONSTITUTIONES EDITAE ... D'URBANE CARD
Contem. Italian binding of red morocco gilt lavishly decorated – arms of Pope Innocent XII in centre of covers – back defective – Rome 1694.
(Moore Allen & Innocent) $460 £220

CONTINENTAL TOURIST, THE
Engraved vignette title – 61 engraved plates – slightly spotted – orig. cloth gilt – lacking spine – g.e. – 8vo. – n.d.
(Sotheby Beresford Adams) $305 £145

CONTRAST, THE or 'Scotland as it was in the Year 1745 and Scotland in the Year 1819'
Cloth backed boards – 1825.
(Bennett Book Auction) $20 £10

CONWAY, MARTIN
'The Alps' – orig. pictorial cloth binding – limited Edn. – signed 1904.
(Lane) $50 £24

COOK, ROBERT J.
'Railway Map of England and Wales' – folding lithographed map mounted on linen – orig. cloth folder – rubbed – 212cm. x 171cm. – 1866.
(Sotheby's) $170 £80

COOKE, E. W.
'Sixty Five Plates of Shipping and Craft' – engraved title loose – cloth gilt – worn – 4to. – 1829.
(Phillips) $925 £440

COOKE, G. A.
'A Topographical Description of the County of Cornwall' – newly bound in full calf.
(Lane) $17 £8
'Modern and Authentic Geography' – 2 vols. – frontis – 100 maps and plates – calf – upper covers detached – 4to. – 1800.
(Phillips) $230 £110

COOKE, GEORGE
'Views in London and Its Vicinity' – 48 engraved proof plates on india paper – half morocco – gilt – g.e. – folio – 1834.
(Phillips) $275 £130

COOKE, W. B.
'Views of the Coloseum' – 14 engraved plates – spotted – contem. morocco backed cloth – rubbed – folio – 1841.
(Sotheby's) $180 £85
'Select Views of Richmond and Hampton Court' – 28 plates – 4to – cloth crudely rebacked – 1846.
(Bonhams) $65 £32

COPPEE, FRANCOIS
'Le Passant' – 1 of 47 copies on papier velin de cuve – watercolours by Boisson – blue morocco by Ruben – a fuschia in four colours on upper cover – silk endpapers – Paris Armand Magnier 1897.
(Sotheby Parke Bernet) $2,415 £1,150

COOPER, A. H. (illustrator)
'The English Lakes' – limited Edn. – signed by illustrator – orig. pictorial cloth – 1905.
(Lane) $55 £26

COOPER, SUSAN FENNIMORE
'Rural Hours' – 4th Edn. – hand col. – litho plates – browning – modern cloth – soiled – 4to. – New York 1851.
(Christie's) $40 £20

COOPER, THOMAS
'A Discourse of the Connexion between Chemistry and Medicine delivered at the University of Philadelphia' – 48 pp new red quarter calf – uncut – 8vo. – Philidelphia 1818.
(Sotheby's) $135 £65

COPINGER, W. A.
'The Manors of Suffolk' – 8 vols including typescript index – inscribed by author – plates – orig. cloth – soiled – 4to. – 1905-11.
(Sotheby's) $525 £250

COPPARD, A. E.
'Clarinda Walks in Heaven' – limited to 1200 copies – orig. cloth backed boards – unopened – dust jacket – 1922.
(Christie's) $40 £20
'Rummy' – Golden Cockerel Press – limited Edn. of 1,000 copies – illus with wood engravings by Robert Gibbings – some foxing – 1932.
(J. Ash) $30 £14

CORDINER, CHARLES
'Antiquities and Scenery of the North of Scotland' – engraved title and 21 engraved plates – 1 do page – contem. calf – gilt – worn – rebacked – 4to. – 1780.
(Sotheby's) $65 £30

CORINDA
'The Thirteen Steps to Mentalism' – 13 parts – illus. – orig. wrappers – 8vo. – 1958-60.
(Sotheby's) $34 £16

CORLESS, REGINALD W.
'Sketches of Hull Authors' – 1879.
(Baitson) $10 £5

Walter de la Mare
from Frances Cornford
Xmas 1923

CORNFORD, FRANCES
'Autumn Midnight' – 1st Edn. – presentation copy – inscribed by author to De La Mare – wood engraved frontis – 17 initials and 7 decorations including cover by Eric Gill – orig. wrappers – uncut – 8vo – Poetry Bookshop, 1923.
(Sotheby's) $125 £60

CORNHILL MAGAZINE, THE
Vol. 1-47 and new series 1-21 – plates – contemporary half calf – worn – 1860-93.
(Christie's S. Kensington) $180 £85

CORNISH PIXIE, THE
Nos. 1-45 – 40 issues only – another set 40 issues only – 301 duplicates – mimeographed text – a few illus. as issued – 4to. – Wolverhampton 1943-46.
(Sotheby's) $85 £40

CORNWALL PARISH REGISTERS
Marriages vol. 1026 and index to vol. 1-6 in 27 vols. – limited Edn. – orig. cloth – slightly soiled – 8vo. – 1900-35.
(Sotheby's) $545 £260

CORNWALL – RILL, HENRY
'Plan of Liskeard Turnpike Roads' – mss on paper – signed – some stains – 2 sheets joined – mounted on linen – 22½ in. x 50½in. – Liskeard Nov. 1855.
(Sotheby's) $115 £55

CORNWALLIS, CHARLES, 1st MARQUESS
AL 1 page – 4to – Mansfield Street, March 1786.
(Phillips) $275 £130

CORONATION
A collection of 7 Coronation and Royalty Souvenir items including issues of Punch and Yorkshire Post.
(Baitson) $4 £2

CORONATION ALBUM, THE
Editor Marquess of Aberdeen – one of 235 copies with UK coins and stamps – mounted photos – orig. morocco – rubbed – oblong 4to. – 1953.
(Sotheby's) $160 £75

CORONELLI, MARCO VINCENZO
'Memoirs Historiques et Geographiques du Royaume de la Moree' – 36 engraved double page maps and plates – contem. calf – gilt spine – 12mo. – Amsterdam 1686.
(Christie's) $670 £320
'Lithuania' – engraved map – historiated title – armorial scale cartouche – coats of arms – stain – 445 mm. x 603 mm. – Venice circa 1696.
(Sotheby's) $75 £35

CORREVON, HENRY
'Fleurs des Champs et des Bois' – illustrated – 1911.
(Laurence & Martin Taylor) $4 £2

CORRY, JOHN
'History of Lancashire' – 2 vols. lacking titles – 18 engraved or litho plates – minor defects – contem. half morocco rubbed – 4to – 1825.
(Sotheby Beresford Adams) $65 £30

CORY, CHARLES B.
'The Birds of Haiti and San Domingo' – map 22 hand col. plates – cloth – 4to. – Boston 1885.
(Phillips) $460 £220

COSMETICS FOR MY LADY AND GOOD FARE FOR MY LORD
Collected recipes – number 47 of 300 copies – orig. cloth – soiled – 1934.
(Christie's) $40 £20

COSTELLO, DUDLEY
'Piedmont and Italy from the Alps to the Tiber' – vol. 2 only of 2 – additional engraved vignette title – 4 portraits – 58 views – 4 coloured maps – several plates waterstained – occas. spotting – contem. half roan – worn – 4to. – 1861.
(Phillips) $295 £140

COSTELLO, LOUISA STUART
''Specimens from the Early Poetry of France' – 1st Edn. – device on title – 4 litho plates – spottings – early 20th cent. polished yellow calf by Riviere – labels – gilt – t.e.g. – 8vo. – William Pickering 1835.
(Sotheby's) $180 £85

COSTIGAN, A. W.
'Sketches of Society and Manners in Portugal' – 2 vols. – calf gilt – worn – 1787.
(Phillips) $65 £30

COSTUME, THE BOOK OF ..... BY A LADY OF RANK
Over 200 engravings – bound in half leather – t.e.g. – 1847.
(Baitson) $15 £7

COTE, C.
'Collection Monnaies de Tarente' – plates orig. wrappers – torn – loose – 4to. – Lugano 1929.
(Sotheby's) $95 £45

COTMAN, JOHN SELL
'Engravings of Sepulchral Brasses in Norfolk, Suffolk' – 2 vols. – 2nd Edn. – col. plates – some folding – contem. half morocco – gilt – slightly rubbed – folio – 1838.
(Sotheby's) $380 £180

COTTAFAVI, GAETANO
'Raccolta della Principali Vedute di Roma e Soui Contorni' – engraved title and 50 plates – spotted – contem. half morocco – rubbed – g.e. – oblong folio – Rome 1843.
(Sotheby's) $190 £90

COTTON LIBRARY (SIR ROBERT BRUCE)
'A Catalogue of the Manuscripts in the Cottonian Library Deposited in the British Museum' – some spotting – half title torn without loss of letters – contemporary half calf – rubbed – upper cover detached – folio – 1802,
(Christie's S. Kensington) $85 £40

COTTON, ROBERT
'Cottoni Posthuma Choice Pieces' – old calf rebacked – 1672.
(Phillips) $45 £22

COUCH, JONATHAN
'A History of the Fishes of the British Islands' – 4 vols. – 250 coloured plates of 252 – orig. cloth – spine torn – 1862-65.
(Christie's S. Kensington) $565 £250

COUNSELL, G.
'The Art of Midwifery' or 'The Midwife's Sure Guide' – 2 plates – 1st Edn. – calf – one joint broken – 1752.
(Bonhams) $115 £55

COUNTRY LIFE
Vol. 65-82 – 18 vols altogether – orig. cloth – 4to. – 1929-37.
(Sotheby's) $485 £230

COURT MAGAZINE, THE
Vols. 2,3,4, 5-37 hand col. plates – engraved views – half calf – gilt – 1833-34.
(Phillips) $125 £60

COURTLEY, MISS M. A.
'Cornish Feasts and Folk Lore' – 1st Edn. – orig. cloth – 1890.
(Lane) $40 £20

COURT GAME OF ASTROPHILOGEON
Complete pack of 60 engraved cards – 30 with maps – 30 with pictorial representations of constellations – all coloured by hand – g.e. – orig. slip case – 95 mm x 63 mm. – Stopforth circa 1830.
(Sotheby's) $440 $210

COVENS, J. AND MORTIER, C.
'Carte de Moscovie' – engraved map – hand col. in outline – margins soiled – mid 18th cent.
(Christie's) $40 £20

COWARD, T. A.
'Birds of the British Isles and Their Eggs' – 4th Edn. – 2 vol. – 455 coloured illus. – 1923.
(Laurence & Martin Taylor) $6 £3

COWLEY, ABRAHAM
'The Works' – portrait – contem. black morocco – gilt – rubbed – 4to. – 1678.
(Phillips) $630 £300

COWPER, WILLIAM
'The Anatomy of the Humane Bodies' – 105 plates – panelled calf – worn – some worming – folio – 1698.
(Irelands) $3,150 £1,500

'Myotomia Refomata' – title in red and black – engr. frontis – 67 engraved plates – numerous other illus. – diagrams and initials – browning – half morocco – folio – 1724.
(Christie's) $1,090 £520

COX, DAVID
'A series of Progressive Lessons, intended to Elucidate the Art of Landscape Painting in Watercolours' – 3rd Edn. – twelve aquatint plates – eight hand coloured – six by a contemporary hand – two crudely by a later hand – browning – contemp. half morocco – rebacked oblong – 4to. – 1816.
(Christie's S. Kensington) $45 £22

COX, REV. THOMAS
'Magna Britannia Antique e Nova' – 6 vols. – 48 folding engraved maps – engraved tables – browned – contemp. calf and a few boards detached – rubbed – sm. 4to. – 1738.
(Sotheby's) $750 £360

COXE, WILLIAM
'Account of the Russian Discoveries Between Asia and America' – 3rd Edn. – 5 folding maps and plans – 1 torn – spotting – modern calf backed boards – 8vo. – 1787.
(Sotheby's) $170 £80

COXE, WILLIAM
'An Historical Tour in Monmouthshire' – 2 vols. – 92 engraved plates – maps – some torn – illus. – some soiled – contem. calf – rebacked – rubbed – 4to. – 1801.
(Sotheby's) $170 £80

CRABBE, GEORGE
'Tales of the Hall' – 2 vols – contem. full calf gilt – hinge split – foxing – 1819.
(J. Ash) $85 £40

CRAIG, EDWARD GORDON
'Ellen Terry and Her Secret Self' – no. 10 of 256 copies – on large paper – signed by author – 'A Plea for G.B.S.' – inserted loosely at end – orig. cloth – a little soiled – t.e.g. – 4to. – 1931.
(Christie's) $105 £50

ACT V SCENE II
THE TRAGICALL HISTORIE OF

King. Our sonne shall winne.
Queene. He's fat and scant of breath.
Heere Hamlet take my napkin rub thy browes,
The Queene carowses to thy fortune Hamlet.
Ham. Good Madam.
King. Gertrud doe not drinke.
Queene. I will my Lord, I pray you pardon me.
King. It is the poysned cup, it is too late.
Ham. I dare not drinke yet Madam, by and by.
Queene. Come, let me wipe thy face.
Laer. My Lord, Ile hit him now.
King. I doe not thinke't.
Laer. And yet it is almost against my conscience.
Ham. Come for the third. Laertes, you doe but dally,
I pray you passe with your best violence,
I am sure you make a wanton of me.
Laer. Say you so, come on. Play.
Osr. Nothing neither way.
Laer. Have at you now. In scuffling they change Rapiers
King. Part them, they are incenst.
Ham. Nay come againe.
Osr. Looke to the Queene there howe.
Hora. They bleed on both sides, how is it my Lord?
Osr. How is't Laertes?
Laer. Why as a woodcock to mine owne springe Osrick,
I am justly kil'd with mine owne treachery.
Ham. How does the Queene?
King. Shee sounds to see them bleed.
Queene. No, no, the drinke, the drinke, O my deare Hamlet,
The drinke the drinke, I am poysned.
Ham. O villanie, how, let the doore be lockt,
Treachery, seeke it out.
Laer. It is heere Hamlet, Hamlet thou art slaine,
No medcin in the world can doe thee good,
In thee there is not halfe an houres life,
The treacherous instrument is in thy hand
Unbated and envenom'd, the foule practise

168

Shakespeare's 'The Tragedy of Hamlet, Prince of Denmark' – No. 214 of 300 copies – 80 wood engraved illus. by Craig – orig linen backed boards – separately bound – editorial notes in pocket inside lower cover – slipcase – folio – Weimer, Cranach Press, 1930.
(Sotheby Bearne) $1,930 £920

CRAMER, JOHN ANDREW
'Elements of the Art of Assaying Metals' – 2nd Edn. – 6 folding plates – contem. calf – ownership inscription – 8vo. – Davis and Reymers 1764.
(Sotheby's) $105 £50

CRANE, STEPHEN
'The Monster and Other Stories' – 1st Eng. Edn. with seven stories – earlier American edition had only three – orig decorative cloth – spine dull – foxing – 1901.
(J. Ash) $55 £25

CRANE, WALTERS
'Cartoons for the Cause' – folio – title and twelve plates by Crane – orig. wrappers – soiled – disbound – 1886-96.
(Christie's S. Kensington) $60 £28

'Queen Summer Number 194 of 250 large paper copies – folio – Cassell & Co. – coloured illustrations by Crane – slight soiling – orig. vellum-backed boards – soiled and bumped – 1891.
(Christie's S. Kensington) $60 £28

CRANTZ, DAVID
'The History of Greenland' – 1st Edn. in Eng. – 2 vols – 9 folding plates including 2 maps – contem. calf – 8vo. – 1767.
(Christie's) $315 £150

CRASTER, SIR E.
'History of the Bodleian Library 1845-1945' – plates – cloth – Oxford, 1952.
(Bennett Book Auctions) $40 £18

CRAWFORD, A.
'The Earldom of Mar' – 2 volumes – cloth – 1882.
(Bennett Book Auctions) $20 £9

CRAWFORD, F. MARION
'A Cigarette Maker's Romance' – 2 vols. – spines slightly faded – 1890.
(J. Ash) $40 £20

CRAWFORD, JOHN
'History of the Indian Archipelago' – 3 vols. – 1st Edn. – 34 engraved plates – 1 coloured – folding map – some foxing and offsetting – cloth – worn – 8vo. – Edinburgh 1820.
(Sotheby's) $230 £110

CREBILLON
'Oeuvres' – Vol. 2 – contem. French mottled calf gilt with arms of Napoleon on each cover – 8vo. – 1797.
(Moore Allen & Innocent) $210 £100

CREMER, W. H. (editor)
'the Secret Out or One Thousand Tricks with Cards' – 1st Edn. – wood engraved illus. – orig. cloth – worn – 8vo. – New York, Dick and Fitzgerald 1859.
(Sotheby's) $40 £20
'The Secret Out' Edinburgh n.d. 'Magic No Mystery' Edinburgh n.d. – illus. – orig. pictorial cloth – slightly faded and worn – 8vo. – 1958-60.
(Sotheby's) $45 £22

CRESWELL, K. A. C. AND OTHERS
'The Mosques of Egypt' – 2 vols. – plates – some col. – illus. – 2 maps and index in pocket – orig. cloth – folio – Giza 1949.
(Sotheby's) $650 £310

CRICKETER, THE
Editor P. D. Warner – vol. 1-2; 4-7 only – illus. – contem. cloth – slightly rubbed – 4to. – 1922-27.
(Sotheby's) $115 £55

CRIKER, T. H. AND OTHERS
The Complete Dictionary of Arts and Sciences' – 3 vols. 1st. Edn. – engraved frontis – numerous plates – 4 maps – some leaves detached contem. speckled calf – worn – folio – 1764-66.
(Sotheby's) $65 £30

CRIMEAN WAR
A collection of 13 papers on the Army before Sebastopol – some folding maps and plans – 8 in contem cloth backed boards – worn – others disbound – folio and 8vo. – 1855-58.
(Sotheby's) $315 £150

CRISP, F. A.
Collection of 32 vols. of Parish Registers – all limited Edn. – orig. vellum parchment backed boards – rather soiled – t.e.g. – 4to.
(Sotheby's) $600 £280

CROFT, WILLIAM (editor)
'Divine Harmony or a New Collection of Select Anthems' – rubricated – soiled – contem. black morocco – gilt panels and monogram of Queen Anne at corners – stamped 'Chapel Royal, Windsor' – rubbed – g.e. – 1712.
(Christie's) $75 £35

CROLY, REV. GEORGE
'Tales of the Great St. Bernard' – 3 vol. – 1st Edn. – slightly spotted – contem. half morocco gilt – slightly rubbed – 12mo. – 1828.
(Sotheby Beresford Adams) $40 £20

CROMBIE, B. W.
'Modern Athenians' – col. plates – half morocco gilt – 4to. – 1882.
(Phillips) $45 £22

CROOKES, SIR WILLIAM
'A Practical Handbook of Dyeing and Calico Printing' – 11 plates – 38 woodcuts and 47 specimens of dyed and printed fabrics – orig. cloth – worn at top and bottom of spine – 8 vo. – Longman Green and Co. 1874.
(Sotheby's) $170 £80

CROOKSHANK, EDGAR M.
'History and Pathology of Vaccination' – 2 vols. – portrait of Benjamin Jesty – col. plates – cloth – 8vo. – 1889.
(Sotheby's) $180 £85

CROSLEIGH, CHARLES
'History of Bradninch' – 1911.
(Laurence & Martin Taylor) $20 £10

CROUCH, NATHANIEL
'Surprising Miracles of Nature and Art' – 3rd Edn. – woodcut frontispiece and illustrations – ads. at end – browning – some margins shaved – old calf – rubbed – 12mo. printed for Nath. Crouch, 1699.
(Christie's S. Kensington) $95 £45

CROW, CAPT. HUGH
'Memoirs' ... together with descriptive sketches of the Western Coast of Africa' – 1st Edn. – litho portrait – 3 plates and a folding map – one leaf of litho music – occas. foxing – orig. cloth backed boards – rebacked – uncut – 8vo. – 1830.
(Sotheby's) $295 £140

CROWLEY, A.
'The Confessions' – limited Edn. – on Japanese vellum – illus. – vols. 1 and 2 – decorated white buckram gilt – t.e.g. – Mandrake Press, 1929.
(Bonhams) $200 £96

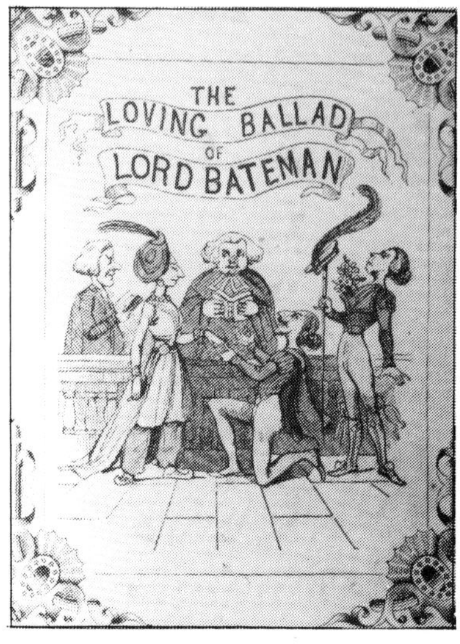

CRUIKSHANK, GEORGE
'The Loving Ballad of George Bateman' – colour plates – full morocco with orig. wrappers bound in – 1st American Edn. with 'The Boy's Story Book' – circa 1850 – Philadelphia.
(Robert Skinner) $170 £80

CRUIKSHANK, GEORGE – HONE, WILLIAM
'Facetiae and Miscellanies' – plates – two mounted and illustrations by Cruikshank – later half morocco – by Ramage – spine faded – 1827.
(Christie's S. Kensington) $80 £38

CRUIKSHANK, ISAAC AND GEORGE
'Munchausen at Walcheren' – 1st Edn. – folding engraved frontis – 4 plates – col. by hand – dark green morocco – gilt – t.e.g. – 12 mo. – J. Johnson 1811.
(Sotheby's) $335 £160

'CRUISE OF THE CHALLENGE LIFEBOAT, – AND VOYAGE FROM LIVERPOOL TO LONDON IN 1852'
sm. 8vo. – orig. cloth – 1853.
(Bonhams) $60 £28

CRUMP, L. M.
'The Severing Seas' – Poems – Oxford 1927.
(J. Ash) $8 £4

CRUNDEN, J.
'Convenient and Ornamental Architecture' – 70 plates – old calf – one joint broken – 1791.
(Bonhams) $105 £50

CRUTTWELL, CLEMENT
'A Tour Through Great Britain' – 6 vol. – contem. tree calf – joints rubbed – spines cracked – 1801.
(Christie's) $60 £28

CRYES OF THE CITY OF LONDON, THE
74 engraved plates including title tipped in – title page damaged – folio album by P. Tempest – circa 1700.
(Phillips) $840 £400

CUITT, GEORGE
'Wanderings and Pencillings amongst Ruins of the Olden Times' – plates – damage by damp – contem. half morocco – worn – g.e. – folio – 1855.
(Christie's) $40 £20
'Etchings of Ancient Buildings in the City of Chester, Castles in North Wales and other Miscellaneous Subjects' – 3 vol. – first with engraved vignette title – subscription list – 20 etched plates by Cuitt – minor defects – loose as issued in orig. wrappers – orig. half gilt folder – folio – Chester 1813.
(Sotheby Beresford Adams) $210 £100

CULPEPER, NICHOLAS
'Complete Herbal' – 4to. – inscribed by the Earl of Essex – engraved portrait – and 40 hand coloured plates – spotted – modern half calf – 1828.
(Christie's S. Kensington) $115 £55
'Works' – 210 coloured plates – 3 vols. – calf.
(Bonhams) $335 £160

CULPEPER, SIR THOMAS, The Younger
'Essayes of Moral Discourses on Several Subjects' – 2nd Edn. – errata leaf – browning and soiling – contem. sheep – worn – one cover detached – sm. 8vo. – 1671.
(Sotheby's) $160 £75

CUMBERLAND, R.
'John De Lancaster' – 1st Edn. – 3 vols. – calf gilt – 1809.
(Phillips) $190 £90

CUMBERLAND, RICHARD
'An Essay towards the Recovery of the Jewish Measures and Weights' – 1st Edn. – 1 folding plate – wormed – calf – 8vo. – Richard Chiswell 1686.
(Sotheby's) $90 £42

CUMING, E. D.
'Squire Osbaldeston, His Autobiography' – orig. buckram binding – 1926.
(Lane) $30 £14

CUNDALL, H. M.
'Birket Foster' – plates – col. – illus. – orig. cloth – spine faded – t.e.g. – sm. 4to. – 1906.
(Christie's) $40 £20

CUNDALL, JOSEPH (editor)
'The Life and Genuis of Rembrandt. The Most Celebrated of Rembrandt's Etchings' – 30 mounted photographs – contemp. red straight-grained morocco – gilt – slightly rubbed – g.e. – 4to. – 1867.
(Christie's S. Kensington) $65 £30

CUNNINGHAM, A.
'The Stupa of Bharut' – actual photographs – mounted illus. – orig. cloth – rubbed – 4to. – 1879.
(Sotheby's) $220 £105

CUNNINGTON, C. W. AND P.
'Handbooks of English Costume – Mediaeval to 20th century' – 7 vols. – plates – orig. cloth – dust jacket – 8vo. – 1952-73.
(Sotheby's) $55 £25

CURIE, MADAME MARIE SKLODOWSKA
'Traite de Radioactivitie' – 2 vol. – 1st Edn. – portrait of Pierre Curie – diagrams in text – half title – half calf – orig. front wrappers bound in – 8vo. – Paris 1910.
(Sotheby's) $295 £140

CURIE, PIERRE
'Oeuvres' – first collected Edn. – portrait – 2 plates – illus and diagrams in text – half title – half calf – 8vo. – Paris 1908.
(Sotheby's) $145 £70

CURLE, J.
'A Roman Frontier Post and Its People' – buckram – plates – map – 4to. – Glasgow, 1911.
(Bennett Book Auction) $75 £36

CURRY, JOHN
'Elements of Bleaching' – half title – contem. half morocco gilt – very worn – owner's name cut from title page – 8vo. – Dublin 1779.
(Sotheby's) $65 £30

CURTAIN DRAWN UP, THE
2 parts in one vol. – 17 engraved erotic scenes inserted – cloth – London 1818.
(Phillips) $525 £250

CURTIUS, BENEDICTUS
'Hortorum Libri Triginta' – 1st Edn. – woodcut printer's device on title – contem. vellum gilt – bookplate of Lord Halifax – folio – 1560.
(Christie's) $600 £280

CURWEN, HENRY
'A History of Booksellers, the Old and the New' – many plates – orig. cloth gilt – expertly restored – bookplate – 1873.
(J. Ash) $75 £35

CUSHING, HARVEY
'The Harvey Cushing Collection of Books and Manuscripts' – 1st Edn. – orig. cloth – 4to. – New York 1943.
(Sotheby's) $65 £30

CUSSANS, JOHN EDWIN
'History of Hertfordshire' part 3 and 4. 'Hundred of Edwinstone' – litho frontis – cloth – orig. wrappers bound in – folio – 1872.
(Sotheby's) $65 £32

CUTLER, THOMAS W.
'A Grammar of Japanese Ornament and Design' – addit. title – plates some chromolith – some soiled – folio – 1880.
(Christie's) $170 £80

CUVIER, G. L. C.
'The Animal Kingdom, Class Aves' – 160 plates – 145 coloured – 3 vols. – cloth 1829.
(Bonhams) $400 £190

CYCLOPAEDIA OF AGRICULTURE
2 vols. – illustrated – some damp stains – thick 8vo. – 1855.
(Irelands) $160 £75

D. T.
'The Complete English Man or the New London School Instructing Children and Elder Persons Speedily to Spell, Read and Write English' – engraved frontis – mss exercises by former owner – stained – cont. sheep – rebacked – 8vo – T. Dawks 1685.
(Sotheby's) $630 £300

DADELEZEN, E. J. VON
'The New Zealand Official Year Book' – 1st Edn. – maps and tables – orig. cloth – 8vo – 1893.
(Sotheby's) $40 £20

DA GAMA, VASCO
'The Three Voyages to India' – translated and edited by Henry Stanley – illus. – author's notes and corrections to text – half morocco – rubbed – 8vo – 1869.
(Sotheby's) $75 £35

DAHL, RAOLD
'Over to You' – slight marks – 1946.
(J. Ash) $40 £20

DAHLBERG, EDWARD
'Bottom Dogs' – precedes American Edn. – 520 copies only – intro. by D. H. Lawrence – author's first book – marks and wrinkles – labels – 1929.
(J. Ash) $65 £32

DAISIE, W. GALSWORTHY
'Architectural Studies in France' – 88 lithographed plates, 13 coloured – occasional slight soiling – orig. half morocco – rubbed – joints worn – folio – B. T. Batsford, 1877.
(Christie's S. Kensington) $60 £30

DALLAS, R. C.
'The History of the Maroons' – 2 vols. – 2 frontis – 2 folding maps – orig. boards – 1803.
(Phillips) $440 £210

DALLAWAY, JAMES
'Constantinople Ancient and Modern' – 1st Edn. – engraved title with vignette – 10 sepia aquatint plates – foxing and spotting – cont. calf – rubbed – 4to – 1797.
(Sotheby's) $275 £130

DALLINGTON, SIR R.
'Aphorismes Civill and Militaire' – 1st Edn. – engraved port. – woodcut device and initials – calf – sm. folio – 1613.
(Phillips) $135 £65

DALTON, JOHN
'Meteorological Observations and Essays' – 1st Edn. – second issue – rough marks – orig. boards – rebacked – uncut – 8vo – T. Ostell 1793.
(Sotheby's) $55 £25

DALTON, RICHARD
'Antiquities and Views in Greece and Egypt' – 5 double page and 37 full page engraved plates – cont. calf backed boards – folio – 1751.
(Christie's) $210 £100

DALY, CESAR
'L'Architecture Privee au XIXe Siecle Troisieme Serie Decorations Interieures Peintes' – 2 vols. in one – 84 coloured lithograph plates – 16 double page – some spotting – cont. half morocco – faded – slightly rubbed – folio – Paris 1877.
(Christie's S. Kensington) $210 £100

DALZIEL, ARCHIBALD
'The History of Dahomey' – 1st Edn. – large paper copy – 6 engraved plates – folding map – modern calf backed marbled boards – spine gilt – uncut – 4to – for the author 1793.
(Sotheby's) $315 £150

DALZIEL, THE BROTHERS
Presentation copy inscribed by Edward Dalziel to Walter Williams – plates – illus. – orig. cloth – soiled – t.e.g. – 4to – 1901.
(Christie's) $75 £35

DAMBOURNEY, L. A.
'Recueil de Procedes et d'Experiences sur les Teintures Solides' – 2 vols. including Supplement – orig. wrappers – soiled – unopened – 8vo – Paris 1786-88.
(Sotheby's) $75 £35

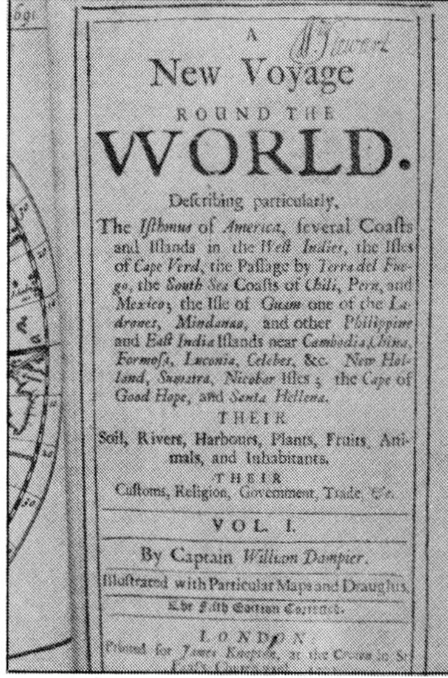

A
New Voyage
ROUND THE
WORLD.
Describing particularly,
The Isthmus of America, several Coasts and Islands in the West Indies, the Isles of Cape Verd, the Passage by Terra del Fuego, the South Sea Coasts of Chili, Peru, and Mexico; the Isle of Guam one of the Ladrones, Mindanao, and other Philippine and East India Islands near Cambodia, China, Formosa, Luconia, Celebes, &c. New Holland, Sumatra, Nicobar Isles; the Cape of Good Hope, and Santa Hellena.
THEIR
Soil, Rivers, Harbours, Plants, Fruits, Animals, and Inhabitants.
THEIR
Customs, Religion, Government, Trade, &c.
VOL. I.
By Captain William Dampier.
Illustrated with Particular Maps and Draughts.
The Fifth Edition Corrected.
LONDON:
Printed for James Knapton, at the Crown in S-

DAMPIER, CAPTAIN WILLIAM
'A Voyage Round the World' – vol. 1 – 2nd Edn. – four maps and 'Voyages and Descriptions' – vol. 2 – 2nd Edn. – three maps – 1703 and 1700.
(Allen & May) $230 £110

DANCE
Rare engraved ticket for M. Fierville's Ball signed and subscribed 'Almack's Tuesday April the 25th' – engraved oval printed in light red showing a woman and putto dancing, docketed Lord J. C. – fold at centre – window mount – 5½ x 4½in.
(Sotheby's) $250 £120

DANCING
'Les Maitres a Danser or the Act of Dancing Quadrilles' – hand col. engraved frontis and double page plate – diagrams in text – 6 pages of music – cont. red straight grained morocco – rubbed – g.e. – sm. 8vo – 1819.
(Sotheby's) $360 £170

DANDIES' BALL, THE OR HIGH LIFE IN THE CITY
1st Edn. – 16 engraved illus. by Robert Cruikshank – col. by hand – soiled – restitched – 12 mo. – John Marshall, 1819.
(Sotheby's) $100 £48

DANDY ANNUALS
3 copies circa 1950's
BEANO ANNUALS
2 copies circa 1950's.
(Baitson) $17 £8

DANDY'S PERAMBULATIONS, THE
1st Edn. – 16 engraved illus. – col. by hand – pencil scoring – torn – spotted – orig. decorated wrappers – resewn – 8vo – John Marshall, 1819.
(Sotheby's) $10 £5

DANIEL, G.
'The Modern Dunciad' – port – inscribed with poem 'To Stella' by author – later morocco gilt – rubbed – 8vo. – 1835.
(Sotheby's) $125 £60

DANIEL, GABRIEL
'Histoire de la Milice Francoise' – 2 vol. – 1st Edn. – woodcut arms on titles – 70 engraved plates – minor defects – contem. sprinkled calf – slightly worn – lacking labels – 4to. – Paris 1721.
(Sotheby Beresford Adams) $335 £160

DANIEL, W. B.
'Rural Sports' – plates – 4 vols. – 8vo – half calf – some leaves loose in binding and edges frayed – 1807-13.
(Bonhams) $210 £100

DANIELL, THOMAS AND WILLIAM
'Oriental Scenery' – 4 parts in 2 vols. – 84 hand col. lithographed plates – contem. half morocco – gilt spines – g.e. – hinges rubbed – elephant folio – 1795-1801.
(Christie's) $22,050 £10,500

DANIELL, WILLIAM
'Illustrations of the Island of Staffa' – 9 col. aquatint plates – half title – spotting – contem. maroon half morocco – worn – oblong 4to. – 1818.
(Sotheby's) $735 £350
'The Adventures of a Hunch Back' – 17 engraved plates on india paper by Daniell – slight spotting – later 19th cent. brown morocco backed boards – folio – 1814.
(Sotheby's) $75 £35

DANKERTS, C.
'Silesia Ducatus' – engraved map – hand col. in outline – historiated title cartouche – coat of arms etc. – fully coloured – 378 mm. x 480 mm. – Amsterdam circa 1700.
(Sotheby's) $115 £55

D'ARBLAY, MADAME FANNY BURNEY
'The Wanderer or Female Difficulties' – 5 vols. – calf gilt – 1814.
(Phillips) $170 £80

DART, J.
'The History and Antiquities of the Cathedral Church of Canterbury' – plates – modern leather – folio – 1726.
(Sotheby's) $65 £30

DARTON, F. J. HARVEY
'English Fabric, a Study of Village Life' – illustrated – 1935.
(J. Ash) $8 £4

DARTON, WILLIAM
'Series of Scripture Prints' – 39 engraved plates – col. by hand – letter press text – loose – contem. half morocco – covers detached – worn – folio – Edward Suter 1851.
(Sotheby's) $40 £20

D'ARUSMONT, FRANCES WRIGHT
'Views of Society and Manners in America' – 1st Edn. – William Beckford's copy – notes in his hand – contem. half calf – gilt spine – bumped – 8vo. – 1821.
(Sotheby's) $200 £95

DARWIN, CHARLES
'The Descent of Man' – 2 vol. – 1st Edn. – first issue 16 pp. of publisher's ads. dated Jan. 1871 at end of each vol. – illustrations.
(Christie's S. Kensington) $360 £170
'The Life and Letters' editor Francis Darwin – 3 vol. – fifth thousand – plates – facsimile letter – orig. cloth – slightly soiled – 1887.
(Christie's S. Kensington) $65 £30

'Journal of Researches into the Natural History and Geology of the Countries Visited during the Voyage of H.M.S. Beagle' – no. 204 of 1500 copies – signed by artist – 55 wood engraved illus. by Robert Gibbings – orig. cloth – slipcase – 4to. – New York 1956.
(Sotheby's) $250 £120

DARWIN, ERASMUS
'Phytologia or the Philosophy of Agriculture and Gardening' – 12 plates – 2 folding – new half calf – uncut – 4to. – J. Johnson 1800.
(Sotheby's) $75 £35

DASENT, G. W.
'The Story of Burnt Najal' – 2 vols. – plates – orig. cloth – gilt – Edinburgh 1861.
(Sotheby's) $75 £35

DAUBENY, CHARLES
'An Introduction to the Atomic Theory' – orig. cloth – uncut – 8vo. – 1831.
(Sotheby's) $65 £32

D'AVENNES, PRISSE
'L'Art Arabe' – reprint of 1877 Edn. – 1 vol. text – 3 vols. plate sm. large folio – half morocco gilt – Beirut, n.d.
(Phillips) $160 £75

DAVENPORT, RICHARD
'The Amateur's Perspective' – pres. copy – 2 vols. incl. supplement – 21 folding plates – orig. boards – 4to. – 1828-29.
(Phillips) $75 £35

DAVID, WILFRID
'Monsoon' – inscribed and signed by author – covers a little dull – 1933.
(J. Ash) $12 £6

DAVIES, RHYS
'The Skull' – 1st Edn. – no. 1 of 110 copies – one of 15 specially bound – signed by author – 15 wood engraved vignettes and cover design by Sylvia Marshall – orig. cream pigskin – black pigskin spine – slightly rubbed – uncut – sm. 4to. – 1936.
(Sotheby's) $135 £65

DAVIES, GERALD S.
'Hans Holbein the Younger' – folio – 1903 – plates – orig. parchment backed cloth – faded – t.e.g.
(Christie's S. Kensington) $40 £18

DAVIES, J.
'Innkeepers' and Butlers' Guide' – orig. board – upper cover detached – 1809.
(Phillips) $65 £30

DAVIES, JOHN
'The Anti Romance or the History of the Shepherd Lysis' – lacks title – binding defective.
(Lane) $30 £14

DAVIES, RHYS
'Print of a Hare's Foot' – Autobiographical – soiled jacket – 1969.
(J. Ash) $8 £4

DAVIES, W. H.
'In Winter' – privately printed – signed – limited Edn. – 250 copies only – orig. boards – worn and loose – 1931.
(J. Ash) $6 £3

DAVILA, H. C.
'The Historie of the Civil Warres of France' – 1st. English Edn. – folio – by R. Raworth – first leaf detached – title slightly torn – without loss – contemp. calf – rubbed – upper cover detached.
(Christie's S. Kensington) $80 £38

DAVY, F. H.
'The Flora of Cornwall' – half morocco – 1909.
(Lane) $50 £24

DAVY, HENRY
'A Series of Etchings Illustrative of the Architectural Antiquities of Suffolk' – 70 etched plates – some spotting – later cloth – rubbed – uncut – folio – Southwold 1827.
(Sotheby's) $170 £80

DAVY, SIR HUMPHRY
'Elements of Agricultural Chemistry' – 1st. Edn. – 10 plates – half calf rubbed – 4to.. – W. Bulmer and Co. 1813.
(Sotheby's) $135 £65

DAVY, JOHN
'Memoirs of Sir Humphry Davy' – 9. vols – orig. cloth binding – good set – 1839.
(Lane) $295 £140

DAVY, N. K.
'Netsuke' – plates – some col. – orig. cloth – dust jacket – 4to. – 1974.
(Sotheby's) $55 £25

DAWE, GEORGE
'The Life of George Morland' – no. 24 of 175 copies – frontis in 2 states – hand col. plates – orig. half vellum – soiled – t.e.g. – 4to. – 1904.
(Christie's) $90 £42

DAWSON, KENNETH
'Marsh and Mudflat' – with 12 others on Natural History – Country Life Edn.
(Laurence & Martin Taylor) $20 £9

DAY, H. E.
'East Anglian Painters' – 3 vols. limited Edn. – plates – calf gilt – 4to. – 1967-69.
(Phillips) $65 £30

'Florigraphia Britannica' – 3 vols. – hand coloured plates – orig. green cloth – 1857.
(Bennett Book Auction) $90 £42

DEAN, BASHFORD
'Catalogue of European Daggers' – limited Edn. – plates – illus. – contem. cloth – rubbed – 4to. – New York 1929.
(Sotheby's) $265 £125

DEANE, A.
'A Tour Through the Upper Provinces of Hindustan between 1804 and 1814' – folding map – inscription by relative – Rivington London 1823.
(Allen & May) $65 £30

DEARN, T. D. W.
'Design for Lodges and Engrances to Parks, Paddocks and Pleasure Grounds – 20 aquatint plates – 1st Edn. – with half title – orig. boards – one joint broken – 1811.
(Bonhams) $460 £220

'Sketches in Architecture; consisting of Original Designs for Cottages and Rural Dwellings' – 19 plates (of 20) – 4to. – orig. boards – back missing – 1823.
(Bonhams) $40 £20

DE BRY, J.T.
'Voyages' – 1 part only engraved title – 14 half page plans – Rio de Janeiro, Japan, Manila, Borneo etc. – binding defective – folio – 1602.
(Phillips) $65 £32

DE BRY, JOHANN THEODOR
'Florilegium Movum' – engraved title and 142 plates – some folding – shaving – water staining – contem. vellum – folio – Oppenheim 1612.
(Christie's) $1,680 £800

DE BURE, F.
'Abrege de la Vie des Plus Fameux Peintres' – 4 vols. in 2 – engraved ports. – no half title to vol. 1 – some minor defects – contem. calf gilt – worn – rebacked – 8vo. – Paris 1762.
(Sotheby Beresford Adams) $25 £11

DE CHAIR, SOMERSET (editor)
'Napoleon's Memoirs' – 2 vols. – no. 67 of 500 copies – frontis – orig. cloth – t.e.g. – The Golden Cockerel Press 1945.
(Christie's) $210 £100

DECKER, PAUL
'Ausfurliche Anleitung sur Civil Bau Kunst' – 2 parts of 3 in 1 vol. – 40 engraved plates incl. titles – some soiled – contem. half vellum – worn – folio – Nuremberg circa 1720.
(Sotheby's) $275 £130

DECREMPS, HENRI
'La Magie Blanche Devoilee' – engraved frontis and title and one woodcut illus. – lacking final leaf – cloth backed boards with library stamp – 8vo. – Paris, 1784.
(Sotheby's) $125 £60

DEE, JOHN
'General and Rare Memorials Pertayning to the Perfect Arte of Navigation' – 1st. Edn. – fine large woodcut on title – woodcut arms of Sir Christopher Hatton – woodcut initials – contem. limp vellum – slightly damaged – folio – John Daye 1577.
(Sotheby's) $9,660 £4,600

DEERING, CHARLES
'Nottinghamia vetus et nova ..... or an historical account of Nottingham' – folding engraved map and 24 plates – several folding – frontis with tear – contem. calf – spine rubbed – 4to. – Nottingham 1751.
(Sotheby Beresford Adams) $145 £70

DE FER, N.
'Des Forces de l'Europe' – 194 town plans etc. – oblong folio – old calf – worn – Paris, 1723.
(Bonhams) $1,470 £700

DEFOE, DANIEL
'Novels and Select Writings' – 14 vol. – limited to 750 copies – orig. cloth – soiled – t.e.g. – Shakespeare Head Press, 1927-8.
(Christie's S. Kensington) $115 £55
'The Political History of the Devil' – 1st Edn. – frontispiece – some slight browning – contemp. panelled calf – re-backed – 1726.
(Christie's S. (Kensington) $65 £30

DEGAS, EDGAR
'Catalogue des Tableaux, Pastels et Dessins' – 4 vol. in 4 – aution catalogue – some prices in pencil – modern cloth – 8vo. – Paris 1918-19.
(Sotheby's) $630 £300

DEGAS, EDGAR – LOUYS, PIERRE
'Mimes des Courtesanes de Lucien' – 22 engraved plates by Maurice Potin, 12 illustrations in text, all after Degas – unsewn in original wrappers,– uncut – no. 302 of 325 copies – A. Vollard, Paris, 1935.
(Sotheby's) $520 £230

DE GRAY, THOMAS
'The Complete Horseman and Expert Farrier' – folio – printed by Thomas Harper – engraved portrait – repaired – margins chewed – soiled – stained – old calf – worn – upper cover lacking.
(Christie's S. Kensington) $170 £80

DE HALSALLE, HENRY
'Treasure Trove in Bookland, The Romance of Modern First Editions' – spine sunned – otherwise nice – 1931.
(J. Ash) $12 £6

DE HAVAS, MOLLY
'Singing Words' – Poems – Reigate 1951.
(J. Ash) $6 £3

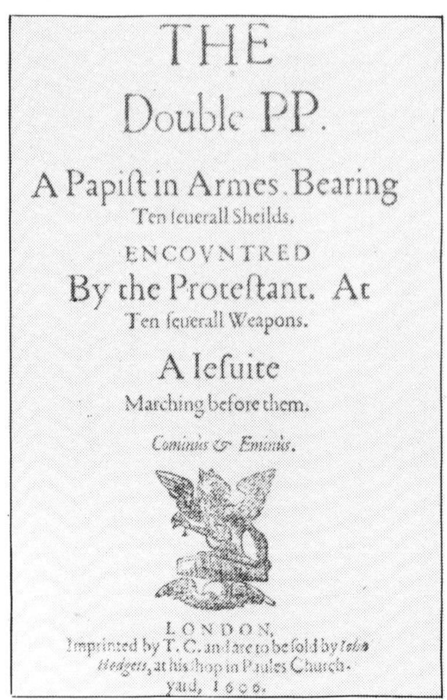

THE
Double PP.
A Papiſt in Armes. Bearing
Ten ſeuerall Sheilds.
ENCOVNTRED
By the Proteſtant. At
Ten ſeuerall Weapons.
A Ieſuite
Marching before them.
Cominus & Eminus.

LONDON,
Imprinted by T. C. and are to be ſold by *Iohn Hodgets*, at his ſhop in Paules Church-yard, 1606.

DEKKER, THOMAS
'The Double PP.' – 1st Edn. – morocco by Mattby – sm. 4to. – 1606.
(Christie's) $2,520 £1,200

DE LA BECHE, HENRY T.
'Report on the Geology of Cornwall, Devon and West Somerset' – contem. cloth – soiled – 1839.
(Christie's) $25 £12

DELACROIX, EUGENE – GOETHE, J. W.
'Von Faust'
13 of 17 litho plates by Delacroix lacking portrait and text – in separate card mounts – folio – Paris, Goyer et Hermet, n.d.
(Sotheby's) $2,100 £1,000

DELACROIX, EUGENE
'Journal de Eugene Delacroix' – 3 vols. – frontis – contem. half morocco – rubbed – g.e. – Paris 1893-5.
(Christie's) $40 £20

DE LA MARE, R.
'A Publisher on Book Production' – 100 copies – orig. boards – dust jackets – sm. 8vo. – 1936.
(Sotheby's) $40 £20

To Walter Sutton
with grateful memories & all good wishes
from W J de la Mare
June 1917.

PEACOCK PIE

DE LA MARE, WALTER
'Peacock Pie' – presentation copy – inscribed by author to Walter Sutton – coloured frontis and illus. by W. Heath Robinson – orig. pictorial cloth – gilt – slight tear on fore-edge – 8vo. – 1916.
(Sotheby's) $95 £45

DELAMOTHE, G. 'G. D. L. M. N.'
'The French Alphabet, Teaching in a very short time, together with the Treasure of the French Tongue' – little frayed some damp staining – contemp. vellum – worn – R. Field, 1592.
(Christie's S. Kensington) £800 £380

DELAMOTTE, W. A. AND OLLIER, C.
'Original Views of Oxford' – partly col. – 25 litho plates – contem. morocco backed cloth – rubbed – folio – 1843.
(Sotheby's) £545 £260

DE L'ART MILITAIRE
Part of a compilation by various authors – 78 full page woodcut illustrations – some leaves torn with loss – stiched – folio – (16th century).
(Christie's S. Kensington) $295 £140

DELASSAUX, V. AND ELLIOT, JOHN
'Street Architecture, a Series of Shop Fronts and Facades' – 22 plates – folio – orig. boards – 1855.
(Bonhams) $420 £200

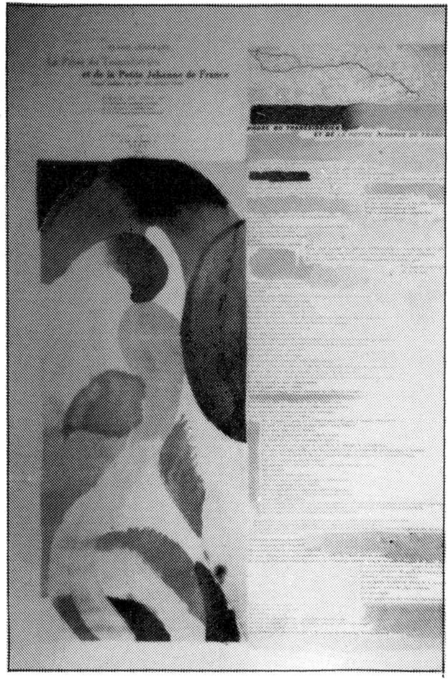

DELAUNEY, SONIA – CENDRARS, BLASE
'La Prose du Transsiberien et la Petite Jehane de France' – some printed in various types and colours – watercolour washes in margins – illus. by Delauney col. through stencils – torn – unbound – large folio – Paris, Editions des Hommes Nouveaux 1913.
(Sotheby's) $505 £240

DE LISLE, G.
'Asia' – partly col. map – torn – circa 1700.
(Phillips) $85 £40

DELKESCAMP, J. W.
'Panorama des Rheins von Mainz bis Colm' folding engraved panorama – soiled – contem. calf backed boards – soiled – slipcase – 4to – Frankfurt am Main 1825.
(Sotheby's) $95 £45

DELLA POETICA DI FRANCESCO PATRICI
Vellum binding – Ferrara 1586.
(Richard Baker & Thomson) $65 £32

DELLON, CHARLES
'Relation de L'Inquisition de Goa' – 2nd Edn. – engraved vignette on title – 6 engraved plates – 3 folding – dampstains – contem. sheep – rubbed – rebacked – spine gilt – 12 mo. – Paris 1688.
(Sotheby's) $65 £30

DE LONG, G. W.
'The Voyage of the Jeanette' – 2 vols. – plates – folding maps – orig. pictorial cloth – 8 vo. – Boston 1884.
(Sotheby's) $85 £40

DELPECH, F. S.
'Iconographie des Contemporains' – 3 vol. – litho portraits – contem. half morocco – rubbed – folio – Paris 1832.
(Sotheby's) $85 £40

DELPHICK ORACLE, THE
'Resolving the Most Curious Questions in Love and Gallantry' – Parts 1-VII complete set – some dampstains – repaired – contem. mottled calf – rebacked – spine gilt rubbed – 8vo. – 1722.
(Sotheby's) $315 £150

DELREIL, LOYS
'Le Peintre-Graveur Illustre' – Vol. 4, 7, 8, 13, 16, 18, 20-29 – 16 vols. only – collectors' edition – illus. original cloth – 4to. – New York, 1969.
(Sotheby's) $400 £190

DEMIDOFF, A. DE
'Travels in Southern Russia and the Crimea' – 2 vols. – pres inscrptn. – portrait – 2 folding maps – 23 plates – illus. – orig. cloth – rubbed – 8vo. – 1853.
(Sotheby's) $220 £105

DENHAM, D. H. CLAPPERTON AND OUDNEY, W.
'Narrative of Travels and Discoveries in Northern and Central Africa' – 2 vol. 3rd Edn. – 13 engraved plates – one col. – 2 folding maps – modern maroon half morocco – spines gilt – t.e.g. – 8vo. – 1828.
(Sotheby's) $135 £65

DENIS, FERDINAND
'Bresil, Colombie et Guyanes' – 2 parts in one – 1st Edn. – 2 double page maps and 100 plates – half title – contem. half morocco – 8vo. – Paris 1837.
(Sotheby's) $115 £55

DENMARK

DENMARK – VISSCHER, N.
'Regni Daniae' – engraved map – hand col. in outline – historiated and armorial cartouche – royal arms – sailing ships etc. – fully col. – 454 mm x 557 mm – Amsterdam circa 1698.
(Sotheby's) $145 £70

DENON, D. V. BARON
'Travels in Sicily and Malta' – calf – gilt – 8vo. – 1789.
(Phillips) $115 £55
'Travels in Upper and Lower Egypt' – 2 vol. 1st English Edn. – 2 folding engraved maps – 59 plates – 15 folding – spotting and off-setting – contem. sprinkled calf – rebacked – 4to. – 1803.
(Sotheby's) $190 £90

DE QUINCEY, THOMAS
'Confessions of an English Opium Eater' – 1st. Edn. – half title – advert leaf at end – 20th cent. maroon levant morocco by Riviere – gilt – g.e. – 12mo. – 1822.
(Sotheby's) $600 £280

DER IN EUROPA UND AMERICA VEREH-LICHE THORN UND KRON GROSS BRITANNIENS
Engraved title and plates – some folding – slight worming – lacking map – title shaved – contemp. vellum – n.d.
(Christie's S. Kensington) $40 £18

DERLETH, AUGUST
'The Shield of the Valiant' – portion of dust wrapper laid down – label removed from rear – New York, 1945.
(J. Ash) $25 £12

DEROME, L.
'La Reluire de Luxe' – limited Edn. – plates – contem. morocco backed boards – rubbed – 8vo. – Paris 1888.
(Sotheby's) $180 £85

DERRIERE LE MIROIR
No. 1-236 in 184, a complete run – lithos by Chagall, Miro, Calder, Braque and others – 16 woodcuts by Arp, Kandinsky and others – one etching by Miro – numerous litho repros and other illus. – most coloured – unsewn in orig. wrappers in 12 folders – 4to. – Paris, Maeght 1946-79.
(Sotheby's) $315 £150

DERRIEY, C.
'Gravure et Fonderie. Specimen Album' – lithographed title and plates – some coloured – orig. morocco backed cloth – gilt spine – slightly rubbed – g.e. – folio – Paris, 1862.
(Sotheby's) $460 £220

DERWENT, REV. C. E.
'The Story of Fish Street Church, Hull' – Illus. – 1899.
(Baitson) $20 £10

DESAGULIERS, J. T.
'A Course of Experimental,Philosophy' – 2 vol. – 3rd Edn. – 78 engraved Plates – browning – contem. calf – rebacked – labels – rubbed – 4to. – 1763.
(Sotheby's) $210 £100

DESCARTES, RENE
'Opera Philosphica' – 2 parts in one vol. – 5th Edn. – numerous illus. in text – some full page – browning and soiling – some leaves loose – contem. calf – worn – 4to. – Amsterdam 1672.
(Sotheby's) $85 £40

DESGODETZ, M.
'Les Edifices Antiques de Rome' – engraved title and illus. – contem. speckled calf – spine gilt – rubbed – folio – Paris 1682.
(Sotheby's) £600 £280

DESNARAIS
'Jeremie, Poeme' – cont. French binding of red morocco gilt with arms of Pope Clement XIV in red cloth case probably by Derome – 8vo. – 1771.
(Moore Allen & Innocent) $2,000 £950

DESNOS, LOUIS CHARLES
'L'Indicateur Fidele ou Guide des Voyageurs ... dresse par le Sieur Michel' – engr. title – dedication – one general map of France – one plan of Paris and 17 road maps – all double page and hand coloured in outline – a few folding – light spotting – contemp. wrappers – backstrip torn with loss 4to. -- Paris 1765.
(Christie's S. Kensington) $275 £130
'Atlas General Methodiqe et Elementaire' – printed and double page engraved titles – 7 double page plates – 60 double page maps – neatly col. – all in engraved borders with text pasted in on either side – contem. green stained vellum backed boards – large 4to. – Paris 1768.
(Sotheby's) $505 £240

DESROCHES-NOBLECOURT, C.
'Tutankhamen' – limited signed Edn. – morocco gilt – overlay on upper cover – g.e. – by Zaehnsdorf – buckram box – 4to. – 1969.
(Phillips) $125 £60

D'ESTOURMEL, COMTE DE
'Journal d'un Voyage en Orient' – 2 vols. – 160 plates – some spotting – orig boards – 1844.
(Phillips) $360 £170

DETMOLD, E. J.
'Fabre's Book of Insects' – 4to. – mounted coloured plates by Detmold – original cloth – New York 1936.
(Christie's S. Kensington) $65 £30

DEUCHAR, DAVID
'A Collection of Etchings after the Most Eminent Masters of the Dutch and Flemish Schools' – vols. II and III of 3 – engraved titles in elaborate borders – 258 plates – occasional spotting – contem. straight grained green morocco – gilt – rubbed – g.e. – folio – Edinburgh 1803.
(Sotheby's) $1,785 £850

DEUTSCH-ENGLISH LEXICON
Title in red and black – one corner torn – some minor defects – contem. calf worn – gilt arms of Johannes Seyfried Graf von Herberstein on covers – Leipzig 1716.
(Sotheby Beresford Adams) $90 £43

DEVEREUX, W.B.
'Views on the Shores of the Mediterranean' – 1st Edn. – 24 tinted litho plates – dedication – spotting – orig. blue half roan – gilt – rubbed – large folio – 1847.
(Sotheby's) $840 £400

DEVIL, THE HISTORY OF THE
Later half calf – joints rubbed – Durham 1822.
(Christie's S. Kensington) $45 £22

DEVRYER, ABRAHAM
'Historie von Francois Eugenius' – 3 vol. – engraved portrait – four folding plates – six folding plans and two folding maps – contemp. half calf – joints rubbed – Amsterdam 1737.
(Christie's S. Kensington) $105 £50

D'HOZIER, J. FRANCOIS
'L'Impot du Sang' – 3 vol. in 6 – spotting – contem. calf backed boards – rubbed – 8vo. – Paris 1874-81.
(Sotheby's) $40 £20

DIBDIN, T. F.
'Reminiscences of a Literary Life' – 2 vol. – engraved plates – contem. calf – gilt – 8vo – 1836.
(Sotheby's) $180 £85

DICKENS, CHARLES
AL to Lloyd. Esq. – framed with engraved portrait – n.d.
(Robert Skinner) $325 £155

'Our Mutual Friend' – 20 parts in 19 – orig. wrappers – chipped and loose – slip-case – London 1864-65.
(Robert Skinner) $475 £225

'The Posthumous Papers of the Pickwick Club' – 20 monthly parts in orig. paper covers – Weller title page – 1836-37.
(Allen & May) $150 £72

'The Nonesuch Dickens' – 24 vol. including case with orig. steel engraved plate by H. K. Browne – limited to 877 copies – plates – illus. – orig. buckram – t.e.g. – 1937-38.
(Christie's) $2,415 £1,150

'A Tale of Two Cities' – 8 in 7 parts – 1st. Edn. – first issue – engraved title and plates – adverts – orig. wrappers – slightly soiled and frayed – 8vo. – 1859.
(Sotheby's) $1,930 £920

'Bleak House' – 20 orig. parts in 19 – 1st. Edn. – 40 plates – adverts – later boards preserving orig. wrappers – 8vo. – 1852-53.
(Sotheby's) $440 £210

DICKENSON'S COMPREHENSIVE PICTURES OF THE GREAT EXHIBITION

2 vols. – 54 col. – litho plates – some torn and repaired – some soiled – vol. 11 slightly damp stained – contem. half morocco – loose – g.e. – folio – 1854.
(Sotheby's) $1,595 £760

DICKINSON, THOMAS

'A Narrative of the Operation of the Recovery of the Public Stores and Treasure sunk in the H.M.S. Thetis at Cape Frio' – 1st Edn. – 3 litho plates – 2 litho maps – orig. cloth – 8vo. – 1836.
(Sotheby's) $190 £90

DICKSON, R. W.

'A Complete Dictionary of Practical Gardening' – 2 vol. in one – 4to. – 1807 – 74 plates – 61 hand coloured – slight browning and damp staining – contemp. calf – worn – lower inner hinges crudely repaired.
(Christie's S. Kensington) $1,010 £480

'Practical Agriculture' – 2 vol. 1st Edn. – 87 engraved plates – 27 hand col. – browning – modern half calf – labels – spines gilt – 4to. – 1805.
(Sotheby's) $460 £220

DICTIONARY OF NATURAL BIOGRAPHY

Vol. 1-24 – orig. cloth – rubbed – 8vo. – 1921-27.
(Sotheby's) $275 £130

DICTIONARY, A NEW ENGLISH

11 vol. in 21 – incl. supplement – contem. half morocco – t.e.g. – orig. wrappers – worn – folio – Oxford 1888-93.
(Christie's) $360 £180

DIEFENBACH, ERNEST

'Travels in New Zealand' – 2 vol. – 5 litho plates – browned – modern calf – 8vo. – 1843.
(Sotheby's) $190 £90

DIE KUNST UNSERER HEIMAT

12 parts various in one vol. – lge. 4to. – plates – some mounted and coloured – contemp. half morocco – joints worn – original wrappers bound in – 1909-10.
(Christie's S. Kensington $30 £15

DIEMERBROECK, ISBRANDUS DE

'De Peste Libri IV' – 1st Edn. – calf – upper cover repaired – crest stamped in blind on sides – 4to. – Arnheim, Johannes Jacob 1646.
(Sotheby's) $85 £40

DIEULAFOY, J.
'A Suse. Journal des Fouilles' – plates – map – illus. – modern morocco backed boards – rubbed – orig. wrappers – t.e.g. – 4to. – Paris 1888.
(Sotheby's) $55 £25

DILETTANTI, SOCIETY OF
'The Unedited Antiquities of Attica' – 1st. Edn. – 78 engraved plates – some foxed – occas. spotting – contem. half russia – spine gilt – joints split – worn – folio – 1817.
(Sotheby's) $380 £180

DILKE, LADY
'French Painters, Furniture and Decoration; Engravers and Draughtsmen of the XVIIIth Century' – 3 vol. – 74 of 150 copies – plates – orig. cloth – rubbed – 1 spine loose – 4to. – 1899-1902.
(Sotheby's) $75 £35

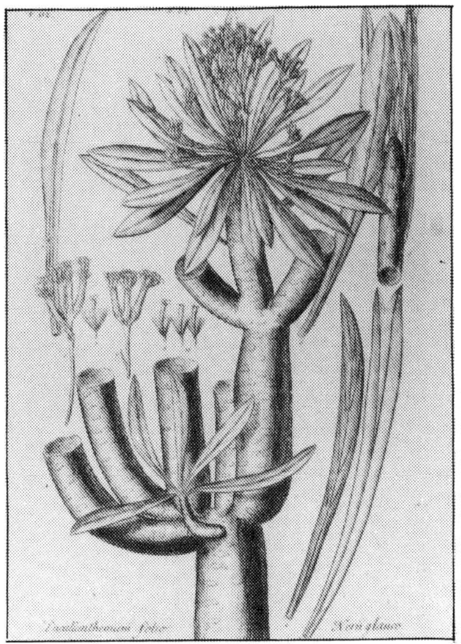

DILLENIUS, JOHANN JAKOB
'Hortus Elthamensis' – 1st Edn. – 2 vols. – 325 plates etched by author – half morocco – folio – 1732.
(Christie's) $2,000 £950

DILLON, P.
'Narrative and Successful Result of a Voyage in the South Seas' – 2 vols. – 1st. Edn. – 3 plates – folding map – slight spotting – modern half calf – spines gilt – t.e.g. – 8vo. – 1829.
(Sotheby's) $630 £300

DIRECTORIUM CHORI
18th cent. Italian binding of black morocco gilt with Papal insignia on each cover – 8vo. – 1665.
(Moore Allen & Innocent) $715 £340

DISNEY, WALT
'Mickey Chercher d'Or' – col. illus. in comic strip form – illus. of Mickey in photographer's studio on title – orig. cloth backed pictorial boards – 4to. – Hachette, Paris, 1931.
(Sotheby's) $95 £45

DISSERTATIONS
A collection of 42 medical dissertations ranging from 1727 to 1862 submitted at Edinburgh, Paris, Montpelier, Gottingen, Halle, Jena and other German Universities – 29 bound – 13 unbound – 4to. and 8vo.
(Sotheby's) $250 £120

DISTON, JOHN
'The Seaman's Guide' – 2 parts in one vol. – 1st Edn. – damp stains – worming – modern calf backed marbled boards – spine gilt – oblong 8vo. – circa 1780.
(Sotheby's) $80 £38

DIVINE HARMONY
Contem. English binding of black morocco gilt – panelled covers with Chapel Royal Windsor on them and royal cypher crowned – 8vo. – 1712.
(Moore Allen & Innocent) $160 £75

DIWAN
Persian mss Loose leaf plus 6 fly leaves – contemporary lacquer binding of birds among flowers – dominant colours red and green on black – folio 16.9 x 10.5cm.
(Christie's) $1,050 £500

DIXON, C.
'Game Birds and Wild Fowl of the British Islands' – 41 col. plates – 2nd Edn. – cloth – 4to. – Sheffield 1900.
(Bonhams) $135 £65

DOBRIZHOFFER, M.
'An Account of the Abipones of Paraguay' – 3 vols. – modern calf backed boards – rubbed – 8vo. – 1822.
(Sotheby's) $125 £60

DOCKER, ALFRED
'Colour Prints of William Dickes Ltd.' – signed Edn. – plates – cloth – 4to. – 1924.
(Phillips) $105 £50

DODDRIDGE, SIR JOHN
'The History of the Ancient and Modern Estates of the Principality of Wales, the Duchy of Cornwall and the Earldome of Chester' – 1st Edn. – dampstaining – 19th cent. red half morocco – rubbed – 4to – 1630.
(Sotheby's) $75 £35

DODDS, JOHN BOVEE
'The Philosophy of Mesmerism and Electrical Psychology' – editor J. Burns – orig. cloth gilt – slightly spotted – 8vo. – 1886.
(Sotheby's) $40 £20

DODGSON, C. L., Lewis Carroll
'Alice's Adventures in Wonderland' – limited Edn. – col. plates by A. Rackham – orig. calf gilt – t.e.g. – 4to. – 1907.
(Phillips) $360 £170

DODGSON, CAMPBELL
'Old French Colour Prints' – no. 834 of 1250 copies – plates – some mounted – coloured – orig. parchment backed cloth – soiled – t.e.g. – 4to. – 1924.
(Christie's) $30 £15

DODSLEY, ROBERT
'The Preceptor' – 2 vol. 1st Edn. – engraved frontis and 28 folding plates – 6 hand col. maps – stained – contem. calf – rebacked – 8vo. – R. Dodsley 1748.
(Sotheby's) $210 £100
'A Select Collection of Old Plays' – 12 vols. – contem. calf – 1780.
(Phillips) $65 £32

DODWELL, E.
'Classical and Topographical Tour Through Greece' – 2 vols. – folding map – 66 plates – 3 col. – woodcuts in text – diced calf gilt – 4to. – 1819.
(Phillips) $400 £190

DOLL, ANTON
'Iconologie fur Dichter, Kunstler und Kunstliebhaber' – engraved title – 75 plates – orig. boards – oblong 4to. – Wien 1801.
(Phillips) $160 £75

DOLMETSCH, H.
'Anthologie de L'Ornement' – col. and plain plates – gold and coloured – illus. in text – orig. cloth backed boards – rubbed – folio – Paris late 19th cent.
(Sotheby's) $135 £65

DOME, THE
Vol. 1 and Nos. 2, 3 and 4 – plates – orig. boards – 1897.
(Phillips) $55 £25

DOMENECH, ABBE E. M.
'Seven Years' Residence in the Great Deserts of North America' – 2 vol. – plates – some col. – folding map – torn – spotting – contem. calf – rubbed – 8vo. – 1860.
(Sotheby's) $170 £80

DONALD, T.
'County of Cumberland' – engraved map – 26 x 32 inches – mounted on linen – margins cropped – stained – 1783.
(Christie's) $20 £10

DONI, A. F.
'La Zucca' – 3 parts in one vol. – woodcuts – some leaves trimmed – half calf – 8vo. – Venice 1551.
(Sotheby's) $250 £120

DONLEAVY, J. P.
'The Onion Eaters' – very good in chipped jacket – 1971.
(J. Ash) $8 £4

DONN, BENJAMIN
'Map of Devon' – 1965.
(Laurence & Martin Taylor) $8 £4

DONNE, JOHN
'Sermons' – 1st Edn. – lacks addit. engraved title – engraved port – tears – rust holes – contem calf – worn – folio – 1640.
(Sotheby's) $55 £25
'Poems ..... with Elegies on the Author's Death' – 1st Edn. – some browning and soiling – early 20th cent. maroon levant morocco by Zaehnsdorf – gilt – g.e. – sm. 4to. – 1633.
(Sotheby's) $965 £460

DONNEAU DE VIZE, JEAN
'The Husband Forced to be Jealous' – 1st. Edn. in Eng. – browning – modern calf backed marbled boards – spine gilt – 8vo. – 1668.
(Sotheby's) $210 £100

DONOVAN, EDWARD
'The Natural History of British Birds' – 5 vols. – 124 hand col. plates – straight grained crimson morocco – g.e. – 1794-98.
(Phillips) $2,730 £1,300

'The Natural History of British Birds' – vol. 3 and 5 only – new Edn. – 48 hand coloured plates – original boards – worn and disbound – 1815-20.
(Christie's S. Kensington) $460 £220

THE WALLS DO NOT FALL

by

H. D.

H. D.
to
Walter de la Mare,
His the Genius in the jar
which the Fisherman finds.

May 14 – 1944.

OXFORD UNIVERSITY PRESS
LONDON NEW YORK TORONTO
1944

DOOLITTLE, HILDA
'The Walls Do Not Fall' – 1st Edn. – presentation copy – inscribed by author to De La Mare – orig. limp boards – 8vo. – 1944.
(Sotheby's) $180 £85

DORE, GUSTAVE – D'AVILLIER, BARON J. C.
'Spain' – plates by Dore – occasional slight spotting – original cloth – soiled – inner hinges – soiled – g.e. – lge 4to. – 1881.
(Christie's S. Kensington) $65 £30

DORNEY, JOHN
'A Briefe and Exact Relation of the Seige Laid Before the City of Glocester' – 1st. Edn. – title in border – browning – modern half calf – spine gilt – sm. 4to. – 1643.
(Sotheby's) $65 £32

DORTU, M. G.
'Toulouse-Lautrec et son Oeuvre' – 6 vol. number 503 of 1500 copies – 4to. – illustrations – orig. – cloth t.e.g. – New York Collector's Editions – 1971.
(Christie's S. Kensington) $315 £150

DOS PASSOS, JOHN
'The Big Money' – 1st Eng. Edn. – covers rubbed – 1936.
(J. Ash) $12 £6

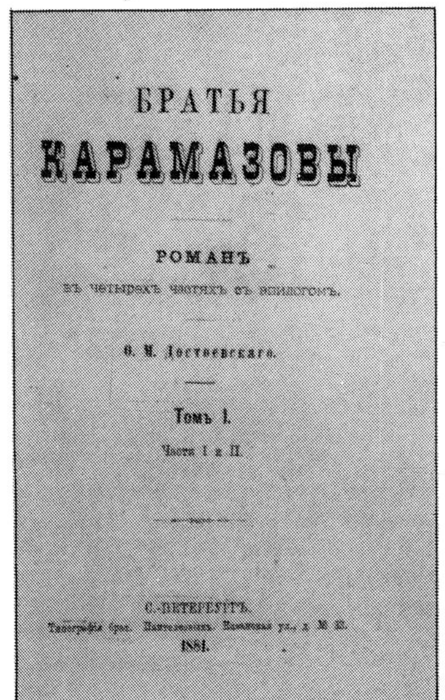
БРАТЬЯ
КАРАМАЗОВЫ
РОМАНЪ
въ четырехъ частяхъ съ эпилогомъ.
Ѳ. М. Достоевскаго.
Томъ I.
Части I и II.
С.-ПЕТЕРБУРГЪ.
1881.

DOSTOEVSKY, F. M.
'Brat'ya Karamazivy' (Brothers Karamazov) – 2 vol. – half titles – spotting – contem, half calf – 8vo. – St. Petersburg 1881.
(Sotheby's) $1,930 £920

DOUGHTY, C. M.
'Arabia Deserta' – one vol. – thin paper vol. – 1926.
(Allen & May) $34 £16

'Travels, Arabia Deserta' – 2 vols., new edition, illustrations with folding map – 1923.
(Christie's S. Kensington) $90 £40

DOUGLAS, NORMAN
'Paneros, Some Words on Aphrodisiacs and the Like' – limited Edn. – frontis – cloth backed boards – 1931.
(Phillips) $55 £25

'Nerinda' – limited signed Edn. – orig. cloth – 1929.
(Phillips) $65 £30

'The Siren Land' – illus. – of the original 1500 around 890 were pulped – orig. decorative cloth – minor marks – scarce – 1911.
(J. Ash) $180 £85

DOUGLAS, SIR ROBERT
'The Peerage of Scotland' – 1st Edn. – 10 engraved plates – list of subscribers – browning – inscription on title – contem. calf – rebacked – worn – large folio – Edinburgh 1764.
(Sotheby's) $40 £20

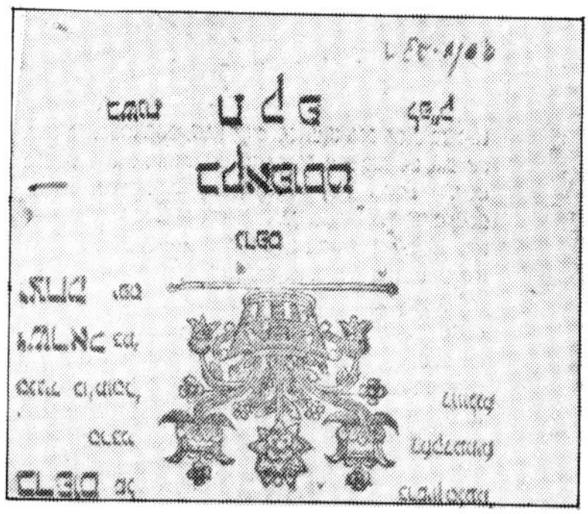

DOV BER BEN SHNEUR SALMAN OF LUBAVITCH
'Ner Mitzvah Ve'torah Or Kuntras Ha'Yichud' – 1st. Edn. – printed on blue paper – printer's mark – orig. leather – 8vo. – Israel, Yaffe 1820.
(Sotheby's) $335 £160

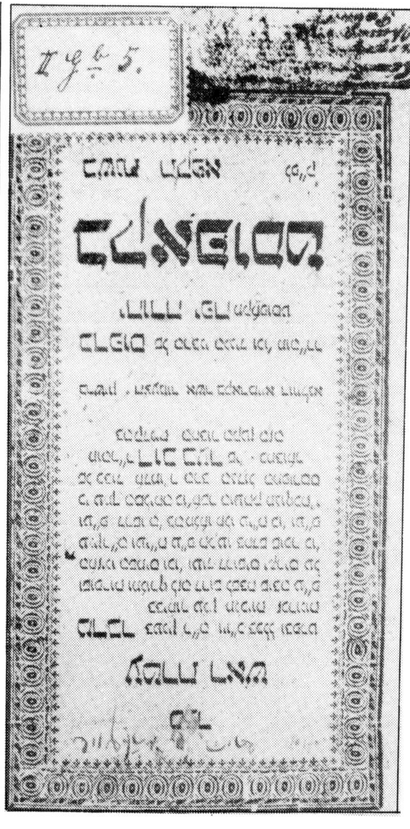

'Ateret Rosh' – 1st Edn. – printed on blue paper – title in typo border – half cloth – 8vo. – 1821.
(Sotheby's) $735 £350

DOVES PRESS
Catalogue Raisonne of books printed and published at the Doves – orig. boards – 1911.
(Phillips) $125 £60

DOWLING, DANIEL
'Mercantile Arithmetic' – 2nd Edn. – browning – soiling – contem. mottled calf – rebacked and rubbed – 8vo. – Dublin 1768.
(Sotheby's) $170 £80

DOYLE, ARTHUR CONAN
'Burgher's Secret' – contained in 'The Sunlight Year Book for 1898' – front endpaper slightly split – pinholes in spine – 1897.
(J. Ash) $12 £6

DOYLE, CHARLES
An early watercolour design for pictorial border showing sleeping soldiers, mother and child etc. – ink and pencil sketches in central area – tears – framed and glazed – 239 mm x 182 mm.
(Sotheby's) $75 £35

DOYLE, R.
'The Foreign Tour of Messrs. Brown, Jones and Robinson' – 1st Edn. – 1855.
(Laurence & Martin Taylor) $8 £4

DOYLE, RICHARD – LEMON, MARK
'The Enchanted Doll' – 1st Edn. – wood engraved frontis – pictorial title – illus. after Doyle – stained – half roan – sm. 4to – Bradbury & Evans 1850.
(Sotheby's) $55 £25

DRABBLE, G. C.
'Catalogue of British Coins' – 2 vol. – plates – orig. wrappers – 4to. – Glendinning 1939-43.
(Sotheby's) $145 £70

DRAKE, SIR FRANCIS
'An Essay on the Art of Engeniously Tormenting' – 5th Edn. – engraved frontispiece after J. Gillray – slightly soiled – margins slightly frayed – original boards – soiled – spine torn – 1811.
(Christie's S. Kensington) $40 £20

DRAKE, JAMES
'Anthropologia Nova: Or a New System of Anatomy' – 2 vol. portrait and 83 plates – some torn and repaired without loss – some spotting – contemp. panelled calf – rebacked – 1707.
(Christie's S Kensington) $135 £65

DRAMATIC CHARACTERS OR DIFFERENT PORTRAITS OF THE ENGLISH STAGE
1st. Edn. – 24 hand col. plates – many of Garrick in celebrated roles – 2 engraved titles in English and French – engraved table of contents and dedication leaf to Garrick – contem. calf – sm. 4to. – for Robt. Sayer 1770.
(Sotheby's) $670 £320

DRAUGHTS BOARD
For use during the First World war – printed on linen with coloured border and illustrations – captioned 'The favourite game of our soldiers in the trenches and our sailors on the sea' – circa 1915.
(Sotheby's) $85 £40

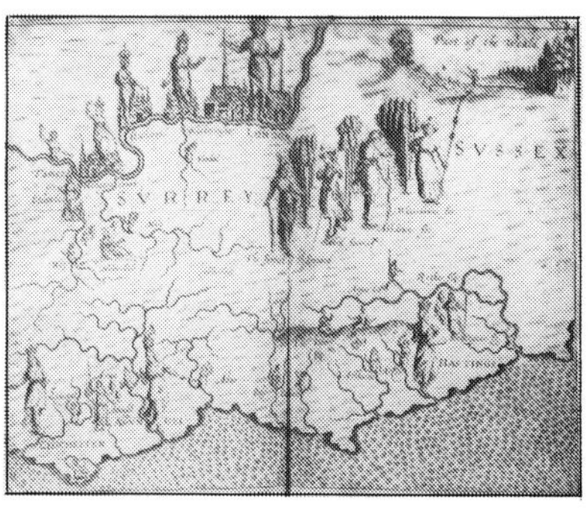

DRAYTON, MICHAEL
'Poly-Olbion – all the Tracts, Rivers, Mountains, Forests and Other Parts of Great Britain' – 1st Edn. – third issue – portrait of Prince Henry – 30 double page engraved maps – some browned – half morocco – rubbed – folio – 1622.
(Christie's) $4,200 £2,000

DRESDEN GALLERY, THE
50 photographic plates – contem. red morocco – green morocco inlaid border – whole ornately gilt – g.e. – folio – 1875.
(Sotheby Beresford Adams) $65 £30

DRESSER, C.
'The Art of Decorative Design' – 28 litho plates – many col. – illus. – slight soiling – some leaves detached – orig. cloth – worn – 4to. – Day & Son 1862.
(Christie's) $80 £38

DRESSER, HENRY E.
'A History of the Birds of Europe' – 9 vols. including supplement – 1st Edn. – 723 litho plates all but two hand col. – contem. green half morocco slightly rubbed – t.e.g. – 4to. – 1871-96.
(Sotheby's) $9,450 £4,500

DRINKWATER, JOHN
'A History of the Late Siege of Gibraltar' – 3rd Edn. – subscription list – 4 engraved folding maps or plans – engraved folding plates by Roberts – a few tears – spotted – Drinkwater's own copy with his bookplate – contem. half russia gilt – upper joint torn – recornered – 4to. – 1786.
(Sotheby Beresford Adams) $170 £80

DRINKWATER, JOHN
'Inheritance' – autobiography – plates – good – 1931.
(J. Ash) $6 £3

'Poems 1908-14' – verse from 'Symbols' inscribed by author on flyleaf – signed August 1932.
(Allen & May) $15 £7

DRINKWATER, JOHN AND RUTHERSTON, ALBERT
'Claud Lovat Fraser' – no. 92 of 450 copies signed by the authors – lge 4to. 1923 – plates – some coloured – orig. cloth – dust-jacket.
(Christie's S. Kensington) $135 £65

DRUMMOND, HENRY
'History of the Noble British Families' – 2 vols. 1st Edn. – large woodcut device on titles – numerous engr. ports, engraved plates – some hand col. – coloured arms – woodcut – illus. in text – contem. half roan – some wear – folio – W. Pickering 1846-52.
(Sotheby's) $230 £110

DRURY, D.
'Illustrations of Natural History' – vol. 1 only – text in English and French – 51 engraved plates – all but one hand col. – contem. calf gilt – rebacked – orig. spine preserved – 4to. – 1770.
(Sotheby Beresford Adams) $135 £64

DRURY, R.
'Adventures ..... during Fifteen Years of Captivity in the Island of Madagascar' – 2 plates – calf gilt – 8vo. – 1807.
(Phillips) $75 £35

DRYDEN, JOHN
'The Comedies, Tragedies and Operas' – 2 vols. – 1st. Edn. – folding engraved portrait torn – dampstains – soiled – contemp. calf – rubbed – hinges split – folio – 1701.
(Sotheby's) $25 £12

'Songs and Poems' – limited to 500 copies, this is no. 7 of 100 specially bound by Sangorski and Sutcliffe and with extra set of plates, decorations and coloured plates by Lavinia Blythe, original morocco, t.e.g., slipcase, folio – 1957.
(Christie's S. Kensington) $430 £190

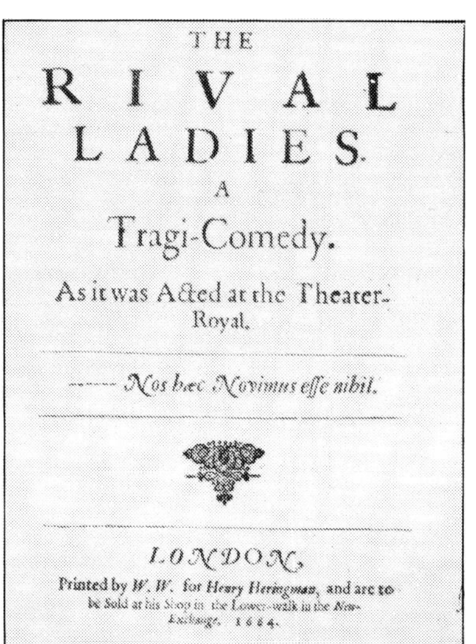
THE
RIVAL
LADIES.
A
Tragi-Comedy.
As it was Acted at the Theater-Royal.
—— Nos hæc Novimus esse nihil.
LONDON,
Printed by W. W. for Henry Herringman, and are to be Sold at his Shop in the Lower-walk in the New-Exchange. 1664.

'The Rival Ladies' – 1st Edn. – modern morocco gilt – g.e. – booklabel of Robert Hoe – sm. 4to. – 1664.
(Christie's) $800 £380

DUBOURG
'Views of Rome and Its Vicinity' – 26 hand col. views – orig. cloth – 4to. – 1844.
(Phillips) $525 £250

DUBREUIL, JEAN
'Perspective Practical' – 1st Edn. – 150 full page engraved illus. in text – 2pp adverts at end – browning – modern polished calf – label – 4to. – 1672.
(Sotheby's) $210 £100

DUBUISSON, A.
'Richard Parkes Bonington' – limited Edn. – plates – orig. cloth backed boards – 4to. – 1924.
(Sotheby's) $145 £70

DU CHAILLU, P. B.
'Explorations and Adventures in Equatorial Africa' – 1st Edn. – folding frontis – map repaired – plates – worn – 1861.
(Phillips) $30 £14
'The Land of the Midnight Sun' – 2 vols. – plates – maps – orig. cloth gilt – 1881.
(Phillips) $65 £32

DUCLOS, CHARLES PINOT
'Considerations sur les Moeurs de ce Siecle' – edition original without dedication to the king – no frontis – contem. calf – rubbed – 12mo. – 1751.
(Sotheby's) $400 £190

DUDLEY, SIR ROBERT
'Carta Omnia Generale D'Affrica' – engraved map – title cartouche – sailing ship – compass rose – one short tear – some perforations – 460mm x 712mm – Florence 1646 or later.
(Sotheby's) $295 £140

DU DOUILLOUX, JACQUES
'La Caccia' – 1st Edn. – in Italian – device on title – woodcut illus. – title in cont. – mss on lower edge – vellum – Milan, 1615.
(Phillips) $335 £160

DUGDALE, THOMAS AND WILLIAM BURNETT
'Curiosities of Great Britain, England and Wales, Delineated' – 10 vols. – engraved titles – 249 plates and 58 double page maps only – some torn – spotting – some leaves detached – orig. cloth – soiled – n.d.
(Christie's S. Kensington) $55 £25

DUGDALE, SIR WILLIAM
'The History of Imbanking and Draining Divers Fens and Marshes' – 2nd Edn. – 11 folding maps – contem. calf – rebacked – ownership stamp of Henry Cavendish (1731-1810) – folio – 1772.
(Sotheby's) $315 £150

DU HALDE, JEAN BAPTISTE
'Description Geographique, Historique et Physique de L'Empire de la Chine et de la Tartarie Chinoise' – 4 vols. – 53 engraved maps, plans and plates – 20 folding – engraved vignettes – some engravings in text – contem. vellum boards – 4to. – The Hague 1736.
(Sotheby's) $1,260 £600
'General History of China' – 4 vol. – 3rd Eng. Edn. – lacks 2 plates – contem. half calf – sm. 8vo. – 1741.
(Sotheby's) $40 £18

DUHAMEL DU MONCEAU
'Traite des Arbres Fruitiers' – 2 vols. – plates – calf gilt – 4to. – Paris 1768.
(Irelands) $840 £400

DULAC, EDMUND
'Rubaiyat of Omar Khayyam' – 4to. – 20 mounted coloured plates by Dulac – soiling – contemp. vellum – gilt – slightly soiled – g.e. – n.d.
(Christie's S. Kensington) $80 £38

DULAC, JEAN – DIDEROT, DENIS
'Les Bijoux Indiscrets' – 2 vol. – limited to 318 copies – this one of ten copies reserved for the artist – presentation copy inscribed twice by the artist – coloured titles and illustrations by Dulac – unbound as issued – in original wrappers – original slip-case. – Paris 1947.
(Christie's S. Kensington) $210 £100

DUMBARTONSHIRE
Double page – hand coloured mounted map – J. Thomson 1823.
(Bennett Book Auction) $20 £10

DUMONT, JEAN AND JEAN ROSSET DE MISSY
'The Military History of the Late Prince Eugene of Savoy and of the late John Duke of Marlborough' – 2 vols. – titles in red and black – engraved vignette – frontis – 32 plates – 53 double page – half titles – some leaves loose – slight dust spotting – contem. speckled calf – joints split – worn – folio – 1736-37.
(Sotheby's) $670 £320

DUNDONALD, ARCHIBALD COCHRANE, TENTH EARL OF
'A Treatise showing the Intimate Connection between Agriculture and Chemistry' – 1st. Edn. – half title – spotting – worming – contem. sprinkled calf – label – joints split – rubbed – 4to. – 1795.
(Sotheby's) $145 £70

DUNKIRK
'Histoire de la Ville de Dunkerque' – by M. Falconier – extrait by David Wells – calf – lower cover detached – 4to. – 1760
(Phillips) $125 £60

DUNNIGER, JOSEPH
'Inside the Medium's Cabinet' plates – New York 1935 – 'How to Make a Ghost Walk' illus. New York 1936 – 1st. Edn. – orig,cloth – slightly faded – 8vo. –
(Sotheby's) $10 £5

DUNSANY, LORD
'Lord Adrian' – limited Edn. – engravings by R. Gibbings – uncut – quarter morocco – Golden Cockerel Press 1949.
(Phillips) $80 £38
'Tales of War' – spine dull with slight split – good – 1918.
(J. Ash) $10 £5

DURET, THEODORE
'Edouard Manet Seinleben und Seine Kunst' – one woodcut and two etched plates – half tone illustrations – orig. cloth – slightly rubbed – t.e.g. – 4to. – Berlin, Paul Cassirer, 1910.
(Christie's S. Kensington) $190 £90

DURFEY, THOMAS
'Songs Compleat, Wit and Mirth' – 6 vol. – reprint – orig. boards – worn – 8vo. – circa 1870.
(Sotheby's) $65 £30

DURHAM – SCHENK, P. AND VALK, G.
'Episcopatus Dunelmensis' – engraved map – col. by hand – historiated initial – separate royal arms – fully col. – parts of adjacent counties col. in outline – verso blank – 402 mm x 503 mm. – Amsterdam circa 1695.
(Sotheby's) £65 £32

DURRELL, LAWRENCE
'Spirit of Place' – very good in dust wrapper – 1969.
(J. Ash) $12 £6
'Pope John'; 'Clea'; 'Justine'; 'Balthazar' – 1st Edn. – in dust jackets.
(Laurence & Martin Taylor) $30 £15
'Prospero's Cell' – orig. yellow cloth – slightly dusty – otherwise very good – 1945.
(J. Ash) $40 £20
'The Alexandria Quartette' – First collected edition, no. 426 of 500 copies, signed by author, original buckram, t.e.g., slipcase – 1962.
(Sotheby's) $190 £85

TEN POEMS

BY

LAWRENCE DURRELL

LONDON:
The CADUCEUS PRESS
GRENVILLE STREET, W.C.1

1932

'Ten Poems' – 1st Edn. – presentation – inscribed by author to De La Mare – orig. wrappers – faded – upper cover split at spine – 8vo. – Caduceus Press 1932.
(Sotheby's) $1,930 £920

DURUY, VICTOR
'Histoire de Romans' – 6 vol. – new Edn. – plates – some chromolith – col. maps – some double page – illus. – slight spotting – orig. red morocco backed cloth – gilt – 4to. – Paris 1879-83.
(Christie's) $75 £35
'History of Greece' – 4 vol. in 8 – one of 250 copies – plates – some col. – illus. – later morocco backed cloth – t.e.g. – 4to. – – 1892.
(Sotheby's) $105 £50

D'URVILLE, M. DUMONT
'Voyage Pittoresque autour du Monde' – maps – plates – quarter morocco – Paris 1834.
(Phillips) $145 £70

DUSSLER, L.
'Signorelli' – plates – cloth gilt – 8vo. – 1927.
(Phillips) $40 £20

DUTCH COSTUME
A folio of 142 decorative drawings – circa 1700.
(Bonhams) $3,150 £1,500

DUTCH NEW TESTAMENT
Gilt and gauffered edges – purple velvet binding with original silver mounts and clasps – Dordrecht 1614.
(Irelands) $755 £360

DUVEEN, DENIS I.
'Bibliothexa Alchemica et Chimica' – one of 200 copies – 16 plates – orig. cloth – 4to. – 1949.
(Sotheby's) $125 £60

DVORAK, MAX
'Pierre Breugel L'Ancien' – 37 coloured plates mounted on 31 sheets – trimmed and spotted – looses as issued in orig. cloth backed portfolio – rubbed – folio – Vienna n.d.
(Sotheby's) $65 £30

DWELLY'S PARISH RECORDS
Vol. 1-15 – Vol. XIV never printed – orig. cloth – slightly soiled – 8vo. – Herne Bay 1913-26.
(Sotheby's) $105 £50

DYKES, W. R.
'The Genus Iris' – col. plates – quarter morocco gilt – t.e.g. – folio – Cambridge 1913.
(Phillips) $630 £300
'Notes on Tulip Species' – col. plates – orig. cloth – 4to. – 1930.
(Phillips) $145 £70

EARDLEY-WILMOT, SIR J. E.
'Reminiscences of the late Thomas Assheton Smith Esq., or the Pursuits of an English Country Gentleman' – 1st Edn. – extra illus. – 8 engraved plates – 47 addit. plates – early 20th cent. maroon morocco by Root & Son – gilt – g.e. – 8vo. – 1860.
(Sotheby's) $250 £120

EARLE, REV. A.
'Essays Upon the History of Meaux Abbey' – 1906.
(Baitson) $15 £7

EARLE, MAJOR CYRIL
'The Earle Collection of Early Staffordshire Pottery' – plates – some col. – orig. cloth – rebacked – rubbed – t.e.g. – 4to. – n.d.
(Sotheby's) $230 £110

EARLE, SIR JAMES
'An Essay on the Means of Lessening the Effects of Fire on the Human Body' – engraved plates – last advert leaf – some spotting – modern morocco backed cloth – 8vo. – 1799.
(Sotheby's) $115 £55

EARLE, JOHN
'Micro-Cosmographie' – number 300 of 400 copies – orig. cloth – dust jacket torn – 4to. – 1928.
(Christie's) $20 £10

EARP, G. B. (editor)
'What We Did in Australia' – 1st Edn. – orig. boards – rebacked – rubbed – cloth folder – sm. 8vo. – 1853.
(Sotheby's) $85 £40

EAST ANGLIAN, THE
Vol. 1-4 new series, vol. 1-13 together 17 vols. – orig. cloth – slightly rubbed – 8vo. – Ipswich and Norwich 1864-1910.
(Sotheby's) $400 £190

EASTBOURNE
18 vignette views – cloth gilt – oblong folio – circa 1800.
(Phillips) $55 £25

EAST INDIES
Large Coll. of Approx. 1000 Blue Books on India, Ceylon, Burma etc. relating to wars, slaves, railways , debts, etc. – some with maps – various bindings – worn – disbound – folio – circa 1800-1860.
(Sotheby's) $3,780 £1,800

To Richard de la Mare

with my thanks for the endless pains he took, & the beautiful result.

from E.R. Eddison

February, 1935.

In addition to the published edition, 12 copies of this book have been printed on hand-made paper, of which this is No. 7.

EDDISON, E.R.
'Mistress of Mistresses, a Vision of Zimiamvia' – 1st Edn. – number 7 of 12 – auto limitation statement by author – presentation copy – decorations by Keith Henderson – maps – orig. parchment gilt – t.e.g. – 8vo. – Faber 1935.
(Sotheby's) $525 £250

EDEN, EMILY
'Portraits of the Princes and People of India' – hand col. title and 24 plates – all mounted – soiled – contem. morocco backed cloth – lacks spine – rubbed – loose – folio – 1844.
(Sotheby's) $1,260 £600

EDGAR, WILLIAM
'Vectigalium Systema or a New Book of Rates .... called Customs' – 2nd Edn. – browning – contem. calf – rebacked – gilt – 8vo. – 1718.
(Sotheby's) $75 £35

EDGEWORTH, MARIA
'Tales and Novels' – 18 vols., engraved frontispieces and additional titles – cont. half calf, spines gilt – 1832-3.
(Christie's S. Kensington) $180 £80

EDGEWORTH, M.
'Patronage' – 1st Edn. – 4 vols errata leaf at end of vol. 4 – calf gilt – 12 mo. – 1814.
(Phillips) $90 £42

EDINBURGH POST OFFICE DIRECTORY CIRCA 1827
Folding map – cloth backed boards – Edinburgh 1827.
(Bennett Book Auction) $50 £24

EDMONDS, BRIGADIER GENERAL SIR JAMES E.
'History of the Great War Based on Official Documents' – 32 vol. only including vol. of maps – original cloth – some rubbed – some worn – 1923-47.
(Christie's S. Kensington) $440 £210

EDMONDS, RICHARD
'The Land's End District' – 1st Edn. – complete with map and pictures – orig. cloth binding – 1862.
(Lane) $60 £28

EDUCATION
The diary of log book of the Board School for Boys, Lansdown Place, Kent Street, Southwark with extracts from H. M. Inspectors' reports – c. 500 pages – half morocco – 1874-88.
(Phillips) $65 £32

EDUCATIONAL CARDS
Complete set of 52 woodcut cards – each with decorative border of flowers etc. – with improving mottoes about learning and gaming – coloured through stencils – 86 mm x 57 mm. – circa 1680.
(Sotheby's) $2,520 £1,200

EDWARD'S BOTANICAL REGISTER ... CONTINUED BY JOHN LINDLEY
14 parts only – 78 hand coloured plates – orig. wrappers – 1842-3.
(Christie's S. Kensington) $485 £230

EDWARDS, BRYAN
'An Historical Survey of the French Colony in the Island of St. Domingo' – 1st Edn. – lacking orig. map – map inserted – browning and soiling – contem. mottled calf – rebacked – rubbed – 4to – 1797.
(Sotheby's) $40 £20
'History, Cival and Commercial of the British Colonies in the West Indies' – 3 vols. – 10 plates – 12 maps – calf gilt – 4to. – 1794-1801.
(Phillips) $525 £250

EDWARDS, J.
'A Companion from London to Brighthelmstone in Sussex' – double page map of Brighton – list of subscribers – 24 charts – maps and engraved views – half calf – 4to. – 1801.
(Phillips) $880 £420

EDWARDS, JOHN
'The British Herbal' – 1st Edn. – 100 fine hand col. engraved plates after drawings by author – marginal tear – red morocco – gilt – worn – folio – for the author 1770.
(Christie's) $10,080 £4,800

EDWARDS, LIONEL
'The Passing Seasons' – col. plates – illus. – orig. boards – slightly rubbed – oblong folio – n.d.
(Sotheby's) $200 £95

'A Leicestershire Sketch Book' – no. 33 of 75 copies – signed by author – col plates – illus. – orig. vellum backed cloth – upper cover soiled – t.e.g. 4to. – 1935.
(Sotheby's) $190 £90

'A Sportsman's Bag' – no. 166 of 650 copies – col plates – illus. – orig. cloth – slightly soiled – spine torn – dust jacket – folio – n.d.
(Sotheby's) $220 £105

EDWARDS, SUTHERLAND
'The Polish Captivity' – 2 vols. – tinted litho plates – orig. cloth – 1863.
(Phillips) $125 £60

EGAN, BERESFORD
'Pollen, A Novel in Black and White' – illustrated by Egan – very good copy – 1933.
(J. Ash) $30 £14

EGAN, PIERCE
'Real Life in London' – 33 coloured plates – 2 vols. – red cloth – soiled – some slight foxing – 1821-31.
(Bonhams) $105 £50

'Life in London' – 1st Edn. – fine full morocco – gilt – inner dentelles – marbled endpapers by Bayntum – slipcase – London 1822.
(Robert Skinner) $735 £350.

EGEDE, HANS
'A Description of Greenland' – vignette title – folding plate – map – calf backed boards – 1818.
(Phillips) $85 £40

EGNATIUS, JOANNES BAPTISTA
'De Exemplis Illustrium Virorum Venetae Civitatis Atque Aliarum Gentium' – large woodcut device on title – woodcut initials – last leaf blank – contemp. limp vellum – lacks ties.
(Sotheby's) $115 £55

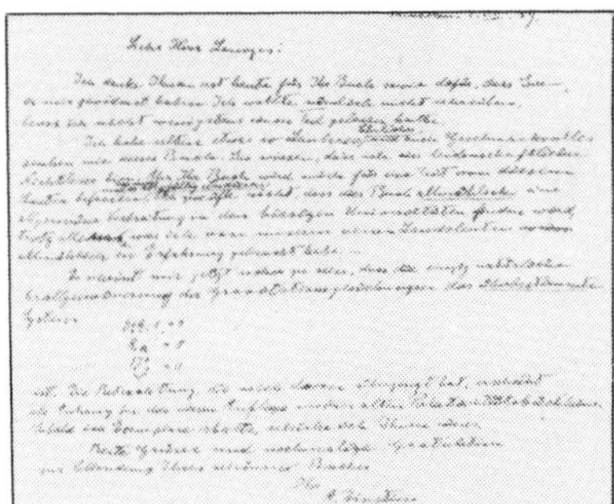

EINSTEIN, ALBERT
Autograph letter signed about relevance of Lanczos' work to Einstein's theories on relativity – 1 page – folio – Princeton 1949.
(Sotheby's) $2,205 £1,050

Typed letter 1 page folio – to Dr. Lanczos expressing pleasure at his recent work and discussing Maxwell's theories of electromagnetism – Old Lyme, Connecticut 1935.
(Sotheby's) $1,260 £600

EISEN, G. A. AND KOUCHAKJI, F.
'Glass' – 2 vol. – plates – orig. parchment backed boards – slipcase – 4to. – New York 1927.
(Sotheby's) $380 £180

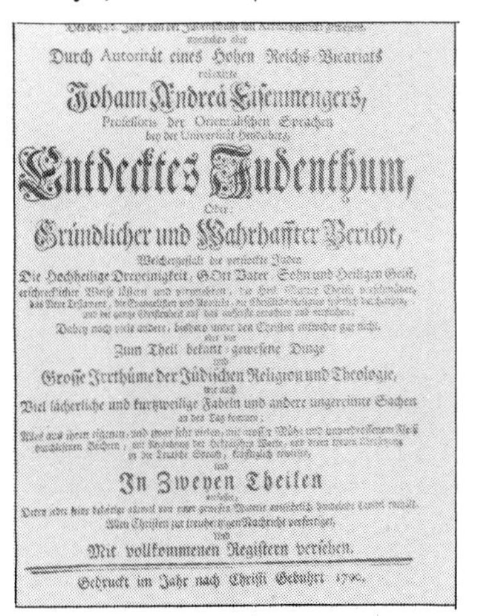

Durch Autorität eines Hohen Reichs-Vicariats
Johann Andreä Eisenmengers,
Entdecktes Judenthum,
Gründlicher und Wahrhaffter Bericht,
Die Hochheilige Dreyeinigkeit, GOtt Vater, Sohn und Heiligen Geist,
Zum Theil bekant-gewesene Dinge
Grosse Irrthüme der Jüdischen Religion und Theologie,
Viel lächerliche und kurtzweilige Fabeln und andere ungereimte Sachen
In Zweyen Theilen
Mit vollkommenen Registern versehen.
Gedruckt im Jahr nach Christi Geburt 1700.

EISENMENGER, JOHANN ANDREAS
'Entdecktes Judenthum' – 2 vols. – 1st. Edn. in German and Hebrew – half leather – 4to. – Koenigsberg, 1700.
(Sotheby's) $1,470 £700

ELGAR, SIR EDWARD
Fine Photo signed on mount and inscribed to Mrs Claude Beddington D. D. B. – mounted – 7½ inches x 6¼ inches – Dec. 1930.
(Sotheby's) $360 £170

ELGAR, F.
'The Royal Navy' – 2nd Edn. – 24 col. litho plates – some soiled – orig. cloth – worn – loose – 4to. – 1873.
(Sotheby's) $390 £185

ELIANA
'A New Romance Formed by an English Hand' – 1st Edn. – browning – contem. sheep – rubbed – folio – 1661.
(Sotheby's) $880 £420

ELIOT, GEORGE
'The Mill on the Floss' – three vols. – orig. cloth – slightly rubbed – library labels on top covers – first vol. a little shaken – 1860.
(J. Ash) $105 £50

ELIOT, T. S.
'Poetry and Drama' – 1st English Edn. – few slight marks to covers – good – 1951.
(J. Ash) $8 £2

(Arms of Diocese)

THE BUILDERS

Song from "The Rock" to R.H.I. de la Mare Esq.

Words by
T. S. ELIOT from T.S. Eliot

Music by
MARTIN SHAW

Sadlers Wells Theatre
May 28th, 1934

Price 4d. net

Published by
J. B. CRAMER & CO., LTD.
139 New Bond Street, London, W.1

ELIOT, T. S.
'The Builders' – song from 'The Rock' with music by Martin Shaw – 1st Edn. – presentation copy inscribed by author to Richard De La Mare – orig. wrappers – 4to. – 1934.
(Sotheby's) $460 £220

ELIOT, W. G.
'Treatise on the Defence of Portugal' – 6 folding maps – calf gilt – 1811.
(Phillips) $40 £20

ELIOTT, GEORGE AUGUSTUS, 1ST. BARON HEATHFIELD
Documents 2 pages – folio – Gibraltar August 1777 – papered seal – contem. endorsement on integral leaf.
(Phillips) $125 £60

ELLING, C.
'Rome' – plates – cloth – 4to. – 1975.
(Phillips) $40 £18

ELLIOT, R.
'Agricultural Changes – Laying Down Land to Grass' – fp. – cloth – Kelso 1905.
(Bennett Book Auction) $30 £14

ELLIOT, W.
'Some Account of Kentish Town' – extra illus. – 41 views – calf gilt – 1821.
(Phillips) $200 £95

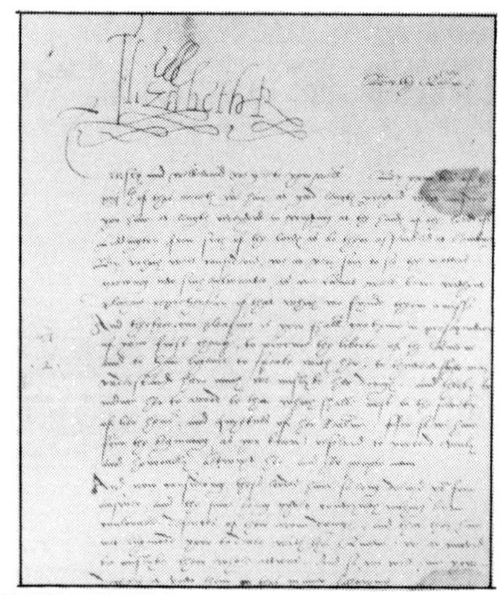

ELIZABETH 1
Important letter signed Elizabeth R at head to Sir Nicholas Throckmorton, her ambassador to Scotland, containing a major statement about Elizabeth's policy towards the fate of Mary Queen of Scots etc. – 5 pages – folio – staining – repairs – integral address leaf – papered seal – Windsor Castle, July 1567.
(Sotheby's) $34,650 £16,500

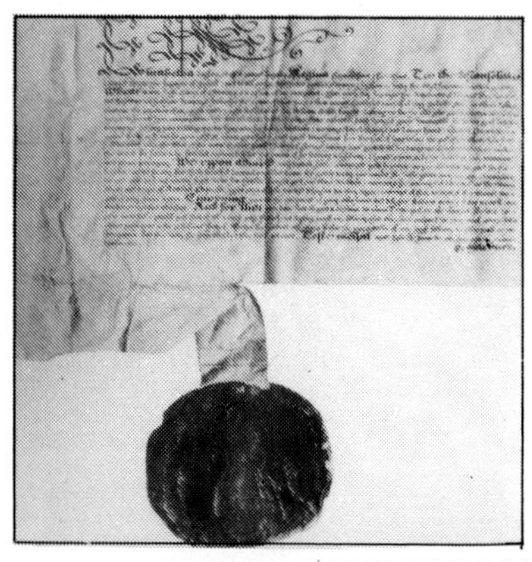

ELIZABETHAN COURT ENTERTAINMENT
The original mock charter by Queen Elizabeth bearing the Great Seal presented to Lord Burghley during a Court entertainment at Theobalds in 1591 on vellum written in fine professional hand – elaborated – signed – soiled and creased – pendant second Great Seal of Elizabeth 1 designed and engraved by Nicholas Hilliard – 10 May 1591.
(Sotheby's) $21,000 £10,000

ELLIOTT, R. AND ROBERTS, E.
'Views in India, China and on the Shores of the Red Sea' – 2 vol. in one – engraved titles and 61 plates – col. frontis by G. Baxter – spotted – contem. calf – worn – 4to. – 1835.
(Sotheby's) $80 £38

ELLIS, F. S. (editor)
'Sir Ysambrace' – limited to 358 copies of which this is no. 350 on paper – printed in red and black – woodcut frontis after Burne Jones – ornamental borders and initials – orig. holland backed boards – uncut – 8vo. – 1897 Kelmscott Press.
(Sotheby's) $275 £130

ELLIS, G. V. AND FORD, G. F.
'Illustrations of Dissections .. of the Human Body' – plate vol. only – 2nd Edn. – folio – 48 col. litho plates – some detached and cut down – some spotting and soiling – contemp. half morocco – soiled – 1876.
(Christie's S. Kensington) $40 £20

ELLIS, WILLIAM
'Narrative of a Tour Through Hawaii' – 1st. Edn. – 7 engraved plates – folding map – modern polished half calf by Root, – labels – t.e.g. – 8 vo. – 1826.
(Sotheby's) $295 £140

ELWOOD, ANNE KATHERINE
'Narrative of a Journey Overland from England ... to India' – 2 vol. – 6 hand tinted aquatints – title of vol. 1 cleanly torn – soiling – modern calf backed cloth – 1830.
(Christie's S. Kensington) $125 £60

EMBLEMS OF MORTALITY
Wood engraved frontis and 51 illus. by Thomas and John Bewick – browned – 19th cent. black morocco – sm. 8vo. – Robert Bassam 1795.
(Sotheby's) $265 £125

EMDEN, A. B.
'A Biographical Register of the University of Oxford to A. D. 1500' – 3 vols. – orig. cloth – dust jackets – 8vo. – Oxford 1957-59.
(Sotheby's) $115 £55

EMDEN – JANSSON, J.
'Emda, vulgo Embden' – double page bird's eye view showing fortified perimeter walls, city arms, shipping on river Ems etc. – Latin text on verso – uncut – 397 mm x 497 mm. – Amsterdam 1657.
(Sotheby's $380 £180

With very kind
regards & recollection,
R. W. Emerson

Mrs G. H. Lewes.

EMERSON, RALPH WALDO
A.L's to George Eliot (Mrs G. H. Lewes) 3 pages introducing a visitor to her – Concord, Nov. 1873.
(Sotheby's) $295 £140

EMERSON, WILLIAM
'The Principles of Mechanics' – 4th Edn. – 4to. – 42 folding engraved plates only – occasional slight soiling – contemp. calf – recornered and rebacked – 1794.
(Christie's S. Kensington) $60 £28

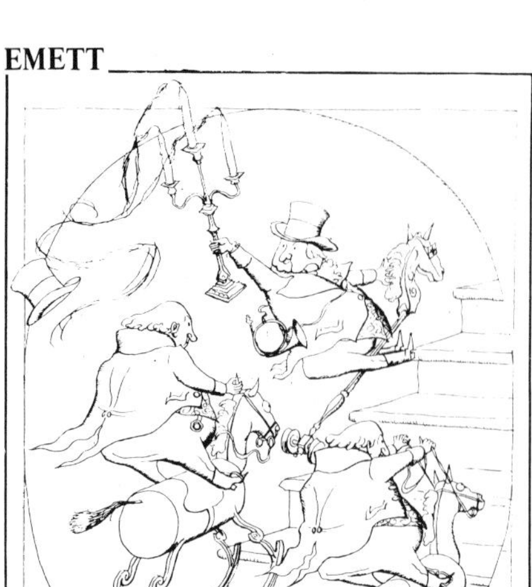

EMETT, F. ROWLAND
The complete set of drawings for 'Peacock Pie' comprising a large design for the pictorial title and 8 smaller illus. – each signed – 1941.
(Sotheby's) $965 £460

EMPSON, WILLIAM
'Some Versions of Pastoral' – Arthur Misenner's copy – with bookplate – slight marks – 1935.
(J. Ash) $20 £10

ENCYCLOPAEDIA BRITANNICA
13 vol. only – including one vol. of plates – 4to. – engraved plates – occasional slight soiling – contemp. calf – rubbed – Dublin 1790-98.
(Christie's S. Kensington) $190 £90
24 vol. – 14th Edn. – orig. cloth – 4to. – 1929.
(Sotheby's) $55 £25

ENCYCLOPAEDIA PERTHENSIS OR UNIVERSAL DICTIONARY OF KNOWLEDGE
24 vol. including one vol. of plates – engraved frontispiece and plates – a few lacking – slight soiling – contemp. calf – rubbed – joints cracked – Perth n.d.
(Christie's S. Kensington) $55 £25

ENFIELD, WILLIAM
'Institutes of Natural Philiosophy Theoretical and Experimental' – 2nd Edn. with considerable additions – 13 folding plates – rustmark – cloth – 4to. – J. Johnson 179
(Sotheby's) $45 £22

ENGELBACH, LEWIS
'Naples and the Campagna Felice' – engraved title – 2 col. maps – 15 hand col. plates by T. Rowlandson – orig. blind stamped cloth gilt – 1815.
(Phillips) $485 £230

ENGLAND STATUTES
Henry III to Henry VIII – vol. 1 of 2 – black letter – browned and soiled – defective – one cover detached folio – 1543.
(Sotheby's) $380 £180

ENGLAND, YEAR BOOKS, EDWARD III
'Liber Assisarum & Placetorum Corone' – French text – black letter – contem. ownership inscription – annotations and underlinings – near contem. London binding – blind stamped calf over wooden boards – folio – London, John Rastell 1514?
(Sotheby's) $590 £280

ENGLISH BIJOU ALMANACK FOR 1840
Engraved throughout – 6 ports. – orig. red roan gilt – g.e. – onlays – decorated slipcase – worn – 20 mm. x 14 mm. – Schloss 1839.
(Sotheby's) $105 £50

ENGRAVINGS
Collection of over 80 hand coloured engravings in 2 vols. – scenes, costumes, animals and ships, some double page – often a few to each page – some damaged, missing or soiled – 19th cent. calf backed boards – worn – folio – Nuremberg, Munich and other places – circa 1700-50.
(Sotheby's) $1,010 £480

ENTICK, JOHN
'The General History of the Late War in Europe, Asia, Africa, America' – 5 vols. – 2nd and 3rd Edn. – portraits – folding maps – soiling – stains – cont. calf – some wear – 8vo – 1765-72.
(Sotheby's) $75 £35

ENSOR, JAMES
'Scenes de la Vie du Christ' – 32 col. lithographs after artist's drawings – lacking title and colophone – unsewn as issued – lacking folder – oblong folio – Brussels 1921.
(Sotheby's) $145 £70

EOTHEN, OR TRACES OF TRAVEL BROUGHT BACK FROM THE EAST
Original cloth gilt rebacked – folding hand coloured frontis and plate – 2nd Edn. – 1845.
(Bennett Book Auction) $25 £12

EPINAY, MADAME DE
'Memoirs et Correspondance' – 3 vols. – orig. Edn. – spotted in places – bookplate – library stamp – contem. half calf – spines faded – 8vo. – Paris 1818.
(Sotheby's) $125 £60

EPSTEIN, J.
'Camera Study of the Sculptor at Work' – Limited Edn. – inscribed by Epstein – photographs by G. Ireland – cloth – 1956.
(Phillips) $40 £20

EQUINOX OF THE GODS, THE, THE OFFICIAL ORGAN OF THE A. A.
Illus. – facsimile ms of liber AL in pocket – vol. III no. III – 4to – buckram gilt – 1936.
(Bonhams) $95 £45

ERIKSEN, SVEND
'Early Neo-Classicism in France' – plates – some col. – orig. cloth – dust jacket – 4to. – 1974.
(Sotheby's) $40 £18

ERNEST, MAX
'Une Semaine de Bonte ou Les Elements Capitaux' – 5 parts – 182 illus. reproducing wood engravings – orig. wrappers – slightly worn – faded – stained – 4to. – Paris, Jean Bucher, 1934.
(Sotheby's) $230 £110

ERSKINE, LADY F.
'Memoirs relating to the Queen of Bohemia' – 19th cent. calf – worn – 8vo. – circa 1772.
(Moore Allen & Innocent) $115 £55

ERSKINE, W.
'The Memoirs and Adventures of the Marquis de Brelague' – 3 vols. – calf gilt – 1743.
(Phillips) $180 £85

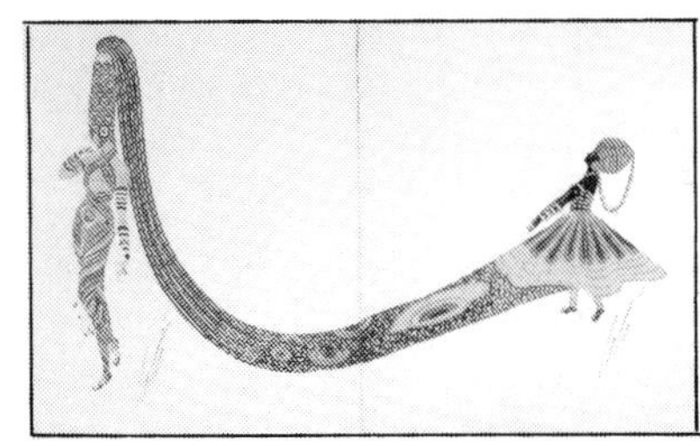

ERTE
Costume design for 'The Favourite' – gouache and gold and silver paint – signed – titled and dated Sept. 1921 on reverse – 33.3 cm. x 26.5 cm.
(Sotheby's) $7,980 £3,800

D'ESPIE, COMTE F. F.
'The Manner of Securing all Sorts of Buildings from Fires' – 2 folding engraved plates – modern boards – 8vo. – n.d.
(Sotheby's) $85 £40

ESSEX
Collection of documents – 20 on vellum and 41 on paper – relating to the manor of Great Coggeshall 1748-1894 – also documents – 5 on vellum – 1 on paper – relating to the manor of Tollesbury Hall 1748-1801.
(Phillips) $125 £60

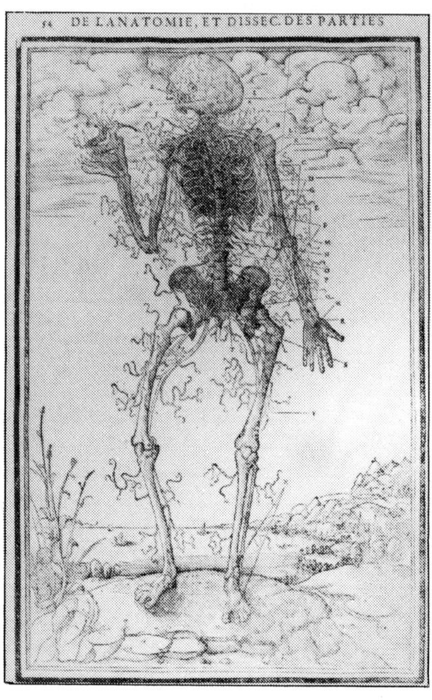

ESTIENNE, CHARLES
'La Dissection des Parties Du Corps' – 1st. Edn. in French – woodcut printer's device – 64 full page woodcuts – half morocco – folio – Paris, 1546.
(Christie's) $5,880 £2,800

ETTMULLE, MICHEL
'Nouvelle Chymie Raisonnee' – woodcut on title – contem. calf – hinges repaired – 12 mo. – Lyons, 1693.
(Sotheby's) $135 £65

EULER, L.
'Methodus Inveniendi Lineas Curvas' – 1st. Edn. – 5 folding plates – later cloth – worn – sm. 4to. – Lausanne & Geneva, 1744.
(Sotheby's) $275 £130

EUSTACE, J. C.
'Tour through Italy' – 2 vols. – 1st. Edn. – calf – gilt – 4to. – 1813.
(Phillips) $40 £20

EVANS, ARTHUR J.
'Through Bosnia and Herzegovina' – 2nd Edn. – frontis – folding map – illus. – orig. cloth – rubbed – 8vo. – 1877.
(Sotheby's) $105 £50

EVANS, SIR ARTHUR
'The Palace of Minos' – 5 vol. incl. index – in seven – all 1st Edn. except index – col. and plain plates – illus. and diagrams in text – numerous pencil notes – stains – orig. cloth – gilt – rubbed – t.e.g. – 4to. – London/New York 1921-64.
(Sotheby's) $335 £160

EVANS, EDITH
'The Papers of Dame Edith Evans' – upwards of 1,000 letters to her from George Bernard Shaw, Ellen Terry, Terence Rattigan, George Moore, William Poel, Seigfried Sassoon, Enid Bagnold, Walter de la Mare and others – with auto drafts of her replies – working notes – corres. with her husband – scripts – typescripts – and much else in 30 boxes and files.
(Sotheby's) $13,860 £6,600

EVANS, GEORGE EWART
'The Pattern Under the Plough' – illustrated by David Gentleman – 1966.
(J. Ash) $12 £6

EVANS, HENRY RIDGELEY
'The Spirit World Unmasked' – illus. – orig. cloth backed boards – slightly worn – rebacked – 8vo. – Chicago 1897.
(Sotheby's) $25 £12

EVANS, I. O.
'The World of Tomorrow' – 24 plates – printed on transparent 'Diophane' plastic – slightly soiled – original cloth backed translucent 'Rhodoid' plastic – spine slightly soiled – Denis Archer, 1933.
(Christie's S. Kensington) $60 £28

EVANS, MARIAN, (George Eliot)
'Romola' – 2 vol. – limited Edn. – plates – contem. half morocco – gilt – 4to. – 1880.
(Sotheby's) $25 £12
'The Mill on the Floss' – 3 vols. – 1st Edn. – half titles – adverts – browning – spotted – orig. cloth – rubbed – hinges repaired – 8vo. – 1860.
(Sotheby's) $210 £100

EVELYN, JOHN
'The Life of Mrs Godolphin' – orig. cloth – expertly restored – new endpapers – 1847.
(J. Ash) $70 £34

EVELYN, JOHN
'Terra' – 6th Edn. – folding table – plate of the Tartarian lamb – calf – rebacked – 4to. – York 1787.
(Sotheby's) $60 £28

EVERITT, G.
'English Caricaturists and Graphic Humourists of the 19th cent.' – 1st Edn. – plates – orig. cloth – rubbed – 4to. – 1886.
(Sotheby's) $60 £28

EXCURSIONS IN THE COUNTY OF NORFOLK
2 vols. – 2 folding maps – engr. views – diced calf gilt – 1818-19.
(Phillips) $250 £120

EXCURSIONS IN THE COUNTY OF SUFFOLK
2 vols. – engraved plates – titles – folding map – contem. half calf – rubbed – 8vo. 1918-19.
(Sotheby's) $200 £95

EXPILLY
'La Topographie de L'Univers' – 2 vols. – contem. French binding of red morocco gilt with unidentified arms – decorated borders – panelled backs – gilt edges – 8vo. – 1758.
(Moore Allen & Innocent) $840 £400

EXQUEMELIN, A. O.
'The History of the Bucaniers of America' – 5th Edn. – 2 vols. – calf – 1771.
(Phillips) $40 £20
'Histoire des Avantiriers Filibustiers' – 2 vol. – new Edn. – 12 mo. – five folding engr. maps – slight clean tears – contemp. calf – spines gilt – joints slightly cracked – Paris, Chez Jacques le Febvre, 1699.
(Christie's S. Kensington) $145 £70

EXTER, ALEXANDRA
Decor designs from a series of pochoirs executed by hand by the artist for the book 'Decors de Theatre' by Alexandra Exter, Paris 1930 – Editions des Quatres Chemins – Decor for Revue Bateau – Decor for Pantomime Espagnol.
(Sotheby's) $505/505 £240/£240

FABER, GEOFFREY
'Elnovia' – some foxing otherwise very good in repaired dust wrapper – 1925.
(J. Ash) $20 £10

FABRICUIS AB AQAPENDENTE, HIERONYMUS
'Oper omnia anatomica & physiologica . . . cum praefaitone Johannis Bohnii' – half title – title in red and black – 61 plates, one folding – double columns – paper discoloured – new boards – cloth spine – folio – Leipzig, Chr. Goetz for J. Fr. Gleditsch, 1687.
(Sotheby's) $682 £350

FADEN, W.
'A Plan of the Attack of Fort Sullivan near Charles Town in South Carolina' – broadsheet with text – plan showing disposition of attacking ships – features col. by hand – water area with light wash – engraving approx. 276 mm x 371 mm – August 1776.
(Sotheby's) $335 £160

FAIRBAIRN, JAMES
Crests of the Families of Great Britain and Ireland – 2 vols. – engraved titles and plates, one lacking, others detached – orig. cloth – rubbed – 8vo – Edinburgh and London, 1860.
(Sotheby Beresford Adams) $59 £30

FAIRBRIDGE, DOROTHEA
'Historic Houses of South Africa' – plates – some coloured – orig. cloth – 4to – 1922.
(Christie's S. Kensington) $77 £42

FAIRFAX, BRIAN
Heavily revised autograph draft of Brian Fairfax's 'Iter Boreale', the account of his hazardous mission to Scotland on behalf of Thomas, third Lord Fairfax, in December 1659 to arrange with General Monck for their joining forces in Yorkshire against Lambert's army to restore Charles II to the throne – 28 pp – folio – July, 1699.
(Sotheby's) $3,700 £2,000

FAIRLESS, MICHAEL
'The Grey Brethren' – 1905.
(J. Ash) $12 £6

LITTLE KING PIPPIN.

FAIRY TALES FROM PAST TIMES
'Mother Goose' 1814, 'King Pippen' 1814, 'Tommy Thumb's Song Book' 1814 – 3 vol. – wood engraved illus. – orig. printed wrappers – 32 mo. – Glasgow 1814.
(Sotheby's) $115 £55

FAIRYLIFE AND FAIRYLAND
'A Lyric poem, communicated by Titania through her secretary, Thomas of Ercildoune' – folio – 16 mounted albumen prints – spotting – orig. morocco backed cloth – gilt – rubbed – g. e.
(Christie's S. Kensington) $45 £22

FAITHORNE, WILLIAM AND OTHERS
A collection of 37 engraved portraits of the seventeenth and eighteenth centuries by Faithorne, including portraits of Queen Elizabeth I and Catherine of Braganza – some cropped – a few minor defects.
(Sotheby Beresford Adams) $117 £60

FALBALAS ET FANFRELUCHES
'Almanach des Modes Presentes, Passes et Futures pour 1924' – vignette on title – 12 plates and cover design by George Barbier – coloured through stencils – unsewn in orig. wrappers – uncut 8vo. – Paris, Jules Meyniel, 1923.
(Sotheby's) $15,120 £7,200

FAMIGLIE CELEBRI ITALIANE
Part 46 only – 29 engr. plates – 1 double page partly hand coloured – contemp. half calf – folio – Milan 1843.
(Sotheby's) $230 £110

FAMILY RECEIPT-BOOK, THE
3rd Edn. – 4to. – some soiling – later half calf – worn – n.d.
(Christie's S. Kensington) $45 £22

FARADAY, MICHAEL
'Chemical Manipulation' – 1st. Edn. – illus. – no errata slip – some discolouration – library – stamps – half calf – worn – 8vo. – W. Phillips 1827.
(Sotheby's) $75 £35
'The Subject Matter of Six Lectures on Non Metallic Elements' – 1st Edn. – woodcut diagrams – spotting – contem. green half calf – rebacked – old spine preserved – spine gilt – rubbed – sm. 8vo. – 1853.
(Sotheby's) $40 £18

FAREY, J.
'Treatise on the Steam Engine' – 25 plates – modern half calf gilt – 4to. – 1827.
(Phillips) $105 £50

FASHION
'World of Fashion' – vol. V – Jan. to Dec. 1828 – 28 hand col. plates – calf gilt – rubbed – sm. 4to. – 1828.
(Phillips) $275 £130

FAUCHE, HIPPOLYTE (trans.)
'Le Maha-Bharata. Poeme Epique de Krishna-Dwaipayana' – 10 vol. – spotting – contem. half morocco – rubbed – t.e.g. – 8vo. – Paris 1863-70.
(Sotheby's) $40 £20

FAULKNER, T.
'Historical and Topographical Description of Chelsea' – 2 vols. – plates – green morocco – gilt – 1829.
(Phillips) $60 £28

FAWCKNER, JAMES
'Narrative of Captain James Fawckner's Travels on the Coast of Benin, West Africa' – 1st Edn. – orig. cloth – slightly marked – 8vo. – 1837.
(Sotheby's) $190 £90

FEARON, HENRY BRADSHAW
'Sketches of America.... A Narrative of a Journey of Five Thousand Miles through the Eastern and Western States of America' – 2nd Edn. – some spotting – modern boards – spine faded – 1818.
(Christie's S. Kensington) $40 £18

FEIBUSCH, HANS (Illustrator)
'The Relevation of Saint John the Divine' – folio – frontis and 12 full page coloured plates.
(J. Ash) $34 £16

FELDBORG, A. ANDERSEN
'Denmark Delineated' – 1st Edn. – addit. engraved title – plates – orig. boards – 8vo. – Edinburgh 1824.
(Christie's) $210 £100

FELIBIEN DES AVAUX, J. F.
'Recueil Historique de la Vie et des Ouvrages de Plus Celebres Architectes' – 4to. – old calf – crudely repaired – Paris, 1696.
(Bonhams) $25 £12

FELKIN, W.
'History of the Machine Wrought Hosiery and Lace Manufactures' – illus. cloth gilt – 1867.
(Phillips) $135 £65

FELLOWES, W. D.
'A Visit to the Monastery of La Trappe' – 4th Edn. – large paper copy – 15 engraved plates – mostly hand col. – contem. half calf – rubbed – large 8vo. – 1823.
(Sotheby's) $145 £70

FENELLOSA, E. F.
'Epochs of Chinese and Japanese Art' – 2 vols. – plates – some col. – some spotting – orig. cloth gilt – 4to. – 1912.
(Phillips) $65 £30

FENELON, FRANCOISE
'The Adventures of Telemachus, Son of Ulysses' – engraved title with vignette – 24 engraved plates – contem. tree calf – label – splits in joints – rubbed – 4to. – 1792.
(Sotheby's) $10 £5

FENN, JOHN
'Original Letters' – 5 vols – engraved frontis – plates – 1 folding – contem. half calf – rubbed – joints cracked – 4to. – 1787-1823.
(Christie's) $55 £25

FENTON, SIR GEOFFREY
'Golden Epistles' – 3rd Edn. – black letter – title in woodcut border – worming – 17th cent. calf – rebacked – rubbed – sm. 4to. 15 October 1582.
(Sotheby's) $360 £170

FER, N. DE
'Les Frontieres de France et des Pays Bas' – engraved title – 22 maps and charts – vellum – folio – circa 1725.
(Phillips) $295 £140

FERGUSON, JOHN
'Bibliotheca Chemica' – 2 vol. reprint of 1906 Edn. – cloth – 8vo. – 1954.
(Sotheby's) $160 £75

FERGUSON, M. AND SMITH, D. B.
'The Printed Books in the Library of the Hunterian Museum' – orig. buckram – folio – Glasgow 1930.
(Sotheby's) $95 £45

FERGUSON, R.
'A Just and Modest Vindication of the Scots Design for the Having Established a Colony At Darien' – 1st. Edn. – browning – contem. sheep – rubbed – 8vo. – Edinburgh 1699.
(Sotheby's) $145 £70

FERGUSSON, ADAM
'An Essay on the History of the Civil Society' – calf – 4to. – Edinburgh 1767.
(Phillips) $440 £210

FERGUSSON, JAMES
'Picturesque Illustrations of Ancient Architecture in Hindostan' – litho title – map and 23 plates – some leaves spotted – orig. morocco backed cloth – worn – loose – folio – 1848.
(Sotheby's) $75 £35

FERGUSSON, R.
'Poems on Various Subjects' – contemp. calf – 3rd Edn. – Edinburgh 1785.
(Bennett Book Auction) $25 £12

FERNANDEZ DE NAVARETE, DOMINGO
'Tratados Historicos, Politicos, Ethicos, y Religiosos de la Monarchie de la China' – 1st Edn. – title in red and black – woodcut arms – typographical border – old limp vellum – folio – Madrid 1676.
(Sotheby's) $115 £55

FERRARIO, GUILIO
'Il Costume Antico e Moderno' – 4 vol. only – two folding maps only – hand coloured – 27 hand coloured plates – some browning and worming – contemp. half vellum – inner hinges split – Livorno 1830-34.
(Christie's S. Kensington) $75 £35

FERRIER, J. P.
'Caravan Journeys and Wanderings in Persia, Afghanistan, Turkistan and Beloochistan' – 3 plates – folding map on linen – modern calf backed cloth – rubbed – 1856.
(Sotheby's) $230 £110

FESTE D'APOLLO, LE
Contem. Italian binding of red morocco gilt with the arms of Mary Amelia daughter of Emperor Francis 1 and Duchess of Parma – gilt back – blue silk endleaves – 4to. – Bodini Press, Parma, 1769.
(Moore Allen & Innocent) $880 £420

FEUILLET, RAOUL AUGER AND ESSEX, JOHN
'For the Further Improvement of Dancing, a Treatise on Chorography' – trans. from French – engraved throughout – many diagrams – dampstains – slightly later half calf – rubbed – 16mo.– Walsh & Randall 1710.
(Sotheby's) $945 £450

FEUQUIERES, ANTOINE DE PAS
'Memoirs Historical and Military with a Military Dictionary' – 2 vols. – 34 woodcut illus. – contem. mottled calf – spines gilt – worn – 8vo. – 1735-36.
(Sotheby's) $55 £25

FIELDING, HENRY
'Tom Thumb' – first issue of this Edn. – wood engraved frontis – 4 full page illus. – 6pp adverts – orig. printed wrappers – lacking backstrip – 12mo. – Thomas Rodd 1830.
(Sotheby's) $20 £9
'Works' – 12 vol. – new Edn. – frontispiece – contemporary marbled calf – rebacked – 1783.
(Christie's S. Kensington) $115 £55

FIELDING, THEODORE
'Cumberland, Westmoreland and Lancashire Illustrated' – 44 hand col. aquatint plates – half title – modern half straight grained morocco – uncut – folio – 1822.
(Sotheby's) $840 £400

FILDES, SIR LUKE (painter)
Series of 32 Als – c 100 pages – 8vo. – 2 auto cards and one telegram – Melbury Road, Kensington, and other places – 1887-1906.
(Phillips) $275 £130

FINDEL, J. G.
'The History of Freemasonry' – Leipzig 1866.
(Baitson) $5 £2

FINDEN AND BARTLETT
'Views of the Ports, Harbours and Watering Places of Great Britain' – 2 vols. – many engraved plates – quarto – green half calf gilt.
(Richard Baker & Thomson) $630 £300

FINDEN, W. AND E. F.
'Illustrations of the Life and Works of Lord Byron' – 3 vol. – 4to. – steel-engraved additional titles and 158 plates, a few slightly stained – contemp. morocco elab. gilt, by Nelson – slightly rubbed – g.e. – 1833-34.
(Christie's S. Kensington) $230 £110

FINGER RINGS
Auto mss account by antiquary Edmund Waterton 1830-87 of his collection of finger rings with a history of rings and ring collecting – 122pp blanks – signed and dated Walton Hall – half morocco – marbled boards – July 1860.
(Phillips) $115 £55

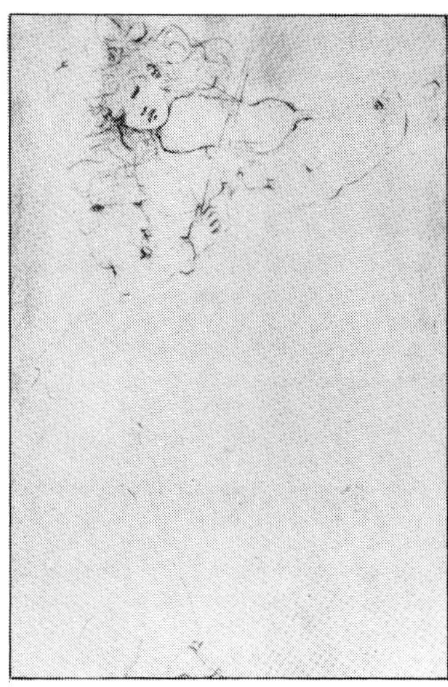

FINI, LEONOR-PINIERO, JUAN BAUTISTA
'Les Descriptions Merveilleuses' – 10 etched plates and 14 headpieces by Leonor Fini – unsewn in orig. wrappers – box – slightly worn – 4to. – Paris, Agori, 1973.
(Sotheby's) $420 £200

FINSCH, OTTO
'On a Collection of Birds from North Eastern Abyssinia and the Bogos Country' – map – 4 col. lithos – circa 1869.
(Phillips) $105 £50

FIRBANK, RONALD
'Extravaganza' – faint mark on top cover – New York 1935.
(J. Ash) $50 £24

FIRESIDE PICTURES
4 full page illus. moving parts operated by levers – orig. cloth backed pictorial boards – corners damaged – 4to. – Raphael Tuck circa 1900.
(Sotheby's) $65 £30

FISCHBACH, F.
'Ornament of Textile Fabric' – 158 coloured plates only of 160 – no text – soiled – orig. calf – portfolio – worn.
(Sotheby's) $220 £105

FISHER SON & CO.
'Country Atlas' – title lacking – 33 engr. maps – hand coloured in outline – two double page – some leaves detached – both covers detached – half morocco – 1842-45.
(Christie's S. Kensington) $115 £55

FITTLER, JAMES
'The Cities and Towns of Scotland' – six plates – disbound – original wrappers – soiled – oblong 4to. – n.d.
(Christie's) $95 £45
'Scotia Depicta' – 1st Edn. – engraved frontis – 48 plates after Nattes – water-stained – short tears – contem. red straight grained morocco – gilt – rubbed – faded – oblong 4to. – 1804.
(Sotheby's) $190 £90

FITZCLARENCE, LIEUT COL. G. A. F.
'Journal of a Route Across India, Through Egypt to England' – 1st Edn. – large folding engraved map – 9 hand col. aquatints – 4 partly col. battleplans – 5 plain plates – occasional foxing – library stamps – modern calf backed boards – 4to. – 1819.
(Sotheby's) $295 £140

FITZGERALD, C. P.
'China' – plates – orig. cloth – dust jacket – 8vo. – 1935.
(Sotheby's) $10 £5

FITZGERALD, F. SCOTT
'The Beautiful and the Damned' – the first issue without the Scribner seal on verso of title – New York 1922..
(J. Ash) $65 £30

AGAMEMNON.

A Tragedy,

TAKEN FROM ÆSCHYLUS.

FITZGERALD, EDWARD
'Agamemnon' – 1st. Edn. – auto corrections by author – orig. blue wrappers – folder – slipcase – 8vo. – Privately printed 1865.
(Sotheby's) $380 £180

FITZHERBERT, SIR ANTHONY
'The New Natura Brevium' – 1st Edn. in English – early 19th cent. calf – joints split – rubbed – 8vo. – 1652.
(Sotheby's) $115 £55

FLAMSTEED, JOHN
'Atlas Coelestis' – 1st Edn. – engraved portrait – 23 of 27 charts of stars – soiling and foxing – some marginal tears – contem. half calf – rubbed – covers detached – large folio – 1729.
(Christie's) $1,575 £750

FLAXMAN, JOHN
'Oeuvres ..... auxquelles on a joint les Tragedies de Sophocle par Giacomelli' – 144 engraved plates only – 126 after Flaxman – 18 by Giacomelli – some slight spotting – one margin torn – modern half morocco – Paris n.d.
(Christie's S. Kensington) $55 £25

FLECKER, JAMES ELROY
'Hassan' – some spotting of edges – slightly rubbed dust wrapper – 1922.
(J. Ash) $20 £10
'Letters from Frank Savery' – limited Edn. – uncut – orig. cloth backed boards – Beaumont Press 1926.
(Phillips) $40 £18

FLEMING, J. AND LEIGHTON, J.
'The Lakes of Scotland, a Series of Views' – 55 steel engraved plates – half morocco – 4to. – 1839.
(Bennett Book Auction) $125 £60

FLEMMING, LEONARD
'A Bard in the Backveld' – slightly torn dust wrapper – Cape Town 1934.
(J. Ash) $6 £3

FLETCHER, GILES
'The History of Russia' – engraved title – lacks prelim leaf – worming – contem. calf – worn – 12 mo.
(Sotheby's) $170 £80

FLETCHER, J. S.
'Picturesque History of Yorkshire' – 3 vols. – 600 illus. – Dent 1899.
(Dacre, Son & Hartley) $115 £54

FLETCHER, JOHN
'The Faithfull Shepheardesse' – 1st Edn. – device on title – browning – modern dark green morocco – sm. 4to. – circa 1610.
(Sotheby's) $460 £220

FLETCHER, W. Y.
'English Bookbinding in the British Museum' – number 95 of 500 copies – plates – orig. cloth – faded – folio – 1895.
(Sotheby's) $440 £210

FLIEGENDE BLATTER
Vols. 1-IXVIII in 8 vol. – illustrations – spotted – the first three in orig. pictorial boards – worn – the others in contemp. cloth – rubbed – 4to. – Munich 1845-54.
(Sotheby's) $200 £95

FLIGHT
Items concerning the early days of – A London to Paris Air Route Map, signed in ink by Charles Lindbergh – June 1924.
(Sotheby, King & Chasemore) $200 £95
A Graham White Aviation Co. catalogue.
(Sotheby, King & Chasemore) $65 £32

A 1920 voucher for a free flight in an Airco Machine.
(Sotheby, King & Chasemore) $10 £5

FLINT, SIR W. RUSSELL
'The Canterbury Tales of Geoffrey Chaucer' – 3 vol. – number 71 of 512 copies – 4to. – mounted coloured plates by Flint – original cloth backed boards – soiled – t.e.g. – 1913.
(Christie's S. Kensington) $115 £55

FLORA'S ALPHABET
24 wood engraved illus. col. by hand – scribbles in pencil – orig. printed wrappers – worn – restitched – 8vo. – Wallis 1822.
(Sotheby's) $65 £32

FLORIAN, J. P. C.
'Fables' – 12 ink and wash drawings by Jean Michel Moreau called Le Jeune – signed with initials and dated 1811-12 – mounted in red morocco album – blue morocco doublures – g.e. by Chambolle-Duru – front joint broken – 8vo. – 1811-12.
(Sotheby Parke Bernet) $8,920 £4,250

FLORINI, MATTEO
'La Gran Citta di Milano' – engr. plan 16 x 21½ inches – cut and laid down – rubbed and soiled early 17th century.
(Christie's S. Kensington) $170 £80

FLORIST'S JOURNAL, THE
3 vols. only – 41 hand col. engraved plates – slight spotting and offsetting – contem. half calf worn – 8vo. – 1845-47.
(Sotheby's) $250 £120

FLOWER, PHILIP W.
'History of the Trade in Tin' – errata – plates – orig. cloth gilt – 1880.
(Phillips) $55 £25

FLOYER, SIR J. AND BAYNARD, E.
'History of Cold Bathing' – 2 parts in one – worming – cloth gilt – 8vo. – 1706.
(Phillips) $75 £35

FOLEY, EDWIN
'The Book of Decorative Furniture' – 2 vol. – mounted coloured plates – original cloth – worn – 4to. – t.e.g. – n.d.
(Christie's S. Kensington) $40 £18

FOLKARD, CHARLES – AESOP
'Fables' – number 29 of 250 copies – signed by publishers – illus. in text by Folkard – orig. pictorial cloth – marked – 4to. – 1912.
(Sotheby's) $145 £70

FONTAINE, LA
'Fables' – illus. by G. Dore – some spotting – orig. cloth gilt – g.e. Cassel – n.d.
(Phillips) $34 £16

FONTANINI, J.
'De Antiquitatibus Hortae Coloniae Etruscorum' – 2nd Edn. – six plates – two double page maps – spotted and dampstained – contemporary calf – worn – Leiden – Sumtibus Pietri Van Der Aa. – n.d.
(Christie's S. Kensington) $160 £75

FOOTBALL PROGRAMMES
23 programmes 1968-74 including 6 F.A. Cup Finals and 17 copies of Football League Review.
(Baitson) $15 £7

FORBES, FREDERICK E.
'Dahomey and the Dahomans' – 2 vols. – 13 plates, 10 chromolithographed – some slight spotting – one section detached – original cloth by Remnant & Edmonds – head and foot of spine bumped – 1851.
(Christie's S. Kensington) $145 £70

'Eleven Years in Selorie' – 2 vols. – 1st Edn. – orig. cloth binding – good copy with uncut leaf edges – 1840.
(Lane) $90 £44

FORBES, H. O.
'Monkeys' – 2 vols. – 41 col plates – 1896-97.
(Laurence & Martin Taylor) $17 £8

'The Natural History of Sokotra and Abd-el-Kuri' – col. – frontis – plates – buckram – soiled – 1903.
(Phillips) $200 £95

FORBES, JAMES
'Letters from France ... including an account of Verdun' – 2 vol. – 1st. Edn. – 2 aquatint plates – half titles – 19th cent. cloth – 8vo. – 1806.
(Sotheby's) $20 £10

FORBES, PROFESSOR EDWARD AND SYLVANUS HANLEY
'A History of British Mollusca and Their Shells' – 4 vols. – litho plates – contem. half morocco – worn – 8vo. – 1853.
(Sotheby Beresford Adams) $100 £48

FORD, FORD MADOX
'Some Do Not' – 1st American Edn. – spine slightly creased – some wear and tear to edges of boards – 1924.
(J. Ash) $20 £10

FORDHAM, GEORGE (jockey)
Two ALs. – 2 pages – 8vo. – Uxbridge – May 1879 to Baron Leopold de Rothschild – 'I trust I may win again for you next Saturday'.
(Phillips) $30 £14

FORE-EDGE PAINTING
'The Diamond Pocket Prayer' – 16mo. – engr. title – plates – contemp. red morocco – gilt – spine rubbed – g.e. with a fore-edge painting depicting the Adoration of the Shepherds.
(Christie's S. Kensington) $135 £65
Campbell, T. 'The Life' and 'The Pleasures of Hope' – 2 vols. in one – spotted – contem. calf – rubbed – edges gauffered and gilt with fore edge painting of river scene with church – 8vo. – 1853.
(Sotheby's) $40 £20
'The Adventures of Gil Blas ... translated .. by Benjamin Heath Malkin' – 4 vol. – 1809 engr. plates – contemp. diced calf – rubbed – rebacked – joints split – spines torn.
(Christie's S. Kensington) $145 £70
Hermans, Felicia. 'Poems' – engraved portrait and additional title – contemp. morocco – gilt – g.e. with a fore-edge painting of Dublin from Phoenix Park – 1862.
(Christie's S. Kensington) $125 £60

FOREIGN FIELD SPORTS, FISHERIES, SPORTING ANECDOTES ETC.
From drawings by Messrs. Howitt, Atkinson, Clark, Manskirch & Co. with a supplement of New South Wales – folio – some stains and spots – contemp. calf rubbed – rebacked with old spine laid down – g.e.
(Christie's S. Kensington) $1,260 £600

FORES
'Sporting Notes and Sketches' – 12 vols. – plates – one torn – orig. cloth – g.e. 1884-95.
(Christie's) $60 £28

FORESTER, C. S.
'Randall and the River of Time' – 1st English Edn. – nice in slightly chipped dust wrapper – 1951.
(J. Ash) $8 £4

FORESTER, THOMAS
'Rambles in the Islands of Corsica and Sardinia' – 1st Edn. – 9 plates – some col. – 2 folding – illus. – orig. cloth – rubbed – 8vo. – 1858.
(Sotheby's) $115 £55

FORMBY, J.
'American Civil War' – 2 volumes – text and maps – cloth – 1910.
(Bennett Book Auction) $10 £5

FORREST, LIEUT COL. C. R.
'A Picturesque Tour along the Rivers Ganges and Jumna' – 1st. Edn. – folding engraved map – col. aquatint vignette – 24 col. aquatints by Hunt and Sutherland – occasional spotting – modern half morocco – 4to. – Ackermann 1824.
(Sotheby's) $1,470 £700

FORESHAW, J. M.
'Parrots of the World' – 158 col. plates by W. T. Cooper – orig. cloth – 4to. – 1973.
(Phillips) $210 £100

FORSTER, EDWARD
'The British Gallery' – 1807.
(Laurence & Martin Taylor) $180 £85

FORSTER, E. M.
'Pharos & Pharillon' – 1st. Edn. – margins slightly browned – original cloth backed boards – rubbed and soiled – The Hogarth Press, 1923.
(Christie's S. Kensington) $65 £30

FORSTER, JOHN R.
'History of the Voyages and Discoveries made in the North' – 3 folding maps – tree calf – rubbed – 4to. – 1786.
(Phillips) $380 $180

FORSYTH, J.
'Beauties of Scotland' – 5 vols. – engravings – calf gilt – 8vo. – 1805-08.
(Phillips) $125 £60

FORTESCUE, SIR JOHN
'A Learned Commendation of the Politique Lawes of England' – 2nd Edn. in Eng, Latin and English text – partly black letter – some early ownership titles – modern polished calf – sm. 8vo. – Richards Tottell 1573.
(Sotheby's) $505 £240

FORTESQUE, HON J. W.
'A History of the British Army' – 13 vol. in 20 – 6 vols. of maps – plates and maps – orig. cloth – rubbed – joints split – 8vo. – 1935.
(Sotheby's) $525 £250

FORTIFICATION
'An Introduction to the Art of Fortification' – 1st Edn. – 3 folding engraved plates – browning and soiling – calf backed marbled boards – label – spine gilt – rubbed – 8vo. – 1745.
(Sotheby's) $90 £42

FOSKETT, DAPHNE
'A Dictionary of British Miniature Painters' – 2 vols. – plates – some col. – orig. cloth – dust jacket – 4to. – 1972.
(Sotheby's) $105 £50

FOSSE, C. H. L. F.
'Idees d'un Militaire Pour La Disposition des Troupes' – hand col. dedication and 11 folding plates – soiling and staining – half title lacking – contem morocco – worn – g.e. 4to. – Paris 1783.
(Christie's) $295 £140

FOSTER, J. J.
'French Art from Watteau to Prud'hon' – 3 vols. – 1 0f 250 copies – plates – calf gilt – t.e.g. – 4to. 1905.
(Phillips) $80 £38
'Miniature Painters, British and Foreign' – 2 vol. – limited Edn. de luxe – signed by author – plates – orig. vellum – rubbed – folio – 1903.
(Sotheby's) $75 £35

FOSTER, BIRKET – MILTON, JOHN
'L'Allegro and Il Penseroso' –steel-engraved illustrations by Birket Foster – text printed in red – slight spotting – original cloth – slightly soiled – g.e. – 1855.
(Christie's S. Kensington) $20 £10

FOSTER, BIRKET; AND OTHERS
'Gems of Scenery from Picturesque Europe' – number 165 of 300 copies – steel engraved plates – mounted on India paper – after Birket Foster and others – a few detached – outer margin of one soiled and worn – original cloth backed boards – soiled – folio – Cassell & Company Limited – n.d.
(Christie's S. Kensington) $525 £250

FOSTER, BIRKET AND H. N. HUMPHREYS – GOLDSMITH, OLIVER
'The Poems' – new Edn. 4to. – frontispiece and illustrations printed in colour by Edmund Evans after Foster and Himphreys – some spotting – original cloth – slightly soiled – spine torn – g.e. – 1869.
(Christie's S. Kensington) $30 £14

FOTHEGILL, GEORGE A.
'Notes from the Diary of a Doctor, Sketch Artist and Sportsman' – coloured frontis, title and plates, illustrations, original cloth, slightly soiled, folio – York, 1901.
(Christie's S. Kensington) $45 £20

FOX-DAVIS, A. C.
'The Art of Heraldry' – illus. – some in colour – cloth gilt – folio – 1904.
(Phillips) $105 £50
'Armorial Families' – 6th Edn. – col. plates – illus. – orig. cloth – rubbed – t.e.g. – 4to. – 1910.
(Christie's) $25 £12

FOXE, JOHN
'Actes and Monuments' – 2 vol. – 5th Edn. – mostly black letter – woodcuts in text – browning and waterstaining – 18th cent. panelled calf – joints split – worn – folio – Peter Short 1596-97.
(Sotheby's) $275 £130

FRANCE
'Rapport de la Commission d'Enquete sur L'Insurrection qui a Eclate dans la Journee du 23 Juin et sur les evenements du 15 Mai' – 3 parts in one – orig. wrappers preserved contem. half roan – arms of Hanover on cover – 4to. – Paris, 1848.
(Sotheby's) $65 £30

FRANCE, ANATOLE
'The Works' – 20 vols. – 1925.
(Lane) $4 £2

FRANCESCO DONATO, DOGE OF VENICE 1545-53
Ducale appointing Lorenzo Bragadin to the military command of Zadar (Jugoslavia) in Italian – mss on vellum – 59 ll written in black ink in fine sloping italic script with calligraphic flourishes – contem. Venetian binding of red brown morocco gilt – extremely fine condition in fitted case – 227 mm x 166 mm. – Venice, May 1547.
(Sotheby's) $1,365 £650

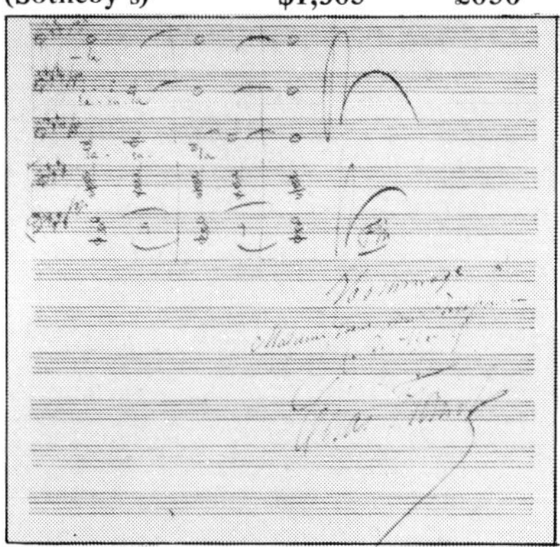

FRANCK, CESAR
Auto mss of an unpublished motet 'O Gloriosa' for 3 part choir – in E major – signed and inscribed at end – 7 pages – folio.
(Sotheby's) $2,100 £1,000

FRANKAU, JULIA
'Eighteenth Century Colour Prints' – plates – unopened – cloth worn – folio – 1900.
(Phillips) $85 £40
'John Raphael Smith' – 50 plates some printed in colours – folio – in portfolio (worn – 1902.
(Bonhams) $115 £55

FRANKLIN, BENJAMIN
'Works' – engraved portrait – browning – contem. calf – damaged – 8vo. – Dublin 1793.
(Sotheby's) $40 £20

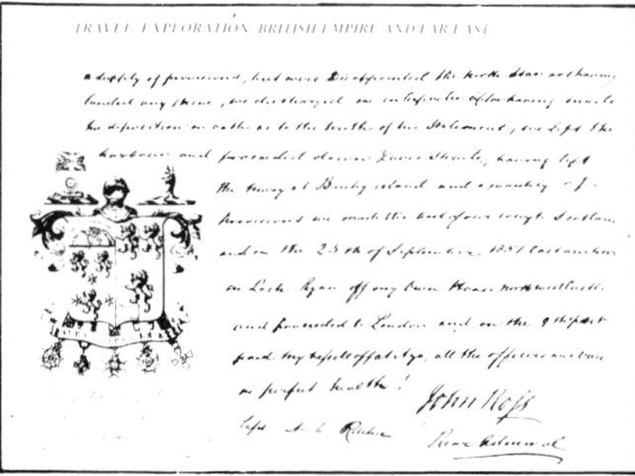

FRANKLIN, SIR JOHN
Auto report signed by Sir John Ross on his search to find Franklin – 3 pages – quarto – Ross's coat of arms in lower left hand corner after 9 Oct. 1851.
(Sotheby's) $715 £340
'Journey to the Shores of the Polar Sea' – 4 vol. – plates – folding map – occasional slight spotting – orig. cloth – spine slightly soiled – sm. 8vo. – 1829.
(Christie's S. Kensington) $25 £12

FRASER, CLAUD LOVAT
A series of 138 ink and watercolour sketches and drawings to illustrate poems by Walter de la Mare mounted in an album one or more to a page with title of poem illustrated – mss title on first page – an alternative title for 'Peacock Pie' – 1912 and one illus. in mount loosely inserted – folio.
(Sotheby's) $6,300 £3,000

FRASER, GEORGE MACDONALD
'Flash for Freedom' – very good in the dust wrapper – 1971.
(J. Ash) $8 £4

FRASER, JAMES
'The History of Nadir Shah' – 1st Edn. – folding engraved portrait – folding map – contem. calf – joints split – 8vo. – 1742.
(Sotheby's) $125 £60

FRASER, JAMES BAILLIE
'Journal of a Tour through Part of the Snowy Range of the Himla Mountains' – 1st Edn. – large engraved folding map – spotted – contem. half russia – spine defective – 4to. – 1820.
(Christie's) $210 £100

FRASER, MRS.
'The Practice of Cookery, Pastry, Pickling, Preserving' – 1st Edn. – 2 engraved plates – some soiling and browning – contem. sheep – joints split – worn – 12 mo. – Edinburgh 1791.
(Sotheby's) $115 £55

FRASER, W.
'The Dukes of Albany and Their Castle of Doune' – 3 plates – cloth gilt – 4to. – 1881.
(Bennett Book Auction) $20 £9

FRAUNHOFER, JOSEPH VON
'Bestimmung des Brechungs-und Farben-zerstreuungs-Vermogens Verschiedener Glasarten in: Denkschriften der Koniglichen Academie der Wissenschaften zu Munchen' – vol. V, 3 plates, 2 folding, wrappers, uncut – Munich, 1817.
(Sotheby's) $790 £350

FREART, ROLAND
'A Parallel of the Ancient Architecture with the Modern' – 4th Edn. – engraved illustrations – 40 full page – engraved title lacking – a few leaves torn – one with a little loss – title laid down – old calf – worn – folio – Printed by T.W. for J. Walthoe, D. Midwinter, etc. – 1733.
(Christie's S. Kensington) $45 £22

FREDERIC II, KING OF PRUSSIA
'Oeuvres Posthumes' – 15 vols. – 1st Edn. – engraved portrait – contem. sprinkled boards – slightly rubbed – 8vo. – Berlin 1877.
(Sotheby's) $115 £55

FREIND, JOHN
'Emmenologia' – in Latin and trans. into English by Thomas Dale – 1st. Edn. in English – engraved vignette on title – advert leaf before title and at end – contem. calf – hinges cracked – 8vo. – T. Cox 1729.
(Sotheby's) $55 £25

FREITAG, ADAM
'Architectura Militaris' – engr. title cut down and mounted – 35 engr. double page plates – slightly spotted – contemp. half vellum – boards worn.
(Sotheby's) $275 £130

FRENCH, GEORGE
'The History of Col. Parke's Administration ... Leeward Islands; with an account of the Rebellion in Antegoa' – portrait – stains – modern calf – 8vo. – 1717.
(Sotheby's) $190 £90

FRERE, J. HOOKHAM
'Works' – 3 volumes – cloth fp. – Pickering 1874.
(Bennet Book Auction) $6 £3

FRESNEL, AUGUSTIN JEAN
'Memoire sur la Diffraction de la Lumiere (Extrait des Annales de Chimie et de Physique)' – 1st Edn., drop title, folding plate, original wrappers, defective, cloth case – Paris, 1815.
(Sotheby's) $385 £170

FREZIER, AMEDEE-FRANCOIS
'Relation du Voyage de la Mer du Sud aux Cotes du Chily et du Perou' – 1st Edn. – 37 maps and plates of which 19 are folding – contem. calf – 4to. – Paris 1716.
(Christie's) $460 £220

FRIEDLANDER, M. J.
'Lucas Van Leyden' – plates – cloth – 4to. – Leipzig 1924.
(Phillips) $45 £22

FRIESZ, EMILE OTHON
Collection of about 50 auto letters and postcards signed many with fine illus. in pencil – ink and washes – c 160 pages folio – quarto and octavo – to his wife Andree, M. Pedron and 'Noel' recording his progress with his paintings and his attempts to sell them – New York, Honfleur and elsewhere 1911-1941.
(Sotheby's) $2,940 £1,400

FRITH, J.
'A Boke made by John Frith answering unto M. Mores Lettur' – calf – worn – sm. 8vo. – Munster, C. Willems 1533.
(Sotheby's) $80 £38

FROGGETT, I. W.
'Survey of the Country Thirty Miles Round London' – folding engraved map – hand col. in outline – mounted on linen – soiled – in orig. slipcase – worn – 106 cm x 132 cm. – 1831.
(Sotheby's) $95 £45

FROHAWK, F. W.
'Natural History of British Butterflies' – 2 vols. – col. plates – orig. cloth – dust jackets – folio – n.d.
(Sotheby's) $240 £115

FROHLICH-BUME, L.
'Ingres' – plates – cloth gilt – t.e.g. – 4to. – 1926.
(Phillips) $60 £28

FROISSART, SIR JOHN
'Chronicles . . . translated . . . by Thomas Johnes' – 12 vols. only, 3rd Edn., 53 aquatint plates, one folding map, cont. russia, joints worn – 1808.
(Christie's S. Kensington) $50 £22

FROSSARD, E. AND J. JOURDAN
'Vues, Prises dans Les Pyrenees Francaises' – addit. litho title – vignette and 24 plates by Engelmann – litho table – contem. half roan – corners worn – folio – Paris 1829.
(Sotheby's) $295 £140

FROST, CHARLES
'Notices Relative to the Early History of the Town and Port of Hull' – half bound copy with catalogue of books sold by J. B. Nichols 1827.
(Baitson) $115 £55

FROST, THOMAS
'The Lives of the Conjurers' – new Edn. – orig. pictorial cloth – 8vo. – 1881.
(Sotheby's) $85 £40

FRY, E.
'Pantographia' – illus. – rebound calf – gilt – t.e.g. – 1799.
(Phillips) $125 £60

FRY, ROGER
'Transformations Critical and Speculative Essays on Art' – 4to. – plates – illustrations – orig. cloth – slightly soiled – 1926.
(Christie's S. Kensington) $45 £22

FRYKE, CHRISTOPHER AND CHRISTOPHER SCHWEITZER
'A Relation of two Voyages made into the East Indies' – 1st Edn. in Eng. – page of notes in neat 18th cent. hand at end – early 20th cent. morocco backed cloth – rubbed – 8vo. – 1700.
(Sotheby's) $420 £200

FUCHS, LEONARD
'De Historia Stirpium' – 1st Edn. – printer's device and full length portrait of author – woodcuts of plants – contem. blind stamped calf – wooden boards – folio – Basle, 1542.
(Christie's) $5,460 £2,600

FULHAME, MRS.
'An Essay on Combustion with a view to a New Art of Painting and Dyeing' – 1st. Edn. – errata slip pasted in – library stamps – cloth – 8vo. – for the author by J. Cooper, 1794.
(Sotheby's) $360 £170

FULLARTON, A. (publisher)
'A Gazetteer of the World' – 7 vol. – numerous engraved plates and maps – latter hand col. in outline – some plates loose – orig. cloth – spines worn – large 8vo. – 1850-57.
(Sotheby's) $20 £10
'The Royal Illustrated Atlas of Modern Geography' – engraved vignette title – 76 col. and tinted litho plates – mostly maps – 46 double page and 30 full page – costume figures – natural history subjects – some plates discoloured – orig. dark red morocco gilt – g.e. – one cover detached – worn – folio – circa 1865.
(Sotheby's) $360 £170

FULLER, THOMAS
'A Pisgah Sight of Jerusalem and the Confines thereof' – 1st Edn. – addit. engraved title – armorial plate – large folding engraved map – 27 double page engraved maps and plates – contem. calf worn – folio – 1650.
(Christie's) $1,220 £580
'The Church History of Britain' – 1st Edn. – browning and soiling – contem. calf – rebacked – worn – folio – 1655.
(Sotheby's) $20 £10

FULTON, ROBERT
'The Illustrated Book of Pigeons' – 50 col. plates – cloth worn – 4to. – n.d.
(Phillips) $135 £65

FUN UPON FUN OR THE HUMOURS OF THE FAIR
2 vols. – each with 8 engraved plates printed in sepia – wood engraved illus. in text – orig. wrappers – 32 mo. – Glasgow circa 1815.
(Sotheby's) $145 £70

FUNCK, M.
'Le Livre Belge a Gravures, Paris and Brussels' – plates – original cloth – slightly faded – t.e.g. – 1925.
(Christie's S. Kensington) $125 £60

FUNNELL, W.
'A Voyage Round the World containing an Account of Captain Dampier's Expedition into the South Seas' – 10 plates – one trimmed – and 5 maps – calf – (rebacked) – 1707.
(Bonhams) $860 £410

FURNISS, HARRY
'Confessions of a Caricaturist'; 'Harry Furniss at Home'; 'More about How to Draw with Pen and Ink'; 'My Bohemian Days' – A.L.s. with sketch loosely inserted – all orig. cloth – soiled – 8vo. – n.d.
(Sotheby's) $115 £55

FURST, HERBERT
'Original Engravings and Engravings, an Appreciation' – plates – orig. cloth – dust jacket – t.e.g. – 4to. – 1931.
(Christie's S. Kensington) $40 £20
'The Modern Woodcut' – col. frontis – plates – cloth – 4to. – 1924.
(Phillips) $65 £30

GADBURY, JOHN
'London's Deliverance Predicted ... showing the Cause of Plagues in General and the probable time when this present pest will have abated' – title and last page soiled – stains – half calf – sm. 4to. – J. C. for E. Calvert 1665.
(Sotheby's) $200 £95

GAFFAREL, JAMES
'Unheard of Curiosities by G.D. for Humphrey Mosely, 1650' – folding table torn and holed – contemporary calf – rebacked – boxed.
(Christie's S. Kensington) $90 £42

GAGE, JOHN
'The History and Antiquities of Suffolk, Thingoe Hundred' – engraved map – plates – contem. half morocco – gilt – slightly rubbed – folio 1838.
(Sotheby's) $125 £60

GAGE, T.
'A New Survey of the West Indies of the English American His Travail by Sea and Land' – 4 full page maps, 2nd Edn., folio, cont. calf, one map slightly defective – E. Cotes and John Sweeting, 1655.
(Bonham's) $450 £200

GALIANI, FERDINANDO
'Dialogues sur le Commerce des Bles' – 2 vols. – half titles – slight browning – modern green morocco – labels – cloth slipcases – 12mo. – Berlin 1795.
(Sotheby's) $230 £110

GALL, FRANZ JOSEPH AND JOHANN CASPER SPURZHEIM
'Anatomie et Physiologie du System Nerveux' – 4 vols. in 2 – atlas – 100 engraved plates – foxing – contem. half calf – upper covers loose – folio – Paris 1810-19.
(Christie's) $1,050 £500

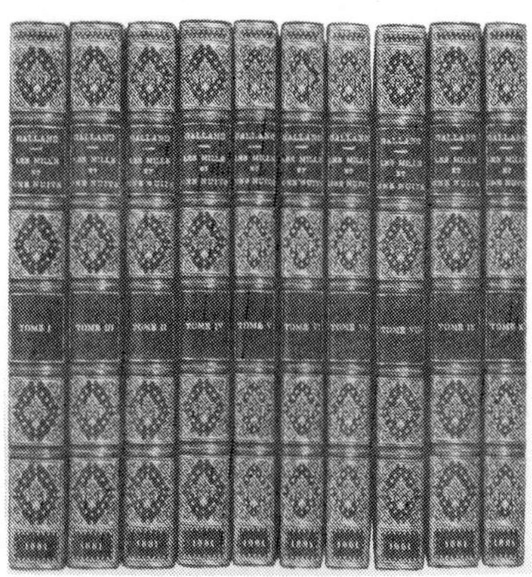

GALLAND, ANTOINE
'Les Milles Nuits et Une Nuit' – 10 vols. – no. 1 of 10 copies sur papier du Japon of an edition of 220 numbered copies – 21 engraved plates in 3 states by Lalauze – brown morocco gilt by Dupre – 8vo. – Paris, Bibliophiles, 1881.
(Sotheby Parke Bernet) $3,160 £1,505

GALLERY OF BRITISH ART
55 steel engraved plates – cloth nd.
(Bennett Book Auction) $6 £3

GALLO, AGOSTINO
'Le Vinto Giornate dell'Agricoltura et de Placeri della Villa' – device on titles – 19 woodcuts – holed – some stains – quarter vellum – 8vo. – Venice 1572.
(Phillips) $525 £250

GALLUP, DONALD
'T. S. Eliot, a Bibliography' – 2nd Edn. – orig. cloth – dust jacket – reprinted 1970.
(Christie's) $20 £10

GALSWORTHY, JOHN
'Over the River' – very good in slightly chipped dust wrapper – 1933.
(J. Ash) $8 £4

GALTON, D.
'Report (Supplement) On the Railways of the United States' – 2 vols. – 34 plates – folding col. map. – soiled – disbound – folio – 1857-58.
(Sotheby's) $335 £160

GALTON, F.
'Inquiries into Human Faculty and its Development' – 1st Edn. – actual photograph mounted – 4 plates – 1 folding coloured – orig. cloth – rubbed – 8vo. – 1883.
(Sotheby's) $230 £110

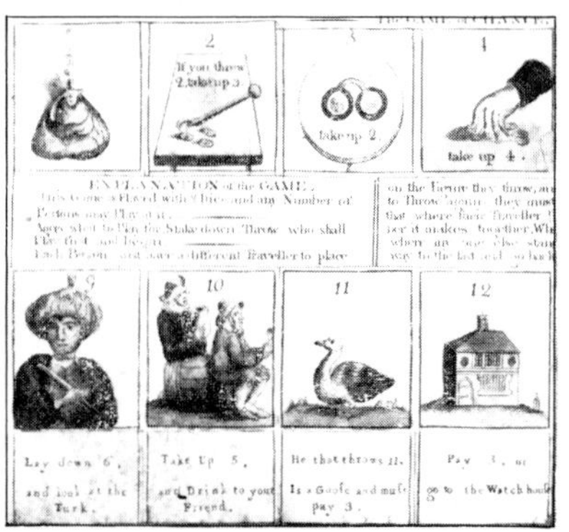

GAME OF CHANCE, THE OR HARLEQUIN TAKES ALL
Engraved sheet mounted on linen – explanation sheet and 32 compartments each with illus. coloured by hand – slightly stained – framed and glazed – 326 mm x 355 mm. – Laurie & Whittle 1794.
(Sotheby's) $170 £80

GARCELON, A.
'Inspirations' – 20 plates by Garcelon – col. through stencils – unsewn as issued in cloth backed portfolio – slightly worn – ties – folio – Paris, Massin, n.d.
(Sotheby's) $230 £110

'GARDEN, AN ILLUSTRATED WEEKLY JOURNAL OF HORTICULTURE, THE'
33 volumes – volume 11, 1877 to volume 47, 1895 (ex. 4 from run) approximately 1000 coloured plates – half calf – 4to. – 1877 to 1895.
(Bennett Book Auction) $325 £155

GARDEN, THE
Vol. 14-24 – coloured plates – contem. cloth – rubbed – 4to. – 1878-83.
(Sotheby's) $230 £110

GARDINER, S. R.
'Oliver Cromwell' – limited Edn. on Japan vellum – lacking duplicate set of plates – silk endpapers – full morocco gilt by Zaehnsdorf – folio – 1899.
(Phillips) $125 £60

GARDNER, G. A.
'Rock Paintings of North West Cordoba' – plates – orig. cloth – folio – Oxford 1931.
(Sotheby's) $125 £60

GARDNER, J. STARKIE
'A New Booke of Drawings invented and designed by John Tijou' – engr. add. title and 19 plates – margins browned – orig. boards – soiled and rubbed – folio – 1896.
(Christie's S. Kensington) $40 £18

GARDNER, T.
'Historical Account of Dunwich, Blithburgh and Southwold' – folding map backed with linen – 8 plates – calf gilt worn – 4to. – 1754.
(Phillips) $400 £190

GARNETT, DAVID
'The Grasshoppers Come' – illustrations and dust wrapper by R. A. Garnett – very good in slightly nicked jacket – 1931.
(J. Ash) $12 £6

GARNETT, RICHARD
'Three Hundred Notable Books Added to the Library of the British Museum under the Keepership of Richard Garnett 1890-99' – title in red and black – portrait frontis – facsimiles in text – orig. maroon morocco backed cloth – slightly rubbed – t.eg. – sm. folio – Privately printed 1899.
(Sotheby's) $75 £35

GARNIER, EDOUARD
'The Soft Porcelain of Sevres' – 50 col. plates – one leaf detached – orig. cloth – g.e. – folio – 1892.
(Christie's) $170 £80

GARRAN, A.
'Picturesque Atlas of Australia' – vol. 1 and 2 only of 3 – plates – maps – spotting – orig. half morocco – rubbed – folio – 4to. – 1886.
(Sotheby's) $315 £150

GARSAULT, FRANCOIS ALEXANDRE PIERRE DE
'Le Nouveau Parfait Marechal' – 2nd Edn. – half title – title in red and black – engraved frontis portrait and 49 engraved plates – many folding – contem. mottled calf – 4to. – Paris Chez Savoye 1746.
(Christie's) $210 £100

GASKELL, MRS. ELIZABETH
'The Works' – 8 vol. – Knutsford Edn. – plates – contem. calf gilt – rubbed – 8vo. – 1788-90.
(Sotheby's) $305 £145
'Elizabeth Gaskell – a Biography' by W. Gerin – plates – Oxford 1976.
(J. Ash) $8 £4

GASPEY, W.
'Tallis's Illustrated London' – 2 vol. – plates in one vol. – the text in the other – two steel-engraved additional titles and 155 plates – 3 folding – some spotting – contemp. half morocco – slightly rubbed –g.e. n.d.
(Christie's S. Kensington) $160 £75

GASTINEAU, HENRY
'Wales Illustrated in a Series of Views' – engraved titles – 86 views only – stains – contem. half morocco – slightly worn – 4to. – 1830.
(Sotheby Beresford Adams) $105 £50

GASTON, ALFRED DE
'Les Marchands des Miracles' – slightly spotted – cloth backed boards – somewhat worn – 12 mo. – Paris 1864.
(Sotheby's) $75 £36

GAULTIER, THE ABBE
'A Course of Geography by Means of Instructive Games' – 14 engraved double page maps – hand col. in outline – torn and repaired – contem. half morocco – 4to. – 1829.
(Christie's) $45 £22

GAUTIER, THEOPHILE
'Mademoiselle de Maupin ... translated by R. & E. Powys Mathers' – No. 359 of 500 copies – 4to. – eight plates by John Buckland Wright – orig. vellum backed cloth – a little soiled – t.e.g. – The Golden Cockerel Press – 1938.
(Christie's S. Kensington) $95 £45
'Une Nuit de Cleopatre' – limited Edn. – illus. by Avril, – crimson morocco – covers tooled in gilt with border of shells and Greek geometric pattern – g.e. – 1894.
(Phillips) $360 £170

GAVARNI, PAUL
'Oeuvres Choisis' 4 vol. in 2 – wood engraved after Gavarni – calf backed boards – slightly worn – t.e.g. – 4to. – Paris 1845-48.
(Sotheby's) $1,470 £700

GAY, JOHN
'Fables' – 2 vols. in one – 2 engraved titles – frontis – 67 plates, 12 by W. Blake – calf gilt – 1793.
(Phillips) $230 £110

GAZETTEER OF THE WORLD
9 volumes – steel engraved plates and maps – cloth – 1886.
(Bennett Book Auction) $20 £10

GEIKIE , WATER
'Etchings Illustrative of Scottish Life and Scenery' – 92 etched plates by Geikie – some mounted on india paper – spotting – contem. morocco – rubbed – g.e. – 4to. – Edinburgh n.d.
(Christie's) $105 £50

GELIS-DIDOT, P.
'La Peinture Decorative en France' – folio – contemp. – half morocco – rubbed – joints – worn – t.e.g. – Paris n.d.
(Christie's S. Kensington) $115 £55

GELL, SIR WILLIAM
'Narrative of a Journey in the Morea' – 9 litho plates – uncut – orig. boards – 1823.
(Phillips) $505 £240
'Pompeiana' – 2 vols in one – port. frontis – 83 full page engravings – vignettes – morocco gilt scuffed – g.e. – 4to. – 1832.
(Phillips) $85 £40

GEMS, THE BOOK OF AND CABINET OF ART
Steel engraved add. title and 55 plates – some slight spotting – orig. cloth – worn – g.e. – 4to. – published by Thomas Holmes.
(Christie's S. Kensington) $95 £45

GEN, THE editor Henry Stanley
Vols. 1-23 no. 3 excepting 38 issues and 74 duplicates in 310 parts – illus. – col. wrappers – 8vo. – 1945-67.
(Sotheby's) $170 £80

GENEALOGISTS' MAGAZINE, THE
Vol. 1-19 – part 11 and an envelope of other publications – 27 vols. together – illus. – modern cloth and orig. wrappers – 8vo. – 1925-79.
(Sotheby's) $190 £90

GENERAL LIST OR CATALOGUE OF ALL THE OFFICES AND OFFICERS ...
In (i) South Britain or England (ii) North Britain or Scotland – modern quarter calf – London 1728.
(Bennett Book Auction) $25 £12

GENERAL STUD BOOK, THE
Vol. 1-34 – various Edn. – contem. calf and half calf – some rubbed and cracked – 1855-61.
(Christie's) $250 £120

GENNETE, C. L.
'Nouvelle Construction de Cheminees' – 13 folding engraved plates – 2 pp adverts at end – contem. mottled sheep – worn – 8vo. – Liege 1760.
(Sotheby's) $200 £95

GENOA
'A Collection of 20 Engraved Views' – all double page including 4 folding – 1 plan – waterstains – dust soiled – occas. browning and spotting – contem. half calf – spine gilt – worn – folio – Genoa circa 1760.
(Sotheby's) $6,090 £2,900

GENTLEMAN'S LIBRARY CONTAINING RULES OF CONDUCT IN ALL PARTS OF LIFE.
Frontis – calf gilt – 1715.
(Phillips) $160 $75

GENTLEMAN'S MAGAZINES
A collection of 16 – engraved plates throughout – orig. green cloth – 1820's-1830's.
(Baitson) $60 £28

GENTLEMEN'S RECREATIONS; TO ALL THE LIBERAL ARTS AND SCIENCES ... HORSEMANSHIP, HAWKING, HUNTING, FOWLING, FISHING, AGRICULTURE ETC.
In three parts – copper plate frontis and 74 plates many sporting and text woodcuts – contemp. panelled calf – jnts. weak – London 1710.
(Bennett Book Auction) $650 £310

GENTRY, T. G.
'Nests and Birds of the United States' – col. litho title and 54 plates – portrait lacking – half morocco – rubbed – Philadelphia n.d.
(Christie's) $105 £50

GENT'S HISTORY OF HULL
In facsimile of original of 1735 – 1869.
(Baitson) $75 £36

GEORGE III
Warrant authorising the Earl of Wilmington to pay Sir William Strickland an allowance of £1000 per annum – integral blank – contem. endorsements – St. James – 23 May 1730.
(Phillips) $230 £110

Fine coloured initial letter portrait of the king on a Royal Letter Patent creating Francis Earl of Bandon as Viscount Bandon of Bandon Bridge in the County of Cork – on vellum – illum. letters in first line – four coats of arms emblazoned – coloured border of bluebells and roses – impression of Great Seal attached to orig. gold ribbon. – October 1795.
(Sotheby's) $1,050 £500

THE GEORGIAN SOCIETY RECORDS
3 vol. – limited to 300, 400 and 550 copies – 4to. – frontispieces – one coloured – plates – some spotting – orig. cloth – soiled – spines torn – stitching weak – Dublin 1909-11.
(Christie's S. Kensington) $115 £55

GERARD, A.
'Account of Koonawur in the Himalaya' – folding map slightly torn – orig. cloth – rubbed – recased – 8vo. – 1841.
(Sotheby's) $240 £115

GERHARDI, WILLIAM
'The Memoirs of Satan' – written with Brian Lunn – 1932.
(J. Ash) $12 £6

GERHARDT, CHARLES
'Traite de Chimie Organique' – 4 vols – 1st Edn. – some text illus. – half titles – errata leaf at end – cloth – spine gilt – 8vo. – Paris, Didot 1853-56.
(Sotheby's) $105 £50

GERMAN BIBLE
2 vols. – the 9th German Bible – 588 leaves – 109 woodcuts with original colouring – orig. blind stamped Nuremberg calf – probably from Koberger workshop – somewhat rubbed – a few repairs – folio – Nuremberg Anton Koberger, 1483.
(Sotheby's) $48,300 £23, 000

GERMANO, DR. GIO
'Additione Apologetico' – 2 vols. in 1 – 18th cent. Italian binding of red morocco gilt with arms of Cardinal Albieri in centre – deep decorative border – gilt – 8vo. – Venice 1675-76.
(Moore Allen & Innocent) $1,050 £500

GERNING, J. J.
'A Picturesque Tour along the Rhine' – map – 24 col. aquatints – recent morocco gilt – 4to. – 1820.
(Sotheby's) $3,150 £1,500

GHILLEBERT DE LANNOY
'L'Instruction d'un Jeune Prince' – in French prose followed by an allegorical poem by Olivier de la Marche on growing old in French verse – illum. mss on vellum – eight large illum. initials in full length borders – 18 large illum. initials with full borders – three very large miniatures – modern pale brown morocco – 250 mm x 175 mm – Southern Flanders and France circa 1485.
(Sotheby's) $63,000 £30,000

GIBB, W. AND R. R. HOLMES
'Naval and Military Trophies' – chromo-lithographed plates – orig. cloth – rubbed.
(Sotheby's) $40 £18

GIBBINGS, ROBERT
'Blue Angels and Whales' – 2nd Edn. – revised and enlarged – contains different and substantially more illustration than the 1938 Pelican – 66 illustrations – some coloured – 1946.
(J. Ash) $10 £5
'The 7th Man' – number 95 of 500 copies – woodcuts by Gibbings – original cloth backed boards – slightly soiled – top and fore-edge gilt.
(Christie's S. Kensington) $95 £45

GIBSON, S.
'Early Oxford Bindings' – Bibliographical Society – no. 10 – illus – cloth backed boards – 4to. – 1903.
(Phillips) $115 £55

GIBSON, THOMAS
'The Anatomy of Human Bodies Epitomized' – 20 engraved plates – contem calf gilt – 1703.
(Phillips) $65 £32

GIBSON, WILLIAM SYDNEY
'The History of the Monastery Founded at Tynemouth' – 2 vols. – plates – 2 col. – some folding – ornamental initials – modern half morocco – 4to. – 1846-47.
(Sotheby's) $135 £65

GIBSON, W. W.
'Home' – limited Edn. – uncut – orig. cloth backed boards – Beaumont Press 1920.
(Phillips) $45 £22

GIDE, ANDRE
'Back from the U.S.S.R.' – 1st English Edn. – spine very slightly creased – 1937.
(J. Ash) $8 £4

GIFFORD, JOHN
'A Residence in France ... 1792-1795' – 2 vols. – calf – 1797.
(Phillips) $60 £28
'History of the Political Life of William Pitt' – 3 vols. – port – half calf – 4to. – 1809.
(Phillips) $40 £20

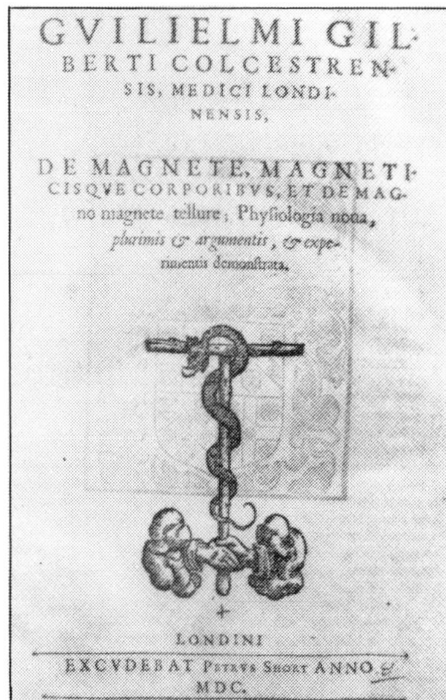

GVILIELMI GIL-
BERTI COLCESTREN-
SIS, MEDICI LONDI-
NENSIS,

DE MAGNETE, MAGNETI-
CISQVE CORPORIBVS, ET DE MAG-
no magnete tellure; Physiologia noua,
plurimis & argumentis, & experimentis demonstrata.

LONDINI
EXCVDEBAT Petrvs Short ANNO
MDC.

GILBERT, C. S.
'An Historical Survey of the County of Cornwall' – 3 vols. – engraved title – 2 frontis and 67 engraved plates – illus. – contem. calf – 4to. – Plymouth Dock, 1817-20.
(Christie's) $545 £260

GILBERT, WILLIAM
'De Magnete' – 1st. Edn. – woodcut device – woodcut arms on verso – contem. limp vellum – later endpapers – bookplate – folio – 1600.
(Christie's) $5,250 £2,500
'On the Magnet, Magnetick Bodies and on the Great Magnet, the Earth' – illus. – orig. limp vellum – soiled – Chiswick Press 1900.
(Christie's) $105 £50

GILCHRIST, A.
'The Life of William Blake' – 2 vols. – illus. – orig. cloth gilt – 8vo. – 1863.
(Phillips) $65 £30

GILCHRIST, JOHN
'A Dictionary, English and Hindoostanee' – 2 vol. – lacking 1 leaf – repairs – minor defects – calf – worn – folio – Calcutta 1786.
(Sotheby's) $105 £50

GILES, H. A.
'A Chinese-English Dictionary' – 4 pages in facsimile – orig. calf backed cloth – rubbed – 4to – 1892.
(Sotheby's) $95 £45

GILLARD, MARTIN
'Home and Other Poems' – inscribed and signed by the author – with a single page letter also inserted – Recipient's bookplate – Ilfracombe 1962.
(J. Ash) $6 £3

GILLES, NICOLAS
'Les Tres Elegantes, Tres Veridiques et Copieuses Annales .....' – 2 vols. in one – architectural woodcut title border – 3 woodcut illus. – one full page and 6 printed genealogical tables – crudely col. – 16th cent. mottled calf – folio – Paris Gaillot du Pre 1525.
(Christie's) $295 £140

GILPIN, WILLIAM
'Observations on Several Parts of Great Britain, Particularly The Highlands of Scotland' – vol. 2 – 3rd Edn. – 34 hand coloured aquatint plates – five slightly shaved – five maps and one table – later half morocco – joints rubbed – 1808.
(Christie's) $60 £28

GIMSON, ERNEST
'His Life and Work' – no. 84 of 500 copies - 9 wood engraved illus. by F. L. Griggs – plates – orig. linen backed boards – uncut – 4to. – 1924.
(Sotheby's) $440 £210

GINNINGWATER, EDMUND
'An Historical Account of the Ancient Town of Lowestoft' – half title – contem. half calf – joints weak – 4to. – 1790.
(Sotheby's) $180 £85

GIONA, J.
'Naissance de L'Odyssee' – limited Edn. – signed by artist and publisher – 26 lithos – uncut – unsewn – orig. vellum backed cloth – 4to. – Lausanne 1963.
(Phillips) $65 £30

GIOVANNI GRASSO
A quantity of material – including post cards – letters – cuttings etc. – collected by Henry Festing Jones – regarding the Sicilian actor.
(Christie's S. Kensington) $420 £200

GISBORNE, THOMAS
'An Inquiry into the Duties of Men' – calf gilt – 4to. – 1794.
(Phillips) $105 £50

GISSING, GEORGE
'The House of Cobwebs' – edges a little foxed – otherwise good copy – 1906.
(J. Ash) $34 £16

GITTINGS, ROBERT
'Famous Meeting' – Poems – very good in jacket – 1953.
(J. Ash) $6 £3

GLAISTER, J. AND OTHERS
'Voyages Aeriens' – litho addit. titles – 6 plates – plans and maps – spotting – contem. morocco backed cloth – slightly soiled – g.e. – large 8vo. – Paris 1870.
(Christie's S. Kensington) $75 £35

GLANCES AT CHARACTER
2st Edn. – 8 hand col. aquatint plates – browning – modern polished yellow calf – label – spine gilt – t.e.g. – sm. 8vo. – 1814.
(Sotheby's) $85 £40

GLASCOCK, CAPT. W. NUGENT
'Naval Sketch Book' – 2 vols. – engraved plates – contem. half calf – 8vo. – 1831.
(Sotheby's) $105 £50

GLASSE, H.
'Art of Cookery Made Plain and Easy' – calf gilt – 8vo. – 1788.
(Phillips) $135 £65

GLAUBER, JOHN RUDOLPH
'The Works ... containing Great Variety of Choice Secrets in Medicine and Alchymy' – 3 parts in 1 vol. – 10 plates only – four woodcut – six engraved – soiled – stained – modern morocco backed boards – printed by Thomas Milbourn .. by D. Newman .. and W. Copper 1689.
(Christie's S. Kensington) $105 £50

GLENCOE, THE MASSACRE OF
1st Edn. – browned – half calf – rebacked – rubbed – sm. 4to. – 1703.
(Sotheby's) $145 £70

GLENDINNING AND CO.
Priced catalogues in 9 vol. – plates – modern cloth – 4to. – 1950-72.
(Sotheby's) $190 £90

GMELIN, JOHANN GEORG
'Flora Sibirica' – 4 vols. – 286 engraved folding plates – some shaved – title spotted – morocco backed boards – 4to. St. Petersburg, 1747-69.
(Christie's) $1,050 £500

GOBINEAU, A.
'Histoires des Perses' – 2 vol. – contem. morocco backed boards – rubbed – folio – 1869.
(Sotheby's) $105 £50

GOBLE, WARWICK – BASILE, GIAMBATTISTA
'Stories from the Penramerone' – limited to 150 copies – 32 col. plates – orig. vellum gilt – lacking ties – rubbed – 4to. – 1911.
(Sotheby's) $190 £90

GODEY'S LADY'S BOOK FOR 1850, 1859 and 1869
3 vols. only – 132 plates – some hand coloured – some torn – various bindings – rubbed – 8vo. – Philadelphia, 1850-69.
(Sotheby's) $65 £32

GODFREY, AMBROSE
'An Account of Extinguishing Fires by Explosion and Suffocation' – modern morocco backed cloth – 8vo. – 1724.
(Sotheby's) $135 £65

GODFREY, M. J.
'Monograph and Iconograph of Native British Orchidaceae' – col. plates – orig. cloth – dust jacket – 4to.. – Cambridge, 1933.
(Sotheby's) $220 £105

GODOFRIDUS, PETRUS
'Dialogues de Amoribus' – half calf – Antwerp 1553.
(Phillips) $40 £20

GODWIN, WILLIAM
'Life of Geoffrey Chaucer' – 2 vols – engraved frontis — contem. calf gilt – 4to. – 1803.
(Phillips) $55 £25

GOEBEL, HEINRICH
'Wandteppiche 1 Teil die Miederlande' – 2 vols. including one of plates – cloth worn – 4to. – Leipzig 1923.
(Phillips) $115 £55

GOETHE, JOHANN WOLFGANG VON
Landscape in grey washes of a mill by a stream inscribed on verso by artist 24 x 33 cms. – slightly foxed and folded – in morocco case – 1831.
(Sotheby's) $14,700 £7,00

GOFFE, THOMAS
'Three Excellent Tragedies viz, The Raging Turk; The Courageous Turk and the Tragedie of Orestes' – 2nd. Edn. – contem. sheep – spine defective – 8vo. – 1656.
(Christie's) $230 £110

GOLD, CAPT. C.
'Oriental Drawings' – 35 of 49 – hand col. aqua plates – lacks title – calf – lacks upper cover – 4to. – 1806.
(Phillips) $335 £160

GOLDEN COCKEREL PRESS
'Chanticleer – a Bibliography of the Golden Cockerel Press' – number 239 of 300 numbered copies – signed by Christopher Sandford, 1936.
'Pertelote, a Sequel to Chanticleer' 1943 – numerous woodcuts by John Buckland-Wright, Lettice Sandford and others – orig. morocco backed cloth – or cloth first by Sangorski and Sutcliffe – 8vo. – Golden Cockerel Press.
(Sotheby Beresford Adams) $250 £120

GOLDING, WILLIAM
'The Pyramid' – 1st American Edn. – nice copy in slightly chipped dust wrapper – 1967.
(J. Ash) $8 £4

GOLDSMITH, OLIVER
'The Works' editor Peter Cunningham – 4 vol. – portrait – addit. titles contemp. calf – spine rubbed – n.d. – 1854.
(Christie's S. Kensington) $45 £22

GOLDSTON, WILL
'Exclusive Magical Secrets' – number 723 of an unspecified limitation – portrait frontis and illus. – many full page – orig. maroon morocco – slightly rubbed with lock and key – 4to. – 1912.
(Sotheby's) $440 £210

GOLF
A collection of 79 vol. on Golf with plates and illus. – most orig. cloth – slightly rubbed – some with dust jackets – 8vo. and 4to. – circa 1910.
(Sotheby's) $440 £210

GOMME, SIR BERNARD – 1620-85, Military Engineer
Auto sketch of two forts on the Medway drawn in pen and ink with auto annotations – creased and soiled – and dated on verso 1669.
(Sotheby's) $1,470 £700

GONSE, L.
'Art Japonais' – 2 vols. – illus. – decor silk boards – upper cover detached – 4to. – Paris 1883.
(Phillips) $160 £75

GOODEN, MONA
'The Poet's Cat - An Anthology' – engraved title and illustration at end by Stephen Gooden – one of 110 copies – signed by the author and the artist – orig. half calf – t.e.g. – 1946.
(Bonhams) $40 £20

GOODLAKE, THOMAS
'The Courser's Manual, or Stud-Book' – engr. portrait on india paper – a few wood-engraved vignettes – contemp. calf – rubbed – Liverpool, 1828.
(Christie's S. Kensington) $80 £38

GOODWIN, FRANCIS
'Domestic Architecture' – 2 vols. – 83 plates – some foxing and offsetting – cloth backed boards – paper labels – worn and soiled – 4to. – 1833-34.
(Sotheby's) $190 £90

GOODY TWO SHOES, THE HISTORY OF
34 of 35 wood engraved illus. – 2 pp adverts – orig. pictorial boards – lacking backstrip – 32 mo. – T. Carnan 1783.
(Sotheby's) $80 £38

GOOS, PIETER
'The Sea Atlas or the Water World' – engraved historiated title – double page map of the world and 39 double page charts on guards – 8 page index and intro in English – contem. calf – 18th cent. rebacking – folio – Amsterdam Pieter Goos 1675.
(Christie's) $11,550 £5,500

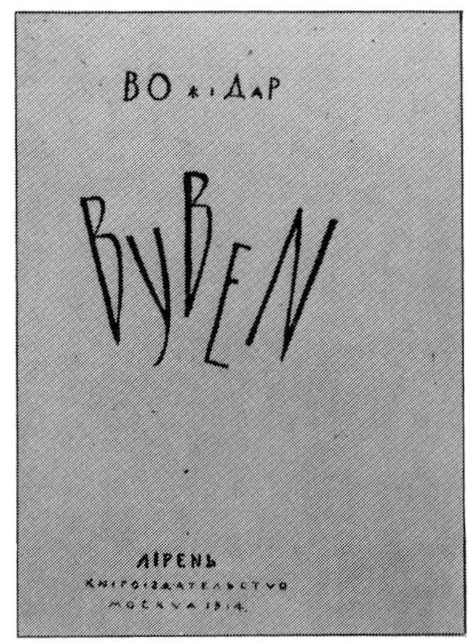

GORDEEV, BOGDAN
'Buben' (Tambourine) – 1st. Edn. – litho ms – orig. wrappers – 4to. – Moscow 1914.
(Sotheby's) $440 £210

GORDON, JOHN
'Engravings of the Skeleton of the Human Body' – 16 plates with explanatory text orig. boards – rebacked – uncut – 8vo. –Edinburgh 1818.
(Sotheby's) $20 £10

GORDON, P.
'Geography Anatomized' – 18th Edn. – 17 folding engraved maps – half title – contem. calf – worn – 8vo. – 1744.
(Sotheby's) $85 £40

GORDON, SETON
'Amid Snowy Wastes' – plates – maps – orig. cloth – spine faded – 1922.
(Christie's) $30 £15

GORDON, W. J.
'Our Home Railway' – 7 orig. parts of 12 – col. plates.
(Baitson) $23 £11

GORLAEUS, ABRAHAM
'Dactyliothecae seu Annulorum Sigillarium' – 2 parts in one – titles in red and black – 2 engraved frontis – 2 portraits – 1 folding – numerous plates – contem. vellum – soiled – 4to. – Leiden 1695.
(Sotheby's) $65 £32

GOSSE, E.
'British Portrait Painters and Engravers of the 18th Century' – 2 vols. – 1 of 100 copies on india paper – duplicate set of prints – orig. wrappers – cloth – slipcase – rubbed – folio – 1906.
(Sotheby's) $200 £95

GOSSE, PHILIP
'An Apple a Day' – illustrations and dust wrapper by Lynton Lamb – very good in worn dust wrapper – 1948.
(J. Ash) $6 £3

GOSTLING, GEORGE (editor)
'Extracts from the Treaties between Great Britain and Other Kingdoms and States' – 1st Edn. – engraved frontis – contem speckled calf – spine gilt – some wear – 4to. – 1792.
(Sotheby's) $40 £20

GOUGH, HENRY
'A Glossary of the Terms Used in British Heraldry' – 1st Edn. – half calf binding – 1847.
(Lane) $40 £20

GOUGH, RICHARD
'British Topography' – 2 vols. – engraved vignette on title – 9 folding maps – contem. calf – rebacked – 4to. – 1780.
(Sotheby's) $65 £30

GOULBURN LOVELL, R.
'Home Interiors' – section one – 30 coloured plates – 2 missing – cloth backed folio – n.d.
(Bennett Book Auction) $10 £5

GOULD, JOHN
'A Monograph of the Trocholidae' – 5 vols. – 1st Edn. – no supplement – 360 hand col. litho plates – contem. green morocco – gilt – spines tooled – slightly rubbed – gilt inside borders – g.e. – a fine copy – large folio – 1861.
(Sotheby's) $27,300 £13,000

GOULD-FREKE, ROBERT
'The History of Freemasonry' - 4 vols. bound in red and gilt morocco – illus. – 1887.
(Baitson) $45 £22

GOWER, JOHN
'Confessio Amantis' – 3 vol. – orig. cloth – soiled – 1857.
(Christie's S. Kensington) $30 £15

GOWER, LORD RONALD SUTHERLAND
'Sir Thomas Lawrence' – one of 200 copies – col. frontis – plates and illus. in 2 states – contemp. levant morocco – spine faded – folio – 1900.
(Sotheby's) $115 £55
'The Lenoir Collection of Original French Portraits at Stafford House' – 186 tinted lithos on 146 sheets – orig. cloth – soiled and dampstained – large folio – 1874.
(Sotheby's) $10 £5

GRAFF, REGNERUS DE
'Tractatus Anatomico-Medicus de Succi Pancreatici Natura et Usu' – addit. engraved title – 3 folding plates – contem calf – upper cover detached – sm. 8vo. – 1671.
(Christie's) $250 £120

GRAHAM, MARIA
'Journal of a Residence in India' – 2nd Edn. – coloured engraved frontis – 15 engraved plates – 2 folding – half title – contem. calf – gilt – rubbed – 4to. – Edinburgh 1813.
(Sotheby's) $65 £32

GRAHAM, R. B. CUNNINGHAME
'The Ipane' – rebound in a very handsome modern quarter calf – preserving the orig. wraps. – 1899.
(J. Ash) $55 £25

GRAHAME, KENNETH
'The Golden Age' – number 216 of 275 copies – signed by author – illus. by E. H. Shepherd – orig. cloth – worn – discoloured – t.e.g. – 8vo. – 1928.
(Sotheby's) $105 £50

GRAINGER, J.
'A Biographical History of England' – 4 vols. – calf gilt – 1779.
(Phillips) $45 £22

GRAND THEATRE AND OPERA HOUSE, HULL
Theatre programme printed on silk for Grand Opening Night – 9th Jan. 1893.
(Baitson) $45 £21

GRAND TOUR ON COACH BOX
Ms corrections and deletions by author – 19th cent. red half morocco – t.e.g. – 12 mo. – 1811.
(Sotheby's) $135 £65

GRANDE DANCE MACABRE, LA
'Des Hommes et Des Femmes' – illus. – contem. morocco – gilt – rubbed – 4to. Paris n.d.
(Sotheby's) $85 £40

GRANDJEAN DE MONTIGHY, A. AND A. FAMIN
'Architecture Toscaneou Palais, Maisons et Autres Edifices de la Toscane' – engraved plates – 1 lacking – contem. morocco backed boards – folio – Paris 1815.
(Sotheby's) $105 £50

GRANDPRE, L. DE
'A Voyage in the Indian Ocean and to Bengal' – 2 vols. – 6 plates – calf gilt – 1803.
(Phillips) $440 £210

GRANT, ANDREW
'History of Brazil' – 1st Edn. – browning – half calf – spine gilt – 8vo. – 1809.
(Sotheby's) $335 £160

GRANT, J.A.
'A Walk Across Africa' – folding map in pocket – spotting – orig. cloth – recased – rubbed – 8vo. – 1864.
(Sotheby's) $210 £100

GRANT, JAMES
'The Tartans of the Clans of Scotland' – coloured plates – orig. cloth – rubbed – split joints – t.e.g. – folio – 1886.
(Sotheby's) $40 £20

GRANTLEY, LORD
'Catalogue of Coins' – 11 vol. – plates – orig. wrappers – 4to. and 8vo. – 1943-45.
(Sotheby's) $400 £190

GRAPHIC, THE
24 vol. various – folio – various bindings – worn – 1870-1918.
(Christie's S. Kensington) $190 £90

GRAPHIC ILLUSTRATIONS OF ANIMALS
19 of 21 double page illus. by W. Hawkins – col by hand – torn repaired – orig. roan gilt – rubbed – folio – Thomas Varty circa 1855.
(Sotheby's) $125 £60

GRAVES, A.
'A Dictionary of Artists' – new Edn. – orig. morocco backed cloth – rubbed – 4to. – 1895.
(Sotheby's) $30 £15

GRAVES, C. AND LONGHURST, H.
'Candid Caddies' – 1935.
(Bennett Book Auction) $15 £7

CAREERS

FATHER is quite the greatest poet
That ever lived anywhere.
You say you're going to write great music—
I chose that first: it's unfair.
Besides, I can't be the greatest painter and do Christ, or angels, or lovely pears and apples and grapes on a green dish, or storms at sea, or anything lovely,
Because *that's been* taken by Claire.

It's stupid to be an engine-driver,
And soldiers are horrible men.
I won't be a tailor, I won't be a sailor,
And gardener's taken by Ben.
It's unfair if you say that you'll write great music, you horrid, you unkind (I simply loathe you though you are my sister) you beast, cad, coward, cheat, bully, liar,
Well? Say *what's left* for me then!

10

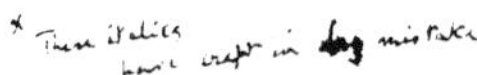

GRAVES, ROBERT
'Goliath and David' – 1st Edn. – limited to 200 copies – presentation copy – inscribed by author to De La Mare – auto note on p. 10 – original red wrappers – uncut – 8vo. – 1916.
(Sotheby's) $780 £370

'The Shout' – limited signed Edn. – orig. boards – 1929.
(Phillips) $60 £28

'Claudius The God' – 1934.
(J. Ash) $20 £10

GRAY, ANDREW
'The Plow-Wright's Assistant' – 1st. Edn. – 16 folding engraved plates – browning – 19th cent. half calf – label – spine gilt – rubbed – 8vo. – Edinburgh 1808.
(Sotheby's) $335 £160

GRAY, G. R.
'A Fasciculus of the Birds of China' – 12 hand col. plates – orig. boards – 4to. – 1871.
(Phillips) $380 £180

GRAY, RHODA
2 orig. pen drawings for the stage set of 'Chase Me Comrade' – at Whitehall Theatre by Rhoda Gray – coloured – one corner torn – 14 in. x 19½ in. – 1964.
(Sotheby Beresford Adams) $45 £22

GRAY, ROBERT
'Letters during .... a tour through Germany, Switzerland, Italy in the years 1791-2' – tree calf – 1794.
(Phillips) $80 £38

GRAY, THOMAS DE
'The Compleat Horseman and Expert Farrier' – title repaired – lacks port – half calf worn – 4to. – 1639.
(Phillips) $115 £55

GREAT MASTERS IN THE LOUVRE GALLERY
4 vol. – limited Edn. – plates – contem. half morocco – rubbed – folio – 1898-1900.
(Sotheby's) $30 £15

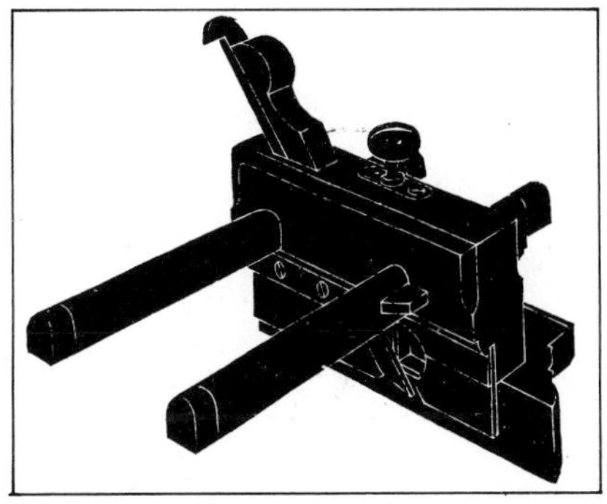

GREEN, A. ROMNEY
'Woodwork in Principle and Practice' – vol. 1 – 1st Edn. – 31 wood engraved illus. – 28 by Eric Gill – 3 by Ralph Beedham – orig. wrappers – uncut – library copy inscription – 8vo. – Douglas Pepler 1918.
(Sotheby's) $135 £65

GREEN, F. L.
'Mist on the Waters' – very good in chipped jacket – 1948.
(J. Ash) $6 £3

GREEN, HENRY
'Nothing' – 1st American Edn. – good – New York 1950.
(J. Ash) $8 £4

GREEN, JAMES AND THOMAS ROWLANDSON
'Poetical Sketches of Scarborough' – 2nd Edn. – 20 hand col. aquatint plates of 21 contem. calf – covers detached – 8vo. – R. Ackermann 1813.
(Sotheby's) $105 £50

GREEN, JOHN
'New General Collection of Voyages' – 4 vol. – plates and maps – half calf – worn – 4to. – 1745-47.
(Phillips) $420 £200

GREEN, THOMAS
'The Universal Herbal' – 2 vols. – 85 hand col. plates – some leaves missing – orig. boards – worn and torn – 4to. – n.d.
(Sotheby Bearne) $335 £160

GREEN, WILLIAM
'The Tourist's New Guide ..... Cumberland, Westmoreland and Lancashire' – 2 vols. – engraved folding map – 36 plates – some aquatint plates – later half green morocco gilt – spine faded – t.e.g. – 8vo. – Kendal 1819.
(Sotheby Beresford Adams) $275 £130

GREENAWAY, KATE
'Puck and Blossom, a Fairy Tale' – mounted illus. by Kate Greeaway printed in colours and gold – originally issued as greetings cards – orig. decorated cloth gilt – rubbed – 4to. – Marcus Ward circa 1875.
(Sotheby's) $170 £80

'A Day in a Child's Life' – Music by Myles B. Foster – coloured illustrations and decorations by Kate Greenaway, original cloth backed pictorial boards, soiled and slightly rubbed – Routledge, 1881.
(Sotheby's) $72 £32

A fine watercolour drawing of young children dancing in a ring – larger sheet with ruled border – signed with initials – discoloured – 80 mm x 130 mm.
(Sotheby's) $630 £300

GREENE, GRAHAM
'The End of the Affair' – covers slightly faded – otherwise a nice copy – 1951.
(J. Ash) $8 £4

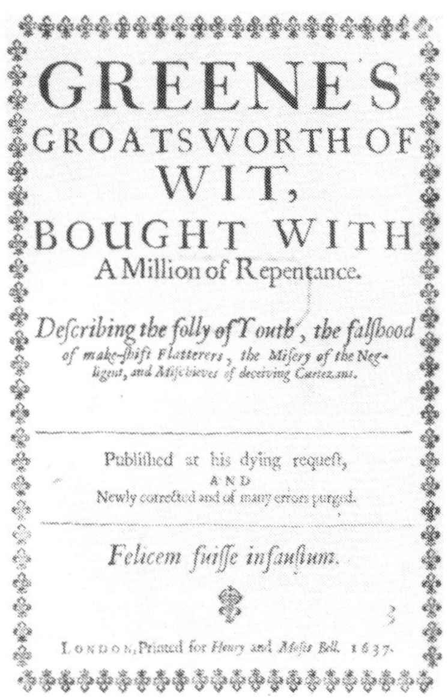

GREENE, ROBERT
'Greene's Groatsworth of Wit' – lacking initial but with final blank – morocco by Sangorski – sm. 4to. – 1637.
(Christie's) $5,250 £2,500

GREENE, W. T.
'Parrots in Captivity' – 3 vols. – 81 hand col. plates – orig. calf gilt – t.e.g. – 8vo. – 1884-87.
(Phillips) $1,155 £550

GREENWOOD, C. J.
'Mansions of England and Wales, County of Lancaster' – 49 lithographed plates – five coloured – some spotted without title or text – contemp. morocco backed cloth – rubbed g.e. disbound – 4to. – n.d.
(Christie's S. Kensington) $115 £55
'Maps of the Principality of Wales' – 5 engraved maps – vignettes – col in outline – mounted in linen – folded in sections – slipcase – each 66 cm x 76 cm – 1831-34.
(Sotheby's) $135 £65

GREENWOOD, J. F.
'Twenty four Woodcuts of Cambridge' – 24 woodcut illustrations – orig. cloth backed boards .
(Christie's S. Kensington) $40 £20

GREENWOOD'S MAP OF LONDON
Coloured with 2 large vignettes in 6 sheets – one corner slightly defective – 1830.
(Bonhams) $335 £160

GREGO, JOSEPH
'Rowlandson the Caricaturist' – 2 vol. – frontispiece – illustrations – slight spotting– contemp. cloth backed boards – soiled – spines worn – g.e. – 4to. – 1880.
(Christie's S. Kensington) $115 £55

GREGORY, I. A. LADY
'The Full Moon' – 1st Edn. – author's own copy – signed and inscribed by her – spotted – orig. wrappers – uncut – unopened – 8vo. – Dublin – by the author at the Abbey Theatre 1911.
(Sotheby's) $360 £170

GREGYNOG PRESS
'Lyfr y Pregeth-wr' – limited Edn. – orig. cloth – slight wear – 4to. – 1927.
(Phillips) $135 £65

GRELOT, W. J.
'A Late Voyage to Constantinople' – 8 folding plates – 6 single page – contem. calf rebacked – 1683.
(Phillips) $190 £90

GRESWELL, W. P.
'Annals of Parisian Typography' – 1st Edn. – title in red and black – 12 woodcut plates – browning – modern half calf – label – spine gilt – 8vo. – 1818.
(Sotheby's) $100 £48

GREVEDON, PIERRE-LOUIS HENRY
'Mosaique de Costumes' – engraved title and 6 only hand col. litho costume portraits – soiled – title foxed – contem. morocco backed boards – large folio – Paris circa 1830.
(Christie's) $170 £80

GREVILLE, CHARLES
'The Greville Memoirs' – 8 vol. including index – one of 630 copies – plates – orig. cloth – t.e.g. – 8vo. – 1938.
(Sotheby's) $440 £210

GREW, NEHEMIAH
'Musaeum Regalis Societatis or a Catalogue & Description of the Natural and Artificial Ratities Belonging to the Royal Society ... Where unto is subjoyned the Comparitive Anatomy of Stomache and Guts' – 2 parts in one – folio – 31 engr. plates – portrait lacking – soiled and dampstained – old calf – worn – Printed by W. Rawlins for the author, 1681.
(Christie's S. Kensington) $180 £85

GRIERSON, P.
'Dumbarton Oaks Collection' – vol. 3 only – plates – orig. cloth – 4to. – Washington 1973.
(Sotheby's) $95 £45

GRIFFITH, SAMUEL YOUNG
'New Historical Description of Cheltenham and Its Vicinity' – large paper copy – engraved title – 50 mounted plates – 1 folding engraved map – 25 other engraved plates – roan backed orig. printed boards – uncut and unopened – 4to. – 1826.
(Christie's) $420 £200

GRIFFITHS, J.
'Travels in Europe, Asia Minor and Arabia' – portrait – map and plates – 1st Edn. – 4to. – boards uncut – 1805.
(Bonhams) $85 £40

GRIGSON, GEOFFREY
'Sad Grave of an Imperial Mongoose' – Poems – very good – dust wrapper – 1973.
(J. Ash) $8 £4
'Samuel Palmer, the Visionary Years' – plates, original cloth, dust jacket, slightly torn – 1947.
(Christie's S. Kensington) $40 £18

GRIMALDI, STACEY
'The Toilet' – 3rd Edn. – engraved pictorial title – 9 plates col by hand – orig. boards – spine worn – 16mo. – Published by author and sold by R. Ackermann 1823.
(Sotheby's) $135 £65

GRIMESTONE, EDWARD
'A Generall Historie of the Netherlands' – 1st. Edn. – title in engraved border – numerous engraved portraits – 19th cent. tree calf – upper cover detached – folio 1608.
(Sotheby's) $315 £150

GRINDLAY, ROBERT MELVILLE
'Scenery, Costumes and Architecture chiefly on the Western Side of India' – 2 vol. in one – 1st Edn. – 2 engraved vignette titles – 18 hand col. aquatint plates – browned – marginal spotting – 19th cent. cloth – spine defective – some wear – folio – 1826-30.
(Sotheby's) $250 £120

GRISET, ERNEST – AESOP
'Fables' – wood engraved illus. after Griset – orig. pictorial cloth – gilt – g.e. – 4to. – Cassell 1870.
(Sotheby's) $95 £45

GROSE, FRANCIS
'The Antiquities of Ireland' – 2 vols. – 1st Edn. – large paper copy – engraved titles and numerous plates – slight browning – 19th cent. green half morocco – rubbed and soiled – g.e. – 4to. – 1791.
(Sotheby's) $160 £75
'The Antiquities of England and Wales' – 8 vols. – numerous engraved plates – quarto – attractively bound in uniform full calf gilt – new Edn. – circa 1785.
(Richard Baker & Thomson) $380 £180

GROSZ, GEORGE
'Gedichte und Gesange' – pictorial title, 4 full page illustrations, tail piece and cover design by Grosz, sewn, loose as issued, original wrappers, uncut, folder and slip-case – Josef Portman, Litomysl, 1932.
(Sotheby's, Chancery Lane) $1,125 £500

GROTESQUES
A series of 7 watercolour drawings of grotesque characters in 17th and 18th cent. costume – 2 with Italian verses below – separate card mounts – average size 245 mm x 175 mm.
(Sotheby's) $250 £120

GROTIUS, H.
'Annotationum in Novum Testamentum' – 3 vols. – titles in red and black – contem. vellum – folio – Paris 1644-50.
(Phillips) $75 £35

'Traite de la Veritie de la Religion' – contem. French binding of red morocco gilt with arms of Madame Adelaide de France – daughter of Louis XV – 8vo. – 1724.
(Moore Allen & Innocent) $545 £260

GRUBE, E. J.
'Islamic Pottery of the 8th to the 15th Century in the Keir Collection' – plates – col. – cloth – 4to. – 1976.
(Phillips) $55 £25

GRUNER, LEWIS
'The Terracotta Architecture of North Italy' – 48 plates mostly colour – quarter morocco gilt – t.e.g. – 4to. – 1867.
(Phillips) $180 £85

GRUTERI
'Animadversiones' – 2 vols. – late 16th cent. Parisian binding dark blue morocco gilt – decorated and tooled with arms of Pietro Duodo – bound in two red morocco cases – vol. 2 restored – Paris 1595.
(Moore Allen & Innocent) $1,890 £900

GUARANA, JACOPO
'Oracoli Auguri, Aruspici, Sibille ...' – 66 leaves – engraved throughout – some soiling – modern half morocco – rubbed – t.e.g. – folio – Venice 1792.
(Christie's) $115 £55

GUARINI
'Il Pastor Fido' – trans. by Sir R. Fanshawe – contem dark blue morocco gilt with royal arms of Charles I and his cypher on each cover – presentation copy from translator to Charles I – signed C. R. in King's hand on flyleaf – blue morocco case with silver medal inset – 4to. – 1647.
(Moore Allen & Innocent) $10,080 £4,800

GUERINIERE, MONSIEUR DE LA
'Ecole de Cavalrie' – 2 vols – 27 plates – 4 folding – browning – later half calf – worn – Paris 1769.
(Christie's) $115 £55

GUESS IF YOU CAN
Wood engraved vignette on title and illus. – decorative borders in various colours – orig. cloth gilt – worn – g.e. – 8vo. – David Bogue 1851.
(Sotheby's) $40 £20

GUISNEE, M.
'Application de L'Algebre a la Geometrie' – 2nd. Edn. – 4to. – eight folding engraved plates – slight soiling throughout – contemp. calf – joints cracked – Paris 1733.
(Christie's S. Kensington) $25 £12

GUMUCHIAN ET CIE
'Les Livres D'Enfance du XVe au XIX Siecle' – 2 vol. – no. 9 of 1000 copies – one of 100 copies on Hollande – mod half morocco – rubbed – spine faded – 4to – Paris 1930.
(Sotheby's) $440 £210

GUNN, JOHN
'An Historical Enquiry Respecting the Performance on the Harp in the Highlands of Scotland' – 3 engraved plates – spotting – cloth back boards – worn – uncut – 4to. – Edinburgh 1807.
(Sotheby's) $210 £100

GUNN, THOM.
'Moly' – very good copy in slightly rubbed jacket – 1971.
(J. Ash) $12 £6

GUNNELL, WILLIAM A.
'Sketches of Hull Celebrities' – half leather binding – 1876.
(Baitson) $4 £2

GURNEY, DANIEL
'The Record of the House of Gourney' – plates and maps – some hand col. – illus. – later morocco by Zaehnsdorf – slightly scuffed – g.e. – 4to. – 1848.
(Christie's S. Kensington) $40 £20

GUSMAN, PIERRE
'Pompei, The City, its Life and Arts' – 4to. – coloured plates – illustrations – orig. cloth – 1900.
(Christie's S. Kensington) $60 £28

GUTHRIE, TYRONE
'Squirrel's Cage and Two other Microphone Plays' – title-label worn – spine little darkened – otherwise nice – 1931.
(J. Ash) $12 £6

GUTHRIE, W.
'A New Geographical, Historical and Commercial Grammer' – maps – sheep – worn – 8vo. – 1783.
(Sotheby's) $85 £40

GUYONNEAU DE PAMPOUR, CHEV. F.M.
'A Practical Treatise on Locomotive Engines upon Railways' – 4 folding plates – spotted – orig. cloth – rebacked – rubbed – 8vo. – 1836.
(Sotheby's) $75 £35

GWINNETT, A.
'The Life, Strange Voyages and Uncommon Adventures of Ambrose Gwinnett' – 4th Edn – engraved frontis – 19th cent. polished yellow calf – rubbed – 12mo. – circa 1773.
(Sotheby's) $85 £40

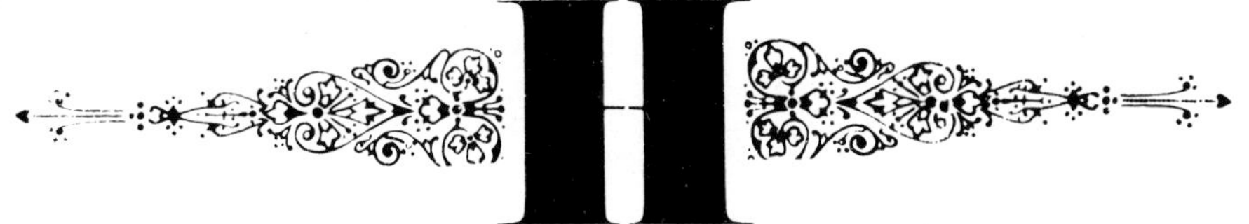

H. A.
'The Life and Letters of John Harris, the Cornish Cocker' – with coloured and other plates of fighting cocks – orig. cloth – 1910.
(Lane) $40 £18

HABINGTON, WILLIAM
'The Historie of Edward the Fourth, King of England' – 1st Edn. – portrait frontis – browning – contem. sheep – worn – folio – 1640.
(Sotheby's) $95 £45

HACHETTE, M.
'Traite Elementaire des Machines' – a 2nd Edn. – 4to – Paris – 32 folding engraved plates – few tears – slight spotting – contemp. half calf – rebacked – ex-library copy – 1819.
(Christie's S. Kensington) $65 £32

HACK, MARIA
'Winter Evening or Tales of Travellers' – four vols. – 1819.
(Allen & May) $12 £6

HADELN, DETLEV VON
'The Drawings of Tiepolo' – 2 vols. – plates – orig. half morocco – worn – t.e.g. – 4to. – Paris 1928.
(Sotheby's) $180 £85

HADEN, SIR FRANCIS SEYMOUR 1818-1910
Early auto diaries and sketch books recording his formative tour of Italy 1843-44 with sketches in pencil, ink and watercolour on 45 pages – c. 250 pages – half calf – worn – sm. and large octavo together with his passport – printed material and some 70 letter.
(Sotheby's) $1,995 £950

HADLEY, GEORGE
'A New and Complete History of the Town and County of Kingston upon Hull' – embellished with superb engravings – Hull 1788.
(Baitson) $160 £75

HAESAERTS, PAUL
'James Ensor' – plates – mounted coloured illustrations – original cloth – dust jacket – 1957.
(Christie's S. Kensington) $25 £12

HAGHE, LOUIS
'Sketches in Belgium and Germany' – 3 vol. – 3 tinted lithographed titles and 76 plates – some slight spotting – most leaves detached – contemporary morocco backed cloth – gilt – slightly damp stained – lower spines slightly rubbed – folio 1840-50.
(Christie's S. Kensington) $400 £190

HAIG, J.
'Topographical and Historical Account of the Town of Kelso' – engraved frontis and plates – original bds – uncut – 1st Edn. – Edinburgh 1825.
(Bennett Book Auction) $95 £46

HAILEY, ARTHUR
'The Final Diagnosis' – very good in dust wrapper – New York 1959.
(J. Ash) $20 £10

HAIN, LUDWIG
'Repertorium Bibliographicum' – 4 vol. – orig. cloth – 8vo. – Milan 1948.
(Sotheby's) $105 £50

HAKEWILL, JAMES
'Eight Views in the Zoological Gardens' – 8 lithographed plates – modern wrappers – orig. wrappers preserved – oblong 8vo. – n.d.
(Sotheby's) $145 £70
'A Picturesque Tour of Italy' – addit. engraved title and 63 plates – contem. calf – spine – covers detached – folio – 1820.
(Christie's) $125 £60

HAKLUYT, R.
'The Principal Voyages ..... of the English Nation' – 12 vol. – limited Edn. – plates and maps – spotting – orig. cloth – rubbed – t.e.g. – 8vo. – Glasgow 1903-05.
(Sotheby's) $190 £90

HALE, SIR MATTHEW
'Contemplations Moral and Divine' – 2 parts in one vol. – 1st Edn. – last leaf blank – contem. calf rubbed – 8vo. – 1676.
(Sotheby's) $55 £25

HALEN, J.
'Narrative of Imprisonment in the Dungeons of the Inquisition' – 2 vol. – 7 plates and maps – contemp. half calf – rebacked – 8vo. – 1827.
(Sotheby's) $65 £30

HALES, STEPHEN
'Some Considerations on the Causes of Earthquakes' – 23 pp lacks half title – new boards – 8vo. – R. Manby and H. S. Cox, 1750.
(Sotheby's) $80 £38

HALFORD, FREDERIC M.
'Modern Development of the Dry Fly' – 2 vol. – number 43 of 75 de luxe copies signed by author – portrait – plates – some col. – specimen flies on sunken mounts – orig. half calf – gilt – rubbed – 4to. – 1910.
(Sotheby's) $1,300 £620

HALL, CAPT BASIL
'Account of a Voyage of Discovery to the West Coast of Corea' – 1st Edn. – 5 engraved maps – 2 folding – one litho plate – one engraved plate and 8 hand col. aquatint plates – lacks half title – dust soiled – contem. roan backed boards – cloth corners – rubbed – 4to. – 1818.
(Sotheby's) $275 £130
'Voyage au Chili, au Perou et au Mexique' – 2 vols. – 1st French Edn. – folding map – half titles – library stamp – 19th cent. half calf – slightly rubbed – 8vo. Paris 1825.
(Sotheby's) $65 £30

HALL, EDWARD
'The Union of the two Noble and Illustre Families of Lancastre and York' – black letter – damp stained and soiled – some leaves defective or missing – 17th cent. calf – very worn – covers detached – folio – 1548?
(Sotheby's) $105 £50

HALL, HENRY (editor)
'The Tribune Book of Open Air Sports' – 1st Edn. – illus. – adverts at end – orig. cloth – worn – 8vo. – New York 1887.
(Sotheby's) $105 £50

HALL, M.
'Commentaries on some of the More Important Diseases of Females' – 8 coloured plates, 1st Edn., boards, uncut, with two others – 1827.
(Bonhams) $180 £80

HALL, REV. PETER
'Picturesque Memorials of Salisbury' – 29 engraved plates – illus. – last errata leaf – contem. half calf – rubbed – 4to. – Salisbury 1834.
(Sotheby's) $65 £30

HALL, RADCLYFFE
'The Well of Loneliness' – 1st Edn. – inscribed by the author – some spotting – orig. cloth – slightly soiled – 1928.
(Christie's S. Kensington) $65 £30

HALL, S. C. (editor)
'The Vernon Gallery of British Art' – 4 vols. – engraved plates – quarto.
(Richard Baker & Thomson) $125 £60
'The Baronial Halls and Picturesque Edifices of England' – 72 lithographed plates after S. Prout and others – some margins soiled – some leaves spotted – contemp. red calf – elaborately gilt – rubbed – 4to. – 1848.
(Christie's S. Kensington) $85 £40
'Selected Pictures from the Galleries and Private Collections in Great Britain' – 4 vol. – engraved plates – contem. half morocco – rubbed – folio – n.d.
(Sotheby's) $1,575 £750

HALL, MR AND MRS S. C.
'Ireland; Its Scenery, Character etc.' – 3 vol. – new Edn. – additional titles and 61 plates – seven coloured – four coloured maps – orig. cloth – faded – New York, n.d.
(Christie's S. Kensington) $85 £40

HALL, W. H.
'New Encyclopaedia' – Vols. 1 and 3 of 3 – plates – calf – covers loose – folio – 1779.
(Phillips) $65 £32

HALLAM, H.
'Views of the State of Europe during the Middle Ages' – 2 vols. – fine bindings – Parish 1835.
(Allen & May) $30 £14

HALLE, JOHANN SAMUEL
'Die Deutsch Giftplanzen, zur Verhutung der Tragischen Vorfalle, nebst den Heilungsmitteln' – engr. vignette on title – 32 hand coloured engr. plates – contemp. half calf.
(Sotheby's) $505 £240

HALLER, ALBRECHT VON
'Bibliotheca Anatomica' – 2 vol. – 1st Edn. – browning – late 19th cent. green half morocco – 4to – Zurich 1774-77.
(Sotheby's) $400 £190
'Physiology' – 2vols. – cover detached of 1 – 1772.
(Phillips) $40 £20

HALLEY, EDMUND
'Catalogus Stellarum Australium' – 1st Edn. – lacks map – five nos. of the Phil Trans 1708-15 bound in at end – 18th cent half calf – upper cover detached – Kenney copy – sm. 4to. – Thomas James for R. Harford 1679.
(Sotheby's) $75 £35

HALLIDAY, T.
'Numerical Games' – half calf – 8vo. – 1819.
(Phillips) $60 £28

HALLIWAY, J. O.
'Rambles in Western Cornwall' – 1st Edn. – 1861.
(Lane) $45 £22

HAMERTON, PHILIP GILBERT
'The Graphic Arts' – plates – mounted illus. – occas. spotting – inner hinges cracked – g.e. – 1854.
(Christie's) $45 £22
'Landscape' – limited Edn. – plates contem. vellum – gilt – folio – 1885.
(Phillips) $105 £50
'Etchings and Etchers' – 1st Edn., 35 plates after Palmer, Haden, Rembrandt and others, some spotting, original morocco backed cloth, rubbed, g.e., large 8vo.
(Christie's S. Kensington) $855 £380

HAMERTON, P. G. AND CAMPBELL DODGSON
'The Etchings of Rembrandt' – no. 193 of 250 copies – etched plates – orig. cloth – rubbed – t.e.g. – folio – 1905.
(Sotheby's) $95 £45

HAMILTON, CHARLES (Frank Richards)
A collection of his works including 14 Billy Bunter titles all but two 1st. Edn. – 11 other titles by Frank Richards and Owen Conquest and 6 duplicates – 31 vol. in all – illus. – orig. cloth – some worn – some dust jackets – with the 'Best of Magnet' and 'Gem' 2 copies – orig. wrappers – n.d. – 4to and 8vo. – 1947-61.
(Sotheby's) $95 £45

HAMILTON, ELIZABETH
'Memoirs of the Life of Agrippina' – 3 vols. half calf gilt – 1804.
(Phillips) $95 £45

My dearest & kind friend
ten thousand thanks for
your goodness. He sent
ten – God bless you
Do not forget that your
friendship is to me invaluable

HAMILTON, LADY EMMA
Three auto letters signed Emma and E. H. – 3 pages – quarto and octavo – from 12 Temple Place and no place to Sir Richard Puleston expressing gratitude to him for alleviating her financial hardship – seal – seal tears – traces of stitching.
(Sotheby's) $600 £280

HAMILTON, ROBERT
'The Natural History of British Fishes' – 2 vols. – 68 hand col. plates – modern half morocco – 8vo. –Edinburgh, 1843.
(Sotehby's) $180 £85

HAMILTON, VEREKER M. J. AND STEWART M. FASSON
'Scenes in Ceylon' – oblong folio – 20 plates – margins soiled – some leaves creased – orig. morocco backed cloth – rubbed – n.d.
(Christie's S. Kensington) $55 £25

HAMILTON, SIR WILLIAM
'Observations on Mount Vesuvius' – 1st Edn. – 5 engraved plates – folding map – foxing and offsetting – map torn – contem. russia – joints rubbed – 8vo. – 1772.
(Sotheby's) $335 £160

HAMILTON, W.
'Vampi Phlegreai' – 59 plates – titles and double page map after Fabris with fine cont. watercolouring of volcanoes, views etc. – orig. quarter leather bindings – ornamental boards – large 4to – Naples, 1776.
(Graves, Son & Pilcher) $12,600 £6,000

HAMLEY, LIEUT. COL. E. BRUCE
'The Story of the Campaign of Sebastopol' – folding litho map – torn – 9 litho plates – 4 coloured – contem. half calf – rubbed – 1855.
(Christie's) $30 £15

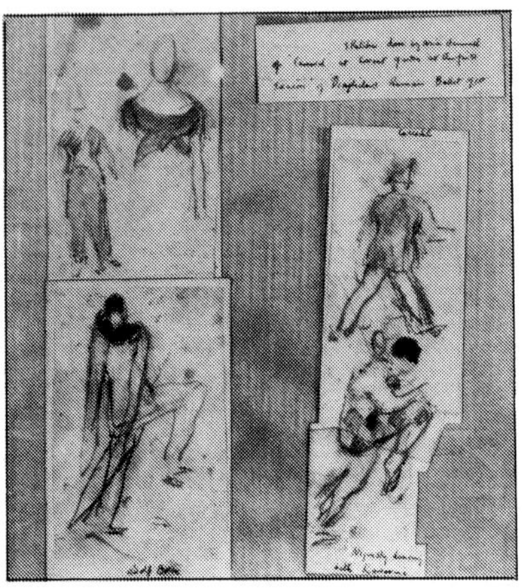

HAMNETT, NINA
'Sketches of Adolf Bolm, Cecchetti and Nijinsky dancing in 'Carnaval' – pencil and watercolour heightened with gouache – one signed and dated 1910 – 9.5 cm x 7 cm.
(Sotheby's) $670 £320

HANCOCK, JOHN
Framed mss with portrait – engraved – 1786.
(Robert Skinner) $650 £310

HANCOCK, THOMAS
'Personal Narrative of the Origin and Progress of Caoutchouc or India Rubber Manufacture in England' – portrait – 19 plates – 3 folding – portraits and title mounted – dampstains – spotting – cloth – 8vo. – Longman etc. 1857.
(Sotheby's) $115 £55

HANDEL, G. F.
'Saul, Samson, Joshua, Theodora' – 4 vols. of scores – engraved throughout – half calf worn – 18th cent.
(Phillips) $135 £65

HANLEY, GERALD
'Gilligan's Last Elephant' – very good in the David Shepherd dust wrapper – 1962.
(J. Ash) $6 £3

HANLEY, JAMES
'Winter Song' – good – 1950.
(J. Ash) $6 £3

HANNOVER, EMIL AND BARNARD RACKHAM
'Pottery and Porcelain, a Handbook for Collectors' – 3 vols. – plates – some col. – illus. – orig. cloth – rubbed – 8vo. – 1925.
(Sotheby's) $95 £45

HANNOVER, NATHAN NATA
'Yeveun Metzelah' – 2nd Edn. – title in border – slight discoloration – signed – half leather and four reprints – 1648-49.
(Sotheby's) $505 £240

HANQAY, JONAS
'A Journal of Eight Days Journey from Portsmouth to Kingston on Thames' – engraved frontis – orig. boards – rebacked – rubbed – 4to. – 1756.
(Sotheby's) $125 £60

HANSHALL, J. H.
'The History of the County Palatine of Chester' – engraved portrait – title – map – 25 plates and one folding plan – spotting – contemp. half calf – worn – 4to. – Chester 1817.
(Christie's S. Kensington) $75 £35

HANWAY, JONAS
'An Historical Account of the British Trade over the Caspian Sea' – 2nd. Edn. – 2 vols. – frontis – 9 folding maps and 15 plates – contem. calf – 4to. – 1754.
(Christie's) $125 £60

'Historical Account of the British Trade over the Caspian Sea' – 4 vols. – 19 plates – 9 maps – calf gilt – 4to. – 1753.
(Phillips) $275 £130

HARDIE, MARTIN
'The Work of Lee Hankey' – number 84 of 350 copies – this is one of 110 of the 'Edition de luxe' (1921) plates – lacking the original signed etching – slight soiling – orig. cloth – soiled.
(Christie's S. Kensington) $95 £45

'Water Colour Painting in Britain' – 3 vols. – col. Frontis – plates – orig. cloth – 4to. – batsford 1967-69.
(Christie's) $125 £60

'Water Colour Painting in Britain' – 3 vol. – plates – orig. cloth – 4to. – 1967-68.
(Sotheby's) $295 £140

HARDING, J. D.
'Harding's Drawing Book for the Year 1841' – 24 sepia litho plates – advert leaf at end – waterstain – orig. half roan – spine gilt – some wear – oblong 4to. – 1841.
(Sotheby's) $115 £55

'Seventy Five Views of Italy and France' – 75 mounted India paper plates, spotting, cont. half morocco, worn, front inner hinge split, g.e., folio – 1834.
(Christie's S. Kensington) $380 £170

HARDY, THOMAS
'Far From the Madding Crowd' – no. 204 of 1500 copies – signed by artist – 19 full page wood engraved illus. and decorations in text by Agnes Miller Parker – another impression of first illus signed by artist loosely inserted – orig. morocco backed boards – slipcase – 8vo. – New York 1958.
(Sotheby's) $360 £170

'Works: The Wessex Novels' – 18 vols., maps, original cloth, spines of eight faded, rubbed – 1902-15.
(Sotheby's) $125 £55

'The Melancholy Hussar' – 1st Edn. in book form of this tale – rebound in attractive near contemporary cloth – very good – 1890.
(J. Ash) $20 £10

HARE, FRANCIS BISHOP
'The Conduct of the Duke of Marlborough during the Present War' – 1st Edn. – browning – contem. panelled calf – rubbed – 8vo. – 1712.
(Sotheby's) $40 £20

HARGRAVE, E.
'The History of the Castle, Town and Forest of Knaresborough with Harrogate' – 4th Edn. – 12mo. – York – 1789 – seven engraved plates – one hand coloured map – illustrations – orig. boards – soiled – backstrip lacking.
(Christie's S. Kensington) $45 £22

HARLEIAN MISCELLANY
8 vol. – intro by Samuel Johnson – browning – contem. calf – joints split – bookplate of Richard Cox – 4to. – 1744-46.
(Sotheby's) $170 £80

HARPER, C.
'English Pen Artists of Today' – plates – cloth – limited Edn. 775 copies – 4to. – 1891.
(Bennett Book Auction) $25 £12

HARRINGTON, JAMES, THE ELDER
'The Commonwealth of Oceana' – 1st Edn. – title in red and black – browning – contem. calf – rebacked – rubbed – folio – 1656.
(Sotheby's) $40 £20

HARRIOT, THOMAS
'Artis Analyticae Praxis' – 1st Edn. – errata leaf at end – half morocco – folio – 1631.
(Christie's) $1,050 £500

HARRIOTT, LIEUT JOHN
'Struggles Through Life ..... in Europe, Asia, Africa and America' – 2 vol. – 1st Edn. – engraved port. – contem. blue half morocco – g.e. – William Beckford's copy – 12 mo. – 1807.
(Sotheby's) $250 £120

HARRIS, JOSEPH
'The Description and Use of the Globes and the Orrery' – title and frontis detached – 7 folding plates – calf – 1751.
(Phillips) $65 £30

HARRIS, MOSES
'Exposition of English Insects' – engraved title frontis – 51 hand col. plates – calf gilt – 4to. – 1782.
(Phillips) $670 £320

HARRIS, THOMAS
'Goya, Engravings and Lithographs' – 2 vols. – plates – mounted – orig. cloth – dust jackets – folio – Oxford 1964.
(Sotheby's) $250 £120

HARRIS, W. C.
'The Highlands of Aethiopia' – 3 vols. – 1st. Edn. – frontis – folding map – chromolith dedication – spotted – orig. cloth – faded – 8vo. – 1844.
(Sotheby's) $275 £130

HARRISON, WILLIAM
'Bibliotheca Monensis. A Bibliographical Account of the Works Relating to the Isle of Man' – 2 vol. – New Edn. – interleaved – contemp. half morocco – slightly soiled – Douglas, Printed for the Manx Society, 1876.
(Christie's S. Kensington) $65 £30

HARROW MEMORIALS OF THE GREAT WAR
6 vol. – portraits – orig. holland backed boards – soiled – t.e.g. – 4to. – 1918-21.
(Sotheby's) $65 £30

HARROW SCHOOL SONG BOOK
Lower endleaf torn – orig. cloth gilt – somewhat worn – 8vo. – with self portrait of Cecil Beaton on recto of upper endleaf with ink and pencil notes and long ink note about his singing during his first term at the school – 1904.
(Sotheby's) $145 £70

HART, MAJOR H.
New Army List etc. – half morocco – 1850.
(Bennett Book Auction) $34 £16

HART, JAMES
'Kainikh or the Diet of the Diseased' – woodcut initials and ornaments – contem. calf – rebacked – spine repaired – folio – John Beale for Robert Allot 1633.
(Sotheby's) $400 £190

HARTGERS, JOAST
'Tragicum Theatrum Actorum & Casuum Tragicorum Londini Publice Celebratorum' – device on title – 8 engraved portraits – 1 folding plate – browned – contem. vellum – inside hinges broken – 12 mo. Amsterdam 1649.
(Sotheby's) $125 £60

HARTLEY, L. P.
'The Hireling' – very good in dust wrapper – 1957.
(J. Ash) $20 £9

HARVEY, GIDEON
'The Vanities of Philosophy and Physick' – 1st Edn. – contem. calf – rebacked – 8vo. – A. Riper and R. Basset 1699.
(Sotheby's) $145 £70

HARVEY, WILLIAM
'Geographical Fun: being Humourous Outlines of Various Countries' – 12 lithographed pictorial maps – slight spotting – unbound – original cloth – corners bumped – 4to. – 1868.
(Christie's S. Kensington) $360 £170

HASLEM, JOHN
'The Old Derby China Factory' – coloured frontispiece – slightly spotted – and plates – original cloth – spine slightly torn – t.e.g. –1876.
(Christie's S. Kensington) $75 £35

HASLUCK, PAUL N.
'The Automobile' – 3 vol. – special Edn. – plates – illus. – orig. cloth – rubbed – 8vo. – 1905.
(Sotheby's) $105 £50

HASSALL, JOHN
Illustrator 'Haden Coffin's Book'.
(J. Ash) $10 £5

HASSELL, J.
'Tour of the Isle of Wight' – 2 vols. – 2 engraved titles – 30 tinted lithos – half calf gilt – 1790.
(Phillips) $100 £48

HASSELQUIST, F.
'Voyages and Travels in the Levant' – folding map – calf gilt – 8vo. – 1766.
(Phillips) $180 £85

HASTED, EDWARD
'The History and Topographical Survey of the the County of Kent' – 12 vol. – 2nd Edn. – 66 engraved plates – maps – engraved vignettes – browning and soiling – contem. mottled calf – rebacked – 8vo. – Canterbury 1797-1801.
(Sotheby's) $485 £230

HASTINGS, HON WARREN
'Of the Means of Guarding Dwelling Houses by the Construction Against Accidents by Fire' – last 2 advert leaves – modern boards – unopened – 8vo. – 1816.
(Sotheby's) $75 £35

HATSELL, JOHN
'Precedents of Proceedings in the House of Commons' – 4 vols. – contem. calf gilt – 4to. – 1796.
(Phillips) $60 £28

HATZFELD, ADOLF VON – LAURENCIN, MARIE
'Sommer' – 4 lithos by Laurencin – signed by artist – etched portrait by Adolf Kaufmann – signed – loose as issued in folder – folio – Dusseldorf – Galerie Flechtheim 1920.
(Sotheby's) $210 £100

HAVARD, H.
'Dictionnaire de l'Ameublement' – 4 vol. – plates – some coloured – orig. wrappers torn – 1 vol loose – 4to. – Paris.
(Sotheby's) $105 £50

HAVERSCHMIDT, F.
'Birds of Surinam' – illus. by P. Barruel – cloth gilt – 4to. – 1958.
(Phillips) $190 £90

HAWKER, R. S.
'Cornish Ballads and Other Poems' – Publisher's presentation copy blind stamp – orig. cloth – expertly restored new endpapers – Oxford 1869.
(J. Ash) $75 £36

HAWKES, JACQUETTA
'Dawn of the Gods' – limited signed Edn. – blue morocco gilt – overlay on upper cover – g.e. by Zaehnsdorf – buckram box – 4to. – 1969.
(Phillips) $60 £28

HAWKESWORTH, JOHN
'An Account of the Voyages in the Southern Hemisphere' – 3 vol. – 2nd Edn. – 51 of 52 engraved plates and charts – some double page or folding – lacks 1 chart – spotting – contem. calf – worn – one cover detached – 4to. – 1773.
(Sotheby's) £485 £230

HAWKINS, E. AND OTHERS
'Medallic Illustrations of the History of Great Britain and Ireland' – 2 vol. – library stamp – orig. cloth – rubbed – 8vo. – 1885.
(Sotheby's) $80 £38

HAWKINS, MARY
'Plymouth Armada Heroes' – bound in full vellum – 1888.
(Lane) $25 £12

HAY, DAVID
'The Clans of Scotland' – 12 hand col. plates in accordion pull out form – orig. boards – worn – Edinburgh n.d.
(Christie's) $55 £25

HAY, GEORGE
'The Book of Hospitalfield' – no. 5 of 14 copies – portrait – plates orig. vellum – soiled – t.e.g. – boxed – 4to – privately printed 1894,
(Christie's $40 £18

HAY, ROBERT
'Illustrations of Cairo' – col. title – dedication – 30 litho illus. – soiled – dampstained – contem. morocco backed cloth – worn – loose – folio – 1840.
(Sotheby's) $525 £250

HAYDEN, ARTHUR (editor)
'The Furniture Designs of Chippendale, Hepplewhite and Sheraton' – plates – modern cloth – 4to – 1910.
(Christie's S. Kensington) $30 £15

HAYES, WILLIAM
'A Natural History of British Birds' – 40 hand col. engraved plates – contem calf – rubbed – covers detached – stitching broken – large folio – 1771-75.
(Christie's) $5,670 £2,700

HAYLEY, W.
'Life and Posthumous Writings of William Cowper' – 3 portraits – 2 plates and a text illus. by William Blake – 3 vols. – orig. boards – badly worn – uncut – Chichester 1803-04.
(Bonhams) $105 £50

HAYLEY, WILLIAM
'An Essay on History' – 2nd Edn. – half title – browning – contem. mottled calf – label – spine gilt – rubbed – 4to. – 1781.
(Sotheby's) $10 £5

HEAD, CAPT. C. F.
'Eastern and Egyptian Scenery, Ruins etc' – litho title and 22 plates on india paper – 3 folding maps – spotting – morocco backed boards – worn – loose – oblong folio – 1833.
(Sotheby's) $420 £200

HEAD, MRS. HENRY
'A Simple Guide to Pictures' – 34 illus. with 24 in colour – 1914.
(Baitson) $4 £2

HEARN, LAFCADIO
'Letters from the Raven' – 1st English Edn. – contemp. half calf – slightly rubbed – good copy – 1908.
(J. Ash) $34 £16

HEARNE, THOMAS
'Antiquities of Great Britain Illustrated in Views' – vol. 1 only of 2 – 50 engraved plates – contem. half calf – orig. printed wrappers – stitched as issued – uncut – oblong 4to.
(Christie's) $85 £40

HEATH, FRANCIS GEORGE
'The Fern Portfolio' – 15 chromolithographed plates – occasional slight spotting – contemporary cloth – slightly soiled –folio – 1885.
(Christie's S. Kensington) $145 £70

HEATH, ROBERT
'A Natural and Historical Account of the Isles of Scilly' – 1st Edn. – good copy in orig. boards with uncut edges – 1750.
(Lane) $105 £50

HEATH, WILLIAM
'The Life of a Soldier' – 1st Edn. – 18 hand col. engraved plates – half title – tears and repairs – orig. boards – very worn – 4to. – 1823.
(Sotheby's) $180 £85

HEDGELAND, J. P.
'A Description of the Splendid Decorations in the Church of St. Neot' – 1st Edn. – with coloured plates – 1830.
(Lane) $115 £55

HEDIN, S.
'Transhimalaja' – 3 vols. – 3 folding maps and illus. – cloth – Leipzig 1909-12.
(Phillips) $95 £45

HEIDE, JAN VAN DER
'Beschryving Der Nieuwluks Uitgevonden en Geoctrojeerde Slang-Brand-Spuiten' – 19 fine engraved plates – some folding depicting fires being fought – 1st Edn. – folio – contemp. vellum – Amsterdam 1690.
(Bonhams) $2,940 £1,400

HEIDELOFF, N.
'Gallery of Fashion' – vol. V-IX 5 vols in 2 – hand col. engraved general titles – 120 hand col. engraved plates – slight spotting – late 19th cent. citron straight grained morocco by Riviere – labels gilt – g.e. – 4to. – April 1798–March 1803.
(Sotheby's) $5,880 £2,800

HEINE, HEINRICH
'Sammtliche Werke' – 21 vols. – 1st complete Edn. – contem. half calf – spines faded – sm. 8vo. – Hamburg 1861-66.
(Sotheby's) $360 £170

HEINECCIUS, IOANNES GOTTLIEB
'Antiquitatum Romanorum Jurisprudentiam Illustratum Syntagme' – 2nd Edn. – engraved frontis – title in red and black – booklabel of Rutherford of Edgerston – old boards rebacked – 8vo. – Strassburg 1724.
(Sotheby's) $75 £35

HEINSIUS, D.
'Resum ad Sylvam-Ducis atque alibi in Belgio aut a Belgis' – folio – engr. title – six plans – three double page – four maps – spotted – contemp. vellum – worn – Ex Officina Elezeviriorum, 1631.
(Christie's S. Kensington) $180 £85

HELYOT, PIERRE
'Histoire des Ordres Monastiques, Religieux et Militaires' – vol. 8 only – 99 engraved plates – occas. soiling – contem calf – joints cracked – 4to. – 1719.
'Album des Costumes de la Cour de Rome' – 2nd Edn. – 80 hand col plates – soiled – contem calf backed boards – rubbed – 4to. – Paris 1862.
(Sotheby's) $85 £40

HENCKEL, J. F.
'Introduction a la Mineralogie' – 2 vol. – contem. calf – gilt spines – 12 mo. – Paris – 1756.
(Sotheby's) $135 £65

HENDERSON, CHARLES
'A History of the Parish of Constantine in Cornwall' – orig. cloth – 1937.
(Lane) $40 £18

HENDERSON, E.
'Iceland or the Journal of a Residence in that Island' – folding map – 16 plates – half calf gilt – 8vo. – 1819.
(Phillips) $135 £65

HENDERSON, GEORGE
'An Account of the British Settlement at Honduras' – 1st Edn. – folding engraved map – advert leaves at end – torn – spotted – soiled – modern speckled calf – 8vo. – 1809.
(Sotheby's) $125 £60

HENDERSON, W. A. AND SCHNEBBELIE, J. A.
'The Housekeeper's Instructor' – 14th Edn. – plates – some folding – some torn – contem. sheep – worn – 1811.
(Christie's) $40 £20

HENDERSON, WILLIAM
'Notes and Reminiscences of My Life as an Angler' – pres copy – photo – portrait – 5 plates – half morocco – gilt – 1876.
(Phillips) $65 £30

HENNEPIN, LOUIS
'Voyage Curieux .... par le Sieur de la Borde' – engraved frontis – 2 large engraved folding maps – 6 folding plates – view of Niagara Falls – marginal worming – contem. calf – 12 mo. – Leiden 1704.
(Christie's) $840 £400

HENRY VIII
'Songs, Ballads and Other Instrumental Pieces' – collected and arranged by Lady Mary Trefusis – plates – half morocco – folio – Oxford, the Roxburghe Club 1912.
(Sotheby's) $190 £90

HENRY, DAVID
'An Historical Account of all the Voyages round the World Performed by English Navigators' – 4 vol. – 1st Edn. – 39 of 44 plates – 5 of 6 folding maps – 19th cent. half calf – 8vo. – 1774.
(Sotheby's) $55 £25
'An Historical Account of the Curiosities of London and Westminster' – title browned – contemp. calf – 1753.
(Christie's) $65 £30

HENRY, G. M.
'Coloured Plates of the Birds of Ceylon' – parts 1 to IV – 64 col. plates – orig. wrappers – parts I-III broken – large 4to. – 1927-35.
(Sotheby's) $200 £95

HENRY, O.
'Short Stories' Folio Society – cover and illustrations by Paul Hogarth – 1960.
(J. Ash) $17 £8

HENTY, G. A.
'Under Drake's Flag' – 1st Edn. – plates – spotted – orig. cloth gilt – 8vo. – 1883.
(Sotheby's) $105 £50

HEPPLEWHITE, A. & CO.
'The Cabinet Maker and Upholsterer's Guide' – 3rd Edn. – folio – 127 engraved plates – one double page – stained – spotted – later morocco – worn – g.e. – 1794.
(Christie's S. Kensington) $250 £120

HEPWORTH, DIXON
'Her Majesty's Tower' – popular Edn. in 2 vols – col. plates etc. – 1901.
(Baitson) $12 £6

HERBERT, GEORGE
'The Temple' – no. 529 of 1500 copies – portrait – orig. decorated cloth – slightly faded – top and fore-edge gilt – The Nonesuch Press – 1927.
(Christie's S. Kensington) $30 £15

HERBERT, SIR THOMAS
'Some Yeares Travels into Divers Parts of Asia and Afrique' – 2nd Edn. – numerous engraved illus. and maps – dampstains – contem. calf – gilt – rubbed – folio – 1638.
(Sotheby's) $360 £170

HERDMAN, WILLIAM G.
'Pictorial Relics of Ancient Liverpool' – Subscriber's copy with all plates – folio – half calf – 1857.
(Richard Baker & Thomson) $630 £300

HERGESHEIMER, JOSEPH
'Tampico' – good copy in chipped John Austen dust wrapper – New York 1926.
(J. Ash) $6 £3

HERMANNIDES, RUTGERUS
'Britannia Magna' – 1st Edn. – 31 folding town plans – general map – vellum repaired – 12 mo. – Amsterdam 1661 circa.
(Sotheby's) $335 £160

HEROINES OF SHAKESPEARE, THE
Engraved under the Direction of ... Charles Heath – 45 hand coloured plates – 2 detached – contemporary morocco – gilt – joints and spine slightly rubbed – g.e. – lge. 8vo. – David Bogue, 1848.
(Christie's S. Kensington) $230 £110

HERON ART BOOKS
27 vols. various – illus. – some col. – orig. cloth – all but one with dust jackets – 1965-70.
(Christie's) $60 £28

HERON, ROBERT
'Elements of Chemistry comprehending all the most Important Facts' – errata leaf – folding table – tree calf – worn – rebacked – 8vo. – Longman 1800.
(Sotheby's) $145 £70

HERRICK, ROBERT
'The Works' – 2 vols. – one of 25 large paer cipies – woodcut portrait – half titles – contem. brown half morocco – rubbed – gilt arms on cover – 4to. – Edinburgh 1823.
(Sotheby's) $105 £50

HERRING, ROBERT
'Paper and Paper Making' – 1st Edn. – frontis – 25 specimens of paper at end – adverts – orig. cloth – 8vo. – Longman, – 1855.
(Sotheby's) $230 £110

HERSCHEL, SIR JOHN FREDERICK WILLIAM
2 ALs 5½ pages – 8vo. – Collingwood – to Rev. Ballack – astronomer – 1866.
(Phillips) $230 £110

HERTFORDSHIRE
11 documents – 6 on vellum – 5 on paper – relating to the manor of Goldingtons – late 16th/18th cent. – with 12 documents – 7 on vellum – 5 on paper – relating to Ware and Thundridge – mid 17th/18th cent.
(Phillips) $160 £75

HERVEY, MRS ELIZABETH
'The Moutray Family' – 4 vols. – 1st Edn. – half titles – orig. boards – 1800.
(Christie's) $380 £180

HETHERINGTON, A. L.
'The Early Ceramic Works of China' – limited Edn. signed by author – plates – some col. – orig. pigskin – 4to. – 1922.
(Sotheby's) $125 £60

HEWITT, N.
'Edinburgh School Atlas' – engraved title and 38 double page maps mainly hand coloured in outline – half morocco – J. Thomson – Edinburgh n.d.
(Bennett Book Auction) $85 £40

HEY, MRS. REBECCA
'The Moral of Flowers' – 3rd Edn. – 23 hand coloured engr. plates – contemp. half morocco – rubbed – t.e.g. – 1836.
(Christie's S. Kensington) $190 £90
'The Spirit of the Woods' – 26 hand col. plates – half morocco rubbed – 1837.
(Phillips) $135 £65

HEYLEYN, PETER
'Cosmographie in Four Books' – 2nd Edn. – addit. engraved title – 4 engraved folding maps – torn – calf – spine missing – folio for Henry Seile, 1657.
(Sotheby's) $380 £180

HEYWOOD, THOMAS
'A Chronographicall History of all the Kings ... with the Life and Predictions of Merlin' – 4to. – engr. portrait – laid down – old speckled calf – corners rubbed – new endpapers – J. Oakes, 1641.
(Christie's S. Kensington) $105 £50

HIBBERD, SHIRLEY
'New and Rare Beautiful Leaved Plants' – 2nd Edn. – hand col. wood engraved plates – illus. in text – some spots – some leaves and plates loose – orig. cloth – rubbed – large 8vo. – 1870.
(Sotheby's) $190 £90
'Favourite Garden Flowers' – 5 vols – coloured plates – half morocco – n.d.
(Bennett Book Auction) $12 £6

HIGGINS, WILLIAM
'Experiments and Observations on the Atomic Theory and Electrical Phenomena' – 1st Edn. – half title – half morocco – 8vo. – 1814.
(Sotheby's) $190 £90

HILARY, SIR WILLIAM
'An Appeal to the British Nation, on the Humanity and Policy of forming a National Institution, for the Preservation of Lives and Property from Shipwreck' – contemporary straight grained morocco – gilt rubbed – g.e. – Bookplate of Augustus Frederick, Duke of Sussex, 1823.
(Christie's S. Kensington) $65 £30

HILL, GEORGE FRANCIS
'A Corpus of Italian Medals' – 2 vols. – plates – orig. cloth – rubbed – folio – 1930.
(Sotheby's) $2,520 £1,200

HILL, SIR JOHN
'A General Natural History' – 55 plates of 56 – stains and discolourations – contem. calf – gilt – spines – folio – 1748-52.
(Christie's) $250 £120
'The Family Herbal' – 54 hand col. plates – soiled – 2 leaves mounted – modern calf – 8vo. – Bungay n.d.
(Sotheby's) $190 £90

HILL, ROWLAND
'Home Colonies; Sketch for a Plan for the Gradual Extinction of Pauperism' – 1 page A.L. from author bound in – 1832.
(Phillips) $95 £45

HILL, THOMAS
'A Profitable Instruction of the Perfect Ordering of Bees' – some shaving and soiling – later calf – 4to. – 1608.
(Christie's) $135 £65

HILLIARD, JOHN NORTHERN
'Greater Magic, a Practical Treatise on Modern Magic' – edited by Carl Jones and Jean Hugard – 1st Edn. – illus. – orig. cloth – 8vo. – Minneapolis Privately Printed 1938.
(Sotheby's) $85 £40

HILLIER, J.
'Japanese Prints and Drawings from the Vever Collection' – 3 vols. – limited Edn. – plates – cloth – t.e.g. – 4to. – 1976.
(Phillips) $135 £65
'The Uninhibited Brush' – limited Edn. – plates – some coloured – 4to. – 1974.
(Phillips) $60 £28

Führen Sie den Degen in Ehren!

HIMMLER, HEINRICH
Document signed – 1 page quarto – awarding the SS sword to Untersturmfuhrer Paul Rohde printed with typescript and mss insertions – edges strengthened – Berlin 20th April 1937.
(Sotheby's) $250 £120

HIND, ARTHUR M.
'Wenceslaus Hollar and his Views of London' – plates – cloth – 4to. – 1922.
(Phillips) $145 £70
'The Etchings of D. Y. Cameron' – limited Edn. – plates – orig. calf backed boards – 4to. – 1924.
(Sotheby's) $65 £32

HINDE, CAPT. R.
'The Discipline of the Light Horse' – frontis – plates – calf gilt – 1778.
(Phillips) $95 £45

HINGSTON, F.C.
'Specimens of the Ancient Cornish Crosses' – bound in half calf – 1850.
(Lane) $40 £20

HINGSTON, J.
'The Australian Abroad' – 2 vol. – plates – maps – ills. – spotting – orig. cloth – rubbed – 8vo. 1879-80.
(Sotheby's) $85 £40

HINTON, J. H.
'The History and Topography of the United States of America' – 2 vol. – 4th Edn. – engraved title and 56 plates of 59 – 7 double page map hand col. in outline – spotting – contem. calf – rubbed – 8vo. – n.d.
(Sotheby's) $170 £80

HINTON, J. W.
'Organ Construction' – 4to. – plates – occasional slight spotting – original cloth 1906.
(Christie's S. Kensington) $40 £18

HIPKINS, A. J.
'Musical Instruments' – 4to. – coloured plates – original cloth – soiled – 1921.
(Christie's S. Kensington) $60 £28

HISTORIE DES OUDEN EN NIEWEN TESTAMENTS
2 vols. – engraved titles – plates – small tears – contem. calf gilt – worn – later wooden case – folio – Amsterdam, Peter Mortier 1700.
(Sotheby Beresford Adams) $285 £135

'HISTORY OF THE SPECULATIVE SOCIETY'
quarter mor. – 1764-1904 – Edinburgh 1905.
(Bennett Book Auction) $34 £16

HISTORY OF THE 33rd BATALLION GUN CORPS
Limited 1st Edn. – vol. and other plates – 1919.
(Lane) $40 £20

HITCHINS, FORTESQUE
'The History of Cornwall' – 2 vols. – engraving illus. quarter calf marbled boards – corners and spine rubbed – Helston 1824.
(May Whetter & Grose) $180 £85

HITLER
2 albums containing scenes showing Hitler and Nazi Germany – compiled by Driver Lockett, Royal Signals, 1947.
(Richard Baker & Thomson) $100 £48

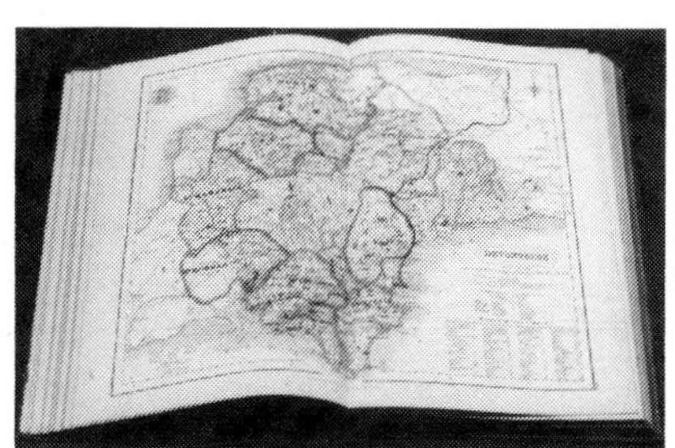

HOBSON'S
'Fox Hunting Atlas' – quarter calf – red gilt dec. boards – spine damaged – rubbed – 1880.
(May Whetter & Grose) $275 £130

HOBSON, G. D.
'Maioli, Canevari and Others' – plates – orig. cloth – rubbed – spine worn – 4to. – 1926.
(Sotheby's) $125 £60
'English Binding Before 1500' – plates – orig. cloth – folio – 1929.
(Sotheby's) $210 £100

HOBSON, R. L.
'Catalogue of the Leonard Gow Collection of Chinese Porcelain' – 1 of 300 copies signed by Gow – full niger morocco gilt – t.e.g. – cloth box – 4to. – 1931.
(Phillips) $545 £260
'The Later Ceramic Wares of China' – illus. some in colour – buckram gilt – 4to. – 1925.
(Phillips) $125 £60
'Worcester Porcelain' – plates – uncut – cloth gilt – slightly soiled – d.w. – 4to. – 1910.
(Phillips) $210 £99
'The Wares of the Ming Dynasty' – number 172 of 256 copies signed by the author – bound in pigskin and with an extra colour plate – plates a few coloured – original pigskin – 4to – t.e.g. – 1923.
(Christie's S. Kensington) $200 £95
'Chinese Pottery and Porcelain' – 2 vol. – limited Edn. – plates – orig. cloth – 8vo. – 1915.
(Sotheby's) $240 £115

HOBSON, R. L. AND MORSE, E. S.
'Chinese Corean and Japanese Potteries' – no. 762 of 500 copies – 4to. – coloured frontispiece – plates – orig. cloth backed boards – corners bumped – New York/ Japan Society 1914.
(Christie's S. Kensington) $95 £45

HOBSON, R. L. AND OTHERS
'Chinese Ceramics in Private Collections' – no. 373 of 625 – col. plates – illus. – orig. cloth – faded – 4to. – 1931.
(Sotheby's) $315 £150

HODGES, SIR BENJAMIN
'An Impartial History of Michael Servetus' – some leaves torn – repaired – soiled – contem. calf – rubbed – 1724.
(Christie's) $65 £32

HODGKIN, J. E. AND E.
'Examples of Early English Pottery' – plates – cloth – 4to. – 1891.
(Phillips) $55 £25

HODGSON, ADAM
'Letters from North America' – 2 vols. – first Edn. – 2 plates – diced calf gilt – 1 cover loose – 1824.
(Phillips) $55 £25

HODGSON, J. E.
'The History of Aeronautics in Great Britain' – one of 1,000 copies – plates – some col. – orig. cloth – rubbed – t.e.g. – 4to. – 1924.
(Sotheby's) $190 £90

HODSON, T. AND DOUGALL, I.
'The Cabinet of the Arts' – plates – some soiling and fraying – extra illus. with 40 extra plates – hand col. – some soiling – contem. half morocco – covers detached – 4to. – 1810.
(Christie's) $420 £200

HOFFMANN, HEINRICH
'The English Struwwelpeter' – 1st Edn. in English – illus. by author – col. by hand – orig. printed boards – covers almost loose – dust jacket – 4to. – Leipsic 1848.
(Sotheby's) $1,720 £820

HOFFMANN, JULIUS
'Das Wunderbare Bilderbuch' – 3rd Edn. – 12 hand col. plates – each with moveable overlay – marks – orig. pictorial boards – detached – 4to. – Stuttgart 1812.
(Sotheby Beresford Adams) $125 £60

HOFFMANN, PROFESSOR A. J. LEWIS
'Conjurer Dick of the Adventures of a Young Wizard' – 1st Edn. – wood engraved illus. 8 pp adverts – orig. cloth – spine worn and discoloured – 8vo. – Warne n.d.
(Sotheby's) $145 £70

HOFMANN, DR. ERNST
'Die Raupen der Gross-Schmetterlinge Europas' – 50 coloured lithographed plates – contemporary half morocco – spine faded – t.e.g. – 4to. – Stuttgart, 1893.
(Christie's S. Kensington) $95 £45

HOFLAND, BARBARA
'Patience and Perseverance or the Modern Griselda' – 4 vol. – half titles – one leaf torn – slightly spotted – later half calf – hinges strengthened – 12 mo. – Minerva Press 1813.
(Sotheby Beresford Adams) $180 £85

HOFSTEDE DE GROOT, C.
'A Catalogue Raisonne of the Works of the Most Eminent Dutch Painters of the 17th cent.' – 8 vol. – orig. cloth – 8vo. – 1908-27.
(Sotheby's) $545 £260

HOGARTH, WILLIAM
'Works' – 2 vol. – engraved portrait – additional titles – one hand coloured – and plates – occasional slight spotting – contemp. half morocco – rubbed – g.e. 4to. – n.d.
(Christie's S. Kensington) $75 £35

HOGG, JAMES
'The Shepherd's Guide' – 1st Edn. – spotting torn – 19th cent. blue half calf – rubbed – 8vo. – Edinburgh 1807.
(Sotheby's) $190 £90

HOGG, T. J.
'The Athenians' – editor Walter Sidney Scott – limited to 350 copies – this number 10 of 50 signed by editor – collotype repros. and specially bound – orig. morocco – t.e.g. – slipcase – 4to. – 1943.
(Christie's) $75 £35

HOLBACH, PAUL HEINRICH DIETRICH VON
'La Politique Naturelle' – 2 vols – half titles – slight browning – early 19th cent. mottled calf – labels – spines gilt – rubbed – 8vo. – Londres 1773.
(Sotheby's) $170 £80

HOLBEIN, HANS
'The Dance of Death' – engraved by W. Hollar – with descriptions in English and French – two portraits – 31 hand coloured plates – some spotting – contemp. morocco – rebacked g.e. – 1816.
(Christie's S. Kensington) $135 £65

HOLCOT, ROBERT
'In Librum Sapientiae Regis Salomonis Pealectiones' – CCXIII – folio – 1586.
(Christie's S. Kemsington) $75 £35

HOLIDAY, GILBERT
'Horses and Soldiers' – mounted title vignette and illus. – some coloured – orig. cloth – 4to. – n.d.
(Christie's) $25 £12

HOLIDAY STROLL, A.
Wood engraved vignette on title and 22 illus. col. by hand – modern boards – engraved frontis bound in – 12 mo. – E. Wallis circa 1830.
(Sotheby's) $50 £24

HOLLAND, H.
'Travels in the Ionian Isles, Albania, Thessaly, Macedonia' – 12 plates – 1 map – calf gilt – 4to. – 1815.
(Phillips) $250 £120

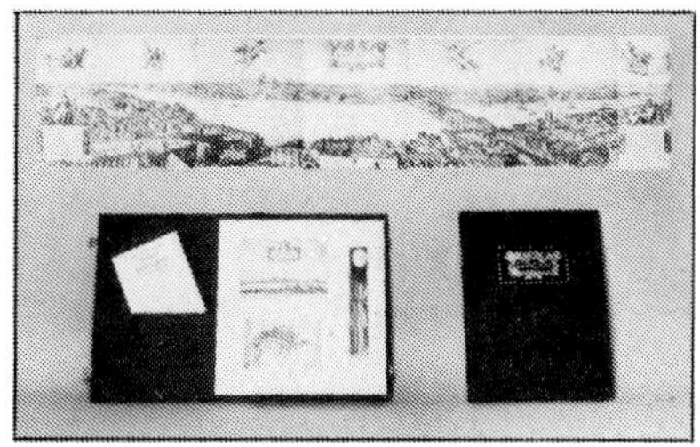

HOLLAR'S LONDON
A collection of facsimile reproductions of 37 etchings by Wenceslaus Hollar of London before and after the Great Fire of 1666 – reproduced to the original size in the British Museum – mounted on 17 boards – accompanied by a separate text and the whole contained in a silk lined solander box bound in leather – set no.1 of a limited Edn. of 150 – 25 in x 20 in.
(Sotheby's) $65 £30

HOLLIDAY, J.
'Life of William Late Earl of Mansfield' – contemp. calf – 4to – 1797.
(Bennett Book Auction) $40 £20

HOLLOWAY, WILLIAM AND BRANCH, JOHN
'The British Museum; Or Elegant Repository of Natural History' – 3 vol. – engraved additional titles and 199 hand coloured plates – occasional slight soiling – vol. 1 lacking
(Christie's S. Kensington) $125 £40

HOLME, CHARLES

'Modern Pen Drawings, European and American' – illus. – limited Edn. of 300 – The Studio, 1901.
(Dacre, Son & Hartley) $75 $36

'English Water Colours. – col. plates mounted – spotted – contemp. half morocco – rubbed – folio – 1902.
(Sotheby's) $60 £28

'Modern Book Production' – plates – some coloured – modern morocco backed cloth – t.e.g. – 4to. – Studio 1928.
(Sotheby's) $65 £32

'Pictures from the Iveagh Bequest' – limited to 100 copies – this unnumbered – plates – contem. half morocco – rubbed – t.e.g. – folio – 1928.
(Christie's) $75 £35

HOLME, CONSTANCE

'He-Who-Came' – spine a shade sunned and worn.
(J. Ash) $8 £4

THE
ACADEMY OF ARMORY,
OR,
A STOREHOUSE
OF
ARMORY
AND
BLAZON.
CONTAINING
The several variety of Created Beings, and how born in Coats of Arms, both Foreign and Domestick.
WITH
The Instruments used in all Trades and Sciences, together with their Terms of Art.
ALSO
The Etymologies, Definitions, and Historical Observations on the same, Explicated and Explained according to our Modern Language.
Very useful for all Gentlemen, Scholars, Divines, and all such as desire any knowledge in Arts and Sciences.
By Randle Holme, of the City of Chester, Gentleman Sewer in Extraordinary to his late Majesty King Charles 2. And sometimes Deputy for the Kings of Arms.
CHESTER,
Printed for the Author, MDCLXXXVIII.

HOLME, RANDLE

'The Academy of Armory' – engraved title – plates – minor defects – later panelled calf – folio – Chester 1688.
(Sotheby Beresford Adams) $250 £120

HOLROYD, JOHN, EARL OF SHEFFIELD

'Observations on the Commerce of the American States' – calf – London 1784.
(Phillips) $85 £40

HOMANN'S HEIRS

'Atlas Compendiarus' – engraved title – double page plate of astronomical and other diagrams – 50 double page engraved maps – variously dated – most hand col. in outline – repairs – orig. limp leather – edges trimmed – folio – Nuremberg 1752 but after 1781.
(Sotheby's) $2,940 £1,400

'Tabula Marchionatus Brandenburgici et Ducatus Pomeraniae' – hand coloured – engraved map – 22 x 19 inches – torn along centrefold – repaired – framed and glazed – (mid 18th century).
(Christie's S' Kensington) $75 £35

'Ducatus Pomeraniae' – hand coloured – engraved map – 23 x 30 inches – torn along centrefold – framed and glazed – (mid 18th century).
(Christie's S. Kensington) $65 £32

'Magna Britannia – Scandinavia – Imperii Moscovitici' – 3 hand coloured maps – all with margins renewed. – circa 1720.
(Phillips) $85 £40

HOME, H.

'Sketches of the History of Man' – 2 volumes – contemp calf – 4to. – 1st Edn. – Edinburgh 1774.
(Bennett Book Auction) $230 $110

HOME, ROBERT

'Select Views in Mysore' – 4 charts – 29 plates – contem. calf gilt – 4to. – 1794.
(Phillips) $190 £90

HOMILIES

'The First (Second) Tome of Homilies' – 2 parts in one – some worming and dampstains – contem. calf – worn – folio – by John Norton, 1633.
(Sotheby's) $40 £20

HOMMAIRE DE HELL, XAVIER

'Les Steppes de la Mer Caspienne, Le Caucase, La Crimee et la Russie Meridionale' – 4 vols. including atlas – 34 litho plates – 5 plans – 1 col. – 1843-44.
(Phillips) $1,090 £520

HONE, WILLIAM
'Ancient Mysteries Described' – 4 full page illus. – one folding – 2 after George Cruikshank – orig. cloth – 8vo. – n.d.
(Sotheby's) $2 £1

HONEY, L. B.
'European Ceramic Art' – plates – some col. – illus. – orig. cloth – 4to. – 1952.
(Sotheby's) $45 £22

HOOKER, JOSEPH DALTON
'The Rhododendrons of Sikkim-Himalaya' – 30 hand col. plates – some soiling and fraying – lacks list of plates and subscribers – orig. cloth – rebacked – slightly rubbed – g.e. – folio – 1849.
(Sotheby's) $1,785 £850

HOOKER, RICHARD
'The Works' – engr. frontis – addit. title – browning and soiling – joints split – rubbed – folio – 1666.
(Sotheby's) $95 £45

HOOKER, SIR WILLIAM JACKSON
'A Century of Ferns' – 98 hand coloured lithographed plates – two double page – contemporary morocco backed cloth – spine lightly rubbed – 4to. – 1854.
(Christie's S. Kensington) $190 £90
'The Journal of Botany' – 4 vol. – portraits – 63 plates – some folding and hand col. – indexes – spotting and soiling – library stamp on title – orig. cloth – rubbed – 8vo. – 1834-42.
(Sotheby's) $65 £30

HOOKER, WILLIAM AND SALISBURY, R.A.
'The Paridisus Londinensis; containing plants cultivated in the vicinity of the Metropolis' – 2 vols. – 119 hand coloured plates, a few folding, occasional spotting – cont. half calf – rubbed, joints cracked – 1806-07.
(Christie's S. Kensington) $3,035 £1,350

HOOPER, W.
'Rational Recreations' – vols. 1-3 of 4 – 2nd. Edn. – 31 folding engraved plates – col by hand – contem. calf backed boards – joints split – 8vo. – L. Davis and others – 1782.
(Sotheby's) £170 £80

HOPE, JAMES
'A Treatise on the Diseases of the Heart and the Great Vessels' – 3rd Edn. – corrected and greatly enlarged – 7 plates – new cloth – 8vo. – 1839.
(Sotheby's) $100 £48

HOPE, W. H. ST. JOHN
'Windsor Castle, an Architectural History' – 3 vols. with portfolio of plans – limited to 1050 copies – this unnumbered – plates – orig. cloth – sm. folio – 1913.
(Christie's) $55 £25

HOPE, SIR WILLIAM
'A New Short and Easy Method of Fencing' – one folding plate – torn – spotted – contem. sheep – worn – rubbed – 4to. – Edinburgh 1707.
(Christie's) $95 £45

HOPKINS, GERALD MANLEY
'Poems' – with notes by Robert Bridges – cloth backed boards – 1st Ed. – London 1918 1918.
(Bennett Book Auction) $75 £36

HOPPER, THOMAS
'Designs for the Houses of Parliament' – 28 plates – four plans – some spotting – margins of title and dedication torn – original half morocco – worn and disbound – oblong folio – n.d.
(Christie's S. Kensington) $230 £110

HOPPUS'S PRACTICAL MEASURER
Folding frontispiece, torn, staining, cont. morocco, rubbed – Manchester, 1847.
(Christie's S. Kensington) $35 £15

HOPSON, CHARLES RIVINGTON
'A General System of Chemistry, Theoretical and Practical' – 2 engraved plates – 4 tables – title spotted – library stamps – half calf – rubbed – 4to. – C. G. J. and J. Robinson 1789.
(Sotheby's) $60 £28

HOPTON, A.
'A Concordancy of Years' – title in woodcut border – partly black letter – worming slightly affecting text – vellum – 1615.
(Sotheby's) $315 £150

HORNBY, REV. JAMES J.
'A Sermon Preached on 27th July 1821 at St. Peter's Church, Liverpool' – binder's personal wood engraved bookplate in an attractive exhibition binding of straight grained red morocco gilt by J. Jones Junior of Liverpool – calf slipcase – 8vo. – Liverpool 1821.
(Sotheby Beresford Adams) $420 £200

HORNE, T. H.
'Landscape Illustrations of the Bible' – 2 vols. bound in full morocco – 1836.
(Lane) $90 £42
'Lakes of Lancashire, Westmorland and Cumberland' – 1st Edn. – 1 folding hand col. map – 43 engravings on india paper after J. Farington – first plate spotted – half morocco – worn – folio – 1816.
(Phillips) $190 £90

HORNER, J.
'View of Buildings in the Town and Parish of Halifax' – lithographed title and 19 plates – one torn – some marginal soiling – orig. wrappers – soiled and torn –oblong folio – 1835.
(Christie's S. Kensington) $295 £140

HORNOT, ANTOINE
'Traite Raisonne de la Distillation' – torn – contem. calf – rubbed – joints cracked – 12 mo. – Paris 1753.
(Christie's) $85 £40

HORREBOW, N.
'The Natural History of Iceland' – 1st Edn. in English – folding engraved map – some browning and soiling – tears – contem. half calf – worn – one cover detached – folio – 1758.
(Sotheby's) $210 £100

HORSFIELD, THOMAS W.
'The History, Antiquities and Topography of the County of Sussex' – 2 vols. – engraved plates – some folding hand col. coats of arms in the text – spotted – contem. half calf – rubbed – Lewes, Sussex Press 1835.
(Sotheby's) $250 £120

HORTUS SANITATIS
3 parts 357 leaves – double column 55 lines – gothic letter – separate title to each part with woodcut on verso – numerous woodcut illus. – all crudely coloured – large capitals in red – contem. marginal notes in ink – library stamp – ownership stamp of Jesuit College, Regensburg, 19th cent. half morocco – folio – Strasburg 1497.
(Christie's) $6,510 £3,100

HORWOOD, R.
'Plan of the Cities of London and Westminster and the Borough of Southwark' – 30 of 32 plates – lacks index map – loose as inserted – soiled – large folio – 1799-1800.
(Sotheby's) $400 £190
'Sloane Street to Chelsea Hospital' – hand col. engraved map – 22 x 21 inches – framed and glazed 1794.
(Christie's) $75 £35

L'HOSPITAL (G. F. A. MARQUIS DE)
'An Analytick Treatise of Conick Sections .... made English by E. Stone' – 4to. – 33 folding engraved plates – contemp. panelled calf – rebacked – joints cracked – 1723.
(Christie's S. Kensington) $60 £28

HOUBRAKEN, ARNOLD
'De Glooteschouburgh Der Nederlautsche Kontschilders En Shilderessen' – 3 vol. – engraved general title – portrait and 47 plates – a few folding – contemp. mottled calf – joints cracked – The Hague, 1753.
(Christie's S. Kensington) $145 £70

HOUGHTON, CLAUDE
'Julian Grant Loses His Way' – some slight foxing – 1933.
(J. Ash) $10 £5

HOUGHTON, W.
'British Fresh-water Fishes' – vol. 1 only – 20 coloured plates – some slight spotting – orig. cloth – slightly soiled – g.e. – lge. 4to.
(Christie's S. Kensington) $230 £110

HOURS OF THE VIRGIN
Use of Rome, in Latin, preceded by a calendar – illum. mss on vellum – 15 large initials with three sided borders – seven large initials with full borders with historiated scenes – 51small miniatures – 14 full historiated borders – 48 small miniatures – 15 full page miniatures – very fine condition – contem. blind stampedbinding perhaps by James Van Gavere of tanned leather over wooden boards – contem. gilt metal enamelled clasps and catches – binding repaired – edges gilt gauffered – 197 mm x 140 mm – Flanders – style of Ghent or Bruges before 1510.
(Sotheby's) $100,000 £48,000

HOURS OF THE VIRGIN, THE
In Latin, preceded by a Calendar – illum. mss on vellum – 168 ll – six large illum. initials – full borders of flowers – insects etc – 10 large historiated initials – six full page miniaturesin arched compartments – red morocco gilt of circa 1600 – probably Spanish – 147 mm x 100 mm. – Ghent or Bruges circa 1500.
(Sotheby's) $23,100 £11,000

HOURS OF THE VIRGIN (Use of Rome)
In Latin, preceded by a Calendar in French – illum. mss on vellum – in dark brown ink in gothic Liturgical hand – panel borders on every text page – 13 small miniatures – 7 large miniatures – some rubbing and staining – 18th cent. French red morocco gilt – orange endpapers – g.e. – 211 mm x 154 mm – Flanders probably Tournai, circa 1475.
(Sotheby's) $21,000 £10,000

HOURS OF ESTIENNE MILET, THE
Comprising the Hours of the Virgin in Latin preceded by a Calendar in French, the Gospel sequences, and other prayers to the Virgin – illum. mss on vellum – three panel borders of coloured acanthus on liquid gold grounds – five full borders – full page armorial achievement and 14 large miniatures in arched compartments – 18th cent. French calf – binding worn – g.e. – 152 mm x 108 mm. – Eastern France circa 1475-1490.
(Sotheby's) $12,180 £5,800

HOURS OF HUGH DE CLUGNY, THE
Comprising the Hours of the Virgin in Latin, preceded by a calendar and one Gospel sequence, followed by the Hours of the Cross and the Holy Ghost – illum. mss on vellum – illum. armorial initials with full length borders – four large historiated initials – six large miniatures with full borders – French 16th cent. calf gilt with interlinked rectangular and lozenge shaped panels – binding worn and defective – lacks ties – 148 mm x 108 mm – Burgundy probably Autun, circa 1560-71.
(Sotheby's) $12,600 £6,000

HOUSE OF LORDS – Legal Cases
A Collection of 79 cases between 1766 and 1796 – in 6 vols. – folio – old boards – calf backs.
(Bonhams) $75 £35

I publish these poems, few though they are, because it is not likely that I shall ever be impelled to write much more. I can no longer expect to be revisited by the continuous excitement under which in the early months of 1895 I wrote the greater part of my other book, nor indeed could I well sustain it if it came; and it is best that what I have written should be printed while I am here to see it through the press and control its spelling and punctuation. About a quarter of this matter belongs to the April of the present year, but most of it to dates between 1895 and 1910.

September 1922.

HOUSMAN, A. E.
The Autograph Manuscript of his Preface to 'Last Poems', marked by the printer 'No Heading', dated by Housman September 1922 – 1 page – folio – identified in two later hands a being by Lewis Carroll.
(Sotheby's) $800 £400

HOUSMAN, LAURENCE
'The Cloak of Friendship' – orig. decorative cloth gilt – very slightly marked – some foxing – 1905.
(J. Ash) $8 £4

HOWARD, DAVID S.
'Chinese Armorial Porcelain' – illus. – orig. cloth – dust jacket – 4to – 1974.
(Sotheby's) $135 £65

HOWARD, JOHN
'An Account of the Principal Lazarettos in Europe' – 2nd Edn. – 21 folding engraved plates of 22 – spotted – later half calf – 4to. – Paris 1862.
(Sotheby's) $105 £50
'The State of the Prisons in England and Wales' – 3rd Edn. – numerous plates – stains – contem. diced russia – worn – three pieces of related ephemera inserted including a 4pp leaflet 'Notes of a Conversation held with Mr Howard' May 1789 – 4to Warrrington 1784.
(Sotheby's) $360 £170

HOWEL, T.
'Journal of a Passage from India .... Asia Minor' – folding map – calf gilt – 8vo. – 1789.
(Phillips) $160 £75

HOWELL, JAMES
'A Survey of the Signories of Venice' – folio – printed for Richard Lowndes, 1651 – two engraved plates – slight marginal worming – spotted later half calf – rubbed – joints worn.
(Christie's S. Kensington) $95 £45
'Londonopolis' – frontis laid down – folding town plan – old calf – sm. folio – 1657.
(Phillips) $190 £90

HOWELL, WILLIAM
'An Institution of General History' – 4 vol. – in three – various Edn. – contemp. calf – worn – folio – 1680-5.
(Christie's S. Kensington) $65 £30

HOWELLS, W. D.
'No Love Lost' – 1st Edn. – presentation copy – inscribed by author – engraved frontis – title – plate and tailpiece by Richardson – orig. cloth – New York 1869.
(Sotheby's) $40 £20

HOWITT, A.
'The Native Tribes of South East Australia' – plates and maps – orig. cloth – 8vo – 1904.
(Sotheby's) $180 £85

HOWITT, SAMUEL
'The British Sportsman' – New Edn. – engraved title and 71 engraved plates – some spots – later half morocco gilt – 4to – 1834.
(Sotheby Beresford Adams) $1,325 £630
'The British Sportsman' – engraved title – 71 plates – half calf – oblong – 4to. – 1806.
(Phillips) $1,300 £620
'British Preserve' – vig. on title and 36 etched plates – 1st Edn. – 4to – cloth – slightly soiled – back repaired – 1824.
(Bonhams) $210 £100

HOWITT, WILLIAM
'Visits to Remarkable Places' – 2 vols. – full tree calf – 1840.
(Baitson) $30 £14

HOYLAND, JOHN
'Historical Survey of the Customs, Habits and Present State of the Gypsies' – 1st Edn. – spotting – modern morocco backed boards – 8vo. – York 1816.
(Sotheby's) $65 £30

HOYLE, E.
'Games Improved' – including treatise on whist – quadrille – piquet – chess – backgammon etc. – calf gilt – 12mo. – 1778.
(Phillips) $55 £25

HOZIER, LOUIS PIERRE D'
'Preuves de la Noblesse de Haut et Puissant Seigneur Antoine-Paul–Jaques de Quelen, Comte de la Vauguoin' – mss – and watercolour on vellum – 40 leaves – coloured and gilt coat of arms on title – signed and sealed by D'Hozier at end – contemporary red morocco – gilt spine – lower gilt dentelles – gilt edges – folio – 1758?
(Sotheby Parke Bernet) $1,860 £885

HUDSON, STEPHEN
'Elinor Colhouse' – good – 1921.
(J. Ash) $8 £4

To my little friend at Carlton Gray school, [illegible] from W. H. Hudson May 13. 1908.

HUDSON, W. H.
'Kith and Kin; Poems of Animal Life' – inscribed by Hudson – original decorated boards – worn – 8vo. – 1901.
(Sotheby's) $90 £44

HUDSON'S BAY COMPANY
Report of the Select Committee – 3 folding maps – contem. cloth backed boards – worn – folio 1857.
(Sotheby's) $275 £130

HUGARD'S MAGIC MONTHLY editor Jean Hugard
Vols. 1-21 in 14 vols. – illus. – vols 1-9 in orig. cloth – remainder boards – 3 with cloth spines – 4to. – New Jersey, Pennsylvania and New York 1945-65.
(Sotheby's) $220 £105

No 6.

Lines Written upon First Observing an Elephant Devoured by a Roc . . . . . .

To Walter de la Mare,
And Family,
With very best wishes for Christmas & the New Year,
From Richard Hughes.
Dec. 1922.

HUGHES, RICHARD
'Lines Written upon First Observing an Elephant Devoured by a Roc' – 1st Edn. – this no. 6 of an unspecified number – presentation copy inscribed by author to De La Mare and family – orig. wrappers – uncut – 8vo. – Golden Cockerel Press 1922.
(Sotheby's) $170 £80

'The Spider's Palace' – spine slightly creased and one stain – 1931.
(J. Ash) $12 £6

HUGHES, TED
'The Earth-Owl and Other Moon People' – illustrated by Brandt. – very good in dust-wrapper – 1963.
(J. Ash) $30 £15

HUGHES, THOMAS
'The Scouring of the White Horse' – 1st Edn. – presentation copy – inscribed by author to his wife – wood engraved double page title – illus. after Richard Doyle – slightly spotted – orig. red cloth gilt – worn – g.e. – 8vo. – 1859.
(Sotheby's) $170 £80

HUGHES, THOMAS
'Ancient Chester' – one of 300 copies' – folio – 29 engr. plates – some slight spotting – contemp. half morocco – slightly soiled – 1880.
(Christie's S. Kensington) $160 £75

HUGHES, W.
'Compleat Vineyard; or a Most Excellent Way for the Planting of Vines' – 1st Edn. – with imprimatur leaf at end – sm. 4to. – 1665.
(Bonhams) $180 £85

HUGO, HERMANUS
'The Siege of Breda' – 1st Edn. in English – engraved title and 14 plates – some browning and soiling – contem. sheep – worn – folio – Ghent 1627.
(Sotheby's) $180 £85

HUGO, VICTOR
'Chatiments' – 1st Edn. – signature of Georges Victor Hugo – orig. wrappers – soiled – upper cover loose – unopened – 12 mo. – Geneva and New York 1853.
(Sotheby's) $360 £170

HUISH, MARCUS B.
'Samplers and Tapestry Embroideries' – number 350 and 600 copies – plates – some col. – illus. – orig. cloth – soiled – spine torn – t.e.g. – 4to. – 1900.
(Christie's) $85 £40

HULBERT, CHARLES
'Memoirs of Seventy Years of an Eventful Life' – one of 500 copies – subscription list – engraved portrait and 8 engraved plates by Tolley and others – orig. wrappers and 2 adverts – later cloth – 4to. – New Shrewsbury – printed by author at private press 1848-52.
(Sotheby Beresford Adams) $400 £190

HULBERT, C.
'The History and Antiquities of Shrewsbury' – 2 vol. in one – engraved plates – spotting and offsetting – contem. half calf – worn – covers detached – 4to. – Providence Grove 1837.
(Sotheby's) $115 £55

HULME, F. EDWARD
'Familiar Wild Flowers' – 5 vol. – coloured plates – contemporary cloth – spines rubbed – n.d.
(Christie's S. Kensington) $40 £18

HUMBER, WILLIAM
'A Record of the Progress of Modern Engineering' – 1 vol. only – actual photo portrait – 36 double page plates – some loose – contem. half roan – worn – folio – 1865.
(Sotheby's) $55 £25

HUMBERT, AIME
'Le Japon Illustre' – 2 vols. – maps – plans – illus. – some spotting – tear – orig. red roan backed cloth – rubbed – g.e. – 4to. – Paris 1870.
(Sotheby's) $115 £55

HUME, F.
'The Man with a Secret' – 3 vol. – lacks half title in vol. 1 and 3 – orig. cloth rubbed – 8vo. – 1890.
(Sotheby's) $30 £15

HUMPHREYS, A. L.
'Old Decorative Maps' – limited Edn. – plates – orig. cloth – faded – 4to. – 1926.
(Sotheby's) $105 £50

HUMPHREYS, HENRY NOEL
'Sentiments and Similes of William Shakespeare' – first page of text chromolithographed – printed throughout in gold and black – occasional slight spotting – original binding – spine slightly rubbed and torn – t.e.g. – 1851.
(Christie's S. Kensington) $95 £45.
'The Genera and Species of British Buuterflies' – col. title and plates – some loose – orig. cloth – gilt – 8vo. – n.d.
(Sotheby's) $190 £90

'The Genera of British Moths' – 2 vol. in one – 62 hand coloured lithographed plates – some leaves – detached – orig. cloth – spine faded – g.e. – 4to. – n.d.
(Christie's S. Kensington) $250 £120

HUMPHREYS, S.
'Nature Displayed' – 7 vols. – 202 plates – calf gilt – 12 mo. – 1750-1749.
(Phillips) $95 £45

HUNT, J.
'British Ornithology' – vol. 1 only – engraved title – 59 hand col. engraved plates – contem. half calf – slightly rubbed – 8vo. – Norwich 1815.
(Sotheby Beresford Adams) $105 £50

HUNT, LEIGH
'The Story of Rimini' – 1st Edn. – later half calf – spine worn – t.e.g. – sm. 8vo. – 1816.
(Christie's S. Kensington) $30 £15

HUNTER, A.
'Culina Famulatrix Medicinae' – 2nd Edn. – engraved frontis – soiled – modern half calf – 12 mo. – York 1805.
(Christie's) $75 £35

HUNTER, GEORGE LEYLAND
'Italian Furniture and Interiors' – 2 vol. – folio – frontispiece and 200 plates – some margins slightly soiled – unbound as issued in orig. cloth portfolio – soiled – n.d.
(Christie's S. Kensington) $75 £35

'Decorative Textiles' – illus. some in colour – cloth gilt rubbed – 4to. – 1919.
(Phillips) $65 £30

HUNTER, HENRY
'The History of London' – 2 vols. – engraved frontis – folding engraved map of the Thames – hand col. in outline – engraved plates and maps – many folding – contem. calf – gilt – 4to. – 1811.
(Christie's) $190 £90

HUNTER, JOHN
'An Historical Journal of the Transactions at Port Jackson and Norfolk Island' – 1st Edn. – engraved title – 5 maps and charts – 10 plates – foxed – modern calf backed boards – 4to. – 1793.
(Sotheby's) $840 £400

'A Treatise on the Blood, Inflammation and Gunshot Wounds' – 2 vols. – 2nd Edn. – portrait – 8 plates on seven sheets lacks half titles – some foxing – red half calf – 8vo. – B. Cox 1812.
(Sotheby's) $135 £65

HUNTER, RACHEL
'Letitia or the Castle without a Spectre' – 4 vol. – 1st Edn. – no half titles – contem. half calf – worn – joints weak – 12 mo. – Norwich 1801.
(Sotheby's) $210 £100

HUNTER, ROBERT (Governor of New York and Jamaica)
ALs – 2 pages – folio – Jamaica March 1730 to Sir William Strickland Sec. for War giving news of the Army in Jamaica.
(Phillips) $40 £20

HUNTER, W.
'Travels Through France, Turkey and Hungary to Vienna' – 2 vols. – folding map – portrait – calf gilt – 8vo. – 1803.
(Phillips) $85 £40

HUNTER, WILLIAM
'The Anatomy of the Human Gravid Uterus' – text in Latin and English – 34 plates – mostly double page – orig. limp green cloth – a little loose – folio – Sydenham Society 1851.
(Sotheby's) $135 £65

HUNTER, WILLIAM S.
'Hunter's Eastern Townships Scenery, Canada East' – addit. litho title – 1 map – some plates loose – orig. cloth – 4to – Montreal, 1860.
(Sotheby's) $1,175 £560

HURLBUTT, FRANK
'Bristol Porcelain' – plates – some col. – orig. cloth – dust jacket – folio – 1934.
(Sotheby's) $170 £80

'Bow Porcelain' – 64 plates – 8 coloured – cloth slightly soiled – 4to. – 1926.
(Bonhams) $60 £28

HURRY, LESLIE
Costume design for Preziosilla – pen and red ink – pastel – watercolour and gouache – signed and titled and dated Edinburgh 1951. – 45.7 cm x 27.6cm.
(Sotheby's) $600 £280

HUTCHINS, JOHN
'The History and Antiquities of the County of Dorset' – 3rd Edn. – 4 vols. – 126 plates – maps – half morocco – gilt panelled – spines – g.e. – folio – 1861-70.
(Christie's) $800 £380

HUTCHISON, L.
'Memoirs of the Life of Col. Hutchison' – 1st Edn. – 2 portraits – plates – including aquatint – half morocco – worn – 4to. – 1806.
(Phillips) $40 £18

HUTCHISON, W.
'History of Cumberland' – 2 vol. – engraved title – folding maps with some repairs – plates – calf – worn – 4to. – 1794.
(Phillips) $60 £28

HUTCHISON, WALTER
'A Pictorial History of the War' – full illus. – 7 vols.
(Baitson) $20 £10

Die New welt, der landschaften unnd Insulen, so bis hie her allen Altweltbeschrybern unbekant/

Gedruckt zu Straßburg durch Georgen Ulricher

An. M. D. XXXIIII.

HUTTICH, JOHANN
'Die New Welt' – 1st Edn. in German – xylographed title – woodcut initials – printer's device – contem. marginalia – vellum ms leaf over boards – folio – Strassburg 1534.
(Christie's) $1,220 £580

HUXLEY, ALDOUS
'The Devils of Loudun' – illustrated – good – 1952.
(J. Ash) $8 £4

HUXLEY, T. H.
'Life and Letters' – editor Leonard Huxley – 2 plates – 1st Edn. – 2 vols. – cloth slightly soiled – 1900.
(Bonhams) $40 £18

HYDE, J. A. LLOYD
'Oriental Lowestoft' – number 424 of 1000 copies – col. frontis – illus. – orig. cloth – soiled – t.e.g. – 4to. – New York 1936.
(Christie's) $115 £55

I

ICONOGRAPHIE FRANCOISE OU PORTRAITS DES PERSONNAGES LES PLUS ILLUSTRE
2 vol. – litho portraits – stained – contem. half morocco – folio – Paris n.d.
(Sotheby's) $40 £20

ILCHESTER, EARL OF
'Letters to Henry Fox, Lord Holland' – orig. calf backed cloth – rubbed – t.e.g. – 4to. – Roxburghe Club 1915.
(Sotheby's) $75 £35

ILLUSTRATED ALPHABET
Wood engr. frontispiece and 31 illustrations – coloured by hand – ornamental borders – orig. pictorial wrappers – backstrip worn – large 8vo. – Albany, NY, Fisk and Little 1860.
(Sotheby's) $65 £30

ILLUSTRATED BOOKS
'Language of Flowers' Boston 1865; 'Language of Flowers' London 1847; Longfellow 'Song of Hiawatha' 1906: 'Fairy Tales from the Arabian Nights' London 1893; Goldsmith's 'The Vicar of Wakefield' London 1896 – 5 vols. – all orig. cloth.
(Robert Skinner) $130 £62

ILLUSTRATED LONDON NEWS
37 vol. various – folio – various bindings – worn – 1870-99.
(Christie's S. Kensington) $735 £350

6 vols. – circa 1846.
(Laurence & Martin Taylor) $85 £40

ILLUSTRATION TO THE BABURNAMA
Oleander and screw pine, birds flocking round pink blossoms, panel of four lines with gold and green margins, attributed 'drawing by Miskina, painted by Bhawani' – laid down on gilt sprinkled album leaf – framed – folio 14 x 9 in. – Mughal circa 1590.
(Christie's) $8,820 £4,200

ILLUSTRATION TO THE BHAGVATA PURANA
Dominant colours green and black – some rubbing – staining and creasing – yellow margin between black rules – black and white rule on red leaf – repaired and restored – 41 cm. x 23.5 cm – Mewar circa 1680-1700.
(Christie's) $1,470 £700

ILLUSTRATION TO THE GITA GOVINDA
Krishna visiting Radha – two lines of black and red devnagari on yellow panel above – yellow margin between black rules – black rule on red border – minor flaking – 25cm x 43.5cm. – Mewar circa 1720.
(Christie's) $735 £350

ILLUSTRATION TO THE RAZMNAMA
Signed Fazl – dominant colours orange, red and mauve, pale yellow ground – some staining and holes – verso 32 lines of black naskh in gold margin with blue and black rules – framed – folio 32.7 x 21.5cm. – Sub Imperial Mughal circa 1616.
(Christie's) $4,620 £2,200

ILLUSTRATION TO THE SHAHNAMEH
Equestrian combat; Bijai defeating a Turkish warrior – dominant colours orange, green and gold, pink ground – lapis sky – miniatures – folio – 29.4 x 16.9 cm.
(Christie's) $1,365 £650

ILLUSTRATION TO AN UNIDENTIFIED MSS
Gold margin between black rules – outer blue rule – some waterstaining – edge repaired – 19 line of black naskh – double column – folio – 28.5 x 18 cm.
(Christie's) $2,100 £1,000

ILLUSTRATIONS OF ARMORIAL CHINA
Limited to 100 copies – 24 col. plates – orig. boards – worn and disbound – sm. folio – 1887.
(Christie's) $125 £60

IMISON, JOHN
'Elements of a Science and Art ... a new Edn. ... by Thomas Webster' – 2 vols. – 32 engr. plates – some folding – some spotted – some soiled – contemp. mottled calf – joints cracked – 1808.
(Christie's S. Kensington) $20 £10

IMP, THE (Edited by H. R. Hauptmann)
Vol. 11 no. 4 - vol. 5 no. 0 – 18 issues only and 30 duplicates – mimeographed text – some illus. – orig. wrappers – some worn – 8vo. – Sydney 1936-39.
(Sotheby's) $6 £3

IMPERIAL GALLERY OF BRITISH ART, THE
48 engraved plates – half morocco worn – folio – circa 1875.
(Phillips) $360 £170

IMPERIAL JOURNAL, THE
3 plates – some folding – half morocco – gilt – 4to. – Manchester circa 1850.
(Phillips) $85 £40

IMPRINT, THE
2 vols. – contemp. half morocco – 4to. – 1913.
(Sotheby's) $160 £75

INCHBALD, E.
'Simple Story' – 1st Edn. – 4 vols. – some pages loose – calf gilt upper cover detached on vol. 1 – 1791.
(Phillips) $230 £110

INDEX LIBRORUM PROHIBITORUM
Contem. Italian binding of red morocco gilt with arms of Medici family – 8vo. – Roma 1681.
(Moore Allen & Innocent) $1,050 £500

INDIAN ARMY
Papers of Lieut General Sir Robert Gordon Rogers KCB (1832-1906) Bengal Staff Corps and 20th Punjab Native Regiment – records of army career – auto memoranda – notes etc. – also 12 pages 8vo. of active service in Egypt (Tel el Kebir).
(Phillips) $115 £55

There has been three small Grain Vessels drove on Shore, Tippo was near Pondicherry and Hyder on his Old Ground.

I hope your Lordship has sent on your Letter to Mr. Holland, it is impossible we can stand long against such a combination of Enemys. I inclose you a report I have just received from the Top of the Mount. And am with great truth

My Lord
Your Lordships
Most Obt. Hum: Servt.
Eyre Coote

Right Honble.
Lord Macartney
&c &c &c

I return the Nabobs Letters

INDIA
Important collection of papers relating to Sir Eyre Coote and the Defeat of Hyder Ali 1780-83,mostly from the papers of Lord Macartney, Governor of Madras.
(Sotheby's) $6,300 £3,000

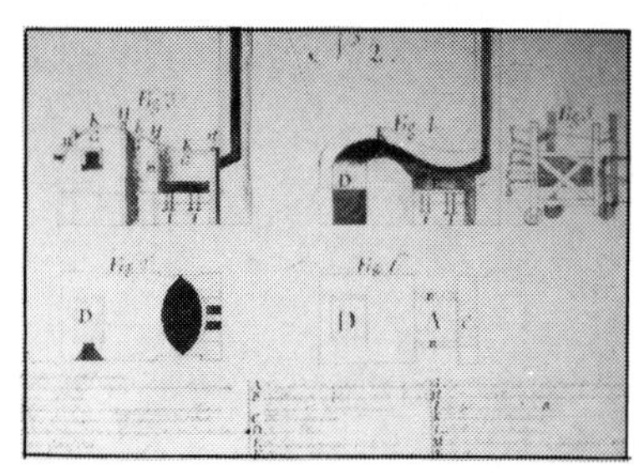

INDUSTRIAL REVOLUTION
Smelting – Exemplification of a patent granted to Robert Albion Cox of Little Britain – illus. with 9 figures drawn in wash – 2 pages of text – folio – with figures on 2 sheets of vellum – signed – duty stamps – 1768.
(Sotheby's) $1,050 £500

INFANT TUTOR, THE
12 woodcut illus. – orig.Dutch floral boards – lacking backstrip – 32 mo. – J. Newbery 1767.
(Sotheby's) $670 £320

INFANTS GRAMMER, THE
Or a Pic-nic of the Parts of Speech – 1st Edn. – 11 wood engr. illustrations coloured by hand – 1p. advertisements at end – slightly stained – orig. printed wrappers – further illustrations on upper cover – soiled and worn – Harris & Son 1822.
(Sotheby's) $115 £55

INFANT'S PATH, THE
Reward Book – 2 corrections by former owner – orig. Dutch floral boards – very slightly rubbed – 32mo. – J. Marshall 1794.
(Sotheby's) $190 £90

INGHIRAMI, FRANCESCO
'Monumenti Etruschi o di Etrusco' – 6 vols. – plus index – plates – some hand col. – half morocco gilt – rubbed – Signet Library copy – 4to. – 1821-26.
(Phillips) $525 £250

INGRAM, JAMES
'Memorials of Oxford' – 3 vols. – 1st. Edn. – 100 plates – woodcut illus. in text – stained and repaired – contem. half roan – faded and worn – 8vo. – 1837.
(Sotheby's) $505 £240

INNERE DES GLASPALASTES IN LONDON DAS (Peepshow)
3 litho sections and front col. by hand – front forming lid of box containing the peepshow – titled in German, French, English and Italian – fitted case – 80 mm x 225 mm extending to 510 mm – Germany 1851.
(Sotheby's) $460 £220

INSECTS AND REPTILES WITH THEIR USES TO MAN
litho frontis – pictorial title and 8 plates – col. by hand – soiled – orig. cloth gilt – stained – 4to. – Darton and Clarke circa 1844.
(Sotheby's) $20 £10

INSTITUTION OF LOCOMOTIVE ENGINEERS
Proceeding – vol. 1-40 in 30 – plates – some folding – illus. – later cloth – 8vo. – 1911-50.
(Sotheby's) $170 £80

INSTRUCTIONS FROM THE ARMY MEDICAL BOARD OF IRELAND, TO REGIMENTAL SURGEONS
Contemp. marbled calf – joints cracked – Dublin – 1806.
(Christie's S. Kensington) $55 £25

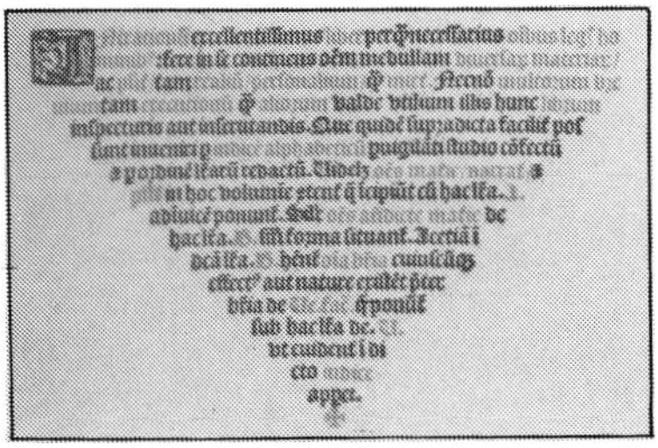

INTRATIONUM EXCELLENTISSIMUS LIBER
Title in red and black – full page woodcut printers device – repairs – 18th cent calf – g.e. folio – Pynson 1510.
(Christie's) $2,940 £1,400

INWOOD, HENRY WILLIAM
'The Erechtheoin Art Athens' – folio – 34 plates – some folding – soiled and dampstained – a few leaves detached – contemp. half morocco – worn – covers detached – 1827.
(Christie's S. Kensington) $40 £18

IRBY, C. L. AND MANGLES, J.
'Travels in Egypt and Nubia, Syria and Asia Minor' – 10 plates and maps – some folding – illus. – contem. calf – rubbed – 8vo. – For Private Distribution 1823.
(Sotheby's) $145 £70

IRELAND

IRELAND
A collection of 6 late 18th cent. pamphlets – 4 relating to Ireland and to Prison Reform, Canal Building and the Church – disbound – 4to. – Dublin and Drogheda 1774-91.
(Sotheby's) $610 £290

IRELAND
Collection of maps and plans of the Irish Bogs – circa 1812.
(Phillips) $460 £220

IRELAND ILLUSTRATED; DEVONSHIRE ILLUSTRATED; LONDON ILLUSTRATED; LONDON IN THE NINTEENTH CENTURY
Extracts from four works in one vol. – 4 engraved titles and 32 plates only – spotted – calf – worn – part of spine lacking – 4to. – 1829-32.
(Christie's S. Kensington) $105 £50

IRELAND, J.
'Hogarth Illustrated' – 2 vols. – illus. – calf gilt – defective – 8vo. – 1791.
(Phillips) $40 £20

IRELAND, S.
'Picturesque Views of the River Medway' – aquatint title – 28 plates – map – some damp-staining – contem. half morocco – rubbed – sm. 4to. – 1793.
(Sotheby's) $170 £80
'Picturesque Views on the River Thames' – 2 vol. – frontispieces – illustrations – occasional slight spotting – orig. cloth – slightly soiled – joints slightly torn – 1848.
(Christie's S. Kensington) $200 £95

IRELAND, W. H.
'Life of Napoleon Bonaparte' – 4 vols. – hand col. plates by Cruickshank – blue morocco gilt with arms on covers by Riviere – lower hinge of 4 cracked – 1828.
(Phillips) $670 £320
'England's Topographer or a New and complete History of ... Kent' – 4 vol. – engraved folding map – title to vol. 1 and 124 plates – 2 detached – some browning – contemporary straight grained calf – spines – rubbed – lower joint of vol 4 broken – 1829-30.
(Christie's S. Kensington) $275 £130

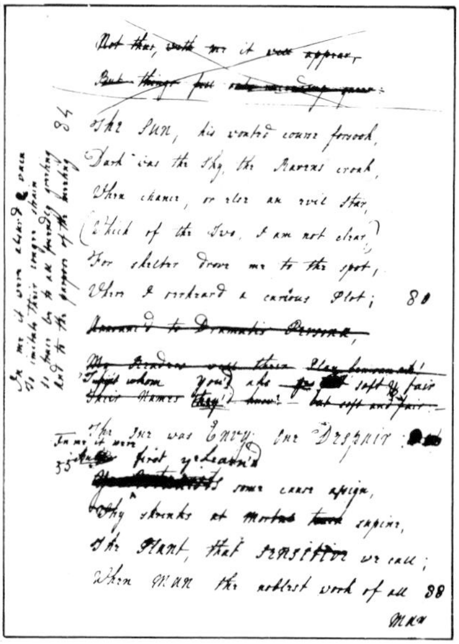
The Sun, his wonted course forsook,
Dark was the sky, the Ravens croak,
Then chance, or else an evil star,
(Which of the two, I am not clear)
For shelter drove me to the spot,
When I rehears'd a curious Plot;
The one was Envy, one Despair
Why shrinks at mortal touch supine,
The Plant, that sensitive we call;
When Man the noblest work of all

IRELAND, WILLIAM HENRY
Important collection of auto literary mss by Ireland's 'Mother' Anna Maria de Burgh Coppinger (Mrs Freeman) many inscribed and signed by Ireland – c 260 pages – dampstained – 4 printed pamphlets – circa 1771-1796.
(Sotheby's) $5,250 £2,500

IRVING, G. AND MURRAY, A.
'The Upper Ward of Lanarkshire' – 3 volumes – maps and plates – large paper copy – quarter mor. – Glasgow 1864.
(Bennett Book Auction) $145 £70

IRWIN, WYLES
'A Series of Adventures, A Voyage Up the Red Sea' – 3rd Edn. – 5 maps (1 loose) – calf – 1787.
(Phillips) $160 £75

ITUC, M.
'Souvenirs d'un Voyages dans La Tartare .. et La Chine' – 2 vol. – folding map – spotting throughout – cloth – Paris, 1850.
(Christie's S. Kensington) $40 £18

JACKSON, SIR C. J.
'English Goldsmiths and their Marks' – frontis loose – 2nd Edn. – cloth – 1921.
(Bonhams) $40 £18
'An Illustrated History of English Plate' – 2 vol. – plates – some coloured – contemp. half morocco – rubbed – 4to. –
(Sotheby's) $105 £50

JACKSON, ELIZABETH
'The Practical Companion to the Work Table' – 11 litho plates – slight dampstains – orig. cloth – spine rubbed – g.e. – sm. 8vo. – 1845.
(Christie's S. Kensington) $20 £10

JACKSON, MRS E. NEVILL
'Silhouette' – plates – some mounted – col. – orig. cloth – faded and soiled – 4to – 1938.
(Christie's) $30 £15

JACKSON, HOLBROOK
'The Anatomy of Bibliomania' – orig. cloth – dust jacket – 1950.
(Christie's S. Kensington) $30 £15

JACKSON, J.
'History of the Scottish Stage' – contemp. calf – 1st Edn. – Edinburgh 1793.
(Bennett Book Auction) $105 £50

JACKSON, JAMES GRAY
'An Account of the Empire of Morocco' – port. – 14 maps and plates – some col. – tree calf – rubbed – 4to. – 1814.
(Phillips) $230 £110

JACKSON, MARIA E.
'The Florist's Manual' – hand col. folding frontis – 4 col. plates – orig. boards – 1827.
(Phillips) $95 £45

JACOB, MAX
Project for a decor – charcoal, indian ink and gouache signed – 37.2cm. x 54cm.
(Sotheby's) $630 £300

JACOB, WILLIAM
'Travels in the South of Spain' – 1st Edn. – 13 engraved plates – 12 hand col. aquatints – 1 folding map with text – cloth – very worn – 4to. – 1811.
(Sotheby's) $275 £130

JACOBS, W. W.
'A Master of Craft' – illustrated by Will Owen – covers a little dull – some foxing – 1900.
(J. Ash) $25 £12

JACQUE-DELAHAYE, XAVROUIN
'Du Retablissement des Eglises de France' – Contem. French straight grained green morocco gilt with arms of Charles X of France surrounded by decorated panels – 4to. – 1822.
(Moore Allen & Innocent) $420 £200

JACQUES, H.
'Sous le Signe du Rossignol' – 19 col. plates and other illus. by Nillsen – limited Edn. – on Japanese vellum – with extra suite of col. plates – 4to. – orig. printed wrapper – Paris, 1923.
(Bonhams) $400 £190

JACQUIN, NICOLAUS JOSEPH VON
'Icones Plantarum Rariorum' – 3 vols. – 649 hand col. plates – tears – dust stained – half morocco – uncut – folio – 1781-93.
(Christie's) $13,020 £6,200

JAGO, F. W. P.
'An English-Cornish Dictionary' – 1st Edn. – rebound in ornamental morocco gilt – 1887.
(Lane) $75 £35

JALOVEC, K.
'German and Austrian Violin-Makers'– 4to. – illustrations – original cloth – 1967.
(Christie's S. Kensington) $40 £18

JAMAICA
Cornwallis, Lieut Col. Stephen – series of 9 ALs 17 pages – folio – Port Royal, Jamaica, April-Dec. 1731 to Sir William Strickland giving account of the difficulties facing officers in Jamaica – contem. endorsement.
(Phillips) $210 £100

Gentle Peter Watson, man of culture,
evinced an interest in this slim green book;
the author seized upon him like a vulture,
and for his copy his pounds seven took.
There were but three bound copies – and none others;
now several more are found, I must confess.
But, though his copy has a suite of brothers,
I trust kind Watson will not like it less.

JAMES, EDWARD
'Opus Septimum' – Limited to 30 copies – pictorial decorations by Rex Whistler – inscribed by author – orig. green morocco – 'Your Name is Lamia' in gilt on upper cover – slightly rubbed – 4to. – 1933.
(Sotheby's) $545 £260

The bearer can give you a full account of my present Circumstances, which are not at all changed from what they were when you heard last from me.
Tho i have charged this honest bearer with messages for you, yet i am glad to tell you hear that i shall always beleeve you a trew friend to my son till you yourself chuse the contrary and that i shall ever be a trew friend to you

JAMES FRANCIS EDWARD STUART
Auto letter unsigned – 1 page octavo – informing correspondent that bearer of letter will provide details of his circumstances – integral leaf with small seal – No place Sept. 1706.
(Sotheby's) $460 £220

JAMES, HENRY
'The Madonna of the Future' – first one vol. Edn. rebound in slightly later half calf by Bickers – 1880.
(J. Ash) $20 £10

JAMES, HOLMAN
'A Voyage Round the World' – 4 vol. – engraved portrait – one folding lithographed map and 21 plates – most by Louis Haghe – some soiling – modern calf backed boards – 1834-35.
(Christie's S. Kensington) $160 £75

JAMES, G. P. R.
'Darnley' – 3 vols. – contemp. half calf gilt – a little worn – 1830.
(J. Ash) $75 £35
'The Commissioner' – 28 steel engravings by Phiz – orig. cloth binding – Curry Dublin 1846.
(Allen & May) $10 £5

JAMES, J. T.
'Journal of a Tour in Germany, Sweden, Russia and Poland' – vig. title – 18 plates calf – 4to. – 1816.
(Phillips) $160 £75

JAMES, MARY B.
'Practical Suggestions in Toy Making for Children' – col. illus. by Irene Heaven – orig. cloth with pictorial cover label – 4to. n.d.
(Sotheby's) $20 £10

JAMES IV, KING OF SCOTLAND
Signet letters signed James R – 1 page – oblong narrow folio – to James Livingstone of Kilsyth requiring him to seize two transgressors – October 1508.
(Sotheby's) $1,680 £800

JAMES V, KING OF SCOTLAND
Signet letters signed James R – 1 page quarto – to Justice, Treasurer, deputies and clerks ordering them to cease any proceedings against William Livingstone of Kilsyth – Stirling February 1529/30.
(Sotheby's) $735 £350

JAMES, WILLIAM
' A Full and Correct Account of the Chief Naval Occurrences of the Late War between Great Britain and the United States of America' – three engr. plates – slightly spotted – margins shaved with loss of a few letters – contemp. half calf – rubbed – 1817.
(Christie's S. Kensington) $60 £28
'The Naval History of Great Britain' – 6 vol. – portraits – folding diagrams – contemp. half calf – rubbed – 8vo: – 1837.
(Sotheby's) $135 £65

JAMIESON, ALEXANDER
'A Celestial Atlas' – engraved title – dedication leaf – 30 celestial maps – 29 hand col. – spotting – orig. half morocco – worn – 4to. – 1822.
(Christie's) $250 £120

JANASHIAN, M.
'Armenian Miniature Paintings of the Monastic Library of San Lazzaro' – colour plates – rexin folio – Venice n.d.
(Phillips) $75 £35

JANE'S FIGHTING SHIPS
In orig. slipcase – 1941.
(Lane) $40 £18

JANE'S OCEAN TECHNOLOGY
1979-80
(Bennett Book Auction) $15 £7

JANIN, JULES
'Un Hiver a Paris' – 1st Edn. – woodcut on title – 18 engraved plates by Eugene Lami – woodcuts in text by Daumier etc. – spotting – contem. half roan – corners and joints worn – 8vo. – Paris 1843.
(Sotheby's) $55 £25

JANSON, J.
'Nottingham' – hand col. map – cartouche – circa 1650.
(Phillips) $115 £55

JARDINE, W.
'Naturalist's Library' – 40 volumes – including Entomology – 7 volumes – Ichthyology 6 volumes – Mammalia 13 volumes – Ornithology 14 volumes – over 1300 hand coloured plates – original cloth – Edinburgh 1833-43.
(Bennett Book Auction) $1,365 £650

JAUFFRET, LOUIS FRANCOIS
'The Little Hermitage' – 3 engraved plates and wood engraved vignette – spotted – morocco backed boards – worn – 12mo. – Birmingham circa 1805.
(Sotheby's) $10 £5

JEAURAT, M.
'Connaissance de Temps ou Exposition du Mouvement des Artes' – folding engr. map – folding tables – orig. wrappers – torn unopened – 8vo. – Paris 1784.
(Sotheby's) $25 £12

JEFFERIES, RICHARD
'Hodge and His Masters' – two vols. – orig. cloth expertly restored – new endpapers – 1880.
(J. Ash) $160 £75

JEFFREYS, JOHN GWYNN
'British Conchology or an Account of the Mollusca' – 5 vols. – most 1st Edn. – numerous plates – 100 coloured – uniform cloth – slightly faded – 12 mo. – 1904 – 1863-69.
(Sotheby Beresford Adams) $210 £100

JEFFREYS, T.
'The County of York' – engraved map on 20 sheets – hand coloured in outline – six town plan vignettes – elaborate dedication and title cartouches with views of Fountains Abbey and Middleton Castle – on guards throughout – two sheets with tears along centre fold – calf backed – worn – lge. folio – 1771-2.
(Christie's S. Kensington) $460 £220

JEFFREYS, T.
'Collection of the Dresses of Different Nations, Ancient and Modern' – 4 vols – 478 of 480 engraved plates – text in English and French – original boards – slightly rubbed – 4to. – 1799.
(Sotheby's) $250 £120

JEKYLL, GERTRUDE
Some English Gardens – fourth impression – coloured plates after drawings by G. S. Elgood – orig. cloth – rubbed – sm. folio – 1906.
(Christie's S. Kensington) $80 £38

'Wall and Water Gardens' – buckram – 3rd Edn. – n.d.
(Bennett Book Auction) $25 £12

Mr Jenner returns the Book & begs his best thanks – He has not finished the Birds he intended for you, but for the present begs your acceptance of the Golden-crested Wren. I wish you much pleasure in the Metropolis & am Dr Sir Yr most sincerely E Jenner [illegible]

JENNER, DR. EDWARD
AL to Dr. Cheston thanking him for a letter and a bird – a magpie – 2 pages – 4to – n.d.
(Sotheby's) $505 £240

JENNER, HENRY
'A Handbook of the Cornish Language' – orig. cloth binding – 1904.
(Lane) $34 £16

JEROME K. JEROME
'Three Men in a Boat' – illus. by A. Frederics – orig. cloth – worn – Bristol 1889.
(Christie's) $20 £10

JEROME, SAINT
'Solitudo sive Vitae Patrum Beremicolarum' – 5 parts in one – 135 engraved plates – title detached – soiled – 18th cent. half calf – upper cover detached – oblong 4to. – circa 1621.
(Sotheby's) $545 £260

JERRARD, PAUL (publisher)
'Butterflies in their Floral Homes ... indited by a Dreamer in the Woods' – hand coloured title and 8 full page illustrations only (of 9) – text printed in red with page headings and decorative borders in gold – one leaf lacking – g.e. – n.d.
(Christie's S. Kensington) $95 £45

JESSE, EDWARD
'Anecdotes of Dogs' – plates, original cloth, t.e.g., soiled – 1846.
(Christie's S. Kensington) $145 £65

JESSE, GEORGE R.
'Researches into the History of the British Dog' – 2 vol – 20 engraved plates by the author – extra-illustrated – contemp. calf – gilt – covers detached and crudely repaired – t.e.g. – 1866.
(Christie's S. Kensington) $125 £60

JESSE, J. HENEAGE
'Literary and Historical Memorials of London' – 2 vol. – nine plates – two folding – margins browned – orig. cloth – rebacked with portion of spines laid down – 1847.
(Christie's S. Kensington) $45 £22

'Works' – 30 vol. – plates – orig. cloth – slightly rubbed – spines – gilt – t.e.g. – 1901.
(Christie's S. Kensington) $40 £20

JEU DES DRAPEAUX
Complete set of 32 engraved cards – undivided sheet – col. by hand – depicting French, Russian, German and English armies – soiled – mounted on thin card – 435 mm x 543 mm. – after 1814.
(Sotheby's) $220 £105

JEWEL, JOHN
'A Replie unto M. Hardings Answeare' – folio – black letter – outer blank margin of last few leaves holed – margins affected by damp – cont. blind stamped calf – rebacked – old spine laid down – lower joint split – clasps lacking – 1565.
(Christie's S. Kensington) $250 £120

JEWELS, A. J.
'Heraldic Church Notes from Cornwall' – 1st Edn. – half calf binding.
(Lane) $40 £20

JEWERS, A. J.
'The Book Plate Annual' – illus. – 1894-96.
(Dacre, Son & Hartley) $17 £8

JEWITT, LLEWELLYNN AND HALL, S. C.
'The Stately Homes of England' – illustrations – orig. cloth – inner hinges weak – g.e. – 1881.
(Christie's S. Kensington) $40 £20

JEWITT, L.
'The Ceramic Art of Great Britain' – 2 vols. – plates – illus. – orig. cloth – rubbed – 8vo. – 1878.
(Sotheby's) $40 £20

JOAD, C. E. M.
'Folly Farm' – slight foxing – very good in dust wrapper – 1954.
(J. Ash) $8 £4

JOB
A fine watercolour drawing of seated figures representing Justice and Mercy below a standing figure in armour – signed – border defective – 350 mm x 274 mm.
(Sotheby's) $230 £110

JOBSON, R.
'The Golden Trade' – no. 218 of 300 copies – later half calf – sm. 4to. – Teignmouth 1904.
(Sotheby's) $75 £35

JOHN, W. D.
'Nantgarw Porcelain' – plates many coloured -- plus supplement in slip. calf – 4to. – 1948.
(Phillips) $180 £85

JOHN, W. D. AND BAKER, WARREN
'Old English Lustre Pottery' – plates – some col. – cloth – 4to. – Newport 1951.
(Phillips) $80 £38

JOHNNY GILPIN'S DIVERTING JOURNEY TO WARE
Wood engraved frontis and 13 illus. – col. by hand – orig. wrappers – ink stain – frontis and title worn – sm. 8vo. – A. K. Newman – 1827.
(Sotheby's) $34 £16

JOHNSON, A.
'Dictionary of American Biography' – 11 vol. – orig. cloth – 4to. – New York 1957-58.
(Sotheby's) $210 £100

JOHNSON, CHARLES
'British Poisonous Plants' – 28 coloured plates – new cloth – 8vo. – 1856.
(Sotheby's) $65 £32

JOHNSON, E. J.
'Journal of a Trip to Paris' – folding menus – sm. engravings stuck down – 5 full page plates – straight grained calf – g.e. – 1822.
(Phillips) $180 £85

JOHNSON, J.
'A Journey from India to England through Persia, Georgia, Russia, Poland and Prussia' – 13 aquatint plates – 5 hand col. – contem. speckled calf – split – 4to. – 1818.
(Sotheby's) $55 £25

JOHNSON, JOHN
'Typographia or the Printer's Instructor' – 2 vols – 1st Edn. – 2 addit wood engraved vignette titles – 2 portraits – illus. in text – original cloth – not uniform – soiled – 16 mo. – 1824.
(Sotheby's) $30 £15

JOHNSON, PAMELA HANSFORD
'The Honours Board' – slightly chipped dust wrapper – 1970.
(J. Ash) $8 £4

JOHNSON, DR. SAMUEL
'Political Tracts' – 1st Edn. – some leaves soiled – contem. boards – rebacked – rubbed – 8vo. – 1776.
(Sotheby's) $200 £95

JOHNSON, SAMUEL
'Jonsoniana, Being Anecdotes and Sayings of Samuel Johnson' – vol. 1 extended to 3 – large paper copy – extra illus. – 45 engraved plates with 240 addit. plates including 10 from Rowlandson's 'Picturesque Beauties of Boswell' – 11 items of poetry and prose – two examples of Johnson's autograph – late 19th cent. red levant morocco by Riviere – gilt – g.e. – 4to. – 1836.
(Sotheby's) $11,550 £5,500

JOHNSON, WILLIAM
'The Imperial Cyclopaidia of Machinery' – folio – engraved portrait – title – dedication and plates – most folding – a few slightly torn – most spotted – contemp. half morocco – worn – n.d.
(Christie's S. Kensington) $145 £70

JOHNSTON, ALEXANDER KEITH
'The Royal Atlas of Modern Geography' – new Edn. – double page maps – coloured in outline – on guards – orig. half morocco gilt – black morocco dust cover – g.e. – folio – Edinburgh and London 1879.
(Sotheby Beresford Adams) $135 £64
'Physical Atlas of Natural Phenomena' – 3rd Edn. – 35 col. or partly col. double page maps – 7 maps and charts – orig. half calf – rebacked – large folio – Edinburgh 1856.
(Sotheby's) $190 £90

JOHNSTONE, W. G. AND CROALL, A.
'The Nature-printed British Sea-Weeds' – plates – 4 vols – orig. cloth text and plates loose in bindings – 1859-60.
(Bonhams) $65 £32

JOLIMONT, F. T. DE
'Vues Pittoresques de la Cathedrale D'Amiens, Orleans, Paris, Reims' – lithos after Chapuy – spotting – half calf – cover detached – 4to – 1824-26.
(Phillips) $95 £45

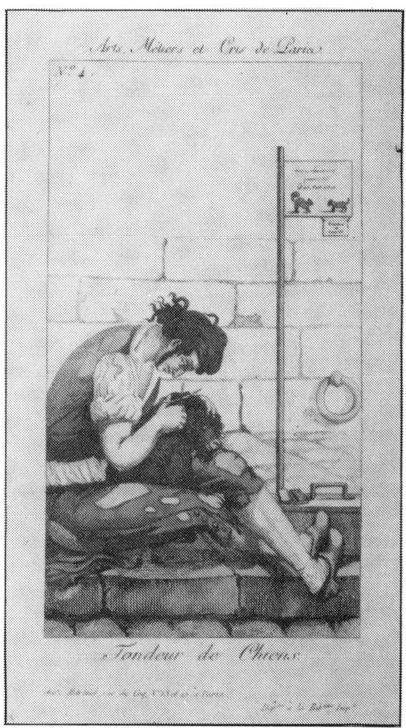

JOLY, ADRIEN
'Les Petits Acteurs du Grand Theatre ou Recueil de Divers Cris de Paris' – engraved title and 60 hand coloured engraved plates – a few by Joly – half title – contemporary red morocco backed boards – gilt and a little rubbed – uncut – binder's gilt monogram inside front cover – 4to. – Paris, Martinet, circa 1815.
(Sotheby Parke Bernet $4,645 £2,212

JOLY, HENRI L.
'Legend in Japanese Art' – illus. incl. 16 col. plates – orig. cloth gilt – g.e. – 4to. – 1908.
(Phillips) $180 £85

JONES & CO'
'Diamond Poets' 35 vols.; 'Diamond Classics' 9 vols. – together 44 vols. – addit. engraved titles – orig. silk bindings – various colours – spines worn and faded – in 2 small glazed bookcases in red leather – prize set from Trinity College, Dublin – gilt arms on back – 16mo. – 1824-32.
(Sotheby's) . $400 £190

JONES, DAVID
Intaglio wood engravings with title 'Omnes de Saba Venient' – showing the three kings – signed and dated – inscribed Christmas 1926 – 125 mm x 100 mm.
(Sotheby's) $230 £110

JONES E. A.
'Catalogue of the Gutmann Collection of Plate' – plates – cloth gilt – t.e.g. – 4to. – 1907.
(Phillips) $145 £70

'The Gold and Silver of Windsor Castle' – number 91 of 285 copies – plates – orig. cloth folio – 1911.
(Sotheby's) $180 £85

JONES, GWYN
'The Green Island' – number 341 of 500 copies – frontis and illus. by John Petts – orig. cloth – t.e.g. – 1946.
(Christie's) $20 £10

JONES, INIGO
'Designs of Plans and Elevations for Public and Private Buildings' – 2 vols. in one – 2 vignettes – 127 of 136 plates – many folding – some repairs – half calf covers detached – folio – 1727.
(Phillips) $180 £85

JONES, LIEUT. R.
'Artificial Fireworks' – 2nd Edn. – eight folding engr. plates – one with large section torn away – title torn without loss – heavily soiled – with a plate depicting the Jubilee Fireworks in 1814 bound at front – later calf – 1776.
(Christie's S. Kensington) $75 £35

JONES, OWEN
'The Psalms of David Illuminated' – chromo-lithographed throughout – original repousse calf – slightly soiled and rubbed – disbound – folio – g.e. (n.d.).
(Christie's S. Kensington) $170 £80
'Grammar of Ornament' – coloured title and 111 plates – half calf – defective – folio – 1856.
(Phillips) $135 £65
'The Sermon on the Mount' – chromolith title and 15 leaves by Jones – orig. purple hand grained morocco – blind stamped – spine and corners worn – g.e. – 1845.
(Christie's) $60 £28
'Gray's Elegy' – lge. 8vo. – chromo. title and 17 leaves by Jones – slightly spotted and soiled – orig. heavily embossed calf by Remnant & Edmonds – rubbed and soiled – g.e. – 1846.
(Christie's S. Kensington) $90 £42

JONES, OWEN AND GOURY, JULES
'Plans, Elevations, Sections and Details of the Alhambra' – 2 vol. – chromolithographed add. titles – 102 engraved – text in English and French – light spotting – contemp. half morocco – slightly rubbed – spines gilt – g.e. – folio – 1842-45.
(Christie's S. Kensington) $2,730 £1,300

JONES, OWEN – LOCKHART, J. G.
'Ancient Spanish Ballads' – new Edn. – chromolithographed additional title – sub-titles – borders and vignettes by Jones – occasional slight spotting – original salmon cloth – upper cover and spine stamped in gilt – slightly soiled – g.e. – 4to. – 1856.
(Christie's S. Kensington) $30 £15

JONES, PHILIP
'An Essay on Crookedness or Distortions of the Spine' – 5 folding plates – new cloth – 8vo. – for the author by S. Gosnell 1788.
(Sotheby's) $105 £50

JONES, T. R.
'Cassell's Book of Birds' – from the text of Dr. Brehm – 4 vol. in two 4to. – 40 coloured plates – one torn at foot – illustrations – spotting – contemp. half morocco.
(Christie's S. Kensington) $80 £38

JONES'VIEWS OF THE SEATS, MANSIONS, CASTLES
4to. – engraved title – and 144 plates – slight spotting and staining – half calf – circa 1829.
(Christie's S. Kensington) $145 £70

JONES, WILLIAM
'Poiklographia' – frontis – calligraphic title – 20 pp alphabets and texts – vignettes – stained – modern cloth preserving orig. cover label - folio – W. Jones circa 1830.
(Sotheby's) $45 £22

JONES, SIR WILLIAM
'Poems ..... Translations from the Asiatick Languages' – calf gilt – 1777.
(Phillips) $75 £35

JONSON, BEN
'A Croppe of Kisses' – number 101 of 250 copies – orig. morocco backed cloth by Sangorski and Sutcliffe – t.e.g. – sm. folio – 1937.
(Christie's) $40 £20
'Works' – folio Edn. – engraved portrait – contemp. mottled calf – rebacked and repaired – rubbed – folio – 1692.
(Sotheby's) $210 £100

JONSTON, J.
'Inscriptiones Historicae Regum Scotorum' – 1st Edn., 11 engraved plates, 10 portraits and royal coat of arms, repaired, good but washed copy in 19th century blue morocco, gilt, g.e., slightly worn, bookplate of Wm. Barr Knox – Amsterdam, Claesson for A. Hart, Edinburgh, 1602.
(Sotheby's Edinburgh) $360 £160

JOUBERT DE L'HIBERDERIE
'Le Dessinateur, Pour Les Fabriques D'Etoffes D'Ore, D'Argent' – woodcut designs – 8vo. –1765.
(Phillips) $250 £120

JOUBERT, F.
'Catalogue of the Collection of European Arms and Armour formed at Greenock by R. L. Scott' – vol. 2 & 3 only (of 3) limited Edn. – plates – orig. half vellum rubbed – folio – 1924.
(Sotheby's) $55 £25

Un peu plus tard, il y eut les tourterelles qu'apprivoisa, pour enchanter mon enfance, mon père qui avait quelque chose d'un poète et d'un oiseleur. Il n'ignorait le chant ni les habitudes d'aucun de nos passereaux. Mon premier acte fut de contrefaire nos tourterelles ; en dode-

JOUHANDEAU, MARCEL AND LAURENCIN, MARIE
'Petit Bestaire' – 8 col. etched illus. by Laurencin – slightly offset – unsewn in orig. wrappers – folder and slipcase – 8vo. – Paris, 1944.
(Sotheby's) $7,350 £3,500

JOURDAIN, M.
'English Decoration and Furniture of the later XVIIIth century 1760-1820' – plates – cloth gilt – Batsford circa 1922.
(Bennett Book Auction) $40 £18

JOURNAL DES DEMOISELLES
Vol. 39-63 – approx. 476 fashion plates – mostly hand col. – contemp. roan backed cloth – gilt – rubbed – 4to. – Paris 1871-95.
(Sotheby's) $1,510 £720

JOUTEL, HENRI
'Journal Historique du Dernier Voyage .... dans la Golfe de Mexique' – 1st.Edn. – large engraved folding map – contem. calf – spine rubbed – 12 mo. – Paris 1713.
(Christie's) $1,470 £700

read we in must book. It tells. He prophets most who bilks the best.

And that salubrated sickenagiaour of vaours have teaspilled all my haz ydency. Forge away, Sunny Sim! Sheepshopp. Bleating Goad, it is the least of things. Eveinstye! Imagine it, my deep dartry dullard! It is hours giving, not more. I'm only out for celebridging over the guilt of the gap in your hiscitendency. You are a hundred thousand times welcome, old wortsampler, hellbeit you're just about as culpable as my woolfell merger would be. In effect I could engage in an energument over you till you were republicly royally toobally prussic blue in the shirt after.[1] *Trionfante di bestia!* And if you're not your bloater's kipper may I never curse again on that pint I took of Jamesons. Old Keane now, you're rod, hook and sinker, old jubalee Keane! Biddy's hair. Biddy's hair, mine lubber. Where is that Quin but he sknows it knot but what you that are my popular endphthisis were born with a solver arm up your sleep. Thou in shanty! Thou in scanty shanty!! Thou in slanty scanty shanty!!! Bide in your hush! Bide in your hush, do! The law does not aloud you to shout. I plant my penstock in your postern, chinarpot. Ave! And let it be to all remembrance. Vale. Ovocation of maiding waters.[2] For auld lang salvy steyne. I defend you to champ my scullion's praises. To book alone belongs the lobe. Foremaster's meed[3] will mark tomorrow when we are making pilscrummage to whaboggeryin with

Finnegan.

[1] From three shellings. A bluedye sacrifice.
[2] Not Kilty. But the manajar was. He! He! Ho! Ho! Ho!
[3] Giglamps, Soaps Geyser, The Smell and Gory Mac Gusty.

305 u

JOYCE, JAMES
'Finnegan's Wake' – 1st Edn. – limited to 425 copies – this marked 'out of series' – disbound and revised for a new Edn. – revisions printed and pasted in, many pencil markings – orig. cloth – t.e.g. – 8vo. – London and New York, 1939.
(Sotheby's) $880 £420

'Ulysses' – 8th printing – orig. wrappers – slightly soiled and torn – sm. 4to. – Paris, Shakespeare and Company – 1926.
(Christie's S. Kensington) $30 £15

'A Portrait of the Artist as a Young Man' – 1st English Edn., original cloth – The Egoist Ltd., 1916.
(Sotheby's) $180 £80

'Exiles' – orig. cloth backed boards – slightly bumped at corners – 1918.
(J. Ash) $170 £80

JUAN, JORGE
'Compendio de Navegacion Para el Uso de los Cavalleros Guardia Marinas' – 1st Edn. engraved title vignette – 12 folding maps and plates – waterstained – contem. mottled sheep – gilt – 4to. – Cadiz 1757.
(Sotheby's) $275 £130

JUDGE, ARTHUR W.
'The Modern Motor Engineer' – 5 vol. illus. – Caxton Publishing Co.
(Baitson) $12 £6

JUDGEND
4 vols. – illus. – orig. wraps – half calf – 1901-2.
(Phillips) $275 $130

JULIEN DE LYON
Portrait of Sarah Bernhardt – pastel – signed and dated – inscribed – 25 inch x 19½ inch.
(Sotheby's) $5,670 £2,700

JULIEN, R. J.
'Atlas Topgraphique et Militaire' – engr. tilte – 46 engr. maps – five flg. remainder double page – slight marginal worming – contemp. calf – 4to. – Paris – 1758.
(Christie's S. Kensington) $210 £100

JUNGMAN, NICO AND BEATRIX
'Holland' – no. 277 of 300 – signed by a artist – coloured plates by N. Jungman – browning – orig. cloth – t.e.g. – 4to. – 1904.
(Christie's) $45 £22

JUST, MICHAEL
'Escape and Other Verse' – orig. wraps. – spine worn through – Leeds 1924.
(J. Ash) $5 £2

JUVENALIS, DECIMUS JUNIUS AND AULUS PERSIUS FLECCUS
'The Satires ... Translated into English Verse by Mr Dryden – folio – inner margin of first few leaves stained – contemp. speckled calf – rebacked – old spine laid down – re-cornered – Jacob Tonson 1693.
(Christie's S. Kensington) $95 £45
'Persii Flacci Satyrae' – contem. English binding of red morocco gilt – black morocco onlays – gilt – 12 mo. – 1744.
(Moore Allen & Innocent) $170 £80

JUVENILE LIBRARY
'A Picture of the Seasons with Anecdotes and Remarks on Every Month of the Year' – wood engraved frontispiece, vignette on title, 4 full page illustrations, very slightly spotted, original roan backed boards, soiled and rubbed – Printed for S. and A. Davis, 1818.
(Sotheby's, Chancery Lane) $55 £25

JUVENILE TRIALS FOR ROBBING ORCHARDS
4th Edn. – wood engraved frontis and 16 illus. – orig. printed boards – 2 illus. on each cover – signed J. Bell – soiled – 12 mo. – T. Carnan 1781.
(Sotheby's) $315 £150

JUVENILIA
Charming coloured rebus letter by Harry Palmer to a child – 3 pages – 4to. – Rudge near Ross, Feb. 1863.
(Sotheby's) $95 £45

KADEN AND NESTAL
'Die Rivere' – 1st Edn. in orig. pictorial cloth – full page coloured plates – book plate of Princess Beatrix – 1884.
(Lane) $55 £25

KALANAG
A collection of 29 programmes, prospectuses, press cuttings and playbills for performances by Kalanag and Gloria in Germany and Great Britain and 10 duplicates – various sizes - circa 1950-55.
(Sotheby's) $315 £150

KALSTONE, DAVID
'Five Temperaments' – New York 1977.
(J. Ash) $6 £3

KAMES, HENRY HOME, LORD
'The Gentleman Farmer' – 3rd Edn. – engraved port. – 3 plates – advert leaf at end – browning – portrait – shaved – 19th cent half calf – spine gilt – rubbed – 8vo. – Edinburgh 1788.
(Sotheby's) $125 £60

KANE, E. K.
'Arctic Explorations' – 2 vol. – 1st Edn. – engraved plates – titles and maps – contem. half calf – gilt – rubbed – 8vo. – Philadelphia 1856.
(Sotheby's) $55 £25

KANE, R.
'Campaigns of King William and the Duke of Marlborough' – folding map – 17 plates – 1 folding – contem. calf gilt – 1747.
(Phillips) $95 £45

KARAMSIN, NICOLAI
'Travels from Moscow Through Prussia, Germany, Switzerland, France and England' – 3 vols. – frontis – folding map – slightly shaved – contem. spotted calf – joints worn – hinges crudely repaired – 12 mo. – 1803.
(Christie's S. Kensington) $95 £45

KAROLIK, M. AND M.
'Collection of American Watercolours & Drawings' – 2 vol. – 4to. – illustrations – original cloth backed boards – slipcase – Boston 1962.
(Christie's S. Kensington) $60 £28

KARR, ALPHONSE
'Voyage Autour de Mon Jardin' – 4to. – eight hand coloured plates – illustrations – seven full page – stained – contemp. half morocco – slightly rubbed and soiled – g.e. – Paris 1851.
(Christie's S. Kensington) $85 £40

KASSEL – JANSSON, J.
'Casselae Vulgo Kassel' – double page engraved view of city intersected by River Fulda – coats of arms – tabular Key – Latin text on verso – uncut – 407 mm x 510 mm – Amsterdam 1657.
(Sotheby's) $420 £200

KATAEV, VALENTINE
'The Embezzlers' – 1st English Edn.
(J. Ash) $6 £3

KAUSLER, F. VON
'Atlas des Plus Memorables Batailles .. Atlas der Wichtigsten Schlacten' – 5 vol. – Carsruche and Freiberg – folding title and prospectus – 152 plans – hand coloured in outline and mounted on cloth – some dampstained – contained in cloth backed slipcases – 1831-37.
(Christie's S. Kensington) $250 £120

KAY, JOHN
'Etchings' – a disbound collection of approximately 108 plates.
(Bennett Book Auction) $40 £18
'Edinburgh Portraits' – part 12 volume 2 – 11 etchings – original wrappers – 1838.
(Bennett Book Auction) $25 £11

KAYE, J.
'History of the Sepoy War in India 1857-1858' – 3 vols. – cloth – 1875.
(Bennett Book Auction) $40 £18

KEATE, GEORGE
'An Account of the Peleu Islands ... composed from the journals ... of Captain Henry Wilson, and some of his officers who ... were there shipwrecked' – 4to. – engr. portrait – 15 plates – one folding – and one folding chart – some light spotting and offsetting a few stains – contemp. calf – rubbed – crudely rebacked – inner hinges cracked – 1788.
(Christie's S. Kensington) $250 £120

KEATS, JOHN
'Endymion' – no. 317 of 500 copies – wood engraved frontis – vignette on title – 2 initials and 53 illus. by John Buckland-Wright – 11 full page – orig. parchment backed cloth gilt – t.e.g. – sm. folio – 1947.
(Sotheby's) $365 £175

KEILL, J.
'Introduction to the True Astronomy' – 26 folding plates – 2 folding maps of the moon – calf gilt – rebacked – 1748.
(Phillips) $60 £28

KEITH, ALEXANDER REV. DR.
'Evidence of Prophecy' – daguerrotype views and other engravings – cloth gilt – new Edn. – 1848.
(Richard Baker & Thomson) $80 £38

KELLY'S DIRECTORY OF HULL, 1929
With folding map.
(Baitson) $25 £13

KELSON, GEORGE M.
'The Salmon Fly' – 8 col. plates – illus. – orig. cloth – rubbed – t.e.g. – 4to.
(Sotheby's) $315 £150

KENDRICK, T.
'The Axe Age' – cloth – n.d. and 18 other books on prehistory circa 1920.
(Bennett Book Auction) $14 £7

KENDON, FRANK
'A Life and Death of Judas Iscariot' – 1926.
(J. Ash) $12 £6

KENILWORTH ILLUSTRATED
Engraved portrait – detached and spotted – and 18 plates – half title detached – contemporary half calf – rubbed – spine lacking – 4to. – Chiswick, 1821.
(Christie's S. Kensington) $40 £20

KENNEDY, A. B. W.
'Petra, Its History and Monuments' – photogravure plates – orig. cloth – 4to. – 1925.
(Sotheby's) $85 £40

KENNEDY, JOHN F.
'While England Slept' – spine a little faded – 1940.
(J. Ash) $17 £8

KENRICK, T.
'British Stage' – 2 vols. – col. plates – half green morocco gilt – 1817-18.
(Phillips) $125 £60

KENSINGTON, LONDON – RHODES, JOSHUA, SURVEYOR: GEORGE BICKHAM, ENGRAVER
' A Topographical Survey of the Parish of Kensington' – fine large scale plan perspective view – cartouche – 12 sections joined – whole mounted on linen – dust soiled – rolled – 42 in x 104 in – for Carington Bowles 1766.
(Sotheby's) $295 £140

KENT, ROCKWELL
'N by E' – very good in worn and slightly defective dust wrapper – New York 1930.
(J. Ash) $40 £20

KENYON, F. G.
'Facsimiles of the Biblical Manuscripts in the British Museum' – plates – orig. cloth – rubbed – folio – 1900.
(Sotheby's) $34 £16

KEPPEL, HON. AUGUSTUS
'Authentic and Impartial Account of the Trial' – calf gilt – 1779.
(Phillips) $40 £20

KEPPEL, MAJOR HON. G.
'Narrative of a Journey Across the Balcan' – 2 vols. – coloured frontis – 3 maps – half calf – gilt – 1831.
(Phillips) $180 £85

KERN, JEROME
Two typed Lls one signed 'Jerry' 2½ pp. - 4to. and 8vo. – 1 and 28 July 1936 to A. E. Leale of Production Services British Ltd. – on film rights of 'Show Boat' and the mss of 'Three Sisters'.
(Phillips) $100 £48

KERNER, J.
'Figures de Plants Economiques' – vols. 5,6,7, only – 4 coloured titles – 300 hand coloured plates – half calf – 4to. – 1792/3/4.
(Phillips) $1,930 £920

KERSBLAKE, JOHN
'Early Georgian Portraits' – 2 vol. – 4to. – plates – original cloth – dust jackets – slipcase – 1977.
(Christie's S. Kensington) $75 £35

KERSSENBROCH, HERMANN VON
'Catalogus Episcoporum Padibronensium' – italics – hand coloured woodcut arms in title – 43 hand col. woodcut arms in text – soiled – ownership inscription and annotations on title – contem. limp vellum – soiled and worn – sm 8vo – 1578.
(Sotheby's) $545 £260

KEULEN, J. VAN
'Engraved Chart of Part of Russia and China with Nova Zembla and Japan' – hand col. in outline – large historiated title vignette – compass roses – sailing ships – fully col. – 519 mm x 595 mm – Amsterdam circa 1770.
(Sotheby's) $105 £50

KEUR, P. AND J.
'De Bet Chryvingh van de Pauli en van de Andere Aposteleu' – hand coloured engraved map – border of Biblical scenes – extracted from Paradisus Canaan, Dutch text on verso – 1648.
(Christie's S. Kensington) $145 £70

KEYES, SIDNEY
'The Iron Laurel' – orig. stiff wraps – slightly chipped dust wrapper – 1942.
(J. Ash) $17 £8

KEYNES, G.
'A Bibliography of William Blake' – limited Edn. – plates – orig. morocco backed cloth – 4to. – Grolier Club New York 1921.
(Sotheby's) $420 £200

KEYNES, GEOFFREY
'John Ray' limited to 650 copies – illus. and facsimiles – orig. cloth – dust jacket 1951 – with 'John Ray' – a handlist to his Works – presentation copy – inscribed by author – orig. wrappers – 8vo. – Cambridge 1944.
(Sotheby's) $85 £40

KEYNES, JOHN MAYNARD
'How to Pay for the War' – 1st Edn. – orig. boards – 8vo. – 1940.
(Sotheby's) $17 £8

KEYS, JOHN
'The Antient Bee-Master's Farewell or, Full and Plain Directions for the Management of Bees' – two engraved plates, one torn and badly repaired, later half calf, slightly rubbed – 1796.
(Christie's S. Kensington) $180 £80

KEYSLEY, J. G.
'Travels Through Germany' – 4 vols. – plates – calf worn – 4to. – 1756-57.
(Irelands) $315 £150

KEYSSLER, JOHANN GEORG
'Neuest Reisen' – 1 of 3 edited by Gottfried Schutze – 5 plates – 2 folding – 19th cent. boards – 4to. – Hannover 1751.
(Sotheby's) $115 £55

KHISL DE KALTENPRUN
'Herbardia Urspergy Baronis' – last 2 leaves blank – ownership inscription deleted – disbound – sm. 4to. – Laibach, Ioannes Manlius 1575.
(Sotheby's) $180 £85

KHLEBNIKOV, V.
'Treonik Troikh' (Service Book for a Trio) – litho plates by Mayakovsky – orig. wrappers – soiled and frayed – sm. 4to. – Moscow 1913.
(Sotheby's) $965 £460

KHOSLA, K. R. AND CHATTERJEE, R. P.
'His Imperial Majesty King George V and The Prince of India and the Indian Empire' – illustrations – mounted – coloured plates – orig. morocco – boxed g.e. – 4to. – Lahore 1937.
(Christie's S. Kensington) $65 £32

KIDDER, D.
'Sketches of Residence and Travels in Brasil' – 2 volumes – original cloth gilt – 33 engraved plates and illustrations – 1st Edn. – Philadelphia, 1845.
(Bennett Book Auction) $75 £36

KILIAN, GEORG CHRISTOPH
'Monumentae Romae Antiquae .....' – engraved title with vignette – 54 plates – some repairs – marginal staining – German Text in pocket at end – orig. boards – worn – rebacked – folio – Augsburg 1767.
(Sotheby's) $200 £95

KINCAID, A.
'History of Edinburgh' – folding map and plan – contemp. calf – Edinburgh 1787.
(Bennett Book Auction) $90 £44

KING OF THE FOREST, THE
Drawing with some colour – blue border with gold floral motif – laid down on a cream album leaf – gilt sprinkled – inscribed 'Anup Chartar' – Mughal circa 1600–1610.
(Christie's) $12,600 £6,000

KING, C. W.
'Antique Gems and Rings' – 2 vol. plates – spotted – orig. cloth – joints split 8vo. 1872.
(Sotheby's) $75 £35

KING, DANIEL
'The Vale-Royal of England or, The County Palatine of Chester Illustrated ... Performed by William Smith and William Webb' – folio – engr. additional title – 16 plates – one double-page – one folding – three double-page maps and plans – illustrations – later mottled calf – rebacked – old spine laid down – joints split – Printed by John Streater – 1656.
(Christie's S. Kensington) $315 £150

KING, EDWARD
'Muniment Antiqua' – 4 vols. – 1st Edn. – half titles – numerous engraved plates – contem. diced calf – gilt spines – folio – 1799-1805.
(Christie's) $210 £100

KING, CAPT. PHILIP P.
'Narrative of a Survey of the Intertropical and Western Coasts of Australia' – 2 vol. – 1st Edn. – 2 folding engraved maps – 3 folding plates and 11 uncol. aquatints – foxing – later blue half morocco – edges and hinges worn – 8vo. – 1827.
(Sotheby's) $800 £380

KING, RONALD – CHAUCER, GEOFFREY
'The Prologue from the Canterbury Tales' – 14 full page screen printed illus. by King – captioned and initialed in pencil – unsewn in orig. buckram folder – slipcase – folio – Editions Alecto, 1967.
(Sotheby's) $14,700 £7,000

KING, WILLIAM
'Chelsea Porcelain' – plates – some col. – orig. cloth gilt – 4to. – 1922.
(Phillips) $80 £38

KINGS OF SCOTLAND, THE
73 engraved portraits – laid down in decorative border – tree calf – gilt – rubbed – Earl of Fife's bookplate – title dated 1781.
(Phillips) $55 £25

KINGSLEY, CHARLES
'The Heroes' – orig. decorative cloth – a little worn – some slight foxing – a little loose – Cambridge 1856.
(J. Ash) $20 £10

KINGSON, AL.
'The Pictorial Word Book' – 22 pp. with numerous wood engraved illus. col. by hand – orig. pictorial wrappers – upper cover stained – 8vo. – Paris circa 1875.
(Sotheby's) $20 £10

KINLOCH, A.
'Large Game Shooting in Thibet and the North West' – map – 12 photo plates – folding plate – half morocco gilt – sm. 4to. – 1869.
(Phillips) $115 £55

KINROSS, JOHN
'Details from Italian Buildings' – number 8 of 300 copies – folio – Edinburgh – plates – orig. buckram – spine bumped t.e.g. – 1882.
(Christie's S. Kensington) $40 £20

KINSEY, W.
'Portugal' – illustrated – half calf – rubbed – large 8vo. – 1829.
(Irelands) $315 £150

KIP, J.
'Nouveau Theatre du Grande Bretagne' – 69 plates of 70 – plate 49 repaired – disbound – folio – 1724.
(Phillips) $1,365 £650

KIPLING, RUDYARD
'The Years Between' – 1919.
(J. Ash) $12 £6
Typed L.S. 1 page – 8vo. from Bateman's – 11 Feb. 1921 – to Miss M. C. Carey regretting he could not write a story for 'Guide's Annual'.
(Phillips) $90 £42

KIRBY, JOSHUA
'The Perspective of Architecture' – engraved frontis – 73 plates – spotting – contem. half calf – worn – upper cover detached – folio – 1761.
(Christie's) $135 £65

KIRCHER, ATHANASIUS
'China Monuments' – engraved title – portrait – 2 engraved folding maps – 23 engraved plates – numerous engraved illus. in text – minor defects – contem. calf gilt – neatly rebacked – folio – Amsterdam 1667.
(Sotheby Beresford Adams) $755 £360

KIRKLAND, JOHN
'The Modern Baker, Confectioner and Caterer' – 4 vols. – colour plates – 1924.
(Baitson) $2 £1

KIRKPATRICK, W.
'An Account of the Kingdom of Nepaul' – 1st Edn. – large folding map – 13 plates – 1 coloured – calf – wormed – 4to. – 1811.
(Sotheby's) $170 £80

KIRWAN, RICHARD
'An Estimate of the Temperatures of Different Latitudes' – green cloth – morocco spine uncut – 8vo. – 1787.
(Sotheby's) $55 £25

KITCHEN, JOHN
'Le Court Leete et Court Baron' – 1st Edn. – a few contem. Ms notes – contem. calf – worn – sm. 8vo. – 1580.
(Christie's) $420 £200

KITCHIN, THOMAS
'A New Universal Atlas' – 2nd Edn. – 68 of 70 plates – hand col. in outline – 19th cent. brown pigskin panelled in blind – stained and rubbed – large folio – Laurie & Whittle 1798.
(Sotheby's) $1,155 £550

KITTON, F. G.
'Dickens and His Illustrators' – 2nd Edn. – mounted portrait – plates – orig. cloth soiled – t.e.g. – 4to. – 1899.
(Christie's S. Kensington) $40 £20

KLASSIKER DER KUNST IN GESAMTAUSGABEN
22 vol. only – plates – illustrations – orig. cloth backed boards – slightly soiled – 4to. – Stuttgart and Berlin 1919-17.
(Christie's S. Kensington) $40 £20

KLOPSTOCK, FRIEDRICH GOTTLIEB
Auto letter signed – 1 page quarto – to A. Schlegel – informing he has sent a large parcel to him – May 1753.
(Sotheby's) $1,300 £620

KNAPTON, JOHN
'Geographia Antiqua' – maps linen backed – extra illus. with 8 maps – Joseph Priestley's copy – three quarter morocco – 1800.
(Robert Skinner) $650 £310

KNATCHBULL-HUGESSEN, E. H.
'Queer Folk' – illus. by S. E. Waller – rebound in handsome modern quarter calf – 1874.
(J. Ash) $55 £25

Tugend Erfahrung und Bescheidenheit Machen den Jüngling zum Manne und beglücken die Menschheit

KNIGGE, ADOLPH FREYHERRN VON
'Uber Den Umgang Mit Menschen' – 3 parts in one vol. – 3rd Edn. – 1 plate – discolouration – boards – rare – 8vo. – Leipzig 1798.
(Sotheby's) $545 £260

KNEWSTUB, JOHN
'A Confutation of Monstrous and Horrible Heresy' – 2 parts in one vol. – 1st Edn. – partly black letter – title in typographical border – waterstaining – disbound – contents loose – 4to. – 1579.
(Sotheby's) $210 £100

KNIGHT, CHARLES (editor)
'A Pictorial Museum of Antiquities' – 2 vols. – half leather – colour illus. and engravings – a.e.g.
(Baitson) $12 £6

'William Caxton' – illus. with 16 vols. of essays and general works – 1844.
(Dacre, Son & Hartley) $90 £42

'London' – 6 vols. – 3 engraved plates – half morocco gilt – virtue – n.d.
(Phillips) $40 £20

KNIGHT, E. H.
'Practical Dictionary of Mechanics' – 3 vols. – illus. cloth worn – backs loose – Cassell n.d.
(Phillips) $40 £20

KNIGHT, F. AND RUMLEY, J.
'Crests of the Nobility' and 'Gentry of the United Kingdom' – engr. title and 29 plates – some slight soiling – orig. boards – soiled – backstrip torn with loss – lge. 4to. – 1827.
(Christie's S. Kensington) $45 £22

KNIGHT, HENRY GALLY
'The Ecclesiastical Architecture of Italy' – vol. 1 of 2 – col. titles – 40 litho plates – spotted – contem. morocco gilt – rubbed – g.e. – folio – 1842.
(Sotheby's) $525 £250

KNIGHT, R. P.
'A Discourse on the Worship of Priapus' – new Edn. – plates – some soiling – contemp. morocco backed boards – rubbed – t.e.g. with bookplate of Duff Cooper – 4to. – 1865.
(Christie's S. Kensington) $55 £25

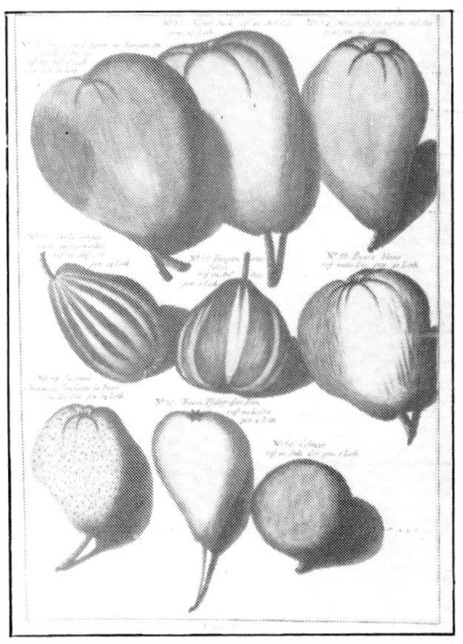

KNOOP, JOAHNN HERMANN
'Pomologia' – 2 vols. in one – 44 hand col. engraved plates by Seligman – contem. calf – worn – cover detached – folio – Nuremberg 1760-66.
(Christie's) $1,050 £500

KNORR, GEORG WOLFGANG
'Deliciae Naturae Selectae' – 2 vols. text in German and French – hand col. engraved title – 91 hand col. engraved plates – 19th cent. calf – folio – 1766-67.
(Christie's) $3,150 £1,500

KNOWLES, VERNON
'The Street of Queer Houses' – illus. by Helen Binyon – 1925.
(J. Ash) $10 £5

KOEHLER, H. A. AND OTHERS
'Medizinal – Pflanzen' – 2 vols. – 203 coloured plates – spotting – contemporary cloth – rubbed – 4to. – Gera-Untemhans – n.d.
(Christie's S. Kensington) $275 £130

KOEHLER, JOHAN DAVID AND WEIGEL, CHRISTOPH
'Descripto Orbis Antiqui' – engraved title and 36 engraved double page maps – hand col. in outline – vignette – stains – cont. calf backed limp marble boards – worn – folio – Nuremberg circa 1720.
(Sotheby's) $315 £150

KOESTLER, ARTHUR – ATKINS, JOHN
'Arthur Koestler' – 1956.
(J. Ash) $8 £4

KOHLHAUSSEN, H.
'Nurnberger Goldschmiedekunst des Mittelalters und der Durerseit 1240 bis 1540' – plates – cloth – d.w. – 4to. – 1968.
(Phillips) $55 £25

KOISUMI, BOKUJO
'The Scenery and Customs of Japan' – 2 vol. – col. plates – orig. Japanese style cloth binding – orig. portfolios – g.e. – oblong folio – Tokyo n.d.
(Christie's) $160 £75

KOLBEN, P.
'Present State of the Cape of Good Hope' – 2 vols. – portrait – plates – panelled calf – 1731.
(Irelands) $315 £150

KOMENSKY, J. A.
'The Labyrinth of the World and the Paradise of the Heart' – limited to 370 copies – this no. 17 of 70 copies spec. bound by Sangorski and Sutcliffe – illus. by Dorothea Braby – orig. morocco – discoloured – t.e.g. – slipcase – the Golden Cockerel Press 1950.
(Christie's) $180 £85

KOORNSTRA, M. T. – BERTRAND, ALOYSIUS
'Gaspard de la Nuit' – 2 vols. – 51 litho illus. by Koornstra – 50 full page – orig. cloth – uncut – slipcase – large 4to. – Utrecht, de Roos, 1956.
(Sotheby's) $735 £350

KOSTER, HENRY
'Travels in Brazil' – 2 vol. in one – 2nd Edn. – 2 folding maps – one cleanly torn – 8 tinted aquatint plates – some margins shaved – soiling – later half morocco – rebacked – 1817.
(Christie's S. Kensington) $210 £100

KOSTUME, ZUR GESCHICHTE DER
124 coloured double page plates – some browned – some loose – orig. cloth – 4to. – Munich n.d.
(Sotheby's) $170 £80

KRUCHENYKH, A.
'10 Ballads o Yade Kormorane' 'Ten Ballads of Poison to Kormoran' – slightly frayed – 4to. – Moscow 1921.
(Sotheby's) $840 £400

KUHAVRT ABD LYDEKKER
'Animals of Portraiture' – folio – 1st Edn. with col. plates – 1912.
(Lane) $25 £12

KUMMEL, OTTO
'Chinesische Kunst' – limited to 300 copies – 150 plates – 18 coloured – half title – slightly dampstained – orig. half cloth – folio – Berlin 1930.
(Sotheby's) $85 £40

KUNHART, C. P.
'Small Yachts, their Design and Construction' – plates – illus. – orig. cloth – rubbed – 4to. – 1887.
(Sotheby's) $105 £50

KUNKEL, JOHANNES
'Philosophia Chemica Experimentis Conformata' – engraved frontis – title in red and black with vignette – contem. panelled calf – rebacked – 12 mo. – Amsterdam, Johannes Walters 1694.
(Sotheby's) $100 £48

KURTH, DR. WILLI
'The Complete Woodcuts of Durer' – limited to 500 copies – plates – spotted – unbound as issued in orig. portfolio – 1927.
(Christie's) $120 £58

KYPSELER, GOTTLIEB
'Les Delices de la Suisse' – 4 vols. addit. engraved title and 74 maps and plates – most folding – contem. calf – gilt – 12 mo. Leiden 1714.
(Christie's) $3,570 £1,700

LABAT, JEAN BAPTISTE
'Nouveau Voyage aux Isles de L'Amerique' – 6 vols – 94 plates and maps – calf gilt – La Haye – 1724.
(Phillips) $40 £20

LACOMBE
'Dictionnaire du Vieux Langage Francois' – 2 vols. – contem. French binding of red morocco gilt with arms of Duke of Savoy on covers – 1766.
(Moore Allen & Innocent) $755 £360

LACRETELLE, JACQUES – LAURENCIN, MARIE
'Lettres Espagnol' – 11 etched illus. by Laurencin – orig. wrappers – uncut – 8vo. – Paris 1926.
(Sotheby's) $670 £320

LACROIX, P.
'Middle Ages' – vol. 2 – 'The Arts, Manners, Customs and Dress' – illus. cloth – 4to. Bickers and Son n.d.
(Phillips) $40 £20
'XVIIIme Siecle Institutions Usages et Costumes France' 1700-1789 – 53 plates – 15 coloured – contemp. half morocco – rubbed – Paris 1875.
(Christie's S. Kensington) $40 £18

LADY BATHING, A
Slightly flaked – small tear – framed – 18.9 cm x 11.9 cm – This miniature shows characteristics of the school of Levni and is probably attributable to Abdullah Boukhari one of the principal artists known to be working during the reign of Sultan Muhammed I (1736-54) – Ottoman circa 1735-45.
(Christie's) $1,155 £550

LA CONDAMINE, CHARLES MARIE DE
'Journal du Voyage' – 1st Edn. – 5 engraved maps and plates – some folding – Paris 1751.
(Christie's) $735 £350

LA FONTAINE, J. DE
'Contes et Nouvelles en Vers' – plates – 2 vols – calf defective – Amsterdam 1764.
(Bonhams) $420 £200
'Tales and Novels in Verse' – 2 vol. – plates – occasional slight spotting – contemp. blue half-morocco – by Sangkorski and Sutcliffe – t.e.g. – 4to. n.d.
(Christie's S. Kensington) $60 £28

LA GELOSIA
Contem Italian binding of brown calf gilt with arms of a cardinal – 8vo. – 1783.
(Moore Allen & Innocent) $210 £100

LAHONTAN, LOUIS-ARMAND BARON DE
'Nouveaux Voyages dans l'Amerique Septentrionale' – 2 vols. – 1st Edn. – third issue of each – engraved frontis – 4 folding maps – 2 plates and plans – contem. mottled calf – gilt spine – 12mo. – Hague chez les Freres l'Honore 1703.
(Christie's) $715 £340

LAIRD, M. AND OLDFIELD, R. A. K.
'Narrative of an Expedition into the Interior of Africa by the River Niger' – 2 vols. – 7 plates – modern half calf – faded – 8vo. – 1837.
(Sotheby's) $170 £80

LAIRESSE, G. DE
'Principles of Drawing' – 2 parts in one vol. – 47 sheets of engravings – one repaired – stained half calf defective – 4to. – 1748.
(Phillips) $125 £60

LAISNE
'Elan du Coeur. Bouquet a Bernard' – mss on paper – 21 leaves – 5 wash drawings – bookplate of Samuel Putnam Avery loosely inserted – contemporary red morocco by Derome le Jeune with his ticket – gilt fillet – spine gilt – pale blue silk liners – gilt edges – sm. 4to. – Paris 1785.
(Sotheby Parke Bernet) $1,765 £840

LAKING, G. F.
'The Furniture of Windsor Castle' – presentation copy from the King – mounted plates – orig. pigskin buckram – rubbed – spotted – t.e.g. – 4to. – n.d.
(Christie's) $145 £70

LAKING, SIR GUY FRANCIS
'A Record of European Armour and Arms Throughout the Seven Centuries' – 5 vol. – 2 frontis – illus. in text – half titles – buckram – soiled – 4to. – 1920-22.
(Sotheby's) $630 £300

'The Armoury of Windsor Castle' – plates – orig. pigskin-backed cloth – rubbed 4to. – 1904.
(Sotheby's) $85 £40

LALAISSE, H. AND BENOIST, F.
'Galerie Armoricane Costumes et Vues Pittoresque' – 3 parts of 5 in one vol. – 3 litho titles and 60 plates – 3 maps – contem. morocco backed boards – rubbed – folio – Nantes 1848.
(Sotheby's) $1,260 £600

LAMB, A. C.
'Dundee' – limited Edn. – plates – some col. – full morocco gilt – t.e.g. – folio – Dundee 1895.
(Phillips) $55 £25

LAMB, LADY CAROLINE
'Glenarvon' – 1st Edn. – 3 vols. – 3 engraved titles – half calf gilt – 1816.
(Phillips) $210 £100

Visit to the Beneficent Fairy

LAMB, CHARLES
'Prince Dorus or Flattery Put out of Countenance' – 1st Edn. – 9 engraved plates – spotted – orig. yellow printed wrappers – slightly worn – cloth case – 16mo. – N. J. Godwin 1811.
(Sotheby's) $670 £320

'A Tale of Rosamund Gray and old Blind Margaret' – number 358 of 500 copies – port – orig. boards – spine soiled – unopened 1928.
(Christie's) $12 £6

LAMB, EDWARD BUCKTON
'Studies of Ancient Domestic Architecture' – 19 of 20 litho plates – spotting – contem. morocco backed cloth – spine rubbed – large 4to. – John Weale 1846.
(Christie's) $65 £30

LAMBARD, WILLIAM
'The Perambulation of Kent' – 4to. – two maps, one slightly shaved, the other folding but torn and repaired – slight soiling – old calf – rebacked – old spine laid down – worn – n.d.
(Christie's S. Kensington) $135 £65

LAMOTTE, A.
'Voyage dans le Nord de L'Europe' – vig. title – folding map – 14 plates – calf – 4to. – 1813.
(Phillips) $275 £130

LANCASTER, F.
'Title and Estate' – three vols. – orig. cloth little loose and spotted – 1871.
(J. Ash) $65 £30

LANCASTER, OSBERT
'Drayneflete Revealed' – illus. by author – slightly chipped dust wrapper – 1949.
(J. Ash) $8 £4

LANCE AND KOEHLER
'Lance's Upper Rhine' – engraved title – 27 engraved plates – some spotting – half calf – circa 1830.
(Phillips) $295 £140

LANDE, LAWRENCE
'The Lawrence Lande Collection of Canadiana in the Redpath Library of McGill University; Rare and Unusual Canadiana, First Supplement to the Lande Bibliography' – 2 vol. together – both limited Edn. signed by Lande – facsimiles – first vol. in orig pigskin backed cloth – slipcase – second in orig. cloth – 4to. and sm. 4to. – Montreal 1965-71.
(Sotheby's) $230 £110

LANDOR, A. H. S.
'In the Forbidden Land' – 2 vol. – plates – some col. – folding map – torn – orig. pictorial cloth – 8vo. – New York 1899.
(Sotheby's) $80 £38

LANDSCAPE ANNUAL FOR 1830, 31 AND 33
3 vols. only – engraved titles and 75 plates – morocco rubbed – g.e. – 8vo. – 1830-35.
(Sotheby's) $220 £105

LANDSCAPE SCENERY ILLUSTRATING SYDNEY AND PORT JACKSON, NEW SOUTH WALES
Vignette title – 37 engraved plates – slightly spotted – contem cloth gilt – slightly worn – g.e. oblong 4to. – 1855.
(Sotheby Bearne) $650 £310

LANDSEER, SIR EDWIN
'The Works' – folio – n.d. – steel-engr. additional title – plates – contemp. morocco – worn – g.e.
(Christie's S. Kensington) $85 £40

'Selections from the Work of Sir Edwin Landseer' – 1 vol. only, 25 coloured mounts, occasional slight browning, original portfolio, soiled, folio – n.d.
(Christie's S. Kensington) $65 £28

LANDT, JORGEN
'A Descriptive of the Feroe Islands' – folding map and 2 folding plates – contem. half sheep – 8vo. – 1810.
(Sotheby's) $95 £45

LANE, A.
'French Faience' – 1948.
(Bennett Book Auction) $17 £8

LANE, E. W. (translator)
'The Thousand and One Nights' – 3 vol. – wood engraved additional titles and illustrations – contemporary calf – spines gilt – spine labels in red and blue morocco – 1859.
(Christie's S. Kensington) $90 £42

LANE, WILLIAM COOLEDGE AND NINA E. BROWNE
'Library of Congress A. L. A. Portrait Index' – orig. cloth – rubbed – 8vo. – Washington 1906.
(Sotheby's) $145 £70

LA NEUVILLE, DE
'An Account of Muscovy as it was in the Year 1689' – 1st Edn. – browning – contem. sheep – rebacked – worn – 8vo. – 1699.
(Sotheby's) $315 £150

LANG, ANDREW
'Prince Charles Edward' – 1st Edn. – one of 350 copies – Japanese paper and plates in duplicate – illus. in text – half title – contem. red levant morocco – gilt – t.e.g. – uncut – 4to. – 1900.
(Sotheby's) $75 £35

'Prince Prigio' – number 5 of an unspecified number of large paper copies – 27 illus. by Gordon Browne – orig. half parchment – soiled – uncut – 4to. – 1889.
(Sotheby's) $55 £25

LANGDON, A. G.
'Old Cornish Crosses' – 1st Edn. – damp marked binding – 1896.
(Lane) $55 £26

LANGLEY, B. & T.
'Gothic Architecture Improved by Rules and Proportions' – engraved title – 64 plates – contem. sheep – rubbed – splits in joints – 4to. – for I. and J. Taylor – n.d.
(Sotheby's) $485 £230

LANSDOWNE, GEORGE GRANVILLE, LORD
'The Genuine Works in Verse and Prose' – engraved head pieces – one leaf cleanly torn – contemp. calf – rubbed – spine gilt – 4to. – 1732.
(Christie's S. Kensington) $145 £70

LAPIQUE, CHARLES - ETIENNE
'O and M. Roman' – 13 illus. by Lapique – orig. vellum – silk screened over design by Lapique – uncut – unopened – sm. 4to. – Paris Le Soleil Noir – 1966.
(Sotheby's) $190 £90

LA PRIMAUDAYE, PIERRE DE
'The French Academie wherein is discoursed the Institution of Maners' – 2nd Edn. – title in typographical border – staining – soiled – contem. calf – blind stamped ornament in sides – sm. 4to. – Eliot's Court Press for G. Bishop 1589.
(Sotheby's) $115 £55

LA QUINTINYE, JEAN DE
'The Complete Gard'ner' – 2 vols. in one – editors George London and Henry Wise – engraved frontis – 9 engraved folding plates – some defects – contem. panelled calf – worn – 8vo. – 1704.
(Sotheby Beresford Adams) $120 £58

LARWOOD, JACOB AND HOTTEN, JOHN CAMDEN
'The History of Signboards' – 4th Edn. – hand coloured frontispiece – 28 plates – occasional slight spotting – contemp. half morocco – rubbed – 1868.
(Christie's S. Kensington) $55 £25

LASINSKT, J. A.
'Croquis Pittoresques, Cinquante-cinq vues du Rhin' – lithographed title – one folding map and 55 plates – slightly spotted – origninal morocco backed boards – rubbed – oblong 4to. – Frankfurt, 1829.
(Christie's S. Kensington) $1,785 £850

LASSO DE LA VEGA, GARCIA
'The Royal Commentaries of Peru' – 2 parts in one vol. – trans. by Sir Paul Rycaut – engraved portrait – 10 plates – contem. panelled calf – bookplate – folio – 1688.
(Sotheby's) $420 £200

LATHAM, B.
'Sanitary Engineering' – plates – half calf – 1878.
(Bennett Book Auction) $6 £3

LATHAM, P. M.
'Lectures on Subjects Connected with Clinical Medicine Comprising Diseases of the Heart' – 2 vols. – 1st Edn. – half titles – 32 pp adverts at end of each – library stamps – orig. cloth – 8vo. – 1845-46.
(Sotheby's) $55 £25

LATHOM, F.
'Men and Manners' – 1st Edn. – 4 vols. – calf gilt – 12mo. – 1799.
(Phillips) $610 £290

LATROBE, .C. I.
'Journal of a Visit to South Africa' – folding map and 16 plates – including 12 aquatints – contem. half calf – rubbed – worn – 4to. – 1818.
(Sotheby's) $925 £440

LAUD, WILLIAM
'The History of the Troubles and Tryal' – folio – engraved portrait – a few slight marginal tears without loss of letters – old calf rubbed – rebacked and recornered – for Ri. Chiswell 1695.
(Christie's S. Kensington) $65 £32

LAUDERDALE, EARL OF
'An Inquiry into the Nature and Origin of Public Wealth' – calf – Edinburgh 1804.
(Phillips) $275 £130

LAUGHTON, L. G. CARR
'Old Ship Figure Heads and Sterns' – No. 210 of 1500 copies – some col. plates – illus. – orig. cloth – gilt – t.e.g. – dust jacket – 4to. – 1925.
(Sotheby's) $250 £120

LAUREL AND HARDY
Good photograph of them in characteristic pose signed by both – 5 x 7 in.
(Sotheby's) $170 £80

LAURENCIN, MARIE – DES OMBIAUX, MAURICE
'Les Belles a Table' – etched by Laurencin – orig. wrappers – uncut – unopened – 8vo. – Paris Budry 1926.
(Sotheby's) $8,400 £4,000

LAURENCIN, MARIE – BLOCH, JEAN-RICHARD
'Dix Filles' – 4 etched plates by Laurencin – morocco backed boards – orig. wrapper bound in – uncut – unopened – 8vo. – Paris 1926.
(Sotheby's) $1,300 £620

LAURI, J.
'Antiquae Urbis Splendor' – engraved title and 160 plates – some hand col. – contem. limp vellum – rubbed – oblong 4to. – Rome 1612.
(Sotheby's) $295 £140

LAURIE, A. P.
'The Brushwork of Rembrandt and his School' – 4 copies – plates – orig. cloth – dust jacket – 4to. – 1932.
(Sotheby's) $210 £100

LAURIE AND WHITTLE
'General Atlas' – engraved title and frontis – 38 hand col. engraved maps – 1 to page – soiled – contem. half morocco – worn – 4to. – 1804.
(Christie's) $275 £130

LAURIE, R. H.
'New Traveller's Companion' – engraved title – 25 engraved maps – hand col. in outline – soiling – orig. morocco wallet – stitching worn – 1828.
(Christie's) $115 £55

LAVER, J.
'A Complete Catalogue of the Etchings and Dry Points of Arthur Briscoe' – plates – 1 etched and signed – orig. cloth – faded – 4to. – 1930.
(Sotheby's) $210 £100

LAVIN, M.
'Second Best Children in the World' – signed by artist E. Ardizzone – colour illus. – pictorial boards – 4to – 1972.
(Phillips) $34 £16

LAVOISIER, ANTOINE LARENT
'Opuscules Physiques et Chimiques' – 2nd Edn. – second issue – 3 folding plates – half title – contem. quarter calf – 8vo. – Paris 1801.
(Sotheby's) $80 £38

LAVOISNE, C. V.
'Complete Genealogical, Historical, Chronological and Geographical Atlas' – 39 hand coloured tables – 26 hand coloured engraved maps with text – all double page and mounted on linen – several torn with loss – some staining – cont. parchment – slightly soiled folio – 1814.
(Christie's S. Kensington) $65 £32

LAW, ERNEST
'Vandyck's Pictures at Windsor Castle' – no. 120 of 375 copies – inscribed by author – plates – stained – orig. cloth – soiled – 1899.
(Christie's) $60 £28

LAW, JOHN
'Considerations sur le Commerce et sur L'Argent' – 1st Edn. in French – 19 pp adverts at end – browning and soiling – contem calf – worn – 12mo. – The Hague.
(Sotheby's) $335 £160

LAWRENCE, – ARCHER, J. H.
'Monumental Inscriptions of the British West Indies' – illus. – spotted – orig. cloth – worn – 4to. – 1875.
(Sotheby's) $40 £20

LAWRENCE, D. H.
'The Lovely Lady' – spine worn and splitting at hinge – 1932.
(J. Ash) $6 £3
'Birds, Beasts and Flowers' – wood engravings by B. Hughes-Stanton – uncut – quarter vellum – t.e.g. – 4to. – Cresset Press 1930.
(Phillips) $135 £65
'Women In Love' – orig. cloth – 1st Edn. – Secker 1921.
(Bennett Book Auction) $12 £6

LAWRENCE, SIR T.
'Engravings from the Works' – spotted – plates – contem. half morocco – rubbed folio – n.d.
(Sotheby's) $40 £20

LAWRENCE, T. E.
'The Letters' – very few faint marks – 1938.
(J. Ash) $20 £10

LAWSON, JOHN PARKER
'Scotland' – 2 copies – litho title and plates – one copy spotted – orig. morocco – gilt – worn – covers detached – g.e. – 4to. – n.d.
(Sotheby's) $200 £95

LAXDAELA-SAGA
1st Edn. – engraved vignette on half title – later wrapper – torn – unopened – 4to. – Copenhagen 1826.
(Sotheby's) $145 £70

LAYARD, E. L.
'Birds of South Africa' – 12 hand col. plates – half morocco gilt – 8vo. – 1874-84.
(Phillips) $250 £120

LEADBETTER, CHARLES
'Astronomy or the True System of Planets' – 1st Edn. – 10 engraved plates – most folding – a few minor defects – contem. panelled calf – slightly worn – sm. 4to. – 1727.
(Sotheby Beresford Adams) $60 £28
'Mechanick Dialling: Or the New Art of Shadows' – 11 folding copper plates – and woodcut text illus. – contemporary calf – London 1737.
(Bennett Book Auction) $105 £50

LEAKE, STEPHEN MARTIN
'An Historical Account of English Money from the Conquest to the Present Time' – 2nd Edn. – 13 plates – contem. calf rubbed – 8vo. – W. Meadows 1745.
(Sotheby's) $55 £25

LEAR, EDWARD
'Views in the Seven Ionian Islands' – litho title and 20 tinted litho plates – orig. green cloth – text and plates loose – folio – 1863.
(Phillips) $2,520 £1,200

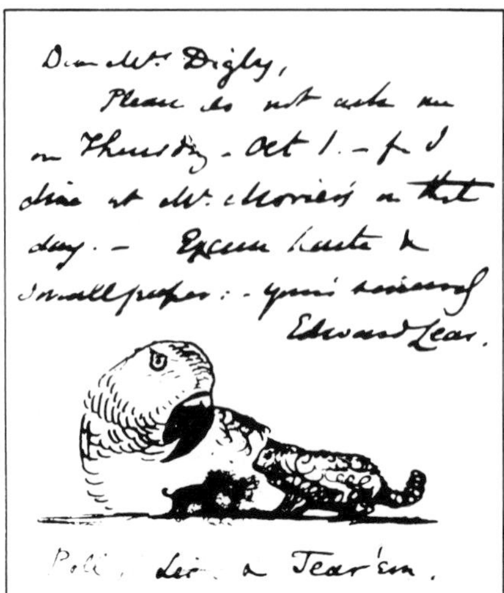

Dear Mrs Digby,
Please do not ask me on Thursday. Oct 1. – for I dine at Mr. Morris's on that day. – Excuse haste & small paper: – yours sincerely
Edward Lear.

Poll, Lear, a Tear'em.

LEAR, EDWARD
Illus. auto letter signed – one page – to Mrs. Digby Watts asking not to be asked to dine on Thursday and illus. with a charming drawing of a giant parrot – diminutive cat and even smaller dog – Sept. 1863.
(Sotheby's) $335 £160

LEAUTAUD, PAUL
'Journal of a Man of Letters 1898-1907' – 1st Edn. English – in dust wrapper – 1960.
(J. Ash) $6 £3

LEAVIS, F. R.
'The Common Pursuit' – covers a little dull – 1952.
(J. Ash) $10 £5

LE BAS, P.
'Allemagne' – vol. 1 – engraved plates – 36 town views – quarter vellum gilt – Paris 1839.
(Phillips) $190 £90

LE BLOND
'Elements de Fortification' – contem. French binding of red morocco gilt with arms of Marie-Adelaide de France – gilt panelled back – 8vo. – 1775.
(Moore Allen & Innocent) $670 £320

LE BLONDE, ALEXANDRE JEAN BAPTISTE
'Neueroffnete Gartner-Akademie' – double page title – engraved frontis – 34 engraved plates – 32 folding – contem. half calf – 8vo. – Augsburg, 1764.
(Sotheby's) $715 £340

LE BRUYN, CORNELIUS
'Voyages au Levant' – 5 vol. – engraved portrait – 5 maps – 4 folding – 84 plates – 12 folding – waterstains – browning – cont. calf – rebacked – corners repaired – 4to. – The Hague 1732.
(Sotheby's) $735 £350

LE CORBEAU, ADRIEN
'The Forest Giant' – wood engraved illus. by Agnes Miller Parker – 1st. Edn. thus translated by 'J.H. Ross' (T.E. Lawrence) – covers slightly soiled and bubbled – 1935.
(J. Ash) $10 £5

LE CORBUSIER, C. AND JANNERET, PIERRE
'Oeuvre Complet' – 3rd Edn. – 2 vol. – illus. – orig. cloth – soiled – oblong 4to. – Zurich 1943-6.
(Christie's) $40 £18

LECKY, W. E. H.
'Works' – 17 vols. – uniform half morocco gilt – t.e.g. – 1865-99.
(Bonhams) $180 £85

LE CLERC, SEBASTIAN
'Practique de la Geometrie sur le Papier et sur le Terrain' – engraved frontis and 82 engravings in text – contem. calf – 8vo. – Paris 1716.
(Sotheby's) $80 £38
'Practical Geometry' – trans Nattes – 44 plates with diagrams and vignettes – half calf gilt – 1805.
(Phillips) $190 £90

LE DRAN, HENRY FRANCOIS
'Observations in Surgery consisting of 115 Different Cases' – 2nd Edn. – 2 folding plates – half title – calf – rebacked – 8vo. – James Hodges 1740.
(Sotheby's) $40 £20

LEE, JAMES
'An Introduction to the Science of Botany' – port. – 12 hand coloured plates – cloth damaged – 1810.
(Phillips) $30 £14

LEE, LAURIE
'The Firstborn' – illustrated with photos by author – in dust wrapper – Hogarth Press 1964.
(J. Ash) $17 £8

LEE, NATHANIEL
'The Works' – 13 parts in one – 2nd collected Edn. – browning – contem. mottled calf – worn – 4to. – 1694.
(Sotheby's) $1,010 £480

LEE, O. A. J.
'Among British Birds in their Nesting Haunts' – 16 vol. – folio – Edinburgh 1897-9 – 160 plates – orig. cloth backed boards – soiled – stitching shaken.
(Christie's S. Kensington) $85 £40

LEE, VERNON
'Limbo and Other Essays' – frontis – slightly stained at edge and lower cover a little damp mark –1897.
(J. Ash) $8 £4

LEECH, JOHN
'Follies of the Year' – hand-finished tinted lithographed title – 21 hand coloured plates after Leech – orig. half morocco – affected by damp – largely disbound – lge. oblong 4to.
(Christie's S. Kensington) $55 £25

LEGAL DOCUMENTS
11 documents including assignment of annuity, 1737 – settlement of South Sea stock, 1740 – will of John Campbell, 1826 – on vellum – 1733-1826.
(Phillips) $45 £22

LEGH, T.
'Narrative of a Journey in Egypt' – 2nd Edn. – 12 plates and maps – some folding – later calf – rubbed – 8vo. – 1817.
(Sotheby's) $45 £22

LE HUEN, NICOLE
'Le Grant Voyage de Jherusalem' – title in red and black – numerous small woodcut illus. in text – large woodcuts and map – worming – early 19th cent. calf backed boards – folio – Paris 1517.
(Sotheby's) $295 £140

LEIGH, CHARLES
'The Natural History of Lancashire, Cheshire and the Peak in Derbyshire' – sub. list – engraved folding map – 23 of 24 plates – minor defects – contem. reversed calf – very worn – folio – Oxford 1700.
(Sotheby Beresford Adams) $60 £28

LEIGH, S.
'New Picture of London' – frontis – coloured title and 23 col. plates – lacks cover – 1834.
(Phillips) $80 £38

LEIGHTON, CLARE
'Tempestuous Petticoat' – endpapers and title page design by the author – 1948.
(J. Ash) $6 £3

LEIGHTON, J.
'Select Views of Glasgow and Its Environs' – engraved by J. Swan – engraved title and 33 plates – blind embossed calf – rubbed – 4to. – 1828.
(Bennett Book Auction) $40 £18

LE KEUX, J.
'Memorials of Cambridge' – 2 vols. – addit. engraved titles – 73 engraved plates – 1 engraved map – spotting – orig. cloth – spines gilt – slightly worn – t.e.g. – 8vo. – 1845.
(Sotheby's) $275 £130

LELAND, JOHN
'The Itinerary' – 9 vol. in three – 2nd Edn. – three engr. plates – one folding – illustrations – spotting – contemp. calf – worn – Oxford 1744-5.
(Christie's S. Kensington) $55 £25

LE LORRAIN, CLAUDE
'Liber Veritatis' – vol. 1 and 11 of 3 – mezzotint portrait – 200 sepia engraved plates after Earlom – foxing – portrait stained – cont. diced russia – very worn – g.e. – folio – J. Boydell 1777.
(Sotheby's) $3,570 £1,700

LE MASSON, EDMOND
'Traite de la Chasse Souterraine du Blaireau et du Renard' – limited signed Edn. of 275 – 5 litho plates – full calf gilt – t.e.g. – Paris 1865.
(Phillips) $145 £70

LENDESIO, E. AND ROSA P.
'Vedute Principali della Villa Borghese' – 34 litho plates – cloth – oblong 4to. – Rome 1842.
(Phillips) $135 £65

LENFANT, JACQUES
'Histoire de la Guerre des Hussites et du Concile de Basle' – 2 vols. – engraved portraits – contem. mottled calf – rubbed – 4to. Utrecht, 1731.
(Sotheby's) $105 £50

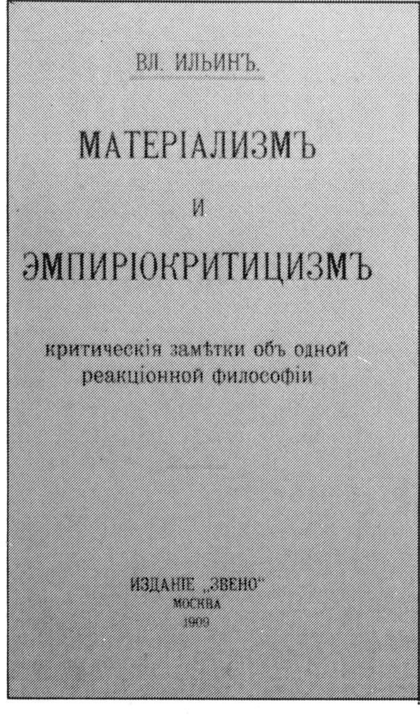

ВЛ. ИЛЬИНЪ.

МАТЕРІАЛИЗМЪ

И

ЭМПИРІОКРИТИЦИЗМЪ

критическія замѣтки объ одной реакціонной философіи

ИЗДАНІЕ „ЗВЕНО"
МОСКВА
1909

LENIN, V. I.
'Materializm i Empirioktritsizm' – one of 2000 copies – orig. cloth – rubbed 8vo. – Moscow 1909.
(Sotheby's) $1,260 £600

LENYGON, F.
'Decoration in England from 1660 to 1770' and 'Furniture in England from 1660-1760' – 2 vol. plates orig. cloth – rubbed – inner hinges worn – 4to. – second impression 1920.
(Christie's S. Kensington) $65 £30

LEPAPE, GEORGES
'Costumes de Theatre, Ballets et Divertissements' – pictorial title and 20 repros of watercolour designs – loose as issued in orig. folder – illus. in silver on upper cover – silver ties – 8vo. – Paris, Lucien Vogel 1920.
(Sotheby's) $460 £220

LEPSIUS, C. R. (editor)
'Denkmaeler Aus Aegyptem Und Aethiopien' – 12 vols. – 904 lithos – maps – some tinted – some printed in colours – 4 folding – spotting – tears and repairs – publisher's half morocco – rubbed – elephant folio – Berlin 1849-58.
(Christie's) $1,785 £850

LERMONTOV, MIKHAIL YUREVICH
'A Hero of Our Times' – 1st. Eng. Edn. – frontis – first leaf and last 12 advert leaves– some soiled – orig. cloth – rubbed – 8vo. – 1854.
(Sotheby's) $200 £95

LE ROUGE, G. L.
'Details des Nouveaux Jardins a la Mode' – cahier 1-4; 6-8 only of 21 – 196 engraved plates –spotting – contem. boards – slightly worn – 4to. – Paris 1774-78 and n.d.
(Sotheby Beresford Adams) $670 £320

LE ROY, J. D.
'Les Ruines des Plus Beaux Monuments de la Greece' – 1st Edn. – 60 engraved plates – contem. morocco – gilt – rubbed – large folio – Paris 1758.
(Sotheby's) $2,730 £1,300

LESLIE, C.
'New and Exact Account of Jamaica' – calf – gilt – 8vo. – 1739.
(Phillips) $360 £170

LESLIE, JOHN (BISHOP OF ROSS)
'De Origine, Moribus, et Rebus Gestis Scotorum Libri Decem' – 2 parts in one – continuous signatures and pagination – 1st Edn. – printed in line borders – folding engraved map – 11 full page illus., genealogical tables – vignette portraits and coats of arms in text – late 17th cent. red morocco – label – split – rubbed – 4to. – Rome 1578.
(Sotheby's) $335 £160

LETAROUILLY, PAUL
'Le Vatican et la Basilique de St. Pierre' – eiditor by Alphonse Simil – 70 plates – slightly brown – cloth – worn and soiled – folio – Cleveland, Ohio, circa 1890.
(Sotheby's) $55 £25

LEUTEMANN, H. – HOLLOWAY, E. W. (Translator)
'Reynard the Fox' – 4to. – steel-engraved additional title and 36 plates after Leutemann – slight spotting – orig. cloth – gilt – spine and corners rubbed – g.e. – n.d.
(Christie's S. Kensington) $40 £20

LEVAILLANT, FRANCOIS
'New Travels into the Interior Parts of Africa' – 3 vols. – folding map – 22 plates – calf gilt – 1796.
(Phillips) $565 £270

LE VARDIN, JACQUES DE
'The Histoire of George Castriot, surnamed Scanderberg, King of Albanie' – some leaves lacking – some detached – some fraying and soiling – old calf – worn – folio – William Posonby 1596.
(Christie's S. Kensington) $55 £25

LEVER, CHARLES
'The Novels' – 37 vol. – copyright Edn. – limited to 1000 copies – some addit. titles – contem. morocco gilt – g.e. – 1897-99.
(Christie's) $250 £120
'Arthur O'Leary: His Wanderings and Ponderings in Many Lands' – 3 vols. – ten etched illus. by George Cruikshank – orig. cloth spines browned and a little worn at tips – some foxing to plates – 1844.
(J. Ash) $75 £36
'The Dodd Family Abroad' – 20 (in 19) orig. parts – 1st edn. – plates – advertisements – orig. wrapper – soiled – some torn and loose – 8vo. – 1852-54.
(Sotheby's) $45 £22
'Works' – copyright Edn. – 37 vols. – half morocco backs worn and faded – 1897-99.
(Bonhams) $65 £30

LEVER, DARCY
'The Young Sea Officer's Sheet Anchor' – 1st Edn. – 110 engraved plates – foxed – waterstained – half calf – worn – contem. ownership inscription – 4to. – 1808.
(Sotheby's) $565 £270

LEVERHULME ART COLLECTIONS
3 vol. – one of 200 copies – plates – some coloured – orig. cloth – slightly rubbed – 4to. – 1928.
(Sotheby's) $400 £190

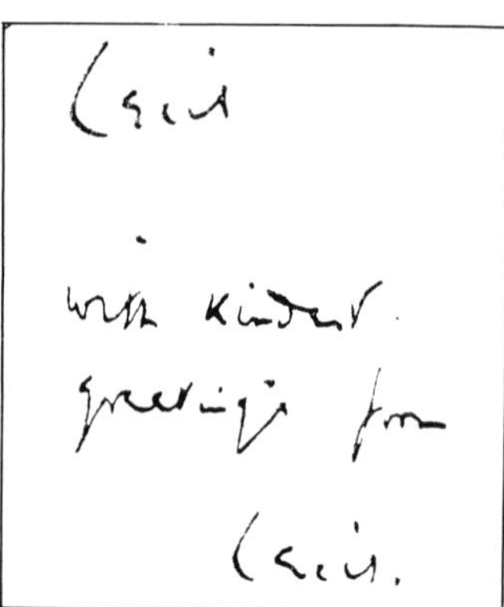

LEWIS, C. DAY
'Word All Over' – 1st Edn. – pres copy – inscribed by author to Cecil Beaton – orig. cloth – 8vo. – 1943.
(Sotheby's) $35 £17

LEWIS, C. T. C.
'The Story of Picture Printing in England During the 19th Cent.' – col. plates – cloth – 4to. – n.d.
(Phillips) $135 £65
'George Baxter the Picture Printer' – 4to. – plates – two lacking – some damaged by damp – a few with loss – orig. cloth – t.e.g. – n.d.
(Christie's S. Kensington) $25 £12

LEWIS, F. C.
'Scenery of the Devonshire Rivers' – orig. cloth binding – large folio.
(Lane) $180 £85

LEWIS, JOHN
'Illustrations of Constantinople' – litho title and 27 views on 25 plates – soiled – contem. morocco backed cloth – lacks spine – loose – folio – n.d.
(Sotheby's) $630 £300
'Sketches of Spain and Spanish Character' – lithographed throughout – tinted title vignette and 25 plates – n.d.
(Christie's S. Kensington) £230 £110

LEWIS, S.
'Atlas comprising the Counties of Ireland' – folding map of Ireland and 32 uncoloured county maps and descriptions – calf – 8vo. – 1736.
(Phillips) $65 £32

LEWIS, WILLIAM
'An Experimental History of the Materia Medica' – 2nd Edn. with corrections – licence leaf at beginning – advert. leaf at end – new cloth – 4to. – R. Baldwin 1768.
(Sotheby's) $85 £40
'A Course of Practical Chemistry' – 1st Edn. – another copy – 9 plates – stamp on title – calf – 8vo. – J. Nourse 1746.
(Sotheby's) $40 £20

LEWIS, WYNDHAM
'The Apes of God' – limited signed Edn. – orig. cloth – 1930.
(Phillips) $115 £55

LEYBOURN, WILLIAM
'Cursus Mathematicus. Mathematical Sciences' – folio – engr, portrait and 94 plates – most folding – illustrations – a few leaves cleanly torn – some blank margins holed without loss – dampstaining and spotting – old calf – worn – Printed for Thomas Basset, Benjamin Tooke, 1690.
(Christie's S. Kensington) $170 £80

LEYLAND, JOHN
'The Yorkshire Coast' – 1892.
(Baitson) $30 £14

LIBER EPISTOLARUM FESTORUM ANNUALIUM
In Latin – illum. mss on vellum – 42 lines – written in dark brown ink in very fine roman hand – full floral borders around every page – 44 floral panels with naturalistic flowers and fruit – very fresh condition – contem. full red velvet with marks of metal fittings – 344 mm x 245 mm. – Paris, 1705.
(Sotheby's) $10,080 £4,800

LIECHTENSTEIN, PRINCESS MARIE
'Holland House' – 2 vol. hand coloured frontispiece and title vignettes illustrations – extra illustrated with views and portraits – some hand coloured – later royal blue levant – gilt by Bayntum – spines slightly faded – g.e. with original bindings – 1874.
(Christie's S. Kensington) $115 £55

LIFE IN PARIS, THE
A Game with characteristic figures – folding litho sheet with panoramic view of shops and 31 litho figures, groups etc. – cut out and mounted on card with wooden stands to form scene depicted on lid – col. by hand – card box – pictorial title in English, French, German – fitted case – Germany circa 1860.
(Sotheby's) $880 £420

LIGHT
'A Journal of Physical, Occult and Mystical Research' – vol. 20-23 only contem. cloth – sm. folio – 1900-03.
(Sotheby's) $55 £25

LIGHT, MAJOR
'Sicilian Scenery' – engraved title and 61 plates – dampstains – contem half morocco – gilt spine – rubbed – g.e. – 8vo. – 1823.
(Sotheby's) $125 £60

LIGON, RICHARD
'True and Exact History of the Island of Barbados' – folding engraved map – neatly repaired – 9 folding plates – 3 folding diagrams – contem. half calf – joints weak – folio – 1673.
(Sotheby's) $545 £260

LILFORD, T. L. P.
'Coloured Figures of Birds of the British Isles' – 7 vols. – col. plates – half red morocco – t.e.g. – 1891-97.
(Phillips) $2,310 £1,100

'Notes on the Birds of Northamptonshire and Neighbourhood' – 2 vol. – plates – lacking map – mod. half morocco – rubbed – t.e.g. – 1895.
(Christie's) $115 £55

L'IMAGE 1896-1897
All published – illus. – orig. coloured wrappers – half calf gilt – 4to. – 1897.
(Phillips) $315 £150

LIMITED EDITIONS CLUB
'The Comedies, Histories and Tragedies of William Shakespeare' – 37 volumes – folio – numbered limited Edn. of 1950 sets only – New York 1939-40.
(J. Ash) $1,155 £550

LINCOLN RECORD SOCIETY
Publications vol. 1-8 orig. boards – slightly soiled – spine torn of one – 8vo. – 1914-23.
(Sotheby's) $180 £85

LINCOLN, W. S.
'Crests and Monograms' – a partially filled album.
(Lane) $10 £5

LINDLEY, J.
'Rosarum Monographia' – 1st. Edn. – 18 hand coloured plates and 1 plain – calf – gilt rebacked – 8vo. – 1820.
(Phillips) $380 £180

LINDLEY, JOHN
'Serium Orchidaceum' – Coloured lithographed half title and 48 hand col. plates after Miss Drake, W. Griffith and others – lithographed by M. Gauci – minor foxing – half morocco – worn – covers detached – folio – 1838.
(Christie's) $5,250 £2,500

LINDSAY, JACK (Translator)
'The Complete Works of Gaius Petronius' – no. 31 of 650 copies signed by translator – plates by Norman Lindsay – some soiling – contem. half calf – rubbed – t.e.g. –FranfrolicoPress n.d.
(Christie's) $145 £70
'Helen comes of Age' – no. 372 of 500 copies signed by the author – orig. cloth – dust jacket – 4to. – The FranfrolicoPress, 1927.
(Christie's S. Kensington) $40 £20
'Men and Gods of the Roman Nile' – slightly chipped dust wrapper – 1968.
(J. Ash) $8 £4

LINDSAY, N.
'Ship Models' – coloured plates – quarter morocco – slipcase – limited Edn. – 146 /150 copies – author signed – 1966.
(Bennett Book Auction) $40 £18

LINDSAY, NORMAN
'Aristophanes. Lysistrata' – number 424 of 725 copies signed by Jack Lindsay – folio – illus. and four plates by Norman Lindsay – orig. half morocco – boxed – Franfrolico Press 1926.
(Christie's S. Kensington) $295 $140

LINKLATER, ERIC
'The House of Gair' – slightly browned dust wrapper – 1953.
(J. Ash) $6 £3

LINSCHOTEN, JAN HUYGEN VAN
'His Discours of Voyages into ye East and West Indies' – 1 folding engraved map only – torn – 3 engraved maps – 4 woodcut maps in text – soiled and spotted – modern leatherette – folio – 1598.
(Christie's) $295 £140

LINTON, E. L.
'The Lake Country' – one double page map – frontispiece – illustrations by W. J. Linton – original cloth – slightly soiled – g.e. – 4to. – 1864.
(Christie's S. Kensington) $20 £10

LINTON, W. J.
'The Masters of Wood Engraving' – number 128 of 500 copies – plates – 1 hand col. – illus. – library stamps – contemp. morocco backed cloth – soiled – folio – 1889.
(Sotheby's) $145 £70

LIPSCOMB, GEORGE
'The History and Antiquities of the County of Buckingham' 8 vols. – large paper copy – numerous engraved plates and maps – some foxed – orig. printed boards – unopened – uncut – 4to. – 1831-47.
(Christie's) $275 £130

LISLE, E.
'Observations in Husbandry' – portrait – plates – calf worn – wormed – 4to. – 1757.
(Irelands) $190 £90

L'ISLE, GUILLAUME DE
'Atlas Nouveau' – engraved and printed title – 54 engraved maps – hand col. in outline – half calf – marbled boards – wanting spine – covers detached – worn – folio – Amsterdam 1730.
(Sotheby's) $3,150 £1,500

'America Septentrionalis' – engraved map – col. by hand – title cartouche – spotted – 452 mm x 579 mm – Augsburg T. C. Lotter circa 1700.
(Sotheby's) $210 £100

'La Pologne' – engraved map – hand col. in outline – historiated title cartouche – fully col. – 478 mm x 624 mm – Paris 1703.
(Sotheby's) $40 £18

LISLE, MAJOR JAMES GEORGE SEMPLE
'The Life ..... Written by Himself' – 1st Edn. – engraved portrait frontis – half title – contem. boards – uncut – 8vo. – 1799.
(Sotheby's) $115 £55

LISSIM, SIMON
Design for the decor 'Tableaux d'Une Exposition' – pencil – watercolour – gouache and indian ink and gold and silver paint – signed and dated 1934 – 41 cm. x 55.2 cm.
(Sotheby's) $380 £180

LISTER, MARTIN
'A Journey to Paris' – 1st Edn. – 6 engraved plates – two folding – 3 pp adverts – dampstains – contem. calf – rebacked – 8vo. – 1699.
(Sotheby's) $105 £50

'Santorii Sanctorii De Statica Medicina Aphorismorum' – 12mo. – engr. frontis – bound at back – slight soiling – contemp. panelled calf – spine worn – Impensis Sam. Smith & Ben. Watford 1701.
(Christie's S. Kensington) $60 £28

LITCHFIELD, FREDERICK
'The Illustrated History of Furniture' – 1893.
(Baitson) $40 £18

LITERARY JOURNAL
Vol. 1 parts 1 and 2 – calf – 1744-45.
(Phillips) $65 £32

LITTLE FOLKS' FUN
Verses by Constance M. Lowe – illus. by Hilda Robinson – 6 full page illus. on discs – orig. cloth backed pictorial boards – 4to. – Ernest Nister 1900.
(Sotheby's) $95 £45

LIVERPOOL TO MANCHESTER RAILWAY
Plan of part of the Estate of Thomas Legh, Esq. – large ms plan on 2 joined sheets indicating proposed route of railway – ms note on verso – slightly frayed and torn – 580 mm x 1900 mm – circa 1821.
(Sotheby Beresford Adams) $170 £80

LIVINGSTONE, DAVID
A. L's arranging to procure beads for next visit to Africa – 4 pages 8vo. to J. B. Horsfall M. P. – Kensington Palace Gardens – Jan 1858.
(Sotheby's) $925 £440

'Missionary Travels and Researches in South Africa' – 1st Edn. – first issue – binding defective – 1857.
(Lane) $30 £14

LIVIUS, TITUS
'Historicorum Romanorum' – 4 parts in 3 vols. – ruled in red – device on title – browning – worming – contem. French red morocco – gilt spines and cover – Pietro Duodo's arms – slightly rubbed – g.e. – 16mo. – 1588.
(Sotheby's) $9,450 £4,500

LIZARS, JOHN
'A System of Anatomical Plates of the Human Body' – litho title 101 litho plates – 15 plates of the brain coloured – no text – half calf – folio – Edinburgh W H. Lizars 1823-27.
(Sotheby's) $420 £200

LLOYD'S
'Lloyd's Register of Shipping and Ship Owners' – 3 vols. – 1963-65.
(Baitson) $25 £13

LLOYD, DAVID
'Memoires of Excellent Personages 1637 to 1660 . . .' – 1st Edn. – title in red and black – browning and soiling – cont. calf – folio – 1668.
(Sotheby's) $40 £20

LLOYD, E.
'Natural History' – 16 vols. – col. plates – buckram gilt – 1896-97.
(Phillips) $145 £70

LLOYD'S ENCYCLOPAEDIC DICTIONARY
7 vols. with numerous illus. – 1895.
(Baitson) $6 £3

LLOYD, L.
'Game Birds and Wild Fowl of Sweden and Norway' – 48 col. lithos – folding map in pocket – cloth gilt – g.e. – 1867.
(Phillips) $230 £110

LLUYD, EDWARD
'Archaeologia Britannica' – 1st Edn. – complete with the Irish–English dictionary – folio – 1707.
(Lane) $250 £120

LOBSTEIN, J. F.
'De Nervi Sympathetici Humani' – 10 plates – some dampstained – orig. boards – soiled – 4to. – Paris 1823.
(Phillips) $135 £65

LOCHER, JACOB
'Spectaculum ... More Tragico Effigiatum' – gothic letter – woodcut on title – woodcut diagram – cont. marginalia and underlining – faded – slightly soiled – 19th cent. half cloth – sm. 4to. – Augsburg 1502.
(Sotheby's) $945 £450

LOCKE, JOHN
'The Reasonableness of Christianity' – 1st Edn. – contem. ms. annotations – calf – spine worn at head – 8vo. – 1695.
(Sotheby's) $190 £90
'Reply to the Bishop of Worcester' – 1697.
(Laurence & Martin Taylor) $65 £30

LOCKMAN, JOHN
'Travels of the Jesuits into Various Parts of the World' – 2 vol. – 1st Edn. – 6 folding engraved maps – torn – spotted – modern morocco backed boards – 8vo. – 1743.
(Sotheby's) $170 £80

LOCOMOTIVE RAILWAY CARRIAGE AND WAGON REVIEW (Formerly Moore's Monthly Magazine)
Vol. 1-65 in 58 – plates – some col. and folding – 6 vol. – contem. half roan – rubbed – remainder orig. cloth – 8to. – 1896-1959.
(Sotheby's) $650 £310

LODGE, E.
'Portraits of Illustrious Personages of Great Britain' – 10 vol. – in 5 engr. plates – spotted – contemp – half morocco – rubbed 8vo. – 1840.
(Sotheby's) $45 £22

LOFFLER, K.
'Der Landgrafenspaalter' – plates – many col. – boards – 4to. – Leipzig 1925.
(Phillips) $85 £40

LOFTIE, W. J.
'Windsor' – inscribed pres copy from Queen Victoria to Lady Waterford – 4to. – Xmas 1885.
(Phillips) $45 £22

LONDON
'Views Consisting of the Most Remarkable Buildings' – title and vignette occasional slight soiling – orig. boards – rebacked – 12mo. – published by Thos. Crabb – n.d.
(Christie's S. Kensington) $30 £15

LONDON ALMANACK FOR THE YEAR 1783
Engraved throughout – orig. red morocco wallet style binding – 33 mm x 34 mm – 1782.
(Sotheby's) $75 £36

LONDON AND COUNTY BREWER, THE
7th Edn. – last advert leaf – contem. calf – worn – 8vo. – 1759.
(Sotheby's) $135 £65

LONDON, BRIGHTON AND SOUTH EAST RAILWAY
A Collection of approx. 250 item of ephemera – including manuscripts of accounts – season tickets – a few maps and specimens of tickets etc. – a few slightly soiled or frayed – cont. half calf – rubbed – folio – 1860-80.
(Sotheby's) $565 £270

LONDON COUNTY COUNCIL
Survey of London – vol. 21, 22, 24, 29-34, 37 and 39 – together 11 vols in 12 – plates orig. cloth – most with dust jackets – 4to. – 1949-77.
(Sotheby's) $275 £130
London County Council Survey of London – 18 vol. – various – and two duplicate vol. lage. 4to. – plates – a few mounted and coloured – illustrations – various bindings – 1921-60.
(Christie's S. Kensington) $460 £220

LONDON GAZETTE, THE
Complete copy for August 7th, 1829.
(Baitson) $4 £2

LONDON AND THE GREAT EXHIBITION 1851
Certificate of thanks by the Mayor and Corporation of the City of London to the 'Illustrious Chief' and the people of France for the hospitality afforded to them on the occasion of the Great Exhibition – borders illuminated and gilt in high relief with arms of the City and Napoleon III with emblems of peace, prosperity and war – signed by H. Dowse and dated 1852 – 31¾ inches x 27½ inches.
(Sotheby's) $670 £320

LONDON INTERIORS
'A Grand National Exhibition' – 2 vol. in one – engraved title – 75 engraved plates – orig. cloth – worn – 4to. – 1841.
(Sotheby's) $65 £30

LONDON MISSIONARY SOCIETY
'Report of the Proceedings against the Late Rev. J. Smith of Demerara on the charge of aiding a rebellion of the Negro Slaves' – some newspaper cuttings inserted – foxed – modern black calf – uncut – 8vo. – 1824.
(Sotheby's) $75 £35

LONDON, SOCIETY OF ANTIQUARIES
Collection of various engraved prints published on behalf of the Society – 11 large folding plates and 16 folio – plates – some with descriptive text – contem. mottled calf – folio – 1713-85.
(Christie's) $840 £400

LONDON THEATRES
186 programmes for London Theatres during 1950's and '60's.
(Baitson) $40 £19

'LONDRES'
Uncol. copper engraved view of London, 17th century.
(Phillips) $65 £30

LONGFELLOW, H. W.
'The Song of Hiawatha' – wood engraved illustrations – occasional slight spotting – original blue cloth – g.e. W. Kent & Co. 1860.
(Christie's S. Kensington) $55 £25
'Keramos and other Poems' – 1st English Edn. – orig. cloth – slightly faded – 1878.
(J. Ash) $10 £5

LONGFELLOW, HENRY WADSWORTH
Fine repro of a head and shoulders photo by Julia Margaret Cameron from the papers of the Tennyson family – mounted – 15 x 10¼inches. – 1868.
(Sotheby's) $170 £80

LONGUEVAL
'Histoire de l'Eglise Gallicane' – 3 vols only – olive morocco gilt with arms of Madame Victoire de France, daughter of Louis XV – 4to. – 1732.
(Moore Allen & Innocent) $275 £130

LOPEZ DE GOMARRA, FRANCISCO
'Histoire Generalle des Indes Occidentales ... traduite en Francois par .. Fumee' – 5th Edn. – title soiled – some leaves detached – stained – contemp. vellum – Paris 1587.
(Christie's S. Kensington) $65 £30

L'ORME, P. DE
'L'Oeuvre' – reprint – orig. wrappers – frayed – folio – Paris 1894.
(Sotheby's) $210 £100

LOUDON, MRS JANE
'The Ladies' Flower Garden of Ornamental Annuals' – 1840.
(Sotheby, King & Chasemore) $1,010 £480

LOUDON, MRS JANE WEBB
'The Ladies' Flower Garden of Ornamental Annuals' – 48 hand col. plates – some spotted – contem. vellum boards – gilt spine – rubbed – g.e. – 4to. – 1840.
(Sotheby's) $1,155 £550

'Hints on the Formation of Gardens and Pleasure Grounds' – 20 folding col. plates – soiling – half morocco – worn – 4to. – 1813.
(Sotheby's) $715 £340

LOUIS XV, KING OF FRANCE
'Cours des Principaux Fleuves et Rivieres de L'Europe. Compose et Imprime par Louis XV, Roi de France .... en 1718' – 1st Edn. – engraved portrait by Audran of the King as a child – woodcut head and end pieces – bookplate of Robert, Marquess of Crewe – 18th cent. red morocco – spine gilt – inner gilt dentelles – gilt edges – slight wear – sm. 4to. – Paris, Dans l'Imprimerie du Cabinet de S. M. 1718.
(Sotheby Parke Bernet) $2,230 £1,060

LOUTHERBURG, P. J. DE
'The Romantic and Picturesque Scenery of England and Wales' – Eng. and French text – 15 hand col. aquatint plates – first title soiled – orig. half roan – spine gilt – some wear – g.e. – folio – 1805.
(Sotheby's) $670 £320

LOW, DAVID
'The Best of Low' – tall 8vo. – slight wear at head of spine – slightly bowed – 1930.
(J. Ash) $15 £8

LOW, FRANCIS H.
'Queen Victoria's Dolls' – pictorial title – 40 col. illus – 33 full page – other illus. and initials by Alan Wright – upper hinge split – orig. pictorial cloth gilt – g.e. – 4to. – Newnes 1894.
(Sotheby's) $40 £18

LOW, HUGH
'Sarawak' – engraved plates – orig. calf gilt – 1848.
(Phillips) $135 £65

LOW, WILL H. – KEATS, JOHN
'Odes and Sonnets' – Plates and title vignette by Low – occasional slight spotting – contemporary morocco – rubbed – folio – g.e. – Philadelphia, 1888.
(Christie's S Kensington) $30 £15

LOWE, CONSTANCE
'See Saw Pictures' – 6 col. illus. – moving parts worked by levers – small tears – orig. cloth backed boards – 4to. – Nister circa 1890.
(Sotheby Beresford Adams) $115 £54

LOWE, E. J.
'Natural History of Rare and New Ferns' – woodcuts and colour illus. – half calf worn – 4to. – 1862.
(Phillips) $60 £28

LOWER, DR. RICHARD
'Eminent Physicians' Receipts' – calf gilt – 12 mo. – 1701.
(Phillips) $115 £55

LOWNDES, WILLIAM THOMAS
'The Bibliographer's Manual of English Literature' – 4 vols. 1st Edn. – interleaved – contem. russia – spines defective – covers loose or defective – 8vo. – 1834.
(Sotheby's) $85 £40

LUCAS, F. L.
'The Homeric Hymn to Aphrodite' – number 573 of 750 copies – frontis and illus. – orig. parchment backed cloth – sm. folio – 1948.
(Christie's) $40 £20

LUCCOCK, JOHN
'Notes on Rio de Janeiro' – 1st Edn. – 2 folding engraved maps – engraved plan – contem. polished calf – 4to. – 1820.
(Christie's) $1,785 £850

LUCRETIUS
'De Rerum Natura' – contem. English binding of black morocco gilt with arms of Count Hoym on each cover – red silk end leaves – 12mo. – 1713.
(Moore Allen & Innocent) $160 £75

LUDLOW, EDMUND
'Memoirs' – 2 parts in one vol. – large paper copy – title in red and black – engraved portrait frontis – slight off-setting to title – contem. panelled calf – spine gilt – slight wear – g.e. – folio – 1751.
(Sotheby's) $30 £15

LUDOLF, J.
'Historia Aethiopica' – plates – marginal stains – calf – repaired – folio – Frankfurt 1681.
(Sotheby's) $65 £30

LUGT, F.
'Inventaire General des Dessins des Ecoles du Nord' – plates – cloth – 4to. – 1936.
(Phillips) $40 £20

LUIS OF GRANADA
'Introductionis ad Symbolum Fidei' 1588 'Dux Peccatorum' 1590.
(Phillips) $45 £22

LUMSDEN, ANDREW
'Remarks on the Antiquities of Rome and Its Environs' – 1st Edn. – engraved portrait – 12 plates and plans – 5 double page or folding – extra illus. – 48 fine original watercolours by Martorana of Rome – fixing – cont. dark blue straight grained morocco gilt – rubbed – 4to. – W. Bulmer sold by G. Nicol 1797.
(Sotheby's) $2,520 £1,200

LURCAT, JEAN – FABRE, J. H.
'Le Monde Merveilleux des Insectes' – 45 lithos by Lurcat – one repeated 4 times – 3 hand coloured – 35 printed in colour – spotted – unsewn in orig. wrappers – decorated folder and slipcase – 4to. – Paris, Societe des Femmes Bibliophiles, 1950.
(Sotheby's) $135 £65

LUTHER, MARTIN
'Operationes in Duas Psalmorum Decades' – title in woodcut border – woodcut device – woodcut initials – some historiated – old boards – corners worn – folio – Basle, 1521.
(Sotheby's) $670 £320

LYALL, ALFRED
'Rambles in Madeira and Portugal, in the Early Part of 1826' – 1st Edn., engraved folding map, lacking first leaf, a few leaves slightly spotted, upper hinge weak, cont. half calf, slightly worn, upper joint just torn – 1827.
(Sotheby's) $65 £30

LYALL, ROBERT
'The Character of the Russians and a Detailed History of Moscow' – 24 engraved plates and maps – some folding – some col. – half title – modern half calf – rubbed – 4to. – 1823.
(Sotheby's) $360 £170

LYDEKKER, RICHARD
'The Deer of All Lands' – ltd. Edn. – signed by publisher – 24 col. litho plates – gilt – soiled – 4to. – 1898.
(Phillips) $670 £320

'Wild Oxen, Sheep and Goats of all Lands' – Ltd. Edn. – signed by publisher – 27 col. litho plates – cloth gilt – soiled – 4to. – 1898.
(Phillips) $800 £380
'Royal Natural History' – plates – 6 vols – pictorial cloth gilt – 1893-96.
(Laurence & Martin Taylor) $60 £28
'The Great and Small Game of Europe, West and Northern Asia and America' – 8 col. plates and other illus. – limited Edn. – 4to. – orig. cloth gilt – slightly worn – 1901.
(Bonhams) $170 £80

LYDIS, MARIETTE
'Lettres de La Religieuse Portugaise' – 8 lithographed illustrations, 7 full page by Lydis, unsewn in original wrappers, uncut, unopened – Hazan, Paris, 1947.
(Sotheby's) $40 £18

LYELL, J. C.
'Fancy Pigeons' – illustrated – 1882.
(Laurence & Martin Taylor) $45 £22

LYLE, OFFICIAL REVIEWS OF ANTIQUES, ARMS AND ART 1977.
(Laurence & Martin Taylor) $10 £5

LYNDSAY, SIR D.
'Facsimile of an Ancient Heraldic Manuscript' – one of 250 copies – plates – orig. cloth – rubbed – 4to. – 1878.
(Sotheby's) $115 £55

LYNE, MICHAEL
'Horses, Hounds and Country' – illustrated – 1938.
(Laurence & Martin Taylor) $10 £5

LYSONS, REV. D. AND S.
'Magna Britannia Vol. II Part II containing The County Palatine of Chester' – one engraved folding map – 34 plates and plans – extra-illustrated with 34 plates and plans – some folding – spotting – contemp. morocco soiled g.e. 4to. – 1810.
(Christie's S. Kensington) $65 £30
'Environs of London' – 3 vols. in 7 – with supplement – extra illus. – half morocco – 1800-11.
(Phillips) $400 £190
'Magna Britannia' The Cornish Volume – 1st Edn. – fine large paper copy – half calf recent binding – 1814.
(Lane) $275 £130
'Topographical and Historical Account of Bedfordshire' – engraved plates – some folding – spotted – contem. calf – rebacked and repaired – 4to. – n.d.
(Sotheby's) $145 £70

LYTTON, E. G. E. B. LORD
'Works' – 28 vol. – Knebworth Edn. – frontispieces – uniform half calf – spines gilt – slightly rubbed – n.d.
(Christie's S. Kensington) $85 £40

MCADAM, J. L.
'Remarks on the Present System of Roadmaking' – orig. boards – 1822.
(Phillips) $80 £38

MACARTHY, MARY
'The Group' – 1st English Edn. – slightly marked dust wrapper – 1963.
(J. Ash) $8 £4

MACAULAY, ROSE
'Orphan Island' – spine slightly dull and rubbed – 1924.
(J. Ash) $12 £6

MACAULAY, T. B. LORD
'Works' – 12 vol. – number 45 of 250 copies – frontispieces – slight browning – orig. cloth – slightly soiled – t.e.g. – 1898.
(Christie's S. Kensington) $80 £38

MACBEAN, FORBES
'Sketches of Character and Costume in Constantinople' – 5 orig. parts – 25 hand col. plates – orig. wrappers – folio – 1854.
(Sotheby's) $565 £270

MACBETH, GEORGE
'The Night of Stones' – 1st Edn. – no. 42 of 110 copies – signed by author – irreg. geometric designes – black – navy and green onlays – signed with initials inside lower cover by Sally Lou Smith – 8vo. – 1968.
(Sotheby's) $420 £200

MACCARTHEY, DESMOND
'The Court Theatre 1904-1907' – the eminent critic's first book – a little foxed – 1907.
(J. Ash) $17 £8

MCCLINTOCK, CAPT.
'The Voyage of the Fox in the Arctic Seas' – plates – illus. – orig. cloth – rubbed – 8vo. – 1859.
(Sotheby's) $55 £25

MACCOLL, D. S.
'Twenty Five Years of the National Art Collection Fund' – plates – orig. cloth – 4to. – 1928.
(Sotheby's) $10 £5

MCCULLOCH, J. R.
'A Treatise on the Principles and Practical Influences of Taxation': 'A Treatise on the Succession to Property Vacant by Death' – 2 works in one vol. – 1st Edn. – half title – contem. blue calf – rubbed – bookplate of Lord Belper – 1845-48.
(Sotheby's) $170 £80

MCCULLOH, JAMES H.
'Researches on America, being an Attempt to Settle some Points Relative to the Aborigines of America' – 2nd Edn. – browning – contem. half calf – Signet arms in gilt on sides – slightly worn – 8vo. – Baltimore 1817.
(Sotheby's) $20 £10

MACCULLOUGH, DR. JOHN
'Remarks on the Art of Making Wine' – 1st Edn. – half title lacks last leaf – contem. half calf – rubbed – 12 mo. – 1816.
(Sotheby's) $460 £220

MCDIARMID, H.
'A Drunk Man Looks at the Thistle' – 1st Edn. – signed by author – cloth gilt – 1926.
(Phillips) $125 £60

'Golden Treasury of Scottish Poetry' – full page letter from author to J. Rothnie 'Lucky Poet' – both 1st Edns. – inscribed by author – cloth gilt – 1940. and 1943.
(Phillips) $75 £35

MACDONALD, GEORGE
'Dealings with the Fairies' – first Edn. – wood engraved frontis – 11 plates after Arthur Hughes – stain rust marks – orig. cloth – worn – g.e. – 16 mo. – 1867.
(Sotheby's) $360 £170

MACDONELL, A. G.
'England Their England' – spine a little sunned – worn and frayed dust-wrapper – 1933.
(J. Ash) $65 £30

MACFALL, HALDANE
'Aubrey Beardsley' – 4to. – plates – occasional spotting – original cloth – spine soiled – 1928.
(Christie's S. Kensington) $40 £18

MACFARLANE AND THOMPSON
'The History of England' – 8 vols. – engravings and maps – 1877.
(Baitson) $6 £3

MCGRATH, R. AND FROST, A. C.
'Glass in Architecture and Decoration' – illus. – orig. cloth – dust jacket – sm. folio – 1937.
(Sotheby's) $40 £18

MACGREGOR, G. METCALFE
'Life and Opinions' – 2 vols. cloth gilt – plates and folding maps – 1888.
(Bennett Book Auction) $8 £4
'Narrative of a Journey Through the Province of Khorassan' – 2 vol. – 1st Edn. – plates – folding map – orig. cloth – 8vo. – 1879.
(Sotheby's) $715 £340

MACGREGOR, JOHN
'British America' – 2 vols. – 1st Edn. – 9 engraved maps – lacking half titles – 19th cent half maroon morocco – covers faded – 8vo. – Edinburgh 1832.
(Sotheby's) $95 £45

MACHEN, ARTHUR
'The Bowmen and Other Legends of the War' – orig. pictorial boards – slight wear and some foxing – 1915.
(J. Ash) $12 £6

MCILWRAITH, W.
'Visitor's Guide to Wigtownshire' – map – calf – gilt – 2nd. Edn. –Dumfries, .1877.
(Bennett Book Auction) $20 £9

MACKAIL, J. W.
'William Morris, an Address' – one of 325 copies on paper orig. limp vellum – 8vo. – Doves Press – 1901.
(Sotheby's) $190 £90
'The History of Painting' – 8 vols. – plates – many col. – cloth gilt – 4to. – 1911.
(Phillips) $115 £55

MCKAY, A.
'History of Kilmarnock' – cloth – 1st Edn. – Kilmarnock 1848 – author's presentation copy
(Bennett Book Auction) $25 £12

MACKAY, C.
'History of the United States of America' – 2 vols. – 2 engraved frontis – titles in vol. 2 – plates – some staining – half calf – 4to. – Virtue n.d.
(Phillips) $80 £38

MCKAY, WILLIAM AND ROBERTS, W.
'John Hoppner, R. A.' – plates orig. cloth – soiled – t.e.g. – 4to. – 1909.
(Christie's) $40 £20

MCKEARIN, C. L. AND H.
'American Glass' – 4to. – plates – original cloth – dust jacket torn – New York 1941.
(Christie's S. Kensington) $30 £15

MACKENNA, F. S.
'Worcester Porcelain' – limited Edn. – plates – orig. cloth – 4to. – 1950.
(Sotheby's) $220 £105

MCKENNEY, T. L. AND HALL, J.
'The Indian Tribes of North America' – 2 maps – plates – 123 coloured – 3 vols. – cloth – Edinburgh 1933.
(Bonhams) $135 £65

MACKENZIE, A.
'Voyages from Montreal on the River St. Laurence ... North America' – port. – 3 folding maps – calf gilt – 4to. – 1801.
(Phillips) $925 £440

MACKENZIE, COLIN
'Five Thousand Recipes in all the Domestic Arts' – 5th Edn. – soiled – a few leaves detached – orig. morocco – worn – 12 mo. – 1825.
(Christie's S. Kensington) $65 £32

MACKENZIE, COMPTON
'Echoes' – chipped dust wrapper – 1954.
(J. Ash) $6 £3

MACKENZIE, SIR JAMES
'Angina Pectoris' – 1st Edn. – orig. cloth – 4to. – 1923.
(Sotheby's) $40 £20

MACKENZIE, M.
'Orcades: or Geographic and Hydrographic Survey of the Orkney and Lewis Islands' – 8 double page maps – large folio – old calf – worn – 1750.
(Bonhams) $210 £100

MACKENZIE-QUIN
'A Method to Multiply or Divide Any Number of Figures' – 4 charts – 2 folding – contem. wrappers – cloth case – folio – Printed for author 1750.
(Sotheby's) $275 £130

MCKERROW, R. B.
'Printers and Publishers' Devices in England and Scotland 1485-1640' – 4to. – illustrations – orig. cloth backed boards – Bibliographical Society, 1949.
(Christie's S. Kensington) $55 £25
'A Dictionary of Printers and Booksellers in England 1557-1775' – orig. buckram backed boards – rubbed – 4to. – Bibliographical Socy. 1910-32.
(Sotheby's) $180 £85

MACKIE, C.
'Norfolk Annals' – 2 vols. – half calf – 1901.
(Irelands) $170 £80

MACKINTOSH, SIR H.
'Early English Figure Pottery' – col. frontis – plates – cloth – 4to. – 1938.
(Phillips) $75 £35

MCLEISH, CHARLES
'Past and Present' by Thomas Carlyle and bound by McLeish inscribed by him 'my first effort at decorative binding' – brown morocco with onlays of green and tooled in gilt – g.e. sm. 8vo. – 1894.
(Phillips) $505 £240

MACLEOD, FIONA
'From the Hills of Dream' – orig. decorative cloth gilt – 1907.
(J. Ash) $17 £8

MCLEOD, JOHN
'Voyage of Alceste along the Coast of Corea' – 2nd Edn. – engraved port. – 5 hand col. aquatint plates – lacks half title – contem. half calf – very rubbed – upper cover detached – 8vo. – 1818.
(Sotheby's) $65 £30

MACLISE, D. – MOORE, THOMAS
'Irish Melodies' – 4to. – engr. additional title and proof impressions of illustrated text after Maclise – slight browning – orig. boards – boxed g.e. – 1846.
(Christie's S. Kensington) $360 £170

MCLOC, J.
'New, Complete, and Universal Natural History of all . . . Quadrupeds, Birds etc.' – frontis and four hundred wood engravings cut by J. Thomson – calf – covers detached – 1813.
(Bennett Book Auction) $40 £20

MACNEICE, LOUIS
'The Burning Perch' – 1st Edn. – blue morocco – gilt diagonal line tooling over panel of coloured onlays – t.e.g. – signed inside lower cover by Elizabeth Greenhill – 8vo. – 1968.
(Sotheby's) $610 £290

MCPHAIL, J.
'The Gardener's Remembrancer' – half calf – 1807.
(Laurence & Martin Taylor) $55 £26

MCPHERSON, DUNCAN
'Antiquities of Kertch' – folio – lithographed additional title and 13 plates – one double page and folding – most coloured – two engraved maps – hand coloured in outline – lacking contents list – some leaves soiled – orig. cloth – spine torn – stitching shaken g.e. – 1857.
(Christie's S. Kensington) $65 £30

MACPHERSON, JAMES
'Temora, an Ancient Epic Poem' – 1st Edn. – title in red and black – engraved vignette – slight browning – modern cloth – uncut – 4to. – 1763.
(Sotheby's) $40 £18

MACQUER, PIERRE JOSEPH
'Elemens de Chymie Theorique' – 1st Edn. – folding plates – half title – contem. French calf – 12 mo. – Paris 1749.
(Sotheby's) $190 £90

MACQUOID, P., AND OTHERS
'A Record of the Collections in the Lady Leverhulme Art Gallery' – 3 vol. – limited to 350 copies – plates – some mounted and coloured – orig. buckram – dust jackets – t.e.g. – folio – 1928.
(Christie's S. Kensington) $160 £75
'The Dictionary of English Furniture' – 3 vols. – folio – coloured plates – illustrations – orig. cloth – t.e.g. – 1924-7.
(Christie's S. Kensington) $400 £190

MACRAY, REV. W. DUNN
'Annals of the Bodleian Library, Oxford' – cloth – Henry Bradshaw's copy, 1868.
(Bennett Book Auction) $20 £10

M., A. D.
'Gamiani' – 2 parts – etched frontis – 15 plates – half morocco gilt – Paris 1864.
(Phillips) $335 £160

MADDEN, SIR FREDERIC
'Illuminated Ornaments Selected from Manuscripts of the Middle Ages' – hand col. addit. title – 59 plates – 2 folding and mounted – modern half morocco – 4to. – 1833.
(Christie's) $145 £70

MADOX, THOMAS
'The History and Antiquities of the Exchequer of the Kings of England' – mss index on fly leafs – contem. panelled calf – hinges cracked – folio – 1711.
(Sotheby's) $20 £10

MADRUS, DR. J. C. (editor)
'Le Livre de Mille Nuits et Une Nuit' – 16 vol. – limited to 100 copies – vol. 2 lacking title – contem. morocco backed boards – spines rubbed – Paris 1903.
(Christie's) $20 £10

MAETERLINCK, MAURICE
'The Blue Bird' – 4to. – 24 mounted coloured plates by F. Caley Robinson – original cloth – joints rubbed – t.e.g. – 1911.
(Christie's S. Kensington) $65 £32

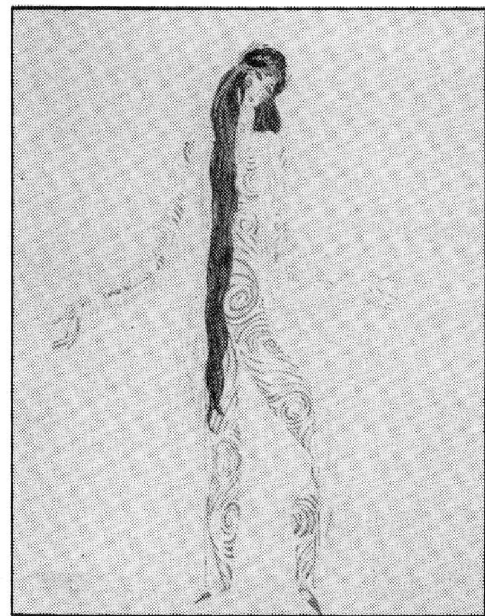

MAETERLINCK, MAURICE – LEPAPE, GEORGES
'Decor et Costumes Pour L'Oiseau Bleu' – 61 plates by Lepape – coloured through stencils – contem. half morocco – t.e.g. – 4to. – Paris Societe d'Edition 'Le Livre' 1927.
(Sotheby's) $295 £140

MAFEKING MAIL, THE
No. 1-152 only of 165 and preface – 'Published by desire' and Special Edn. of 8th March 1900 – bound in one vol. – some tears – contem. half calf – rubbed – folio – 1899-1900.
(Sotheby's) $145 £70

MAGALLANIUS
'Tractatus Theologicus' – contem. Roman binding of red morocco gilt with arms of Pope Clement X in half red morocco slip-case – sm. 4to. – 1666.
(Moore Allen & Innocent) $7,560 £3,600

MAGALOTTI, LORENZO
'Letters Scientifiche' – occasional alight spotting contemporary vellum – soiled – Venice, 1756.
(Christie's S. Kensington) $20 £10

MAGIC, editor Ellis Stanyon
Vol. 1, vols. 3-15 in 154 parts lacking 22 issues – as issued – some worn – one defective – 4to. – Dec. 1900 to May 1920.
(Sotheby's) $115 £55

MAGIC CARDS
12 litho cards each with illus. col. by hand with concealed image – in orig. box – pictorial label on lid – 115 mm x 76 mm – H. G. Clarke and Co. circa 1850.
(Sotheby's) $170 £80

MAGICIAN ANNUAL, THE – (Editor Will Goldston)
Vols. 2-5 plates – some col. – illus. – orig. cloth gilt – spines faded – 4to. – 1908-12.
(Sotheby's) $115 £55

vol. 1-5 plates – some col. – illus. – vol. 1 lacking title and wrappers – remainder in orig. cloth – gilt – rather worn – vol. 2 with orig. wrappers bound in – 4to. – 1907-12.
(Sotheby's) $145 £70

MAGNA CARTA
Trans. by George Ferrers – black letter – hand col. woodcut initials – 19th cent. calf rubbed – Sir William Fairfax's copy (1609-44) with ownership inscription and his signature – 8vo. – Elizabeth widow of Robert Redman 1541?
(Sotheby's) $145 £70

MAGNUS, JOHANNES (archbishop of Upsala)
'Gothorum Sueonum Que Historia' – 1st Edn. – woodcut title page – full page map of Scandinavia – many smaller woodcuts through text – historiated initials and large woodcut device at end – some paper flaws – stains and a tear – 17th cent. calf – gilt border – red label – worn and torn – folio – Rome 1554.
(Sotheby's) $1,050 £500

MAIDENS WORSHIPPING GANESH
Minor flaking – white rules on dark blue border with double white lines and outer rules in red leaf – some flaking – 36.1 cm x 48.8 cm. – Guler circa 1800.
(Christie's) $4,830 £2,300

MAIGRET, MONSIEUR
'A Treatise on the Safety and Maintenance of States by the Means of Fortresses' – translated from the original French by J. Heath – cont. calf – worn – 1747.
(Christie's S. Kensington) $85 £40

MAILLOL, AIRSTIDE
'Les Eclogues' of Virgil – 43 woodcut illustrations by Maillol – spotted – with prospectus inserted – unsewn – uncut – unopened – original vellum backed folder – slightly damaged ties – 4to. – Weimar, Cranach Press, 1926.
(Sotheby's) $95 £45

MAILLOL, ARISTIDE – OVID
'L'Art D'Aimer' – 12 litho plates – 11 woodcut illus. and 4 initials by Maillol – unsewn in orig. wrappers – uncut – folder – upper joint weak – slipcase – soiled – folio – Lausanne, Philippe Gonin 1935.
(Sotheby's) $1,010 £480

MAILLOL, ARISTIDE – LONGUS
'Daphnis et Chloe' – woodcut illustrations and initials by Maillol – slightly spotted – unbound as isssued in original – Paris, Philippe Gonin, 1937.
(Christie's S. Kensington) $525 £250

MAIMBOURG
'Histoire de la Ligue' – Vol. 1 only 18th cent. French binding of citron morocco gilt with arms of Madame Sophie, daughter of Louis XV – 12 mo. – 1683.
(Moore Allen & Innocent) $380 £180

MAINTENON, M. DE
'Memoires' – 16 vols. – 1789.
(Moore Allen & Innocent) $250 £120

MAITLAND, W.
'The History and Survey of London from its Foundation to the Present Time' – maps and plates – some folding – folio – reversed calf worn – map of London torn – 1756.
(Bonhams) $335 £160

MALAVOLTI, ORLANDO
'Historia . . . De'fatti and Guerre de'Sanesi' – 3 parts in one vol. – 4to – woodcut portraits on verso of title of parts one, two and three – old vellum soiled – Sienna, Per Salvestro Marchetti Libraro, 1599.
(Christie's S. Kensington) $45 £22

MALCOLM, J. P.
'Historical Sketch of the Art of Caricaturing' – illus. – foxing – rebound – cloth gilt – 4to. – 1813.
(Phillips) $85 £40

MALCOLM, JAMES PELLER
'Anecdotes of the Manners and Customs of London during the Eighteenth Century' – 2 vol. – 2nd Edn. – 45 engr. plates – including 12 hand coloured fashion plates – some slight spotting – contemp. marbled calf – spines rubbed and slightly chipped – 1810.
(Christie's S. Kensington) $95 £45

MALCOLM, COL. SIR J.
'Sketches of Persia' – 2 vols. – half calf – gilt - 8vo. – 1827.
(Phillips) $65 £30

MALET, CAPT. H.
'Annals of the Road' – coloured plates – orig. cloth – gilt – spine faded – 8vo. – 1876.
(Sotheby's) $170 £80

MALHAM, J.
'Naval Gazeteer' – vol.1 of 2 – 11 folding maps – calf gilt – 8vo. – 1799.
(Phillips) $100 £48

MALINOWSKI, B.
'Argonauts of the Western Pacific' – 1932.
(Allen & May) $25 £12

MALLET, A. M.
'Description de L'Univers' - vol. 3 only – 107 maps and plates disbound – sm. 4to. – 1683.
(Phillips) $170 £80

MALORY, SIR THOMAS
'Morte D'Arthur' – Illus. by Beardsley – one of 1,500 – fine orig. publisher's Art Nouveau Binding – orig. wrappers bound in – 2 vols. – London 1893.
(Robert Skinner) $375 £178

'Birth, Life and Acts of King Arthur' – 2 vols., illustrated by Aubrey Beardsley, cloth gilt – 1893.
(Phillips) $180 £80

'Lancelot and Guinevere' – illustrated by Lettice Sandford – orig. silver cloth – some slight marks – Folio Society 1953.
(J. Ash) $10 £5

'The Noble and Joyous Boke Entytled le Morte d'Arthur' – 2 vol. – number 366 of 370 copies – illus. - orig. morocco – t.e.g. – folio – Shakespeare Head Press 1933.
(Christie's) $335 £160

MALTON, T.
'A Compleat Treatise on Perspective in Theory and Practice' – engraved frontis and 47 plates of 48 – some folding – old calf – joints weak – folio – 1778.
(Bonhams) $115 £55

MALVEZZI, VIRGILIO MARCHESE
'Discourse upon Cornelius Tacitus' – 1st Edn. in English – title in woodcut border – dampstains – contem. calf – rubbed – folio – 1642.
(Sotheby's) $40 £20

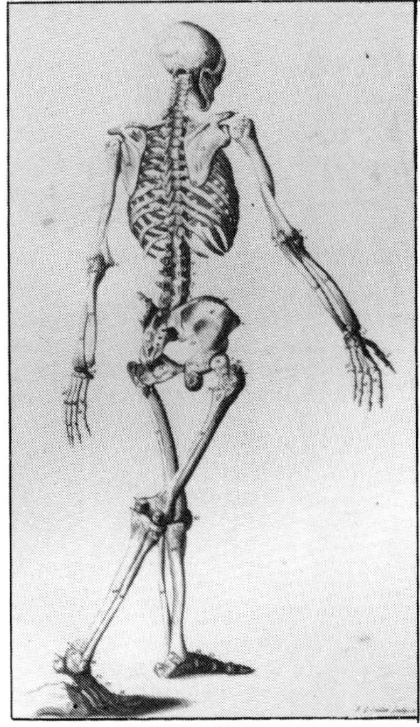

MANGET, JOHN JACOB
'Theatrum Anatonicum' – 2 vols. – engraved frontis – half title – engraved illus. after Seiller – 136 engraved plates after Seiller and others – incl. 4 folding and 21 Eustachian plates – tears – shaved and soiled browning – half morocco – folio – Geneva and Cologne, 1717.
(Christie's) $735 £350

MANN, THOMAS
Erika Mann 'The Last Years of Thomas Mann' – slightly marked dust wrapper – 1958.
(J. Ash) $6 £3

MANNING, H. E.
'Sermons Preached before the University of Oxford' – orig. cloth – title label slightly chipped – some foxing – Oxford 1844.
(J. Ash) $50 £24

MANNLICH, J. C.
'Verfuch uber Gebrauche, Kleidung und Wallen der alteften Volfer' – 29 engraved plates – some slight spotting – contemporary half calf – spine gilt – joints cracked – 4to. – Munich 1802.
(Christie's S. Kensington) $45 £22

MANSTEIN, BARON C. H. DE
'Memoirs of Russia' – calf gilt – 8vo – Dublin, 1770.
(Phillips) $60 £28

MANTZ, PAUL
'Antoine Watteau' – limited Edn. – plates – green morocco – gilt – t.e.g. – 4to. – Paris 1892.
(Phillips) $55 £25

MAOUT, E. LE
'Histoire Naturelle des Oiseaux' – 2nd Edn. – plates – some tinted – 15 hand coloured – some slight spotting – orig. cloth – spine holed and chipped at head and foot – g.e. – 4to. – Paris, 1855.
(Christie's S. Kensington) $105 £50

MAP OF INTENDED RAILWAY LINE FOR LIVERPOOL TO LEEDS AND THE HUMBER
Engraved map – 17 x 34 inches – framed and glazed – 1830.
(Christie's S. Kensington) $30 £15

MARCET, MRS J.
'Conversations on Botany' – 20 hand col. plates – one double page – some spotting – modern cloth – 8vo. – 1817.
(Phillips) $80 £38

MARCH, RICHARD
'The Mountain of the Upas Tree' – spine a little dull – Editions Poetry London 1948.
(J. Ash) $6 £3

MARCHAIS, CHEVALIER RENAUD DES
'Voyage en Guinee, Isles Voisines et a Cayenne' – 4 vols. – 1st Edn. – addit. engraved title – 5 folding maps and 25 plates – mostly folding – contem. calf rubbed – 12 mo. – Paris 1730.
(Christie's) $400 £190

Der gantz Jüdisch glaub
mit sampt eyner gründtlichenn
vnd warhafftigen anzeygunge / aller satzungen / Cere-
monien / gebetten / heymliche vnd öffentliche gebreüch, deren sich die
Juden halten, durch das gantz Jar / mit schönen vnnd gegründten
Argumenten wider iren glauben / durch Anthonium Margari-
tham, Hebreyschen Leser, der löblichen Universitet vnd
Fürstlichen Stat Leypzigk / beschryben vnd
an tag gegeben.

Durch in selbst gemehrt vnd gebessert / M. D. XXXI.

MARGARITHA, ANTONIUS
'Der Gantz Juedisch Glaub Mit Sampt Eyner Grundslichen und Warhaftigen' – 2nd Edn. – woodcuts on title – and in text – light staining – signature – vellum – sm. 4to. – with an xerox copy of the work. – Augsburg 1531.
(Sotheby's) $3,570 £1,700

MARIANA, JUAN DE
'The General History of Spain' – 2 parts in one – 1st Edn. in English – large paper copy – calf – worn – folio – 1699.
(Sotheby's) $145 £70

MARIE, ABBE J. F.
'Traite de Mechanique' – 12 folding plates – cont. calf – rubbed – small 4to. – Paris, 1774.
(Phillips) $40 £20

MARIETTE, PIERRE JEAN
'Traite des Pierres Gravees' – 2 vols. 2 engraved titles – dedication leaf – 5 vignettes – contem. French dark blue morocco – gilt decorative border – arms of Comte Henri de Calenberg (1685-1772) – gilt decorations – red morocco labels – gilt edges – 19th century bookplate of Francis Hutchison – folio – Paris, Imprimerie de l'Auteur 1750.
(Sotheby's) $965 £460

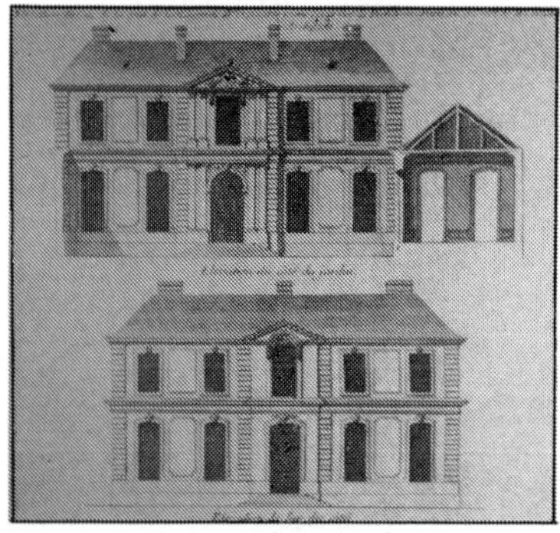

MARIETTE, JEAN (publisher)
'Architecture Francaise' – 2 vols. – 2 engraved titles – 256 engraved plates – many double page and folding – some discoloured – contem. sprinkled calf – gilt spines – folio – Paris, chez Jean Mariette 1727.
(Christie's) $1,155 £550

MARIVAUX, P. C. DE
'Oeuvres' – 12 vols. – port. – contem. tree calf – gilt – Paris 1781.
(Phillips) $335 £160

MARKHAM, COL. F.
'Shooting in the Himalayas' – wood engraved addit title and illus. – 8 col. litho plates folding – litho map – contem. half morocco – joints rubbed – 1854.
(Christie's) $125 £60

MARLBOROUGH'S VICTORIES
52 engraved cards each with scene relating to War of the Spanish Succession – captions below – some rhyming – orig. wrapper with illus. of Great Mogul and embossed stamp duty – 92 mm x 61 mm Christopher Blanchard, circa 1708.
(Sotheby's) $5,460 £2,600

MARLOTH, RUDOLF
'The Flora of South Africa' – 4 vols. in six – 4to. – plates some coloured – some with portions excised – original cloth – some soiled – vol 2 and 3 with dust jackets – t.e.g. – Capetown circa 1913.
(Christie's S. Kensington) $135 £65

MAROT, CLEMENT
'Oeuvres' – 2 vols. – number 42 of 100 copies – portrait – modern blue half morocco by St. Michael's Abbey – orig. wrappers bound in – t.e.g. – Lyons, 1869-70.
(Christie's S. Kensington) $55 £25

MARRYAT, JOSEPH
'Collection towards a History of Pottery and Porcelain' – illus. – coloured litho plates – browning – half morocco – rubbed – g.e. – 1850.
(Christie's) $45 £22

MARSDEN, WILLIAM
'The History of Sumatra' – 3rd. Edn. – 28 engraved plates – folding map – errata slip – tears – spots – contem. calf – rebacked – 4to. – 1811.
(Sotheby's) $275 £130

MARSH, LT. COL. W. LOCKWOOD
'Aeronautical Prints and Drawings' – no. 18 of 100 copies – plates – some col. – original pigskin – rubbed – t.e.g. – 4to. – 1924.
(Sotheby's) $315 £150

MARSHALL, A.
'Fancy Ices' – cloth – circa 1894.
(Bennett Book Auction) $14 £7

MARSHALL, A.
'Specimens of Antique Carved Furniture and Woodwork' – 50 plates – half leather – folio – 1888.
(Bennett Book Auction) $14 £7

MARSHALL, C. E. DENDY
'A History of British Railways Down to the Year 1830' – plates – one folding – illustrations – orig. cloth – dust jacket – lge. 8vo. – 1938.
(Christie's S. Kensington) $55 £25

MARSHALL, H. R.
'Coloured Worcester Porcelain' – limited Edn. – plates – orig. cloth – 4to. – Newport 1954.
(Sotheby's) $180 £85

MARSTON, JOHN
'The Metamorphosis of Pigmalion's Image' – number 258 of 325 copies – 2 plates by Rene Ben Sussan – orig. cloth backed boards – 1926.
(Christie's) $12 £6

MARTIN, BENJAMIN
'The Young Gentleman and Lady's Philosophy' – 2 vol. – engraved frontispiece and 50 plates only – many folding – some spotted and slightly torn – some leaves spotted – contemp. calf – rubbed – covers of vol. 2 – detached – 1759-63.
(Christie's S. Kensington) $40 £18

'A New and Compendious System of Optics' – 34 folding plates – half title – some discolourations and dust soiling – contem. calf rubbed – 8vo. – James Hodges 1740.
(Sotheby's) $160 £75

MARTIN, C. W.
'The History and Description of Leeds Castle' – 8 actual photographs mounted – many leaves strengthened – dampstains – orig. cloth – rubbed – sm. folio – 1869.
(Sotheby's) $85 £40

MARTIN, F. R.
'The Miniature Paintings and Painters of Persia, India and Turkey' – one of 300 copies – plates – some col. – illus. – original cloth – dust jacket – large 4to. – Holland Press 1969.
(Sotheby's) $115 £55

MARTIN, J.
'Account of the Natives of the Tonga Islands' – 2 vols. – front. – half calf gilt – 1817.
(Phillips) $210 £100

MARTIN, M.
'A Description of the Western Isles of Scotland' – 1st Edn. – folding engraved map and plate – browning – contem. calf – upper cover detached – worn – 8vo. – 1703.
(Sotheby's) $180 £85

MARTIN, R. MONTGOMERY
'Tallis Illustrated Atlas' – engraved frontis and addit. title – 83 engraved maps with vignettes – town and city plans – one folded and mounted on linen – 2 vols. uniformly bound in contem. half calf – worn – folio – circa 1851.
(Sotheby's) $1,575 £750
'Australia. – parts 1-3 only – 8 double page maps – hand col. in outline – 7 portrait and plates – soiled – orig. cloth – rubbed – 4to. – n.d.
(Sotheby's) $380 £180
'The British Colonies' – 2 vols. – div. 2 and 6 only – 5 maps by Tallis – 6 plates – cloth gilt – worn – n.d.
(Phillips) $75 £35

MARTINE, GEORGE
'Essays and Observations on the Construction of Thermometers' – 3rd Edn. – folding engraved table – calf – 8vo. – Edinburgh Alexander Donaldson, 1780.
(Sotheby's) $85 £40

MARTINEAU, H.
'English Lakes' – plates – 2 col. – folding – hand col. map – cloth gilt – g.e. – 4to. – circa 1855.
(Phillips) $105 £50

MARTINELLI, FIORAVANTI
'Rome Ricercata Nel Suo Sito' – woodcut frontis – 40 woodcuts in text – leaves stained – contem. limp vellum – stitching broken – 8vo. – Rome 1750.
(Sotheby's) $40 £18

MARTY, A.
'Architecture Pittoresque et Moderne ....' – 12 numbered plates – litho in colour by Lallemand fils and Ch. Walter – country villas on the outskirts of Paris – with ground plans – contem. blue half calf – corners worn – folio – Paris 1880.
(Sotheby's) $170 £80

MARTYN, THOMAS
'Thirty eight plates with Explanations; intended to illustrate Linnaeus's System of Vegetables' – 38 hand coloured plates – a few slightly soiled – modern boards – new Edn. – 1817.
(Christie's S. Kensington) $90 £42

MARY QUEEN OF SCOTS
Remarkable auto letter written at the age of 11 to her mother Mary of Guise announcing her intention to make her first communion – 1 page – folio – Meudon Easter 1554.
(Sotheby's) $10,920 £5,200

MARZIALS, T.
'Pan Pipes' – illus. by W. Crane – orig. pictorial boards – oblong 4to. – Routledge n.d.
(Phillips) $40 £20

MASEFIELD, JOHN
'With the Living Voice' – orig. wraps. – Prelims a little foxed – glassine jacket – 1925.
(J. Ash) $8 £4

MASKELL, A.
'Ivories' – plates – orig. cloth – 4to. – 1905.
(Phillips) $40 £18

MASON, A. E. W.
'The Dean's Elbow' – bookplate – 1930.
(J. Ash) $8 £4

MASON, CHARLOTTE
'The Lady's Assistant for Regulating and Supplying the Table' – 8th Edn. – some spotting – contem. sheep – joints split – covers loose – 8vo. – 1801.
(Sotheby's) $75 £35

MASON, G. H.
'The Punishments of China' – 22 col. plates - rather soiled – contem. half leather – worn – folio – 1801.
(Sotheby's) $95 £45

MASON, R. HINDRY
'The History of Norfolk' – 2 vol. – double page map – plates – some col. – contem. half morocco – rubbed – t.e.g. – folio – 1884.
(Christie's) $115 £55

MASPERO, G.
'The Dawn of Civilisation' – folding map and illus. – presentation copy by translator – SPCK 1901.
(Baitson) $20 £10

MASSE, E. M. M.
'Camp de la Gironde' – 12 litho plates after Masse – spotting – frayed – orig. wrappers – partly disbound – folio – 1845.
(Christie's) $75 £35

THE
EMPEROVR
OF
THE EAST.
A Tragæ-Comœdie.
The Scæne Constantinople.
As it hath bene diuers times acted, at the *Black-friers*, and *Globe* Play-houses, by the *Kings Maiesties Servants.*
Written by PHILIP MASSINGER.

LONDON,
Printed by THOMAS HARPER, for *Iohn Waterson*, ANNO 1632.

MASSINGER, PHILIP
'The Emperour of the East' – 1st Edn. – morocco by Sangorski – g.e. – sm. 4to. – 1632.
(Christie's) $735 £350

MASTERS, JOHN
'Bhowani Junction' – very good in dust wrapper – 1954.
(J. Ash) $12 £6

MASTERS OF ETCHING
Vol. 1-19, 21-28, 32 and 33 only – plates – some spotted – cloth – oblong folio – Studio 1924-32.
(Sotheby's) $170 £80

MATHERS, E. POWYS
'Procreant Hymn' – number 84 of 200 copies – plates by Eric Gill – orig. cloth – dust jacket – soiled – frayed – 1926.
(Christie's) $275 £130

MATISSE, HENRI – JOYCE, JAMES
'Ulysses' – 6 lithos by Matisse – each with repros of preparatory drawings – orig. buckram – gilt – uncut – 4to. – New York, Limited Editions Club 1935.
(Sotheby's) $130 £62

MATTHEW, PATRICK
'Emigration Fields' – 1st Edn. – 2 folding engraved maps – half title – orig. cloth – faded – spine worn – 8vo. – 1839.
(Sotheby's) $125 £60

MATTHEWS, H.
'Diary of an Invalid' – calf gilt – 1820.
(Phillips) $30 £14

MATTHIOLI, P. A.
'Opera' – title in woodcut border – woodcuts throughout – half vellum – worn – library stamp – foxing – folio – Basle 1674.
(Bonhams) $1,155 £550

MAUCHLINE BINDING
'Longfellow's Poetical Works' – picture of vase of flowers on cover – n.d.
(Bennett Book Auction) $6 £3

MAUCHLINE, R.
'Mine Foreman's Handbook' – cloth – Philadelphia 1905.
(Bennett Book Auction) $10 $5

MAUCLAIR, CAMILLE
'Ames Bretonnes' – no. 4 of 10 copies sur Japon – coloured illus. by Wely – original water colour of old woman seated – fine light green morocco binding by Noulhac – original wrappers bound in – chemise and slipcase – sm. 4to. – Paris, Piazza, 1907.
(Sotheby Parke Bernet) $1,485 £710

MAUGHAM, W. S.
'The Circle' – orig. wraps – slightly worn and nicked – 1921.
(J. Ash) $20 £10

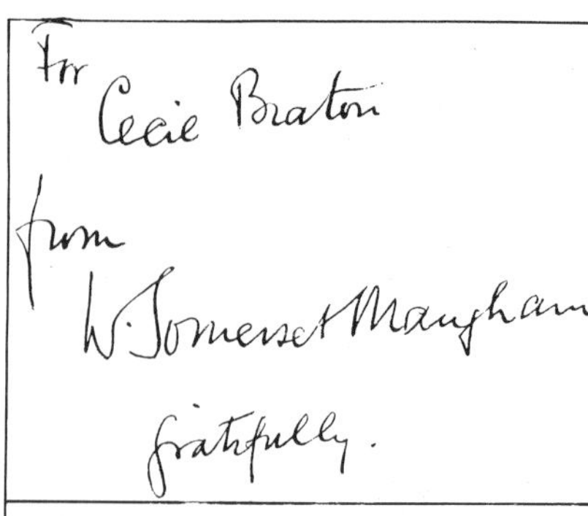

'Ah King' – second issue – pres copy – inscribed by author to Cecil Beaton – orig. cloth – slightly worn – 8vo. – 1933.
(Sotheby's) $95 £45

MAUGIS, M.
'Description of the Cartoons of Raphael Urbino' – 43 of 45 plates – half calf gilt – oblong 4to. – n.d.
(Phillips) $145 £70

MAUND, B.
'The Botanic Garden' – vol. 1 only – 25 hand col plates – half calf – circa 1840.
(Phillips) $250 £120

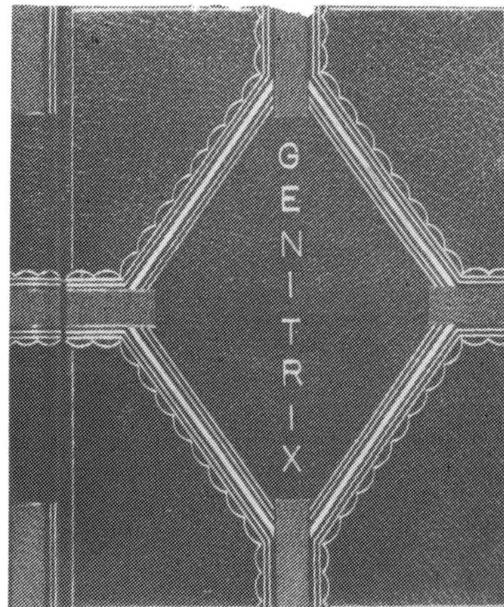

MAURIAC, FRANCOIS
'Genitrix' – 1 of 25 copies on Japon imperial – blue morocco by Leroy-Dor – title and name of author in gold – Paris, La Cite des Livres 1926.
(Sotheby Parke Berne') $1,395 £665

MAURICE, THOMAS
'A Modern and Ancient India' – 2 vols. – quarto 1st Edn. – folding and other plates – both marked – 1798 and 1803.
(Lane) $105 £50
'Indian Antiquities or Dissertations Relative to Hindostan' – 7 vols. – new Edn. – engraved plates and maps – majority folding – light browning – speckled calf – spines gilt – joints split – slight wear – dispersal stamp of Ely Cathedral Library – 8vo. – 1800-1801.
(Sotheby's) $30 £15
'Grove Hill .... with an Ode to Mithras' – 1st Edn. – wood engraved illus. – slight offsetting – leaf loose – disbound – 4to. – T. Bensley, 1799.
(Sotheby's) $75 £35

MAVOR, WILLIAM
'The English Spelling Book' – 15th Edn. – engraved frontis with 2 illus. – wood engraved picture aphabet – 12 illus. of animals – 6 of fables – orig. sheep – worn – 12mo. – Richard Phillips 1805.
(Sotheby's) $30 $14

MAXWELL, SIR HERBERT
'British Freshwater Fishes' – illus. 12 col. plates – gilt dec. dark green cloth – t.e.g. – boards loose – Hutchison and Co. 1904.
(May Whetter & Grose) $40 £20

MAXWELL, MARIUS
'Stalking Big Game With A Camera' – limited Edn. – signed – plates – cloth soiled – 4to. – 1924.
(Phillips) $65 £32

MAYER, AUGUST L.
'Veleazques, A Catalogue Raisonne of the Pictures and Drawings' – plates – orig. cloth – faded – t.e.g. – 4to. – 1936.
(Sotheby's) $315 £150

MAYER, LUIGI
'Views in Palestine' – 24 hand col. aquatint plates – text in English and French – cont. morocco backed calf – gilt – rubbed – folio – 1804.
(Sotheby's) $860 £410
'Views in Egypt, Views in the Ottoman Empire' – 2 parts in one – 72 hand col. aquatint plates – contem. diced russia – gilt chipped – folio – 1801-03.
(Christie's) $1,300 £620
'A Selection of the Most Interesting of Ainslie's celebrated . . . views in Turkey . . . Syria, Sicily, the Eolian Islands . . . etc' – 16 hand coloured aquatint plates after Mayer only – occasional spotting – stains – half morocco – limp covers – soiled and rubbed – folio – R. Bowyer, 1811.
(Christie's S. Kensington) $250 £120

MAYNARD, GEORGE HENRY
'The ... Works of Flavius Josephus' – engraved frontispiece – plates and two maps – hand coloured in outline – contemporary calf – joints cracked – folio – n.d.
(Christie's S. Kensington) $40 £18

MAYOW, JOHANNES
'Opera Omnia Medico Physica' – 7 plates – titles in red and black – lacks portrait – half calf – 8vo. – The Hague, 1681.
(Sotheby's) $55 £25
'La Belle Magie ou Science de l'Esprit' – 1st Edn. – woodcut arms – portrait of author – 2 plates – folding diagrams – browning – soiled – contem. calf – spine worn – 12 mo. – Lyon 1669.
(Sotheby's) $135 £65

MAYUYAMA, J. (editor)
'Art in the West' – illus. – orig. cloth – slipcase – 4to. – Tokyo 1966.
(Sotheby's) $135 £65

MAZARIN, CARDINAL
'Letters to Lewis XIV' – engraved portrait – contem. calf gilt – 4to. – 1752.
(Phillips) $65 £30

MAZOIS, F.
'Les Ruines de Pompei' – engraved title – plates – some folding – contem. half morocco – rubbed – folio – Pàris, 1812.
(Sotheby's) $95 £45

MEAD, R.
'Medica Sacra or a Commentry on the Most Remarkable Diseases' – trans. R. Stack – calf – upper cover detached – 8vo. – 1704.
(Phillips) $40 £18

MEDAILLES SUR LES PRINCIPAUX EVENEMENTS DU REGNE DE LOUIS LE GRAND
1st quarto Edn. – engraved frontis – 296 engraved medels with text – signature of title – slight browning – cont. calf – lacking spine – very worn – Cirencester bookplate – 4to. – 1702.
(Sotheby's) $85 £40

MEE, ARTHUR
'Yorkshire, North, West and East Ridings' – 3 vols.
(Baitson) $8 £4

MEE, MARGARET
'Flowers of the Brazilian Forests' – 1 of 500 copies signed by author – col. plates – quarter morocco gilt – t.e.g. – folio – 1968.
(Phillips) $210 £100

MEERZA, H. R. H. NAJAF KOOLEE
'Journal of a Residence in England and of a Journey from and to Syria' – 2 vols. – cloth gilt – 1839.
(Phillips) $105 £50

MEGILLAT ESTHER, THE SCROLL OF ESTHER
In Hebrew – mss on a vellum scroll – 6 membranes stiched together – complete – 21 lines arr. in 25 columns – written in black ink in Hebrew script – large decorative panel in full colour – benediction for the reading of the Megillah – separate mss on vellum scroll – text in ornamental painted arches – full floral border – worn – margins defective – 355 mm x 900 mm – 1651-52.
(Sotheby's) $12,600 £6,000

MEIER-GRAEFE, J.
'Corot' – plates – orig. half vellum – soiled – 4to. – Berlin 1930.
(Sotheby's) $65 £30

MEISS, M. AND KIRSCH, E. W.
'The Visconti Hours' – number 51 of 55 copies signed by Di Modrone – col. plates – orig. vellum – gilt inner dentelles – g.e. 4to. – Arcadia Press 1973.
(Christie's) $105 £50

MEMORIALS OF RUGBY
24 lithos – some foxing – half morocco gilt – folio 1843 – 'Memorials of Shrewsbury School' – litho title and 13 litho plates – half morocco gilt – worn – g.e. – folio – 1843.
(Phillips) $125 £60

MENCKEN, JOHANN BURCHARD
'De Charlataneria Eruditorum .....' – 2 vol. 1st Edn. – 1st Edn. in French – titles in red and black – vignette – 2 frontis – contem. calf – worn – upper cover nearly detached – sm. 8vo. – Leipzig and the Hague 1715 and 1721.
(Sotheby's) $10 £5

MENDELSOHN BARTHOLDY, FELIX
A. L.'s to Herr Sachse giving advice about travelling in France and England – 1 page 4to. – address on verso with seal – Frankfurt, May 1841.
(Sotheby's) $715 £340

MENZIES, WILLIAM
'The History of Windsor Great Park and Windsor Forest' – 20 actual photographs mounted – 2 folding maps – soiled – some marginal tears – orig. half morocco – worn – loose – folio – 1864.
(Sotheby's) $335 £160

MERCATOR, G.
'Scotiae Regnum (North)' – hand col. – map – wide margins – circa 1600.
(Phillips) $160 £75

MEREDITH, GEORGE
'Works' – 22 vol. Surrey Edn. – frontispiece – occasional slight spotting – contemp. maroon half calf – by Riviere – some vol. rubbed – spines gilt – t.e.g. – 1912.
(Christie's S. Kensington) $145 £70

MEREDITH, LOUISA ANNE
'Some of My Bush Friends in Tasmania' – chromolith addit. title – 11 plates and 3 illus. – soiling and fraying – orig. cloth – disbound – g.e. – folio – Day & Son 1860.
(Christie's) $200 £95

'Flora's Gems' – hand col. title and 10 of 11 col. plates – original cloth – gilt – g.e. – folio – 1830.
(Phillips) $420 £200

MERIAN, MARIA SIBYLLA
'Histoire Generale des Insectes de Surinam et de Toute L'Europe' – 325 hand col. engraved plates on 188 leaves – contem. mottled calf – worn – detached – folio – Paris, 1771.
(Christie's) $11,550 £5,500

MERIGOT, JAMES
'A Select Collection of Views and Ruins in Rome' – large paper copy – text in Eng. and French – 63 col. aquatint plates – slight spotting – recent black half calf – preserving orig. boards – worn – uncut – folio – 1826.
(Sotheby's) $880 £420

MERION, M.
'Topographia Helvetiae' – 2 maps and 67 fine engraved views on 53 sheets including view and map of Zurich – large double page view of Basle – vellum – some foxing – small folio – Francofurti 1642.
(Bonhams) $6,720 £3,200

MERRY, TOM
A Collection of 42 coloured lithographs issued as supplements to the 'St. Stephen's Review' the majority satirical cartoons on the subject of Home Rule – a few short tears – folio – 1884-91.
(Sotheby's) $115 £55

METCALFE, JOHN
'The Smoking Leg' – 1925.
(J. Ash) $34 £16

METEREN, EMANUEL VAN
'Nederlandische Historien' – map lacking – engr. title – fore margin shaved with a little loss – some spotting and staining – contemp. vellum – soiled 4to. – 1611.
(Christie's S. Kensington) $65 £30

MEXICO – BLAEU, W. AND J.
'Nova Hispani and Nova Galicia' – engraved map – hand col. in outlone – historiated and armorial title cartouche – compass rose and sailing ship – fully col. – thick paper – verso blank – stains – 347 mm x 482 mm. – Amsterdam circa 1640 or later.
(Sotheby's) $210 £100

MEYER, FRANZ SALES
'A Handbook of Ornament' – full page illustrations – some spotting original cloth – B. T. Batsford – 1894.
(Christie's S. Kensington) $20 £10

MEYER, H. J.
'Universum' – vol. 1 only – engraved title and 48 plates – spotting – damp-stains – orig. cloth – rubbed – oblong 4to. – New York n.d.
(Sotheby's) $230 £110

MEYNIER, JOHANN HEINRICH
'Erzahungen Fur Kinder' – 1st Edn. – 8 engraved plates – coloured by hand – spotting – orig. boards – worn – 8vo, – Nuremberg Campe 1812.
(Sotheby's) $285 £135

MEYRICK, SIR SAMUEL RUSH
'A Critical Inquiry into Ancient Armour' – 3 vols. – 2nd Edn. – 80 plates – mostly hand col. – contem. half morocco – spines gilt – g.e. – 4to. – 1842.
(Sotheby's) $840 £400

MICHAEL, ANDRE
'Histoire de L'Art' – 9 vols. incl. index in 18 – plates – illus. 4 vols. in orig. wrappers – others in contem. half morocco – faded t.e.g. – 8vo. – Paris 1905-29.
(Sotheby's) $85 £40

MICHAEL, JOHN
'The Old Stones of Land's End' – limited Edn. – signed by author – 1973.
(Lane) $30 £15

MICHAEL SCOTUS
'Liber Phsyiognomiae' – 1st Edn. – 36 leaves – 23 lines – roman letter – initials – chapter marks and intiails strokes in red – dampstained – contem. limp vellum – worn – upper hinge broken – sm. 4to. - Venice, Jacobus de Fivizano, 1477.
(Sotheby's) $125 £60

MIDDIMAN, S.
'Select Views in Great Britain' – engraved title – 53 plates – morocco gilt – oblong 4to. – 1812.
(Phillips) $210 £100

MIDDLESEX, HACKNEY
9 documents – 8 on vellum – 1 on paper – the majority relating to the manor of Hackney and the grant of vaults of Hackney churchyard. – 18th cent.
(Phillips) $95 £45

MIDDLETON, CONYERS
'The Miscellaneous Works' – 4 vols. – port. – contem. calf gilt – 4to. – 1752.
(Phillips) $100 £48

MIDDLETON, ERASMUS AND OTHERS
'The New Dictionary of Arts and Sciences' – 2 vols. in 1 – engraved frontis – repaired – plates – contem. calf – 1778.
(Sotheby's) $145 £70

MIDGET MAGICIAN, THE
Editor Wilf Huggins – vol. 1 no. 1 – vol. 2 no. 4 – number 10 of unspecified limitation – each signed by author – unsewn in orig. wrappers – 32 mo. – 1951-54.
(Sotheby's) $545 £260

MIEGE, G.
'A Relation of Three Embassies from CharlesII to the Great Duke of Muscovie' – 1st Edn. – 2 engraved ports. – modern half calf – 8vo. – 1669.
(Sotheby's) £160 £75

MIGEON, GASTON
'1900 L'Expostion Retrospective de L'Art Decoratif Francais' – 10 original parts number 123 of 200 copies – mounted coloured plates – some slight spotting – original wrappers – two contemporary morocco portfolios – Paris n.d.
(Christie's S. Kensington) $335 £160

MILES, HENRY DOWNES
'Pugilistica or the History of British Boxing' – 3 vol. – numerous illus. – slight spotting – orig. cloth gilt – faded – 8vo. – Edinburgh 1906.
(Sotheby Beresford Adams) $105 £50

MILES, W. J.
'Modern Practical Farriery' – 5 parts – plates – some col. – orig. boards – 4to. – W. Mackenzie n.d.
(Phillips) $25 £12

MILET-MURDEAU, M. L. A.
'Voyage de la Perouse autour du Monde' – 2 vols. – no. atlas – port. – calf gilt – 4to. – 1799.
(Phillips) $250 £120

MILITARY
Collection of 19 large Manuscript plans of Battles, camps, fortifications etc., all finely drawn and col. on paper – battle plans showing dispositions of opposing forces – entrenchments etc. – several mounted on linen – 4 detached – calf backed boards – worn – large folio – approx. 600 x 430mm. – 18th century.
(Sotheby's) $1,890 £900

MILITARY COSTUME OF TURKEY, THE
Hand col. aquatint vignette title – frontis – 29 hand col. plates – contem. maroon morocco – gilt – contents loose – g.e. – folio – 1818.
(Sotheby's) $295 £140

MILTARY TRANSACTIONS ... In Indostan, History of the
2 vols. – 36 plates and maps – many folding – calf gilt – 4to. – 1775-8.
(Phillips) $135 £65

MILITARY UNIFORMS
108 col. plates folio size from 'Supplement to the Army and Navy Gazette' – 1890-1900.
(Phillips) $275 £130

MILL, JAMES AND WILSON, H. H.
'The History of British India' – 10 vol. in 9 – 5th Edn. -contem. half morocco – rubbed – spines gilt – 1858.
(Christie's) $135 £65

MILLAIS, JOHN GUILLIE
'Game Birds and Sporting Sketches' – plates – some hand col. – orig. half morocco – slightly rubbed – t.e.g. – large 4to. – 1892.
(Sotheby's) $250 £120
'Natural History of the British Surface-Feeding Ducks' – limited edn. – plates many coloured – orig. cloth gilt – t.e.g. – 4to. L.P. – 1902.
(Phillips) $485 £230
'British Deer and Their Horns' – 185 text and full page illus. frontis – coloured 4to. – orig. buckram – soiled – 1897.
(Bonhams) $105 £50
'The Life and Letters of Sir J. E. Millais' – 3 vol. incl. plates – limited Edn. – orig. cloth – rubbed – 8vo. and 4to. – 1899.
(Sotheby's) $60 £28

MILLAR, ERIC G.
'English Illuminated Manuscripts from the X to the XVth century' – 2 vols. – plates – 2 coloured – orig cloth – soiled – t.e.e. – folio – Paris and Brussels 1926-28.
(Sotheby's) $360 £170

MILLAR, GEORGE HENRY
'A New, Complete and Universal Body, or System of Natural History' – plates – first few leaves with slight marginal soiling – contemp. – half calf – worn – folio – n.d.
(Christie's S. Kensington) $105 £50

MILLAR, JOHN
'Observations Concerning the Distinctions of Ranks in Society' – calf – 4to. – 1771.
(Phillips) $315 £150

MILLER, HENRY
'The Cosmological Eye' – very good in dust wrapper – Editions Poetry London 1945 (1946).
(J. Ash) $40 £20

MILLER, JOHN
'Illustratio Systematis Sexualis Linnaei' – 1st Edn. – engraved title and text in Latin and Eng. – frontis and 212 engraved plates – incl. 4 hand col. plates of leaves and 104 plates in 2 states – half morocco – rubbed – joints cracked – large folio – 1777.
(Christie's) $11,550 £5,500

MILLER, PHILIP
'The Gardener's Dictionary' – 2nd Edn. – four plates – one slightly shaved – one detached – some contemp. manuscript notes and corrections – contemp. panelled calf – joints worn – folio – 1733.
(Christie's S. Kensington) $105 £50

MILLES, THOMAS
'Archaio-Ploytoe Containing Ten following Books to the former Treasurie of Ancient and Moderne Times' – engraved title – laid down and slightly shaved – illus. panelled calf – rebacked – old spine laid down – Printed by William Jaggard, 1619.
(Christie's S. Kensington) $115 £55

MILLS, ALFRED
'Pictures of Roman History' – 1st Edn. – 48 engraved plates – inscription on back of first – orig. red roan – worn – 61 mm x 57 mm – Carton and Harvey 1809.
(Sotheby's) $55 £25

MILNE, A. A.
'Winnie the Pooh' 1st Edn. – 'Now we are Six' 1st. Edn. – 'The House at Pooh Corner' – 2nd Edn.
(Laurence & Martin Taylor) $30 £15

MILNE, CHRISTOPHER
'The Enchanted Places' – dust wrapper – 1974.
(J. Ash) $8 £4

MILNER, A.
'Bustle' – red morocco – orig. wrappers bound in – by Riviere – upper joint split – 8vo. – privately printed – 1897.
(Sotheby's) $6 £3

MILTON, JOHN
'Poems' – 2nd Edn. – adverts at end – modern red morocco – g.e. – 8vo. – For Tho. Dring 1673.
(Sotheby's) $360 £170

'Angli pro Populo Anglicano Defensio' – engraved title – vellum – 1651.
(Phillips) $65 £32

'The Poetical Works' – Notes by Edward Hawkins – 4 vols. – later calf – rubbed – Oxford 1824.
(Christie's S. Kensington) $65 £32

MILTON, THOMAS AND OTHERS
'The Chimney Piece Maker's Daily Assistant of a Treasury of New Designs for Chimney Pieces' – 1st Edn. – engraved frontis – 2 advert leaves at end – browning – soiled – contem. calf – upper cover stained black – worn – 8vo. – 1766.
(Sotheby's) $630 £300

MINER, H. S.
'Orchids' – 24 colour plates – orig. cloth soiled – g.e. – 4to. – 1885.
(Phillips) $145 £70

MINIATURE
Written in Arabic 23 mm x 16 mm in brass case with magnifying glass set in – crimson morocco gilt – 1860.
(Bennett Book Auction) $40 £20

MINIATURE BOOK – SCHLOSS'S ENGLISH BIJOU ALMANAC FOR 1840
Engraved throughout – illustrations – orig. boards – rebacked – contained in slipcase with magnifying glass in fitted silk and velvet lined morocco box.
(Christie's S. Kensington) $250 £120

MINIATURE BOOK – SHAKESPEARE WILLIAM
'Works' – 39 vols. – 2 x 1¼ inches – original uniform binding – faded – in a wooden bookcase – n.d.
(Christie's S. Kensington) $100 £48

MINIATURE BOOK – TAYLOR, JOHN
'The Booke of Martyrs' – part 2 only – soiled and dampstained – rubbed – crudely bound in 17th century kid and brown silk – worn – 1 x 1½in. – n.d.
(Christie's) $210 £100

MINING
A collection of approx. 60 Parliamentary Blue Books on Mines and Mining accidents etc. – some with maps and plans – soiled – mostly disbound – folio and 8vo. – 1826-56.
(Sotheby's) $1,365 £650

MIREUR, HIPPOLYTE
'Dictionnaire Des Ventes D'Art' – 7 vol. – morocco backed boards – original wrappers bound in – lge. 8vo. – Paris 1911-12.
(Christie's S. Kensington) $230 £110

Here begynneth
the thyrde parte of oure Ladyes Myr-
roure. that ys of youre Masses.
AD.COMPLETORIV
Orate celi de-
super; Dewe ye heuens from
aboue. & cloudes mote rayne
the rightwise. erthe mote be opened

MIRROUR OF OUR LADY
Woodcuts on title and verso – five other woodcuts – woodcut device – small tears and stains – 19th cent. calf – bookplate of Daniel Caron – folio – 1530.
(Christie's) $5,250 £2,500

MISHIMA, YUKIO
'Death in Midsummer' – 1st English Edn. – slightly shipped dust wrapper – 1967.
(J. Ash) $12 £6

MISSALE ROMANUM
Printed in red and black – illus. – original holland backed boards – soiled – folio – Bremen Press 1931.
(Sotheby's) $115 £55

MISSELDEN, EDWARD
'Free Trade or the Meanes to Make Trade Flourish' – 1st Edn. – 19th cent. green morocco – gilt – stamp of Alexander Gardyne, 1883 – 8vo. – J. Legatt for S. Waterson 1662.
(Sotheby's) $1,680 £800

MITCHELL, T. L.
'Three Expeditions into the Interior of Eastern Australia' – 2 vol. – 2nd Edn. – 51 plates – folding or coloured – lacks map – modern cloth – faded – 8vo. – 1839.
(Sotheby's) $80 £38

MITCHELL-COTTS, CAMPBELL
'The Lute Player in Avalon' – inscribed and signed by the author to Wilfred Gibson – 1937.
(J. Ash) $6 £3

MITE, THE
8 illus. – orig. red cloth gilt – 21 mm x 17 mm – Grimsby – 1891.
(Sotheby's) $210 £100

MITFORD, MARY RUSSELL
'Dramatic Scenes, Sonnets and Other Poems' – modern half-morocco – occasional light browning of the text – 1827.
(J. Ash) $65 £32

MITFORD, NANCY
'The Sun King' – limited signed Edn. – red morocco gilt – overlay on upper cover – g.e. by Zaehnsdorf – buckram box – 4to. – 1969.
(Phillips) $105 £50

MITFORD, WILLIAM
'The History of Greece' – 10 vol. in 5 – some stains – contem. diced calf – very worn – 8vo. – 1814-20.
(Sotheby's) $2 £1

MODEL RAILWAY NEWS, THE
Vol. 1-16 in 8 – illus. – contem. cloth rubbed – 8vo. – 1925-40.
(Sotheby's) $40 £18

MODELES DE MENUISERIE, CHOISIS PARMI CE QUE PARIS OFFRE DE PLUS NOUVEAU
addit. engraved title – 73 plates – spotting – contem. half calf – worn – folio – Paris, Bance aine, 1825.
(Sotheby's) $190 £90

MOE, EMILE A.
'L'Apocalypse de Saint Sever' – limited Edn. – col. plates loose as issued in orig. board portfolio – folio – Paris, 1942.
(Sotheby's) $25 £12

MOFFETT, THOMAS
'Insectorum Sive Minimorum Animalium Theatrum' – title torn with loss – soiled – stained – old sheep – worn – folio – Thos. Cotes 1634.
(Christie's S. Kensington) $190 £90

MOGG, EDWARD
'Survey of the High Roads of England and Wales' – engraved vignette title – first part – hand coloured general map – 233 hand coloured road maps on 112 sheets – half calf worn – D. Lloyd-George's bookplate – 1817.
(Phillips) $1,220 £580
'Paterson's Roads' – nine folding maps – one neatly repaired one slightly shaved and creased – some slight spotting – later half morocco – rubbed – 1826.
(Christie's S. Kensington) $25 £12

MOISESSO, FAUSTINO
'Historia della Ultima Guerra nel Friuli' – 4to. – engr. title – holed with loss of two characters – one folding map – holed – torn and repaired – contemp. vellum – soiled – torn – Venice, Appresso Barezzo, 1623.
(Christie's S. Kensington) $65 £30

MOLEVILLE, B. DE
'The Costume of the Hereditary States of the House of Austria' – 50 col. plates – calf – worn – folio – 1804.
(Sotheby's) $485 £230

MOLIERE. J. B. P. DE
'Le Misanthorpe' – limited to 350 – this no. 34 – plates – olive green levant morocco – covers with inlays – g.e. – slipcase – 4to. – Paris 1907.
(Christie's) $250 £120

MOLL, H.
'New Map of Great Britain' – outline hand colouring – large folio – late 18th century.
(Bennett Book Auction) $45 £22

Facsimile of 1725 Edition. 'Thirty Six New and Correct Maps of Scotland' – cloth backed boards – oblong folio – 1896.
(Phillips) $45 £22

MOLLARD, J.
'The Art of Cookery' – plates – some spotting – 8vo. – 1807.
(Phillips) $135 £65

MONIER, PIERRE
'The History of Painting, Sculpture, Architecture, Graving' – 1st Edn. – in English – engraved frontis – advert leaves – contem. panelled calf – hinges cracked – 8vo. – T. Bennet 1699.
(Sotheby's) $40 £20

MONKHOUSE, W. COSMO
'The Works of Sir Edwin Landseer' – 2 vols. vols. – engraved vignette title in vol. 2 engraved plates after Landseer – numerous wood engraved illus. in text – contem. half morocco – joints and spines torn – 4to. – n.d.
(Sotheby Beresford Adams) $145 £70

MONRO, HAROLD
'The Silent Pool and Other Poems' – orig. stiff wraps. – worn at foot of spine – chipped dust wrapper – 1942.
(J. Ash) $6 £3

MONTAGUE, C. E.
'Right off the Map' – signed limited Edn. of 260 copies only – spine slightly sunned – 1927.
(J. Ash) $12 £6

MONTAGUE, M. WORTLEY
'Letters of ...' – 3 vols. – vol. 3 lacks half title – calf gilt – 1767.
(Phillips) $55 £25

MONTFAUCON, BERNARD DE
'Antiquity Explained' – 7 vols. including 5 vol. Supplement in 2 vols – first Edn. in English – titles in red and black – numerous engraved plates – majority folding – occasional browning and spotting – contem. speckled calf – joints and several spines split – folio – 1721-25.
(Sotheby's) $315 £150

MONTGOMERIE, N. & W.
'Sandy Cane and Other Scottish Nursery Rhymes' – illus. by Norah Montgomerie – Hogarth Press 1948.
(J. Ash) $8 £4

MONTGOMERY, B. L., 1st VISCOUNT MONTGOMERY OF EL ALAMEIN
'History of Warfare' – limited signed Edn. – black morocco gilt – with overlay on upper cover – g.e. – by Zaehnsdorf – buckram box – 4to. – 1969.
(Phillips) $95 £45

MOORCROFT, W. AND TREBECK, G.
'Travels in the Himalayan Provinces of Hindustan and the Punjab' – 2 vols. – frontis – folding map – orig. cloth – rubbed – 8vo. – 1841.
(Sotheby's) $565 £270

MOORE, GEORGE
'Celibate Lives' – 1st Edition thus – with new preface etc. very slightly sprung – 1927.
(J. Ash) $8 £4

MOORE, HENRY
'Heads, Figures and Ideas' – coloured litho plates – quarter cloth – folio – 1958.
(Phillips) $95 £45

MOORE, J.
'Narrative of the Campaign of the British Army in Spain' – port. – 2 folding maps – 1 plate – calf gilt – 4to. – 1809.
(Phillips) £75 £35

MOORE, JOHN HAMILTON
'A New and Complete Collection of Voyages and Travels' – folio – plates and maps – some leaves torn with loss – soiled – contemporary calf – worn – n.d.
(Christie's S. Kensington) $65 £30

MOORE, THOMAS
'Lalla Rookh' – illus. – spotted – inscribed by Queen Victoria to her niece Augusta – orig. cloth – gilt – rubbed – joints split – g.e. – sm. 4to. – 1860.
(Sotheby's) $85 £40

MOORHOUSE, EDWARD
'The Romance of the Derby' – 2 vols. – 1st. Edn. – 1908.
(Lane) $12 £6

MORAIS, C. DE
'Le Veritable Fauconnier' – 1st Edn. – spotted – blue morocco gilt – rubbed – g.e. – 12 mo. – Paris 1683.
(Sotheby's) $460 £220

MORANT, P.
'History and Antiquities of the County of Essex' – 2 vols. – 6 folding maps – 25 plans and plates – some folding – calf – folio – 1768.
(Phillips) $630 £300

MORAVIA, ALBERTO
'Agostino' – 1st English Edn. – 1947.
(J. Ash) $6 £3

MORDEN, ROBERT
'Scotland' – hand coloured framed early map.
(Bennett Book Auction) $75 £36
'Worcester, Oxford, Gloucester' – 3 uncol. maps – circa 1695.
(Phillips) $100 £48

MORE, HANNAH
'Strictures on the Modern System of Female Education' – 2 vol. – 1st Edn. – orig. boards – rather worn – uncut – 8vo. – 1799.
(Sotheby's) $145 £70

MORE, SIR THOMAS
'Utopia' – 1st Edn. of trans by Gilbert Burnet – contem. calf – worn – 8vo. – 1684.
(Sotheby's) $105 £50

MOREAU-NELATON, ETIENNE
'Jongkind Raconte par Lui Meme' – no. 546 of 600 copies – plates – orig. wrappers – 4to. – Paris 1918.
(Sotheby's) $325 £155

MORELLIUS, A.
'Specimen Universae Rei Numerae' – contem. French binding of red morocco gilt – panelled covers with arms of Count Hoym, 8vo. – Paris 1683.
(Moore Allen & Innocent) $840 £400

MORERI, L.
'Le Grand Dictionnaire Historique' – frontis – 10 vols. – old calf worn – folio – Paris 1759.
(Bonhams) $105 £50

MORGAN, LADY SYDNEY
'France' – half calf gilt – 4to. – 1817.
(Phillips) $55 £25

MORISON, DOUGLAS
'Views of the Ducal Palaces and Hunting Seats of Saxe Coburg and Gotha' – litho title and 20 plates – soiled – orig. calf backed cloth – rubbed – loose – folio – 1846.
(Sotheby's) $525 $250

MORISON, STANLEY
'Type Designes of the Past and Present' – illustrations – original cloth – dust jacket – The Fleuron Limited – 1926.
(Christie's S. Kensington) $25 £12
'Four Centuries of Fine Printing' – plates – orig. cloth – dust jacket – 1949.
(Christie's S. Kensington) $25 £12
'The History of the Times' – 4 vols. in 5 – illus. – cloth – gilt – 1935-52.
(Phillips) $40 £20
'The Typographic Book' – Facsimiles – orig. cloth – dust jacket – slipcase – 4to. – 1963.
(Sotheby's) $55 £25

MORISON, S. AND CARTER, H.
'John Fell' – one of 1000 copies – plates – orig. cloth – folio – Oxford 1967.
(Sotheby's) $200 £95

MORLAND, SAMUEL
'History of the Evangelical Churches in Piedmont' – title in red and black – plan – engravings – calf worn – 4to. – 1658.
(Phillips) $105 £50

MORLEY, CHRISTOPHER
'The Haunted Bookshop' – covers a little marked – some pencilled markings in text – 1920.
(J. Ash) $8 £4

MORLEY, JOHN
'The Life of Richard Cobden' – 2 vol. – portrait – spotted – contem. half calf – covers rubbed – 1881.
(Christie's) $20 £10

MORNAY
'Picture of St. Petersburg' – 20 hand col. aquatint plates – lacking frontis – contem. straight grained red morocco – spine gilt – some wear – folio – 1815.
(Sotheby's) $735 £350

MORNING CHRONICLE, THE
4 Edn. – framed – 1799.
(Laurence & Martin Taylor) $20 £10

MORRIS, BEVERLEY R.
'British Game Birds and Wild Fowl' – 60 col. plates – orig. cloth gilt – slightly worn – 4to. – 1891.
(Phillips) $715 £340

MORRIS, REV. F. O.
'The History of British Birds' – 8 vols. col. – plates – cloth – Groombridge – n.d.
(Phillips) $565 £270
'A Series of Picturesque Views of Seats of the Noblemen and Gentlemen of Great Britain and Ireland' – 6 vol. – additional titles and 234 plates – printed in colours from wood blocks – occasional slight spotting – original red morocco, by 'John Leighton' gilt – joints worn – g.e. – 4to. William McKenzie – n.d.
(Christie's S. Kensington) $145 £70
'A History of British Butterflies' – 5th Edn. – 72 hand coloured plates – occasional slight spotting – original cloth – spine bumped and slightly soiled – 4to. – 1870.
(Christie's S. Kensington) $115 £55

'A History of British Birds' – 6 vols – 5th Edn. – coloured illus. – gilt decorated green boards – dampstained – John C. Nimmo 1903.
(May Whetter & Grose) $670 £320

MORRIS, L.
'Plans of the Principal Harbours, Bays and Roads in St. George's and the Bristol Channels' – editor W. Morris – new Edn. – engraved maps – one folding – modern cloth – sm. folio – Shrewsbury, 1801.
(Sotheby's) $420 £200

MORRIS, WILLIAM
'The Story of the Glittering Plain' – 1st trade Edn. Chiswick Press – small 4to. – bookplate and occasional stamps of the London Joint Stock Bank – slightly loose – 1891.
(J. Ash) $30 £15

MORRISON, ALFRED
'The Collection of Autograph Letters.... the Hamilton and Nelson Papers' – 2 vols. – original cloth backed boards – unopened – 8vo. – for Private Circulation 1893-94.
(Sotheby's) $40 £20

MORROW, GEORGE
Eight large watercolour drawings to illus. 'The Crusaders' – by A. J. Church – all but one signed – margins soiled – 380 mm x 245 mm. – circa 1904.
(Sotheby's) $295 £140

MORTON, JOHN
'The Natural History of Northamptonshire' – 2 engraved double page folding maps – 14 engraved plates – cont. calf – gilt – folio – 1712.
(Christie's) $335 £160

Imprinted at Newcaſtle upon TYNE,
by ROBERT BARKER, Printer to the
Kings moſt Excellent Majeſtie: And by
the Aſſignes of JOHN BILL.
1639.

MORTON, THOMAS, BISHOP OF DURHAM
'A Sermon Preached Before the King's Most Excelent Majesty' – lacking final blanks – woodcut device on title – minor defects – disbound – morocco backed case – sm. 4to. – Newcastle upon Tyne 1639.
(Sotheby Beresford Adams) $180 £85

MOSELEY, H. N.
'Notes of a Naturalist on the 'Challenger" – folding map – 2 chromolith plates – woodcut illus. in text – slightly spotted – orig. cloth – just rubbed – 8vo. – 1879.
(Sotheby Beresford Adams) $70 £34

MOSES, HENRY
'A series of 29 Designs of Modern Costume' – engraved title – 29 plates – boards – 4to. – 1823.
(Phillips) $105 £50

'Visit of William IV as Lord High Admiral to Portsmouth' – engraved title and dedication leaf with vignettes – 17 plates one dampstained – contem. calf – rubbed – folio – 1840.
(Sotheby's) $315 £150

'Vases from the Collection of Sir H. Englefield' – engraved title – 40 plates by Moses – one hand col. – text in French and English – soiling – contem. half morocco rubbed – g.e. – 1819-20.
(Christie's) $45 £22

MOSS, FLETCHER
'pilgrimages to Old Homes' – 7 vols. – numerous illus. – orig cloth gilt – minor defects – t.e.g. – 8vo. – Didsbury and Manchester 1901-20.
(Sotheby Beresford Adams) $135 £65

MOTIF
No. 1-13 all published – plates – orig. boards and wrappers – 4to. – 1958-67.
(Sotheby's) $145 £70

MOTTELAY, P. F.
'Bibliographical History of Electricity and Magnetism chronologically arranged' – 1st. Edn. – plates – orig. cloth – 8vo. – 1922.
(Sotheby's) $95 £45

MOULE, T.
'Great Britain Illustrated' – engraved title – 115 plates on 59 pages – quarter morocco gilt – 4to. – 1830.
(Phillips) $200 £95

MOUNT, WILLIAM AND RICE, THOMAS
'The Sea Coasts of France' – engraved title and Royal arms – 15 engraved double page charts – contem. calf backed boards – folio – circa 1715.
(Christie's) $600 £280

MUCHA, ALPHONSE
Design for 'Medee' – Sarah Bernhardt wearing a Bat headdress – pencil – 26 cm. x 16.5 cm. –
(Sotheby's) $1,575 £750

MUCHA, ALPHONSE
Designs for Mercury – pencil – inscribed – 39.3 cm. x 24.2 cm.
(Sotheby's) $1,470 £700

MUDGE, LIEUT.-COL.
'General Survey of England and Wales' – part 2 Devon and Cornwall – 5 folding maps on linen – calf gilt – n.d.
(Phillips) $295 £140

MUDIE, ROBERT
'The Feathered Tribes of the British Islands' – 2 vol. – title vignettes wood engraved and printed in colours by George Baxter – 19 hand coloured plates – some slightly spotted – orig. cloth – worn – 1834.
(Christie's S. Kensington) $65 £32

MUIR, PERCY
'English Children's Books' – plates – illus. – orig. cloth – dust jacket – 4to. – 1954.
(Sotheby's) $95 £45

MUIR, RAMSAY
'A History of Liverpool' – heavily extra illus. with 35 engraved and wood engraved plates – spots – later red half morocco – gilt – t.e.g. – 8vo. – Liverpool 1907.
(Sotheby Beresford Adams) $135 £65

MUIRHEAD, L.
'Journals of Travels in parts of .... France .... The Pays de Vaud and Tuscany' – orig. boards – 1803.
(Phillips) $135 £65

MULLER, WILLIAM
'Sketches of the Age of Francis 1st' – folio – litho title – dedication and 25 plates – spotting – a few marginal tears – orig. morocco backed cloth – worn and disbound – 1841.
(Christie's S. Kensington) $40 £20

MULOCK, DINAH MARIA
'John Halifax Gentleman' – three vols – superb modern full calf gilt by Bayntun – specially made slipcase – 1856.
(J. Ash) $295 £140

MULSANT, E.
'Lettres a Julie sur L'Ornithologie' – 15 hand col. plates – quarter morocco gilt Laplace Sanchez et Cie, Paris, n.d.
(Phillips) $85 £40

MULTZER, MARCEL
Design for 'La Vierge d'Avila ou Saint Therese' – design in pencil, pen and indian ink and watercolour on heavy paper – inscribed and annotated with instructions to the dressmakers.
(Sotheby's) $125 £60

MUN, THOMAS
'England's Treasure by Forraign Trade' – 2nd Edn. – contem sheep – rubbed – 8vo. – J. Fletcher for Robert Horne 1669.
(Sotheby's) $1,010 £480

MUNICIPAL CORPORATION BOUNDARIES
Report of the Commissioners – 3 vol. only col. maps – contem. cloth backed boards – worn – sm. folio – 1837.
(Sotheby's) $400 £190

MUNNINGS, A. J.
'Pictures of Horses and English Life' – cloth dust wrapper – 4to. – 1927.
(Irelands) $335 £160

MUNSTER, SEBASTIAN
Set of six uncoloured maps comprising 3 of the world and the 4 continents – all clean with good margins – circa 1540.
(Phillips) $3,570 £1,700
'Tabula Assiae IX' – woodcut map – hand coloured in outline – Latin text on verso – 12 x 13 inches (mid 16th century.
(Christie's S. Kensington) $40 £18

MURCHISON, SIR RODERICK IMPEY
'Siluria; the History of the Oldest Known Rocks' – 1st Edn. – 37 litho plates – 3 folding – 1 hand col. folding map – woodcut diagrams in text – orig. cloth – rubbed and soiled – 8vo. – 1854.
(Sotheby's) $170 £80

MURDOCH, IRIS
'An Unofficial Rose' – slight mark at head of spine – 1962.
(J. Ash) $10 £5

MURPHY, J. AND SOUSA, FR. LUIS DE
'Plans, Elevations, Sections and Views of the Church of Batalha in Portugal' – engraved title – engraved dedication 25 views – 2 double – waterstain half calf – new spine and corners – folio – 1795.
(Sotheby's) $125 £60

MURRAY, ALEXANDER D. D. (Orientalist)
'Account of the Life and Writings of James Bruce of Kinnaird' – 1st Edn. – large paper copy – 18 engraved plates – 2 folding engraved maps – browning – orig. boards – rebacked – rubbed – soiled – 4to. – Edinburgh 1808.
(Sotheby's) $180 £85

MURRAY, A. S. AND WHITE, A. H.
'White Athenian Vases in the British Museum' – folio – 27 plates – contem. half morocco – rubbed – 1896.
(Christie's) $45 £22

MURRAY, E. C. GRENVILLE
'The Member for Paris' – 3 volumes – contemp. half leather – little rubbed – 1871.
(J. Ash) $115 £55

MURRAY, H.
'Historical Account, Discoveries and Travels in Africa' – 2 vols. – 6 maps – calf gilt – 1817.
(Phillips) $85 £40

MURRAY, JOHN FISHER
'A Picturesque Tour of the River Thames in its Western Course' – engraved frontispiece – three maps – illustrations – slight spotting – modern half calf – 1853.
(Christie's S. Kensington) $60 £28

MURRAY-OLIVER, A.
'Captain Cook's Artists in the Pacific' – limited Edn. – col. plates – illus. – orig. half rexine – slipcase – oblong folio. – Christchurch New Zealand 1969.
(Sotheby's) $110 £52

MUSAEUS, J. K. A.
'Popular Tales of the Germans' – trans. by William Beckford – 2 vol. – contem. speckled calf – gilt – 12mo. – 1791.
(Sotheby's) $275 £130

MUSEE ROYALE DE NAPLES
Copy number 189 – engraved addit title and 57 plates – most hand col. – staining and soiling – contem. half morocco with gilt metal clasp – rubbed and soiled – 4to. – Paris 1857.
(Christie's) $115 £55

MUSGRAVE, REV. GEORGE
'A Ramble into Brittany' – 2 vols. in leather – London 1870.
(Baitson) $8 £4

MUSKETT, JOSEPH J.
'Suffolk Manorial Families' – 3 vols. – contem. cloth – slightly faded – 4to. – Exeter, privately printed 1900-14.
(Sotheby's) $200 £95

MUSSET, ALFRED DE
'La Mouche' – no. 48 of 200 copies – green morocco by Marius Michel – gilt spine – Paris 1892.
(Sotheby Parke Bernet) $1,951 £930

MUSSET, PAUL DE
'Voyage Pittoresque en Italie partie Septentrionale' – 23 engravings – some spotting – orig. cloth gilt – upper cover detached – g.e. – Paris n.d.
(Phillips) $100 £48

MYER, REGINALD
'Chats on Old English Tobacco Jars' – plates – orig. cloth – affected by damp – 4to. – n.d.
(Christie's) $40 £20

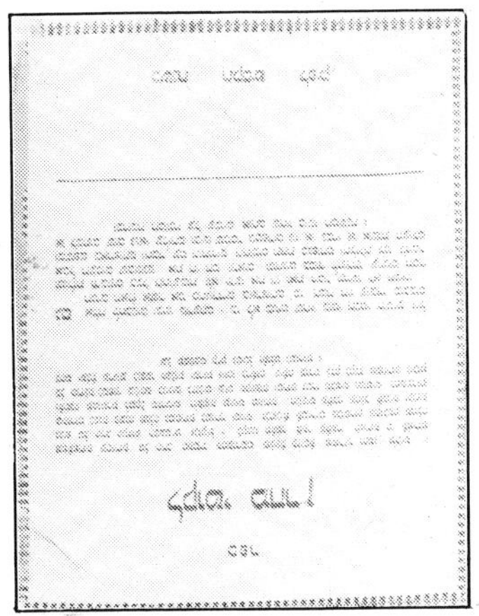

NACHMAN OF BRAZLAV
'Likutei Maharan Tinyana' – 1st Edn. – browned – shaved half leather – 4to. – 1809.
(Sotheby's) $670 £320

NAGLER, G. K.
'Die Monogrammisten' – 6 vol. including index – contem. half morocco – rubbed – 8vo. – Munich and Leipzig, 1879-1920.
(Sotheby's) $525 £250

NAISMITH, J.
'General View of the Agriculture of the County of Clydesdale' – original bds. - uncut – folding map – 1806.
(Bennett Book Auction) $65 £30

NALSON, JOHN
'An Imperial Collection of the Great Affairs of State 1639-49' – 2 vol. – 1st Edn. – engraved frontis – browning – contem. mottled calf – rubbed – folio – 1682-83.
(Sotheby's) $115 £55

NANCE, R. MORTON
'A New Cornish-English Dictionary' – 1st Edn. – 1938.
(Lane) $20 £10

'Sailing Ship Models' – limited Edn. – col. frontis – plates – cloth gilt – t.e.g. – 4to. – 1924.
(Phillips) $145 £70

NANSEN, FRIDTJOF
'In Northern Mists' – 2 vol. – mounted coloured frontispieces – illustrations – orig. cloth – 1911.
(Christie's S Kensington) $95 £45

'Farthest North' – portrait and coloured and other illus. 2 vols. – cloth torn, a few leaves foxed – 1897.
(Bonhams) $45 £22

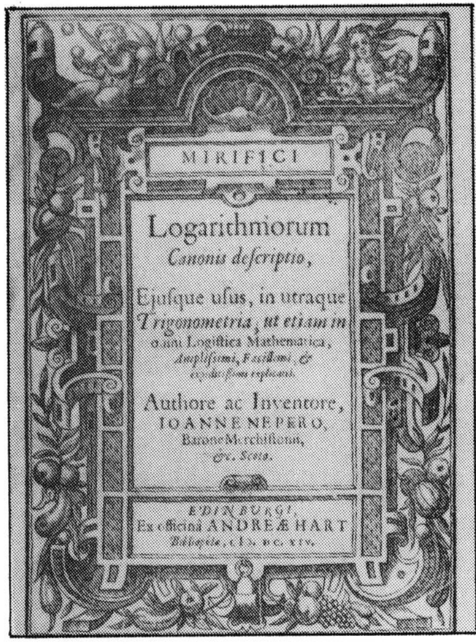

MIRIFICI
Logarithmorum
Canonis descriptio,
Ejusque usus, in utraque
Trigonometria, ut etiam in
Authore ac Inventore,
IOANNE NEPERO,

NAPIER, JOHN
'Mirifici Logarithorum Canonis Descriptio ..... ut etiam in omni Logistica Mathematica ... explicato' – !st Edn. – first issue – some pages misnumbered – woodcut border – diagrams in text – slight browning – marginal annotations – bound in a leaf of a 14th cent. Italian mss on vellum – worn – half red morocco case – ownership inscriptions – sm 4to. – Edinburgh 1614.
(Sotheby's) $6,300 £3,000

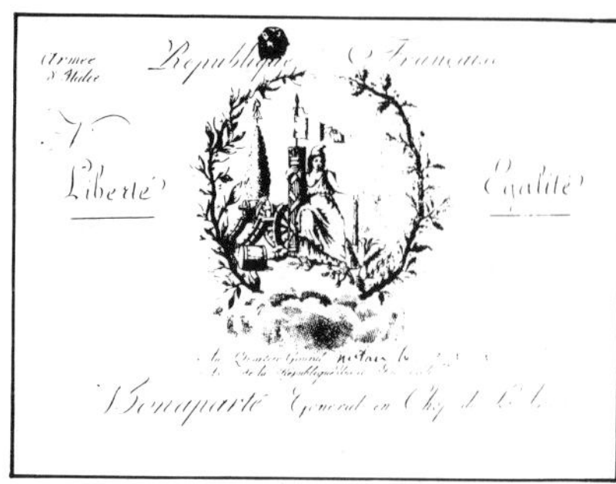

NAPOLEON I
Letter signed Bonaparte, 1 page – folio to Archbishop of Milan attractive vignette heading showing female figure – Milan 13 December 1796.
(Sotheby's) $590 £280

15 word autograph note of approval to end of note by Berthier Minister of War, requesting a grant of 1,500 francs to 30 officers in Grand Armee to let them buy horses – 3 pages folio – Augsburg 12 October 1805.
(Sotheby's) $650 £310

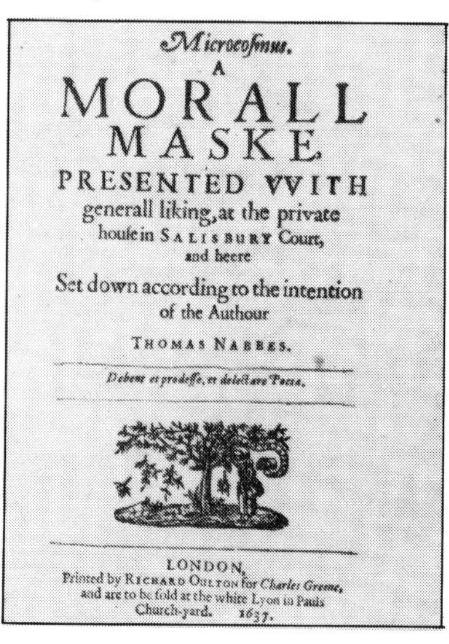
Microcosmus.
A
MORALL
MASKE
PRESENTED VVITH
generall liking, at the private
house in SALISBURY Court,
and heere
Set down according to the intention
of the Authour
THOMAS NABBES.

Debent et prodesse, et delectare Poeta.

LONDON,
Printed by RICHARD OULTON for Charles Greene,
and are to be sold at the white Lyon in Pauls
Church-yard. 1637.

NARBES, THOMAS
'Microcosmos, a Morall Maske' – 1st Edn. – printer's woodcut device on title – some inkstains – 19th cent half morocco – sm. 4to. – 1637.
(Christie's) $360 £170

NARDINI, FAMIANO
4to. – 15 engraved plates and plans – some folding – one double page and folding – a few leaves torn and neatly repaired – loss of a few letters – some browning – old vellum – Rome 1666.
(Christie's S. Kensington) $115 £55

NARES, E.
'Thinks I to Myself' – 2 vols. in one – calf gilt – 1811.
(Phillips) $34 £16

NARES, G.
'Narrative of a Voyage to the Polar Sea' – 2 vols. – 1st Edn. – plates and maps – orig. cloth – soiled – 8vo. – 1878.
(Sotheby's) $160 £75

NASH, FREDERICK, JOHN SCOTT AND M. P. B. DE LA BOISSIERE
'Picturesque Views of the City of Paris and Its Environs' – 2 vol. in one – Supplement – large paper copy – Eng. and French text – 57 engraved plates – contem. half red morocco – spines gilt – worn – folio – 1823.
(Sotheby's) $230 £110

NASH, JOSEPH
'The Mansions of England in Olden Times' – 4 parts in one vol. – litho titles and 100 plates – some leaves spotted – orig. morocco – gilt – rubbed – g.e. – folio – 1875.
(Sotheby's) $180 £85

NASH, PAUL
'The Tragedie of King Lear' – one of 500 copies on pure rag paper – 4to. – printed at the Shakespeare Head Press – illustrations and coloured plates by Nash – original cloth backed boards – soiled and a little rubbed – 1927.
(Christie's S. Kensington) $95 £45

NASH, TREDWAY RUSSELL
'Collection for the History of Worcestershire' – 2nd Edn. with additions – 2 vols. with supplement – engraved title vignettes folding engraved map – 76 engraved plates – 13 facsimiles of Domesday and 25 tables – contem. russia – gilt – rubbed – folio – 1799.
(Christie's) $335 £160

NAT RAGINI
Flaked slightly stained and smudged – gold margin and red leaf applied – 31.5 cm x 22.6 cm – Sub Imperial Mughal possibly Ajmar, circa 1640-60.
(Christie's) $1,155 £550

NAT RAGINI
Two lines in black sanskrit on natural leaf above identifying raga – gold, red and blue margins between black rules – red leaf – numbered – 38.5 cm x 26 cm. – North Deccan probably Aurungabad circa 1660-1680.
(Christie's) $1,470 £700

NATIONAL ART GALLERY, SOFIA
Limited Edn. – col. plates mounted – loose as issued in orig. cloth backed board portfolio – folio – Sofia, 1964.
(Sotheby's) $40 £20

NATIONAL BIOGRAPHY, DICTIONARY OF
22 vol. includes 1st supplement – India paper Edn. 1921-22; second supplement vol. 1 of 2 – binding worn 1912; supplements 1901-40 – 4 vol. 1927-49 – 8vo.
(Sotheby's) $335 £160

NATIONAL GALLERY CATALOGUES
Earlier Italian Schools – 2 vols. – some plates – some col. and mounted – orig. cloth – dust jackets – folio – 1953.
(Sotheby's) $50 £23

NATURAL HISTORY OF QUADRUPEDS FOR CHILDREN
1st Edn. – 26 engraved plates – each with two or three illus. – orig. roan backed boards – worn – 12mo. – Darton Harvey and Darton 1813.
(Sotheby's) $30 £14

NAVAL LIBRARY, MINISTRY OF DEFENCE, CATALOGUE OF, LONDON
5 vol. – folio – orig. cloth – Boston 1967.
(Christie's) $100 £48

NAVAL LOG BOOKS
Kept by Midshipman John Blandy on HMS Alexandra and Active in North European, Mediterranean and Caribbean waters – c. 750 pages – charts and watercolour drawings – 1882-86.
(Phillips) $420 £200

NAZARI, GIOVANNI BATTISTA
'Della Tramutatione Metallica Sogni Tre' – 2nd Edn. – anchor device on title – author's arms woodcut on verso – curious woodcuts in text some full page – woodcut initials – stained and discoloured – contem. limp vellum – very soiled – half blue morocco case – ownership inscript. – Brescia, 1572.
(Sotheby's) $800 £380

NAVARINO, A.
'Armiranda Orbis Christiani' – 2 vol. in one – editor J. B. Bagatta – title in red and black – leaves browned – spotting contem. blind stamped pigskin boards – soiled – spine worn – from the College of the Society of Jesus Landshuth – folio – Venice 1680.
(Sotheby's) $105 £50

NEAL, DANIEL
'The History of New England' – 2 vols. – 1st Edn. – titles in red and black – 1 folding engraved map – browning – 18th cent. calf gilt – Signet arms on side – one cover detached – 8vo. – 1720.
(Sotheby's) $85 £40

NEALE, JAMES
'The Abbey Church of Saint Alban Hertfordshire' – folio – chromolithographed title – 59 photolithographed plates and plans – two double page – some soiling and small marginal tears – contemp. morocco backed cloth – soiled spine rubbed t.e.g. – n.d.
(Christie's S. Kensington) $30 £15

NEBELSPALTER
Vol. 51-57 only – contemp. cloth backed boards – rubbed – a few wrappers lacking – 4to. – Zurich, 1925-31.
(Sotheby's) $170 £80

NECKER, JACQUES
'Lettre et Rapport' Paris 1789 'Memoire' 1789 'Memoire' Mai 1790 'Memoire' Aout 1790 – third browned – others slightly browned – modern boards – 8vo.
(Sotheby's) $135 £65

NEEDLEWORK BINDING
Holy Bible – design of a spray of tulips in gilt oval with fruit – birds and insects as border – panelled spine – worn – in morocco case – 1642.
(Irelands) $3,675 $1,750

Victory Jany. 20th. 1804

My own dear beloved Emma I send a very neat watch for our God child and you will see it is by a good maker that is I suppose it will Tick for a year instead of a month or two you will I suppose tell her that it is only to be worn when she behaves well and is obedient, I am very sorry that your comb is not arrived the Brig is at

NELSON, HORATIO
Fine auto letter signed Nelson and Bronte to Emma Hamilton – 4 pages – quarto – sending a watch for their child and mentions that a comb. is on its way to Emma etc. – 4 pages – quarto – Victory 20 January 1804.
(Sotheby's) $5,250 £2,500

NELSON, J.
'History and Antiquities of the Parish of Islington' – 23 plates – including folding map – half calf gilt – worn – 8vo. – 1823.
(Phillips) $65 £30

NERSESSIAN, S. D.
'The Chester Beatty Library. A Catalogue of the Armenian Manuscripts' – 2 vol. – plates – orig. cloth – folio – Dublin 1958.
(Sotheby's) $230 £110

NESBIT, EDITH
'The Magic City' – 1st Edn. – pictorial cloth gilt – 1910.
(Laurence & Martin Taylor) $34 £16

NESBITT, ALEXANDER
'A Descriptive Catalogue of the Glass Vessels in the South Kensington Museum' – col. plates – half morocco gilt – 1878.
(Phillips) $80 £38

NESFIELD, W. EDEN
'Specimens of Mediaeval Architecture' – litho title – 100 plates – one col. – some detached – margins torn – orig. morocco backed cloth – worn – g.e. – folio – 1862.
(Christie's) $85 £40

NEUMANN, A. H.
'Elephant Hunting in East Equatorial Africa' – plates – maps – cloth – 1898.
(Phillips) $180 £85

NEW CRIES OF LONDON, THE
1st Edn. – engraved frontis and 10 plates – orig. roan backed boards – rubbed – 12 mo. – Harvey and Darton 1823.
(Sotheby's) $275 £130

NEW EPICUREAN OR THE DELIGHTS OF SEX, THE
2 parts – extra illus. with 30 early photos – 1875.
(Phillips) $1,470 £700

NEW PEERAGE, THE
3 vol. – 3rd Edn. – plates – some spotting – modern half cloth slightly soiled – 1785.
(Christie's S. Kensington) $40 £20

NEW STORY ABOUT LITTLE JACK HORNER, AND AN ACCOUNT OF THE MANY NICE THINGS OF WHICH HIS MINCE PIE WAS MADE
Wood engraved frontispiece and 7 illustrations coloured by hand – orig. pictorial wrappers – covers loose and stained – large 8vo. – Albany NY. E. H. Bender – 1850.
(Sotheby's) $30 £15

NEW TOM THUMB, THE
'With an Account of his Wonderful Exploits, as related by Margery Meanwell' – 2nd Edn. – wood engraved vignette on title and 23 illustrations on 8 pages coloured by hand – page of advertisements inserted inside lower cover – fitted case – 8vo. –J. Harris & Son 1822.
(Sotheby's) $360 £170

NEW YORK (Peepshow)
5 litho sections and front col. by hand – slightly worn – fitted case – 136 mm x 226 mm extending 260 mm – Germany circa 1840.
(Sotheby's) $780 £370

NEW YORK – HOMANN, J. B.
'Nova Anglia' – engraved map – principal area col. by hand – pictorial title cartouche – 489 mm x 582 mm – Nuremberg circa 1740 or later.
(Sotheby's) $295 £140

NEW ZEALAND
Hand col. map – coloured cartouche – A. Zatta 1778.
(Phillips) $460 £220

NEW ZEALAND ATLAS
Editor Ian Wards – limited to 500 de luxe copies – orig. calf – gilt – slipcase – 4to. – Wellington 1976.
(Sotheby's) $40 £18

NEWCASTLE
A collection of 42 playbills for the Theatre Royal, Newcastle – minor defects – 1820-21.
(Sotheby Beresford Adams) $135 £65

THE

PHILOSOPHICAL

AND

Phyſical Opinions,

Written by her Excellency, the Lady MARCHIONESSE of NEWCASTLE.

LONDON

Printed for *J. Martin* and *J. Alleſtrye* at the Bell in St. *Pauls* Church-Yard 1655.

NEWCASTLE, MARGARET CAVENDISH, DUCHESS OF
'The Philosophical and Physical Opinions' – 1st Edn. – some browning – some tears – half red morocco gilt – g.e. – bookplate – folio – for J. Martin and J. Allestrye, 1655.
(Sotheby's) $880 £420

NEWDIGATE, BERNARD
'The Art of the Book' – plates – illustrational orig. cloth – slightly soiled – 4to. – The Studio Limited, 1938.
(Christie's S. Kensington) $40 £18

NEWFOUNDLAND
'An Act to Encourage Trade to Newfoundland' – modern wrappers – folio – by Charles Bill 1699.
(Sotheby's) $125 £60

NEWGATE
'Diary of Henry Baylis of Newgate listing Names of Malefactors sentenced to Death or Transportation' – mss on paper – 130pp vellum – circa 1755-75.
(Phillips) $565 £270

NEWLANDS, JAMES
'The Carpenter's and Joiner's Assistant' – folio – 1880.
(Lane) $15 £7

NEWMAN, J. H.
'Dream of Gerontius' – limited Edn. of 525 – number 10 – 1909.
(Laurence & Martin Taylor) $19 £9

NEWNES, GEORGE (publisher)
16 vols. on drawing and etching – Van Dyck, Holbein etc. – plates – orig. cloth backed boards – 4to. – n.d.
(Phillips) $125 £60

NEWTON, C. T.
'Travels and Discoveries in the Levant' – 2 vols. – 41 maps and plates – some leaves spotted – half crimson morocco gilt – t.e.g. – 8vo. – 1865.
(Phillips) $125 £60

NEWTON, SIR ISAAC
'Mathematical Principle of Natural Philosophy' . . . translated . . . by Robert Thorpe – 2nd Edn. – 22 folding engraved plates – occasional slight spotting – contemporary half calf – spine chipped – joints cracked – 4to. – 1802.
(Christie's S. Kensington) $55 £25

'Philosopiae Naturalis Principia Mathematica' 3rd Edn. – editor Henry Pemberton – engraved portrait by Vertue – title in red and black – diagrams – contem. diced russia gilt – joints split – 4to. – W. and J. Innys, 1726.
(Sotheby's) $1,050 £500

'The Method of Fluxions and Infinite Series' – translated from authors's Latin – 1st Edn. – engraved plate and diagrams in text – errata and advertisement leaf – contem. panelled calf – lower cover detached – 4to. – Henry Woodfall, 1736.
(Sotheby's) $1,470 £700

NICERON, JEAN FRANCOIS
'La Perspective Curieuse ou Magie Artificiele des Effets Merveilleux' – 1st Edn. – addit. engraved title – 25 plates – one double page – text brown – worming – contem limp vellum – stained – folio – Paris, Pierre Billaine 1638.
(Sotheby's) $800 £380

NICHOLS, BEVERLEY
'A Book of Old Ballads' – 16 colour illus. by H. M. Brock – 1934.
(Baitson) $10 £5

NICHOLS, JOHN
'The History and Antiquities of the County of Leicester' – 4 vols. in 8 – 521 portraits – plates and maps – cont. diced russia – gilt – folio – 1795-1811.
(Christie's) $2,205 £1,050

NICHOLS, R.
'The Smile of the Sphinx' – limited Edn. – uncut – orig. cloth backed boards – Beaumont Press 1920.
(Phillips) $40 £18

NICHOLSON, FRANCIS
'The Practice of Drawing and Painting Landscape from Nature in Watercolours' – 1st Edn. – 1 folding and coloured – some foxing – cloth – worn – 4to. – 1820.
(Sotheby's) $65 £30

NICHOLSON, GEORGE (editor)
'The Illustrated Dictionary of Gardening' – 8 vols. – coloured plates and engravings – decorated bindings – L. Upcott-Gill n.d.
(Baitson) $24 £11

NICHOLSON, J. AND BURN, R.
'History and Antiquities of Westmorland and Cumberland' – 2 vols. – 2 folding maps – calf gilt – 4to. – 1777.
(Phillips) $125 £60

NICHOLSON, M. A.
'Dictionary of the Science and Practice of Architecture, Building, Carpentry' – 2 vol. – new Edn. – numerous engraved plates – spotting – contem. half calf – some defects – 4to. – n.d.
(Sotheby Beresford Adams) $34 £16

NICHOLSON, PETER
'Practical Carpentry, Joinery and Cabinet Making' – 2 parts in one vol. – 90 engraved plates – including frontis – some leaves spotted – modern calf backed boards – 4to. – 1826.
(Sotheby's) $230 £110

NICHOLSON, W.
'History of the Wars Occasioned by the French Revolution' – 21 hand coloured plates – lacks frontis – calf covers detached – folio – 1817.
(Phillips) $250 $120

NICOLAS, SIR NICHOLAS H.
'History of the Orders of Knighthood of the British Empire' – 4 vol. – chromo-lithographed title – portrait and 24 plates – some col by hand – later red morocco – elaborately gilt – g.e. – some spotting – 4to. – 1841-42.
(Sotheby's) $1,595 £760

NICOLAS, P. F.
'Methode de Preparer et Conserver Les Animaux' – 10 engraved plates – creased half title repaired – some soiling – later half morocco – spine gilt – rubbed – Paris 1800.
(Christie's S. Kensington) $65 £30

NICOLSON, BENEDICT
'Joseph Wright of Derby' – 2 vol. – 4to. – mounted frontis – illustrations – some coloured – original cloth – dust jackets – 1968.
(Christie's S. Kensington) $115 £55

NIEBURR, CARSTEN
'Description de l'Arabie' – 2 parts in one – engraved title with vignette – 25 engraved maps – 8 folding – contem. boards – rubbed – uncut – 4to. – Amsterdam and Utrecht 1774.
(Sotheby's) $335 £160

NIEDIECK, PAUL
'Cruises in the Bering Sea' – plates – cloth – 1909.
(Phillips) $40 £20

NIELSEN, KAY – ANDERSEN, HANS
'Fairy Tales' – 8 col. plates – illus. in text – orig. cloth – dust jacket – 8vo. – New York 1932.
(Sotheby's) $85 £40

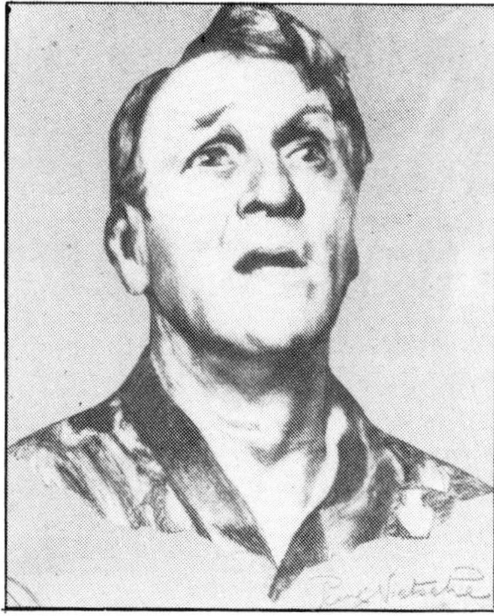

NIETSCHE, PAUL
'Portrait of Chaliapine' – red crayon and collage with photograph of Chaliapine signed and dated and dedicated to Lady Curzon – July 1913.
(Sotheby's) $210 £100

NIHELL, ELIZABETH
'A Treatise on the Art of Midwifery' – 1st Edn. – contemp. calf – 1760.
(Bonhams) $170 £80

NILE, THE
'Notes for Travellers in Egypt' – 4to. – full blue calf gilt – map – plans – 1892.
(Baitson) $100 £48

NIXON, H. M.
'Five Centuries of English Bookbinding' – large 8vo. – 100 fine plates with definitive text – 1978.
(J. Ash) $37 £18

'Broxbourne Library Style and Designs of Book Bindings' – 1 of 500 copies – illus. – quarter parchment – 4to. – 1956.
(Phillips) $965 £460

NIZAMI: KHAMSEH
Persian mss – 267 ff plus 2 fly leaves – some waterstaining and soiling – illuminated headings principally in lapis and gold – 18 miniatures – later brown tooled morocco binding – folio – Turkman circa 1480.
(Christie's) $1,365 £650

NOBILITY OF ENGLAND
The original petition signed by 33 of the 'nobilitie of England' – addressed to James I in 1621 including Earl of Essex, Earl of Warwick, Richard Dacre, Thomas Wentworth etc. against the prejudice caused to the English peerage by the lavish grant of Irish and Scottish titles of nobility – large double folio sheet partly mounted – minor repairs – one signature – contemp. endorsement – undated.
(Sotheby's) $840 £400

NOBLE, T.
'Blackheath. A Poem ... and various other Poems' – engraved title – plates – occasional slight spotting – contemporary diced calf – rubbed – joints worn – g.e. – 4to. – 1808.
(Christie's S. Kensington) $115 £55

NOBLE, T. AND ROSE, T.
'The Counties of Chester, Derby, Leicester, Lincoln and Rutland' – 70 plates on 35 leaves – by T. Allom – half calf gilt – 4to. – 1836.
(Phillips) $210 £100

NOCQ, HENRY AND DREYFUS, CARLE
'Tabatieres Boites et Etuis .... des collections du Musee du Louvre' – plates – half morocco – a little rubbed – 4to. – Paris 1930.
(Christie's S. Kensington) $145 £70

NODIER, CHARLES
'Paris Historique' – 3 vols. – two lithographed frontis – lithographed plates – occasional slight spotting – cont. calf boards – spines faded – Paris – bookplates of Duff Cooper – 1838-9.
(Christie's S. Kensington) $180 £85

NOEHDEN, GEORGE HENRY
'Specimens of Ancient Coins of Magna Graecia and Sicilly ' 1st Edn. – 21 engraved plates – 19th cent. half green morocco – rubbed – partly uncut – folio – 1826.
(Sotheby's) $170 £80

NOGUCHI, YONE
'Hiroshige' – limited Edn. – orig. wrappers – cloth folder – 4to. – 1934.
(Sotheby's) $135 £65

NOLAN, J.
'History of the War Against Russia' – 8 vols. – orig. cloth binding – 1857.
(Lane) $34 £16

NOLLET, ABBE JEAN ANTOINE
'Lettres sur l'Electricite' – 2 vols. in one – 8 folding plates – contem. calf gilt – Paris 1764.
(Phillips) $145 £70

NORDEN, JOHN (topographer)
Docs. – also by his son John – 1 page folio – 1621 claiming payment for surveying – signed by five of the Prince's council and receipted by Norden senior – December 1621.
(Phillips) $1,050 £500
'Speculum Britanniae; An Historical and Chorographical Description of Middlesex and Hertfordshire' – 2 parts in 1 – engraved title – 2 fly titles and 4 folding maps – engraved arms and woodcut illus. in text – contem. calf – gilt spine – rubbed – sm. 4to. – 1723.
(Sotheby's) $670 £320
'Manuscript Maps of Cornwall' – fine copy – 1972.
(Lane) $20 £10

NORFOLK PARISH REGISTERS
Marriages Vol 1-12 – limited Edn. – orig. cloth – slightly soiled – 8vo. – 1899-1936.
(Sotheby's) $160 £75

NORGE
'A Complete Epitomy of Practical Navigation' – full calf binding – 1860.
(Lane) $30 £14

NORONHA FREYRE
'Istoria delle Guerre del Regno del Brasilie' – 2 vols in one – portrait – 26 engraved folding maps – plans and views – worming – half morocco – rubbed – Rome 1700.
(Christie's) $4,200 £2,000

NORRIS, FRANK
'The Responsibilities of the Novelist' – New York 1903.
(J. Ash) $17 £8

NORTH, I. W.
'A Week in the Isles of Scilly' – 1st Edn. – orig. cloth binding – good copy – 1850.
(Lane) $90 £42

NORTH, ROGER
'Examen or an Enquiry into the Credit and Veracity of a Pretended Complete History' – 1st Edn. – portrait – browning – contem. calf – worn – covers – detached – 4to. – 1740.
(Sotheby's) $65 £30

NORTH AND SOUTH AMERICA
Collection of 50 maps – mostly hand col. – many with tears – various cartographers and dates before 1850.
(Phillips) $210 £100

NORTHCOTE, JAMES
'One Hundred Fables' – portrait – wood engraved additional title and illustrations – occasional slight spotting – orig. cloth – faded – spine torn – n.d.
(Christie's S. Kensington) $25 $12

NORTHCOTE, LADY ROSALIND
'Devon' – illus. by Widgery – 1914.
(Laurence & Taylor) $17 £8

NORWAY, A. H.
'Highways and Byways in Devon and Cornwall' – 1898.
(Lane) $12 £6

NORWAY – GOOS, P.
Engraved chart – hand col. in outline – title cartouche – compass roses fully col. 428 x 525mm. – Amsterdam 1650.
(Sotheby's) $230 £110

NORWAY ILLUSTRATED
Text in English and Norwegian – 40 plates – incl. 8 coloured – quarter calf – upper cover detached – oblong folio – New York n.d.
(Phillips) $400 £190

NOTT, S. C.
'Chinese Jade' – 1st Edn. – plates – some col. – cloth – 4to. – 1936.
(Phillips) $55 £25

NOUVERRE, JEAN GEORGES
'Lettres sur la Danse, sur les Ballets et les Arts' – 4 vol. – large paper – errata leaf in each – lacks portrait of Saunders – bookplate of Arnold Haskell – slightly later glazed boards – rubbed – 4to. – St. Petersbourg 1803-04.
(Sotheby's) $840 £400

NUMISMATIC SOCIETY, AMERICAN
Museum Notes – nos. 1-21 – plates – orig. wrappers – 8vo. – New York 1946-76.
(Sotheby's) $460 £220

NUNEZ, PEDRO
'De Crepusculus' – 1st Edn. – title in woodcut border -diagrams – in text – woodcut device – modern vellum backed boards – half blue morocco case – sm. 4to. – Lisbon, L. Rodericus 1542.
(Sotheby's) $1,890 £900

NUREMBERG TRIALS
The Trial of German Major War Criminals – 26 vols. including Opening and Closing Speeches and Judgements – mod. cloth – 8vo. – 1946-51.
(Sotheby's) $345 £165

OAKESHOTT, W.
'Some Woodcuts by Hans Burgkmair' – orig. morocco backed cloth – 4to. – Oxford, Roxburghe Club 1960.
(Sotheby's) $220 £105

OAKLEY, E.
'The Magazine of Architecture, Perspective and Sculpture' – frontis – and 93 plates – folio – half calf – 1730.
(Bonhams) $275 £130

OBERTUS DE HORTO AND GERARDUS, CACAPISTUS
'De Feudis Libri V' – 2 parts in one – ornamental initials – dampstains – worming – 17th cent. vellum boards – soiled – title inscribed 'Holland House' – sm. 8vo. – Mons Regalis 1567.
(Sotheby's) $85 £40

O'BRIEN, HON DONOUGH
'Miniatures of the XVIIIth and XIXth Centuries' – 15 copies – plates – 1 col. – orig. cloth – dust jackets – 4to. – 1951.
(Sotheby's) $170 £80

O'CASEY, SEAN
'The Silver Tassie' – 1st Edn. – port. – orig. cloth – slightly soiled – 1928.
(Christie's) $60 £28

OCKLEY, S.
'An Account of South West Barbary' – folding coloured map – crisp copy in contem. calf – broken – 8vo. – J. Bowyer 1713.
(Sotheby's) $200 £95

O'DONAGHUE, F. AND HENRY M. HAKE
'Catalogue of Engraved British Portraits in the British Museum' – 6 vol. – orig. cloth – 8vo. – 1908-25.
(Sotheby's) $220 £105

L'OEIL, REVUE D'ART MENSUELLE
No. 1-144 in 8 vols. – plates and illus. – some coloured – modern half morocco – gilt ornament on spines – 4to. – 1955-66.
(Sotheby's) $170 £80

OFFICE DE L'EGLISE EN FRANCOIS ET EN LATIN
Engraved frontis and contemporary bookseller's ticket of J. P. Labottiere, Bordeaux – contemporary French inlaid binding – Dutch white and gilt endpapers – one corner slightly worn – citron morocco case by Riviere – 12 mo. – Paris, Theodore de Hansy, 1754.
(Sotheby Parke Bernet) $2,975 £1,415

OFFICE DE LA SEMAINE SAINT
Contem. French binding of red morocco gilt with the arms of Louis Phillips, brother of Louis XIV on each cover – 8vo. – 1729.
(Moore Allen & Innocent) $420 £200

OFFICERS
'List of the Officers of the Army and Marines etc.' – calf – monthly Army list – morocco gilt – 1914 – and an Indian Army List – wrappers – 1938 – 1794.
(Bennett Book Auction) $40 £20

O'FLAHERTY, LIAM
'The Pedler's Revenge' – dust wrapper.
(J. Ash) $12 £6

OGILVY, J. S.
'Relics and Memorials of London Town' – 1911.
(Allen & May) $15 £7

OGILVIE-GRANT, W. R. AND OTHERS
'The Gun at Home and Abroad, British Game Birds and Wildfowl' – number 763 of 950 copies – 4to. – plates – some coloured – orig. morocco – slightly rubbed – t.e.g. – 1912.
(Christie's S. Kensington) $135 £65

OLD DAME TROT
8 pp each with lithographed verse and illustrations coloured by hand – unbound – Glasgow 1840.
(Sotheby's) $65 £30

OLD GRAND-PAPA AND OTHER POEMS
For the Instruction and Amusement of Children – 36 wood engraved illustrations – including one on title and 3 on covers – slightly discoloured – orig. pictorial wrappers – backstrip worn – joints stitched – 12 mo. – Samuel Wood & Sons 1818.
(Sotheby's) $60 £28

OLD MAN YOUNG AGAIN, THE
Engraved title – limited Edn. – morocco gilt – t.e.g. – 1898.
(Phillips) $85 £40

OLD MASTER DRAWINGS
14 vols. Collector's Edn. – illus. – orig. cloth – 4to. – New York 1970.
(Sotheby's) $115 £55

OLD WATER COLOUR SOCIETY'S CLUB
Vol. 6-27 – plates – some col. – orig. cloth backed boards – 4to. – 1929-49.
(Sotheby's) $735 £350

OLDENBOURG – JANSSON, J.
Double page bird's eye view – coat of arms – cartouches etc. – Latin text on verso – stains – 348 mm x 465 mm – Amsterdam 1657.
(Sotheby's) $440 £210

OLDENBOURG, R.
'Rubens' – plates – cloth – 8vo. – 1921.
(Phillips) $34 £16

OLDHAM, J. BASIL
'English Blind Stamped Bindings' – one of 750 copies – 'Blind Panels of English Bindings' – together 2 vols. – plates – illus – original cloth – folio – Cambridge, 1893-94.
(Sotheby's) $275 £130

OLDHAM, JOHN
'Works' – 4 parts in one vol. – old calf rebacked – 1692.
(Phillips) $65 £30

OLINA, GIOVANNI PIETRO
'Ucceliera Opero Discorso della Natura' – 2nd Edn. – title within engraved border – 55 full page engr. illust. only – 4to. – Rome presso M. Angelo de Rossi 1684.
(Christie's S. Kensington) $180 £85

OLIVER, CHARLES AND JAMES LAVER
'Original Views of London As It Is' – 2 vol. – coloured plates after T. S. Boys – orig. wrappers – upper cover of one vol. slightly soiled – folio – Guildford, 1972.
(Christie's S. Kensington) $180 £85

OLIVER, R. A.
'A Series of Lithographic Drawings from Sketches of New Zealand' – limited facsimile Edn. – col. plates – orig. half morocco – card slipcase – folio – Waiura Martinborough 1977.
(Sotheby's) $75 £35

OLIVER, V. L.
'The History of the Island of Antigua' – illus. and maps – 3 vols – folio – cloth (soiled) – 1894-99.
(Bonhams) $160 £75

OLLIER, CHARLES, (Publisher of Keats and Shelley)
Indenture of apprenticeship of Charles Ollier – signed to Phillip Drake – a notary public and scrivener – on vellum – 20.5 cm x 18.5 cm – 1 August 1802.
(Phillips) $135 £65

OLSCHKI, LEO
'Incunabula Typographica A Catalogue of the books printed in the fifteenth century ... in the library of Henry Walters' – coloured frontispiece – orig. calf – t.e.g. – 4to. – Baltimore, 1906.
(Christie's S. Kensington) $80 £38

OLSEN, O. T.
'The Piscatorial Atlas of the North Sea, English and St. George's Channels' – 50 double page coloured maps – orig. cloth – rubbed – spine worn – folio – Grimsby 1883.
(Sotheby's) $145 £70

OLYMPIC GAMES
Text in German – 1936.
(Lane) $30 £14

OMAR, KHAYYAM
'Rubaiyat' – trans by Edward Fitzgerald – no. 50 of 300 copies – 8 full page engraved illus. by John Buckland-Wright – orig. morocco backed cloth – gilt – sm. folio – 1938.
(Sotheby's) $380 £180

OMPHALIUS, JACOBUS
'De Elocutionis imitatione ac apparatu ... ad Cardinalem Bellaium' – italics – woodcut device on title – woodcut initials – slightly soiled or dampstained in places – old boards – slightly worn – sm. 8vo. – Paris, Guillaume Julien 1555.
(Sotheby's) $65 £30

ONGANIA, FERDINANDO (Editor)
'Calli e Canali in Venezia' – folio – lithographed title – 100 plates – some detached – some spotting – original morocco backed cloth – slightly rubbed – t.e.g. – 1890-91.
(Christie's S. Kensington) $145 £70

ONIONS, OLIVER
'Arras of Youth' – 1949.
(J. Ash) $8 £4

OPIE, MRS A.
'Temper' – 3 vols. – half titles – calf – 1812.
(Phillips) $105 £50

OPTIQUE COMPLETE DE VERSAILLES (peepshow)
5 engraved sections and front with 3 peepholes coloured by hand – orig. slip-case – fitted case – 133 mm x 190 mm extending 500 mm – Paris circa 1830.
(Sotheby's) $545 £260

ORACLE, THE COOK'S
1823.
(Richard Baker & Thomson) $75 £36

ORANGE, JAMES
'The Chater Collection' – limited Edn. – port. – plates – original cloth – 4to. – 1924.
(Phillips) $460 £220

ORCUTT, W. D.
'The Book in Italy' – limited Edn. – plates – some mounted and coloured – parchment backed boards – soiled – 4to. – 1928.
(Sotheby's) $125 £60

ORIENTAL CERAMIC SOCIETY, TRANSACTIONS OF
5 vol. only – limited to 1000 – 1100 and 1200 copies – plates – orig. cloth – 4to. – 1954-74.
(Christie's) $160 £75

ORLEANS, F. P. DUC D'
'Lettres 1825-42' – no. 8 of 40 copies on Japon – portrait – modern red morocco by Nupre – lavishly gilt – morocco and silk doublures – orig. wrappers – g.e. – 8vo. – Paris 1889.
(Sotheby's) $125 £60

ORLERS, J. J. AND H. DE HAESTENS
'The Triumphs of Nassau or, a descriptions .. of all the victories ... under Prince Maurice of Nassau', translated out of French by W. Shute – folio – soiled – dampstained – old calf – rubbed – joints split – printed by Adam Islip 1613.
(Christie's S. Kensington) $100 £48

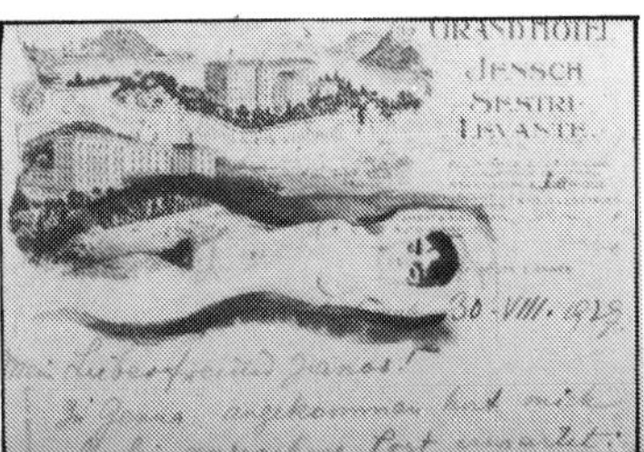

ORLIK, EMIL
Illustrated autograph letter signed – 4 pages octavo to Janos Plesch giving an account of his cruise on the Mediterranean and the pictures he has painted with watercolour sketch of a nude. – Jensch Sestri-Levante 1927.
(Sotheby's) $200 £95

ORME, EDWARD
Orme's collection of 'British Field Sports' – coloured title and plates after S. Howitt – orig. wrappers – slightly soiled – oblong folio – Guildford.
(Christie's S. Kensington) $145 £70

ORME, EDWARD
'An Essay on Transparent Prints' – text in Eng. and French – engraved title – 15 engraved plates – 10 hand coloured – one plate of specimen papers – without subscription list – minor defects – orig. boards – slightly worn – 4to. – 1807.
(Sotheby Beresford Adams) $460 £220

ORMEROD, GEORGE
'The History of the County Palatine and the City of Chester' – 3 vols. – 2nd Edn. – revised and enlarged by Thomas Helsby – portrait double page map – coloured – numerous engraved maps and plans – orig. cloth backed boards – very worn – folio – 1882.
(Sotheby Beresford Adams) $315 £150

ORTA, GARCIA DE AND NICOLO MONARDES
'Dell'Historia de i Semplici Aromatim et Akre Cose: Che Vengono Portate Dall' Indie Orientali Pertinenti All'Uso Della Medicina' – 2 parts in 1 vol. – woodcut device on title – woodcuts in the text – slightly rotted or dampstained in places – contemp. limp vellum – repaired and recased – sm. 8vo. – Venice 1589.
(Sotheby's) $125 £60

ORTEGA, JUAN DE
'Suma de Arithmetica' – 1st Edn. – Italian text – woodcut borders – Spanish royal arms – diagrams in text – device at end – some foxing – contem. vellum boards – stained – upper cover detached – lacking ties – folio – Rome 1515.
(Sotheby's) $1,090 £520

ORTELIUS, A.
'Africa Tabula' – hand col. map 2 tears affecting plate upper left corner – 1606.
(Phillips) $200 £95

ORWELL, GEORGE
'The Road to Wigan Pier' – 1st Edn. – orig. orange colour – 1937.
(Lane) $8 £4
'The Lion and the Unicorn' – orig. white cloth – spine very slightly soiled – 1941.
(J. Ash) $20 £10

OSBORN, FRANCIS
'Advice to a Son' and 'A Miscellany of Sundry Essayes' – two works in one vol. – 12 mo. – old calf – rebacked – Oxford, 1658/9.
(Christie's S. Kensington) $65 £32

OSBORNE, JOHN
'The World of Paul Slickey' – 1959.
(J. Ash) $20 £10

OSBORNE, W. G.
'The Court and Camp of Runjeet Sing' – 1st Edn. – plates – orig. cloth – 8vo. – 1840.
(Sotheby's) $275 £130

OSLANDER
'Harmoniae Evangelicae' – 19th cent. French binding of straight grained red morocco gilt by Simier – signed at foot of spine – 12 mo. – Paris 1545.
(Moore Allen & Innocent) $380 £180

OSLER, SIR WILLIAM
'Incunabula Medica' – port. – 16 plates – orig. holland backed boards – soiled – 4to. – Bibliographical Socy. 1923.
(Sotheby's) $210 £100

OSMASTON, F. P. B.
'The Art and Genius of Tintoret' – 2 vols. – plates – cloth gilt – t.e.g. – 4to. – 1915.
(Phillips) $60 £28

OSTELL, THOMAS
'A New General Atlas' – 30 engraved maps – hand coloured in outline – half calf – rubbed – covers detached – 4to. – 1807.
(Christie's S. Kensington) $170 £80

OTTLEY, W. J.
'Italian School of Design' – 71 plates – some spotting and repairs – some loose – binding defective – folio – 1823.
(Phillips) $380 £180

OTWAY, THOMAS
'Works' – limited Edn. – 3 vols. uncut – orig. cloth backed boards – 4to. – Nonesuch Press 1924.
(Phillips) $65 £30

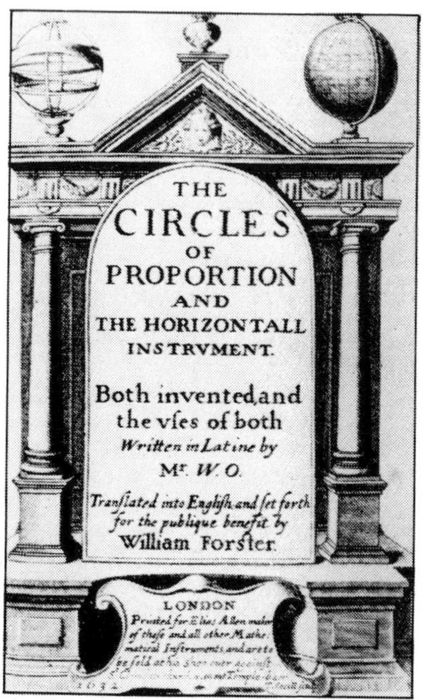

OUGHTRED, WILLIAM
'The Circles of Proportion and the Horizontal Instrument' – 2 parts in one – printed title to each part – 3 plates – woodcut diagrams – errata leaf – staining – contem. sheep rebacked – half red morocco case – bookplate – sm. 4to. – 1633.
(Sotheby's) $2,205 £1,050

OVER, CHARLES
'Ornamental Architecture in the Gothic, Chinese and Modern Taste' – 53 engraved plates only – number 32 lacking – damp-staining – contemp. calf – worn – 1758.
(Christie's S. Kensington) $105 £50

OVERBEKE, BONAVENTURA AND MICHAEL
'Reliquae Antiquae Urbis Romae' – 1st Edn. – 3 vols in one – title in red and black – engraved portrait frontis – contem. calf – gilt spine – slightly rubbed – folio – 1708.
(Christie's) $1,260 £600

OVID
'Opera' – 5 vols. – contem. English binding of red morocco gilt with serpentine edge – 12 mo. – 1745.
(Moore Allen & Innocent) $200 £95

OWEN, MAJOR C. H.
'Sketches in the Crimea' – hand coloured lithographed title and five plates after Owen – on four leaves – one folding but separated along fold – some spotting and soiling – orig. morocco backed cloth – worn and disbound – oblong folio – 1856.
(Christie's S. Kensington) $210 £100

OWEN, E.
'Old Stones and Crosses' – illus. half morocco gilt – folio – 1886.
(Phillips) $65 £30

OWEN, MRS HENRY
'The Illuminated Book of Needlework ... Preceded by a History of Needlework .. Editor Countess of Wilton' – chromolithographed additional titles – plates – most hand coloured – occasional spotting – original cloth – soiled – 1847.
(Christie's S. Kensington) $60 £28

OWEN, J. AND E. BOWEN
'Britannia Depicta or Ogilby Improve'd' – engraved title – four page table of contents and 273 pages of road maps and text – the last spotted – contemp. calf – rebacked – joints split – 1720.
(Christie's S. Kensington) $755 £360

OWEN, JOHN
'Latine Epigrams Englished by Tho. Harvey' – 12 mo. – three printed titles – lower margin of first title torn and repaired – contemp. sheep – worn – 1677.
(Christie's S. Kensington) $45 £22

OWEN, ROBERT
'The Book of the New Moral World' – 1st Edn. – presentation copy – inscribed to the Queen of Portugal – orig. cloth – marked – unopened – 8vo. – 1836.
(Sotheby's) $1,010 £480

OXFORDSHIRE
Garsington Manor – Royal Letters Patent with initial portrait of James I in Latin in vellum – 26 x 30 inches – upper margin decorated with heraldic beasts and emblems – Westminster 1612.
(Sotheby's) $115 £55

OZANNE, NICOLAS
'Recueil de Combats et D'Expeditions Maritimes' – engraved vignette on title – 39 engraved plates and plans – spotting – contem. half calf – worn – folio – Paris 1797.
(Sotheby's) $1,995 £950

P

PACIOLI, LUCA
'Somma de Aritmetica Geometria Proporzioni e Proporzionalita' – 1st. Edn. – 308 leaves – 56 lines and headline – gothic letter – red and black with strapwork border – some marginal diags., notes and calculations – holes – browning and staining – modern vellum boards – half red morocco case – folio – Venice, Paganini de Paganini, 1494.
(Sotheby's) $20,580 £9,800

PACKER, THOMAS
'The Dyer's guide being an Introduction to the Art of Dying Linen, Cotton, Wool, Dresses ..... Furniture etc.' – half title – short tear – new cloth – 8vo. – Sherwood, Neely and Jones 1816.
(Sotheby's) $85 £40

PADEREWSKI, IGNAZ JAN
Auto musical quotation of three bars – signed – 1 page – 4to. – with photographic pcs. and a bookmarker depicting the pianist as a young man – 19 July 1905.
(Phillips) $75 £35

PADUANIUS, FABRICIUS
'Tractatus duo alter de Ventis' – 1st Edn. – device on title – 39 engravings in text – 5 full page – some browning – repairs – contem. limp vellum – lacking ties – folio – Bologna, 1601.
(Sotheby's) $1,785 £850

PAGANINO, A.
'Libro de Rechami' – Part 1 only – facsimile Edn. – contem. vellum – gilt – 4to. – Venice, 1878.
(Sotheby's) $10 £5

PAGE, JOHN
'An Exploration of Dartmoor' – 1892.
(Lane) $15 £7

PAGE, WILLIAM (Editor)
'The Victoria History of the County of Durham' – 3 vol. – plates – maps and plans – some coloured – some folding – original cloth – lge. 4to. – 1905-28.
(Christie's S. Kensington) $105 £50

PAGES, VICOMTE DE
'Travels Round the World' – 3 vols. – 1 folding plate – 1 folding table – calf gilt – 8vo. – 1791-2.
(Phillips) $630 £300

PAGET, F. E.
'The Pageant; Or Pleasure and its Price' – contemp. half calf – 1843.
(J. Ash) $40 £20

PAINE, THOMAS
'Common Sense' 1776; 'Remarks on Common Sense' 1776 – 2 works in one vol. – slight browning – modern boards 8vo.
(Sotheby's) $105 £50

PALAEONTOGRAPHICAL SOCIETY
Publications – 24 vol. – plates – some leaves defective – orig. wrappers – 4to. – 1848-70.
(Sotheby's) $380 £180

PALATINO, G. B.
'Compendio del Gran Volume de L'Arte del Benescriuere' – lacks title – water-staining and soiling – sm. 4to. – Rome 1566.
(Sotheby's) $85 £40

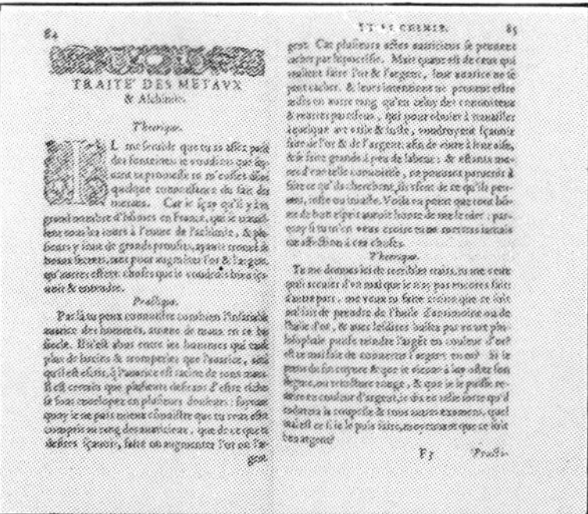

PALISSY, BERNARD
'Discours Admirables, de la Nature des Eaux et Fonteines' – 1st Edn. – upper margins of some renewd – modern red morocco – g.e. by Godillot – 8vo. – Paris, Martin le Jeune, 1580.
(Sotheby's) $3,570 £1,700

PALL MALL MAGAZINE, THE
29 vol. various – coloured plates – illus.-trations – uniform half morocco – some rubbed and faded – spines gilt – 1894-1910.
(Christie's S. Kensington) $250 £120
Vols. 8 and 9 - 1896 – STRAND MAGA-ZINE Vol 7 - 1894 – GOOD WORDS 1893.
(Laurence & Martin Taylor) $2 £1

PALLADIO, ANDREA
'Five Orders of Architecture' – editor Colen Campbell – engraved title and 36 plates – spotting – ownership inscriptions including Cecil Beaton – contemp. calf – rebacked – sm. folio – 1729.
(Sotheby's) $335 £160
'Architecture' – 2 vols. in one – port. – engraved title – 158 plates – morocco backed boards – worn – folio – 1742.
(Phillips) $630 £300

PALLAS, P. S.
'Travels through the Southern Provinces of the Russian Empire' – 2 vol. – 2nd. Edn. – vignettes and 51 plates – the majority hand coloured – some folding – three folding maps – frontispiece – half calf – rubbed – 4to. – John Stockdale, 1812.
(Christie's S. Kensington) $380 £180

PALLISER, MADAME BURY
'Histoire de la Dentelle' – plates – browned – orig. cloth – g.e. – 4to.– Paris 1892.
(Christie's) $55 £25

PALMER, A. H.
'Samuel Palmer, A Memoir' – etched frontispiece by Samuel Palmer – autotype and wood engraved plates – after Palmer – some leaves creased and slightly soiled – contemp. morocco backed boards – worn – disbound – 4to. – The Fine Art Society, Limited – 1882.
(Christie's S. Kensington) $125 £60

PAMPHLETS
A collection of pamphlets issued by Bezalel of Jerusalem in German and Hebrew and seven other pamphlets some printed on paper – three with Art Nouveau covers – one richly illus. – various sizes – Jerusalem 1906.
(Sotheby's) $230 £110

PANOFSKY, E.
'Albrecht Durer' – 2 vol. – plates – orig. cloth – 4to. – Princeton 1943.
(Sotheby's) $115 £55

PANORAMA OF LONDON AND THE RIVER THAMES
Extending hand col. panorama in orig. cloth folder – illus. London News – circa 1850.
(Phillips) $145 £70

PANORAMA OF THE RHINE
By Delkescamp, F. G.
Engraved panoramic map with small vignettes – torn – separate title in French and German – text in German – in orig. roan backed boards – 91.75 in x 10.25 in. – large 8vo. – Frankfurt am Main 1837.
(Sotheby's) $135 £65

PANORAMA VON POTZDAM
Coloured chromolith in six sections – backed with linen – Berlin circa 1870.
(Bonhams) $200 £95

PANORAMA, THE , OF THE WORLD
Etched frontis – title and 7 plates – col. by hand – orig. roan backed boards – spine worn – upper joint split – 12 mo. – R. Millar circa 1820.
(Sotheby's) $40 £18

PANVINIO, ONOFRIO
'De Ludis Circensibus' – engraved title – 2 small engraved portraits – 29 plates most double page – contem. vellum – gilt – fleurons at corners – arabesque centrepieces – folio – Padua, Paolo Frambotti 1642.
(Sotheby's) $840 £400

PAPE, FRANK C. AND FRANK FOX
'The Gateway to Spenser' – 16 col. plates – 1918.
(Baitson) $40 £18

PAPEWORTH, JOHN B.
'Rural Residences' – 27 hand col. plates – publisher's adverts at end – some text loose – orig. boards – lacks spine – 4to. – Ackermann 1818.
(Phillips) $420 £200
'Poetical Sketches of Scarborough' – 21 hand col. plates by Rowlandson – diced calf gilt – 1813.
(Phillips) $180 £85

PAPIRUS TAKEN FROM A MUMMY OF THEBES IN THE COLLECTION OF THE EARL OF BELMORE
Hand col. litho scroll after G. Schark – torn – orig. pictorial boxwood drum – soiled – 24 cm x 360 cm. – C. Hullman-dell, n.d.
(Sotheby's) $360 £170

PAPON, JEAN
'Corpus Iuris Francici' – title in red and black with woodcut device – old ownership inscription – worming – boards worn and very wormed – folio – Geneva 1624.
(Sotheby's) $20 £10

PARACELSUS, P. A. T.
'Astronomica et Astrologica' – 1st Edn. – editor Balthasar Floter – 2 full page woodcut portraits of author – 18th cent. vellum boards – half red morocco case – armorial plate – sm. 4to. – Cologne 1567.
(Sotheby's) $2,940 £1,400

'Prophecien und Weissagungen' – 89 woodcuts – some browned – stained – wrappers – half red morocco case – sm. 4to. – 1549.
(Sotheby's) $1,720 £820

PARDIES, IGNACE
'Globi Coelestis .... Opus Postumum' – 2nd Edn. – 6 double page star maps – large folding engraved table – lacks portrait – soiling and discolouration – contem calf – worn – French Jesuit inscription – very rare – large folio – Paris 1693.
(Sotheby's) $1,365 £650

PARAGUAY – BLAEU, W. AND J.
Engraved map – hand col. in outline – cartouches and sailing ships – fully col. – Latin text on verso – discoloured – 449 mm x 546 mm.
(Sotheby's) $85 £40

PARIS, J.A.
'The Life of Sir Humphrey Davy' – 2 vols. – 1st Edn. – newly bound in half morocco 1831.
(Lane) $65 £30

PARIS NOUVEAU ET SES ENVIRONS D'APRES LES PHOTOGRAPHIES
44 litho plates only – spotted – orig. cloth – gilt – rubbed – g.e. – folio – Paris 1859.
(Sotheby's) $230 £110

PARIS THEATRES
9 programmes for Theatres including Folies Bergere, Casino de Paris and Tabarin circa 1940's and '50's'.
(Baitson) $8 £4

PARIVAL, JEAN DE
'Les Delices de la Hollande' – derniere Edn. – engraved title – folding view – 19 folding plans and map – browning – contem. vellum – 12 mo. – Amsterdam 1685.
(Sotheby's) $200 £95

PARK, J. J.
'The Topography and Natural History of Hampstead' – engraved frontispiece and 12 portraits and plates – one folding map – slight spotting – cloth backed boards – rubbed – inner hinges cracked – 1818.
(Christie's S. Kensington) $170 £80

PARK, MUNGO
"Travels in the Interior Districts of Africa' – 9 engraved plates and maps – some folding – 2 leaves of music – browned – modern half calf – 4to. – 1799.
(Sotheby's) $170 £80
'Journal of a Mission to the Interior of Africa .. 1805' – double page folding map – calf cover detached – lacks backstrip – 4to. – 1815.
(Bennett Book Auctions) $105 £50

PARK'S NEW TWELFTH NIGHT CHARACTERS
'King of Hearts and others' – wood engraved illus. of 28 characters – coloured by hand – with conundrums – folded in orig. engraved pictorial wrapper lettered 'The Droll Story' – coloured by hand – large folio – circa 1840.
(Sotheby's) $105 £50

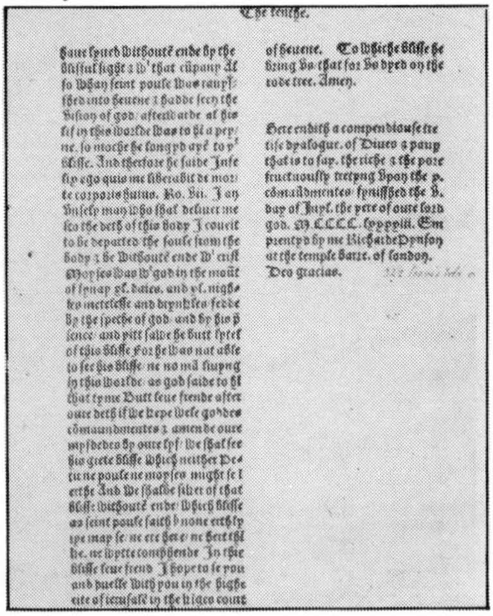

PARKER, HENRY
'A Compendiouse Tretise of Dives and Pauper' – 1st Edn. – 241 leaves of 244 – 36 lines gothic letter – waterstains – late 18th cent. red morocco – spine gilt – roll tooled borders – g.e. – bookplates – folio – Richard Pynson July 1493.
(Christie's) $16,800 £8,000

PARKER, CHARLES
'Villa Rustica' – 64 lithographed plates and plans – some spotting – contemp. half morocco – rubbed – g.e. – 4to. – 1832.
(Christie's S. Kensington) $95 £45

PARKES, SAMUEL
'Chemical Essays principally relating to the Arts and Manufactures of the British Dominions' – 5 vols. – 1st Edn. – 23 plates – orig. boards – spines rubbed – uncut –12 mo. – Richard Taylor for the author 1815.
(Sotheby's) $115 £55

PARKINSON, JOHN
'Paradisi in Sole' – reprint of 1629 Edn. – orig. holland backed boards – rubbed – folio – 1904.
(Sotheby's) $115 £55

'Paradise in Sole' – 2nd Edn., engraved additional title, illustrations, cont. calf, rubbed, spine chipped, folio – 1656.
(Christie's S. Kensington) $290 £130

PARKS, FANNY
'The Wanderings of a Pilgrim during Four and Twenty Years in the East' – 2 vol. – 50 litho plates – some folding – some spotting – orig. cloth gilt – recased – soiled – 8vo. – 1850.
(Sotheby's) $565 £270

PARLIAMENTARY LISTS OF THE PEERS OF ENGLAND ELECTED 26 APRIL 1768
2nd Edn. – full illus.
(Dacre, Son & Hartley) $85 £40

PARLOUR MAGIC
1st Edn. – wood engraved title – illus. in text and decorations by E. Landells – orig. cloth gilt worn – 8vo. – Whitehead 1828.
(Sotheby's) $55 £25

PARRISH, MAXFIELD
'The Knave of Hearts' – col. illus. mostly full page by Parrish – orig. cloth backed pictorial boards – stitching shaken – 4to. – New York 1925.
(Christie's) $275 £130

PARRISH, MAXFIELD – WHARTON, E.
'Italian Villas and their Gardens' – plates, one detached, the coloured ones by Parrish, original cloth, stitching worn – 1904.
(Christie's S. Kensington) $110 £50

PARROT ON A PERCH
Orange head, green, blue and purple wings, dark grey beak – natural ground slightly stained – and two house sparrows – laid down – smudged – mounted together on a buff album leaf – pale orange border – stamped 'Sohrab Khan Khanazad Badsh Alamgir' – Mughal circa 1660.
(Christie's) $2,100 £1,000

PARTINGTON, JAMES RIDDICK
'A History of Chemistry' – 4 vol. – cloth – 8vo. – 1961-70.
(Sotheby's) $180 £85

PARUTA, PAOLO
'Politick Discourses ... by Henry Earl of Monmouth' – 1st Edn. in English – engraved portrait frontis – browning and soiling – contem. calf – worn – g.e. – folio – 1657.
(Sotheby's) $20 £10

TRAITEZ
DE
L'EQVILIBRE
DES LIQVEVRS,
ET
DE LA PESANTEVR
DE LA
MASSE DE L'AIR.
Contenant l'explication des cauſes de divers effets de la nature qui n'avoient point eſté bien connus juſques ici, & particulierem̃et de ceux que l'on avoit attribuez à l'horreur du Vuide.

Par Monſieur PASCAL.

A PARIS,
Chez GVILLAUME DESPREZ, ruë S. Iacques, à l'Image S. Proſper.
M. DC. LXIII.
AVEC PRIVILEGE DV ROY.

PASCAL, BLAISE
'Traitez de l'Equilibre et de la Pesanteur de la Masse de l'Air' – 1st Edn. – 2 folding plates – woodcut – red morocco gilt – g.e. – old ownership inscription – 12 mo. – Paris, Guillaume Desprez 1663.
(Sotheby's) $2,000 £950

PASS, CRISPEN VAN DE
'Hortus Floridus' – 2 vol, vol. 1 number 74 of 530 copies – vol. 2 number 333 of 530 copies – oblong 4to. – additional titles and full page illustrations – orig. morocco backed boards – spines worn – The Cresset Press 1928-9.
(Christie's S. Kensington) $80 £38

PASSAGES FROM MODERN BRITISH POETS
2 copies – different Edn. – etched plates by Whistler, Millais and others – orig. cloth – gilt – soiled – g.e. – 8vo. – n.d.
(Sotheby's) $145 £70

PASSIO DOMINI NOSTRI JESU CHRISTI
Number 231 of 250 copies – 6 wood engraved illus. by Eric Gill – orig. cloth – uncut – dust jacket – 4to. – 1926 Golden Cockerel Press.
(Sotheby's) $365 £175

THÈSES

DE

PHYSIQUE ET DE CHIMIE,

présentées

A LA FACULTÉ DES SCIENCES DE PARIS,

LE AOUT 1847.

Par M. L. PASTEUR.

PARIS,

IMPRIMERIE DE BACHELIER.

Rue du Jardinet, 12.

1847.

PASTEUR, LOUIS
'Theses de Physique et de Chimie' – 40 pages – slight spotting – orig. printed wrappers – soiled – 4to. – Paris, Bachelier, 1847.
(Sotheby's) $2,310 £1,100

PASTEUR, LOUIS
'Etudes sur le Vin' – 1st Edn. – 32 plates – most col – illus. in text – stamp on title – modern French half calf – uncut – 8vo. – Paris 1866.
(Sotheby's) $275 £130

PATIN, CHARLES
'Imperatorum Romanorum Numismata' – 1st Edn. – title in red and black – engraved vignette – frontis – portrait – 6 plates – 2 folding maps – contem. vellum boards – rebacked – folio – Strassburg 1671.
(Sotheby's) $80 £38

'Thesaurus Numismatum e Museo Caroli Patini ... sumptibus autoris' – engraved portrait frontis – engraved vignette on title – numerous engravings of coins and head pieces in text – contem calf – worn – 4to. – Amsterdam 1672.
(Sotheby's) $40 £20

Ad sacratiſſimam cæſaream maieſtatem, libri de die paſſionis domini noſtri Ieſu Chriſti dedicatio.
Paulus de Middelburgo, dei & apoſtolicæ ſedis gratia epiſcopus foroſempronieñſis, ſereniſſimo romanorum regi Maximiliano imperatori electo ſemper auguſto fœlicitatem optat.

Ogitanti mihi Maximiliane rex inclyte cuinam principi lucubratiũculas meas de die paſſionis domini noſtri Ieſu Chriſti conſcriptas dedicarem, uenit in mentem quod iã pridem a ueridicis & fide dignis acceperim, te in lucem huius mundi primum fuiſſe æditum ipſo die quo Chriſti ſaluatoris paſſio a chriſtianis recolebatur, quem diem ueneris ſanctum appellant: cũ ergo dies iſte a diuina prouidentia fuerit dicatus genio tuo, æquum atq; honeſtum putaui lucubratiunculas meas de eodem die cõſcriptas (quaſi tuo genio congruentes) eidem dedicare. ad quod accedit, quia apud priſcos, dies natalis regis a populo obſeruari & feſta deuotione ac ſtrenis celebrari ſolet, cum ergo non modo natalis mei ſoli princeps exiſtas, & iunioris noſtri ducis auus, uerum etiam romanorũ & germanorũ rex, quinimmo totius chriſtianæ reipublicæ imperator, Chriſtiq; ſaluatoris paſſionis cultor præcipuus ſemper fuiſti, uiſa eſt mihi tua maieſtas apprime digna cui hanc noſtram lucubratiunculam quaſi ſtrenã natali eius cõſentaneã dedicarem: ſolent enim

A

PAULUS, DE MIDDELBURGO
'De Recta Paschae Celebratione ....' – 1st Edn. – woodcut borders – full page woodcut device at end – several leaves printed in red and black – occas. foxing worming – contem. vellum boards – rebacked – folio – Fossombrone, 1513.
(Sotheby's) $925 £450

PAUZAUREK, G. E.
'Guter und Schlechter Geschmack im Kuntsgewerbe' – plates – cloth gilt – t.e.g. – 1912.
(Phillips) $65 £32

PAXTON, SIR J. AND J. LINDLEY
'Flower Garden' – 108 coloured plates – 3 vols. – 4to. – orig. cloth – 1882-84.
(Bonhams) $190 £90

PAYNE, A. H.
'Royal Dresden Gallery' – 2 vol. – engraved titles – plates – spotted – orig. cloth – rubbed – 4to. – n.d.
(Sotheby's) $400 £190

PAYNE-GALLWEY, R.
'The Book of Duck Decoys' – coloured plates – 1 folding – spotted – orig. cloth – rubbed – 8vo. – 1886.
(Sotheby's) $170 £80

PEACOCK AT HOME, THE
'A Merry Game' – complete set of 36 litho cards with illus. of Mrs Dorset's characters and 4 forfeit cards col. by hand – folding pictorial sheet – stained and split – orig. wooden box – pictorial label – John Nichols circa 1850.
(Sotheby's) $230 £110

PEACOCK, THOMAS LOVE
'The Genius of the Thames' – 2nd Edn. – engraved frontis – advert leaf at end – some browning and soiling – orig. boards – rebacked – worn – spine detached – uncut – book label of Bristol Athenaeum library – sm. 8vo. – 1812.
(Sotheby's) $65 £30

With gratefulness for your fruitful help.

Mervyn Peake.
Nov – 1941

PEAKE, MERVYN
'Shapes and Sounds' – 1st Edn. – presentation copy – inscribed by author – orig. cloth backed boards – dust jacket with design by author – 8vo. – 1941.
(Sotheby's) $135 £65

John Batchelor 'Mervyn Peake, A Biographical and Critical Exploration' – slightly rubbed dust wrapper – 1974.
(J. Ash) $8 £4

PEAKE, MERVYN – GRIMM, J. C. L. AND W. C.
'Household Tales' – col. double page and 4 plates – illus. by Mervyn Peake – some full page – orig. cloth – discoloured – dust jacket torn – 4to. – 1946.
(Sotheby's) $40 £22

PEARCE, THOMAS
'The Laws and Customs of the Stanneries in the Counties of Cornwall and Devon' – folio – full calf binding – 1725.
(Lane) $360 £170

PEARCH, G.
'A Collection of Poems in Several Hands' – 4 vols. – half titles – engraved vignettes contem. calf – labels – slightly rubbed – 8vo. – 1775.
(Sotheby Beresford Adams) $25 £12

PEEL, C.
'Somaliland; Two Expeditions into the Far Interior' – map – plates – illus. – cloth – poor – 1900.
(Bennett Book Auction) $35 £16

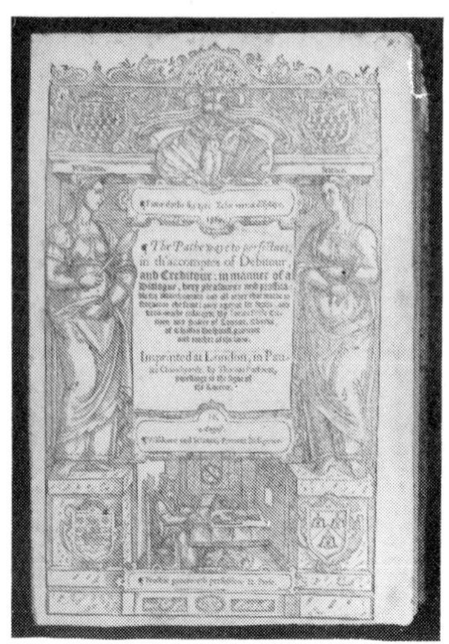

PEELE, JAMES
'The Pathe Way to Perfectnes' – title within woodcut border with portrait – partly black letter – worming – folio – T. Purfoote 1569.
(Phillips) $1,300 £620

PEETERS, J.
'Cabinet de L'Archduke Leopold 1st' – 12 portraits – 11 on horseback – 10 scenes – 138 plans on 127 sheets – old calf – oblong folio – Antwerp circa 1650.
(Phillips) $1,365 £650

PELHAM, CAMDEN
'The Chronicles of Crime' – 2 vol. – engraved addit. title – plates – some spotting – orig. cloth – worn – 1886.
(Christie's) $40 £20

PELHAM, CAVENDISH
'The World' – 2 vols. – engraved frontis – engraved maps and numerous engraved plates – contem. calf – rubbed – 4to. – 1810.
(Christie's) $170 £80

PELLIOT, PAUL
'Jades Archaiques de Chine Appartenant a M.C.T. Loo' – plates – contem. cloth – orig. front wrapper bound in at end – folio – Paris and Brussels, 1925.
(Sotheby's) $230 £110

PEMBERTON, HENRY
'A View of Sir Isaac Newton's Philiosphy' – 4to. – twelve folding engraved plates – some margins slightly browned – contemp. mottled calf – rebacked – S. Palmer, 1728.
(Christie's S. Kensington) $200 £95

PENALUNA, W.
'Historical Survey of the County of Cornwall' – 2 vols. – coloured and folding plates – orig. boards with paper labels – 1838.
(Lane) $115 £55

PENLEY, AARON
'The English School of Painting in Water Colours' – 25 chromolithographed plates – some leaves loose – orig. cloth – gilt rubbed – folio – 1868.
(Sotheby's) $40 £22

PENNANT, THOMAS
'Some Account of London' – 2nd Edn. – 4to. – engr. portrait – title vignette – 13 plates – a few folding and one folding plan – slight spotting – one leaf detached – contemp. calf – joints cracked – 1791.
(Christie's S. Kensington) $65 £30
'Tours in Wales' – 3 vol. – plates – some folding – occasional slight spotting – contemporary straight grained calf – 1810.
(Christie's S. Kensington) $125 £60
'A Tour in Scotland' – 2 vols. – full calf – 1775.
(Baitson) $40 £17

PENNEL, JOSEPH
'Pictures of the Wonders of Work' – drawings – etching and lithos – 1916.
(Baitson) $17 £8
'Pen drawings and Pen Draughtsmen' – plates and illustrations – 4to. – paper bds. – 1895.
(Bennett Book Auction) $35 £16

PENROSE ANNUAL
Vol. 25-35; 37-42-47; 51; 53; 56-63 and 65 – together 29 vol. – plates – orig. bindings – rubbed – 4to. – 1923-72.
(Sotheby's) $275 £130

PENTON, STEPHEN
'The Guardian's Instruction' – 'New Instructions to the Guardian' – 2 works in one – contem. calf – joints cracked – 12 mo. – 1688 and 1694.
(Christie's) $115 £55

PENTZ, G.
'Triumphs of Human Life' – 6 engraved plates only – cropped and mounted and 18 other engraved mounted portraits by Lombart, Vertue, Pranker and others – all mounted.
(Sotheby Beresford Adams) $90 £42

PEOPLE'S GALLERY OF ENGRAVINGS, THE
3 vols. – numerous engravings – quarto – calf gilt.
(Richard Baker & Thomson) $80 £38

PEPLER, H. D. C.
'In Petra' – preface and notes by Eric Gill and Hilary Pepler – 9 wood engraved illus. or decorations – 3 by David Jones – rest by Gill – orig. linen – paper label on upper cover – sm. 4to. – S. Dominic's Press 1923.
(Sotheby's) $180 £85

PEPYS, SAMUEL
'Diary and Correspondence' – editor Lord Braybrooke – 4 vol. – 4th Edn. – 9 engraved plates – 2 folding – contem. calf – gilt – spines rubbed – faded – g.e. – 8vo. – 1854.
(Sotheby's) $95 £45

PERCIVAL, R.
'Account of the Island of Ceylon' – 4 folding maps – calf gilt – upper cover detached – 4to. – 1803.
(Phillips) $170 £80

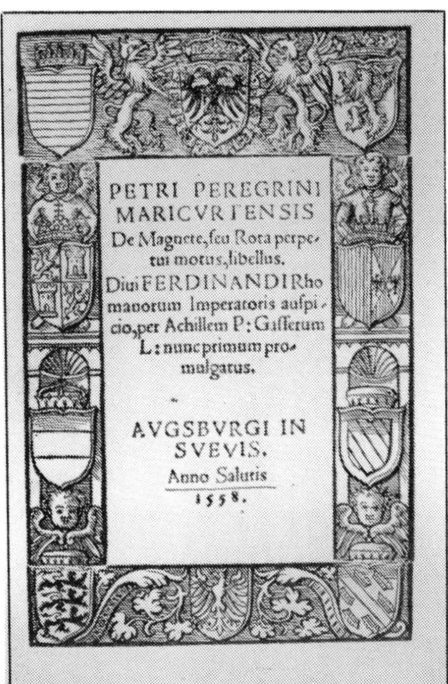

PETRI PEREGRINI MARICVRTENSIS De Magnete, seu Rota perpetui motus, libellus. Diui FERDINANDI Rhomanorum Imperatoris auspicio, per Achillem P. Gasserum L. nunc primum promulgatus.

AVGSBVRGI IN SVEVIS. Anno Salutis 1558.

PEREGRINUS, PETRUS
'De Magnete, seu Rota Perpetua Rotis' – title within woodcut armorial border – 4 woodcut diagrams – some passages underscored – Augsburg 1558.
'De Naturae Mirabilis Opusculum' – 1st Edn. – title with device in woodcut borders – 2 works in one vol. – 18th cent. calf – gilt panelled sides with arms of Jean Bouhier 1673-1746 – half red morocco case, sm. 4to.
(Sotheby's) $2,100 £1,000

PERELLE, G.
'Vues des Belles Maison de France' – 30 engraved plates of Versailles only – including fountains and gardens – without prelims – 18th cent. parchment backed boards – worn – oblong 4to. – Paris n.d.
(Sotheby Beresford Adams) $440 £210

PERRAULT, CLAUDE
'Cinderella and the Two Gifts' – col. illus. to text by E. de Beaumont – contem. red calf – joints split – rubbed – g.e. – folio – Paris 1886.
(Sotheby's) $10 £5

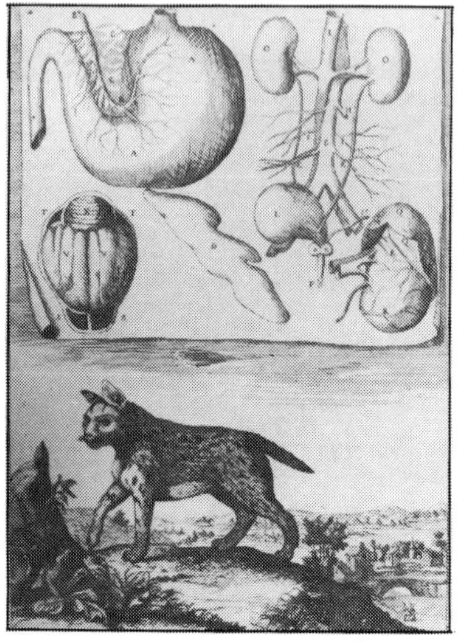

'Memoirs for a Natural History of Animals' – 1st English Edn. – title in red and black – engraved frontis – 35 plates – a few neat ms corrections – contem. red morocco panelled in gilt – slightly worn – g.e. – folio – Joseph Streater 1688.
(Sotheby's) $925 £440

PERRY, CHARLES
'View of the Levant, particularly of Constantinople, Syria, Egypt and Greece' – 1st Edn. – 20 engraved plates – 7 folding – contem. calf – rubbed – corners – worn – folio – 1743.
(Sotheby's) $210 £100

PERRY, M. C.
'Narrative of the Expedition of an American Squadron to the China Seas and Japan' – 96 plates including nude bathing scene – some coloured and folding – rebound – cloth gilt – 4to. – 1856.
(Phillips) $295 £140

'PERSIA, THE SECRET HISTORY OF'
calf gilt – 12 mo. – 1745.
(Phillips) $210 $100

PERU – BLAEU W. AND J.
Engraved map including sailing ships – compass rose and sea monsters – Latin text on verso – stained and discoloured – 376 mm x 493 mm.
(Sotheby's) $40 £18

PETERS, HARRY T.
'Currier and Ives'; 'America on Stone'; 'California on Stone' – 4 vols – some coloured – orig. cloth – 4to. – New York, 1976.
(Sotheby's) $230 £110

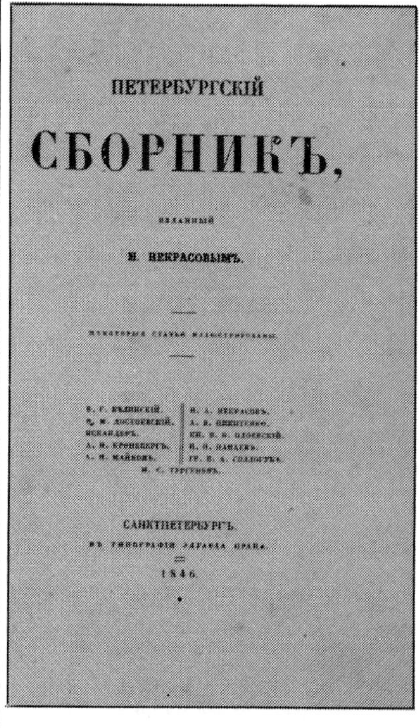

ПЕТЕРБУРГСКІЙ

СБОРНИКЪ,

Н. НЕКРАСОВЫМЪ.

САНКТПЕТЕРБУРГЪ.

1846.

PETERSBURGSKY ABORNIK
(Petersburg collection, editor N. Nekrasov) illus. by Agin and Gavarni – spotting – contem. half calf – rubbed – 8vo. – St. Petersburg 1846.
(Sotheby's) $1,260 £600

PETIT COURTIER DES DAMES
2 vol. – numerous col. plates – half morocco – 8vo. – Paris 1839-40.
(Sotheby's) $295 £140

PETIT NEPTUNE FRANCAIS, LE; OR, FRENCH COASTING PILOT
4to. – engraved frontispiece – slightly soiled and 41 charts – most folding – contemp. marbled calf – corners bumped – rebacked – 1793.
(Christie's S. Kensington) $380 £180

PETIT, VICTOR
'Bagneres de Luchon et Ses Environs' – litho title vignette and 30 litho plates – orig. cloth gilt – oblong folio – Bagneres de Luchon n.d.
(Bennett Book Auction) $160 £75

'Souvenire des Pyrenees' – coloured litho title and 44 litho plates – including title illustrations – original quarter calf – spine worn and rubbed – small folio – Paris n.d.
(Bennett Book Auction) $295 £140

PETITJEAN, C. AND WICKERT, C.
'Catalogue de L'Oeuvre Gravee de Robert Nanteuil' – 2 vols. -including 1 of plates – limited Edn. – 4to. – 1925.
(Phillips) $95 £45

PETRIDES, PAUL
'L'Oeuvre Complet de Maurice Utrillo' – 4 vols. – one of 1,000 copies – plates – original covers – slipcases – 4to. – Paris 1959-66.
(Sotheby's) $755 £360

PETTIGREW, T. J.
'A History of Egyptian Mummies' – 13 litho plates – spotted – orig. cloth backed boards – rubbed – 4to.– 1834.
(Sotheby's $135 £65

PETTUS, SIR JOHN
'Fleta Minor. The Laws of Art and Nature in Metals' – 2 parts in one – 1st Edn. – presentation copy – illus. in text – ornamental initials – browning and soiling – 19th cent. calf backed marbled boards – worn – folio – for the author 1683.
(Sotheby's) $170 £80

PEURBACH, GEORGE
'Theoricarum Novarum Planetarum' – Petit's device on title – full page woodcut sphere – woodcut diagrams in text – worming – modern cloth – folio – Paris, 1515.
(Sotheby's) $800 £380

PHELPS
'A Short History of English Literature' – – illustrated account – orig. quarter calf – very slightly rubbed – 1962.
(J. Ash) $8 £4

PHIL MAY
'The Folio' – no. 52 of 250 copies – portrait – illus. – spots – orig. parchment cloth – slightly rubbed – t.e.g. – folio – n.d.
(Christie's) $45 £22

PHILIDOR, A. D.
'Analysis of the Game of Chess' – contem. calf gilt – 1790.
(Phillips) $145 £70

PHILIP, H.R.H. THE DUKE OF EDINBURGH
'World Wildlife Crisis' – number 151 of 265 copies – signed by Prince Philip – col. plates – illus. – orig. blue morocco – g.e. – 4to. – Arcadia Press 1971.
(Christie's) $115 £55

PHILIP IV, KING OF SPAIN
'Carta Executoria de Hildalguia' in favour of three brothers of Seville in Spanish – illum. mss on vellum 102 11 – written in dark brown ink in very fine rounded gothic script – capitals calligraphically written – every page in full illum. border – very large illum initials – four full page miniatures – contem. binding of red velvet over wooden boards – seal of Philip IV in lead – all extremely fine fresh condition – in contem. fitted box of wood covered with vellum – 389 mm x 270 mm – Granada, 9 May 1626 with additions dated Seville 2 June 1626.
(Sotheby's) $18,900 £9,000

PHILLIP, A.
'Voyage to Botany Bay' – 1st Edn. – vig. title – 53 plates – some-pages loose and torn – 4to. – 1789.
(Phillips) $460 £220

PHILLIPS
'Mexico Illustrada' – no. 397 of 1000 copies – facsimile reprint – plates – text in English and Spanish – orig. calf – folio – Mexico 1965.
(Sotheby's) $460 £220

PHILLIPS, J. C.
'A Natural History of the Ducks' – 4 vols. – 74 col. plates – half red morocco gilt – t.e.g. – 4to. – 1922.
(Phillips) $2,835 £1,350

PHILLIPS, J. M.
'Jamaica; Its Past and Present State' – 1st Edn. – cloth – slightly worn – 1843.
(Bonhams) $55 £25

PHILLIPS, SIR RICHARD
'The Book of English Trades' – 72 wood engraved plates – slight browning – contem. sheep – rubbed – 12 mo. – 1821.
(Sotheby's) $335 £160

PHILOSOPHICAL THERESA, THE
2 vols. – 16 col. litho plates – early photo inserted at end – cloth – 8vo. – n.d.
(Phillips) $525 £250

PHILPOTTS, EDEN
'The Girl and the Faun' – illus. by Frank Brangwyn – signed by author – 304/350 copies – dedication by author – 1917.
(Laurenece & Martin Taylor) $40 £21
'The Dartmoor Novels' – 6 vols. – limited Edn. of 1500 copies – frontis – quarter vellum – 1927.
(Richard Baker & Thomson) $65 £30
'A Dish of Apples' – Ltd. Edn. of 500 – signed by author and artist – col. plates – by A. Rackham – orig. cloth gilt – t.e.g. – 1921.
(Phillips) $440 £210

'PHOTOGRAPHY, BRITISH JOURNAL OF'
5 volumes nos. 24 – 1877, 25 – 1878, 26 – 1879, 27 – 1880 and 33 – 1886. – with some autotype notes – half calf – marbled bds. – 4to.
(Bennett Book Auction) $75 £36

PICART, BERNARD
'The Ceremonies and Religious Customs of the Various Nations of the Known World' – 7 vols. in six – titles in red and black – engraved vignette – numerous engraved plates – half titles – occas. worming – contem. speckled calf – gilt – joints split – folio – 1733-39.
(Sotheby's) $1,155 £550

PICASSO – JACOB, MAX
'Le Siege de Jerusalem' – no. 22 of 85 copies on papier de Hollande – signed by Picasso and Jacob – 3 plates by Picasso – original wrapper – Paris, Henry Kahnweiller 1914.
(Sotheby Parke Bernet) $2,975 £1,420

PICASSO, PABLO
'Avant Garde, Picasso's Erotic Gravures' – illustrations after Picasso – original wrappers – 4to. – New York, 1969.
(Christie's S. Kensington) $30 £15

Mounted portrait after Man Ray – signed by photographer – illus. – one col. errata lead – orig. wrappers – soiled – spine torn – 4to. – Paris n.d.
(Christie's) $100 £48

Full length photograph of Picasso in bathing trunks – signed in ballpoint – 7¼ x 5 inches.
(Sotheby's) $315 £150

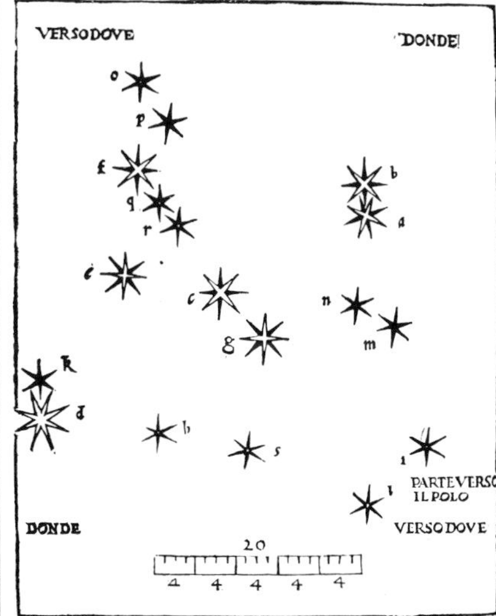

PICCOLOMINI, ALESSANDRO
'De La Stella del Mondo ....' – 2 parts in one vol. – 1st Edn. – device on titles – woodcut diagrams – full page star maps – dampstaining – marginal notes – underscoring – ownership inscriptions – contem. vellum – stained – modern bookplate – half red morocco case – sm. 4to. – Venice, 1540.
(Sotheby's) $1,155 £550

PICCOL PASSO, CIPRIANO
'The Three Books of the Potter's Art' – 1 of 750 plates – orig. cloth – dust jacket – folio – 1934.
(Sotheby's) $180 £85

PICIONI, MATHEO
'A Series of Plates Depicting the Arch of Constantine' – folio – 21 engr. plates – mounted on guards – one torn and neatly repaired modern vellum – slightly soiled – Rome circa 1650.
(Christie's S. Kensington) $95 £45

PICTORIAL HISTORY OF ENGLAND, THE
7 vol. – new Edn. – engraved plates – some spotting – coloured maps – contemp. calf – spines gilt – joints slightly rubbed – 1855-58.
(Christie's S. Kensington) $105 £50

PICTURE POST
Vol. 1-75 – complete set – some special numbers included – first 7 in publisher's cloth – remainder orig. wrappers – some soiled – 4to. – October 1 1938 – June 1 1957.
(Sotheby's) $565 £270

'PICTURESQUE EUROPE'
5 volumes – steel engraved plates – half morocco gilt – n.d.
(Bennett Book Auction) $240 £115
Odd Volume – 'British Isles' – 13 steel engraved plates, inc. Edinburgh – cloth – 4to. – circa 1878.
(Bennett Book Auction) $17 £8

PICTURESQUE REPRESENTATIONS OF THE DRESS AND MANNERS OF THE ENGLISH
1st Edn. – 50 hand col. aquatint plates after Pyne – contem. straight grained green morocco – spine gilt – slight wear – 8vo. – 1814.
(Sotheby's) $210 £100

PICTURESQUE ROUND GAME OF THE PRODUCE AND MANUFACTURES OF THE COUNTIES OF ENGLAND AND WALES
Engraved sheet mounted on linen with aquatint pictorial map – col by hand – slightly soiled – book of rules in orig. folder – splits in joints – 660 mm x 516 mm – E. Wallis circa 1830.
(Sotheby's) $315 £150

PICTURESQUE VIEWS OF THE PRINCIPAL SEATS OF THE NOBILITY AND GENTRY IN ENGLAND AND WALES
98 plates – some stained – sm. oblong folio – old calf – 1787-88.
(Bonhams) $275 £130

PIGANIOL DE LA FORCE, JEAN AIMAR
'Nouvelle Description de la France' – 7 vols. 2nd Edn. – red and black – engraved frontis – numerous folding engraved plates – maps – hand col. in outline – red morocco labels – contem. mottled calf – spines gilt – 8vo. – Paris chez Theodore Legras 1722.
(Christie's) $275 £130

PIJOAN, J.
'History of Art' – 2 vols. – plates – cloth – 1933.
(Phillips) $40 £20

PINELLI, BARTOLOMEO
'Istoria Romana Incisa all Acqua Forte' – engraved frontis – 100 plates – spotted and dampstained – contem. half morocco – rubbed – joints split – oblong folio – Rome n.d.
(Sotheby's) $145 £70
'Cinquanta Vedute dei Costumi Popolari e Piu Interessanti di Roma' – 50 engraved plates only – some soiled – contem. wrappers – torn – folio – Rome circa 1836.
(Sotheby's) $630 £300

PINERO, ARTHUR W.
'The Second Mrs Tanqueray'- orig. cloth slight marks etc. – 1895.
(J. Ash) $34 £16

PINKERTON, ALLAN
'Claude Melnotte as a detective and other stories' – fifteen thousand, manuscript dedication on front free-end paper by the author to Sir John Duke, Baron Coleridge, Lord Chief Justice, plates, original decorated cloth, soiled – 1880.
(Christie's S. Kensington) $27 £12

PINKERTON, J.
'Petralogy, a Treatise on Rocks' – 2 vols. – engraved title vignettes – contem. calf – joints cracked – 1811.
(Christie's) $45 £22

PINKERTON, JOHN
'A General Collection of the Best and Most Interesting Voyages and Travels in all Parts of the World' – 17 vols. – numerous engraved plates and maps – some folding – contem. calf – spine rubbed – 4to. – 1808-14.
(Christie's) $565 £270

PINNA
'Defensio' – 18th cent. Italian binding of brown morocco gilt with arms – folio – 1729.
(Moore Allen & Innocent) $715 £340

PINNOCK, W.
'The Golden Treasury' – 72 engravings on 18 leaves – staining – quarter morocco worn – 12 mo. – 1842.
(Phillips) $60 £28

PINTER, HAROLD
'Five Screenplays' – limited Edn. of 150 copies only – signed and numbered by the author – 1971.
(J. Ash) $65 £32

PIOZZO, HESTER LYNCH
'Anecdotes of the Late Samuel Johnson' – 1st Edn. – half title – spotting – contem. half calf – rubbed – 8vo. – 1786.
(Sotheby's) $250 £120
'Letters to and from the Late Samuel Johnson' – 2 vols. – 1st Edn. – full tree calf – 1788.
(Lane) $135 £65

PIPER, JOHN
'The Quest' – design for a backdrop – gouache and brush and ink – 31.2 cm x 60.3 cm.
(Sotheby's) $2,100 £1,000

PIPER, JOHN – ANTHONY WEST
'John Piper' – one of 136 copies – this 1 of 10 with orig. watercolour by Piper – signed and numbered – tipped in frontis – col. plates – illus. – orig. morocco – t.e.g. – slipcase – 4to. – 1979.
(Christie's) £420 £200

PIRELLI PIN UP CALENDAR
12 col. photographic illus. – folio – 1973.
(Sotheby Beresford Adams) $20 £10

Lucien arrive de sa conférence avec Bensusan
il lui a dit ce qu'il m'avait dit; il ne désire attendre
6 mois que pour que Lucien ait le temps de réfléchir à
sa conversion, décidément il nous prend pour des
imbéciles. Je ne sais ce qui va se décider. Moi je crois
qu'il ne faut pas attendre 6 mois, vu que d'un
côté comme de l'autre cela n'avancera à rien.
Ecris moi quelle est la personne qui veut bien
te prêter l'argent et combien.
nous t'embrassons tous les trois
embrasses les enfants et crois moi ton
mari affectionné
C. Pissarro

PISSARRO, CAMILE
Good auto letter signed 3 pages quarto, to his wife Julie describing the progress of his work – London June 1892.
(Sotheby's) $800 £380

PITCHFORD, DENYS WATKINS
8 scraper board designs depicting dwarfs by a river – signed – card mounts – 209 mm x 148 mm – 1942.
(Sotheby's) $345 £165

PITMAN, SIR ISAAC
'The Art and Practice of Printing' – 26 parts and 3 binders – 1932/3.
(Baitson) $4 £2

PITT, MOSES
'The English Atlas' – 4 vols. – calf very worn – portrait and 170 maps – mostly double page – some stained – 2 covers loose – folio – 1680-83.
(Irelands) $9,240 £4,400

PITT, MOSES AND STEPHEN SWART
'Bohemia' – 2 engraved maps – title cartouches – armorials – various sizes – 1680.
(Sotheby's) $20 £10

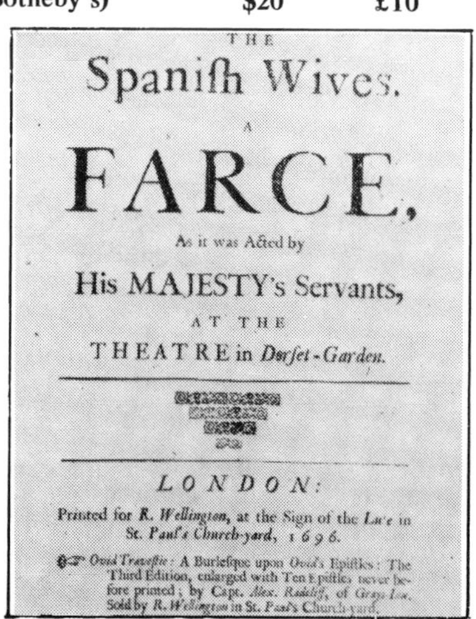

THE

Spanish Wives.

A

FARCE,

As it was Acted by

His MAJESTY's Servants,

AT THE

THEATRE in *Dorset-Garden.*

LONDON:

Printed for *R. Wellington*, at the Sign of the *Lute* in St. *Paul's Church-yard*, 1696.

Ovid Travestie: A Burlesque upon *Ovid's* Epistles: The Third Edition, enlarged with Ten Epistles never before printed; by Capt. *Alex. Radcliff*, of *Grays Inn.* Sold by *R. Wellington* in St. *Paul's* Church-yard.

PIX, MARY
'The Spanish Wives' – 1st Edn. – stains – recent morocco backed boards – sm. 4to. – 1696.
(Christie's) $190 £90

PLANCHE, J. R.
'A Cyclopaedia of Costume' – 2 vol. – 4to. – 42 plain and 24 chromolithographed plates – a very few affected by adherance of tissue guards – morocco backed cloth – slightly soiled – upper – cover of vol. 2 affected by damp – 1876-9.
(Christie's S. Kensington) $115 £55

PLANTA DELLA CITTA DI ROMA
With 16 views on 32 sections mounted on linen – folded – Rome 1827.
(Bonhams) $55 £25

PLATH, SYLVIA
'Crystal Gazer and Other Poems' – no. 272 of 400 – frontis piece by author – grey morocco – geometric design – navy suede doublures – palladian edges – fitted case – signed with initials inside lower cover by Sally Lou Smith (1978) – Rainbow Press, 1971.
(Sotheby's) $965 £460

PLATTES, GABRIEL
'A Discovery of Subterranean Treasure' – 22 pp paper discoloured – stains – new cloth – uncut – 8vo. – sold by booksellers of London and Westminster 1715.
(Sotheby's) $20 £10

PLIMSOLL, SAMUEL
'Our Seamen – An Appeal' – 1st Edn. – most leaves loose – orig. cloth – 1873.
(Lane) $55 £26

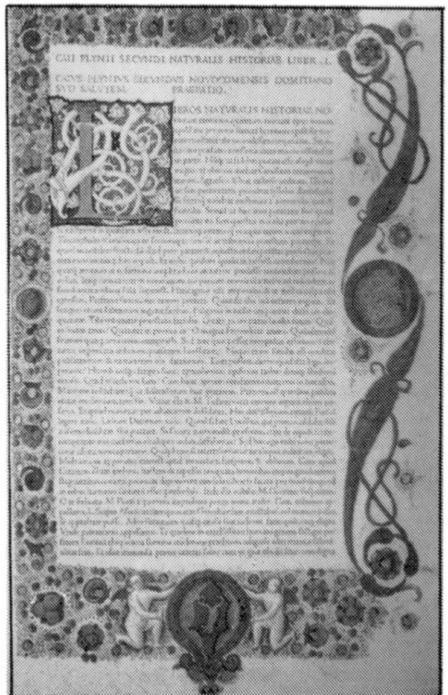

PLINIUS SECUNDUS, GAIUS
'Historia Naturalis' – 355 leaves and 50 lines – roman letter – very fine renaissance border of flowers and fruit etc. – marginal stains and minor wormholes – exceptionally large and clean copy – 18th cent. red morocco panelled in gilt – splits – rubbed – folio – Venice 1472.
(Sotheby's) $19,320 £9,200

PLINY THE ELDER
'Naturalis Historiae' – 3 vol. – engraved frontis – cloth – soiled – Leiden and Rotterdam 1669.
(Christie's) $65 £30

PLOMER, H. R.
'Wynkyn de Worde' – illus. cloth – t.e.g. – 1925.
(Phillips) $65 £30

PLOMER, WILLIAM
'Museum Pieces' – repaired dust wrapper – 1952.
(J. Ash) $12 £6

PLON, E.
'Benvenuto Cellini' – illus. by P. le Rat – 4to. – half morocco (worn) – Paris, 1883.
(Bonhams) $100 £48

PLOT, ROBERT
'The Natural History of Oxfordshire' – 2nd Edn. – plates – no map – contem. panelled calf – joints split – rubbed – folio – Oxford 1705.
(Sotheby's) $105 £50

PLUCHE, N.A.
'Spectacle de la Nature or Nature Displayed' – vols. 3-6 only – 106 plates mostly folding – of plants, ships etc. – calf – 8vo. – 1740-48.
(Phillips) $80 £38

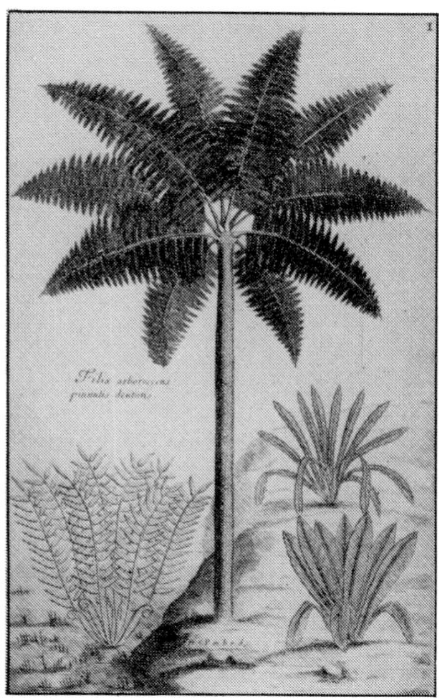

PLUKENET, LEONARD
'Phytographia' – 7 works bound in 5 vols. – 1st Edn. – portrait – engraved titles – 454 botanical plates – half morocco or calf – rebacked – folio and 4to. – 1691-1705.
(Christie's) $1,430 £680

PLUMIER, CHARLES
'L'Art de Tourner' – French and Latin text – title in red and black – engraved vignette – addit. engraved title – 72 plates – 1 folding – browning – contem. calf – rebacked – worn – from library of Earl of Essex with his monogram gilt – folio – Paris, Claude Jombart 1701.
(Sotheby's) $840 £400

PLUTARCH
'Les Vies des Hommes' – 6 vols. – 'Decade Contenant les Vies des Empereurs' – 'Les Oeuvres Morales' – 7 vols. – 14 vols. – altogether – rubricated – illustrated by 22 plates after Marillier and others from 1783 Edn. – a very nice copy in late 18th cent. French red morocco gilt – g.e. – 8vo. – 1567/1567/1574.
(Sotheby Parke Bernet) $5,390 £2,570

PLUTARCH'S MORALS
5 vol. four engraved frontispiece – contemp. calf – joints worn – 1685-90.
(Christie's S. Kensington) $65 £32

PLUVINEL, ANTOINE DE
'L'Exercice de Monter a Cheval' – engraved port. frontis – 5 folding plates – contem calf – gilt spine – 8vo. – Paris 1660.
(Christie's) $210 £100

POCHAT, G.
'Figur und Landschaft' – plates – cloth – 4to. – 1973.
(Phillips) $40 £20

POCOCKE, RICHARD
'A Description of the East and Some Other Countries' – 2 vols. – 2 parts in vol 11 – 1st Edn. – titles with engraved vignettes – 178 engraved plates – maps and plans – folding – engraved dedication – browning – contem. calf – spines gilt – folio – 1743-45.
(Sotheby's) $800 £380

POE, E.A.
'Tales of Mystery and Imagination' – plates – some col. – by Harry Clarke cl. – some wear – 4to. – 1928.
(Phillips) $65 £30

POETRY LONDON – NICHOLAS MOORE (Editor)
'The PL Book of Modern American Short Stories' – titling on spine faded – Editions Poetry London 1945 (1946).
(J. Ash) $8 £4

POGANY, WILLY – WAGNER, RICHARD
'The Tale of Lohengrin' – coloured plates and illustrations by Pogany – orig. cloth – slightly soiled – boxed.
(Christie's S. Kensington) $95 £45
'The Rime of the Ancient Mariner' – 20 col. plates – illus – decorations and ornamental text by Pogany – orig. cloth – gilt – rubbed – t.e.g. – 4to. – 1910.
(Sotheby's) $125 £60

POGRABSKI, ANDREJ
'Poloniae Litvaniae Descriptio' – hand coloured engraved map – 13½ x 19 inches – framed and glazed – 1570 or later.
(Christie's S. Kensington) $105 £50

POINSETT, J. R.
'Notes on Mexico' – folding map on linen – half title – modern calf backed boards – rubbed – 8vo. – 1825.
(Sotheby's) $190 £90

POLE, MATTHEW
'Synopsis Criticorum Aliorumque Sacrae Scripturae' – 5 vols. – titles in red and black – woodcut device – contem. blind stamped vellum – vol. 1 not uniform – gilt arms added on sides of vols. II-V – spines rubbed and soiled – folio – Utrecht 1684-86.
(Sotheby's) $125 £60

POLEHAMPTON, E. AND J. M. GOOD
'The Gallery of Nature and Art' – 6 vol. – 93 engraved plates – contem. calf – rubbed – 1821.
(Christie's) $55 £25

POLEY, A. F. E.
'St. Paul's Cathedral' – 2nd Edn. – inscribed by author – plates and illus. – half morocco – gilt – t.e.g. – folio – 1932.
(Phillips) $65 £30

POLITICAL SKETCHES
Album containing 83 uncol. satirical cartoons published by Fores, McLean and others – half calf – oblong folio – circa 1840.
(Phillips) $95 £45

POLLARD, A. W. AND REDGRAVE G. R.
'A Short Title Catalogue of Books' – original cloth backed boards – 4to. – The Bibliographical Society, 1946.
(Christie's S. Kensington) $65 £30

POLLOCK, ALSAGER
'The Cockpit of Europe' – slight staining along fore-edges of covers – 1913.
(J. Ash) $12 £6

POLWHELE, R.
'Traditions and Recollections' – 2 vols. – 1st Edn. in half calf – 1826.
(Lane) $100 £48

POLYEN AND SEXTUS JULIUS FRONTIUS
'Les Ruses De Guerre .. Avec Les Stratagesmes' – 2 vol. – contem. mottled calf – gilt – spines slightly chipped – Paris 1739.
(Christie's S. Kensington) $45 £22

POLYNESIA
Hand col. map with vignettes – mounted – J. Tallis circa 1850.
(Phillips) $40 £20

PONOFSKY, ERWIN AND OTHERS
'Die Deutsche Plastik' – 5 vol. – various – plates – orig. boards and uniform cloth – 4to. – Leipzig, Florence and Munich, 1924-6.
(Christie's S. Kensington) $160 £75

PONSONBY, THE LADY EMILY
'Violet Osborne' – three vol. – rebound in contemp. half morocco – very slightly rubbed – some foxing – 1865.
(J . Ash) $75 £36

POOR LAW COMMISSIONERS' REPORT...
'On an Inquiry into the Sanitary Conditions of the Labouring Population of Great Britain' – plates and plans – some folding – some leaves browned – orig. cloth – rubbed – 8vo. – 1931.
(Sotheby's) $335 £160

POPE, ALEXANDER
'An Essay on Man' with notes by William Warburton – engraved frontispiece after the author – advertisement leaf at end – contemp. calf – rubbed – 1745.
(Christie's S. Kensington) $65 £30

POPE, A. UPHAM
'An Introduction to Persian Art' – plates – orig. cloth – 8vo. – 1930.
(Sotheby's) $17 £8
'A Survey of Persian Art' – 7 vols. including index – plates – some col. – illus. – orig. cloth – slightly faded – folio and 8vo. – 1938-58.
(Sotheby's) $1,575 £750

PORNY, M. A.
'The Elements of Heraldry' – 5th Edn. – 24 engraved plates – cont. marbled calf – rebacked – old spine – laid down – 1795.
(Christie's S. Kensington) $40 £20

ASPICIT ET INSPICIT
IO. BAPT. PORTAE
NEAPOLITANI
MAGIAE NATVRALIS
LIBRI XX.
Ab ipso authore expurgati, & superaucti, in quibus scientiarum Naturalium diuitiæ, & delitia demonstrantur

I De mirabilium rerum causis.
II De varijs animalibus gignendis.
III De nouis plantis producendis.
IIII De augenda supellectili.
V De metallorum transmutatione
VI De gemmarum adulterijs.
VII De miraculis magnetis.
VIII De portentosis medelis.
IX De mulierum cosmetice.
X De extrahendis rerum essentijs.
XI De myropœia.
XII De incendiarijs ignibus.
XIII De raris ferri temperaturis.
XIIII De miro conuiuiorum apparatu.
XV De capiendis manu feris.
XVI De inuisibilibus literarum notis.
XVII De catoptricis imaginibus.
XVIII De staticis experimentis.
XIX De pneumaticis.
XX Chaos.

CVM PRIVILEGIO.
NEAPOLI, Apud Horatium Saluianum. D. D. LXXXVIIII.

PORTA, GIOVANNI BATTISTA DELLA
'Magiae Naturalis' – title in woodcut border with portrait of author – woodcut illus. and diagrams – numerous woodcut initials and headpieces – spotting – staining – notes – half red morocco case – folio – Naples, 1589.
(Sotheby's) $800 £380

PORTER, KATHERINE ANNE
'Collected Stories' – New Edn. with preface by author – dust wrapper – 1967.
(J. Ash) $6 £3

PORTER, P. E. B.
'Around and About Saltash' – 1st Edn. – limited – long presentation description from author – 1905.
(Lane) $90 £44

PORTER, ROBERT KER
'Travelling Sketches in Russia and Sweden' – 2 vols. in one – 41 engraved and aquatint plates – some hand col. – folding – some offset – modern half calf – earlier spine laid down – rubbed – 4to. – 1809.
(Sotheby's) $650 £310

THE PORTFOLIO, AN ARTISTIC PERIODICAL editor P. G. Hamerton
Numerous plates – 75 vols. – blue cloth – gilt – one vol. waterstained – folio – 1876-1881.
(Bonhams) $380 £180

PORTRAIT OF A COURTIER
Inscribed to Manohar, slightly rubbed and creased – laid down – border of nasta'liq calligraphy applied in gold and polychrome ground on a Shahjehan muraqqa folio decorated with birds and animals – minor staining and edges defective – Mughal circa 1590-1605.
(Christie's) $9,450 £4,500

PORTRAIT OF A DAPPLED GREY STALLION
Attributable to Sheikh Muhammed Amir – inscribed in English below 'Sheikh Muhammed Amir , Calcutta at Koryah 1840' – black division and margin – white leaf – 22.9 cm x 28.8 cm. – Calcutta circa 1840.
(Christie's) $670 £320

PORTRAIT OF A EUROPEAN LADY
Wearing low necked white dress and feathered cap – blue ground – oval format – gold margin – black leaf trimmed – 24.1 cm x 18.3 cm – Mewar circa 1770.
(Christie's) $545 £260

PORTRAIT OF NUR JEHAN
Richly jewelled with pearls, rubies and emeralds and holding a wine glass – drawing with colour – a few small holes – trimmed – laid down – 36 cm x 25.5 cm – Bikaner circa 1750.
(Christie's) $2,310 £1,100

PORTRAIT OF AN OLD MULLAH
Drawing with touches of colour – minor worming and staining – inscribed Farrokh Beg – broad black nasta'liq inscribed on gold and polychrome floral ground – on a Shahjehan muraqqa folio decorated with sprays of flowers – clouds – blooms and green foliage outlined in gold – slightly stained and defective – Mughal circa 1620-50.
(Christie's) $6,720 £3,200

PORTRAIT OF A PRINCE
Holding a sarpach – drawing with touches of colour on the face upper right corner restored – rebacked – 26.5 cm x 20.4 cm – Kishangarh circa 1750.
(Christie's) $545 £260

POSSOZ, MILY – LARBAUD, VALERY
'Caderno' – 8 etched plates by Possoz – slightly spotted – original wrappers – uncut – 8vo. – Paris. Au Sans Pareil. 1927.
(Sotheby's) $420 £200

POSTCARDS
Bundle Tuck Oilettes (39) – including Harry Payne military – and 100 unused views in original envelopes.
(Bennett Book Auction) $40 £20

POST OFFICE
Collection of approx. 200 Parliamentary Blue Books on Postage, Stamp Duty etc. – a few folding maps – soiled – disbound – folio – circa 1820-60.
(Sotheby's) $3,045 £1,450

POSTLETHWAYT, MALACHY
'The Universal Dictionary of Trade and Commerce' – 2 vols. – 3rd Edn. – trans. from Savary des Brulons – titles in red and black with engraved vignettes – frontis – 24 folding maps – contem. speckled calf – gilt – worn – folio – 1766.
(Sotheby's) $145 £70

POTTER, BEATRIX
Margaret Lane: 'The Tale of Beatrix Potter' – plates – some coloured – 1948.
(J. Ash) $8 £4

POTTER, BEATRIX – WEATHERLEY, FREDERICK
'A Happy Pair' – 6 col. illus. by Potter with initials H. B. P. – orig. pictorial wrappers – slightly soiled and worn – g.e. – 16 mo. – Hildesheimer and Faulkner, circa 1890.
(Sotheby's) $3,885 £1,850

POTTER, STEPHEN
'The Theory and Practice of Gamesmanship' – chipped dust wrapper – 1947.
(J. Ash) $12 £6

POTTS, THOMAS
'The British Farmer's Cyclopaedia' – 2nd Edn. – engr. additional title and 41 plates – 22 hand coloured – one detached – some spotting – contemp. half calf – worn – 4to. – 1807.
(Christie's S. Kensington) $115 £55

POULET, W.
'Atlas on the History of Spectacles' – vol. 1 only of 2 De Luxe Edn. – orig. half morocco – 4to. – Bonn, 1978.
(Sotheby's) $45 £22

POULSON, GEORGE
'The History and Antiquities of Holderness' – 2 vols. – engravings – folding maps etc. – 1840.
(Baitson) $380 £180
'The History and Antiquities of Beverley' – 2 vols. in one – engravings – folding pedigrees – 1829.
(Baitson) $125 £60

POUPEE ..... LES DIMANCHES DE LA
Engraved title – 16 col. plates with text orig. pictorial boards – oblong 8vo. – circa 1840.
(Phillips) $90 £42

POWELL, J.
'Views in Egypt' – 24 folding litho plates – some torn – folding engraved map – no text – orig. boards – worn – folio – circa 1810.
(Sotheby's) $210 £100

POWELL-COTTON, MAJOR
'In Unknown Africa' – plates 2 maps – orig. cloth – 1904.
(Phillips) $90 $42

Microſcopical Obſervations.

OBSERVAT. XXIII.

Of the little greeniſh Graſshopper or Locuſt, bred upon the backside of green leaves, eſpecially the leaves of Gooſberries, Sweet briar, and golden Mouſear, in April *and beginning of* May.

POWER, HENRY
'Experimental Philosophy in Three Books' – 1st Edn. – 1 folding plate – woodcuts in text – soiling and staining – 19th cent. calf over which has been laid an early 16th cent. Flemish blind stamped binding – rather wormed – half red morocco case – contem. ownership inscription – 1664.
(Sotheby's) $1,510 £720

POWYS, JOHN COWPER
'In Defence of Sensuality' – 1st English Edn. – 1930.
(J. Ash) $20 £10

POWYS, LLEWELYN
'A Baker's Dozen' – covers a little dull and soiled – good – 1941.
(J. Ash) $8 £4

'Glory of Life' – no. 66 of 277 copies – wood engraved frontis – 13 illus. by Robert Gibbings – orig. vellum backed cloth – soiled – t.e.g. – 4to. – 1934.
(Sotheby's) $4,620 £2,200

POWYS, T. F.
'Rosie Plum' – illustrations and dust wrapper by John Ward – 1966.
(J. Ash) $12 £6

POYNTING, F.
'Eggs of British Birds' – col. plates – contem. half morocco rubbed – 4to. – 1895-96.
(Sotheby's) $40 £20

POZZO, ANDREA
'Rules and Examples of Perspective Proper for Painters and Architects' – folio – engraved frontispiece – two titles – one full page illustration – 100 plates only – text in Latin and English – a few leaves detached – old half calf – worn – printed for J. Senex and R. Gosling – n.d.
(Christie's S. Kensington) $200 £95

PRAISSAC, LE SIEUR DU
'Les Discours et Questions Militairs' – new Edn. – woodcut title – laid down with a little loss – plans and decorations – soiling – worming and a few tears – with loss – margins frayed – contemp vellum – rubbed – stitching shaken – Rouen, 1636.
(Christie's S. Kensington) $55 £25

PRATT, ANNE
'Flowering Plants, Grasses, Sedges and Ferns of Great Britain' – 6 vols. – colour plates – half morocco gilt – F. Warne – n.d.
(Phillips) $14 £7

PRATTENT, THOMAS AND M. DENTON
'The Virtuoso's Companion and Coin Collector's Guide' – 8 vols. in one – engraved titles – frontis – 238 of 240 engraved plates – orig. boards – disbound – 8vo. – 1797.
(Sotheby Beresford Adams) $40 £18

PRENTICE, A.
'Renaissance Architecture and Ornament in Spain' – 60 plates – cloth – folio – Batsford circa 1893.
(Bennett Book Auction) $30 £14

PRESCOTT, WILLIAM H.
'History of the Conquest of Peru' – 2 vol. portraits – map – contemporary half morocco – joints cracked – 1847.
(Christie's S. Kensington) $10 $5

PRESENTS FOR GOOD GIRLS
12 engraved illus. col. by hand – stained – torn and frayed – orig. printed wrappers – soiled and worn – 12 mo. – Tabert and Co. 1804.
(Sotheby's) $65 £32

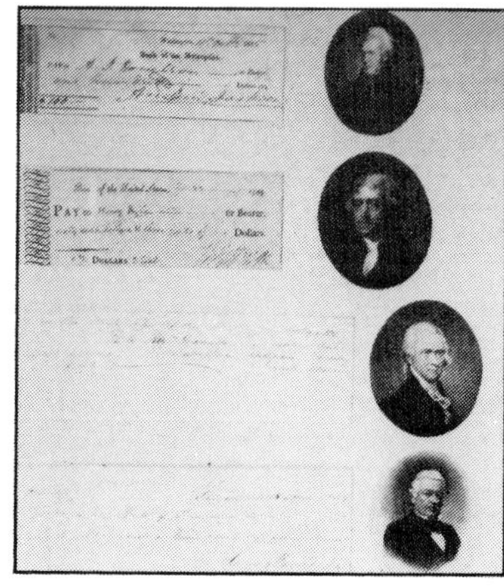

PRESIDENTIAL CHECKS
Andrew Jackson, 1835; Thomas Jefferson, 1793; Alexander Hamilton 1794; James Buchanan, 1834.
(Robert Skinner) $3,300 £1,570

PRESLEY, ELVIS
Photograph of Presley in military uniform in a car, signed in blue ball point – with another – 5½ x 3½ inches.
(Sotheby's) $210 £110

PRESTON, SIR LIONEL
'Sea and River Painters of the Netherlands' – plate – orig. cloth – faded – 8vo. – 1937.
(Sotheby's) $85 £40

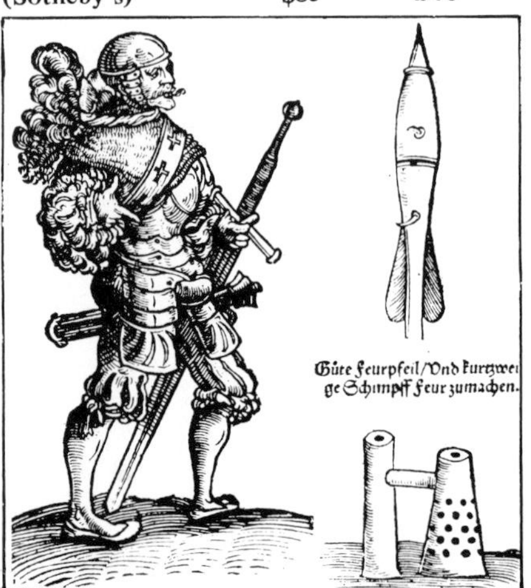

PREUSS, JACOB
'Ordnung, Namen, und Regiment alles Kreigs Volcks' – 1st Edn. – 4 leaves – gothic letter – 3 woodcuts on title – modern boards – bookplate of the Prince of Liechenstein – sm. 4to. – Strassburg 1530.
(Sotheby's) $630 £300

PRETTY PORTRESS, THE OF WINDSOR LODGE
3 engraved plates – presentation leaf – morocco backed boards – worn – 12 mo. – William Darton circa 1825.
(Sotheby's) $25 £12

PRICE, LAKE
'Exteriors and Interiors in Venice' – 11 mounted hand col. plates of 25 – soiled – orig. morocco backed cloth – worn – folio – 1843.
(Sotheby's) $95 £45

PRICE, RICHARD
'Observations on Reversionary Payments' – 1st Edn. – contemporary calf – rubbed – 8vo. – 1771.
(Sotheby's) $200 £95

'Observations on Reversionary Payments' – 2nd Edn. – calf gilt – 1772.
(Phillips) $125 £60

'Additional Observations on the Nature and Value of Civil Liberty and the War With America' – sheep – defective – 12 mo. – Dublin 1777.
(Sotheby's) $360 £170

PRICE, WILLIAM
'Archaeologia Cornu Britannica' – 1st Edn. very fine uncut copy – rebound in full calf gilt – 1790.
(Lane) $190 £90

PRICHARD, H. H.
'Through the Heart of Patagonia' – col. frontis – maps – plates – orig. cloth gilt – 1902.
(Phillips) $65 £32

PRICHARD, J. C.
'Natural History of Man' – 50 coloured plates – half calf gilt – worn – 1848.
(Phillips) $85 £40

PRICKE, ROBERT
'An Excellent Introduction to Architecture' – woodcut device on title – 7 full page engravings – adverts – 18th cent. parchment backed boards – slightly worn – spine torn – folio – 1670.
(Sotheby Beresford Adams) $460 £220

PRIESTLEY, JOSEPH
'The History and Present State of Electricity with Original Experiments' – 2nd Edn. – corrected and enlarged – 8 plates – 2 charts – errata slip at end – 3 pp catalogue of books on electricity – 2 pp of works of Priestley – contem. calf worn – hinges cracked – 4to. – J. Dodsley 1769.
(Sotheby's) $145 £70

'Heads of Lectures on a course of Experimental Philosophy, particularly including chemistry' – 12 mo. – contemp. marbled calf – worn – Dublin, 1794.
(Christie's S. Kensington) $95 £45

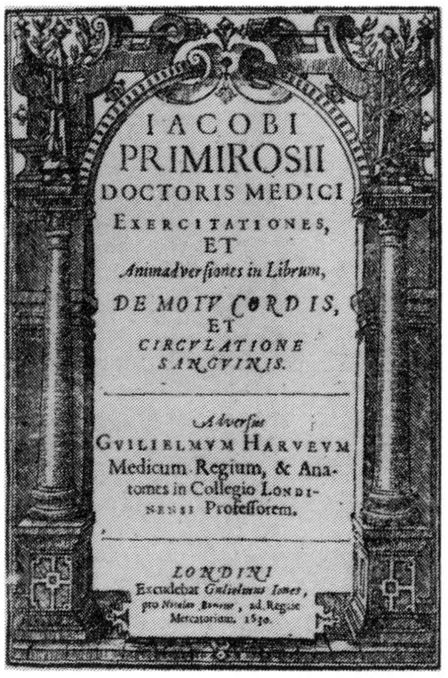

PRIMEROSIUS, JACOBUS
'Exercitationes, et Animadversiones in Librum de Motu Cordis' – 1st Edn. – title in woodcut border – tears and holes – red morocco gilt by Zaehnsdorf – sm. 4to. – 1630.
(Sotheby's) $1,300 £620

PRINCE, JOHN
'Worthies of Devon' – uncut leaf edges – good copy – 1810.
(Lane) $40 £20

PRINGLE, JOHN
'Observations on Diseases of the Army, in Camp and Garrison' – 3 parts in one vol. – 1st. Edn.. – contem. calf gilt – rubbed – 8vo. – 1752.
(Sotheby Beresford Adams) $250 £120

PRINT COLLECTORS' QUARTERLY, THE
Vol. 2 no. 2-3; vol.. 3 no.1-3; vol. 4 no. 1 & 4; vol. 8 no. 1-8; vol. 19 no. 2-3; vol. 20; vol. 21 no.1-2; vol. 23 no. 1 & 3 and 2 indexes and 5 duplicates – together 67 vols. – orig. wrappers – some torn and loose – 8vo.- 1912-36.
(Sotheby's) $400 £190

PRIORATO, G. G.
'Historia di Ferdinando Terzo Imperatore' – title in red and black – 62 engraved portraits – dampstains – vellum – folio – Vienna 1672.
(Phillips) $135 £65

PRISSE D'AVENNES, E.
'The Oriental Album' – col. title – 31 litho plates – spotted – contem. half morocco – rubbed – folio – 1846.
(Sotheby's) $460 £220

PRITCHARD, JAMES COWLES
'The Natural History of Man' – 3rd Edn. – 52 plates only – 46 hand col. – spotting – contem. calf – rubbed – t.e.g. – 1848.
(Christie's) $65 £30

PRITCHARD, W.
'Picturesque Scenery in North Wales' – 10 lithographed plates – 29 extra illustrations – several dampstains – half morocco – – worn – hinges cracked – part of spine lacking – 4to. – n.d.
(Christie's S. Kensington) $285 £135

PRITT, T. E.
'Book of the Grayling' – 3 col. plates – orig. calf gilt – 4to. – Leeds 1888.
(Phillips) $105 £50

PROCTOR, R.
'Bibliographical Essays' – no. 79 of 200 copies – orig. morocco backed cloth – 8vo. – 1905.
(Sotheby's) $180 £85

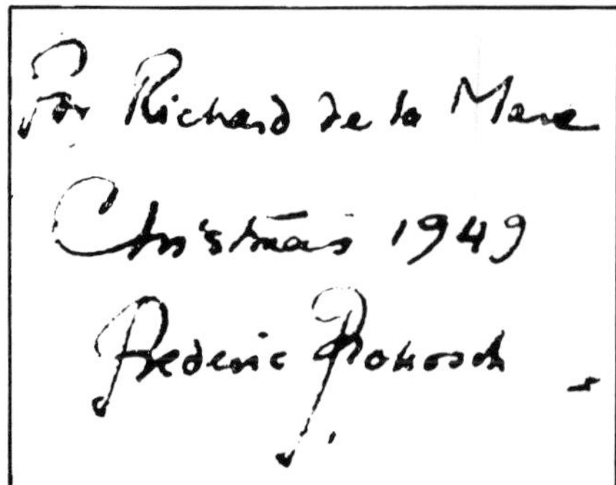

PROKOSCH, FREDERICK
'Snow Song' – 1st Edn. – limited to 44 copies of which this is 4 of 10 – bound in Florentine paper – presentation copy – inscribed by author to Richard de la Mare – orig. wrappers – 8vo. – Paris 1949.
(Sotheby's) $45 £22

PROPERT, W. A.
'The Russian Ballet' – plates – orig. cloth backed boards – rubbed – 4to. – 1921.
(Sotheby's) $220 £105

PTOLEMY
'Almagestum' – 1st complete Edn. – gothic letter – woodcut diagrams in margins – fine woodcut initials – printer's device in red and black – small repair – modern half brown morocco – folio – Venice 1515.
(Sotheby's) $2,520 £1,200

PROUT, SAMUEL
'Prout's Microcosm' – 'The Artist's Sketch Book' – 24 litho plates – advert leaf at end – orig. cloth – spine faded – joints split – folio – 1841.
(Sotheby's) $135 £65

PUNCH
Vol. 1-100 and various later vol. in 51 vol. various bindings – most worn – 4to. – 1841-1920.
(Christie's S. Kensington) $230 £110

Vol. 1-100 and Spielmann's 'History of Punch' – in 26 vol. – contemp. half morocco – worn – some covers and spines loose – in fitted slipcase – 4to. – 1841-95.
(Sotheby's) $315 £150

PUTEO, PARIS DE
'Duello Libro de Re Imperatori' – woodcut title – repaired without loss – soiling – worming – vellum soiled – 8vo. –Venice 1521.
(Christie's) $55 £25

PYE, CHARLES
'Provincial Copper or Tokens Issued between the years 1787 and 1796, London and Birmingham' – engr. title – spotted and 36 plates after Pye – some spotting – contemp. half calf – rubbed – rebacked with old spine laid down – n.d.
(Christie's S. Kensington) $125 £60

PYNE, J. B.
'Lake Scenery of England' – chromolithographed title and 24 plates – some slight spotting and dampstaining – original cloth by Leighton Son & Hodge – slightly soiled – g.e. – sm. Folio – n.d.
(Christie's S. Kensington) $95 £45

PYNE, W. H.
'Etchings of Rustic Figures' – 60 plates – half calf – 1815.
(Phillips) $135 £65

'Microcosm or a Picturesque Delineation of the Arts, Agriculture, Manufactures etc.' – vol. 2 only – 62 plates – orig. boards – oblong folio – 1806.
(Phillips) $315 £150

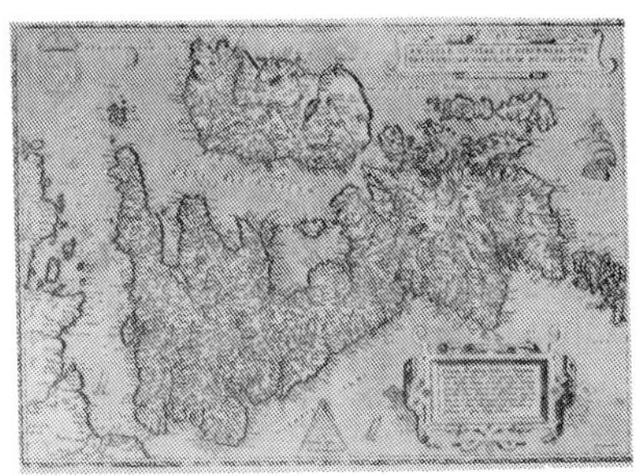

QUAD, MATTHEW AND J. BUSSEMECHER
'Europae Totius Orbis Terrarum Partis Praestantissimae' – engraved architectural title – 66 double page engraved maps – text in Latin on versos – medallion portraits – etc – some hand col. – early mss note – calf – line and roll tooled borders – centre ornaments – traces of gilding – gauffered and gilt edges – sm. folio – Cologne 1594-96.
(Sotheby's) $6,300 £3,000

QUARLES, FRANCIS
'Divine Fancies Digested into Epigrammes Meditations and Observations' with the initial and final blanks – some spotting and staining – modern calf – sm. 4to. – 1641.
(Sotheby's) $145 £70

'Emblems' – engraved title and plates – soiled – leaves torn – contem. calf – worn – 1669.
(Christie's) $40 £18

THE QUARTERLY REVIEW
58 vol. various in 57 – contemp. – half calf – rubbed – spine chipped – ex-library copies – 1824-66.
(Christie's S. Kensington) $65 £30

QUAYLE, ERIC
'The Collectors' Book of Books' and 'The Collectors' Book of Detective Fiction' .. –
(Laurence & Taylor) $30 £14

QUEEN'S THEATRE
Bill for Queen's Theatre, Hull, for 1st June 1868.
(Baitson) $65 £30

QUESTION AND ANSWER CARDS
40 engraved cards of 50, each with a question or answer – lacking 3, 4, 5, 11 and 21 and answers no. 11, 14, 16, 20 and 23 – slightly soiled – 55 mm x 45 mm – Germany circa 1700.
(Sotheby's) $230 £110

QUESTIONS–DEVINETTES
Series 1, 2, 3, and 4 (11 parts) – 14 vol. in all – each with 9 illustrations including one on upper cover – 5 coloured – orig. pictorial wrappers – 8vo. – Epinal circa 1910.
(Sotheby's) $30 £15

QUINCY, J.
'Compleat English Dispensatory' – calf gilt – 8vo. – 1722.
(Phillips) $125 £60

QUINTINYE, J. DE LA
'Complete Gard'ner' – 2 vols. in one – frontis – 10 folding plates – some worming – calf gilt – 8vo. – 1701.
(Phillips) $115 £55

QUINTUS, CURTIUS
'De Rebus Gestis Alexandri' – 18th cent. red morocco binding with brown morocco quatrefoil centrepiece – 16 mo. – Amsterdam 1628.
(Moore Allen & Innocent) $135 £65

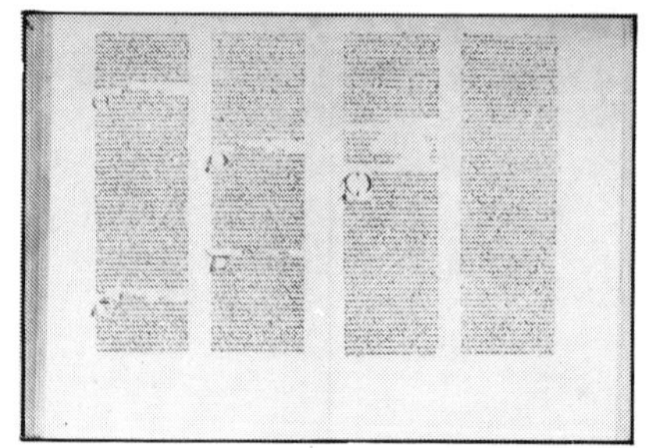

RABANUS, MAURUS
'De Universo' – 1st. Edn. – 168 leaves of 170 – 56 lines roman letter – 2 columns – some worming – but generally excellent copy – 18th cent. Dutch calf – panelled in gilt – slightly rubbed – g.e. – half red morocco case – folio – Strassburg 1467.
(Sotheby's) $19,320 £9,200

RABBULA GOSPELS (editor by C. Ceccheli and others)
Limited Edn. – plates – orig. calf – folio – Olten and Lausanne 1959.
(Sotheby's) $170 £80

RACINET, M.A.
'Le Costume Historique' – 6 vols. – 500 plates – some coloured – later morocco backed boards – very slightly rubbed – sm 4to. – Paris, 1888.
(Sotheby's) $755 £360

RACING CALENDAR
Vol. 1-199 – contem. calf – earlier vols. rubbed and cracked – later vols. faded – 1773-1971.
(Christie's) $630 £300

RACKHAM, ARTHUR
'Peter Pan Portfolio' – limited Edn. – signed by publisher and engraver – 11 coloured mounted plates of 12 – half vellum gilt – folio – n.d.
(Phillips) $400 £190

'The Legend of Sleepy Hollow' by Washington Irving – many illus. by Rackham – coloured and others tipped in – col. dust cover cloth gilt – 1928.
(Richard Baker & Thomson) $75 £36

'Some British Ballads' – 4to. – 16 mounted coloured plates – by Rackham – orig. cloth – slightly soiled – n.d.
(Christie's S. Kensington) $55 £25

'The Fairy Tales of the Brothers Grimm' – 4to. – 40 mounted coloured plates by Rackham – one slightly creased – orig. cloth – spine faded and slightly torn – 1909.
(Christie's S. Kensington) $115 £55

Ink and watercolour drawing of Puck with Bottom's head – signed and dated 1908 – framed and glazed – 134 mm x 184 mm.
(sotheby's) $2,625 £1,250

RACKHAM, ARTHUR – BARRIE, J. M.
'Peter Pan in Kensington Gardens' – 4to. – mounted coloured frontispiece and plates by Rackham – orig. cloth – slightly rubbed and soiled – 1906.
(Christie's S. Kensington) $105 £50

RACKHAM, ARTHUR – BIANCO, MARGERY WILLIAMS
'Poor Cecco' – 4to. – 7 mounted coloured plates by Rackham – orig. cloth – slightly soiled – 1925.
(Christie's S. Kensington) $65 £32

RACKHAM, ARTHUR – LA MOTTE FOUQUE, F. H. C. DE
'Undine' – 15 mounted coloured plates by Rackham – one detached – some leaves slightly spotted – orig. cloth – spine faded and rubbed – 4to. – 1909.
(Christie's S. Kensington) $60 £28

RACKHAM, ARTHUR – SHAKESPEARE WILLIAM
'A Midsummer Night's Dream' – 4to. – 39 mounted coloured plates by Rackham – only original cloth – joints rubbed – 1919.
(Christie's S. Kensington) $60 £28

RACKHAM, ARTHUR – SWINBURNE, A. C.
'The Springtide of Life' – 4to. – eight coloured plates by Rackham – orig. cloth – spine slightly faded – 1918.
(Christie's S. Kensington) $45 £22

RACKHAM, BERNARD
'Islamic Pottery and Italian Majolica' – plates – some col. – orig. cloth – dust jacket – 8vo. – 1959.
(Sotheby's) $125 £60

RADCLIFFE, A.
'Mysteries of Udolpho' – 4 vols – 2nd Edn. – some pages loose – calf gilt – 12 mo. – 1794.
(Phillips) $90 £42

RADCLIFFE, ALEXANDER
'The Ramble' – 1st Edn. – red morocco by Riviere – upper joint split – 8vo. – for the author 1682.
(Sotheby's) $180 £85

RADCLIFFE, JOHN
'Ashgill or the Life and Times of John Osborne' – 1900.
(Baitson) $2 £1

RADCLIFFE, M.
'A Modern System of Domestic Cookery' – 2 parts in one vol. – engraved title – frontis – 11 engraved plates – some defects – contem. calf gilt – worn – 8vo. – Manchester 1824.
(Sotheby Beresford Adams) $65 £32

RADCLYFFE, C. W.
'Memorials of Westminster School' – litho title – 11 plates – spotted – orig. half calf – worn – folio – n.d.
(Sotheby's) $210 £100

'Memorials of Charter House' – title and 13 lithoplates – folio – half morocco worn – 1844.
(Bonhams) $65 £30

RADEMAKER, ABRAHAM
'Kabinet van Nederlandsche Outheden en Gezichten' – 2 vols – engraved and printed titles – first in French – text in Dutch, French and English – 300 engraved views – later russia gilt – joints torn – 4to. – Amsterdam 1725-31.
(Sotheby Beresford Adams) $2,520 £1,200

RADEN, WOLDEMAR
'Switzerland' – illus. by A. Closs – orig. cloth gilt – 4to. – 1878.
(Phillips) $545 £260

RADER, MATTHEW
'Bavaria Sancta' – 3 parts in one vol. – 3 engraved titles and plates by R. Sadeler – full crimson morocco gilt – g.e. – folio – 1615-27.
(Phillips) $180 £85

RADFORD, G.
'Rambles by Yorkshire Rivers' – no. 4 of 12 copies – plates in 2 states signed by artist – orig. parchment boards – rubbed – sm. 4to. – Leeds n.d.
(Sotheby's) $85 £40

RAFFALD, ELIZABETH
'The Experienced English Housekeeper' – 12th Edn. – engraved title – three folding plates – slightly torn – spotting and soiling – modern half calf – 1799.
(Christie's S. Kensington) $65 £32

RAFFLES, SIR THOMAS STANFORD
'Antiquarian, Architectural and Landscape Illustrations of the History of Java' – 1st Edn. – complete with all full page col. and other plates – orig. cloth binding – 1844.
(Lane) $180 £85

RAILWAY MAGAZINE, THE
Vols. 1-121 lacking 92 and 93 – in 119 vols. – plates – illus. – orig. or cont. cloth – few rubbed – 8vo and 4to – 1897-1975.
(Sotheby's) $2,100 £1,000

RAILWAY MAP OF CENTRAL EUROPE
Railways from Edinburgh, London and Dublin – litho – orig. colour – 410 x 510mm. – Bartholomew 1860.
(Tooleys) $20 £10

RAILWAYS later RAILWAY WORLD
Vols. 1-32 – plates – illus. – some coloured – modern cloth – 4to and 8vo – 1939-71.
(Sotheby's) $170 £80

RAIMONDO, EUGENIO
'Le Caccie delle Fiere Armate ... et deigli Animali Quadrupedi, Volatili, and Acquatici' – 1st Edn. – 7 full page woodcuts – full calf gilt – 8vo. – Brescia, 1621.
(Phillips) $610 £290

RAINBOW ANNUAL, THE
for 1937, 1939 and 1940 – 3 vols.
TIGER TIM'S ANNUAL
1939 and 1940 – 2 vols. – plain and col. illus. – orig. cloth backed pictorial boards – with 22 others.
(Sotheby's) $65 £30

RAINE, JAMES
'The History and Antiquities of North Durham' – engraved frontis – numerous plates – some foxing – cont. calf – t.e.g. – folio – 1852.
(Christie, Manson & Woods) $85 £40

RALEIGH, WALTER
'Historie of the World' – 5 books – 2 titles – one engraved – 8 double page maps – cont. panelled calf rebacked – thick folio – 1st Edn. – 1614.
(Bennett Book Auction) $180 £85

RAMELLI, AGOSTINO
'Le Diverse et Artificiose Machine' – 1st Edn. – text in Italian and French – engraved title with portrait of author – 195 full and double-page engravings – some staining and discolouration – cont. limp vellum – gilt – soiled – folio – Paris, 1588.
(Sotheby's) $5,670 £2,600

RAMSAY, ALLEN (Editor)
'The Evergreen, being a Collection of Scots Poems Wrote by the Ingenious before 1600' – 1st Edn. – 2 vols. – soiling – booklabel of John Rutherford of Edgerston – cont. calf – rubbed – 8vo – Edinburgh, 1724.
(Sotheby's) $210 £100

RAMSAY, ANDREW MICHAEL
'Histoire de Vicomte de Turenne' – 2 vols. – engraved portrait – 12 folding plates – dampstains – cont. mottled calf – worn – 4to – Paris, 1735.
(Sotheby's) $125 £60

RAMSDEN, LADY GWENDOLEN
'A Smile within a Tear and Other Fairy Stories' – plates by Bertha Newcombe – orig. decorative cloth – 1897.
(J. Ash) $10 £5

RANJITSINGH, K. S.
'The Jubilee Book of Cricket' – plates – orig. cloth – soiled – 1897.
(Christie's) $55 £25

RANKING, JOHN
'Historical Researches on the Conquest of Peru, Mexico . . . by the Mongols' – without supplement – 4 engraved plates – 2 folding maps – author's inscription – text repaired – modern half morocco – 1827.
(Christie's) $115 £55

RANSOME, ARTHUR
'The Imp and the Elf and the Ogre' – illustrated – spine a little faded – covers stained at edges – nice copy – 1910.
(J. Ash) $40 £18

RAPIN, RENE
'Gardens . . . four books made English by John Evelyn Junior' – 1st Edn. in English – second issue – arms of Lord Arlington – John Evelyn's bookplate – 19th century panelled calf – g.e. – 8vo – 1673.
(Sotheby's) $460 £220

RASTALL, W. DICKINSON
'A History of the Town and Church of Southwell' – engraved plates – some spotted – cont. calf – rebacked – 4to – 1787.
(Sotheby's) $125 £60

RAVEN, SIMON
'The Feathers of Death' – nice copy – 1959.
(J. Ash) $10 £55

RAVILIOUS, ERIC
'The Wood Engravings' – limited Edn. – no. 11 of 188 – illus. – orig. grey buckram with design by Ravilious on upper cover – folio – 1972.
(Sotheby's) $115 £55
'The Wood Engravings' – limited Edn. – facsimiles – orig. cloth – slipcase – folio – Lion and Unicorn Press, 1972.
(Sotheby's) $145 £70

RAY, JOHN
'Methodus Plantarum' – 1st Edn. – bound in full calf – good copy – 1733.
(Lane) $55 £26

RAY, PRAPHULLA CHANDRA
'A History of Hindu Chemistry from the Earliest Times to the Middle of the Sixteenth Century' – 2 vols. – 2nd Edn. of vol. 1, 1st Edn. of vol. 2 – slip with reviews – presentation copy – half roan – 8vo – Calcutta and London 1903-09.
(Sotheby's) $75 £35

RAYE, CHARLES
'A Picturesque Tour Through the Isle of Wight' – 1st Edn. – 24 hand col. plates – orig. half red roan – label on upper cover – slight wear – oblong 4to – 1825.
(Sotheby's) $735 £350

RAYET, OLIVIER AND COLLIGNON, MAXIME
'Histoire de la Ceramique Grecque' – 16 col. plates – illus. – spotted – cont. vellum backed boards – soiled – orig. wrappers preserved – 4to – Paris, 1888.
(Sotheby's) $55 £25

RAYLEIGH, LORD AND RAMSAY, SIR WILLIAM
'Argon, a new Constituent of the Atmosphere' – 1st American Edn. – 43pp new cloth – 4to – Washington, Smithsonian Institute, 1896.
(Sotheby's) $10 £5

RAYNAL, G. T. F.
'Histoire Philosophique et Politique' – 7 vols. – 7 frontis – 7 folding maps – errata leaves – waterstains – 2 maps with tears – cont. calf – gilt – rubbed – bookplate of Lord Forbes – The Hague, 1774.
(Sotheby's) $95 £45

RAYNER, S.
'The History and Antiquities of Haddon Hall' – 30 lithographed plates only of 32, 29 mounted on india paper – some spotting – original cloth – worn – g.e. – large 4to – Derby, Robert Moseley, 1836.
(Christie's S. Kensington) $25 £12

READE, CHARLES
'The Cloister and the Hearth' – illus. by Byam Shaw – 1909.
(Baitson) $10 £5

REAGAN, RONALD (40th President of the U.S.A.)
Photograph of Reagan when a film star – signed and inscribed 'Good Luck' – postcard 5½ x 3½in.
(Sotheby's) $115 £55

REAUMUR, R. A. F. DE
'The Art of Hatching and Bringing Up Domestick Fowls' – 15 folding plates – modern calf backed boards – London, 1750.
(Phillips) $360 £170
'Natural History of Bees' – trans. from French – 12 folding plates – cont. calf gilt – 1744.
(Phillips) $160 £75

REBUS CARDS
24 of 25 engraved cards each with motto – 5 key cards – orig. case – ink stained – Paris, circa 1830.
(Sotheby's) $85 £40

RECEUIL DES MEDITATIONS SUR LES MYSTERES DE LA RELIGION
Ms on 330pp with decorative title incorporating royal arms in watercolour – French binding – 8vo – blue morocco slipcase.
(Moore Allen & Innocent) $1,995 £950

RECORDE, ROBERT
'The Castle of Knowledge' – 1st Edn. – fine allegorical woodcut title – numerous diagrams – slight soiling – cont. marginal notes in English – modern half blue morocco – early signature of William Gyfford – folio – Reginald Wolfe, 1556.
(Sotheby's) $3,715 £1,770
'Arithmetick or the Grounds of Arts' – slightly spotted and soiled – lacks first leaf – cont. calf – joints split – 8vo – 1654.
(Sotheby's) $135 £65

RECORD OF THE UNIVERSITY BOAT RACE COMMEMORATION DINNER 1881
No. 17 of 250 copies – three plates – orig. cloth – rubbed – 4to – 1883.
(Christie's S. Kensington) $95 £45

RECORDING BRITAIN
4 vols. – illus. after Russell Flint, John Piper and others – orig. cloth – spine slightly faded – sm. 4to – 1946-49.
(Sotheby's) $30 £15

RECUSANCY
Collection of 17th century pamphlets mostly concerned with Roman Catholic recusancy.
(Phillips) $170 £80

RED RIVER SETTLEMENT, PAPERS RELATING TO
3 maps, 2 folding – disbound – folio – 1819.
(Sotheby's) $275 £130

REDDING, CYRUS
'An Illustrated Itinerary of the County of Cornwall' – 1st Edn. in fine morocco binding – heavily gilt.
(Lane) $80 £38

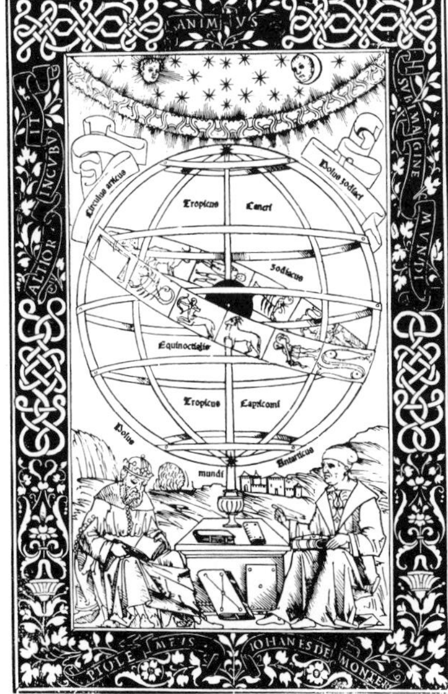

REGIOMONTANUS, JOHANNES
'Epitoma in Almagestum Ptolemaei' – 1st Edn. – 108 leaves of 110 – 48 lines and headline – gothic letter – woodcuts – diagrams – initials – worming – 19th century half russia gilt – folio – Venice, 1496.
(Sotheby's) $6,300 £3,000

REEVE
'England's Restitution'; 'England's Backwardness'; 'A Cedar's Sad and Solemn Fall' – 3 vols. in one – cont. English binding of brown morocco gilt with the royal arms on the cover – traces of ties – 4to – 1661.
(Moore Allen & Innocent) $840 £400

REGULATIONS AND INSTRUCTIONS RELATING TO HIS MAJESTY'S SERVICE AT SEA
Cont. tree calf – slightly worn – 4to – 1808.
(Sotheby Beresford Adams) $115 £55

Walter de la Mare
from
Forrest Reid

27 Oct. 1916.

REID, FORREST
'The Spring Song' – 1st Edn. – presentation copy, inscribed by author to Walter de la Mare – orig. cloth – spine rubbed – 8vo – 1916.
(Sotheby's) $95 £45
'Young Tom' – orig. cloth boards – very faintly spotted – 1944.
(J. Ash) $10 £5

REID, JOHN
'Turkey and the Turks' – hand coloured illus. – orig. cloth – soiled – 1842.
(Baitson) $30 £15

REINHARD, JOSEPH
'A Collection of Swiss Costumes' – 30 finely col. plates – cont. half morocco gilt – 4to – circa 1830.
(Sotheby's) $2,520 £1,200

REISH, J. D.
A collection of 76 coloured lithographs issued as supplementary cartoons with 'United Ireland' – a few slightly spotted and frayed – various sizes – 1884-94.
(Sotheby's) $115 £55

AEPITOMA OMNIS PHYLOSOPHIAE. ALI|AS MARGARITA PHYLOSOPHICA TRACTANS
de omni genere scibili: Cum additionibus: Quę in alijs non habentur.

REISCH, GREGORIUS
'Aepitoma Omnis Phylosophiae' – 2nd Edn. – 287 leaves – large woodcut on title – numerous woodcut illus. – diagrams – some full page and several coloured by hand – folding map of the world with Hebrew grammar of C. Pellicanus – red morocco gilt – g.e. – sm. 4to – Strassburg, 1504.
(Sotheby's) $2,100 £1,000

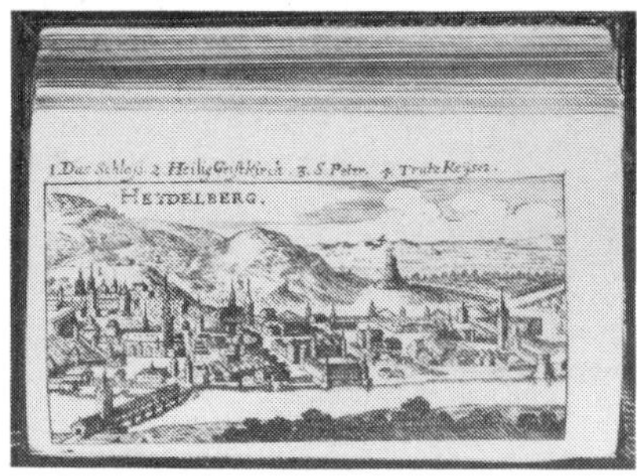

REISS GESERT DURCH OBERUND DEUTSCHLAND
Double page engraved title – 116 town plans, Antwerp, Baden, Berlin, Bonn, Dresden etc. – full morocco gilt – g.e. – 12 mo. – Christoff Riegels, Nuremberg, 1686.
(Phillips) $8,820 £4,200

RELANDUS, HADRIANUS
'Palestina ex Monumentis Veteribus Illustrata' – title in red and black – device – engraved portrait – 10 maps, 3 folding – 3 engraved plates – folding table – cont. vellum boards – 4to – Nuremberg, 1716.
(Sotheby's) $505 £240

RELIGIOUS TRACTS
'A Collection of 29 Tracts' – in 7 vols. – including two major works by such authors as Comber and Bossuet – majority cont. calf – one modern half calf – several worn – 4to and folio.
(Sotheby's) $315 £150

REMARQUE, E. M.
'All Quiet on the Western Front' – Charles Keeping illustrations – Folio Society – 1966.
(J. Ash) $10 £6

REMEMBRANCES FOR ORDER AND DECENCY IN THE UPPER HOUSES OF PARLIAMENT
Ms on 191pp. – cont. straight grained red morocco gilt with arms of George III – 8vo – 1803.
(Moore Allen & Innocent) $210 £100

RENAN, ERNST
'Priere sur L'Acropole' – one of 45 copies – brown morocco – gilt edged – from the library of Marcel Pognon – Paris Pelletan, 1899.
(Sotheby Parke Bernet Monaco) $1,765 $950

RENNELL, JAMES
'Memoir of a Map of Hindoostan' – 4 engraved maps – spotting – cont. calf – rubbed – joints split – 4to – 1788.
(Christie's S. Kensington) $55 £25

REPORT OF COLLEGE OF ENGINEERING IMPERIAL UNIVERSITY OF TOKYO, No. 7 DECORATION OF PALACE BUILDINGS OF PEKING
No. 110 of 1,000 copies – oblong folio, Tokyo, 1906 – plates – some mounted and coloured – unbound as issued – in orig. portfolio.
(Christie's S. Kensington) $180 £85

REPORT OF THE COMMITTEE OF THE SOCIETY OF ARTS . . . RELATIVE TO THE MODE OF PREVENTING THE FORGERY OF BANK NOTES
6 engraved plates, one folding – orig. boards – soiled – backstrip torn – 1918.
(Christie's S. Kensington) $85 £40

REPORT OF THE CRUISE OF THE U.S. REVENUE CUTTER 'BEAR' AND THE OVERLAND EXPEDITION FOR THE RELIEF OF WHALERS IN THE ARCTIC OCEAN
Plates – orig. cloth – 8vo – Washington, 1899.
(Sotheby's) $40 £20

REPTON, H.
'Observations on the Theory and Practice of Landscape Gardening' – 1st Edn. – 27 plates, 13 hand col., 14 with overslips including 2 text illus. – some repairs – 2 plates mounted on linen – one extra plate inset – modern half morocco – 4to – 1803.
(Phillips) $1,680 £800

RESTIF DE LA BRETONNE, NICHOLAS EDME
'Monument du Costume Physique et Moral de la Fin du Dix Huitieme Siecle' – 1st Edn. – 26 engraved plates by Moreau and Freudeberg – plates mounted – some soiled – red morocco by Pagnant – gilt – large folio – Neuwied, 1789.
(Sotheby's) $7,350 £3,500

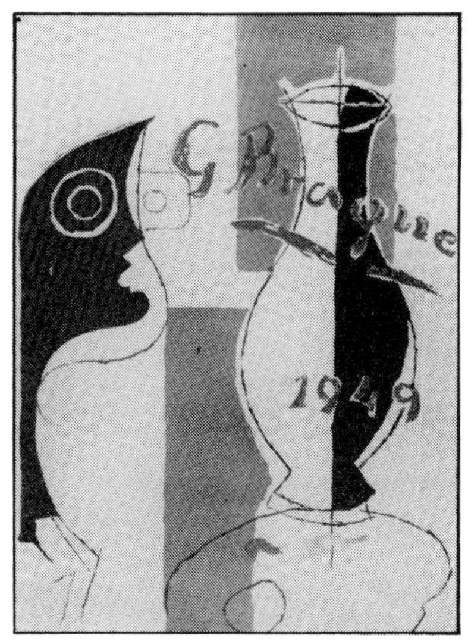

REVERDY, PIERRE – BRAQUE, GEORGES
'Une Aventure Methodique' – 27 lithos in black by Braque – 11 col. – half vellum – orig. wrappers bound in – uncut – folio – Paris, Maeght, 1950.
(Sotheby's) $360 £170

REYNOLDS, JAMES (Publisher)
'Pictorial Atlas of Arts, Sciences, Manufactures and Machinery' – coloured title, vignette and frontis – 32 plates only, most coloured, one detached – a few cleanly torn – cont. half morocco – slightly rubbed.
(Christie's S. Kensington) $55 £25

REYNOLDS, SIR JOSHUA
'Engravings from the Works' – 3 vols. – plates – spotted – cont. half morocco – rubbed – folio – n.d.
(Sotheby's) $505 £240

REYNOLDS, S. W.
'Engravings from the Pictures & Sketches painted by Sir Joshua Reynolds' – one vol. only – engraved title – dedication – portrait – detached and 116 plates – some spotting and light dampstains – cont. half morocco – worn – upper cover detached – spine torn with loss – folio – Bayswater, July 1820.
(Christie's S. Kensington) $315 £150

REYNST, GERARD
'Variorum Imaginium' – engraved title and 34 plates – names of artists and engravers inserted in ms – mostly engraved by Cornelius Vischer – cont. mottled calf – spine rubbed – folio – Amsterdam, circa 1661.
(Christie Manson & Woods) $1,365 £650

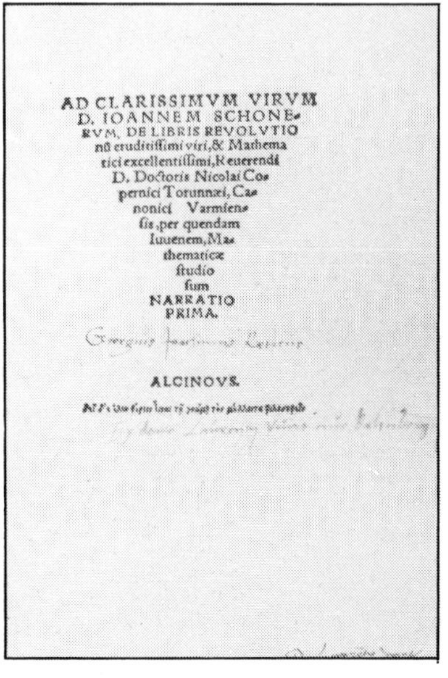
AD CLARISSIMVM VIRVM
D. IOANNEM SCHONE-
RVM, DE LIBRIS REVOLVTIO
nũ eruditissimi viri, & Mathema
tici excellentissimi, Reuerendi
D. Doctoris Nicolai Co-
pernici Torunnæi, Ca-
nonici Varmien-
sis, per quendam
Iuuenem, Ma-
thematicæ
studio
sum
NARRATIO
PRIMA.

ALCINOVS.

RHETICUS, GEORG JOACHIM
'De Libris Revolutionum . . . Doctoris Nicolae Copernici' – 1st Edn. – 38 leaves – limp vellum – half red morocco case – sm 4to – Danzig, 1540.
(Sotheby's) $157,500 £75,000

RHIND, WILLIAM
'A History of the Vegetable Kingdom' – engraved portrait – additional title and 41 plates, 32 hand coloured – slight soiling – cont. half morocco – rubbed – 4to – Glasgow, 1860.
(Christie's S. Kensington) $125 £60

RIBEYRO, J.
'Histoire de L'Ile de Ceylan' – title in red and black – folding map – 7 folding plates – cont. calf, gilt – Amsterdam, 1701.
(Phillips) $115 £55

RICCARDI, PIETRO
'Biblioteca Matematica Italiana' – 2 vols. – Milan, Gorlich editore – orig. cloth – 1952.
(Christie's S. Kensington) $80 £38

RICCIOLI, GIAMBATTISTA
'Almagestum Novum Astrononiam Veterem Novamque Complectens' – in 2 vols. – 1st Edn. – engraved frontis by F. Curtus to each vol. – 2 double page engraved lunar maps – numerous woodcut diagrams – some browning – worming – cont. calf – gilt – rebacked – old spines laid down – folio – Bologna, 1651.
(Sotheby's) $1,720 £820

RICE, HAROLD
'Encyclopaedia of Silk Magic' – 3 vols. – illus. by Francis Martineau – orig. cloth – 8vo – Armore and Wynnewood, Pa 1948-62.
(Sotheby's) $40 £18

RICH, CLAUDIUS JAMES
'Narrative of a Residence in Koordistan' – 2 vols. – 13 plates – maps – some folding – one torn – later calf backed boards – recased – 8vo – 1836.
(Sotheby's) $200 £95

RICHARD II
Vellum deed with original seal, 1400 – Henry VII part of vellum document, circa 1485, with seal (broken) and 2 nos. Suite des Nouvelles Ecclesiastiques – 1799.
(Bennett Book Auction) $45 £22

RICHARDS, WALTER
'Her Majesty's Army' – Parts 1, 3 (2 copies) and 4 of 4 – coloured titles and 28 plates – orig. cloth – rubbed – g.e. – 4to – n.d.
(Sotheby's) $65 £30

RICHARDS, WILLIAM
'The Universal Library of Trade and Commerce' – 7 parts in one – engraved title and 93 plates – 3 folding of 'the Compleat Penman' – staining – cont. calf – worn – 4to – 1747-53.
(Sotheby's) $145 £70

RICHARDSON, C. AND OTHERS
'Racing at Home and Abroad' – limited Edn. – 3 vols. – plates – orig. morocco – rubbed – 4to – 1923-31.
(Sotheby's) $145 £70

RICHARDSON, CHARLES JAMES
'Studies from Old English Mansions' – 4 vols. – litho titles and 132 plates – folding – hand coloured – cont. morocco backed cloth – rubbed – loose – folio – 1841-48.
(Sotheby's) $170 £80
'Studies of Ornamental Design' – 2 parts in one – litho title and plates – spotting – library stamps – orig. cloth – rebacked – worn – folio – 1851.
(Sotheby's) $75 £35

RICHARDSON, GEORGE
'A Book of Ceilings' – title and text in English and French – 48 engraved plates by George Richardson – cont. boards – uncut – soiled – folio – 1776.
(Christie Manson & Woods) $800 £380

RICHARDSON, HENRY HANDEL
'Maurice Guest' – very slightly rubbed endpapers worn at hinges – good copy – 1908.
(J. Ash) $8 £4

RICHARDSON, J.
'Travels in the Great Desert of Sahara' – 2 vols. – 3 plates of 4 – folding map – illus. – spotting – cont. calf – rubbed – 8vo – 1848.
(Sotheby's) $40 £18

RICHARDSON, SIR JOHN AND OTHERS
'The Museum of Natural History' – 2 vols. – chromolith titles – addit. pictorial title in vol. 1 – plates, some coloured – gilt – t.e.g. – 8vo – circa 1850.
(Sotheby Beresford Adams) $85 £40

RICHARDSON, JONATHAN
'The Works' – 10 engraved plates – vignette – spotting – cont. morocco – gilt spine rubbed – g.e. – sm 4to – Strawberry Hill Press, 1792.
(Sotheby's) $55 £25

RICHARDSON, WILLIAM AND CHURSTON, REV. EDWARD
'The Monastic Ruins of Yorkshire' – 2 vols. in one – litho title and plates – illus. – some leaves loose – cont. half calf – worn – folio – 1843.
(Sotheby's) $380 £180

RICHEPIN, JEAN
'Nouvelle Mythologie' – 3 vols. – plates, some coloured – quarter morocco gilt – t.e.g. – 4to – Paris, 1920.
(Phillips) $105 £50

RICKARD, T. A.
'Through the Yukon and Alaska' – frontis cloth – slightly soiled – San Francisco, 1909.
(Phillips) $60 £28

RICKETS, MAJOR
'Narrative of the Ashantee War' – 4 litho plates – later half calf – rubbed – 8vo – 1831.
(Sotheby's) $160 £75

RICKETTS, CHARLES
'The Parables from the Gospels' – 310 copies printed – 10 wood engraved illus. by Ricketts – orig. limp vellum – The Vale Press, 1903.
(Christie's) $210 £100
'The End of Hand and Soul' by Rossetti with decorations by Ricketts – cont. light green morocco by De Sauty – inlaid with red – t.e.g. – 12mo – 1899.
(Christie's) $90 £42

RIDDELL, ROBERT
'The Carpenter and the Joiner, Stair Builder and Hand-Railer' – plates – including cardboard cut out models – some spotting – cloth – soiled – 4to.
(Christie's) $40 £18

RIDLEY, T.
'View of Civile & Ecclesiasticall Law' – cont. vellum – 2nd Edn. – 4to – Oxford, 1634 – loose in binding.
(Bennett Book Auction) $75 £36

RIDPATH, GEORGE
'The Border History of England and Scotland' – 1st Edn. – cont. calf – joints weak – 4to – 1776.
(Sotheby's) $145 £70

RIEDRER, FRIEDRICH
'Spiegel der Wahren Rhetorik' – 1st Edn. – 188 leaves – 44 lines and headline – woodcut flanked by two angels – full page woodcut by Matthes Maler on verso – wormed throughout – dampstained – calf over wooden boards – rubbed – folio – Freiburg, Friedrich Riedrer, 1493.
(Sotheby's) $3,360 £1,600

RIENAECKER, V.
'John Sell Cotman' – no. 241 of 500 copies – plates some mounted and coloured – orig. cloth – dust jacket – 4to – Leigh-on-Sea, 1953.
(Christie's S. Kensington) $55 £26

RIGHETTI, P.
'Descrizione del Campidoglia' – 2 vols. – 390 plates – half calf – gilt – folio – Rome, 1833-36.
(Phillips) $115 £55

RIOU, STEPHEN
'The Grecian Orders of Architecture' – 1st Edn. – engraved vignette on title – 28 plates – folding – engraved headpieces – browning and soiling – half calf – rebacked – folio – 1768.
(Sotheby's) $380 £180

RISDAN, TRISTRAM
'The Chorographical Description of the County of Devon' – 1st Edn. – with continuation Vol. 2 – bound in full panelled calf – 1714.
(Lane) $75 £35

RITCHIE, LEITCH
'Scott and Scotland' – engraved frontis – title vignette and 19 plates after George Cattermole – occasional spotting – cont. morocco – rubbed – g.e. – 1835.
(Christie's) $40 £18

RITCHIE, R.
'Railways, their Rise, Progress. . . Railway Accidents' – woodcuts – orig. cloth – 1846.
(Bennett Book Auction) $40 £20

RITTER, C.
'The Comparative Geography of Palestine And the Sinaitic Peninsula' – 4 vols. – orig. cloth – rubbed – spines worn – mostly unopened – 8vo – Edinburgh, 1866.
(Sotheby's) $125 £60

RIVERO, MARIANO EDUARDO AND DON JUAN DIEGO DE ISCHUDI
'Antiguedades Peruanas' – Atlas Vol. only – coloured lithograph title and 59 plates – orig. cloth backed boards – soiled – rubbed – oblong folio – Vienna, Leopoldo Muller, 1851.
(Christie's S. Kensington) $420 £200

RIVERS OF GREAT BRITAIN
'Thames from Source to Sea' – 2 vols. 1891.
'Rivers of the South and West Coasts' – 1879.
'Thames' – 1891 – all 4to.
(Phillips) $125 £60

RIVIERE, G.
'Renoir et Ses Amis' – plates – cloth – 4to – 1921.
(Phillips) $190 £90

ROBBERDS, J. W. AND STARK, JAMES
'Picturesque Views Near the Eastern Coast of England' – large paper – 24 plates and 12 vignettes by Cooke, others after Stark – early cloth – worn – folio – London and Norwich, 1843.
(Sotheby's) $275 £130

ROBBINS, ALFRED
'Launceston, Past and Present' – orig. cloth bindings – 1884.
(Lane) $25 £12

ROBERT-HOUDIN, JEAN-EUGENE
'The Secrets of Stage Conjuring Translated and Edited by Professor Hoffmann' – 1st English Edn. – illus. – orig. pictorial cloth – gilt – slightly worn – 8vo – 1881.
(Sotheby's) $100 £48

ROBERTS, DAVID
'The Holy Land, Syria, Idumea, Egypt and Nubia' – 3 vols. in 2 – frontis portrait – 2 tinted litho titles and 120 tinted litho plates after Roberts – without map – half morocco – folio – 1842-45.
(Christie's) $5,250 £2,500

ROBERTS, LEWES
'The Merchant's Map Of Commerce' – 1st Edn. – engraved frontis – addit. engraved title – 5 full page maps – cont. calf – cont. signature of George Legatt on endpaper – folio – 1638.
(Christie Manson & Woods) $4,410 £2,100

ROBERTS, DAVID
'Picturesque Sketches in Spain' – tinted lithographed title and 25 plates – some slight spotting – cont. morocco backed cloth – slightly rubbed – disbound – folio – Published by Henry Graves & Co. n.d., Prospectus 1827.
(Christie's S. Kensington) $800 £380

ROBERTS, COL. DAVID
'The Adventures of Johnny Newcombe' – 15 hand coloured plates by Rowlandson – disbound – 1815.
(Phillips) $190 £90

ROBERTS, MARY
'Voices from the Woodlands' – 20 hand col. litho plates – orig. cloth – rebacked – modern endpapers – 1850.
(Christie's) $65 £30

ROBERTSON, D.
'Tour Through the Isle of Man' – 2nd Edn. – map and 7 sepia aquatints of 8 – some browning – half calf – rubbed – 1794.
(Phillips) $40 £20

ROBERTSON, G.
'General View of the Agriculture of the County of Midlothian . . .' – 1st Edn. – fldg. col. map and 9 plates – cont. calf – Edinburgh, 1795.
(Bennett Book Auction) $105 £50

ROBERTSON, WILLIAM
'The History of Scotland' – 3 vols. – 1800.
(Laurence & Martin Taylor) $4 £2
'A Tour Through the Isle of Man' – 1st Edn. – large paper copy with the seditious passage later supressed – 8 tinted aquatints – some spotting – cont. calf – rebacked – covers worn – large 8vo – 1794.
(Christie's S. Kensington) $145 £70
'The History of the Reign of Charles V' – 3 vols. – cont. calf – spines gilt – cracked – one cover detached – 4to – 1769.
(Christie's) $30 £15

Astrolabii quo primi mo bilis motus deprehen duntur Canones.

Instrumentum Astrolabii etiam Impressum est Venetiis in officina Petri Liechten stein Coloniensis Germani ano 1512

ROBERTUS, ANGLICUS
'Astrolabii quo Primo Mobilis Motus Deprehenduntur Canones' – Gothic letter – woodcut diagrams and initials – bound in a fragment of a 14th century Italian medical mss on vellum over boards – rare – sm 4to – Venice, Petrus Liechtenstein, 1512.
(Sotheby's) $925 £440

ROBINSON, B.
'New Elements of Conick Sections' – illus. in text – calf – 1704.
(Phillips) $65 £30

ROBINSON, C. E.
'A Royal Warren or Picturesque Ramble in the Isle of Purbeck' – presentation copy – etched plates – illus. – orig. cloth – rubbed – 4to – 1882.
(Sotheby's) $30 £15

ROBINSON, C. N.
'Old Naval Prints; Their Artists and Engravers' – col. and other illus. – limited Edn. – 4to. – buckram, slightly stained – 1924.
(Bonhams) $75 £35

ROBINSON, CHARLES – SHELLEY, P. B.
'The Sensitive Plant' – illus. and 18 mounted plates by Robinson, mostly col. – some soiling – orig. vellum gilt – t.e.g. – 4to – n.d.
(Christie's) $105 £50

ROBINSON, CHARLES – SHAKESPEARE, WILLIAM
'Songs and Sonnets' – 12 col. plates and decorations in text by Robinson – orig. pictorial cloth – gilt – rubbed – 4to – 1917.
(Sotheby's) $105 £50

ROBINSON, EDWARD ARLINGTON
'The Town Down The River' – attractive copy – New York, 1910.
(J. Ash) $45 £22

ROBINSON, WILLIAM E., 'Chung Ling Soo'
'Spirit Slate Writing and Kindred Phenomena' – 1st Edn. – 66 illus. – Martinka & Co. label on title – orig. pictorial cloth – stained and worn – 8vo – New York, 1898.
(Sotheby's) $250 £120

ROBINSON, W. HEATH
'Fairy Tales' by Hans Christian Andersen – no. 4 of 100 copies – 16 col. plates and illus. in text by Heath Robinson – orig. vellum gilt – stained – t.e.g. – 4to – 1913.
(Sotheby's) $735 £350

ROBINSON, W. HEATH – RABELAIS, FRANCOIS
'The Works' – 2 vols. – frontis and illus. by Heath Robinson – orig. cloth – soiled – t.e.g. – 4to – 1904.
(Christie's S. Kensington) $17 £8

ROBINSON, F. CAYLEY – MAETERLINCK, MAURICE
'The Blue Bird' – 25 col. plates by Robinson – orig. cloth gilt – stained – 4to – 1912.
(Sotheby's) $95 £45

ROBJIN, J.
'Paskaert Vande Kust Genehoa en Rio de Senegal' – engraved chart of the mouth of the Senegal River – hand col. in outline – pictorial title vignette – historiated scale cartouche – 2 compass roses – compass lines on land and water areas – verso blank – 414 x 514mm.
(Sotheby's) $20 £10

ROBY, J.
'Traditions of Lancashire' – 4 vols. – large paper copy – engraved plates in 2 states – cont. calf – rebacked – 8vo – 1829-31.
(Sotheby's) $95 £45

RODD, EDWARD H.
'The Birds of Cornwall' – 1st Edn. – orig. cloth binding – 1880.
(Lane) $35 £17

ROE, F. GORDON
'Sea Painters of Britain' – 2 vols. – one of 500 copies – plates, some col. – orig. cloth – dust jackets – 8vo – Leigh on Sea, 1947-48.
(Sotheby's) $170 £80

ROEMER, JOANNE JACOBO
'Genera Insectorum Linnaei et Fabricii' – hand col. engraved title, vignette and 36 plates – margins browned – cont. half calf – rebacked – 4to – Wintertur, 1789.
(Christie's S. Kensington) $315 £150

ROESEL VON ROSENHOF, AUGUST JOHANN
'Historia Naturalis Ranarum Nostratium' – text in Latin and German – hand col. engraved frontis and 24 engraved plates, in two states, one hand col. – half morocco – rubbed – folio – Nuremberg, 1753-58.
(Christie's) $1,220 £580

ROESSLER, BALTHAZAR
'Speculum Metallurgiae Politissimum' – 1st Edn. – title in red and black – 25 engraved plates – half title – browning – boards – rebacked with cloth – worn – half red morocco case – folio – Dresden, J. J. Winckler, 1700.
(Sotheby's) $1,050 £500

ROESSLIN, EUCHARIUS
'The Birth of Mankind' – woodcut title with border – lacks leaf – 4 plates – 4 leaves inserted with early woodcuts – old panelled calf – 8vo – 1545.
(Phillips) $440 £210

ROGER, P.
'Percement de L'Isthme Americain par un Canal Interoceanique' – orig. wrappers – torn and loose – 4to – Paris, 1864.
(Sotheby's) $40 £20

ROGERS, C.
Rental Book of the Cistercian Abbey of Cupar-Angus – 2 vols. – circa 1880.
(Bennett Book Auction) $17 £8

ROGERS, CHARLES
'A Collection of Prints in Imitation of Drawings' – 2 vols. – 2 frontis – engraved title by Bartolozzi – 106 plates on 103 leaves – cont. half calf – spines defective – large folio – 1770.
(Christie Manson & Woods) $1,575 £750

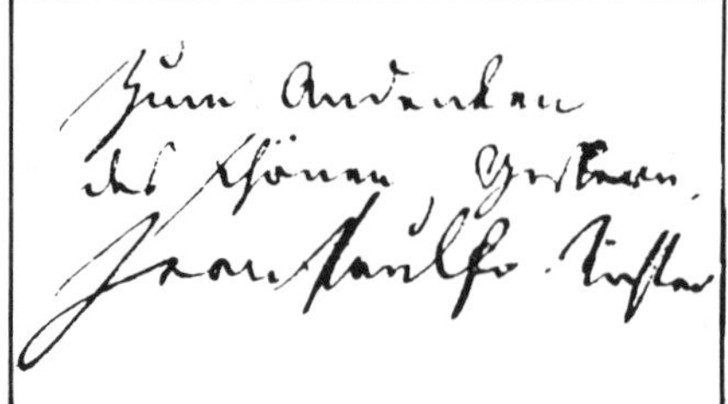

ROGERS, SAMUEL
AL 2 pages – 6vo. – no place, to a Whig hostess, Lady Holland, promising to come to dinner – July, 1826.
(Sotheby's) $65 £30
'Human Life, A Poem' – orig. boards – expertly rebacked – 1819.
(J. Ash) $20 £10
'Italy, A Poem' – numerous engraved vignettes in text after Turner and Stothard – spots and stains – cont. morocco gilt – slightly worn – hinges weak – 8vo – 1830.
(Sotheby Beresford Adams) $75 £36

ROGET, J. L.
'A History of the Old Watercolour Society' – 2 vols. – spine torn – cloth – gilt – 1891.
(Phillips) $95 £45

ROHDE, ELEANOUR SINCLAIR
'The Old English Herbals' – col. frontis – plates – orig. cloth – sm 4to – 1922.
(Sotheby's) $55 £25

ROIZMAN, MATVEI
'Khevronskoe Vino' (Hebron Wine) – one of 1,000 copies – orig. wrappers by G. Eieistov – soiled – 8vo – Moscow, 1923.
(Sotheby's) $115 £55

ROLT, RICHARD
'The Lives of the Principal Reformers' – 1st Edn. – 21 mezzo portraits – some spotting – modern half calf – folio – 1759.
(Sotheby's) $95 £45

ROMAINS, JULES
'The Body's Rapture' – limited to 1,000 numbered copies – nice copy – Boriswood, 1933.
(J. Ash) $19 £9

ROMANCE OF SYDRACH, THE
'La Fontaine de Toutes Sciences' – in French prose – illum. mss on vellum – three large illum. initials – almost full page diagram of the world – one small miniature and very large miniature with full border of bar design sprouting ivy leaves in blue, red and green – 18th century French calf – spine gilt in compartments – marbled endpapers – 290 x 220mm – France, perhaps Paris, circa 1350-75.
(Sotheby's) $15,750 £7,500

ROMANO, GUILIO
'Frieze depicting the Entry of Emperor Sigismund into Mantua' – 25 engraved plates by Antoinette Bouzonet Stella including pictorial dedication to Colbert without title – 18th century calf backed boards – very worn – oblong folio – Paris, 1675.
(Sotheby Beresford Adams) $250 £120

RONALDS, A.
'The Fly Fisher's Entomology' – 6th Edn. – 20 col. plates – slightly soiled – orig. cloth – rubbed – 8vo – 1862.
(Sotheby's) $105 £50

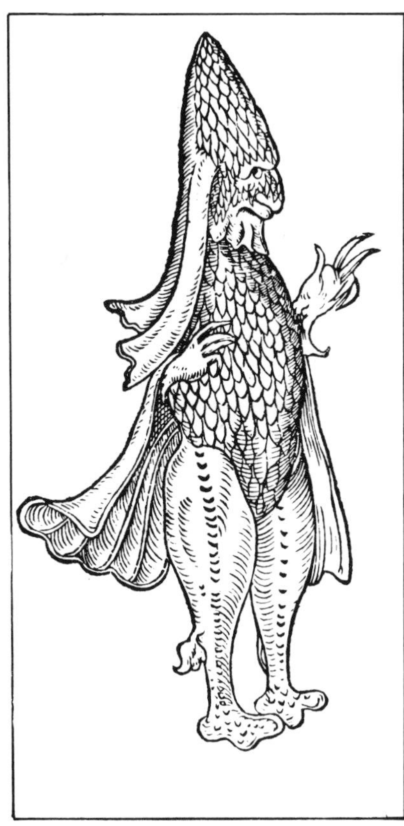

RONDELET, GUILLAUME
'Libri de Piscibus Marinis' – 1st Edn. – 2 parts in one vol. – device on titles – woodcut portrait of author – 400 woodcuts in text – slight staining or browning – 18th century French mottled calf – gilt spine – worn – folio – Lyon, Mayhias Bonhomme, 1554-55.
(Sotheby's) $2,100 £1,000

RONGEAT, A.
'An Amusing and Attractive Geography dedicated to the Youth of England' – complete set of 11 litho cards, with explanation – 10 cards printed on both sides with map and view col. by hand – g.e. – orig. case – pictorial label on side with title – 100 x 71mm – Ackermann, circa 1835.
(Sotheby's) $160 £75

RONSARD, P. DE
'Choix de Sonnets' – limited to 226 copies – wood engraved frontis – woodcut border – orig. decorated boards – soiled – uncut – Artist Lucien Pissarro – 8vo – Eragny Press, 1902.
(Sotheby's) $210 £100

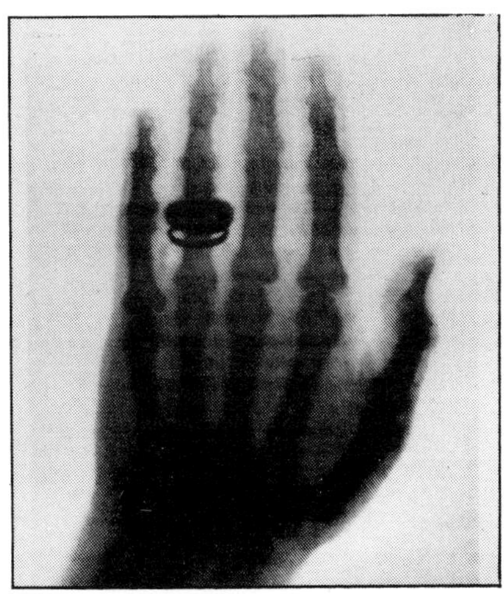

RONTGEN, WILHELM CONRAD
'Eine Neue Art von Strahlen' – Parts I and II – orig. printed wrappers – slightly soiled – half brown morocco case – 8vo – (the first announcement of the accidental discovery of X-rays) – Wurzburg, 1895-96.
(Sotheby's) $6,090 £2,900

ROOS, FRANK
'Bibliography of Early American Architecture' – orig. cloth – dust jacket – University of Illinois Press, 1968.
(Christie's) $20 £10

ROOSES, MAX
'Dutch Painters of the 19th Century' – 4 vols. – plates – orig. cloth – gilt – t.e.g. – 4to – 1898-1901.
(Phillips) $105 £50
'Christophe Plantin' – plates – cont. half morocco – rubbed – folio – Paris, n.d.
(Sotheby's) $95 £45

ROOSEVELT, THEODORE, PRESIDENT OF U.S.A.
3 typed Ls., 9½ pages, 4to – one on White House paper but written from Oyster Bay, N.Y., and other places, to Governor of Sudan with auto corrections and related material – menu, printed speech of welcome to Roosevelt etc. – 1908-09.
(Phillips) $755 £350

ROSCOE, T.
'Wanderings in South Wales including the River Wye' – frontis – vignette title – 44 engravings and 2 maps – modern half calf – t.e.g. – C. Tilt – n.d.
(Phillips) $65 £32

ROSCOE, WILLIAM
'The Butterfly's Ball and the Grasshopper's Feast' – 15pp engraved throughout – 14 illus. – frontis col. by former owner – stained – rebound in Dutch floral paper – cloth case – 16mo – J. Harris, 1807.
(Sotheby's) $85 £40
'Illustrations . . . of the Life of Lorenzo de Medici' – large paper copy – 4to – inscribed 'Dr. Alexander Monro, Edinburgh, with the sincere esteem and grateful respect of The Author' – plates, some spotting – later half morocco – worn – 1822.
(Christie's S. Kensington) $60 £28

ROSE, ALFRED
'Register of Erotic Books' – orig. cloth – 2 vols. – New York, Jack Brussel, 1965.
(Christie's S. Kensington) $170 £80

ROSE ANNUAL, THE
28 vols. – lacking those for 1948, '49, '51, '54 and '61 – plates – orig. cloth – 8vo – 1946-80.
(Sotheby's) $30 £15

ROSE, THOMAS
'Westmoreland, Cumberland, Durham and Northumberland' – engraved title – 80 engraved views on 40 sheets – some foxing – half calf – gilt – 4to – 1832.
(Phillips) $90 £42

ROSENTHAL, L.
'The Kingdom of the Pearl' – Limited Edn. – col. plates by E. Dulac – orig. decorated boards – cloth backed – 4to – n.d.
(Bonhams) $60 £28

ROSS, ALEXANDER
'A View of All the Religions in the World' – calf – 1653.
(Richard Baker & Thomson) $65 £30

ROSS, FREDERICK
'The Ruined Abbeys of Britain' – 2 vols. – illus. – William Mackenzie.
(Dacre, Son & Hartley) $34 £16

ROSS, SIR JOHN
'Narrative of a Second Voyage in Search of a North-West Passage' – 25 plates, 6 hand coloured lithographs – 4to – A. W. Webster, 1835.
(Christie's S. Kensington) $210 £100

ROSS-CRAIG, STELLA
'Drawings of British Plants' – 7 vols. – parts 1-27 illus. – buckram – gilt – 1948-70.
(Phillips) $75 £35

ROSSEL, FREDERIC
'Francis Laine, Son Cahier d'Esquisses' – no. 169 of 300, signed by author – 68 plates – loose as issued – orig. cloth portfolio – slightly rubbed – 4to – Montbeliard, 1923.
(Sotheby's) $34 £16

ROSSETTI, CHRISTINA
'Sing Song, a Nursery Rhyme Book' – 1st Edn. – wood engraved frontis – vignette and illus. by the Dalziels – spotted – orig. pictorial cloth – rubbed – g.e. – 8vo – Routledge, 1872.
(Sotheby's) $105 £50

ROSSI, GIOVANNI GIACOMO AND FALDA, GIOVANNI BATTISTA
'Il Nuovo Teatro Della Fabriche et Edifici in Prospettiva di Roma Moderna' – 4 parts in one – 142 engraved plates, including titles and dedications – cont. sprinkled calf – slightly worn – oblong folio – Rome, 1699.
(Sotheby Beresford Adams) $965 £460

ROSSINI, LUIGI
'Viaggio Pittoresco Da Roma a Napoli' – engraved title and 80 plates – cont. half vellum – gilt – slightly rubbed – large folio – Rome, 1839.
(Sotheby's) $3,570 £1,700

ROSTAND, EDMOND
'Cyrano de Bergerac' – 1st English Edn. – orig. cloth – nice copy – 1898.
(J. Ash) $34 £16

ROTH, H. LING
'Oriental Silverwork, Malay and Chinese' – plates – orig. cloth – 4to – 1910.
(Sotheby's) $40 £20
'The Natives of Sarawak and British North Borneo' – 2 vols. – one of 700 copies – folding map, illus. – orig. cloth – rubbed – joints split – 8vo – 1896.
(Sotheby's) $230 £110

ROTHSCHILD, LORD
'The Rothschild Library' – 2 vols. – plates – orig. cloth – 8vo – 1969.
(Sotheby's) $210 £100

ROUSSEAU, JEAN-JACQUES
Important collection of mss written partly by Rousseau and partly by Madame Dupin comprising approx. 149 pages in Rousseau's hand and 50 in Mme. Dupin's hand with a few pages in other hands, 326pp in all – mostly large 4to – modern brown morocco gilt with brown morocco and green silk cover gilt and a brown morocco and green silk slipcase gilt – circa 1746-1750.
(Sotheby Parke Bernet Monaco) $26,020 £14,000

ROWE, REV. HENRY
'Fables in Verse' – 30 wood engraved plates – embossed library stamp – cont. green straight grained morocco – gilt – repaired – g.e. – 8vo – J. J. Stockdale, 1810.
(Sotheby's) $40 £18

ROWE, S.
'Perambulation of the Antient and Royal Forest of Dartmoor' – Limited Edn. – plates – maps – cloth rubbed – uncut and unopened – 8vo – 1896.
(Phillips) $75 £35

ROXBURGH AND BERWICK
An Act for . . . amending certain Roads, 1806, An Act for amending the Laws concerning High-ways, Bridges and Ferries in Scotland 1845, An Act for . . . maintaining certain Roads in the Counties of Roxburgh and Berwick 1849, An Act for making a Railway from . . . Jedburgh to the Kelso Branch . . . 1855, Valuation Book of the County of Roxburgh, Hawick, 1811, and mss lists of lands, Proprietor, tenant and annual value of Jedburgh Parish – n.d. mid 19th century – all bound together.
(Bennett Book Auctions) $65 £30

ROXBURGHE CLUB
Johnstone, H. 'Letters of Edward, Prince of Wales' – original morocco bound cloth – rubbed – 4to – 1931.
(Sotheby's) $75 £35

ROY, WILLIAM
'The Military Antiquities of the Romans in Britain' – 1st Edn. – 50 engraved plates – 3 engraved page maps – large engraved page folding plate – 1 printed table – spotting – cont. half calf – joints split – wear – large folio – 1793.
(Sotheby's) $190 £90

ROYAL ACADEMY PICTURES
2 vols. with a collection of coloured prints – 1892-93.
(Lane) $8 £4
'Royal Academy Pictures 1892' – illustrating the 124th Exhibition of the Royal Academy – Cassell & Co.
(Baitson) $12 £6

ROYAL ACADEMY OF ARTS
'Exhibition of British Primitive Paintings from the 12th to the 16th Centuries' – plates – cloth – t.e.g. – 4to – 1924.
(Phillips) $45 £22

ROYAL ANTHROPOLOGICAL INSTITUTE JOURNAL
Vols. 70-95, in 41 vols. – plates – orig. wrappers – 4to – 1940-65.
(Sotheby's) $170 £80

ROYAL ARTILLERY WAR COMMEMORATION BOOK
Plates – orig. cloth – slightly soiled – t.e.g. – 4to – 1920.
(Christie's S. Kensington) $40 £18

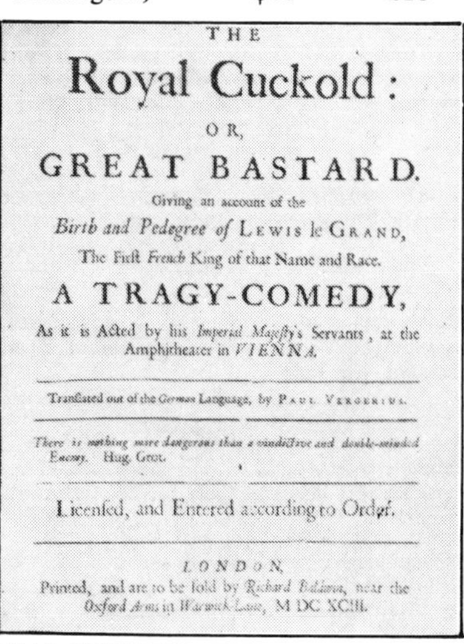

THE
Royal Cuckold:
OR,
GREAT BASTARD.
Giving an account of the
Birth and Pedegree of LEWIS le GRAND,
The First *French* King of that Name and Race.
A TRAGY-COMEDY,
As it is Acted by his *Imperial Majesty's* Servants, at the Amphitheater in *VIENNA*.

Translated out of the *German* Language, by PAUL VERGERIUS.

There is nothing more dangerous than a vindictive and double-minded Enemy. Hug. Grot.

Licensed, and Entered according to Order.

LONDON,
Printed, and are to be sold by *Richard Baldwin*, near the *Oxford Arms* in *Warwick Lane*, M DC XCIII.

ROYAL CUCKOLD, THE
A tragi-comedy – 1st Edn. – morocco by Sangorski – sm 4to – 1693.
(Christie's) $1,010 £480

ROYAL GEOGRAPHICAL SOCIETY JOURNAL
Vol. IV part 2, Vol. VII part 2, Vol. VIII parts 2 and 3, Vol. LX part 1, Vol. X parts 1 and 3, Vol. XI part 1, Vol. XII part 5 1, Vol. XIII part 1, Vol. XIV part 2, Vol. XV part 1, Vol. XVI part 1, Vol. XXVII parts 42, 43, 46, 64 and 69; together 19 vols. – folding plans – orig. wrappers – or cloth – and 35 issues of the Proceedings of the Society – 8vo – 1834-1957.
(Sotheby's) $545 £260

ROYAL SPECIAL TRAIN
Programme and letters relating to Royal Train from Market Weighton to King's Cross, 28th October 1905.
(Baitson) $15 £7

'ROYAL VARIETY SHOW' PROGRAMMES
18 vols. – various – orig. wrappers – slightly soiled – 1954-75.
(Christie's S. Kensington) $65 £30

ROYAUMONT, SIEUR DE
'The History of the Old and New Testaments' – numerous engraved plates – some leaves frayed – calf – worn – rebacked with cloth – folio – R. Blome, 1705.
(Sotheby's) $115 £55

RUDBECK, OLAUS
'Atland Eller Manheim Dedan Japhets Afkomne Utgange . . .' – 1st Edn. – 2 vols. and folio atlas – engraved frontis to both parts – numerous maps – plates and woodcuts on 40 leaves – marginal repairs – 19th century quarter calf – gilt – folio – Upsala, H. Curio 1679-89.
(Sotheby's) $1,470 £700

RUDDER, SAMUEL
'A New History of Gloucestershire' – 8 plates only – title detached – cont. calf – worn – rebacked – folio – Cirencester, 1779.
(Christie's S. Kensington) $60 £28

RUELLIUS, JOANNES
'De Nature Stirpium' – 1st Edn. – title in woodcut border – half morocco – folio – 1536.
(Christie's) $670 £320

RUGGIERI, FERDINANDO
'Studio d'Architettura Civile' – 3 parts in one vol. – 2 engraved titles to each part – 162 engraved plates – 65 plates from numerical sequence – waterstains – cont. half calf – covers worn – large folio – Florence –1722-28.
(Christie Manson & Woods) $170 £80

RULES AND REGULATIONS FOR THE SWORD EXERCISE OF THE CAVALRY, FOR THE WAR OFFICE
29 engraved plates, most slightly creased – cont. tree calf – rubbed – upper cover detached – 1810.
(Christie's S. Kensington) $45 £22

RUNDELL, MRS. MARIA ELIZA
'A New System of Domestic Cookery' – engraved frontis – addit. title and 9 plates – margins browned – orig. cloth – spine torn – 1843.
(Christie's) $55 £25

RUPIN, ERNEST
'L'Oeuvre Limoges' – plates – illus. – cont. half morocco – rubbed – 4to – Paris, 1890.
(Sotheby's) $115 £55

RUSKIN, JOHN
'The Seven Lamps of Architecture' – 14 plates by Ruskin – later issue with adverts – orig. decorated blind stamped cloth – some wear to spine – 8vo – 1849.
(J. Ash) $65 £32
'Notes on His Collection of Drawings by J. M. W. Turner' – large paper copy – plates – folding map – orig. morocco backed cloth – rubbed – t.e.g. – 4to – 1878.
(Sotheby's) $105 £50
'Essays on Political Economy' – cont. morocco – spine slightly torn – g.e.
(Christie's S. Kensington) $65 £32

RUSSELL, BERTRAND
'New Hopes for a Changing World' – very good in slightly rubbed dust wrappers – 1951.
(J. Ash) $6 £3

RUSSELL, J.
'Atlas of the World' – 34 engraved plates – 33 maps, hand col. in outline – one torn – stains – cont. calf – covers detached – 4to – circa 1830.
(Sotheby's) $170 £80

RUSSELL, LADY R.
'Letters' – calf – 4to – 1783.
(Bonhams) $40 £20

RUSSELL, W. H.
'A Memoir of the Marriage of H.R.H. Prince Edward Albert, Prince of Wales' – chromolithographed plates and title – loose – spotting – orig. cloth – gilt – folio – n.d.
(Sotheby's) $125 £60

RUSSIAN ALPHABET CARDS
Complete set of 28 engraved cards, 27 with an illus. of a street seller, col. by hand, caption with initial letter and street cry, pencil trans. on back, pictorial label from orig. box – 186 x 118mm – Moscow, circa 1830.
(Sotheby's) $2,205 £1,050

CHRONICA.

Der Prouintz Lyfflandt/darinne vermeldet werdt,

Wo dath sülnige Landt ersten gefunden / vnde thom Christendome gebracht ys: Wol de ersten Regenten des Landes gewesen sind: van dem ersten Meyster Düdesches Ordens in Lyfflandt beth vp den lesten / vnde van eines ydtliken Daden.

Wat sick in der voranderinge der Lyfflendisschen Stende / vnd na der tydt beth in dat negeste 1583. Jar / vor seltzame vnd wänderlike Geschefft im Lande tho gedragen hebben: nütte vnde angenehme tho lesende korth vnd loffwerdich beschreuen.

Dorch
BALTHASAR RVSSOVVEN
Reualiensem.

Thom andern mal mith allem flyte auersehen / corrigeret / vorbetert/vnd mith velen Historien vormehret dorch den Autorem sülueſt.

Gedrücket tho Bart / in der Förstliken Drückerye / Dorch Andream Seitnern.
1584.

RUSSOW, BALTHASAR
'Chronica Der Provintz Lyfflandt' – 1st Edn. – title in red and black – some orig. notes in 18th century hand – cont. calf – gilt arabesque on both covers – worn and wormed – 4to – Barth, 1584.
(Sotheby's) $880 £420

RUTH, THE BOOK OF
Limited to 250 copies – orig. stiff wrappers – slipcase – The Nonesuch Press, 1923.
(Christie's) $90 £42

RUTHERFORD, LORD ERNEST
'Radioactivity' – 1st Edn. – half title – Radcliffe Library duplicate with stamps – orig. cloth – 8vo – Cambridge, 1904.
(Sotheby's) $160 £75

RUTHERFORD ESTATE
A Collection of Family Papers Addressed to the American Heirs
Plates – map and a few photographs – wrappers – 4to – circa 1890-1895.
(Bennett Book Auction) $20 £10

RUTTER, J.
'Delineations of Fonthill and Its Abbey' – large paper copy – hand col. title and frontis – folding map – orig. half calf – rubbed – 4to – For the Author, 1823.
(Sotheby's) $420 £200

RYCAUT, PAUL
'The Present State of the Ottoman Empire' – 3rd Edn. – engraved frontis – 2 plates and many engravings in text – title reinforced – cont. sheep – gilt spine – sm folio – 1670.
(Sotheby's) $230 £110

RYFF, WALTER HERMANN
'Der Furnembsten, Notwnedigsten, der Gantzen Architectur Angehorigen, Mathematischen und Mechanischen . . .' – 1st Edn. – title in red and black – full page emblematic woodcut – numerous fine woodcut illus. and diagrams – some worming and soiling – cont. blindstamped pigskin over wooden boards – rubbed and soiled – folio – Nuremberg, 1547.
(Sotheby's) $9,240 £4,400

SACKVILLE-WEST, VITA
'The Garden' – no. 588 of 750 copies – signed by author – orig. cloth – t.e.g. – Michael Joseph 1946.
(Christie's) $115 £55
'Selected Poems' – contains five previously uncollected poems – slightly browned dust wrapper – Hogarth Press 1941.
(J. Ash) $12 £6

SACROBOSCO, JOHANNES DE
'Sphaera Mundi' – 69 leaves – 35 lines – roman letters – fullpage woodcut – woodcut diagrams and initials – device at end – contem. annotations – soiling – stains – 2 works in one vol. – 19th cent. vellum – soiled – sm. 4to. – 1488/89.
(Sotheby's) $1,930 £920
'Textus de Sphaera' – editor Jacobus Faber Stapulensis – large woodcut on title – woodcut diagrams and initials – modern half calf – folio – Paris, Simon de Colines, 1527.
(Sotheby's) $880 £420

SADE, D. A. F. MARQUIS DE
'La Nouvelle Justine' – 10 vols – 6 frontis and 99 engraved plates – 8 half titles – morocco – 12 mo. – Hollande (Paris?) 1797.
(Phillips) $1,850 £880

SAGE, B. DE
'Le Diable Boiteux' – 2 vols. in one – 13 plates – rebound calf gilt – 12 mo. – Amsterdam 1739.
(Phillips) $85 £40

SAGES IN RELIGIOUS DISCUSSION
Laid down on a contemporary album leaf – pale orange and dark blue border with gold floral motif – buff leaf with stylised flower sprays in gold – water-stained – small split in side – Mughal circa 1680.
(Christie's) $15,750 £7,500

SAIL AND STEAM SHIPS, LIGHT-HOUSES ETC.
Collection of approx. 74 Parliamentary Blue Books – some with plates – soiled – most disbound – folio – circa 1800-60.
(Sotheby's) $945 £450

SAINT IGNY, SIEUR DE
'Elemens de Portraiture' – engraved title – 32 plates engravings in text – contem mottled calf – 8vo. – Paris 1630.
(Sotheby's) $20 £10

SAINT NON, ABBE DE
'Voyage Pittoresque ou Description du Royaumes de Naples et de Sicilie' – 4 vols. in 5 – 275 engraved plates – maps – vignettes – illus in text – woodcut fleurons – half titles – doubles medailes – half morocco rubbed – covers detached – large folio – Paris 1781-86.
(Christie's) $630 £300

SAINT-PIERRE, J. H. B. DE
'Etudes de la Nature' – 4 vols. – vol. 1-3 2nd Edn. – a few engraved plates – contemporary calf – a little rubbed – joints and spine slightly cracked – 12mo. – Paris 1786-8.
(Christie's S. Kensington) $40 £20

SALA, ANGELO
'Opera Medico-Chymica' – 1st. collected Edn. – additional engraved titles – some woodcuts in text – Frankfurt – J. Beyer, 1647 'Tracatus Duo. De Variis tum Chymicorum' 1649 – bound in one vol. – browned – stained – contem. vellum boards – soiled – half red morocco case – rare – 4to.
(Sotheby's) $880 £420

SALAMAN, MALCOLM C.
'The Etchings of James McBey' – no. 14 of 100 copies signed by McBey – 4to. – plates – orig. vellum backed buckram – slightly soiled.
(Christie's S. Kensington) $135 £65
'The New Woodcut' – illus. – some coloured by over 180 artists – nice clean copy-book-plate – 4to – Studio Special, 1930.
(J. Ash) $65 £30
'French Colour-Prints of the XVIII Century' – 4to. – coloured plates – some spotting – original cloth – soiled inner hinges worn – 1913.
(Christie's S. Kensington) $25 £12
'British Book Illustration, Yesterday and Today' – cloth – Studio 1923.
(Bennett Book Auction) $34 £16

SALE, LADY FLORENTIA. 1790-1853
Diarist who survived the British retreat from Kabul 1842. Auto journal of her tour in Northern India in 1832-33 – c. 140 pages with about 50 Company School watercolours of architectural scenes including the Taj Mahal signed Florentia Sale – slightly browned – indian tree calf – gilt – quarto – together with a similar album comprising 65 Company school watercolours of mosques.
(Sotheby's) $1,260 £600

SALLUSTIUS CRISPUS, CAIUS
'La Conjuracion de Catilina y la Guerra de Jugurta' – engraved title – nine plates – one map contemporary marbled sheet – large sections excised from covers – folio – Madrid, Joachin Ibarra, 1772.
(Christie's S. Kensington) $545 £260

SALMON AND SEA FISHERIES, THE
'Reports on the Natural History and Habits of Salmonoids' – half morocco gilt – 1867. – Dublin 1852.
(Phillips) $55 £25

SALMON, WILLIAM
'Polygraphice or the Arts of Drawing, Limning and Painting' – 3rd Edn. – engraved title – 15 plates – lacks title and portrait – stains – tears – plates shaved – calf – rebacked – 8vo. – I. Crumpe 1675.
(Sotheby's) $40 £20
'Pharmacopaeia Londinensis' – soiling – contem. calf – crudely rebacked – Thos. Dawks 1678.
(Christie's) $45 £22
'Compleat English Physician or the Druggists' Shops Opened' – calf – 8vo. – 1693.
(Phillips) $295 £140

SALMONENSEN, F.
'The Birds of Greenland' – col. plates – text in Danish and English – half calf gilt – 4to. – 1950.
(Phillips) $250 £120

SALMONS, V.
'Charles Eisen' – limited Edn. – plates – orig. cloth – 8vo. – 1914.
(Sotheby's) $40 £20

SALTER, T. F.
'The Angler's Guide' – vignette title – frontis – plates – uncut – orig. boards – cover detached – 1823.
(Phillips) $80 £38

SALVIN, F. H. AND BRODRICK, W.
'Falconry in the British Isles' – 24 hand col. plates – half morocco gilt – t.e.g. with auto letters by Francis Henry Salvin 2½ pp 1866 on natural history matters.
(Phillips) $715 £340

SALVIN, O. AND GODMAN, F. D.
'Biologia Centrali Americana' – 4 vols. – 84 vol. plates – mod. cloth gilt – t.e.g. – 4to. – 1879-1904.
(Phillips) $755 £360

SAMMES, AYLETT
'The Antiquities of Ancient Britain' – vol. 1 – title in red and black – map – engraved illus. in text – some browning and soiling – modern half cloth – rubbed – folio – 1676.
(Sotheby's) $55 £25

SAMOUELLE, GEORGE
'The Entomologist's Useful Compendium' – 12 hand coloured plates – occasional light spotting – contemporary calf – joints split – 1819.
(Christie's S. Kensington) $95 £45

SAMS, W.
'Studies from the Stage or the Vicissitudes of Life' – 19 hand col. engraved plates of 20 – lacks title – soiled – pencil marks and tears – orig. half roan – worn – oblong 4to. – 1823.
(Sotheby's) $85 £40

SAMSON, G. B.
'Japan, a Short Cultural History' – plates – orig. cloth – dust jacket – 8vo. – 1931.
(Sotheby's) $30 £15

SANDBURG, C.
'Early Moon' – illustrated by James Daugherty – cloth – 1st Edn. – New York, 1930.
(Bennett Book Auction) $4 £2

SANDBY, P.
'Virtuosis Museum Select Views of England, Scotland' and Wales' – 108 plates – calf gilt – oblong 4to. – 1778.
(Phillips) $590 £280

SANDERSON, SIR WILLIAM
'A Compleat History of the Life and Raigne of King Charles' – 1st Edn. – 2 engraved ports – browning and soiling – contem. calf – worn – folio – 1658.
(Sotheby's) $20 £10

SANDYS, GEORGE
'A Relation of a Journey Begun 1610' – 3rd Edn. – engraved title – folding plate – illus. in text – lacking map – 18th cent. mottled calf – worn – folio – 1627.
(Sotheby's) $115 £55

'Anglorum Speculum' – 1st. Edn. – half title – slight browning – contem. mottled calf – splits in joints – rubbed – 8vo. – 1684.
(Sotheby's) $60 £28

SANDYS, W.
'Specimens of Cornish Provincial Dialect' – half morocco binding – 1846.
(Lane) $30 £15

SANGORSKI, E. AND SUTCLIFFE, G.
'Rubaiyat of Omar Khayyam' – 4to – n.d. – calligraphy – plates and illuminations by Sangorski and Sutcliffe – some spotting – orig. cloth – gilt – soiled – t.e.g.
(Christie's S. Kensington) $55 £25

SANNAZARO, JACOPO
'El Parto de la Virgen .... traduzido en Castellana por Gregorio Hernandez' – 2nd Edn. in Castellan – woodcut device on title – wormed – soiled – 18th cent. calf – slightly worn – sm. 8vo. – Salamanca 1569.
(Sotheby's) $170 £80

SANSOM, WILLIAM
'Something Terrible, Something Lovely' – very good copy in dust wrapper – Hogarth Press 1948.
(J. Ash) $12 £6

SANSON, NICHOLAS
'Basse ou Grande Pologne' – engraved map – hand coloured in outline – 22 x 17 inches – framed and glazed – 1665.
(Christie's S. Kensington) $65 £32

SANTO BARTOLI, PIETRO
'Receuil des Peintres Antiques' – 2 works in 1 vol. first Edn. – limited to 30 copies – 40 hand coloured engraved plates in first work including 7 extra plates – Pierre Jean Mariette's copy with his signature – Paris 1757-60.
(Sotheby Parke Bernet) $8,920 £4,250

'Receuil de Peintres Antiques Trouvees a Rome' – 2 works in 3 vols. – printed on vellum – 61 engraved plates all but 8 superbly hand coloured – 2 folding – contemp. dark blue morocco by Derome le Jeune with his ticket – gilt borders – spines gilt – gilt edges – pink silk liners – folio – Paris, Didot L'Aine, 1783-87.
(Sotheby Parke Bernet) $7,435 £3,540

SARPI, PAOLO
'Historia del Concilio Tridentino ... di Pietro Soave Polano' – folio – spotted – later sheep backed boards – Londra, Appresso Giovan 1619.
(Christie's S. Kensington) $60 £28

SARRATT, J. H.
'A New Treatise on the Game of Chess' – 2 vols. – worn – 1821.
(Bonhams) $45 £22

PART EIGHT: MIGRATION TO THE MIDLANDS

WHEN DIXON ARRIVED AT THE PACKLESTONE Kennels in the middle of October, with my four hunters and a man under him, he was realizing an ambition which must often have seemed unattainable. To break away from Butley for a season in a country which adjoined such notable names as the Quorn, the Pytchley, and Mr. Fernie's—well might he have wondered how it had been brought about! But there we were; and Aunt Evelyn had been left to drive through a lonely winter with Harkaway and the stable-boy—now nearly eighteen and promoted to the dignity of wearing Dixon's top-hat and blue livery coat.

From the moment when Denis had first suggested my going with him, I had made up my mind to do it. Nevertheless, the fact remained that I couldn't afford it. I was putting myself in a false position in more ways than one: financially, because I should be spending my whole year's income in less than six months; and socially, because the people in the Packlestone Hunt quite naturally assumed that I was much better off than I really was. I had discussed it all with Denis in April. Denis was good at making fifteen shillings do the work of a pound, and he was fond of talking about money. But when I divulged my exact income he

[211]

SASSOON, SEIGFRIED
'Memoirs of a Fox Hunting Man' – proof copy of 1st Illus. Edn. – ink or pencil sketches by William Nicholson indicating the position of 21 pictorial vignettes – proofs of the blocks pinned or clipped to the appropriate pages – original wrappers – 8 vo. – 1929.
(Sotheby's) $1,850 £880

SATCHWELL, RICHARD
'Scripture Costume with Biographical Sketches' – 20 hand col. engraved plates – advert leaf at end – spotting – contem. half straight grained morocco – slightly worn – t.e.g. – folio – 1819.
(Sotheby's) $95 £45

SATURDAY BOOK, THE
Editor Leonard Russell and others – vol. 1-34-plates – illus. – orig. cloth – 3 without dust jackets – soiled – 18 boxed – 8vo. – 1941-75.
(Sotheby's) $145 £70

VOYAGES
DANS LES ALPES,
PRÉCÉDÉS
D'UN ESSAI
SUR L'HISTOIRE NATURELLE
DES ENVIRONS
DE GENEVE,
Par HORACE-BÉNEDICT DE SAUSSURE, *Profeſſeur de Philoſophie dans l'Académie de Geneve.*
TOME PREMIER.

Nec ſpecies ſua cuique manet, rerumque [illegible]
Ex aliis alias reparat Natura figuras.
Ovid.

A NEUCHATEL,
CHEZ SAMUEL FAUCHE, IMPRIMEUR ET LIBRAIRE DU ROI.
M. DCC. LXXIX.

SAUSSURE, HORACE BENEDICT DE
'Voyages dans les Alpes' – 4 vols. – 1st Edn. – engraved vignettes on titles – 22 folding plates – 2 folding maps – engraved headpieces – some tears and holes – browning – contem. boards – worn – largely unopened – 4to. – Neuchatel and Geneva 1779-96.
(Sotheby's) $1,850 £880

SAVAGE, W.
'Dictionary of the Art of Printing' – rebound – half calf – gilt – 1841.
(Phillips) $190 £90

SAVARY, JACQUES
'The Universal Dictionary of Trade and Commerce' – 2 vol. – engraved frontis – 24 folding maps – tears repaired – folding tables – some soiling – contem. half calf – worn – folio – 1751-55.
(Sotheby's) $295 £140

The Miners Friend;
OR, AN
ENGINE
TO RAISE
WATER
BY
FIRE,
DESCRIBED.
AND
Of the manner of Fixing it in
MINES.
WITH
An Account of the ſeveral other Uſes it is applicable unto; and an
ANSWER
To the OBJECTIONS made againſt it.
By *THO. SAVERY* Gent.

Pigri eſt ingenii contentum eſſe his, quæ ab aliis inventa ſunt. Seneca.

LONDON: Printed for *S.Crouch* at the Corner of *Popes-Head-Alley* in *Cornhil.* 1702.

SAVERY, THOMAS
'The Miner's Friend or An Engine to Raise Water by Fire' – 1st Edn. – folding engraved plate – title loose and soiled – recent half calf – 8vo – S. Crouch, 1702.
(Sotheby's) $2,520 £1,200

SAVIGNY, J. B. H. AND CORREARD, A.
'Narrative of a Voyage to Senegal' – hand col. frontis – plate – half title – spotted – contem. calf backed boards – rubbed – 8vo. – 1818.
(Sotheby's) $85 £40

Eugenio di Savoya

SAVOY, PRINCE EUGENE OF
Letter signed in Italian – one page – folio – to Marchese Ficino Pepoli of Bologna congratulating him on wife's delivery of first child – Vienna 1731.
(Sotheby's) $170 £80

SAXE, MAURICE COMTE DE
'Mes Reveries' – 2 vol. – 4to. – 84 engraved plates and plans – 61 folding – three hand coloured – contemp. mottled calf – rubbed – spines worn – joints slightly split – Amsterdam and Leipsig, 1757.
(Christie's S. Kensington) $230 £110

SAXTON, CHRISTOPHER
'Cantii, Southsexiae, Suriae, et Middlesia Comitat' – hand coloured engraved map – 22 x 16½ inches slightly stained – framed and glazed – 1575.
(Christie's S. Kensington) $1,470 £700
'Glamorgan Commitatus' – engraved map – hand coloured in outline – 13 x 19 inches – one small hole – marginal staining – 1579.
(Christie's S. Kensington) $2,730 £1,300
'Glamorgan' – engraved map hand coloured in outline – 11 x 13½ inches – framed and glazed 1610 or later.
(Christie's S. Kensington) $90 £42

SAYER, ROBERT
'The Russian Discoveries' – engraved map extending into the Arctic, Baffin Bay to China and Japan and with part Of North America – all hand col. in outline – slight offsetting – 452 mm x 611 mm – 1775.
(Sotheby's) $135 £65

A joint production – Dorothy Sayers & me – may it amuse you!
Helen Simpson.
Christmas 1937.

SAYERS, DOROTHY L.
'Papers relating to the Family of Wimsey' – 1st Edn. – limited to 500 copies – presentation copy – inscribed by Helen Simpson – frontis – plate – limitation slip loosely inserted – orig. wrappers – spine faded – 8vo. – Privately printed 1936.
(Sotheby's) $170 £80

'Catholic Tales and Christian Songs' – Author's second book – orig. decorative stiff wrappers – spine chipped – some wear and marks – Oxford 1918.
(J. Ash) $115 £55

SCALE, BERNARD
'An Hibernian Atlas' – vignette on engraved title and dedication leaf – 37 engraved maps and index leaf – col. by hand – text to each map – all versos blank – 19th cent. parchment – gilt – green morocco label – sm. 4to. – R. Sayer and J. Bennett, 1776.
(Sotheby's) $630 £300

SCANDINAVIA
32 maps – all 19th cent.
(Phillips) $85 £40

SCANDINAVIA – JAILLOT, H.
'La Scandinavie et les Royaumes de Suede, de Danemark et de Norwege' – engraved map – hand col. in outline – historiated and armorial title cartouche – full col. – some discolouration – 455 mm x 647 mm – Paris circa 1700.
(Sotheby's) $170 £80

SCELTA DI FACEZIE
'Tratti, Buffonerie, Motti ...' – woodcut printer's device on title – spotting – inscription on fly leaf probably in Heber's hand 18th cent. red morocco by Padeloup le Jeune with his ticket – triple gilt fillet – double fillet round spine – gilt dentelles – gilt edges cracked – small abrasion – 8vo. – Florence, Apresso i Giunti, 1586.
(Sotheby Parke Bernet) $670 £320

SCERE, MAURICE
'Microcosmo' – number 94 of 650 copies – Maestricht, 1928 – woodcut frontispiece and illustrations – later morocco backed boards – soiled – original wrappers bound in.
(Christie's S. Kensington) $20 £10

SCHILLER, FRIEDRICH VON
'Sammtliche Werke' – 12 vols. – portrait frontis – spotted in places – contem. half calf – rubbed spines worn – sm. 8vo. – Stuttgart and Tubingen 1838.
(Sotheby's) $230 £110

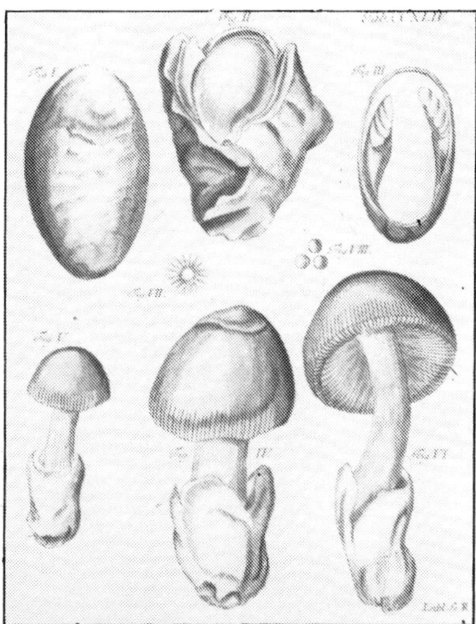

SCHAEFFER, JACOB CHRISTIAN
'Fungorum' – 1st. Edn. – 4 vols. – 2 engraved frontis – title vignette in vol. IV in red – 330 hand coloured engraved plates – text in Latin and German – half morocco – rubbed – 4to. – Regensburg 1762-74.
(Christie's) $3,780 £1,800

SCHILLER GALLERY
From the original drawings of E. W. Kaulbach and others, a series of photographs with text – embossed cover over boards – folio – London circa 1870.
(Bennett Book Auction) $6 £3

SCHILLINGS, C. G.
'With Flashlight and Rifle' – 2 vols. illus. – cloth gilt – 1906.
(Phillips) $40 $18

SCHKUHR, CHRETIEN
'Histoire des Carex ou Laiches' – engr. portrait and 54 hand coloured plates – occasional slight staining – contemp. calf – worn – 4to. – Leipzig, 1802.
(Christie's S. Kensington) $105 £50

SCHLIEMANN, DR HENRY
'Troy and Its Remains' – plates and maps – some folding – illus. – pencil marginalia – orig. cloth – worn – t.e.g. – 8vo. – 1875.
(Sotheby's) $65 £30

SCHMID, HERMAN AND STIELER, KARL
'Aus Deutschen Bergen' – plates – illus. – orig. decorated cloth – gilt – rubbed – g.e. – 4to. – Stuttgart 1873.
(Sotheby's) $160 £75

SCHMIDT, ROBERT
'Early European Porcelain as Collected by Otto Blohm' – limited Edn. – col. plates – illus. – orig. cloth – dust jacket – 4to. – Munich 1953.
(Sotheby's) $125 £60

SCHMIDTMEYER, P.
'Travels into Chile' – 25 of 30 plates – a few coloured – some spotting – half morocco worn – 4to. – 1824.
(Phillips) $210 £100

SCHMIT, ROBERT
'Eugene Boudin' – 3 vol. – no. 460 of 1300 copies – illus. – orig. cloth – t.e.g. – 4to. – Paris 1973.
(Christie's) $275 £130

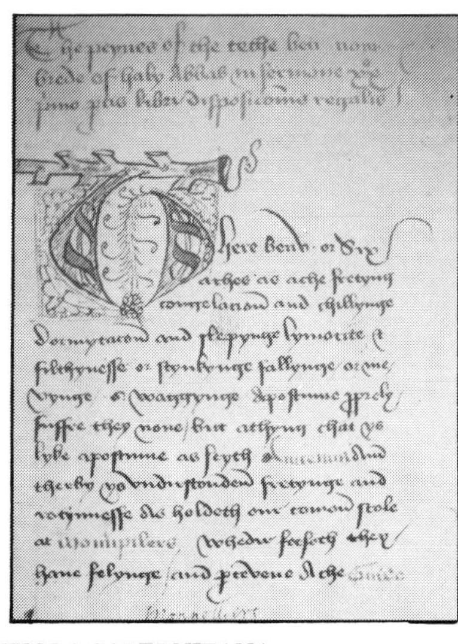

SCHOLA SALERNITANA
'Regimen Salernitanum' – in Latin with section in Eng. – mss on paper – 262 leaves – 16-19 lines in dark brown ink – occas. initials in red – excellent cond. except for some waterstaining – 15th cent. blindstamped calf over wooden boards – rebacked in 19th cent. – 148 x 105 cm – England mid 15th cent.
(Christie's) $8,400 £4,000

SCHOMBERG, F. & A. AND MARQUIS H. DE RUVIGNY
'The Humble Petition of the Protestants of France' – 4 leaves – frayed – modern boards – folio – for L. Curtis, 1681.
(Sotheby's) $10 £5

SCHOOL BOOKS
A collection of 152 books designed for use in schools – some with plates and illus. – various bindings – many worn – various sizes – 1763-1903.
(Sotheby's) $160 £75

SCHOOL MISTRESS, THE
42 wood engraved illus. – stained – morocco backed cloth – orig. pictorial wrappers bound in – 32 mo. – Robert Bassam circa 1790.
(Sotheby's) $145 £70

SCHREIBER, C.
'Journals' – 2 vols. – plates – orig. cloth – rubbed – 8vo. – 1911.
(Sotheby's) $115 £55

SCHREINER, OLIVE
'Dream Life and Real Life' – orig. cloth – spine darkened – slightly loose – 1893.
(J. Ash) $20 £10

SCHWERDT, C. F. G. R.
'The Hampshire Hunt in a Series of Five Plates' – no. 35 of 200 copies – col. addit. title – mounted plates loosely inserted – 4 col. map and illus. – orig. wrappers slightly soiled – torn – oblong folio – Privately printed 1929.
(Christie's) $75 £35

SCOT, D.
'Engineer and Machinist's Assistant' – engraved title – illustrations and 132 plates – 4to. – half calf – plates and text foxed – Glasgow etc 1849.
(Bennett Book Auction) $19 £9

SCOTLAND, SOUVENIR OF
120 chromo views – Nelson 1895.
(Bennett Book Auction) $50 £24

SCOTT, J.
'History of the Life and Death of John, Earl of Gowrie ..' – original boards – uncut – Edinburgh 1818.
(Bennett Book Auction) $17 £8

SCOTT, PETER
'The Eye of the Wind' – inscribed and with sm. water col. sketch by Peter Scott – smudged – plates – some col. – orig. leatherette – g.e. – 1961.
(Christie's) $40 £20

SCOTT, R. F.
'The Voyage of the Discovery' – 2 vol. – plates – folding maps – spotting – orig. cloth – rubbed – 8vo. – 1905.
(Sotheby's) $180 £85

SCOTTISH HISTORY AND TOPOGRAPHY
8 vols. including Maxwell (H) – 'Scottish Land Names' – cloth – 1894.
(Bennett Book Auction) $34 £16

SCOTTISH HISTORY SOCIETY
First and Third Series – 31 vol. only – orig. cloth – 8vo. – various dates.
(Sotheby's) $240 £115

SCOURGE, THE (editor Thomas Lewis)
Nos. 1-XLIII – a complete set bound in one vol. – some damp stained – soiled – first two issues torn and repaired – contem. calf worn – folio – Nov. 1717.
(Sotheby's) $400 £190

SEAGO, EDWARD
'High Endeavour' – 20 plates by author – good copy – 1944.
(J. Ash) $10 £5

SEBA, ALBERTUS
'Locupletissimi Rerum Naturalium Thesauri Accurata Descriptio' – 4 vols. – engr. portrait – 448 engraved plates – contem. diced russia – later spines – g.e. – rubbed – covers detached – folio – Amsterdam, 1734-65.
(Christie's) $2,520 £1,200

SEDDON, JOHN
'Rambles In the Rhine Provinces' – 14 actual photographs mounted – plates – illus. – orig. cloth – rubbed – loose – g.e. – 4to. – 1878.
(Sotheby's) $180 £85

SEE, R. R. M.
'English Pastels' – 1750-1830 number 15 of 750 copies – mounted plates – a few coloured – occasional slight spotting – orig. parchment – soiled lge. 4to. – 1911.
(Christie's S. Kensington) $40 £18

SEITZ, DR. A.
'Macrolepidoptera of the World: The African Rhopalocera' – vol. 13 in 2 vols. – incl. one of plates – 4to. – 1925.
(Phillips) $145 £70

SELBY – PRIDEAU, JOHN
'Plates to Selby's Illustrations of British Ornithology' – 2 vol. – engraved titles and 222 plates all uncoloured – spotting – mid 19th century half calf – rubbed covers – detached – g.e. – lge. folio – Edinburgh and London, circa 1834.
(Christie's S. Kensington) $3,360 £1,600

SELDEN, JOHN
'Table Talk' – 2nd Edn. – some leaves foxed – contem. panelled calf – spine repaired – worn – 8vo. – 1696.
(Sotheby's) $105 £50

A SELF INDULGENT MAIDEN
Green floral robe trimmed with gold and red – floral design on blue ground – silver and gold arabesques on yellow leaf – four verses on verso – folio 34.5 x 23 cm. – Isfahan circa 1600.
(Christie's) $4,620 £2,200

SELOUS, F. C.
'Travel and Adventure in South East Africa' – map – illus. – orig. cloth gilt – 1893.
(Phillips) $115 £55

SEMMES, ADMIRAL RAPHAEL
'Memoirs of Service Afloat during the War between the States' – port. plates – orig. cloth defective – Baltimore 1869.
(Phillips) $55 £25

SEMPLE, MISS
'The Costume of the Netherlands' – Eng. and French text – engraved title with hand col. aquatint vignette – 30 col. aquatint plates – some browned – contem. boards – worn and loose – sm. folio – Ackermann 1818 or later.
(Sotheby's) $505 £240

SEMPLE, ROBERT
'Observations on a Journey through Spain and Italy to Naples' – 2 vol. – calf gilt – 1807.
(Phillips) $115 £55

SENAULT, L.
'Heures Nouvelles Tirees de la Sainte Ecriture' – engraved throughout – frontis and 6 plates in line borders with gold – ornamental vignettes – borders – initials – soiling and discolour – contem. red morocco – gilt – worn – 8vo. – Paris 1690.
(Sotheby's) $65 £30

SENECA
'Tragoediae' – contem. dark blue morocco gilt with stamp of golden fleece – in quarter red morocco slip case – 8vo. – 1661.
(Moore Allen & Innocent) $1,575 £750

SENEX, I. AND HARRIS, I.
'New Mapp of Rome' – uncol. town plan – 4 insets – early 18th cent.
(Phillips) $65 £30

SENIOR, NASSAU W.
'Four Introductory Letters on Political Economy' – 1st. Edn. – a little spotting – contem. blue calf backed marbled boards – rubbed – bookplate of Baker Library, Harvard Business School, – 8vo. – 1852.
(Sotheby's) $115 £55

SEQUIERIO, J. F. AND BUMALDI, J.A.
'Bibliotheca Botanica' – title in red and black – contem. calf gilt – 4to. – The Hague 1740.
(Phillips) $190 £90

SERA, YOSUKE
'Old Imari Blue and White Porcelain' – plates – some col. – folding maps – orig. boards – slipcase – 4to. – Kyoto 1959.
(Sotheby's) $125 £60

SERY VOLK (Grey Wolf editor S. A. Iznar)
First year no. 1-26; second year no. 1-23 in 22 – 8vo. – 1907-08.
(Sotheby's) $800 £380

SEUTTER, M.
'Lower Austria' – hand col. map – cartouche – circa 1730.
(Phillips) $85 £40

SEVERIM DE FARIA, M.
'Noticias de Portugal' – 1st Edn. – browned – contem. calf – rubbed – sm. folio – Lisbon 1655.
(Sotheby's) $210 £100

SEVIGNE, MADAME DE
'Lettres' – 12 vols. – 1818.
(Moore Allen & Innocent) $250 £120

SEYER, S.
'Memoirs, Historical and Topographical of Bristol and its Neighbourhood' – 2 vols. – engraved plates – 1 loose – contemp. calf – rubbed – 4to. – Bristol 1821-23.
(Sotheby's) $95 £45

SHACKLETON, E. H.
'The Heart of the Antarctic' – 2 vol. – 1st. Edn. – plates – folding maps – illus. – orig. cloth – t.e.g. – dust jackets – 4to. – 1909.
(Sotheby's) $230 £110

SHADBOLT, SIDNEY H.
'The Afghan Campaigns' – 2 vols. – cloth gilt – t.e.g. – 4to. – 1882.
(Phillips) $95 £45

SHAFFNER, T. P.
'History of the United States of America' – 2 vol. – plates and maps – some folding – some torn or loose – contem. half morocco – worn – 4to. – n.d.
(Sotheby's) $10 £5

SHAFTESBURY – ANTHONY ASHLEY COOPER, EARL OF
'Characteristicks of Men, Manners, Opinions, Times' – 3 vol. – 5th (but 7th) Edn. – engraved – portrait – margin cleanly torn – contemp. tree calf – worn – Birmingham, John Baskerville, 1773.
(Christie's S. Kensington) $20 £10

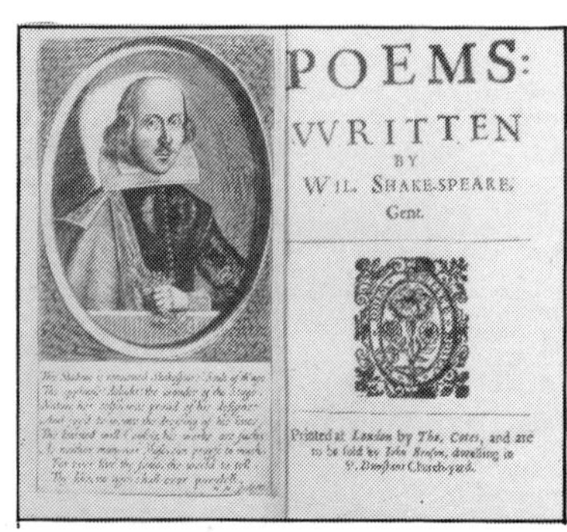

SHAKESPEARE, WILLIAM
'Poems' – dated and undated titles – engraved frontis by Marshall – morocco gilt by C. Smith – rebacked with orig. spine – sm. 8vo. – 1640.
(Christie's) $11,550 £5,500

'The Plays' – Editor Samuel Johnson and George Steevens – 21 vols. – engraved portrait – browning and spotting – contem. calf – worn – covers detached – 8vo. – 1803.
(Sotheby's) $105 £50

SHARP, SAMUEL
'A Treatise on the Operations of Surgery' – 4th Edn. – 14 engraved plates – some soiled – contemp. calf – rebacked – 1743.
(Christie's S. Kensington) $65 £32

SHARPE, C. K.
'Etchings' – nine mounted plates – 27 engraved plates – some spotting – margins browned – original cloth – rubbed – spine torn – t.e.g. – 4to. – Edinburgh and London, 1869.
(Christie's S. Kensington) $65 £32

SHARPE, R. BOWDLER
'Sketch Book of British Birds' – col. frontis and illus. by A. F. and C. Lydon – orig. cloth – slightly soiled – spine rubbed – 8vo. – 1898.
(Christie's S. Kensington) $40 £20

SHAW, G. BERNARD
'The Works' – vol. 1-30 of 33 – no. 870 of 1025 – orig. cloth – t.e.g. – dust jackets – 8vo. – 1930-32.
(Sotheby's) $115 £55
'Saint Joan' – 1st published Edn. – good copy – attractive bookplate – 1924.
(J. Ash) $8 £4

SHAW, GEORGE
'General Zoology' – 24 vol. only – uncol. engraved plates – spotting – contem. half morocco rubbed – 1800-26.
(Christie's) $360 £170

SHAW, HENRY
'Alphabets, Numerals and Devices of the Middle Ages' – title in red and black – 24 plates – 14 in colours – some leaves detached – spotting – orig. cloth backed boards – scuffed – folio 1845.
(Christie's) $80 £38
'Dresses and Decorations of the Middle Ages' – 2 vol. – large paper copy – plates – illus. – some hand col. – contem. half morocco – rubbed – folio – 1843.
(Sotheby's) $360 £170

SHAW, HENRY AND MEYRICK, SIR SAMUEL RUSH
'Specimens of Ancient Furniture' – 4to. – 73 engr. plates – ten hand-coloured – some soiling, a few torn – repaired without loss – no. 62 misbound – contemp. morocco backed cloth – worn – inner hinges split – 1836.
(Christie's S. Kensington) $75 £35

SHAW, H. AND MOULE, T.
'Details of Elizabethan Architecture' – engraved title and 59 plates – some coloured – spotting – cloth – 4to. – 1839.
(Phillips) $55 £25

SHAW, JAMES
'Sketches of the History of the Austrian Netherlands' – 2nd Edn. – calf gilt – 1788.
(Phillips) $145 £70

SHAW, RICHARD NORMAN
'Architectural Sketches from the Continent' – litho title and plates – browned – spotted – orig. roan backed cloth – worn – g.e. – folio – 1872.
(Sotheby's) $230 £110

SHAW, S.
'An Accurate Alphabetical Index of the Registered Entails in Scotland' – boards – covers detached – 4to. – uncut – Edinburgh, 1784.
(Bennett Book Auction) $34 £16

SHAW, S.
'Physiognomy' – tree calf – 18th cent.
(Laurence & Martin Taylor) $17 £8

SHAW, STEBBING
'The History and Antiquities of Staffordshire' – vols. I and II – 2 folding maps – 2 folding tables – 82 plates – later half morocco – gilt – uncut – folio – 1798-1801.
(Christie's) $545 £260

SHAW, THOMAS
'Travels or Observations of Barbary and the Levant' – maps and plates – con. calf – folio – Oxford 1738.
(Phillips) $180 £85

SHAW, THURSTAN
'Igbo-Ukwa, an Account of the Archaeological Discoveries in Nigeria' – 2 vols. – illus. – orig. cloth – dust jacket – 4to. – 1970.
(Sotheby's) $34 £16

SHEARER, THOMAS
'The Cabinet Maker's London Book of Prices' – 29 engraved plates – old sheep – 4to. – 1793.
(Phillips) $460 £220

SHEE, MARTIN ARCHER
'Rhymes on Art or the Remonstrance of a Painter' – 1st. Edn. – spotting – stitching loose – orig. boards – spine defective – uncut – 8vo. – 1805.
(Sotheby's) $65 £30

SHEEHAN, J. J.
'History of the Town and Port of Hull' – illus. and folding maps – 2nd Edn. – lacks spine and part of index.
(Baitson) $40 £20

'History of the Town and Port of Kingston upon Hull' – 2nd Edn. – illus. with folding plans – engravings etc. – Beverley 1866.
(Baitson) $85 £40

SHEPHERD, J. C. AND JELLICOE, G. A.
'Italian Gardens of the Renaissance' – illus. – half morocco gilt – folio – 1925.
(Phillips) $160 £75

SHEPHERD, T. H.
'London Interiors with Their Costumes and Ceremonies' – engraved title – 49 plates – contem. gilt – rubbed – g.e. – 4to. – 1841.
(Sotheby Beresford Adams) $145 £70

'Metropolitan Improvements of London in the 19th Century' – addit. engraved title – 79 plates on india paper – 1 map – foxing – green half calf – gilt spine – rubbed – 4to. – 1827.
(Sotheby's) $170 £80

SHEPPARD, W.
'Faithful Councellor or the Marrow of the Law in English' – calf gilt – 1651.
(Phillips) $65 £32

SHERER, JOHN
'The Classic Lands of Europe' – 2 vols. – engraved titles and 121 plates – contem. half calf – rubbed – 4to. – n.d.
(Sotheby's) $315 £150

SHERER, MAJOR MOYLE
'Tales of the Wars of Our Times' – 2 vols. – orig. boards – 1829.
(Phillips) $85 £40

SHIRTCLIFE, R.
'Theory and Practice of Gauging' – 7 folding plates – calf gilt – 1740.
(Phillips) $100 £48

SHOBERL, FREDERIC, (Editor)
'The World in Miniature ... Africa' – 4 vol. – hand coloured add. title and two folding maps – 45 plates – all but one hand coloured – some aquatint – some folding – some leaves detached – orig. boards – worn – 12 mo. – n.d.
(Christie's S. Kensington) $115 £55

SHORTHOUSE, J. H.
'John Inglesant' – author's first and most important novel – rebound in full half levant morocco by Sangorski and Sutcliffe – fine copy – Privately printed, Birmingham 1880.
(J. Ash) $250 £120

SHOWER, SIR BARTHOLOMEW
'Cases in Parliament Resolved and Adjusted upon Petition ...' – 1st. Edn. – signature 1698 – notes by Joseph Keble, (1662-1710) – contem. calf – rubbed – folio – 1698.
(Sotheby's) $190 £90

SHOWMAN, THE
Nos. 2-62 lacking nos. 5, 11, 18 and 57 – illus. – orig. wrappers – a few torn – 4to. – 1900-1902.
(Sotheby's) $275 £130

SIBLY, E.
'An Illustration of the Celestial Science of Astrology' – 1817.
(Dacre, Son & Hartley) $100 £48

SIBREE, REV. JAMES
'Fifty Years Recollections of Hull' – engravings – 1884.
(Baitson) $20 £10

SIDNEY, S.
'The Book of the Horse' – 25 col. plates – spotting – contem. half calf – rubbed – inner hinges cracked – 4to. – n.d.
(Christie's) $125 £60

'The Three Colonies of Australia' – 2 copies – plates – illus. – spotting – orig. cloth – rebacked – rubbed – 8vo. – 1852.
(Sotheby's) $65 £30

SIGNATURE
New series no. 1-18 – plates – orig. wrappers – 6 cloth backed portfolios – 8vo. – 1946-54.
(Sotheby's) $190 £90

SILTZER, F.
'The Story of British Sporting Prints' – illustrations – slight spotting – original cloth – rubbed – n.d.
(Christie's S. Kensington) $105 £50

SIMEONI, G.
'Commentarii all a Tetrarchia di Venegia, di Milano, di Mantova' – portrait on title – device on last leaf – Venice 1849.
(Sotheby's) $135 £65

SIMMS, F. W.
'Public Works of Great Britain' – 153 engraved plates – woodcut vignettes – some double page – spotted – contem. half morocco – worn – folio – 1838.
(Sotheby's) $210 £100

SIMON, ANDRE
'Wines of the World' – limited signed Edn. – crimson morocco gilt – gilt overlay in upper cover – g.e. by Zaehndorf – buckram box – 4to. – 1969.
(Phillips) $85 £40

SIMON, O.
'A Specimen Book of Types and Ornaments at Use in the Curwen Press' – limited Edn. – orig. cloth – 4to. – 1928.
(Sotheby's) $380 £180

SIMONS, LOUIS
'Journal of a Tour and Residence in Great Britain' – 2 vols. – 21 aqua plates – calf – Edinburgh 1815.
(Phillips) $40 £20

SIMPLICISSIMUS
14 Edn. only – orig. wrappers – frayed – 4to. – Munchen 1904-43.
(Sotheby's) $145 £70

SIMPSON, J.
'Letters to Sir Walter Scott ... Effects of the Visit to Scotland ... His Majesty King George IV' – original boards – uncut – Edinburgh 1822.
(Bennett Book Auction) $25 £12

SIMPSON, THOMAS
'The Doctrine of Annuities and Reversions' – 2 works in 1 – modern boards – 8vo. – 1742-43.
(Sotheby's) $180 £85

SIMPSON, WILLIAM
'The Seat of War in the East' – second series only – litho title and 38 plates only – spotting – fraying – orig. cloth – worn and disbound – folio – 1856.
(Christie's) $95 £45

SINCLAIR, GEORGE
'Hortus Gramineus Woburnensis or an Account of the Results of Experiments on Different Grasses' – 4th Edn. – 43 hand col. plates – orig. cloth – recased – soiled – n.d.
(Christie's S. Kensington) $55 £25

SINCLAIR, SIR JOHN
'The Code to Health and Longevity' – 4 vols. – 3 engraved frontis – contem. half calf – spines lacking – some covers detached – Edinburgh 1807.
(Christie's) $40 £20

SINCLAIR, JOHN
'The History of the Public Revenue of the British Empire' – 1st Edn. – calf gilt – 4to. – 1785-90.
(Phillips) $275 $130

SINGER, GEORGE JOHN
'Elements of Electricity and Electro-Chemistry' – 1st. Edn. – 4 engraved plates – 4 pp adverts without three samples of coloured oxides – new cloth – 8vo. – Longman 1814.
(Sotheby's) $65 £30

SINGER, HANS WOLFGANG
'Rembrandt's Samtliche Radierungen' – 3 portfolios – 312 mounted plates – orig. boards – Munich 1915.
(Phillips) $65 £30

SINGER, SAMUEL WELLER (Editor)
'Early English Poetry' – 8 vols. of 9 in 7 – 4 engraved ports – lacks the vol. of Hall's Satires – some offsetting – contem. red half morocco – gilt – g.e. – 12 mo. – Chiswick Press 1817-23.
(Sotheby's) $125 £60

SIRET, HENRI AND LOUIS
'Les Premiers Ages du Metal dans le Sud Est de L'Espagne' – 2 parts in one vol. – 27 plates – orig. morocco backed cloth – rubbed – spine torn – 4to. – Antwerp 1887.
(Sotheby Beresford Adams) $170 £80

SISMONDI, J. C. L. SIMONDE DE
'Nouveaux Principes d'Economie Politique' – 2 vols. – 2nd Edn. – half titles – spotting – modern calf backed marbled boards – slightly rubbed – 8vo. – Paris 1827.
(Sotheby's) $210 £100

RUSTIC ELEGIES
FOR
TAPLOW de la MARES.
*
'Tis a note of enchantment; what ails her? she sees
A mountain ascending, a vision of trees...'

SITWELL, DAME EDITH
'Rustic Elegies' – 1st. Edn. – inscribed by Siegfried Sassoon on half title – orig. cloth – dust jacket – 8vo. – 1927.
(Sotheby's) $135 £65

For
Walter de la Mare
with homage from
Edith Sitwell

'Green Song and Other Poems' – Presentation copy – inscribed by author to De La Mare – orig. cloth – discoloured – dust jacket – 8vo. – 1944.
(Sotheby's) $115 £55

SITWELL, SIR OSBERT
'England Reclaimed' – 1st Edn. – pres copy inscribed by author for Cecil Beaton – orig. cloth – somewhat faded – 8vo. – 1927.
(Sotheby's) $75 £35

SITWELL, SACHEVEREL
'Monks, Nuns and Monasteries' – 1st American Edn. – many plates – some coloured – dust wrappers – 4to. – New York 1965.
(J. Ash) $12 £6

SKEAT, W. AND BLAGDEN, C.
'Pagan Races of the Malay Peninsula' – 2 col. – plates – orig. cloth – 1906.
(Sotheby's) $160 £75

SKELTON, JOHN
'Pithy, Pleasant and Profitable Works' – 2nd Edn. – advert leaf at end – waterstains – contem. mottled calf – gilt spine – 8vo. – 1736.
(Sotheby's) $85 £40

SKENE, J.
'Series of Sketches of the Existing Localities' – 21 parts – 19 etched plates – 2 parts without plates or wraps – 1st. Edn. – Edinburgh 1829.
(Bennett Book Auction) $15 £7

SKENE, SIR JOHN OF CURRIEHILL
'Regiam Majestatem' – 1st. Edn. in English translated by author – woodcut device – woodcut initials and ornaments – title slightly soiled – 17th cent. calf – folio – Edinburgh 1609.
(Sotheby's) $230 £110

SKETCH, THE
'A Journal of Art and Actuality' – vols. 1-4; 64-84; 91-102 – together 37 vols. in 29 – some contemp. calf roan and some original cloth gilt – 6 in half morocco gilt – with name of Sir Cecil Beaton stamped on foot of spine – sm. folio – 1893-1918.
(Sotheby's) $95 £45

SKINNER, JOSEPH
'The Present State of Peru' – 1st Edn. – 20 hand col. engraved plates – some tears – half calf – spine crudely repaired – 4to. – 1805.
(Sotheby's) $335 £160

SLATER, J. H.
'Engravings and Their Value' – 6th Edn. – plates – a few coloured – orig. cloth dust jacket – lge 4to. – n.d.
(Christie's S. Kensington) $40 £18

SLAVERY
Highly important and extensive archive of some 8,000 letters and papers relating to the West Indian estate of the Codrington family particularly Antiqua and Barbados from the 17th to the 20th century – 40 maps and plans of islands and plantations – 130 deeds and mortgages – 250 inventories of slaves and stock – 9 vols. of commercial papers – 24 letter books – 400 legal documents and a number of printed pamphlets about slavery in 17 cardboard boxes and 1 tea chest – 1668-1944.
(Sotheby's) $191,100 £91,000

SLOANE, W. M.
'The Life of Napoleon' – 4 vols. – plates – many col – half morocco gilt – 4to. – 1906.
(Phillips) $65 £30

SMEATON, JOHN
'A Narrative of the Building of the Eddystone Lighthouse' – 2nd Edn. – engraved vignette title and 23 plates – spotted – contem. half morocco – worn – covers detached – folio – 1813.
(Sotheby's) $295 £140

SMELLIE, WILLIAM
'The Philosophy of Natural History' – 2 vols. – calf – rebacked – 8vo. – Dublin 1790.
(Sotheby's) $30 £15

SMITH, A. H.
'The Place Names of the North Riding' – 1928.
(Baitson) $10 £5

SMITH, AARON
'The Atrocities of the Pirates' – number 356 of 500 copies – frontis and illus. by Clifford Webb – orig. cloth – faded – sm. folio – 1929.
(Christie's) $75 £35

SMITH, ALBERT AND REACH, ANGUS B.
'The Man in the Moon' – 5 vols. – 24 folding plates – some torn – illus. – soiled – modern morocco by Root and Son – orig. wrappers and adverts preserved – sm. 4to. – 1847-49.
(Sotheby's) $30 £15

SMITH, C. J.
'Historical and Literary Curiosities' – engraved plates – some spotted – contem. half morocco – rubbed – 4to. – 1845.
(Sotheby's) $25 £12

SMITH, CHARLES HAMILTON
'The Ancient Costume of Great Britain' – addit. col. engraved title – 60 col. plates – marginal stain – contem. green half morocco – spine defective – folio – J. Dowding n.d.
(Sotheby's) $335 £160

SMITH, CHARLOTTE
'Rural Walks in Dialogues' – 2 vol. in one – spotted – lacking endleaves – contem. sheep – spine rubbed – 12 mo. – Cadell and Davis 1795.
(Sotheby's) $10 £5
'Ethelinde' – 1st Edn. – 5 vols. – calf – 1789.
(Phillips) $335 £160

SMITH, EDWARD
'Account of a Journey Through North Eastern Texas in 1849 for the Purposes of Emigration' – 2 folding maps – orig. green cloth – spine torn – 8vo. – London and Birmingham 1849.
(Sotheby's) $460 £220

SMITH, G. B.
'The Life of Gladstone' – 3 vols. – colour plates – half morocco binding.
(Lane) $8 £4

SMITH, G. E.
'The Royal Mummies' – plates – modern half morocco – orig. upper wrapper preserved – folio – Cairo 1912.
(Sotheby's) $265 £125
'Egyptian Mummies' – plates – orig. cloth – 4to. – 1924.
(Sotheby's) $65 £30

SMITH, GEORGE
'The Cabinet Maker and Upholsterer's Guide' – engraved addit. title – 48 plates – contem. cloth – worn – 4to. – 1826.
(Christie's) $65 £30

SMITH, GEORGE
'A Complete Body of Distilling explaining the Mysteries of that Science' – 3rd Edn. – engraved frontis of a lab – index leaf – inner margin of frontis – title and some pages soiled – contem. calf – worn – 8vo. – Henry Lintot 1738.
(Sotheby's) $75 £35

SMITH, GODFREY
'The Laboratory or the School of Arts ... Secrets of Jewellery ... Arts of making Glass etc.' – trans from German – 1st Edn. – frontis – 5 plates – ornaments – contem. calf – Lord Minto bookplate – 8vo. – John James 1739.
(Sotheby's) $135 £65

SMITH, J. J.
'Remarks on Rural Scenery' – 20 etched plates only 5 orig. – watercolours by author bound in at end – half calf – upper cover detached – 4to. – 1797.
(Phillips) $230 £110

SMITH, SIR JAMES EDWARD
'A Grammar of Botany' – 1st. Edn. – 21 hand coloured plates – a few slightly soiled – some leaves spotted – modern boards – 1821.
(Christie's S. Kensington) $85 £40

SMITH, JOHN
'A Catalogue Raisonne of ... the most eminent Dutch, Flemish and French Painters' – 9 vol. including the supplement – limited to 1250 copies – plates original cloth – soiled – Reprinted for Sands & Co., London and Edinburgh, 1908.
(Christie's S. Kensington) $145 £70

SMITH, J. T.
'Vagabondiana' – Etchings of remarkable beggars – 48 etched plates – half morocco covers detached – 4to. – 1817.
(Phillips) $135 £65

SMITH, JOHN THOMAS
'Antiquities of Westminster' – 38 plates – 15 coloured – occasional slight soiling – half title and vindication lacking – 1807 – 'Sixty two Additional Plates to Smith's Antiquities of Westminster' – coloured title vignette – 62 plates – some spotted (1809) – bound in one volume – margins slightly browned – contemp. russia – bumped – joints split g.e. 4to.
(Christie's S. Kensington) $200 £95

SMITH, MADELEINE
13 auto letters signed to her lover Emile L'Angelier who was afterwards poisoned – c. 75 pages – many cross written – octavo – postmarked with 2 contem. printed accounts of her trial – a letter – 2 playbills and other papers – folio – Edinburgh June 1857.
(Sotheby's) $1,890 £900

SMITH, R.
'Universal Directory for Taking Alive and Destroying Rats' – 5 plates – mostly folding – modern boards – uncut – 8vo. – 1786.
(Phillips) $40 £20

SMITH, MRS R. SOUTHWOOD
'Panoramic View of the city of Funchal in the Island of Madeira' – large folding hand tinted litho in 3 parts by L. Haghe – cloth leather backed with original label – oblong folio – list of subscribers – Weymouth 1844.
(Bennett Book Auction) $115 £55

SMITH, T. (Editor)
'Poetica Erotica' – 2 vols. – limited Edn. – cloth backed boards – New York 1927.
(Phillips) $30 £14

SMITH, T. J.
'Nollekens and His Times' – 2 vol. – extra illus. with 135 portraits and plates – 2 hand col. – 2 orig. water colours – modern morocco by Riviere – 8vo. – 1829.
(Sotheby's) $335 £160

SMITHERAN, P. H.
'Infantry Uniforms of the British Army' – 3 vol. – all signed by author – coloured plates – original cloth – dust jackets – folio – 1965-70.
(Christie's S. Kensington) $40 £20

SMYTH, W. H.
'Memoir Descriptive of Sicily and Its Islands' – folding map – 13 hand col. plates – some leaves soiled – modern half morocco – 4to. – 1824.
(Sotheby's) $210 £100

'Aedes Hartwellianae, The Cycle of Celestial Objects' – 2 vol. – plates – illustrations – contemp. calf – rubbed 4to. – for private circulation only – 1851-60.
(Sotheby's) $40 £20

SMYTHIES, B. E.
'The Birds of Burma' – col. plates – buckram – 1953.
(Phillips) $180 £85

SNELLING, THOMAS
'Silver Coin and Coinage of England 1762'
'Gold Coin and Coinage of England 1763'
'Copper Coin and Coinage of England 1766'
'Silver Coin and Coinage of Scotland 1774'
– duplicates of all but second – 7 vols. in 2 – engraved plates – contem. half calf – – rubbed – 4to.
(Sotheby's) $220 £105

SNOW, DAVID AND OTHERS
'Raymond Ching, the Bird Paintings' – limited to 360 copies signed by artist – signed print loosely inserted – plates – illus. – contem. morocco – gilt – folio – 1978.
(Sotheby's) $200 £95

SNOWMAN, A. KENNETH
'Eighteenth Century Gold Boxes of Europe' – plates – some col. – orig. cloth – dust jacket – 4to. – 1966.
(Sotheby's) $60 £28

SOCIETY FOR THE DIFFUSION OF USEFUL KNOWLEDGE, MAPS
2 vol. – 154 engraved maps – 28 of the Americas – 51 city plans – plates of stars all uncoloured except hand col. geological map of England and Wales – contem. half russia – covers detached – worn – large 4to. – Chapman and Hall 1844.
(Sotheby's) $420 £200

SOCIETY FOR PROMOTING CHRISTIAN KNOWLEDGE, A COLLECTION OF TRACTS
Modern wrappers – in 2 slipcases – 12mo. – 1797-1807.
(Sotheby's) $55 £25

SOLA, A. E.
'Klondyke, Truths and Facts of the New El Dorado' – 1st Edn. – plates and 4 maps – orig. cloth gilt – insert Yukon Mining Co. 1897 share certificate for 100 shares of $1 each – London 1897.
(Phillips) $125 £60

SOLE, WILLIAM
'Menthae Britannicae' – 2 pp Als from author inserted – 23 of 24 plates – covers detached – 4to. – Bath 1798.
(Phillips) $95 £45

SOLON, M. L.
'The Ancient Art Stoneware' – 2 vol. – limited Edn. – plates – orig. wrappers – rubbed – folio – 1892.
(Sotheby's) $125 £60

'Inventions Decoratives' – engraved additional title and 49 plates by Solon – some spotting and soiling – unbound as issued in original portfolio – Paris 1866.
(Christie's S. Kensington) $65 £30

SOLVYNS, FRANCOIS BALTHAZAR
'The Costume of Hindostan' – Eng. and French text – 60 hand col. engraved plates – lacking covers – spine worn folio – 1807.
(Sotheby's) $335 £160

SOME SHORT STORIES WRITTEN BY A LADY TO AMUSE A YOUNG FRIEND
2nd Edn. – frontis and 7 plates – col. by hand – orig. roan backed boards – rubbed – 16 mo. – J. Harris 1825.
(Sotheby's) $210 £100

SOMERVILLE, E. O. E.
'Slipper's A B C of Hunting' – coloured illus. – 1st. Edn. – 1903.
(Laurence & Martin Taylor) $30 £14

SOMERVILLE, THOMAS
'The History of Political Transactions' – 2 vols. – contem. calf – 4to. – 1792-98.
(Phillips) $90 £42

SONNERAT, PIERRE
'Voyage aux Indes Orientales' – 5 vols. – including Atlas – 140 plates – 3 folding maps – text 8vo. – Atlas 4to. – 1806.
(Phillips) $400 £190

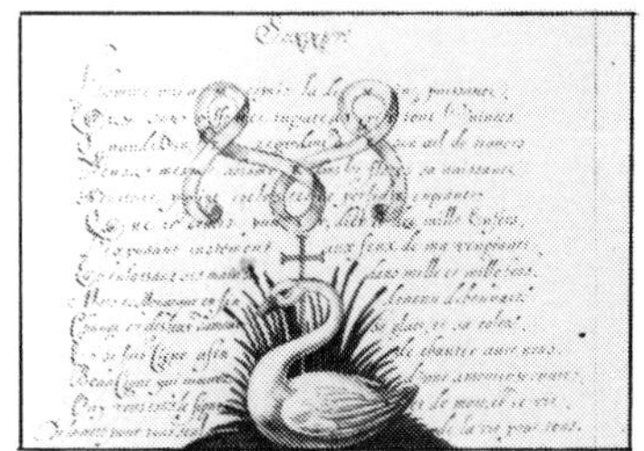

SONNETS SUR LA PASSION DE JESUS
A series of 69 French sonnets on the Passion of Christ followed by a short poem on the Passion, a second series of 36 sonnets on religious themes, and 21 six line stanzas, all in French – illum. mss on vellum – illum. title within full page decorated scheme – 68 miniatures – 8 full page miniatures – contem. Parisian dark red morocco gilt – panelled sides – two ties lacking – 197 mm x 227 mm. France, second quarter of the 17th cent.
(Sotheby's) $5,040 £2,400

SONNINI, C. S.
'Travels in Upper and Lower Egypt' – engraved port. – folding map – torn but repaired – 27 plates – advert leaf at end – browning – contem. half calf – 4to. – 1800.
(Sotheby Beresford Adams) $65 £32

SOPWITH, T.
'Eight Views of Fountains Abbey' – folio – some dampstaining – mostly marginal – orig. wrappers – soiled – Ripon n.d.
(Christie's S. Kensington) $105 £50

SORCAR
A collection of 9 souvenir programmes with several postcards and other publicity for Sorcar's performances in U. S. A. and Great Britain – various sizes – 1950-57.
(Sotheby's) $65 £30

SOTHEBY CATALOGUES
50 Old Master drawings, paintings, engravings and etchings – plates – 1960-74.
(Phillips) $55 £25

SOTHEBY'S
Catalogues of 24 book sales – many hard backs – 1933-69.
(Bennett Book Auction) $30 £14

SOTHEBY'S REVIEW
20 vol. various – 4to. – 1956-78.
(Christie's S. Kensington) $190 £90

SOTHEBY, SAMUEL LEIGH
'Ramblings in the Elucidation of the Autograph of Milton' – two mounted photographs of portraits – lithographed plates of facsimile hand writing – some spotting – original morocco – rubbed – the covers with sunken paper panels depicting respectively Paradise Lost and Paradise Regained – t.e.g. – sm. folio – 1861.
(Christie's S. Kensington $85 £40

SOTOMEYOR
'A Shamefull Revenge' – Eric Fraser illustrations – spine very slightly sunned – folio Society 1963.
(J. Ash) $10 £5

SOUTH AMERICA
34 maps – mostly hand col. including Vaugondy, Pinkerton, Bowen, Thomson, Johnson etc. – various dates.
(Phillips) $115 £55

SOUTH KENSINGTON MUSEUM, ART HANDBOOKS
Illus. 17 vols. – cloth.
(Bonhams) $45 £22

SOUTHERN AFRICA – BLAEU W. AND J.
'Aethiopia Inferior vel Exterior' – engraved map of central and southern Africa – hand col. in outline – historiated title cartouche – animals, sailing ships – full col. – French text on verso – 379 x 484 mm.
(Sotheby's) $210 £100

SOUTHEY, ROBERT
'History of the Peninsular War' – 3 vol. – modern half calf – scuffed – 4to. – 1823-32.
(Christie's) $65 £30

SOUTHEY, T.
'Chronological History of the West Indies' – 3 vols. half polished calf – 8vo. – 1827.
(Irelands) $145 £70

SOWERBY, G. B.
'Illustrated Book of British Shells' – 24 col. plates – cloth gilt – 1859.
(Phillips) $85 £40

SOWERBY, MILLICENT
A series of 10 watercolour drawings of young children at breakfast, feeding kittens etc. – all but one signed – some captioned in pencil – average size 260 mm x 205 mm.
(Sotheby's) $780 £370

SPAIN
'Retrotos de Los Espanoles Illustres con un Epitome de sus Vidas' – engraved portraits, limp leather, some leaves stained – Madrid, 1791.
(Bonham's) $200 £90

SPARK, MURIEL
'The Abbess of Crewe' – inscription on fly – slightly chipped dust wrapper – 1974.
(J. Ash) $8 £4

SPARRMAN, ANDREW
'A Voyage to the Cape of Good Hope' – 2nd Edn. – folding map – 10 engr. plates calf – rubbed – 4to. – 1786.
(Phillips) $335 £160

SPARROW, W. SHAW
'Sir John Lavery and His Work' – no. 25 of 160 copies – orig. vellum backed boards – soiled – folio n.d.
(Sotheby's) $125 £60

'Angling in British Art' – coloured frontis and plates – buckram – 4to. – 1st. Edn. – 1923.
(Bennett Book Auction) $95 £46

'George Stubbs and Ben Marshall' – plates – some col. – orig. cloth – bleached – 4to. – 1929.
(Phillips) $65 £32

'Henry Alken ... with Intro by Theodore Cook' – number 61 of 250 copies – signed by Cook – plates – some col – orig. cloth – spotted – t.e.g. – 4to. – 1927.
(Sotheby's) $135 £65

SPECTACLES DE PARIS
Contem. French binding of red morocco gilt with arms of Marie Antoinette in dark blue morocco case – 12 mo. – 1782.
(Moore Allen & Innocent) $925 £440

SPECTATOR, THE
8 vols., engraved frontispieces and titles, cont. marbled calf, repaired – n.d.
(Christie's S. Kensington) $70 £32

SPEECHES
'By a Member of the Parliament .. at Edinburgh' .. 1703 – contemporary calf – with, 'An Account of a Conversation ... Regulation of Goverments for the Common Good of Mankind In a Letter to the Marquis of Montrose' ... 1703 – Edinburgh 1704.
(Bennett Book Auction $40 £20

SPEECHLY, WILLIAM
'A Treatise on the Culture of the Vine' – 2nd Edn. – 6 folding plates – cont. calf gilt – 1789.
(Phillips) $115 £55

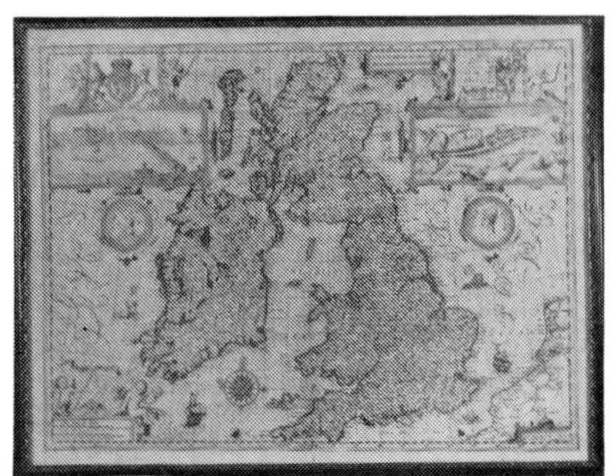

SPEED, JOHN
'Dorsetshyre' – engraved map – hand coloured in outline – 13½ x 19 ½ inches framed and glazed – 1614-16 Sudbury and Humble.
(Christie's S. Kensington) $360 £170

'Sussex' – engraved map – hand coloured in outline – framed and glazed – 13½ x 19½ inches – Henry Overton 1743.
(Christie's S. Kensington) $250 £120

'The Kingdome of Great Britain' – hand col. map – 2 inset plans framed and glazed – Sudbury and Humble, 1611.
(Phillips) $755 £360

'Cambridge' – hand col. map – inset town plan – margins trimmed – 1611.
(Phillips) $295 £140

'Oxfordshire' – hand coloured map, inset town plan, arms – 1611.
(Phillips) $495 £220

SPEER, A.
'Die Neue Reichskanzlei' – plates – cloth gilt – worn 4to. – Munich n.d.
(Phillips) $105 £50

SPEIGHT, HARRY
'Upper Wharfedale' – photographic illus. – 1900.
(Dacre, Son & Hartley) $70 £34

SPEKE, J. H.
'Journal of the Discovery of the Source of the Nile' – 2nd Edn. – frontis – folding map – plates – cloth gilt – 1864.
(Phillips) $90 £42

SPELMAN, SIR HENRY
'The English Works' – 2 parts in one vol. – first collected Edn. – subscription list – without portrait – contem. panelled calf – slightly worn – folio – 1723.
(Sotheby Beresford Adams) $35 £17

SPENCE, H. D. M.
'Cloister Life in the Time of Coeur de Lion' – illus. H. Railton – 1st. Edn. – 1892.
(Laurence & Martin Taylor) $5 £2

SPENCE, JOSEPH
'Polymetis' – 1st. Edn. – engraved portrait frontis – 41 engraved plates – occasional spotting and offsetting – contem. speckled calf – gilt – joints split – some wear – folio – 1747.
(Sotheby's) $40 £20

'Polymetis: or an Enquiry concerning the Agreement Between the Works of the Roman Poets and the Remains of the Ancient Artists' – 2nd Edn. – engraved portrait and 41 plates – four folding – damp stains – later half pigskin – worn – folio – 1775.
(Christie's S. Kensington) $95 £45

SPENCER, B. AND GILLEN, F.
'The Arunta' – 2 vol. – plates – orig. cloth – dust jacket – 8vo. – 1927.
(Sotheby's) $275 £130

SPENCER, STANLEY
Als 1½ pages – 8vo. Cliveden View, Cookham, 25 Sept. 1958 to Miss Susan Bennett.
(Phillips) $65 £32

SPENCER, SIR W. B.
'Native Tribes of the Northern Territory of Australia' – plates – half morocco gilt – t.e.g. – 1914.
(Phillips) $115 £55

'Wanderings in Wild Australia' – 2 vols. – plates and folding maps – orig. cloth d.w.s. – 1928.
(Phillips) $105 £50

'Native Tribes of Central Australia – plates and 2 folding maps – orig. cloth gilt – 8vo. – 1899.
(Phillips) $105 £50

SPENDER, STEPHEN
'European Witness' – very good in slightly marked dust wrapper – 1946.
(J. Ash) $8 £4

SPENSER, EDMUND
'The Shepherd's Calendar' – first Latin Edn. – titles in red and black – text in Eng. and Latin – 19th cent. half morocco – slightly rubbed – 8vo. – for M.M.T.C. and G. Bedell 1653.
(Sotheby's) $80 £38

SPHERE, THE
Vol. 1-3 only – folio – plates – illustrations – a few leaves detached – orig. cloth – worn – 1900.
(Christie's S. Kensington) $45 £22

SPIELMANN, M. H.
'British Portrait Painting' – 2 vols. – no. 112 of 376 copies – plates – spotting – orig. half vellum – t.e.g. – folio – 1910.
(Christie's) $95 £45
'The Iconography of Andreas Vesalius' – plates – 2nd Edn. 1555 – printed from orig. woodblock – inserted in pocket – illus. in text – orig. cloth – dust jacket – 4to. – 1925.
(Sotheby's) $105 £50
'The History of Punch' – number 166 of 250 copies – large paper Edn. – frontis – illus. – orig. cloth – faded – t.e.g. – 4to. – 1895.
(Christie's) $20 £10
'Henriette Ronner' – portrait – 12 plates – original cloth soiled – 4to. – 1891.
(Phillips) $170 £80

SPIELMANN, M. H. AND JERROLD, W.
'Hugh Thomson' – illus. cloth stained – 1931.
(Phillips) $30 £14

SPILSBURY, F. B.
'Picturesque Scenery in the Holy Land and Syria' – 20 col. plates – half morocco gilt – folio – 1803.
(Phillips) $840 £400

SPILSBURY, J.
'A Curious and Exact Plan of the Environs of Warsaw' – hand coloured engraved map – 15 x 11 inches – framed and glazed – 1763.
(Christie's S. Kensington) $45 £22

SPINDLER, WALTER
One of a pair of studies of Sarah Bernhardt as Theodora – pen, ink and water colour – signed and dated – 35.5 cm x 22.2 cm – 1890.
(Sotheby's) $420/440 £200/210

SPITZER COLLECTION
6 vol. – one of 600 copies – plates – 1 lacking and 1 duplicated – loose as issued in orig. cloth portfolios – 1 worn – lacks ties – folio – Paris, 1890-92.
(Sotheby's) $315 £150

SPON, JACOB
'The History of the City and State of Geneva' – 1st Edn. in English – addit. engraved title – 4 engraved plates – browning and soiling – contem calf – rubbed – folio – 1687.
(Sotheby's) $210 £100

SPORTING REPOSITORY, THE
Limited Edn. – 22 col. plates – orig. cloth gilt – t.e.g. – 1904.
(Phillips) $95 £45

SPRAT, THOMAS
'The History of the Royal Society of London' – 1st Edn. – 2 folding plates – errata leaf – also added the Evelyn frontis in photostat facsimile – contem. calf – rebacked – 4to. – T. R. for R. Martyn 1667.
(Sotheby's) $85 £40

SQUIER, E. G.
'Travels in Central America' – 2 vol. – plates – some col. – some folding – illus. – spotting – orig. cloth – rubbed – 8vo. – New York 1853.
(Sotheby's) $145 £70

STABLES, GORDON
A collection of his works comprising 52 titles with several variant issues or Edn. – 82 vol. in all – orig. pictorial cloth – worn – 8vo. – 1890-1910.
(Sotheby's) $25 £12

STACK, RICHARD
'An Introduction for the Study of Chemistry' – folding table at end – contem. half calf – 8vo. – Dublin, Wm. Jones 1802.
(Sotheby's) $75 £35

STAHL, GEORGE ERNST
'Experiments, Observationes, Animadversiones' – paper discoloured in places – contem. calf – 8vo. – Berlin 1731.
(Sotheby's) $85 £40

STANEWELL, L. M.
'Calendar of the Ancient Deeds, Letters etc. in the Archives of the Corporation of the City of Hull' – 1951.
(Baitson) $6 £3

STANLEY, SIR H. M.
'In Darkest Africa' – 2 vols. – plates – maps – 1 loose – orig. cloth gilt – 1890.
(Phillips) $65 £32

STANLEY, THOMAS
'The History of Philosophy' – 1st. Edn. – second issue – 17 engraved ports. – browning – early 18th cent. calf – worn – folio – 1656.
(Sotheby's) $55 £25

STARK, A. C. AND SCLATER, W.
'The Birds of South Africa' – 4 vols. - illus. – orig. cloth – t.e.g. – 1900-06.
(Phillips) $755 £360

STARKE, L.
'Deutsche Geschichte' – 2 vol. – chromolitho addit. title – plates – some chromolith maps – some double page contem. half morocco – rubbed – Bielfield and Liepzig 1880-81.
(Christie's) $40 £20

STARKEY, GEORGE
'A True Light of Alchemy' – rather browned throughout – small tear – half roan – 12 mo. – J. Dawkes for author, 1709.
(Sotheby's) $420 £200

STARKIE - GARDNER, J.
'Old Silverwork' – 1903.
(Laurence & Martin Taylor) $55 £25

STATE TRIALS
8 vols. – panelled calf – gilt – folio – 1719.
(Irelands) $230 £110

STATISTICAL HISTORY OF SCOTLAND, AN ABRIDGED
Dawson (J. Hooper) – cloth – Edinburgh 1853.
(Bennett Book Auction) $15 £7

STAUNTON, SIR GEORGE
'An Authentic Account of the Embassy from the King of Great Britain to the Emperor of China' – 2 vols. only – lacking atlas – 1st Edn. – engraved portrait frontis – illus. in text – adverts – modern cloth backed boards – spines faded – 4to. – 1797.
(Sotheby's) $115 £55

STEDMAN, C.
'The History of the Origin .... The American War' – 2 vols. – 15 maps and charts – tree calf gilt – 4to. – 1794.
(Phillips) $840 £400

STEEL'S ORIGINAL AND CORRECT NAVY LIST 1789-92
Bound in 1 vol.
(Richard Baker & Thomson) $95 £45

STEILER, KARL; WACHENHUSEN, H., HACKLANDER, F. W.
'The Rhine from its Source to the Sea' – plates – illustrations – original cloth – slightly soiled – t.e.g. folio – 1878.
(Christie's) $735 £350

STEIN, GERTRUDE
'First Reader and Three Plays' – 1st Edn. – pres copy – inscribed by artist to Cecil Beaton – pen and ink portrait – illus. and decorations by Francis Rose – orig. cloth backed boards – 8vo. – Dublin and London 1946.
(Sotheby's) $180 £85

STEIN, M. A.
'On Alexander's Track to the Indus.' – plates – orig. cloth – 8vo. – 1929.
(Sotheby's) $275 £130

STEINBECK, JOHN
'East of Eden' – 1st Eng. Edn. – covers dull and soiled – 1952.
(J. Ash) $6 £3

STEINLEN
'Chats et Autres Betes' – Texte de Georges Lecomte – no. 14 of 35 copies on Japon imperial – mounted coloured plates and numerous illustrations – half morocco – original wrappers bound in – 4to. – Paris, Rey, 1933.
(Sotheby Parke Bernet) $1,300 £620

STEP, EDWARD AND WATSON, WILLIAM
'Favourite Flowers of Garden and Greenhouse' – 4 vol. – 314 coloured plates only – contemp. half morocco – rubbed – t.e.g. – 1896-7.
(Christie's S. Kensington) $315 £150

STEPHEN, JAMES
'War in Disguise' – 3rd Edn. – half calf – 1806.
(Phillips) $55 £25

STEPHEN, W.
'History of the Queen's City of Edinburgh Rifle Volunteer Brigade etc.' –cloth backstrip faded and detached on one side – 1881.
(Bennet Book Auction) $12 £6

STEPHENSON. RUSSELL
'Eighty Sketches in Watercolour from Nature' – no. 66 of limited Edn. of 220 – 1926.
(Laurence & Martin Taylor) $40 £19

STEVENSON, ROBERT LOUIS
'A Child's Garden of Verses' – illus. by George Robinson – one of 250 large paper copies on vellum – cloth – slipcase – New York 1896.
(Robert Skinner) $240 £115

STEVENSON, ROBERT LOUIS
'Records of a Family of Engineers' – very good copy in dust wrapper – 1912.
(J. Ash) $25 £12
'The Pentland Rising' – 1st Edn. of author's first book – orig. green wrappers – in morocco solander box – 8vo. – Andrew Elliot 1866.
(Christie's) $755 £360
'Works' – 25 vol. – Swanston Edn. – number 1659 of 2,060 copies – frontispiece – occasional slight spotting – original cloth – t.e.g. – 1911-12.
(Christie's S. Kensington) $80 £38

STEVENSON, THOMAS GEORGE
(Publisher)
'Edinburgh in the Olden Time' – number 1 of 350 copies – plates – orig. morocco backed cloth – rubbed – spine detached – t.e.g. – folio – Edinburgh 1880.
(Sotheby's) $17 £8

STEVENSON, WILLIAM
'Historical Sketch of the Progress of Discovery, Navigation and Commerce' – half calf gilt – 1824.
(Phillips) $65 £32

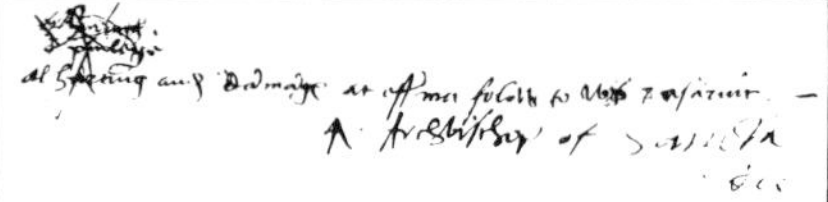

STEWART, ALEXANDER 1493-1513
Natural son of James IV and Archbishop of St. Andrews – letter signed with auto ps – 1 page – oblong octavo – traces of former mounting.
(Sotheby's) $380 £180

STEWART, D.
'Sketches of the Character, Manners .. of the Highlanders of Scotland' – 2 volumes – folding hand coloured map and table – contemp. calf – Edinburgh 1822.
(Bennett Book Auction) $60 £28

STILLINGFLEET, B.
'Miscellaneous Tracts ... Natural History, Husbandry and Physick' – calf gilt – 8vo. – 1759.
(Phillips) $80 £38

STIRLING-MAXWELL, SIR WILLIAM
'Don John of Austria' – 2 vol. – 12 copies – limited to 115 copies – plates – illus. orig. morocco backed cloth – t.e.g. – dust jackets – large 4to. – 1883.
(Sotheby's) $95 £45
'The Works' – limited Edn. – 6 vols. – orig. cloth gilt – 1891.
(Phillips) $65 £30
'Examples of the Ornamental Heraldry of the Sixteenth Century, first and second series' – 2 vol. in 1 – 32 copies – illus. orig. bindings – slightly soiled – spines torn – t.e.g. – folio – 1867-68.
(Sotheby's) $440 £210

STOCKDALE, JOHN
'A Geographical, Historical and Political Description of Germany, Holland .... Sardinia' – index map – 3 folding maps – 23 town plans – Amsterdam, Geneva, Berne, Berlin, etc. – calf – 4to. – 1800.
(Phillips) $545 £260

STODART, R. R.
'Scottish Arms' – 2 vol. – limited Edn. – coloured plates – orig. cloth – rubbed – folio – Edinburgh 1881.
(Sotheby's) $190 £90

STODDART, T.
'Angler's Companion to the Rivers and Lochs of Scotland' – 4 plates illus. and map – cloth gilt – 1847.
(Bennett Book Auction) $45 £22

STOKER, BRAM
'Dracula' – 1st Edn. – slightly soiled – original cloth – soiled – spine worn – inner hinges cracked – free endpapers lacking – 1897.
(Christie's S. Kensington) $65 £32

STOLBERG, COUNT FREDERICK
'Travels Through Germany, Switzerland etc.' – 4vols. bound in half calf – 1797.
(Lane) $60 £28

STONEY, CAPT. H. BUTLER
'A Residence in Tasmania' – 8 lithographed plates – one folding map – wood engraved illustrations – slight spotting – contemp. calf – slightly rubbed – 1856.
(Christie's S. Kensington) $180 £85

STONHAM, C.
'Birds of the British Islands' – 5 vols. – map and plates after Medland – cloth gilt – rubbed – slight spotting – large 4to. – 1906.
(Phillips) $210 £100

STORER, J. AND H. S.
'Views in Edinburgh' – 2 vol. – engraved titles – 97 plates – 2 folding maps – soiled – contem. half morocco – rubbed – t.e.g. – 8vo. – 1820.
(Sotheby's) $30 £15

STORER, JAMES
'History and Antiquities of the Cathedral Churches of Great Britain' – 4 vols. – engraved titles – engraved plates – half calf gilt – 1818-19.
(Phillips) $105 £50

STORER, WILLIAM AND GOUGH, H.
'Topographical Notes on Churches' – 2 vols. in ms – embellished by numerous watercolours by Storer – half calf – 1858-62.
(Phillips) $135 £65

STOTHARD, C. A. AND BASIRE, J.
'The Bayeux Tapestry' – 17 hand coloured engraved plates by Basire after Stothard – soiled and dampstained – contemporary half calf – worn – spine and upper cover lacking – folio – published by the Society of Antiquaries, 1819-23.
(Christie's S. Kensington) $145 £70

STOW, JOHN
'The Abridgement of the English Chronicle' by E. Howes, for the Company of Stationers – text printed in black letter – some stains – later calf – joints rubbed – 1611.
(Christie's S. Kensington) $40 £20

STOWE, HARRIET BEECHER
'Uncle Tom's Cabin' – wood engraved port. – vignette on title – 27 plates after Cruikshank – torn – hinge split – half calf – rubbed – 8vo. – John Cassell 1852.
(Sotheby's) $30 £15

STRAET, JAN VAN DER (JOHANNES STRADANUS)
'Venationes Ferarum, Avium, Piscium' – 101 engraved plates only – lacking title – additional 17 plates after Straet – margins torn and soiled – some rebacked – other defects – later calf backed boards – very worn – oblong folio – Antwerp 1580.
(Sotheby Beresford Adams) $2,520 £1,200

STRAFFORD, ELIZABETH
'The Captain's Little Daughter' – 3 hand col. litho plates – orig. cloth gilt – soiled – 4to. – Dean and Son circa 1855.
(Sotheby's) $65 £30

STRAHAN, EDWARD (Editor)
'A Collection of the Works of J. L. Derome' – 2 vol. – number 864 of 1000 copies – folio – 99 mounted plates only – orig. morocco – gilt – rubbed g.e. – New York 1881.
(Christie's S. Kensington) $55 £25

STRAITS OF MAGELLAN – BLAEU, W. AND J.
Engraved map – hand col in outline – title cartouche – coat of arms – full col. – sailing ships partly col. – Dutch text on verso – 411 mm x 532 mm – Amsterdam 1642 or later.
(Sotheby's) $145 £70

STRAND MAGAZINE
Volumes 1 to 7 – original cloth – 1891-1894.
(Bennett Book Auction) $16 £8
Vol. 1 – original cloth binding – 1891.
(Lane) $4 £2

STRAND MUSICAL PORTFOLIO, THE
Complete 20 vol. issue – 1910-11.
(Baitson) $6 £3

STRANGE, E. F.
'The Colour-Prints of Hiroshige' – number 47 of 250 copies – plates – orig. vellum boards.
(Sotheby's) $265 £125

STRANGE, T. A.
'English Furniture Woodwork Decoration during the 18th Cent' – 3,000 illus.
(Baitson) $35 £17

STRATTON, ARTHUR
'The English Interior' – subscript list – numerous plates – some col. – contem. vellum backed cloth – gilt – t.e.g. – folio – 1920.
(Sotheby Beresford Adams) $100 £48

STRICKLAND, AGNES
'Lives of the Queens of England' – 12 vols. – half calf.
(Irelands) $40 £20

'Lives of the Queens of England' – 16 vols. – number 30 of 39 sets of Royal Edition – plates in 3 states – very fine full crushed morocco – title gilt – edges gilt – doublures of multi coloured leathers with armorial shields – slipcases – Philadelphia 1902.
(Robert Skinner) $600 £285

STRICKLAND, W. G.
'A Dictionary of Irish Artists' – 2 vol. – plates – soiling – orig. cloth – 1913.
(Christie's) $80 £38

STRING, A. OF BRITISH PEARLS, BEING A MORAL TALE
3 vol. in one – 10 engraved plates – damp-stained – repaired – contem. calf – spine loose – 8vo. – 1812.
(Sotheby's) $34 £16

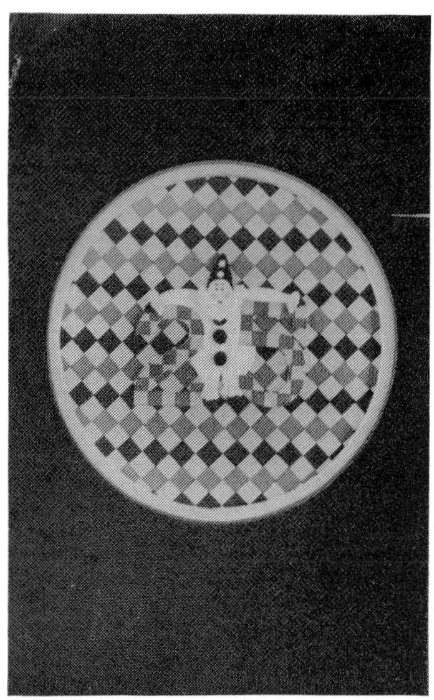

STRONG, L. A. G.
'The Hansom Cab and the Pigeons' – no. 132 of 212 – signed by author – wood engraved frontis and 16 pictorial decors by Eric Ravilious – black morocco – circular inset – black calf doublures – palladian edges – signed inside lower cover by Angela James – 8vo. – Golden Cockerel Press 1935.
(Sotheby's) $1,050 £500

STRUTT, JOSEPH
'A Complete View of the Dress and Habits of the People of England' – 2 vols. – plates – some hand col. – loose – contem. half morocco – rubbed – 4to. – 1842.
(Sotheby's) $210 £100

'The Baronial and Ecclesiastical Antiquities of England' – coloured plates – some loose – contemp. half morocco – worn – 4to. – 1842.
(Sotheby's) $65 £30

STRUWWELPETER, DER ... UND DROLLIGE BILDER FUR KINDER VAR 3-6 JAHREN
Special 100th Edn. – 4to. – stiff 11 – cloth – backed boards – circa 1876.
(Bennett Book Auction) $15 £7

STUART, GILBERT
'A View of Society in Europe' – calf gilt – 4to. – 1778.
(Phillips) $250 £120

STUART, JAMES AND REVETT, NICHOLAS
'The Antiquities of Athens' – 1st Edn. – 4 vols. – without supplement – engraved title – illus. and numerous plates – contem. polished russia – gilt spines – folio – 1762-1816.
(Christie's) $1,785 £850

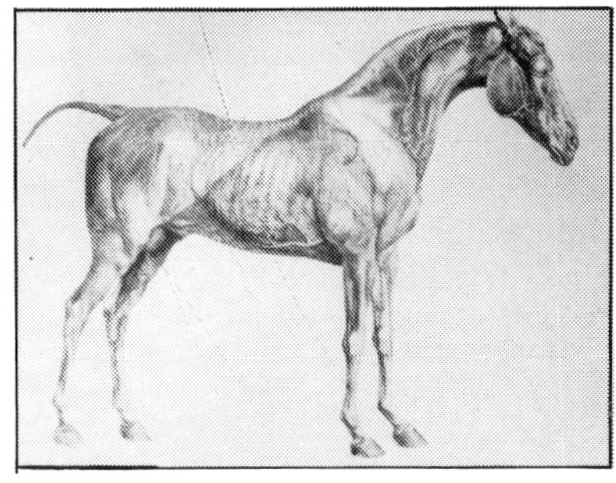

STUBBS, GEORGE
'The Anatomy of the Horse' – 1st. Edn. – 24 engraved plates – contem. diced russia – worn – oblong folio – J. Purser for author, 1766.
(Christie's) $3,150 £1,500

STUDIO, THE
Vol. 30-33 – plates – some coloured – illustrations – uniform cloth – 1903-04.
(Christie's S. Kensington) $40 £18

STUDIO LIBRARY, THE
'English Water Colours / Coloured Plates of Works of Eminent Painters'.
(Laurence & Martin Taylor) $17 £8

STUDIO PUBLICATIONS
18 vols. including Modern Etchings, Old English Mezzotints, etc. – plates – 4to. – 1901-35.
(Phillips) $380 £180

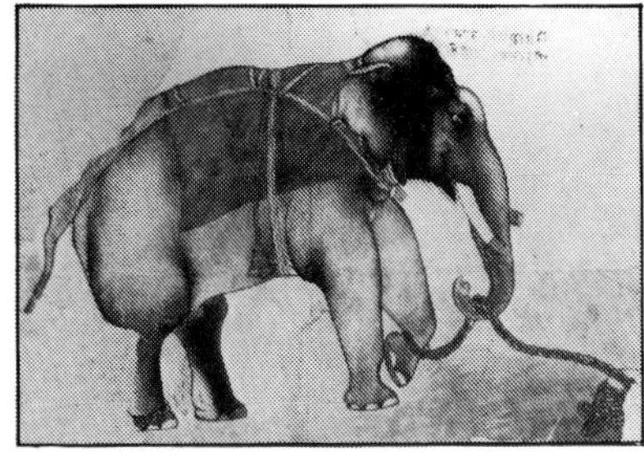

STUDY OF A TETHERED ELEPHANT
Ink drawing in colour – principally maroon and gold – green wash inscription illegible – slight staining – repaired – rebacked – 28.5 cm x 42 cm. – Kotah circa 1720-40.
(Christie's) $735 £350

STUKELEY, WILLIAM
'Itinerarium Curiosum' – 2 vols in one – 2nd Edn. – engraved frontis – portrait and numerous engraved plates – maps – some folding by Stukeley and others – contem. calf – gilt – g.e. – folio – 1776.
(Christie's) $420 £200

STURMY, SAMUEL
'The Mariners' Magazine' – engraved and printed title in facsimile – plates illus. in text – half calf – 4to. – 1684.
(Phillips) $125 £60

STYLISED ROSE BUSH, A
Pink blooms and green foliage edges with gold – laid down on album leaf – panels of nasta'liq applied – polychrome border on cream leaf – various floral sprays and floral trellis design on a single strip of cotton – laid down on similar album leaf – Mughal circa 1700-1750.
(Christie's) $1,470 £700

SUCKLING, REV ALFRED
'Memorials of the Antiquities and Architecture of the County of Essex' – 3 vols. – limited Edn. – index – litho plates – some col. – a few in 2 states – tables – some spotting – contem. half calf – rubbed – orig. cloth – 4to. – 1846-48.
(Sotheby's) $125 £60
'The History and Antiquities of the County of Suffolk' – 2 vol. – plates – some col. – spotted – contem. morocco – rebacked – rubbed – 8vo. – 1846-48.
(Sotheby's) $160 £75

SUCKLING, JOHN
'A Ballad Upon a Wedding' – number 70 of 375 copies – illus. by Eric Ravillious – orig. cloth backed boards – dust jacket – 1927.
(Christie's) $85 £40

SULLIVAN, J.
'The History of the District of Maine' – folding engraved map – browned – contem. calf – rebacked and repaired – 8vo. – Boston 1795.
(Sotheby's) $125 £60

SULLY, MAXIMILLIEN DE BETHUNE
'Memoires' – 3 vols. – 2nd Edn. – engraved portrait – frontis – titles in red and black – half titles – 1 leaf loose – contem. calf – worn – rebacked – 2 covers detached – 4to. – 1747.
(Sotheby's) $115 £55

SUNDEVALL, C. J. AND KINBERG, J. G. H.
'Svenska Foglarna' – 2 vols. – 84 plates – quarter morocco gilt – oblong 4to. – 1856-57.
(Phillips) $525 £250

SURR, T. S.
'The Magic of Wealth' – 3 vols. – calf gilt – 12mo. – 1815.
(Phillips) $160 £75

SURREY-GREENWOOD, C. AND H.
'Map of the County of Surrey' – hand col. – engraved map in 32 sections – large inset of Kew Palace – soiled – mounted on linen – edges bound – calf pull off case – 40 inches x 48 inches – George Pringle Jnr 1 Sept 1823.
(Sotheby's) $335 £160

SURTEES, R. S.
'Plain or Ringlets' – n.d. – 'Mr Romford's Hounds' – n.d. 'Handley Cross' – n.d. – 'Ask Mamma' – n.d. – 'Mr Sponge's Sporting Tour' – n.d. – hand coloured frontispieces – title vignettes and plates after John Leech and H. K. Browne – uniform half morocco – spines gilt – slightly rubbed.
(Christie's S. Kensington) $180 £85

SURTEES, ROBERT
'The History and Antiquities of ... Durham' – 4 vol. – 18 engraved plates – later half morocco – rubbed – t.e.g. – folio – 1816-40.
(Christie's S. Kensington) $275 £130

SURTEES, REV SCOTT F.
'Waifs and Strays of North Humber' – London 1864.
(Baitson) $15 £7

SUTCLIFFE, G. LISTER (Editor)
'The Modern Carpenter, Joiner and Cabinet-maker' – 8vo, 4to – plates – illustrations – orig. cloth – slightly soiled and rubbed – 1903.
(Christie's S. Kensington) $95 £45

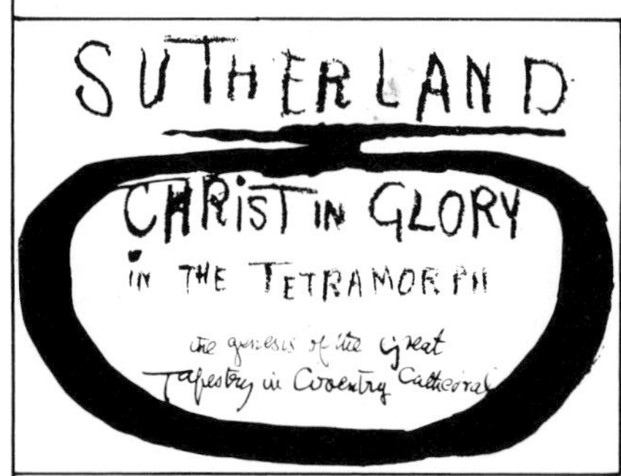

SUTHERLAND, GRAHAM
The original text of his dissertation on the Great Tapestry at Coventry Cathedral – auto designs and the annotated proof for the title and five tapes of the conversation – c. 120 pages quarto and folio.
(Sotheby's) $1,175 £560

SVETLOV, V.
'Ballet Contemporain' – no. 389 of 520 copies – plates – some col. – illus. – modern cloth – t.e.g. – 4to. – St. Petersburg 1912.
(Sotheby's) $295 £140

SWAINSON, W.
'New Zealand and Its Colonisation' – folding hand col. map – orig. cloth – rubbed – 8vo. – 1859.
(Sotheby's) $65 £30

SWAN, ABRAHAM
'The British Architect; or The Builder's Treasury of Stair-Cases' – folio – 60 engraved plates – some with letter press descriptions on the same leaf – title soiled – later half morocco – worn – 1745.
(Christie's S. Kensington) $275 £130

SWANN, H. K. AND WETMORE, A.
'A Monograph of the Birds of Prey' – 2 vols. – plates some col. – half crimson morocco gilt – t.e.g. – 4to. – orig. wrappers bound in – 1930-45.
(Phillips) $505 £240

SWARBRECK, S. D.
'Sketches in Scotland' – litho title and 25 views on 24 plates – spotted – contem. morocco backed cloth – worn – loose – folio – 1839.
(Sotheby's) $440 £210
'Stirling Castle' – lithograph – coloured – mounted and framed.
(Bennett Book Auction) $40 £20

SWAYSLAND, W.
'Familiar Wild Birds' – 4 vols. – col. plates – light spotting – orig. cloth – worn – t.e.g. – n.d.
(Christie's) $65 £32

SWINBURNE, A. C.
'Atalanta in Calydon' – only 100 copies made – full crushed morocco gilt – silk doublures – 4to. – 1865.
(J. Ash) $370 £175

SWINBURNE, HENRY
'Travels through Spain' – 13 engraved plates – extra illustrated with five additional plates – some folding – 1779.
(Christie's S. Kensington) $115 £55

SWINDEN, H.
'History of Great Yarmouth' – calf – 4to. – 1772.
(Irelands) $170 £80

SWITZERLAND
'Its Mountains, Valleys, Rivers and Lakes' – new Edn. – illus. – orig. cloth – rubbed – g.e. – 4to. – 1903.
(Christie's) $85 £40

SYDENHAM SOCIETY
'Publications' – 45 vol. – 1 vol. contemp. calf – rubbed – remainder orig. cloth – rubbed – 8vo. – 1844-83.
(Sotheby's) $380 £180

SYDENHAM, THOMAS
'The Entire Works Newly Made English - the third edition by John Swan' – advertisement leaf bound at beginning, cont. calf gilt – E. Cave, 1753.
(Sotheby's) $157 £70

SYMONDS, MARY AND PREECE, LOUISA
'Needlework Through the Ages' – plates – some col. – orig. cloth – spine faded – large 4to. – 1928.
(Christie's) $125 £60

SYMONDS, R. W.
'Furniture Making in the Seventeenth and Eighteenth Century' – plates – some coloured – cloth gilt 4to. – 1955.
(Phillips) $115 £55
'English Furniture from Charles II to George II' – limited Edn. – plates – cloth – 4to. – 1929.
(Phillips) $135 £65
'Thomas Tompion, his Life and Work' – 4to. – plates – a few coloured – orig. cloth – dust jacket – 1969.
(Christie's S. Kensington) $55 £25

SYMONS, JOHN
'High Street Hull and Biographical Sketches' – 1862.
(Baitson) $70 £34

SYNODUS LARINENSIS
Contem. Italian binding of brown morocco gilt with large arms of Cardinal Orsini in the centre – gilt and gauffered edges – 4to. – Roma 1728.
(Moore Allen & Innocent) $1,890 £900

TABLEAUX VIVANTS
Limited Edn. – 20 plates plus 3 extra illus. – orig. parchment – gilt – t.e.g. – Erotike Biblion Society – n.d.
(Phillips) $440 £210

TACITUS, PUBLIUS CORNELIUS
'Opera' – folio – apud Christophorum Plantimum – folding table – lacking final blank – soiled – early 19th century half calf – joints slightly split – 1585.
(Christie's S. Kensington) $85 £40

TAGEREAU, VINCENT
'Discours sur L'Impuissance de L'Homme et de la Femme' – 1st Edn. – device on title – slight browning – some worming – repaired – modern calf backed marbled boards – sm 8vo – Paris 1611.
(Sotheby's) $20 £10

TAILLEPIED, F. H.
'Traite de L'Apparition des Esprits' – engraved title – old calf – gilt back – 8vo – Rouen, 1602.
(Bonhams) $90 £42

TALLIS, J.
'History and Description of the Crystal Palace' – 2 vols. – plates – some foxing – morocco gilt – g.e. – 4to – n.d.
(Phillips) $105 £50

TANCRED, G.
'Rulewater and Its People' – plates – cloth – Edinburgh, 1907.
(Bennett Book Auction) $30 £14

TANNER, THOMAS
'Bibliotheca Britannica Hibernica' – 1st Edn. – title with engraved vignette – portrait frontis – offsetting on title – slight spotting – cont. speckled calf – joints split – worn – folio – 1748.
(Sotheby's) $105 £50

TANNER, THOMAS HAWKES
'The Practice of Surgery' – 2 vols. – 1875.
(Baitson) $4 £2

TANSILLO, L.
'The Nurse, a Poem' – translated by Wm. Roscoe – presentation copy – cont. straight grained morocco – rubbed – 4to – Liverpool, 1798.
(Sotheby's) $180 £85

TARBELL, HARLAN
'The Tarbell Course in Magic' – 7 vols. – portraits and numerous illus. – orig. cloth – 8vo – New York, 1953-72.
(Sotheby's) $90 £42

TARN, NATHANIEL
'A Nowhere for Vallejo; Choices; October' – First thus with new material – very good – 1972.
(J. Ash) $8 £4

TASSO, TORQUATO
'La Gerusalemme Liberata' – wood engraved title and twenty full page illus. – some slight spotting – old calf – corners repaired – joints slightly cracked – 4to – Venice all' insegna della Sapienza, 1673.
(Christie's S. Kensington) $170 £80

TATHAM, C. H.
'Etchings' – 126 plates, including no 47 bis – no plate 101 – dark blue morocco backed cloth – folio – 1843.
(Sotheby's) $155 £55
'Etchings' – 2nd Edn. – examples of Ancient Ornamental Architecture – 101 plates only – a little soiling and staining – cont. half morocco – worn and rebacked – 1803.
(Christie's S. Kensington) $30 £15

TATLER, THE
4 vols. – nos. 1-270 of 1709-10 – Sharpe, 1804.
(Dacre, Son & Hartley) $12 £6
Vols. 1-68 – 65 vols. altogether – some leaves loose – some vols. orig. cloth – cont. half roan – cont. cloth – rubbed – folio – 1901-18.
(Sotheby's) $670 £320

TATTERSALL, C. E. C.
'A History of British Carpets' – plates – some col. – orig. cloth – soiled – large 4to – Benfleet, 1934.
(Christie's) $85 £40

TATTERSALL, GEORGE
'Sporting Architecture' – plates – some foxing – orig. cloth – 4to – 1841.
(Sotheby's) $230 £110

TAUBERT, SIGFRED
'Bibliopola' – 2 vols. – plates – some coloured – illus. – orig. cloth – slipcase – 4to – 1966.
(Sotheby's) $65 £32

TAYLOR, ALISTER AND GLEN, JAN
'C. F. Goldie, His Life and Painting; Prints, Drawings and Criticism' – Ltd. Edn. – 2 vols. – plates – some col. – orig. morocco backed cloth – preserved in cloth boxes – 4to – Waiure Martinborough, 1977-78.
(Sotheby's) $105 £50

TAYLOR, GEORGE LEDWELL AND CRESY, EDWARD
'The Architectural Antiquities of Rome' – 1st Edn. – 2 vols. – 130 plates, one double page – spotted – cont. calf gilt – rubbed – large folio – 1821-22.
(Sotheby Beresford Adams) $85 £40

TAYLOR, GEORGE AND SKINNER, ANDREW
'Survey and Maps of the Roads of North Britain, or Scotland' – engraved title – 62 maps – frayed and chewed – general map lacking – cont. limp leather – rubbed – 8½ x 20in. – 1776.
(Christie's S. Kensington) $135 £65
'Maps of the Roads of Ireland' – engraved title with vignette – large folding map of Ireland torn – 288pp road maps – list of subscribers – cont. half calf – rubbed – hinges cracked – 8vo – London and Dublin, 1778.
(Sotheby's) $335 £160

TAYLOR, ISAAC
'Scenes in Asia for the Amusement and Instruction of Little Tarry at Home Travellers' – 2nd Edn. – folding engraved map – 28 plates – orig. roan backed boards – worn – 12mo – J. Harris and Son, 1821.
(Sotheby's) $40 £18

TAYLOR, JAMES (Editor)
'A Family History of England' – illus. with maps, portraits, views and other engravings – 12 vols.
(Baitson) $10 £5

TAYLOR, JEREMY
'Doctor Dubitantium' – 1st Edn. – printed title in red, addit. title – portrait frontis – advert leaf at end – slight browning and soiling – small hole – cont. calf – worn – one cover detached – folio – 1660.
(Sotheby's) $55 £25
'The Rule and Exercises of Holy Living' – 1st Edn. – engraved title – 19th century tree calf – gilt spine – 12mo – for Richard Royston, 1650.
(Sotheby's) $10 £5

TEATE, FAITHFUL
'Ter Tria or the Doctrine of Father, Son and Spirit' – in verse – 2nd Edn. – lacks final blank – soiled – cont. sheep – worn – sm 8vo – 1669.
(Sotheby's) $125 £60

TECHNOLOGY AND CULTURE
Vols. 1-6 Detroit and Chicago 1960-65; Vols. 8-20 Chicago 1967-75; index to vols. 1-10 – orig. wrappers.
(Phillips) $75 £35

TEESDALE, H. J.
'New British Atlas' – engraved title – 45 hand coloured engraved maps – 3 folding – remainder double page – two torn – few small tears – two spotted – half calf – one cover detached – 4to – 1832.
(Christie's S. Kensington) $460 £220

TEESDALE, HENRY & CO.
'A New General Atlas of the World' – engraved vignette title – 46 col. engraved maps, all full page except one double page – repaired – orig. calf backed boards – morocco label – spine defective – folio – 1831-32.
(Sotheby's) $275 £130
'A Map of the County Palatine of Lancaster' – large engraved folding map – title cartouche with engraved view – col. 48 sections – mounted on linen – 8vo – 1830.
(Sotheby Beresford Adams) $135 £64

TEMPLE, A. G.
'The Wallace Collection of Paintings' – Ltd. Edn. – 2 vols. – plates – half morocco gilt – t.e.g. – folio – 1902.
(Phillips) $160 £75

TEMPLE, SIR JOHN
'The Irish Rebellion' – 1st Edn. – cont. calf – rubbed – sm 4to – 1646.
(Sotheby's) $105 £50

TEMPLE, SIR RICHARD
'Palestine Illustrated' – 34 illus. plates – 32 col. – some detached – 4 maps – 2 double page – orig. cloth – soiled – t.e.g. – 4to – 1888.
(Christie's) $40 £20

TEMPLE, SIR WILLIAM
'Memoirs of what Passed In Christendom from 1672 to 1679' – 2nd Edn. – cont. sheep – spine worn – 12mo – 1692.
(Christie's) $40 £20

TENNYSON, LORD ALFRED
Fine photo by Julia Margaret Cameron, inscribed by her, albumen print – facsimile signature of sitter – 10 x 8½in. – framed and glazed.
(Sotheby's) $800 £380
'In Memoriam' – No. 960 of 2,000 copies – orig. boards – slightly rubbed – unopened – slipcase – Nonesuch Press, 1933.
(Christie's S. Kensington) $30 £15
'The Works' – 8 vols., 1872-73 – portrait – cont. red morocco – gilt – with the arms of Exeter College, Oxford, stamped in gilt on upper and lower covers – slightly faded – corners bumped – g.e.
(Christie's S. Kensington) $105 £50
'Idylls of the King' – first issue with verso of title blank – orig. cloth – 1859.
(J. Ash) $12 £6

TENNYSON, ALFRED AND HALLAM
'Poems by Two Brothers' – 1st Edn. – cont. calf – rebacked – 8vo – 1927.
(Sotheby's) $420 £200

TERRARI, SYBIL
'Old Plymouth' – 1913.
(Lane) $8 £4

THACKERAY, W. M.
'Our Street' – Tipped in is an orig. pencil sketch by Thackeray of a young lady with a negro page – 16 plates by author all hand col. – rebound in full morocco by Bradstreet – orig. wrappers preserved – some wear and repairs – 1848.
(J. Ash) $250 £120

THEATRE, LE
1-16th year lacking 2 and 1 duplicate, together 30 vols. – col. plates – illus. – orig. cloth – rubbed – g.e. – folio – Paris, 1898-1913.
(Sotheby's) $630 £300

THEATRUM DANUBII EXHIBENS VARIOS PERSPECTUS . . . QUAE DANUBIO ADJACENT
Engraved title and 62 engraved plates – cont. wrappers – spine slightly torn – oblong folio – Augsburg, Haeredes Jeremiae Wolffii, circa 1750.
(Sotheby Beresford Adams) $6,720 £3,200

THEIRS, A.
'Histoire de la Revolution Francaise' – 10 vols.
'Histoire du Consulat et de L'Empire' – 22 vols. includ. atlas – 32 vol. altogether – plates – folding maps – atlas in orig. cloth backed boards – remainder half morocco – gilt spines – rubbed – one cover detached – 8vo and 4to – 1845-80.
(Sotheby's) $75 £35

THEIRY, A.
'Album de la Colonie Agricole de Mettray' – lithographed title – 20 lithographed plates – spotted – orig. cloth – rubbed – almost disbound – oblong 4to.
(Christie's S. Kensington) $85 £40

THEOCRITOS
'The Complete Poems translated by Jack Lindsay' – no. 113 of 500 copies – woodcut plates by Lionel Ellis – orig. green parchment – faded – sm folio – t.e.g. – Fanfrolico Press, 1929.
(Christie's S. Kensington) $55 £25

'THEORY AND PRACTICE OF ARCHITECTURE OR VITRUVIUSAND VIGNOLA ABRIDG'D . . . by Mr. PERRAULT . . . and . . . JOSEPH MOXON'
engraved frontis – plates – some lacking – illus. – margins shaved with loss of letters – cont. calf – rubbed – 1703.
(Christie's S. Kensington) $40 £20

THERSNER, ULRIC
'Fordna Och Narvarande Sverige. La Suede Ancienne et Moderne' – 358 full page views, 10 half page – earlier soft ground etchings or aquatints – later are lithographed and some tinted – text in Swedish and French – 3 bound vols. in half calf – rubbed – folio – Stockholm, 1817-67.
(Sotheby's) $4,620 £2,200

THEURIET, ANDRE
'Le Secret de Gertrude' – 8 of 25 copies on papier de chine – green morocco by Marius Michel – decorated in gilt – Paris, Launette & Cie, 1890.
(Sotheby Parke Bernet) $5,200 £2,800

THIBAULT, J. A. F.
'The Novels and Short Stories of Anatole France' – 19 vols. – no. 21 of 300 copies – plates – orig. morocco – slightly rubbed – t.e.g. – New York and London – n.d.
(Christie's S. Kensington) $65 £32

THIMME, J.
'Art and Culture of the Cyclades' – plates – cloth – 4to – 1977.
(Phillips) $55 £25

THIRD CHAPTER OF ACCIDENTS, THE
1st Edn. – 15 engraved illus., 5 full page – some tears – orig. marble paper wrappers – worn – restitched – 12mo – Darton and Harvey, 1801.
(Sotheby's) $95 £45

THOMAS, A. H. AND THORNLEY, I. D.
'The Great Chronicle of London' – no. 174 of 500 copies – plates – orig. morocco – spine faded – 4to – 1938.
(Sotheby's) $180 £85

THOMAS AQUINAS CALENDAR 1926
16 wood engraved illus., including cover design, 4 by Eric Gill, 2 by David Jones – fraying – modern cloth – orig. upper wrapper bound in – folio – 1925.
(Sotheby's) $180 £85
'Summae Theologicae' – 5 parts in 2 vols. – 5 titles – vellum over wooden boards – folio – C. Plantin, Antwerp, 1585; one folio 1634.
(Phillips) $90 £42

THOMAS, B.
'Shooters' Guide . . . Natural History of Dogs of Breeding, Pointers, Setters etc.' – 1st Edn. – orig. boards – uncut – 1809.
(Bennett Book Auction) $95 £46

THOMAS, CAITLIN
'Leftover Life to Kill' – auto of poet's widow – good in rubbed dust jacket – 1955.
(J. Ash) $8 £4

THOMAS, DYLAN
'A Prospect of the Sea' – nice clean copy in chipped dust wrapper – 1955.
(J. Ash) $25 £12

THOMAS, EDWARD
'Lafcadio Hearn' – Proof copy, presentation copy, inscribed by author to De La Mare – orig. wrappers – 8vo – 1911.
(Sotheby's) $695 £330

THOMAS, FREDERICK
'Humourous and Other Poetic Pictures of Devon' – orig. cloth binding.
(Lane) $34 £16

THOMAS, H.
'Early Spanish Bookbindings' – Bibliographical Society no. 23 – 98 plates – cloth backed boards – t.e.g. – 4to – 1939.
(Phillips) $75 £35

THOMAS, JERRY
'How to Mix Drinks or the Bon Vivant's Companion' – illus. – some browning – spine chipped – joints cracked – New York, 1862.
(Christie's) $65 £32

THOMAS, JOSEPH
'Randigal Rhymes' – 1st Edn. – orig. cloth binding – 1895.
(Lane) $25 £12

THOMAS, TH.
'Design for Sarah Bernhardt as Theodora' – pencil, watercolour and gouache – 52 x 31.2cm.
(Sotheby's) $840 £400
'Designs for a girl carrying flowers, an incense bearer and a standard bearer' – pencil, indian ink and watercolour – 33 x 51cm.
(Sotheby's) $85 £40

THOMAS, WILLIAM
'The Historye of Utalye' – 2nd Edn. – black letter – soiled – repaired – antique style calf – sm 4to – 1561.
(Sotheby's) $210 £100

THOMASON, EDWARD
'Enamelled Impressions struck off from the Splendid Series of Medal Dies, illustrative of the Holy Scriptures' – 2 vols. – stitched medallic impressions and letterpress contained in two morocco boxes – rubbed – 4to – g.e. – n.d.
(Christie's S. Kensington) $80 £38

THOMPSON, FRANCIS
'Poems' – Ltd. Edn. of 500 copies – frontis, title and cover design by Laurence Housman – orig. decorative boards – spine rubbed and worn – nice copy – 1893.
(J. Ash) $105 £50

THOMPSON, JAMES
'Life of James Allan, the Celebrated Northumberland Piper' – text incomplete but 6 hand col. engravings from Cruikshank – Newcastle upon Tyne, 1828.
(Baitson) $20 £9

THOMPSON, WINFIELD M. AND LAWSON, THOMAS
'The Lawson History of the America's Cup' – Ltd. Edn. – plates – orig. cloth – gilt – rebacked – soiled – t.e.g. – 4to – Boston, 1902.
(Sotheby's) $60 £28

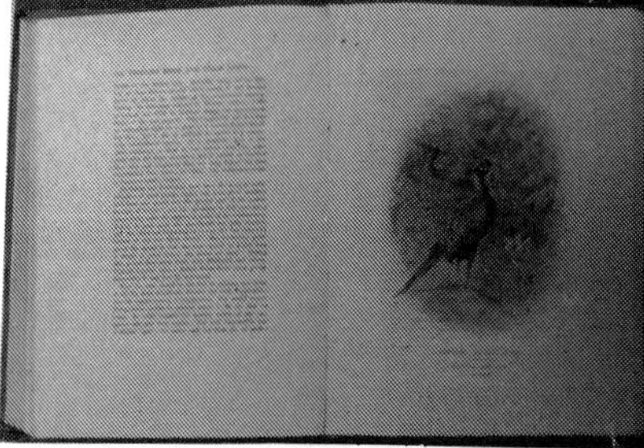

THOMSON, A. LANSBOROUGH
'Britain's Birds and Their Nests' – 132 col. illus. by George Rankin – gilt decorated red cloth boards – W. and R. Chambers, 1910.
(May Whetter & Grose) $125 £60

THOMSON, HUGH
'Jack the Giant Killer' – 16 full page col. illus. and pictorial borders by Thomson – orig. pictorial wrappings – split – 4to – 1898.
(Sotheby's) $55 £25

THOMSON, HUGH AND GOLDSMITH, OLIVER
'She Stoops to Conquer' – no. 77 of 350 copies signed by the artist – 4to – mounted col. plates by Thomson – orig. vellum – soiled – t.e.g. – tie lacking – n.d.
(Christie's S. Kensington) $40 £20

THOMSON, JOHN
'A General Atlas' – engraved title and 40 maps – hand col. in outline – one double page – two tables – slightly spotted – modern calf – slightly soiled – 4to – Edinburgh, 1819.
(Christie's S. Kensington) $420 £200

THOMSON, SIR JOSEPH JOHN
'Conduction of Electricity Through Gases' – 1st Edn. – half titles – orig. cloth – 8vo – Cambridge, 1903.
(Sotheby's) $125 £60

THOMSON, THOMAS
'A System of Chemistry' – 2nd Edn. – 4 vols. – 4 plates – lacks half titles – cont. calf – spine and hinges worn – 8vo – Edinburgh, 1804.
(Sotheby's) $30 £15

THOMSON, W. G.
'Tapestry Weaving in England from the Earliest Times to the End of the XVIII Century' – plates – cloth – gilt – 4to – 1928.
(Phillips) $135 £65

THOREAU, H. D.
'Where I Lived and What I Lived For' – no. 330 of 380 copies – illus. by Robert Gibbings – orig. vellum backed boards – rubbed – 16mo – 1924.
(Christie's) $30 £15

THORNBURY, W. AND WALFORD, E.
'Old and New London' – 6 vols. – illus. map in pocket at end – half morocco gilt – 4to – n.d.
(Phillips) $90 £42

THORNDIKE, LYNN
'A History of Magic and Experimental Science' – vols. I-VI of 8 – 1st Edns. – orig. cloth – some rubbed and faded – 8vo – New York, 1923-41.
(Sotheby's) $115 £55

THORNDIKE, LYNN AND KIBRE, PEARL
'A Catalogue of Incipits of Mediaeval Scientific Writings in Latin' – 2nd Edn. – orig. buckram – marked – 4to – 1963.
(Sotheby's) $65 £30

THORNTON, R. J.
'Elements of Botany' – 2 vols. – orig. cloth – 168 plates – uncut – 1812.
(Bennett Book Auction) $50 £24

THORNTON, T.
'Present State of Turkey' – calf gilt – 4to – 1807.
(Phillips) $80 £38

THORNTON, WILLIAM
'The New Complete and Universal History, Description and Survey of the Cities of London and Westminster' – engraved plates and maps – frayed or torn – cont. half morocco – rebacked – rubbed – folio – 1784.
(Sotheby's) $160 £75

THOROTON, ROBERT
'The Antiquities of Nottinghamshire' – 2nd Edn. – 3 vols. – engraved titles and 95 plates only of 97 – folding – torn and repaired – illus. – cont. half morocco – rubbed – one cover detached – t.e.g. – 4to – 1790-96.
(Sotheby's) $115 £55

THORPE, JAMES AND WALTON, IZAAK
'The Compleat Angler' – no. 47 of 250 copies signed by the artist – mounted col. plates by Thorpe – occasional slight spotting – cont. morocco – spine faded – t.e.g. – 4to – n.d.
(Christie's S. Kensington) $105 £50

THROSBY, JOHN
'Thoroton's History of Nottinghamshire' – 3 vols. – engraved titles – 95 plates only and 1 map – spotting – cont. diced calf – worn – 4to – 1797.
(Christie's) $95 £45

THUNBERG, CARL PETER
'Voyages au Japon' – 4 vols. – trans. by L. Langes – engraved port, engraved vignette – 28 engraved plates, 7 folding – cont. calf gilt – spine worn – Paris, 1796.
(Sotheby's) $460 £220

THURLOW, EDWARD LORD
'Moonlight' – dark blue straight grain morocco – gilt – g.e. – silk liners – fore edge painting riverside scene – later leather slipcase – 8vo – 1814.
(Sotheby's) $400 £190

TICKELL, REV. JOHN
'The History of the Town and County of Kingston upon Hull' – folding frontis and engravings – leather bound – 1796.
(Baitson) $160 £75

TIEGUS, WALTER
'Cornish Worthies' – 1st Edn. – 2 vols. – bound in half morocco – 1884.
(Lane) $30 £15

TILLER, TERENCE
'Notes for a Myth and Other Poems' – fine in dust wrapper – Chatto and Windus, 1968.
(J. Ash) $8 £4

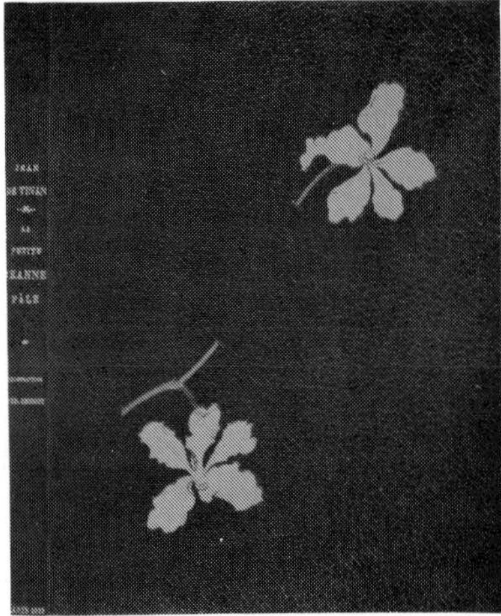

TINAN, JEAN DE
'La Petite Jeanne Pale' – 1 of 8 copies with original designs by the artist – black morocco – gilt – Paris Le Livre d'Art, 1922.
(Sotheby Parke Bernet) $5,200 £2,476

TINDAL, N. AND RAPIN, P.
'History of England' – atlas only – 62 engraved maps all double page – soiled and browned – covers lacking – folio – 1745 or later.
(Christie's) $840 £400

TIPPING, H. A.
'Grinling Gibbons and the Wood-work of his Age' – illus. – cloth buckram – slightly soiled – folio – 1914.
(Bonhams) $80 £38

TISSANDIER, GASTON
'Popular Scientific Recreations, A Storehouse of Instruction and Amusement' – New Edn. – illus. – orig. pictorial cloth gilt – slightly worn – large 8vo – circa 1890.
(Sotheby's) $90 £42

TISSOT, J. J.
'The Life of Christ' – 2 vols. – chromoliths by Lemercier of Paris.
(Laurence & Martin Taylor) $8 £4
'Avis au Peuple sur sa Sante' – cont. French binding of olive morocco gilt with arms of Victoire-Louise-Marie-Therese, daughter of Louis XV – 12mo – 1767.
(Moore Allen & Innocent) $630 £300

TODD, C. S.
'Incidents in the History of Kingston upon Hull' – London, 1869.
(Baitson) $25 £12

TODD, JOHN HENRY
'Historical Tablets and Medallions Illustrative of an Improved System of Artificial Memory' – engraved title and 20 plates with hand col. backgrounds – some loose – orig. cloth backed boards – engraved label – soiled – 4to – George Cowie, 1828.
(Sotheby's) $55 £25

TOLAND
'Life of John Milton' – cont. English binding of red morocco gilt – Republican symbols on covers – 8vo – 1761.
(Moore Allen & Innocent) $1,050 £500

TOLKEIN, J. R. R.
'The Lord of the Rings' – 1st Edn. – 3 vols. – vol. 1 signed by author with a greeting in Feanorian script – red morocco inlays in concentric circles on each cover – line tooling around spines – author's orig. titles and owner's sub titles on covers – g.e. – by Bayntum – 8vo – 1954-55.
(Sotheby's) $5,670 £2,700
'The Lord of the Rings' – 3 vols. – 1955.
(Allen & May) $365 £175

TOLMER, A.
'Mise en Page; the Theory and Practise of Layout' – illus. – some coloured – orig. printed boards – in case – 4to – Paris, 1931.
(Bonhams) $40 £20

TOLSTOY, LEO
Postcard photograph signed in black ink in English script.
(Sotheby's) $420 £200

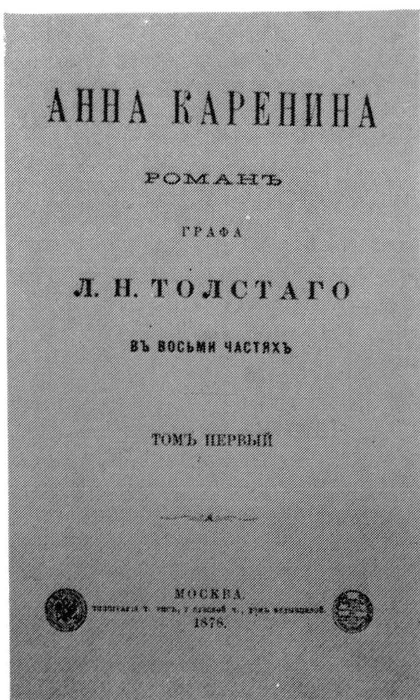

АННА КАРЕНИНА
РОМАНЪ
ГРАФА
Л. Н. ТОЛСТАГО
ВЪ ВОСЬМИ ЧАСТЯХЪ
ТОМЪ ПЕРВЫЙ
МОСКВА.
1878.

TOLSTOY, L. N.
'Anna Karenina' – 1st Edn. – 3 vols. – soiling – cont. half calf – 8vo – Moscow, 1878.
(Sotheby's) $5,760 £2,700

TOM TIT, ARTHUR GOOD
'La Science Amusante' – 3 vols. – numerous wood engraved illus. – vol. I and II slightly spotted – leaves almost loose – first 2 in orig. cloth – gilt edged – third rebound – 8vo – Paris, 1890-93.
(Sotheby's) $85 £40

TOMBLESON, W. AND FEARNSIDE, W. G.
'Eighty Picturesque Views of the Thames' – frontis – engraved title and 77 engravings – orig. cloth – gilt – g.e. – 4to – n.d.
(Phillips) $715 £340

TOMKINS, C. F. AND PLANCHE, J. R.
'Twelve Designs for the Costume of Shakespeare's Richard the Third' – litho title and 12 plates – col. by hand and heightened by gold – morocco half roan – worn – uncut – folio – 1830.
(Sotheby's) $190 £90

TOMLINE, GEORGE
'Memoirs of the Life of William Pitt' – 2 vols. – cont. calf gilt – 4to – 1821.
(Phillips) $65 £32

TOMLINSON, H. M.
'The Sea and the Jungle' – 1st Illus. Edn. – with 16 woodcuts by Claire Leighton – new preface by author – 1930.
(J. Ash) $12 £6

TOPHAM, REV. JOHN
'An Epitome of Chemistry wherein the Principles of the Science are Illustrated' – 1st Edn. – advert leaf at end – cloth roan spine – uncut – ownership inscription – 8vo – Longman, 1822.
(Sotheby's) $10 £5

TOPLIS, WILLIAM A. AND OXENHAM, JOHN
'The Book of Sark' – no. 345 of 500 signed by author and artist – col. plates – orig. vellum boards – lacking 2 ties – t.e.g. – folio – 1908.
(Sotheby's) $200 $95

TOPSEL, EDWARD (Editor)
'The History of Four Footed Beasts and Serpents' – general title and two divisional titles – woodcut illustrations – soiling – browning – later morocco – slightly rubbed – folio – Printed by E. Cotes for G. Sawbridge . . T. Williams . . T. Johnson, 1658.
(Christie's S. Kensington) $505 £240

TORIO, TORQUATO
'Arte de Escribir' – 2nd Edn. – addit. engraved title – 57 plates of 58 – slight staining – cont. Spanish calf – rubbed – 4to – Madrid, 1802.
(Sotheby's) $95 £45

TORRENS, H. D.
'Travels in Ladak, Tartary and Kashmir' – 12 col. plates – some folding – folding map – soiled – orig. cloth – rubbed – 8vo – 1862.
(Sotheby's) $210 £100

TORREY, JOHN
'A Flora of the State of New York' – 2 vols. – addit. engraved titles – 162 col. litho plates – marginal stains – half roan – very defective – 4to – Albany, 1843.
(Sotheby's) $275 £130

TOSCANELLA, ORAZIO
'Historiche, Aggiante, delle Vite di Plutarco' – 2 vols. in one – woodcut printers devices on titles and one tailpiece – first few leaves slightly soiled – old vellum – soiled – 4to – Venice, Appresso Gabriel Giolito de Ferrari – 1567.
(Christie's S. Kensington) $60 £28

TOSSANO, P.
'Dictionarium Hebraicarum' – some browning in text – old calf – worn – Basle, 1615.
(Phillips) $85 £40

TOULONGEON, F. EMMANUEL
'Histoire de France' – 3 vols. – maps, charts and tables – half calf gilt – 4to – Paris, 1806.
(Phillips) $65 £30

TOURNEFORT, JOSEPH PITTON DE
'A Voyage into the Levant' – 3 vols. – 149 plates, lacks 3 – calf – gilt – w.a.f.– 1746.
(Phillips) $230 £110
'Institutiones rei Herbariae' – 3 engraved titles and 489 engraved plates – 2 vols. – old calf gilt – 4to – 1719.
(Bonhams) $600 £280

TOURREIL, JACQUES DE
'Oeuvres' – 2 vols. – port. – engraved titles – cont. calf – 4to – Paris, 1721.
(Phillips) $75 £35

TOVEY, CHARLES
'Champagne' – map – litho – title and 7 litho plates – 1870.
(Phillips) $65 £32

TOWLE, TIM
'The Seven Deadly Sins' – sm folio illus. by Clarke Hutton – designed and printed by Edward Burrett – Ltd. Edn. of 70 copies – printed on col. papers throughout – signed by author, publisher and artist – Penmiel Press, Esher, 1980.
(J. Ash) $55 £25

TOWN PLANS
42 uncoloured plans, mostly German of Frankfurt, Bonn etc. – circa 1696.
(Phillips) $715 £340

TOWNSON, ROBERT
'Travels in Hungary' – hand col. folding map – 16 plates – calf – gilt – 1797.
(Phillips) $200 £95

TOY BOOK OF BIRDS AND BEASTS, THE
24 coloured wood-engraved plates after Harrison Weir – orig. cloth – paper panel on upper cover torn with some loss – g.e. – 4to – n.d.
(Christie's S. Kensington) $45 £22

TRADE CARDS – MILITARY UNIFORMS
An album containing 56 Liebig meat extract cards, mainly VG/EX, 23 mainly French similar trade cards, circa 1910? 84 cigarette cards, mainly circa 1920, and 38 modern trade cards all military uniforms and vehicles, and a flat Will's album – Military Uniforms of the British Empire (2 albums).
(Bennett Book Auction) $65 £30

TRADE CATALOGUES
Carron Company Architect's Catalogue – many illus. – cloth – circa 1925-30 – Sheffield Plate – T. Bradbury & Sons – n.d. – circa 1900 – Slingsby Trucks – boards – circa 1920 – General Brass Foundry – circa 1920? and one other Tools Catalogue – 1955.
(Bennett Book Auction) $30 £14

TRAILL, C. P.
'Canadian Wild Flowers' – ten hand col. lithographed plates after Agnes Fitzgibbon – soiling – title lacking – leaves spotted – orig. cloth – rubbed – folio – Montreal, 1869.
(Christie's S. Kensington) $85 £40

TRAINS ILLUSTRATED
Vols. 1-14 – another vol. – 14 altogether – illus. – some coloured – cont. cloth – 8vo – 1946-68.
(Sotheby's) $295 £140

TRAVEN, B.
'The Creation of the Sun and the Moon' – 1st English Edn. – illus. by Alberto Beltran – 1971.
(J. Ash) $12 £6

TREDGOLD, THOMAS
'On the Steam Engine' – 2 vols. – plates – half calf gilt – 4to – Virtue – n.d.
(Phillips) $180 £85

TREGONING, J.
'The Laws of the Stanneries of Cornwall' – 1st End. – full morocco binding – new – 1808.
(Lane) $160 £75

TRELAWNY, COLLINS
'Perranzabuloe; the Lost Church Found' – presentation copy from author – orig. cloth binding – 1843.
(Lane) $40 £18

TREVOR-BATTYE, AUBYN (Editor)
'Lord Lilford on Birds' – portrait – plates by Thorburn – browning – orig. cloth – soiled – t.e.g. – 1903.
(Christie's) $30 £15

TREW, CHRISTOPH JAKOB
'Hortus Nitidissimus' – 2 vols in one of 3 – titles and text in Latin and German – 118 hand col. engraved plates, lacking 2 by M. Seligmann – old vellum backed boards – worn – one detached – large folio – Nuremberg, Seligmann, 1768-72.
(Christie's) $12,600 £6,000

TRIMEN, HENRY
'Hand Book to the Flora of Ceylon' – 6 vols. including 4to folder of plates, without supplement of 1931 – 88 hand col. litho plates – slight spotting – orig. cloth – rubbed and soiled – 8vo and 4to – 1893-1900.
(Sotheby's) $335 £160

TRIMMER, SARAH
'A History of Quadrupeds' – engraved frontis – 35 wood engraved illus. – 29 after Bewick – spotting – cont. half calf – joints split – worn – 12mo – Tegg and Castleman, 1803.
(Sotheby's) $12 £6

TRIPP, F. E.
'British Mosses' – 2 vols. – 39 plates, lacks no. 16 – cloth gilt – 4to – 1874.
(Phillips) $45 £22

TRISTRAM, H. B.
'Survey of Western Palestine . . . Flora and Fauna' – 13 hand col. plates – buckram gilt – 4to – 1884.
(Phillips) $315 £150

TROLLOPE, ANTHONY
'The Vicar of Bullhampton' – 1st Edn. in book form – illus. by Woods – cont. half calf – rubbed – foxing – lacks half title and advert leaves – 1870.
(J. Ash) $115 £55

TROLLOPE, FRANCES (Translator)
THOMAS (Editor)
'Italy from the Alps to Mount Etna' – plates – illus. – occasional spotting – orig. cloth – slightly soiled – large 4to – 1877.
(Christie's S. Kensington) $75 £35

TROUBLES, THE, OF HARRY CARELESS or GOING TOO FAR
Wood engraved frontispiece and 7 illus. coloured by hand – orig. pictorial wrappers – backstrip worn – large 8vo – Albany, NY. E. H. Bender – 1850.
(Sotheby's) $45 £22

TRUSLER, JOHN
'The Progress of Man and Society' – 1st Edn., issue with vignette at foot of page 241, illustrations, slight staining, cont. sheep, joints cracked – 1791.
(Christie's S. Kensington) $110 £48

TRUSLER, JOHN
'Proverbs in Verse' – wood engraved vignette on title – 48 illus. all by John Bewick – orig. boards – lower cover stained – partly unopened – sm 8vo – I. Souter, 1814.
(Sotheby's) $200 £95

TRYTHALL, W. J.
'The Three Town Directory' – folding map – orig. cloth – 1881.
(Lane) $30 £14

TUCKEY, JAMES HUNGSTON
'An Account of a Voyage to Establish A Colony at Port Philip in Bass's Strait' – 1st Edn. – half title – browning – staining – orig. boards – covers loose – uncut – 8vo – 1805.
(Sotheby's) $1,260 £600

TUCKEY, J. K.
'Narrative of an Expedition to the River Zaire' – 13 engraved plates, one hand col. – folding map – illus. spotted – modern cloth – rubbed – 4to – 1818.
(Sotheby's) $275 £130

TUER, ANDREW W.
'Bartolozzi and His Works' – 2 vols. – plates – orig. parchment – soiled – t.e.g. – 4to – n.d.
(Christie's S. Kensington) $90 £42

TUGRA AND FIRMAN OF SULTAN AHMET II
Tugra black sprinkled with gold, sefine style, divani jali script, alternately black and red, chancery signature at beginning and end – minor staining – creased when folded – slightly defective – framed – Ottoman, circa 1691-95.
(Christie's) $1,365 £650

TULLY, MISS
'Letters Written During a Ten Years' Residence at the Court of Tripoli' – 3rd Edn. – 2 vols. – 1819 – folding map – 7 hand col. aquatint plates – soiled – modern calf backed cloth.
(Christie's S. Kensington) $105 £50

TULLY, RICHARD
'Narrative of Ten Years' Residence at Tripoli' – 1st Edn. – folding engraved map – 5 hand col. aquatint plates – modern polished calf – spine faded – 4to – 1816.
(Sotheby's) $125 £60

TUNNICLIFFE, C. F.
'Shorelands Summer Diary' – illus. and 16 coloured plates by the author – orig. cloth backed boards – slipcase.
(Christie's S. Kensington) $230 £110

TUPPER, M. F.
'Proverbial Philosophy' – illus. by Tenniel – 1867.
(Laurence & Martin Taylor) $1 50p

TURKEY, MILITARY COSTUME OF
Addit. engraved title and col. aquatint vignette – 30 col. aquatint plates – cont. half roan – uncut – upper cover detached – folio – T. McLean, 1818.
(Christie, Manson & Woods) $210 £100

TURNBULL, GEORGE
'A Treatise on Ancient Painting' – 1st Edn. – large copy – title in red and black – 54 engraved plates – cont. speckled calf – spine gilt – joints split – bookplate of Sir James Dashwood – folio – 1740.
(Sotheby's) $210 £100

TURNBULL, J. R.
'Sketches of Delhi' – litho title – dedication and 14 plates – orig. cloth – rubbed – loose – folio – 1858.
(Sotheby's) $220 £105

TURNBULL, JOHN
'A Voyage Round The World in 1800-4' – mottled calf – gilt – 4to – 1813.
(Phillips) $840 £400

TURNER, D.
'Account of a Tour in Normandy' – 2 vols. – plates – some marginal stains – orig. cloth – rubbed – 8vo – 1820.
(Sotheby's) $105 £50

TURNER, DAWSON AND DILLWYN, LEWIS WESTON
'The Botanist's Guide through England and Wales' – 1st Edn. – 2 vols. – browning – orig. boards – uncut – 8vo – 1805.
(Sotheby's) $55 £25

TURNER AND GIRTIN
'Picturesque View of English, Scotch and Welsh Scenery A Hundred Years Ago' – frontis – 2 facsimiles and 31 steel engraved plates – orig. cloth – 1873.
(Bennett Book Auction) $60 £28

TURNER, J. M. W.
'The Rivers of France' – large paper copy – 61 steel engraved plates on india paper – spotted – no text – later half morocco – folio – n.d.
(Christie's) $180 £85

TURNER, J. M. W. AND OTHERS
'An Antiquarian and Picturesque Tour Round the Southern Coast of England' – engraved frontispiece and 46 plates only after Turner and others – mounted illus. on india paper – occasional spotting – cont. half morocco – worn – g.e. – large 4to – 1849.
(Christie's S. Kensington) $210 £100

TURNER, J. M. W. AND WHITAKER, REV. T. DUNN
'A Series of Views . . . in Richmondshire' – 32 steel engraved plates on india paper – large paper copy – quarter morocco – folio – 1843.
(Bennett Book Auction) $65 £30

TURNOR, CHRISTOPHER HATTON
'Astra Castra, Experiments and Adventures in the Atmosphere' – 1st Edn. – presentation copy, inscribed by author – col. frontis – 41 photozincographic plates – orig. cloth – worn – large 4to – 1865.
(Sotheby's) $265 £125

TUSSER, THOMAS
'Five Hundred Points of Good Husbandry' – one of 500 copies – orig. calf – soiled – 4to – 1931.
(Sotheby's) $85 £40

TWINING, ELIZABETH
'Illustrations of the Natural Order of Plants' – 2 vols. – 160 hand col. lithographed plates – occasional slight spotting – cont. half morocco – rubbed – g.e. – folio – 1849-55.
(Christie's S. Kensington) $4,410 £2,100

TWYFORD, H. P.
'He Came to Our Door' – 1946.
(Lane) $8 £4

TYAS, ROBERT
'Beautiful Birds' – 2 vols. – 12 hand col. plates – orig. cloth – 1850.
(Phillips) $230 £110
'Favourite Field Flowers' – second series – 12 col. plates – inscription on title – orig. cloth – gilt – worn – 8vo – 1850.
(Sotheby's) $105 £50

TYBURN CHRONICLE', 'THE: or 'VILLAINY DISPLAY'D'
4 vols. – engraved frontispieces and 35 plates – some soiling – cont. calf – joints cracked – three covers detached.
(Christie's S. Kensington) $40 £20

TYLOR, E. B.
'Anthropology' – full calf – 1881.
(Laurence & Martin Taylor) $6 £3

TYMMS, W. R. AND WYATT, W. D.
'The Art of Illuminating' – chromolithographed title – 95 plain and chromo plates – modern half morocco – a few leaves badly bound in – Day and Son – n.d.
(Christie's S. Kensington) $65 £30

TYPES OF THE BRITISH ARMY
11 col. plates on board – half morocco – Army and Navy Gazette – 1893.
(Phillips) $60 £28

TYRELL, HENRY
'The History of the War with Russia' – 6 parts – portraits – 33 views – 4 maps with vignettes – cloth worn – circa 1856.
(Phillips) $40 £18

UDE, LOUIS EUSTACE
'The French Cook' – 14th Edn. – engraved portrait – dampstained – some spotting – modern half calf – 1841.
(Christie's S. Kensington) $65 £30

'The French Cook' – 7th Edn. – portrait – 8 plates – one detached – margins frayed – browning – contem. half calf – upper cover detached – spine torn – 1822.
(Christie's) $60 £28

UFFIZIO DELLA SETTIMAN SANTA
Contem. Italian binding of red morocco gilt with the arms of Camillo Borghese in centre of cover and his bookplate – blue silk endleaves – decorated back – 8vo. – Roma 1794.
(Moore Allen & Innocent) $315 £150

UHLAND, LUDWIG
Fine auto letter signed discussing the nature of his poetic inspiration – 3 pages – octavo – to novelist Otto Heinrich, Graf von Loben – Tubingen August 1812.
(Sotheby's) $1,010 £480

ULITA, (Almanach of the Ural Literary Association)
One of 300 copies – orig. wrappers – 8vo. – Leningrad by the author, 1927.
(Sotheby's) $105 £50

ULLOA, ANTONIO DE
'Physikalische und historische Nachrichten vom sudlichen und nordostlichen America' – 2 parts in one vol. – 1st German Edn. – translated and edited by J. A. Dieze – slightly spotted – cont. boards – 8vo – Leipzig, 1781.
(Sotheby's) $30 £15

UNITED STATES GEOLOGICAL SURVEY TO THE SECRETARY OF THE INTERIOR – vols. III, IV and VI-XXVI in 64 vols. excluding a vol. of coloured folding maps and a duplicate of vol. IV – copiously illustrated with plates and illustrations – all but two in cont. red calf leather – rubbed – 4to – Washington, 1883-1904.
(Sotheby's) $240 £170

UNIVERSAL HISTORY, MODERN PART OF
44 vol. – contem. mottled calf – gilt spines – 8vo. – 1759-66.
(Sotheby's) $315 £150

UNLUCKY JOHN AND HIS LUMP OF SILVER – JUVENILE COMIC TALE
Wood engraved frontis – 14 illus. col. by hand – soiled – orig. printed wrappers – spine gilt – sm. 8vo. – Dean and Munday 1825.
(Sotheby's) $95 £45

Mögen uns Allen der Vollmond der [illegible] klar und unumwölkt aufgehen!
Mit Achtung und Liebe
Der Ihrige
L. Uhland.

UNTERMYER COLLECTION, IRWIN
'Chelsea and other English Porcelain Pottery and Enamel' – text by Yvonne Hackenbroch – 4to. – plates – some coloured – orig. cloth backed boards – dust jacket – Cambridge, Massachusetts, 1957.
(Christie's S. Kensington) $65 £30

UNTRODDEN FIELDS OF ANTHROPOLOGY
2 vol. – 2nd Edn. – plates in pocket – cont. cloth – worn – orig. wrappers preserved – 4to. – Paris, 1898.
(Sotheby Parke Bernet) $44 £22

UNWIN, GEORGE
'Letters and Remarks on Cornish Tin' – 1st Edn. – full morocco – 1730.
(Lane) $55 £26

UPCOTT, WILLIAM
'Bibliographical Account of the Principal Works relating to English Topography' – 3 vols. – engraved frontispiece in vols. 1 and II spotted throughout – contemporary calf rebacked – 8vo. – 1818.
(Christie's) $95 £50
Catalogue of the Library (manuscripts and autographed letters; prints, pictures and curiosities) – sold by auction by Messrs. S. Leigh Sotheby & Co. – June 15, 22, 25, 1846 – 3 parts in one vol. – as issued – large paper copy – original cloth worn – folio – 1846.
(Christie's) $180 £90

UPDIKE, D. B.
'Printing Types' – 2 vol. – 2nd Edn. – plates – illustrations orig. cloth – dust jacket – 1937.
(Christie's S. Kensington) $55 £25

USHER, J. W.
'Art Collector's Treasures' – plates – calf gilt – t.e.g. – 4to. – 1916.
(Phillips) $55 £25

USTINOV, PETER
'The Loser' – author's first novel – slightly worn dust wrapper – 1961.
(J. Ash) $8 £4

UTKIN, IOSIF
'Povest o Ryzhem Motele' (Story of the Ginger Motel) – illus. and orig. wrappers – trimmed – by K. Rotov – later cloth – sm. 4to. – Moscow 1926.
(Sotheby's) $105 £50

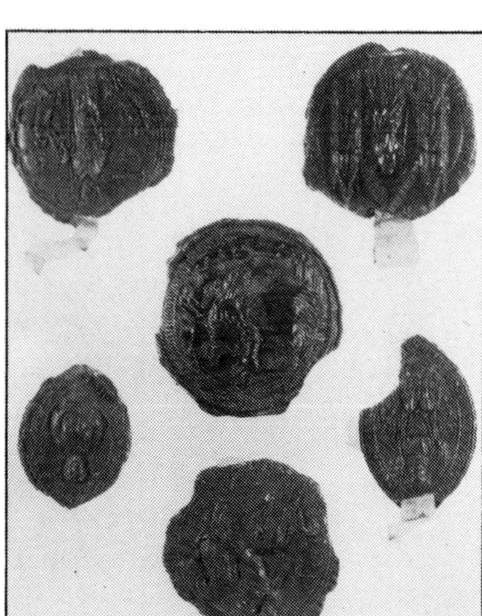

UTRECHT SEALS
A very large and notable collection of approx 550 detached from public record offices in Utrecht and elsewhere in the Netherlands, including approx. 320 mediaeval seals – at least 16 of the 12th or early 13th cent. and about 50 13th cent. seals – some labelled – many worn and defective but generally good – in 5 large half calf boxes – worn and most covers detached with a printed list – 12th – 18th cents.
(Sotheby's) $8,400 £4,000

UWINS, THOMAS
'The Costume of the University of Oxford' – 1st Edn. – 17 hand col. engraved plates – half titles – spotting – contem. calf rebacked – worn – 4to. – R. Ackermann 1815.
(Sotheby's) $160 £75

UZANNE, OCTAVE
'Fashion in Paris 1797 to 1897' – 100 hand coloured plates – illustrations – orig. cloth – spine faded – 4to. – 1898.
(Christie's S. Kensington) $115 £55

VACHON, M.
'La Renaissance Francaise' – plates – half morocco – t.e.g. – 4to. – 1910.
(Phillips) $55 £25

VAENIUS, E.
'Tractatus Physiologicus de Pulchritudine' – eng. vignettes – 18th cent. red morocco – gilt – Brussels, 1662.
(Sotheby Parke Bernet) $180 £90

VALENTIA, GEORGE ANNESLEY VISCOUNT
'Voyages and Travels to India, Ceylon, The Red Sea, Abyssinia, and Egypt' – 1st Edn. – 3 vols. – small stamp on titles – 69 engraved maps and plates – maps all folding – large engraved vignette at the beginning of each vol. – contemporary vellum gilt – blindstamped arms on covers – head of one spine slightly torn – 4to. – 1809.
(Christie's) $800 £400

'Voyages and Travels to India, Ceylon, the Red Sea and Egypt' – 3 vols. – 3 vigs. – 69 engr. plates, maps and charts some folding – orig. calf gilt – 4to. – 1809.
(Phillips) $1,090 £520

VALENTINE, BASILIUS
'The Last Will and Testament' – 4th Edn. – folding table – 113 woodcuts in text – 19th cent. half calf – rubbed – 8vo. – 1671.
(Sotheby's) $180 £85

VALENTINE, J. (Photographer)
'Photographic Groups of Eminent Personages' – cloth gilt – circa 1875.
(Tessa Bennett, Edinburgh) $18 £8

VALERIANI, D. AND SEGATO, G.
'Atlanto Monumentale del Basso e Dell Alto Egitto' – 161 engraved plates – some col. – some folding – some torn – soiling – orig. cloth – lacks spine – worn – loose – folio Florence 1840.
(Sotheby's) $420 £200

VALERIO, SAMUEL
'Yad ha'Melech' – 1st Edn. – title within architectural woodcut border –library stamp on title – antique-style morocco – sm. 4to. – Venice, Giovanni Griffio, 1586.
(Christie's) $440 £220

VALERIUS, M.
'Dictorum Factorumque' – browned – cont. pigskin with metal clasps – worn – Lyons, 1536.
(Sotheby's) $60 £30

VALIN, RENE-JOSE
'Nouveau Commentaire sur L'Ordinnance de la Marine .... 1681' – 2 vols. – margins dampstained – contem. mottled calf – worn – 4to. – La Rochelle 1766.
(Sotheby Beresford Adams) $40 £20

VALK, G.
'Pars summa, seu Australis Superioris Rheni Circuli; Pars altera, seu Borealis Circuli Rheni . . . Hassiae Lantgraviatus . . . Lothargingiae Ducatum etc.' – engraved maps of countries on the upper and lower Rhine – hand coloured in outline – decorative title cartouches – each sheet approx. 490 x 595mm – Amsterdam, circa 1700.
(Sotheby's) $100 £50

VALK, G. AND SCHENK, P.
'Middlesexiae' – hand col. map – cartouche – circa 1650.
(Phillips) $230 £110

VALLANCE, AYMER
'Old Crosses and Lychgates' – illus. – orig. cloth – gilt – slightly soiled – B. T. Batsford, 1920 – and 16 others. – 4to and 8vo.
(Sotheby's) $80 £40

VALLARDI, P. AND J.
'Itineraire D'Italie' – 16 folding maps – one table – slight soiling – contemporary half calf – worn – Milan 1817.
(Christie's S. Kensington) $40 £20

VALLISNIERI, ANTONIO
'Opere diverse ... I. Istoria del Camaleonte Affricanno ..., II. Lezione academica intorno all'origine delle fontane, III. Raccolti di Vari Trattati' – 3 parts in one vol. – each with separate title – engraved frontispiece portrait and 30 folding plates – by A. Luciani – contemporary paper boards – 4to. – G. G. Ertz 1715; 'Istoria della Generazione dell'uomo e degli Animali' – 13 engraved plates – paper wrappers – sm. 4to. – G. G. Hertz 1721.
(Christie's) $380 £190

'Opere Fisico-Mediche' – 3 vols. – engraved title vignette by A. dalla Via – portrait of the author within architectural vignette border – 91 illustrations on 84 plates – 3 folding – by A. Luciani et al. – and another illustration in the text – wormhole in title and first leaves of first vol. – uncut in original paper boards – in buckram slipcase – folio – S. Coleti 1733.
(Christie's) $320 £160

VALSAVALA, A. M.
'De Aure Humana Tractatus' – title in red and black – 10 folding engraved plates – browning and soiling – contem. panelled calf – rubbed – sm. 4to. – Utrecht 1727.
(Sotheby's) $250 £120

VAMBERY, A.
'Travels in Central Asia' – 1st Edn. – plates – folding map – orig. cloth – 8vo. – 1864.
(Sotheby's) $180 £85

VAN DE VELDE, C. W. M.
'Le Pays D'Israel' – col map – 99 tinted litho views – some views of Jerusalem – half morocco gilt – large oblong folio – Paris 1858.
(Phillips) $1,680 £800

VAN GOIDSENHOVEN, J. P.
'La Ceramique Chinoise sous les T'Sing' – limited Edn. – col. plates – morocco gilt – 4to. – 1936.
(Phillips) $180 £85

VAN KEULEN, J.
'The English Channel' – coloured map – 495 mm x 570 mm – Amsterdam 1704.
(Tooleys) $505 £240

VANCOUVER, GEORGE
'Voyage of Discovery to the North Pacific Ocean and round the World' – 6 vols. – 1 folding map of 2 – torn – 4 of 17 folding plates – cont. half calf – 3 vols. slightly smaller – very worn – 3 spines missing – some covers detached – 1801 – and 3 others – 8vo.
(Sotheby's) $90 £45

VANITY FAIR
6 vols. only – col. plates – half calf – worn – w.a.f. – folio – 1896-98.
(Sotheby's) $640 £320

VANITY FAIR CARTOONS
A collection of 96 caricatures by Ape, Spy and others of Lord Roberts, Lord Baden-Powell, Queen Victoria and other military and political leaders of the period – some in duplicate – some with accompanying text – folio – circa 1869-1902.
(Sotheby's) $170 £80

VANLAIR, C.
'La Guerre aux Microbes' – Brussels, 1887, 'Sur la Persistance de l'Aptitude Regeneratice des Nerfs' – Brussels, 1888, 'Le Mesoneurite Noduleuse' – Paris, 1894 – off-prints – orig. wrappers – soiled; and other medical pamphlets – w.a.f.
(Sotheby's) $16 £8

VAN MARLE, R.
'The Development of the Italian Schools of Painting' – 19 vols. – reprint – orig. cloth – 8vo. – New York 1970.
(Sotheby's) $315 £150

VANE, C. W. MARQUESS OF LONDONDERRY
'Narrative of the War in Germany and France' – 2 engraved maps – hand col. in outline – 1 folding – contem. mottled calf – gilt – rubbed – 4to. – 1830.
(Sotheby's) $40 £20

VANUCCIUS, ROBERTUS
'Sermocinales artes ... eiusdem dialogus de arte sermocinali eiusdem carmina' – woodcut device on title – woodcut initials – lacks last leaf wormholes – dampstaining – sm. 8vo. – Venice, Cominus de Tridino 1545.
(Sotheby's) $55 £25

VARAGNAC, ANDRE
'French Costumes designed by Lapagne-Mecvey' – sm. folio – 40 coloured plates – original wrappers – worn – Hyperion Press 1939.
(Christie's S. Kensington) $30 £15

VARENIUS, BERNARDUS
'Descriptio regni Japoniae et Siam' – 1st English Edn. – title printed in red and black – 19th century half calf – worn – slight dampstaining – 8vo – 1673.
(Sotheby's) $140 £70
'Geographia generalis . . . aucta & illustrata ab Isaaco Newton' – 2nd Edn. of Newton's Edn. – 5 folding engraved plates – slight browning and soiling – cont. mottled calf – rubbed – 8vo – 1681.
(Sotheby's) $30 £15

VARLOT, L.
'Xylographie de l'Imprimerie Troyenne', 'tire a petit nombre' – woodcuts – quarter cloth – spine chipped – 4to – Troyes et Paris, 1859.
(Sotheby's) $56 £28

VASON, GEORGE
'An Authentic Narrative of Four Years' Residence at Tongataboo' – 1st Edn. – engraved frontispiece by Parkyns – engraved map – errata leaf – outer margins of plate and map slightly shaved, small tear in title – contemporary calf rebacked – 8vo – 1810.
(Christie's) $300 £150

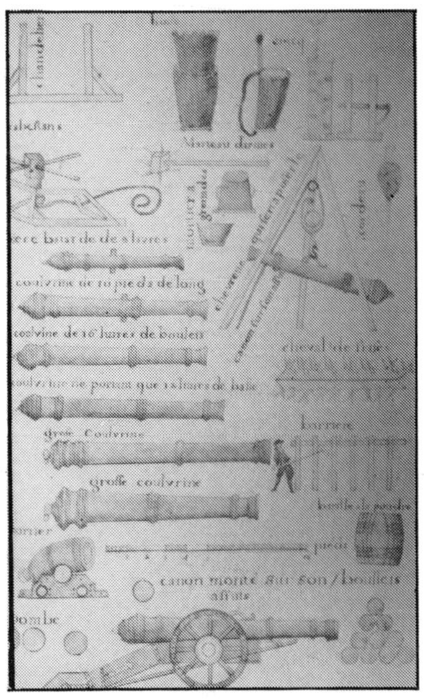

VAUBAN, SEBASTIEN LE PRESTRE, MARQUIS DE, 1633-1707
Fine early 18th cent. mss of his celebrated work 'Trait de L'Attaque de Places' – 243 pages of text with 32 superbly drawn hand col. folding plates – contem. calf – bookplate – with Albemarle coat of arms – large folio.
(Sotheby's) $2,520 £1,200

VAUGHAN, HILDA
'Pardon and Peace' – good – 1942.
(J. Ash) $6 £3

VAUGONDY, ROBERT DE
'Amerique Septentrionale' – hand col. map – some foxing – 1750.
(Phillips) $125 £60

VAURIE, C.
'Tibet and Its Birds' – signed limited Edn. – illus. – half red morocco gilt – t.e.g. by Sangorski – 8vo. – 1972.
(Phillips) $105 £50

VAUXHALL GARDENS
Album containing engraved views, posters for theatre, concerts, ascent of the Royal Nassau Balloon Races, music scores etc. – cloth defective – folio.
(Phillips) $210 £100

VECCHIETTI, H.
'De Anno Primitivo' – later morocco – gilt – rubbed – folio – Augsburg, 1621.
(Sotheby's) $30 £15

VECELLIO, CESARE
'Habiti Antichi' – 3rd Edn. – device on title – 415 woodcuts of costumes – orig. red morocco – rubbed – g.e. – 8vo. – Venice 1664.
(Sotheby's) $775 £370
'Corona delle Nobili, et Virtuose Donne' – 4 parts in one vol. – numerous full page woodcuts of lace patterns – browned – vellum – stained – sm. oblong 4to. – Venice 1592-1608.
(Sotheby's) $30 £15

VECHER
'Triremy' (Evening of the Trireme) – one of 600 copies – marginal stains – modern cloth backed boards – orig. wrappers preserved – 8vo. – Petrograd 1916.
(Sotheby's) $210 £100

VEDUTE DI ROMA E SUOI CONTORNI
100 engraved plates – orig. wrappers – soiled – oblong 8vo. – Rome circa 1820.
(Sotheby's) $95 £45

VEER, GERRIT DE
'Tre Navigationi Fatte Dagli Olandesi, E. Selandesi' – 1st Italian Edn. – trans by Giovanni Giunio – engraved vignette on title – 32 engraved maps and scenes in text – disbound – sm 4to – Venice, G. B. Ciotti, 1599.
(Sotheby's) $1,000 £500

VELLY, L'ABBE
'Histoire de France' – 32 vol., vol. 8 lacking – browning – contemporary mottled calf – joints cracked – one cover detached – Paris 1761-81.
(Christie's S. Kensington) $60 £28

VELPEAU, A. A. L. M.
'Nouveaux Elements de Medicine Operatoire' – 5 vol. – including atlas vol. of plates – 2nd Edn. – 22 engraved plates – red morocco backed marbled boards – spines gilt – slightly rubbed – atlas vol. roan backed cloth – 8vo. – Paris 1839.
(Sotheby's) $95 £45

VENERES UTI OBSERVANTUR IN GEMMIS ANTIQUIS
Two parts in one – 'Lugd Baravorum' two engr. titles and seventy plates – text in French and English – outer margin of one leaf repaired – later marbled calf – gilt – g.e.
(Christie's S. Kensington) $125 £60

VENETTE, NICHOLAS
'The Art of Pruning Fruit-Trees' – some dampstaining and working with loss of a few letters – old calf – spine lacking – upper cover detached – for Tho. Basset, 1685.
(Christie's S. Kensington) $135 £65

VENGROV, NATAN
'Khvoi' – limited Edn. – this no. 40 – illus. and orig. wrappers by E. Yurova – spine torn – 8vo. – Petrograd 1919.
(Sotheby's) $160 £75

VENICE
'Il Gran Teatro di Venezia' – 2 vols. in one – titles in red and black – 102 double page engraved plates – including 66 views – many by Zucchi after Tiepolo, Manaigo and others – two other views inserted from another work – contem. half calf – large folio – circa 1720.
(Christie's) $7,980 £3,800

VENNING, M. A.
'A Geographical Present' – 2nd Edn. – 60 hand coloured plates – one torn cleanly – soiling and staining – orig. roan backed boards – worn – 12mo. 1818.
(Christie's S. Kensington) $65 £30

VENTENAT, E. P.
'Description Des Plantes Nouvelles . . . Dans Le Jardin De J. M. Cels' – 100 engraved plates mostly after Redoute – cont. French half red morocco – partly uncut – the Plesch copy – folio – Paris, 1800.
(Sotheby's) $1,600 £800

VENTURI, A.
'Storia dell'Arte Italiana' – 11 vol. in 25 – illus. – modern morocco – gilt spines – slipcases – 8vo. – Milan, 1901-40.
(Sotheby's) $2,205 £1,050

VENTURI, LIONELLO
'Cezanne, Son Art, Son Oeuvre' – 2 vols. – including 1 vol. of plates – one of 1,000 copies – original printed wrappers – partly unopened – uncut slightly soiled – 4to. – Paris 1936.
(Christie's) $1,700 £850

VENUS ATTIRING THE GRACES
A Poem – modern wrappers – J. Dodsley – 1777; and another.
(Sotheby's) $60 £30

VERE, SIR FRANCIS
'The Commentaries' – 1st Edn. – edited by Wm. Dillingham – printed with line borders throughout – 3 engraved portraits – 7 double page plates, maps and plans – cont. mottled calf – recased and rebacked – some leaves waterstained from inner margins, a few spots – sm folio – Cambridge, 1657.
(Sotheby's) $300 £150

'The Commentaries . . . published by Wm. Dillingham' – 1st Edn. – 10 engraved plates and maps, some double page – half title – dampstained – 18th century tree calf – rebacked – rubbed – folio – 1657.
(Sotheby's) $90 £40

VERGIL, POLYDORE
'Adagiorum Opus' – title within historiated woodcut border – printer's device at end – title and last leaf a little dust-soiled – paper boards – Signet library gilt stamp on covers g.e. stamp of Bibliotheca Heberiana – 8vo. – Jena, sumptibus Blasius Lobenstein, 1632.
(Christie's) $140 £70

VERGILIUS, MARO P.
'Buccolica, Georgica et Aeneas' – frontis – browned – cont. half morocco – rubbed – 4to – Cambridge, 1701.
(Sotheby's) $20 £10

VERLAINE, PAUL
'Parallelement' – no. 12 of 23 copies on Japon ancien – 23 plates by Chimot – with 2 original designs – blue morocco – gilt – Paris 1934.
(Sotheby Parke Bernet) $2,415 £1,150

'Dedicaces' – new Edn. – one of 55 copies on holland – contemporary morocco backed boards – slightly rubbed – original wrappers bound in – bookplate of John Quinn – t.e.g. – Paris 1894.
(Christie's S. Kensington) $40 £20

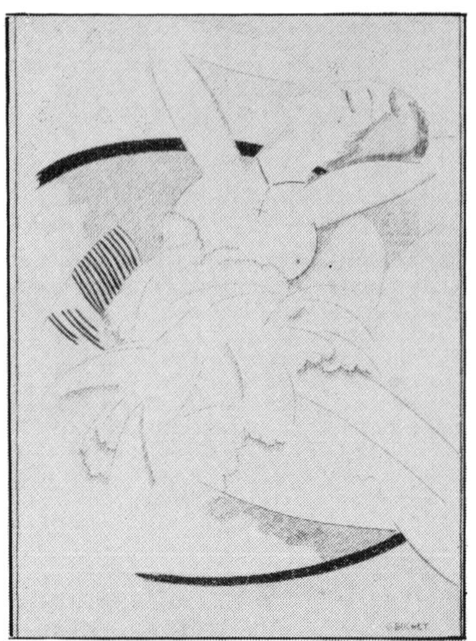

VERLAINE, PAUL – BUCHET, GUSTAVE
'Les Amies' – 13 etched plates by Buchet – coloured by hand – unsewn in orig. wrappers – backstrip damaged – uncut – 4to. – Paris, Le Livre, 1921.
(Sotheby's) $360 £170

VERLAINE, PAUL – LAURENCIN, MARIE
'Fetes Galantes' – 10 etched plates by Laurencin – red morocco – embossed cover tooled in gilt – orig. wrappers bound in – t.e.g. – calf backed folder – slipcase by Bonfils, 4to. – Paris Messein 1944.
(Sotheby's) $670 £320

VERLET, P., GRANDJEAN, S., BRUNET, M.
'Sevres' – 3 vols – including prospectus – plates – some col. – mounted – orig. cloth – dust jackets – prospectus original ring backed rexine – 4to. – Paris 1953.
(Sotheby's) $420 £200

VERNE, JULES
'Twenty Thousand Leagues Under the Sea' – 1st Eng. Edn. – illus. – orig. pictorial cloth – gilt – Very good – 1875.
J. Ash) $230 £110

VERNER, WILLOUGHBY
'History and Campaigns of the Rifle Brigade 1800-13' – 2 vols. – ports. – maps – orig. cloth slightly worn – small 4to. – 1912-19.
(Phillips) $105 £50

VERNER, CAPT. W.
'Sketches in the Sudan' – 38 lithographed plates and one map – orig. boards – worn – oblong 4to. – 1885.
(Christie's S. Kensington) $105 £50

VERNET, C.
'Cris de Paris' – 50 hand coloured lithographed plates – margins soiled – slight dampstaining – lacking coloured title – orig. morocco backed boards – rubbed – folio – Paris n.d.
(Christie's S. Kensington) $600 £280

VERSAILLES GARDEN STATUARY
56 engraved plates depicting statues and ornaments in the gardens of Versailles by Le Potre, Edelinck and one by Chaveau – versos blank – 18th cent. calf backed boards – worn – edges uncut – folio – 1672-81.
(Christie's) $505 £240

VERSTEGAN, OR ROWLANDS, RICHARD
'A Restitution of Decayed Intelligence in Antiquities' – sm. 4to. – engr. illust. – modern speckled calf by Bayntun – g.e. – John Norton, Joyce Norton and Richard Whitaker, 1634.
(Christie's S. Kensington) $170 £80

VERTUE, GEORGE
'Medals, Coins, Great Seals, Impressions from the Elaborate Works of Thomas Simon, Chief Engraver to the Mint' – engraved title – 48 plates – new half calf – 4to – G. Vertue, 1753.
(Sotheby's) $65 £30

VERWER, PIETER ADRIAEN
'Historie van het Verlatene en Gelukkige Weesiut, Charlotte Summers' – 2 vols., 2nd Edn., engraved plates, soiled, a few pages torn with loss, soiling, cont. calf, extremities rubbed, inner hinges split – Amsterdam, 1751.
(Christie's S. Kensington) $45 £20

VESME, A. DE AND MASSAR, P. D.
'Stefano Della Bella' – Catalogue Raisonne – 2 vol. – 4to. – reprinted New York – plates – orig. cloth – Collectors Editions, 1971.
(Christie's S. Kensington) $45 £22

VESPERSTUNDE, DIE
Col. Illus. – 22 full page and decorations orig. cloth backed pictorial boards – worn – 4to. – Berlin, Asher n.d.
(Sotheby's) $55 £25

VEVER, HENRI
'Catalogue of Highly Important Japanese Prints, Illustrated Books, Drawings and Fan Paintings' – vol. 2 and 3 only – plates – some folding – some col. – illus. – orig. boards – dust jackets – 4to. – Sotheby 1975-77.
(Sotheby's) $115 £55

'La Bijouterie Francaise' – 3 vols., plates, illustrations, unopened, original wrappers, soiled – Paris, 1906-08.
(Christie's S. Kensington) $270 £120

VICARY, THOMAS
'The English Mans Treasure, With the True Anatomie of Mans bodie . . . now sixtly augmented and enlarged' – black letter – full page woodcut – 19th century half green morocco – spine rubbed – slightly rubbed – sm 4to – 1613.
(Sotheby's) $400 £200

VICKY
A series of 12 orig. pen and crayon sketches on one sheet comprising Old Vicky's Almanac for 1962 including one showing Harold Macmillan on the grouse moor – all partly hand col. – some with artist's proof corrections – framed – approx. 21 in. x 27 in. – 1962.
(Sotheby Beresford Adams) $210 £100

VICTOIRES, CONQUETES, DESASTRES, REVERS ET GUERRES CIVILES DES FRANCAIS DE 1792 A 1815
27 vols. – plates and maps – some folding – some leaves spotted – contem. calf backed boards – rubbed – 8vo. – Paris 1817-21.
(Sotheby's) $160 £75

VICTORIA
The official Diamond Jubilee photograph signed and dated by the Queen inscribed on reverse by her private secretary, Sir Arthur Bigge, to the photographer Downey – original mount – 13 x 7½ inches – April 1897.
(Sotheby's) $1,300 £620

VICTORIA
'Leaves from the Journal of our Lives in the Highlands' – 1st. Edn. – presentation copy – inscribed by author – 4 engraved plates – 11 mounted photographs – 3 wood engraved illus. – spotted – orig. cloth – gilt – slipcase – 8vo. – Privately Printed 1865.
(Sotheby's) $460 £220

ALs 3 pages 8vo Holyrood, 28 August 1856 to her favourite son 'My darling little Arthur' – later the Duke of Connaught – with vignette heading of Holyrood.
(Phillips) $295 £140

VICTORIA COUNTY HISTORIES
16 odd volumes for Nottingham, Gloucester, Durham, Devon, Kent, Lincoln, Surrey, Sussex and Warwick including 4 duplicates – plates – illus. – orig. cloth – 4 with dust jackets – 4to. – 1905-69.
(Sotheby's) $295 £140

VICTORIA COUNTY HISTORY
Hertfordshire – vols. I-IV and index. vol. – half morocco – spines gilt – index vol. in cloth – t.e.g. – colour plates, photographic plates, maps, plans and black and white illus. in text – 1902-23.
(Lawrence) $160 £80

VICTORIAN ILLUSTRATORS
Collection of 78 vols. concerning or illus. by Doyle, Tenniel, Caldecott, Leech, Keene, Dore, Cruikshank, May, Daumier, Beardsley – orig. bindings – rubbed – various sizes.
(Sotheby's) $440 £210

VIDA, M. G.
'Poematum' – 2 parts in 1 vol. – engraved portrait – Oxford, 1722; 'Hymni de Rebus divinis' – 19th century roan – Oxford, 1733.
(Sotheby's) $84 £42

VIELLOT, L. P.
'Histoire Naturelle Des Oiseaux De L'Amerique Septentrionale' – 2 vols. – 131 plates printed in colours and finished by hand – cont. double engraved map of America – coloured in outline – bound in – some foxing – cont. half red morocco – gilt spines – folio – Paris, 1807.
(Sotheby's) $8,000 £4,000

'Histoire Naturelle Des Plus Beaux Chantiers De La Zone Torride' – 72 plates after drawings by J. G. Pretre – printed in colours and finished by hand – some foxing – large copy – green calf – gilt – uncut – folio – Paris, 1805.
(Sotheby's) $8,000 £4,000

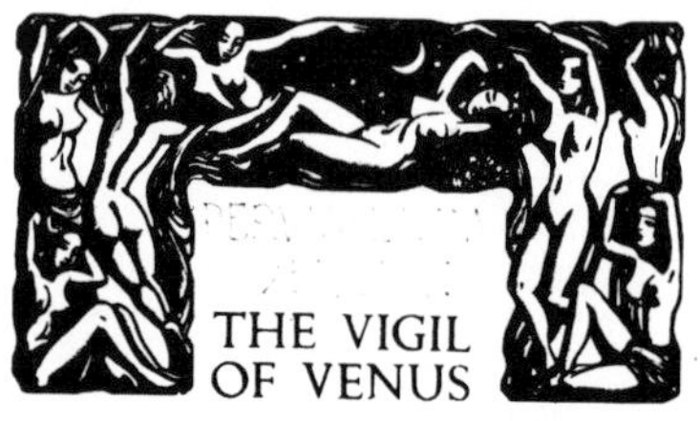

VIGIL OF VENUS, THE
'Pervigilium Veneris' – no 1 of 100 copies – engraved and aquatint borders and vignettes to double page title – 12 illus. – 2 pictorial tailpieces – by John Buckland-Wright – orig. blind tooled morocco – uncut – 4to. – 1939.
(Sotheby's) $3,990 £1,900

VIGNE, G.
'A Personal Narrative of a Visit to Ghunzi, Kabul and Afghanistan' – 1st. Edn. – litho frontis – hand col. – tinted plates – folding map – orig, cloth – 8vo. – 1840.
(Sotheby's) $220 £105

VIGNOLA, JACOPO, BAROZZI DA
'Regole della prospettiva prattica ... con i commentari del ... Egnatio Danti' – title in red and black with engraved architectural border – 16 full page engraved plates by Giorgio Fossati – several woodcut head and tailpieces – small marginal stain to one plate – contemporary paper boards – uncut slightly worn – large folio – Pietro Bassaglia 1743.
(Christie's) $440 £220

VILLA AND COTTAGE ARCHITECTURE
'Select Examples of Country and Suburban Residences Recently Erected' – folio – Blackie and Sons 1868.
(Christie's) $115 £55

VILLANI MATTEO
'Istoria di Cittadino Florentino' – vellum binding – Firenza 1581.
(Richard Baker & Thomson) $90 £44

VILLARS, LOUIS HECTOR DUC DE
'Vie du Marechal Duc de Villars ecrite par lui meme' – 4 vol. – 1st Edn. – engraved portrait and 4 folding engraved maps – head pieces – 1 leaf loose – library stamps – contem. mottled calf – spines gilt – rubbed – 12 mo. – Paris 1784.
(Sotheby's) $105 £50

VILLON, FRANCOIS
'Les Oeuvres' – 1st Edn. – 18th cent. French red morocco – gilt – slightly rubbed – g.e. – 8vo. – Paris 1532.
(Sotheby's) $7,140 £3,400

VINCE, S.
'Treatise on Practical Astronomy' – 8 folding plates – calf gilt – 4to. – 1790.
(Phillips) $90 £42

VINCENT, B.
'Haydn's Dictionary of Dates 1881'; and 'Dictionnaire des Sciences Philosophiques' 1875 – Paris.
(Baitson) $6 £3

VINES, SHARARD
'The Pyramid' – poems – signed by author – fine copy – 1926.
(J. Ash) $10 £5

VINNE, T. E. DE
'The Plantin-Moretus Museum' – no. 162 of 425 copies – portrait – limp vellum – Grabhorn Press, 1929; 'The Gorleston Psalter' – Presentation copy – cloth backed boards – worn – dampstains – 1907; and 5 others.
(Sotheby's) $70 £35

VIOLLET-LE-DUC, E. E.
'Histoire d'un Dessinateur' – frontis – light foxing – quarter morocco – gilt spine – hinges rubbed – Paris, circa 1878.
(Sotheby's) $40 £20

VIRGIL
'Georgica' – large copy – polyglot edn. – edited by W. Sotheby – cont. russia – gilt – front cover detached – 4to – W. Nicoll, 1827.
(Sotheby's) $10 £5

'Le Georgica ... in ottava rima' – engraved title with heraldic vignette – 4 engraved plates by Cristoforo dell'Acqua after Antonio Vecchia – stamp on title margin soiling to some margins – vellum backed paper boards – uncut – 4to. – Vicenza, Francesco Modena, 1780.
(Christie's) $70 £35

VIRTUE & CO.
'The Shakespeare Gallery' – plates – leather – worn – circa 1850; and 21 others – some in calf.
(Sotheby's) $90 £45

VIRGINIA – BLAEU, W. AND J.
'Nova Virginia Tabula' – engraved map – hand col. in outline – cartouches – coats of arms – figure of Indian inset engraving – full col. – French text on verso – 374 mm x 480 mm – Amsterdam circa 1645.
(Sotheby's) $420 £200

VIRGINIA, COLONY OF
Five indentures on paper with schedule of property and related material – 1775-1783.
(Phillips) $85 £40

VISCONTI, G. B. A.
'Description des Antiques du Musee Royal' – contem. red morocco gilt with arms of Louis XVIII in gilt on front cover – g.e. –Neuilly library stamp – 8vo. – Paris 1817.
(Phillips) $85 £40

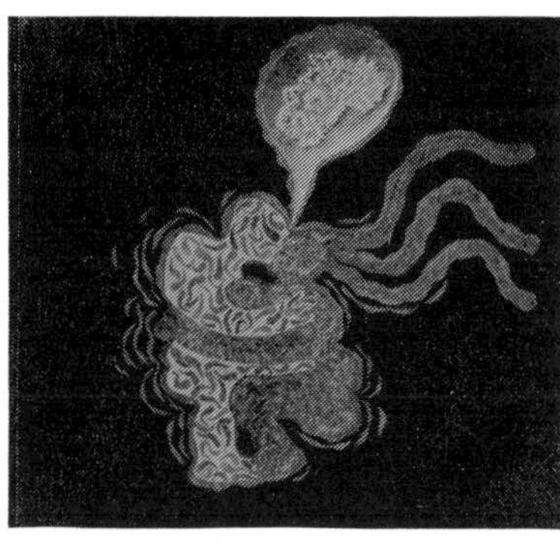

VISITORS' BOOK
100 leaves of blank goatskin parchment – green morocco – design on upper cover in form of 2 embracing figures – all edged in emerald green – red paper doublures – g.e. – upper edge tooled – signed in blind on lower cover and dated 1968 by Philip Smith – oblong 4to. – 1968.
(Sotheby's) $1,765 £840

VISSCHER, C. J.
'Tabula Germaniae Emendata Recens' – engraved map – hand col. in outline – historiated title cartouche – fully col. – 471 mm x 555 mm – Amsterdam circa 1650.
(Sotheby's) $105 £50

VISSCHER, NICOLAUS
'The Travels of St. Paul' – uncol. map – insects – Amsterdam, circa 1690.
(Phillips) $85 £40

Ireland – 'Hiberniae Regnum' – engraved map – hand coloured in outline – armorial and pictorial title and scale cartouches etc. – fully coloured – engraved tables at sides of map – framed – 560 x 738mm – Amsterdam, circa 1700.
(Sotheby's) $220 £110

Gibraltar – 'Plan de la ville de Gibraltar ... 1706' – engraved plan and view of Gibraltar, with perspective view of the town and rock and plan of Ceuta – 3 engravings on one plate, coloured by hand – title in French and Dutch – 433 x 528mm – Amsterdam, circa 1708 or later.
(Sotheby's) $180 £90

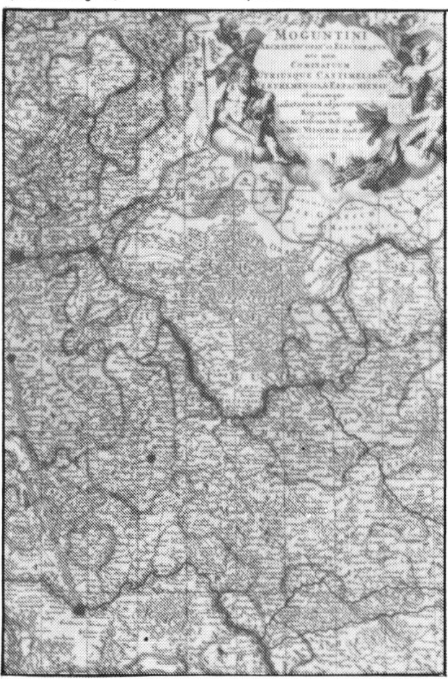

'Atlas Minor sive totius orbis terrarum: Variae Tabulae Geographicae in quibus loca in orbe bello flagrantia conspiciuntur' – sepia engraved allegorical general title by G. de Lairesse – printed title in Latin, French and Dutch – 36 hand coloured double-page engraved maps only of 40 – some folding – foremargin of engraved title with small tears repaired – printed title laid down – contemporary calf – a little rubbed and worn – folio – Amsterdam, N. Visscher – n.d. (after 1705).
(Christie's) $4,800 £2,400

VITA DI S. FILIPPO NERI
Fine engraved title with putti – 60 full page engraved plates by Innocente Alessandri after Pietro Antonio Novelli – contemporary half calf – worn, head of spine chipped – folio – Innocente Alessandri, 1793.
(Christie's) $120 £60

VITRUVIUS, POLLIO MARCUS
'Les Dix Livres d'Architecture . . .' Second Edition revue . . . par M. Perault – engraved frontispiece – numerous text engravings, many full or double page – some dampstaining – old calf, very defective – folio – Paris, 1684.
(Sotheby's) $240 £120

'Architectura . . . cum exercitationibus . . . Joannis Poleni et commentariis variorum, additis nunc primum studiis Simonis Stratico'– 8 parts in 4 vols. – 141 plates, the majority engraved – g.e. – stamp of the Dominican Fathers, Edinburgh, on blank sides of two plates – 'Ralph Sneyd' gilt stamped on covers – 4to – Udine – 1825-30.
(Sotheby's) $560 £280

'Architecture Generale' – engraved plates – cont. calf – rubbed – some dampstains – 12mo – Paris, 1681.
(Sotheby's) $130 £65

'I Dieci Libri Dell'Architettura' – 2 woodcut plates – woodcut illus. – a few stains – 19th cent. calf – worn – 4to. – Venice, A. de'Vecchi, 1629.
(Sotheby Parke Bernet) $170 £85

VIVALDUS, J. L.
'Aureum Opus de Veritate Contritionis' – Gothic letter – device of Fr. Regnault on title and of Jean Barbier at end – old inscriptions partly deleted on title and verso of last leaf – soiling – cont. calf – repaired – 8vo – Paris, Jean Barbier for Fre. Regnault – 1509.
(Sotheby's) $140 £70

VIVIAN, GEORGE
'Views from the Gardens of Rome and Albano' – tinted lithographed frontispiece and 24 plates – by J. D. Harding after Vivian – engraved vignettes in text – original morocco backed cloth – spine scuffed – folio – 1848.
(Christie's) $760 £380

VOIGT, CHARLES ADOLPH
'Rouge et Noir' – plates – orig. cloth gilt – slightly worn – 8vo. – 1898.
(Sotheby's) $40 £20

VOINA KOROLEI
'War of Kings' – 16 col. litho plates – orig. wrappers – frayed and soiled – loose – oblong folio – Moscow 1918.
(Sotheby's) $210 £100

VOITURE, V. DE
'Works' – 2 vol. – portrait – calf – worn – 8vo. – 1736.
(Sotheby's) $40 £20

VOLKMANN, HANS VON
'Afrika, Studien und Einfaelle' – coloured pictorial title and 12 plates by the author – orig. half cloth – pictorial covers – lower corners slightly bruised – oblong 4to. – Leipzig, Breitkopf & Hartel 1895.
(Sotheby's) $85 £40

VOLKOVYSKY, ARNOLD
'Solnsta Potselui' (Kiss of the Sun) – illus. by N. Al'tman – orig. wrappers – torn and soiled – 8vo. – St. Petersburg 1914.
(Sotheby's) $170 £80

VOLLAND, AMBROISE (Publisher)
'Lettres de Vincent Van Gogh a Emile Bernard' – orig. calligraphic wrappers – colour frontis – colour plate and 100 other reproductions, handwriting facsimile etc. – 4to – Paris, 1911.
(Lawrence) $30 £15

VOLLARD, AMBROISE
'Paul Cezanne' – one of 200 copies 'sur velin a la forme, ... avec le filigrane Paul Cezanne' of an Edn of 1,000 – original frontispiece etching 'Tete de Femme' in bistre – numerous other plates – original wrappers bound in – t.e.g. – others uncut – 4to. – Paris, Galerie A. Vollard, 1914.
(Christie's) $560 £280

VOLNEY, C. F.
'Travels through Syria and Egypt' – 2 vols. – 5 plates – calf gilt – 8vo. – 1788.
(Phillips) $145 £70

'Travels Through Syria and Egypt . . . 1783-85' – 2 vols., 2nd Edn. in English, 3 folding engraved plates, 2 folding engraved maps, slight browning, cont. tree calf, worn, upper covers detached – 1788.
(Sotheby's) $65 £30

'L'Alfabet Europeen Applique Aux Langues Asiatiques' – folding tables, half title, cont. calf backed boards, worn – Paris, 1819.
(Sotheby's) $100 £45

VOLPI
'Annali della Tipografia Volpi-Cominiana' – large paper copy – engraved portrait frontispiece and title vignette – original wrappers – uncut – 8vo. – Padua, 1809.
(Christie's) $440 £220

VOLT, ALESSANDRO
Document signed being a prospectus for the University of Pavia for academic year 1817-18, printed on both sides with mss. insertions, oblong folio.
(Sotheby's) $450 £200

VOLTAIRE, FRANCOIS MARIE AROUET DE
'La Pucelle' – a suite of 22 fine ink and wash drawings by Charles Monnet prepared for an edition which never appeared – mounted in an album – red morocco elaborately gilt – blue morocco doublures – silk liners g.e. – The Savigny de Moncorps copy with arms – folio – 1777-79.
(Sotheby Parke Bernet) $180,265 £85,840

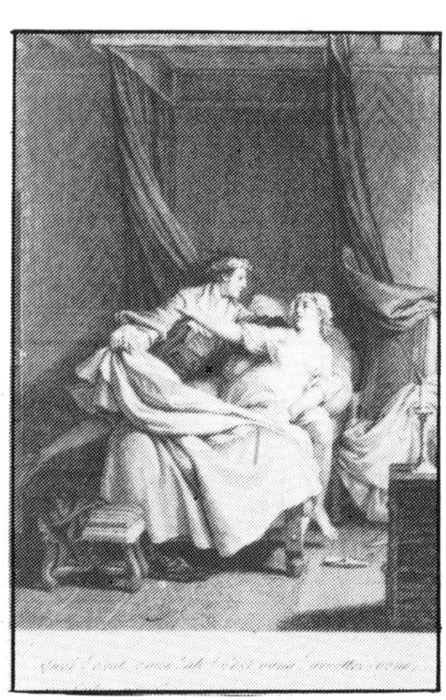

'Oeuvres Completes' – 70 vols. – half titles, engraved portraits and plates after Moreau – bookplates of the Earl of Wicklow – cont. tree calf gilt – a few vols. slightly worn 8vo. – De l'Imprimerie de la Societe Litteraire-Typographique – 1785-89.
(Sotheby's) $1,600 £800

'La Henriade' – frontis and plates – old red morocco gilt – worn – 4to. – Londres 1728.
(Bonhams) $90 £42

'Epistles sur le Bonheur, la Liberte, et l'Envie' – Amsterdam (Paris?), 1738; 'Reponse a toutes les Objections . . . . contre la Philosophie de Neuton' – ib – cloth – 1740.
(Sotheby's) $90 £45

VON FALKE, OTTO
'Decorative Silks' – 1922.
(Christie's) $177 £85

The lyue of saynt James thappostle

But toke it & threwe it in the vysage of the Juge/ and smote out therwyth one of his eyen· Thenne was Julyan wro-
the/and made to shote at her: And she was smeten wyth one arowe in to the si
de: And wyth a nother vnto the herte
And she soo smyten yelded vp her soule vnto god/ and thus suffred martirdom/ aboute the yere of our lorde two hōdred foure score & seuen. Her body was beried in a castell bulsena· bytwene tholde towne & viterbe/ and tyrus whiche was not ferre fro that castell: whyche is now dest-
royed/

Here begynneth the lyfe of saynt James the more and Apostle and first of thīterpretaciō of his name

This James thappostle is sayd James the sone of zebedee/bro-
ther of saynt Johan theuange-
lyst/And boanarges/ that is the sone of thonder/ And James the more he was

sayd James the sone of zebedee: not one ly in flessh: but in theyposicōn of the na-
me·/ For zebedee is interpreted gyuyng or gyuen/and James gaaf himselfe to god by martirdom of deth/ And he is gi-
uen to vs of god for a specyal patron/he is sayd iames broder of John not oonly by flesh: but by semblaūce of maners.
For they bothe were of one loue/ of one estudye/and of one wylle/ They were of one loue for to auenge our lorde / For whan the samarytanes wold not recey-
ue Jhesu cryst/James & John sayd: yf it plese the lorde/ lete fyre descende fro he-
uen & destroye theym/ They were of like studye for to lerne/ for thyse two were they that demaūded of our lorde of ẏ day of Jugement/& of other thynges to co-
me· And they ayed that one of them mi-
ghte sitte at right syde of him/ and that other on his lyft side/ He was sayd the sone of thonder/by cause of the sowne of his predycacyon/ For he fered the euylle and exyted the slowfull/ And by the hie-
nes of his prechyng he dyde merueylles in conuertyng them to the fayth· to wreof bede sayth of saint John/that he thondred soo hie/that yf he had thondred a lytyl hi-
er/all the worlde myghte not haue com-
prysed him/He is sayd James the mo-
re/lyke as that other James is sayd ẏ lasse/ Fyrste by reason of his callynge / For he was fyrst called of Jhesu cryst Secondly by reason of famylyaryte/ for Jhū cryst was seen to haue gretter famy-
lyarite wyth him than wyth the lasse Ja-
mes/lyke as it apereth at reysing of the mayde & at his holy transfyguracōn/ Thyrdly by reason of his passion for e-
mōge all other thapostles he was the first he that suffred deth. & he maye be sayd mo-
re/by cause he was fyrst called to be apos-
tle: soo he was fyrste called to the Joye perdurable.

VORAGINE, JACOBUS DE
'The Golden Legend' trans by Caxton – 3rd Edn. in Eng. – 401 leaves of 436 – gothic letter – numerous woodcuts – waterstains – 16th cent. notes in ink – 19th cent morocco over wooden boards – folio – Wynkyn de Worde May 1493.
(Christie's) $10,500 £5,000

'The Golden Legend' – translated by William Caxton – 3 vol. – one of 500 copies – illustrations – original holland backed boards – rubbed – 4to. – Kelmscott Press, 1892.
(Sotheby's) $440 £210

VOSMAR, A.
'Description d'un Nouvelle . . . Porc a large groin, ou Sanglier Afrique' – 18 hand coloured plates, morocco gilt – Amsterdam, 1767.
(Phillips) $405 £180

VOSSIUS, ISAAC DE LUCIS
'Natura et Proprietate' – 1st Edn., woodcut device on title, woodcut diagrams in the text, cont. calf, rubbed, Willems 1296, small 4to – Amsterdam, L. & D. Elzevir, 1662.
(Sotheby's) $270 £120

VOYAGES
'A Compendium of Authentic and Entertaining Voyages – digested in a Chronological Series' – 2nd Edn. – 7 vols. – 23 maps , of which 15 folding, and 24 plates, of which 17 folding – some slight spotting, paper faults or tears in 3 leaves slightly affecting text – contemporary calf – some joints cracked, spines a little chipped, some labels missing – (Sabin 20518) – 12mo. – 1766.
(Christie's) $200 £100

VRIES, DAVID PIETERSZ DE
'Korte Historiael' – 1st Edn. – gothic letter – 18 half page copperplate illus. – modern citron morocco – spine discoloured – g.e. – sm. 4to. – Hoorn and Alkmaar 1655.
(Sotheby's) $1,785 £850

VUILLEMIN, A. A.
'La France et Ses Colonies' ... – engr. additional title – 108 hand coloured maps, five folding and slightly torn – some spotting – contemp. morocco backed boards – slightly rubbed – folio – Paris J. Migeon 1877.
(Christie's S. Kensington) $230 £110

WAAGEN, G. F.
'Treasures of Art in Great Britain' – 4 vols. including Supplement – cont. half calf – gilt – 8vo – 1854-57.
(Sotheby's) $135 £65

WADDINGTON, G. AND HANBURY, B.
'Journal of a Visit to some Parts of Ethiopia' – 15 plates of 16 – 2 maps – some spotted – half calf – rubbed – w.a.f. – 4to – 1822.
(Sotheby's) $36 £18

WAFFENUBUNGEN
54 litho illus. of gun carriages, cavalry and various soldiers – col. by hand and mounted on wooden block – lacking some – 3 litho sheets of plans and illus. of maneouvres – col. by hand – instructions in German and French – orig. box – pictorial label on lid – worn – Germany circa 1840.
(Sotheby's) $410 £195

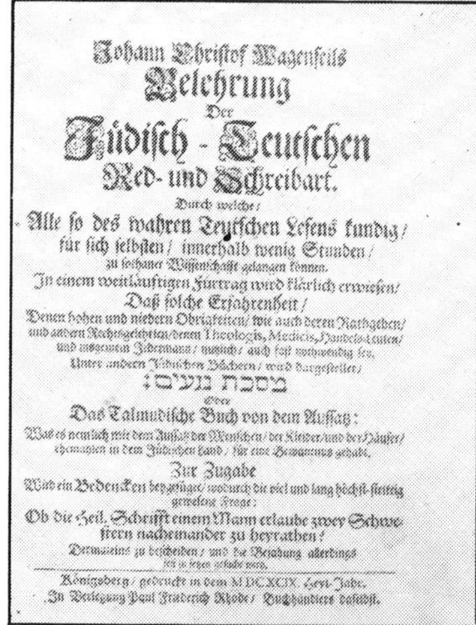
Johann Christof Wagenseils
Belehrung
Der
Jüdisch - Teutschen
Red- und Schreibart.
Durch welche/
Alle so des wahren Teutschen Lesens kundig/
für sich selbsten/ innerhalb wenig Stunden/
zu sothaner Wissenschafft gelangen können.
In einem weitläufftigen Fürtrag wird klärlich erwiesen/
Daß solche Erfahrenheit/
מסכת נגעים
Oder
Das Talmudische Buch von dem Aussatz:
Zur Zugabe
Ob die Heil. Schrifft einem Mann erlaube zwey Schwestern nacheinander zu heyrathen?
Königsberg/ gedruckt in dem MDCXCIX. Heil-Jahr.

WAGENSEIL, JOHANN CHRISTOF
'Belehrung Der Juedisch Teutschen Red und Schreibart' – plates – slight staining – half leather – 4to – Koenigsberg, 1699.
(Sotheby's) $1,050 £500

WAGHENAER, LUCAS JANSZ
'Speculum Nauticum Super Navigatione Maris Occidentalis Confectum, continens omnes oras maritimas Galliae, Hispaniae et praecipuarum partium Angliae in diversis mapps martimis comprehensum' – title repeated in Dutch – 2 parts in 1 vol. – 45 double page engraved maps by Baptista and Joannes van Deutecom – dedication in Latin to Queen Elizabeth I – 20 other prelim. leaves – full page woodcut diagrams – printed tables etc. – cont. cream pigskin – blind tooled borders – very worn – restored – folio – 398 x 282mm – Leiden, typis Plantinianis Franciscus Raphelengius, pro Luca Ioannis Aurigario, 1586.
(Sotheby's) $38,000 £19,000

'The Sea Coastes betweene Dover and Orfordnes . . .' – engraved map of East Coast with mouth of Thames and other rivers – col. by hand, coats of arms, cartouches – compass rose, sailing ships etc. – stained – framed – 320 x 500mm – Amsterdam, 1588.
(Sotheby's) $460 £220

WAGNER, SIR ANTHONY
'Heralds of England – a History of the Office and College of Arms' – illus. – H.M.S.O., 1967.
(Dacre, Son & Hartley) $40 £18

WAGNER, RICHARD
Facsimile of Wagner's score for 'Tristan und Isolde' at Leipzig used by Sir George Solti in Vienna, New York, Covent Garden and elsewhere between 1947 and 1971 – annotated by him with comments in coloured pencil – signed with dates and places of performances – grey paper wrappers – quarto.
(Sotheby's) $190 £90

'Siegfried and the Twilight of the Gods' – plates by Rackham – spotted – 4to – 1911.
(Sotheby's) $44 £22

'The Tale of the Lohengrin' – no. 23 of 525 copies – plates by Pogany – orig. vellum boards – rubbed – 4to – 1913.
(Sotheby's) $36 £18

WAIT, W. E.
'Coloured Plates of the Birds of Ceylon' – 4 parts – 64 colour plates by Henry – orig. wrappers – 2 Als from the artist to Dr. Drummond and signed woodcut – 4to – 1927-35.
(Phillips) $230 £110

WAKEFIELD, E. J.
Illustrations to 'Adventure in New Zealand" – Ltd. facsimile Edn. – col. plates – some folding – orig. half morocco – folio – Wellington, 1968.
(Sotheby's) $65 £32

WALBANK, ALAN (Editor)
'Queens of the Circulating Library' – illus. samplings of Yonge, Wood, Oliphant, Braddon, Ouida etc. – nice copy – 1950.
(J. Ash) $8 £4

WALCOTT, J.
'Flora Britannica Indigena: or plates of .. Plants of Great Britain etc.' – frontis and copper plates – half morocco – Bath, 1778.
(Bennett Book Auction) $100 £48

'Flora Britannica Indigene': or 'Plates of the Indigenous Plants of Great Britain' : with their descriptions taken from Linnaeus's Systema Naturae – cont. stained calf – engraved frontispiece portrait – 168 engraved plates – Printed for the author, 1778 – 8vo – Henrey, 1472.
(Lawrence) $96 £48

WALEY, ARTHUR
'An Introduction to the Study of Chinese Painting' – no. 14 of 50 copies signed by the author – plates – slightly spotted – pig skin – rubbed.
(Sotheby's) $135 £65

WALFORD, EDWARD AND THORNBURY, WALTER
'Old and New London; Greater London' – together 8 vols. – illus. – cont. cloth – rubbed – 4to – 1897-98.
(Sotheby's) $85 £40

WALKER, A.
'The Rifle, its Theory and Practice' – woodcuts – cloth – 1st Edn. – Westminster, 1864.
(Bennett Book Auction) $40 £18

WALKER, ALEXANDER
'Beauty in Woman' – litho plates of drawings from life by Henry Howard – Bohn London, 1846.
(Baitson) $4 £2

WALKER, D.
'Exercises for Ladies' – illus. – morocco gilt – worn – 12mo – 1837.
'Manly Exercises' – engraved title – frontis – illus. – orig. cloth – gilt – 1847.
(Phillips) $75 £35

WALKER, GEORGE
'The Costume of Yorkshire' – Ltd. Edn. – col. plates – spotted – orig. parchment – worn – loose – folio – Leeds, 1885.
(Sotheby's) $250 £120

'The Costume of Yorkshire' – titles and text in English and French – 40 hand coloured aquatint plates – contemporary half calf – gilt – morocco labels corners scuffed – folio – 1814.
(Christie's) $2,400 £1,200

WALKER, J. AND C.
'The British Atlas' – 46 of 47 engraved maps – hand col. in outline – cont. half morocco – rubbed – 4to – 1835-37.
(Sotheby Beresford Adams) $275 £130

Complete set of 42 English County Maps (including Monmouth and one of each of the Ridings of Yorkshire), showing railways, boundaries etc. – linen backed folding engraved maps, hand coloured in outline – orig. cloth boards with paper labels – each approx. 13.5 x 17in. Together with maps of North Wales and South Wales from the same series – each 16.75 x 26in.
(Lawrence) $250 £125

A Geological Map of England, Wales and a part of Scotland – large engraved map, coloured by hand – slight staining – mounted on linen – extending to approx. 55 x 38½in. folding into cloth pull-off. – 8vo – 1835 or later.
(Sotheby's) $80 £40

WALLACE, A. R.
'The Geographical Distribution of Animals' – 1st Edn. – 2 vols. – maps – illus. – orig. cloth – some wear – 1876.
(Phillips) $95 £45

WALLACE, EDGAR
'The Thief in the Night' – foolscap – spine worn and rubbed – 1928.
(J. Ash) $6 £3

WALLACE, J.
'An Account of the Islands of Orkney' – folding map and folding plate – calf – gilt – London, 1700.
(Bennett Book Auction) $180 £84

WALLACE, W.
'Ye Actis and Deidis' – 3 vols. – calf – Perth, 1790.
(Bennett Book Auction) $25 £12

WALLER, ERIK
'Bibliotheca Walleriana' – 2 vols. – another vol. – portrait – 55 plates – orig. buckram – dust jackets – 8vo – Stockholm, 1955.
(Sotheby's) $180 £85

WALLICH, NATHANIEL
'Plantae Asiaticae Rariores' – 3 vols. – double page engraved map and 295 hand col. litho plates – one large double page folding plate – later black cloth – large folio – Treuttel and Wurtz, 1830-32.
(Christie's) $5,250 £2,500

WALLIS, J.
'Grammatica Linguae Anglicanae' – vellum – sm 8vo – 1672.
(Phillips) $105 £50
'British Atlas' – engraved title and 31 hand col. maps only – 13 lacking – slightly stained – some leaves disbound – half morocco – upper covers detached – 1814.
(Christie's S. Kensington) $180 £85

WALMSLEY, EDWARD
'Physiognomical Portraits; One Hundred Distinguished Characters' – 2 vols. – large paper copy – English and French text – addit. engraved titles – 107 portraits – spotting – 19th century green morocco – gilt – rubbed – 4to – 1824.
(Sotheby's) $190 £90

WALPOLE, F.
'The Ansayrii or Assassins with Travels in the Further East' – 3 vols. – frontis – modern calf backed cloth – rubbed – 8vo – 1851.
(Sotheby's) $200 £95

WALPOLE, H.
'Historic Doubts on the Life and Reign of King Richard the Third' – 1st Edn. – 2 plates – orig. wrappers – uncut – loose – 1758; and another – 4to.
(Sotheby's) $80 £40
'The Castle of Otranto' – Jeffery's Edn. – 7 col. plates – cont. calf – rebacked – rubbed – 1800.
(Sotheby's) $80 £38
'A Catalogue of the Royal and Noble Authors of England' – 2 vols – 1st. Edn. – frontis – spotted – cont. calf – worn – Strawberry Hill Press, 1758.
(Sotheby's) $76 £38

WALPOLE, ROBERT
'Travels in Various Countries of the East' – 1st Edn. – 2 engraved maps and 11 plates – a few folding – cont. diced calf – rebacked with original spine preserved – slightly rubbed – 4to – 1820.
(Sotheby's) $100 £50

WALPOLE SOCIETY
Vols. I-XXVII – original cloth backed boards – 4to. – Oxford, 1912-39.
(Christie's) $560 £280

WALPOLE-BOND, JOHN
'The History of Sussex Birds' – 3 vols. – col. plates – buckram gilt – t.e.g. – 1938.
(Phillips) $230 £110

WALPOOLE, GEORGE AUGUSTUS
'The New British Traveller' – engraved frontis – folding engraved map – numerous engraved plates, maps – cont. sprinkled calf – folio – circa 1800.
(Christie Manson & Woods) $525 £250

WALSH, JOHN HENRY
'Stonehenge' – presentation copy – engraved frontis – illus. – adverts at end – orig. boards – rebacked – 1853.
(Phillips) $100 £48

WALSH, REV. ROBERT
'Narrative of a Journey from Constantinople to England' – folding map – 6 plates – half calf – gilt – 8vo – 1828.
(Phillips) $45 £22
'Constantinople' – 2 vols. – map – engraved views – some foxing – half calf – gilt – 4to – n.d.
(Phillips) $160 £75
'Constantinople and the Scenery of the Seven Churches of Asia Minor' – first and second series – 2 parts in one vol. – frontispiece – additional engraved titles and numerous engraved plates after T. Allom and others – small dampstain to corner of plates – mainly not affecting engraved areas – occasional minor spotting – contemporary green morocco – gilt – spine gilt – rubbed, corners worn – 4to. – circa 1840.
(Christie's) $90 £45
'Constantinople and the Scenery of the Seven Churches of Asia Minor' – first and second series – 2 vols. – 2 engraved titles and 94 plates – double-page map – titles and frontispiece a little browned – contemporary half russia – 4to. – 1839.
(Christie's) $220 £110

WALSINGHAM, THOMAS
'Histoire Tragique et Memorable de Pierre de Gaverston' – ruled in red throughout – slight browning – calf gilt by Antoine Chaumont – g.e. – Hamilton Palace copy – sm. 8vo. – Paris?, 1588.
(Christie's) $200 £100

WALTERS, HENRY
'Incunabula Typographica' – plates – illus. – orig. calf – rubbed – 4to – Baltimore, 1906.
(Sotheby's) $55 £25

WALTHAMSTOW ANTIQUARIAN SOCIETY
Official publications, nos. 1-38 with index and 2 duplicates, together 41 vols. – plates – orig. wrappers – 4to – 1915-40.
(Sotheby's) $85 £40

WALTON, CECILE
Watercolour drawing of a youth in a stormy landscape, lightning etc. – framed and glazed – 228 x 235mm.
(Sotheby's) $145 £70

WALTON, E.
'Flowers from the Upper Alps' – chromolitho plates – cloth, gilt – 4to – 1869.
(Bonhams) $105 £50
'Alpine Vignettes' – 4th Edn. – 12 chromolithographed plates – slightly spotted – orig. cloth – rubbed and disbound – 4to – 1882.
(Christie's S. Kensington) $60 £28

WALTON, I. AND COTTON, C.
'The Compleat Angler' – edited by J. Major – plates – cont. green morocco gilt – g.e. – 1844.
(Bonhams) $95 £45
'The Compleat Angler' – plates by E. H. New – 4to – 1897.
(Sotheby's) $30 £15

WALTON, TONY
Design for a front cloth – indian ink and gouache – signed and dated '58 – 37.5 x 62cm.
(Sotheby's) $1,890 £900

WANG YU CH'UAN
'Early Chinese Coinage' – plates – orig. wrappers – 8vo – New York – 1951.
(Sotheby's) $55 £25

WARBERG
'Charta Ofver Staden Warbergs' made 1750 by Jacob Kanters, showing fire of 1767 – col. mss plan, divided into streets – diagrammatic compass rose, descriptive key – perforations at fold – a few marginal tears – 487 x 374mm – Stockholm, 1796.
(Sotheby's) $190 £90

WARD, H. G.
'Mexico in 1827' – 2 vols. – 13 litho and aquatint plates – some folding – one col. – 2 folding maps – stains and spots – cont. half calf – rubbed – spines torn – 1828.
(Christie's) $180 £85

WARD, HUMPHRY AND ROBERTS, W.
'Romney. A Bibliographical and Critical Essay with a Catalogue Raisonne' – 2 vols. – plates – some spotting – orig. cloth – soiled and rubbed – inner hinges weak – 4to – 1904.
(Christie's S. Kensington) $75 £35

WARD, JOHN
'The Lives of the Professors of Gresham College . . . with a Life of the Founder, Sir Thomas Gresham' – appendix portrait and 4 plates – cloth – calf spine – folio – John Moore, 1740.
(Sotheby's) $40 £20

WARD, LYND (Illustrator)
'An Almanac for Moderns' – 1st English Edn. – illus. and cover by Ward – 1936.
(J. Ash) $17 £8

WARD, R. P.
'Tremaine' – 3 vols. – frontis in vol. 1 – half calf gilt – 1825.
(Phillips) $55 £26

WARD, ROLAND
'A Naturalist's Life Study' – plates – orig. cloth – 4to – 1913.
(Phillips) $105 £50

WARD, SAMUEL
'A Modern System of Natural History' – 2 vols. – 113 plates – 7 hand col. – cont. half calf – worn – stitching broken – 12mo – 1775-76.
(Christie's) $0 £15

WARD, WILFRID
'The Life of John Henry, Cardinal Newman' – 2 vols. – extra illus. copy – 70 portraits including 2 of Newman and Als by Newman, Gladstone, Henry Manning, Matthew Arnold etc. – cont. red morocco by MacDonald – elaborate gilt – purple morocco doublures – watered silk endleaves – t.e.g. – others uncut – 8vo – 1912.
(Sotheby's) $460 £220

WARDELL, JAMES
'A Catalogue of Tradesmen's Tokens' – illus. – paper bound – Leeds, 1852.
(Dacre, Son & Hartley) $40 £20

WARDEN, FLORENCE
'A Prince of Darkness' – 3 vols. – orig. cloth – soiled and shaken – but a good set – 1885.
(J. Ash) $85 £40

WARE, ISAAC
'A Complete Body of Architecture' – engraved frontis – numerous engraved plates – many folding – cont. sprinkled calf – folio – 1767.
(Christie Manson & Woods) $630 £300

WARING, EDWARD SCOTT
'A Tour to Sheeraz . . . to which is added a History of Persia' – 2 plates – text browned – purple half calf – rubbed – upper inside hinge broken – 4to – 1807.
(Sotheby's) $700 £350

WARING, J. B.
'Art Treasures of the United Kingdom' – chromolithographed title and plates – cont. morocco – rubbed – edges gauffered and gilt – 4to – 1858.
(Sotheby's) $220 £105
'Illustrations of Architecture and Ornament' – 70 plates – spots – orig. cloth – gilt – g.e. – folio – London, 1865.
(Phillips) $65 £30
'Masterpieces of Industrial Art and Sculpture' – 3 vols. – text in English and French – chromolith plates and titles – orig. red morocco – gilt – g.e. – folio – 1863.
(Christie Manson & Woods) $380 £180

WARING, J. B. AND MACQUOID, T. R.
'Examples of Architectural Art In Italy and Spain' – litho title and 63 plates – soiled – orig. cloth – rubbed – lacks spine – loose – folio – 1850.
(Sotheby's) $65 £30

WARMSTRY, T.
'The Baptised Turk' – 1st Edn. – calf gilt – upper cover and spine detached – 8vo – 1658.
(Phillips) $90 £42

WARNER, SIR GEORGE
'Queen Mary's Psalter' – plates – spotted – orig. half morocco – gilt – 4to – 1912.
(Sotheby's) $100 £48

WARNER, RALPH
'Dutch and Flemish Flower and Fruit Painters of the XVIIth and XVIIIth Centuries' – plates – cloth – t.e.g. – folio – 1932.
(Phillips) $170 £80

WARNER, RICHARD
'A Walk Through Wales; A Second Walk Through Wales' – 2 vols. – illus. and plans – half calf – joints cracked – 1798-99.
(Christie's S. Kensington) $65 £32

WARRE, COL. H. J.
'Sketches in the Crimea' – litho title – 10 plates of 14 – cloth gilt – oblong 8vo – circa 1850.
(Phillips) $105 £50

WARREN, J. B. L.
'A Guide to the Study of Bookplates' – plates – orig. cloth – Manchester, 1900.
(Christie's S. Kensington) $40 £20

WARTON, THOMAS
'The History of English Poetry' – 3 vols. – lacks supplement – cont. calf gilt – 4to – 1775-81.
(Phillips) $100 £48

WASS, VERRALL
'32 New Drawing Room Deceptions' – orig. wrappers – worn – n.d.
'Essence' 1931 and 'Astound Your Audience' – 2 vols. – 2 copies 1936 – illus. – all but first in orig. cloth – 4 with dust jackets – worn – 8vo.
(Sotheby's) $8 £4

WATERTON, CHARLES
'Wanderings in South America' – New Edn. – numerous wood engraved illus. in text – orig. cloth – gilt worn – 1879 – and 11 others.
(Sotheby's) $60 £30

WATHEN, JAMES
'A Series of Views Illustrative of the Island of St. Helena' – 1st Edn. – first issue – engraved title with hand col. portrait – 9 col. aquatint plates – soiled – cont. calf – rubbed – 4to – 1821.
(Sotheby's) $715 £340
'Journal of a Voyage, in 1811 and 1812, to Madras and China' – 1st Edn. – 24 hand coloured aquatint plates – lacking first leaf of plate list – occasional spotting and soiling – cont. half russia – very worn – upper cover and title detached – 4to. – 1814.
(Sotheby's) $600 £300

WATSON, RICHARD, BISHOP OF LLANDAFF
'Chemical Essays' – 1st Edn. – 5 vols. – general half title in vol. 3 – cont. calf – sm 8vo – Cambridge 1780-86.
(Sotheby's) $200 £95

WATT, JAMES
'Supplement to the Description of a Pneumatic Apparatus for Preparing Factitious Air' – one plate – cloth – uncut – 8vo – Birmingham, Thomas Pearson, 1796.
(Sotheby's) $190 £90

WATT, ROBERT
'Bibliotheca Britannica' – 1st Edn. – 4 vols. – errata leaf at end – spotting and staining – modern brown half morocco – 4to – Edinburgh, 1824.
(Sotheby's) $160 £75

WATTEAU, JEAN ANTOINE
'Figures des Differents Caracteres, des Paysages & d'Etudes' – 2nd Edn. – engraved frontis, title, portrait – 8pp of text and 351 subjects on 213 plates – some tears on lower margins – one or two plates lightly soiled – late 19th/early 20th century tan morocco – gilt – g.e. – folio – Paris, Huquier, circa 1740.
(Sotheby Parke Bernet) $8,360 £4,500

WATTS, I.
'Logick: or, The Right Use of Reason' – New Edn. – calf – London by C. Whittingham, 1801.
(Bennett Book Auction) $10 £5

WATTS, W.
'Seats of the Nobility and Gentry' – 84 plates – half calf gilt – oblong 4to – 1779.
(Phillips) $360 £170

WAUGH, EVELYN
'The Ordeal of Gilbert Penfold' – 1st Edn. – presentation copy, inscribed by author for Cecil Beaton – orig. cloth – uncut – 8vo – 1957.
(Sotheby's) $780 £370

'Scoop' – 1st American Edn. – presentation copy, inscribed by author – Als by Waugh loosely inserted – soiled – without dust jacket – Boston 1938 and another by Waugh – 8vo.
(Sotheby Beresford Adams) $145 £70

WEALE, JOHN
'The Theory, Practice and Architecture of Bridges' – 4 vols. in 3 – plates, mostly folding – cont. morocco backed cloth – rubbed – 1843.
(Sotheby's) $640 £320

'Quarterly Papers on Architecture' – 8 parts in 4 – many lithos – some coloured – cont. half morocco – 4to – 1844-45.
(Christie Manson & Woods) $190 £90

'The Theory, Practice and Architecture of Bridges' – 3 vols. – binding defective – 1843.
(Lane) $25 £12

WEATHERLY, FRED. E.
'Goosey Gander'; 'Holly Boughs' and 'Little Pickle'; 'Little Pussy Cat'; 'Tens and Elevens'; 'Twilight Land' – 6 vols each with 8 illus. col. and full page and illus. in text – orig. cloth backed pictorial boards – slightly rubbed – sm 4to – New York, circa 1890.
(Sotheby's) $100 £48

WEAVER, LAURENCE
'Houses and Gardens' by E. L. Lutyens – numerous plates – orig. cloth backed boards – slightly stained and rubbed – folio – 1913.
(Sotheby's) $60 £30

WEBB, JOHN
'A Vindication of Stone Henge Restored' – engraved illus. – cont. calf – rubbed – joints cracked – folio.
(Christie's S. Kensington) $230 £110

WEBB, MARY
'The Chinese Lion' – no. 127 of 350 copies – orig. cloth backed boards – slipcase – 1937.
(Christie's) $25 £12

'The Golden Arrow' – author's scarce first book – rebound in handsome half morocco – very good – 1916.
(J. Ash) $115 £55

WEBBER, BYRON
'James Orrock' – 2 vols. – no. 322 of 500 copies – plates – orig. cloth – soiled – t.e.g. – 4to – 1903.
(Christie's) $65 £30

WEBSTER, J.
'The Judgement Set' – browned – cont. sheep – rubbed – 4to – 1654.
(Sotheby's) $30 £15

WEBSTER, JOHN W.
'A Description of the Island of St. Michael . . . with remarks on the other Azores' – 1st Edn. – 2 folding engraved maps – folding chart and 3 aquatint plates – some slight foxing and spotting – later cloth – 8vo – Boston, Mass, 1821.
(Sotheby's) $76 £38

WEBSTER, W.
'Websters Tables' – 3rd Edn. – some leaves shaved – browned – modern cloth – 1634.
(Sotheby's) $200 £100

WEDGEWOOD, JOSIAH
'Catalogue of Cameos, Intaglios, Medals etc.' – 6th Edn. with additions – colour printed plates – orig. wrappers – re-backed – cloth case – Holland House copy – 8vo – Etruria, 1787.
(Sotheby's) $840 £400

WEDMORE, FREDERICK
'Turner and Ruskin' – Edn. de luxe – 2 vols. and folder of plates – cloth – gilt – 4to – 1900.
(Phillips) $105 £50

WEIDNERS, JOHANN
'Glauber Kinder Gottes Kreuk-Schule' – 4th Edn. – plates – soiled – cont. blind stamped vellum – 1738.
(Christie's) $85 £40

WEIGELT, C. H.
'Giotto' – plates – cloth – gilt – 8vo – 1925.
(Phillips) $30 £14

WEINHART, F. C.
'Medicus Officiosus ... Aphoristica' – frontis – cont. vellum – Venetia, 1724.
(Phillips) $60 £28

WEISS, J. H.
'Nouvelle Carte Hydrographique et Routiere de la Suisse' – engraved map on two sheets – 22 x 34in. – marginal tears – circa 1800.
(Christie's S. Kensington) $60 £28

WEITZMANN, K.
'Monastery of Saint Catherine at Mount Sinai . . . the Icons' – plates – cloth – 4to – 1976.
(Phillips) $60 £28

WELD, CHARLES RICHARD
'A History of the Royal Society' – 1st Edn. – 2 vols. – engraved frontis – offsetting – cont. calf – gilt – 8vo – 1848.
(Sotheby's) $95 £45

WELD, ISAAC
'Travels Through the States of North America and the Provinces of Upper and Lower Canada, during the years 1795-97' – 1st Edn. – engraved folding map – hand coloured in outline – and 15 engraved plates – maps and plans – erratum slip pasted at the foot of the list of plates – contemporary tree calf – gilt – 4to. – for John Stockdale, 1799.
(Christie's) $560 £280

'Travels Through the States of North America' – 15 engraved plates and maps of 16 – some folding – browned – library stamp – cont. calf – rebacked and repaired – rubbed – 4to – 1799.
(Sotheby's) $135 £65

WELLCOME ARCHAEOLOGICAL RESEARCH EXPEDITION TO THE NEAR EAST
7 vols. – plates – orig. cloth – 4to – 1938-53.
(Sotheby's) $105 £50

WELLS, EDWARD
'The Young Gentleman's Astronomy, Chronology and Dialling' – 1st Edn. – 3 parts in one – 25 engraved plates – browning – repaired – modern calf – 8vo – 1712.
(Sotheby's) $80 £38

WELLS, H. G.
'Kipps' – 1st Edn. – signed by the author on bookplate – rubbed – 1905.
(Sotheby's) $60 £30
'The Wonderful Visit' – 1st Edn. – orig. red cloth gilt – t.e.g. – uncut – 8vo – 1895; 'The Wheels of Change' – orig. red cloth gilt – t.e.g. – uncut – 8vo – 1896.
(Lawrence) $80 £40

WELLS, J.
'The Charm of Oxford' – 1st Edn. – 1920.
(Laurence & Martin Taylor) $10 £5

To W. J. de la Mare
from
Dunsany
Aug: 24. 1951.
To look at these, the most neglected poems of our time.

WENTWORTH, LADY
'Drift of the Storm' – Intro. by Lord Dunsany – 1st Edn. – presentation copy, inscribed by Dunsany – orig. cloth – spine faded – dust jacket – 8vo – Oxford, 1951.
(Sotheby's) $30 £14

WENTWORTH, T.
'The West India Sketch Book' – 1st Edn. – 2 vols. – 10 plates, 3 col., 2 tinted, map and chart – illus. in text – spotting and offsetting – 19th century mauve half calf – bound at the Mayo Constitution Office with ticket – faded – 8vo – 1834.
(Sotheby's) $210 £100

WENTWORTH, WILLIAM CHARLES
'A Statistical Historical and Political Description of the Colony of New South Wales' – 1st Edn. – contemporary half calf rebacked – 1819, 'A Statistical Account of the British Settlements in Australasia' – 3rd Edn. – 2 vols. – engraved frontispiece and two folding maps, one with small tears, occasional foxing, sometimes severe – contemporary calf – Signet Library gilt stamp on covers – 8vo. – 1824.
(Christie's) $400 £200

WESLEYAN METHODISM
Extensive collection of letters addressed to the Sagar family, prominent Methodist family in Lancashire – 150 Als by Wesleyan ministers, circa 1780-circa 1840; printed circular of Wesley's itinerary in 1790, printed petition in favour of Wm. Wilberforce, six auto lines of poetry by Charles Wesley and Sagar family correspondence.
(Phillips) $840 £400

WEST, CHARLES
'Lectures on the Diseases of Childhood and Infancy' – 1st Edn. – 16pp adverts – orig. cloth – rubbed – 8vo – 1848.
(Sotheby's) $190 £90

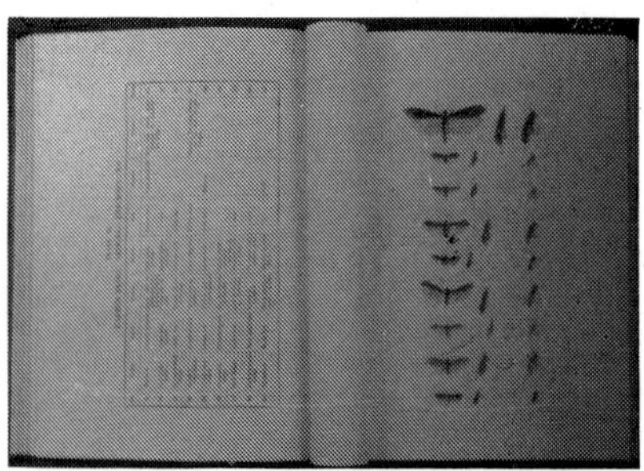

WEST, LEONARD
'The Natural Trout Fly and Its Imitations' – illus. col. plates – gilt lettered brown cloth boards – staining and rubbing – 2nd Edn. – W. Potter, 1921.
(May Whetter & Grose) $75 £35

WESTALL, WILLIAM AND MOULE, THOMAS
'Great Britain Illustrated' – 1st Edn. – large paper copy – 118 views on 59 plates – majority on india paper – spotting – cont. half red morocco – spine gilt – covers faded – t.e.g. – 4to – 1830.
(Sotheby's) $420 £200
'Great Britain Illustrated' – engraved title and 58 plates of 59 – cont. half morocco – rubbed – spotted – 4to – 1830.
(Sotheby's) $120 £60

WESTAMACOTT, C. M.
'The English Spy' – 1st Edn. – first issue – woodcut plate – hand col. frontis – 70 col. plates, by Cruikshank – full olive morocco gilt – g.e. – by Riviere – 1825-26.
(Phillips) $1,300 £620

WESTELL, W. P.
'Circling Year' – 5 vols.
(Laurence & Martin Taylor) $6 £3

WESTGARTH, W.
'Victoria, Late Australia Felix' – folding map – slightly torn – errata slip – orig. cloth – rubbed – 8vo – 1853.
(Sotheby's) $180 £85

WESTON, JESSIE L.
'King Arthur and His Knights; a Survey of Arthurian Romance' – orig. wrappers – nice copy – 1899.
(J. Ash) $17 £8

WESTROPP, M. S. D.
'Irish Glass' – plates – orig. cloth – soiled – 4to – n.d.
(Phillips) $65 £32

WESTWOOD, J. O.
'Illuminated Manuscripts of the Bible copied from Select Manuscripts of the Middle Ages' – plates spotted – hinges broken – cont. half morocco – rubbed – 4to – 1843-45.
(Sotheby's) $45 £22
'The Butterflies of Great Britain' – hand col. title and 19 plates – 2 plain plates – some soiled – orig. cloth – rebacked – rubbed – h.e. – 8vo – 1857.
(Sotheby's) $115 £55
'The Butterflies of Great Britain' – 1st Edn. – plates – 19 hand coloured – half calf – rubbed – 1855.
(Sotheby's) $180 £90
'Illuminated Illustrations of the Bible copies from Select Mss of the Middle Ages' – half title – title in red and black – addit. colour printed title and 39 protected plates in gold colours – leather backed green cloth – spine gilt – a.e.g. – 1846 – new endpapers.
(Lawrence) $100 £50

WET NURSE SUCKLING AN INFANT, A
Trimmed – edges slightly stained – framed – 25.5 x 17.8cm. – Golconda – circa 1680.
(Christie's) $1,785 £850

WETENHALL, EDWARD
'Enter into Thy Closet or a Method and Order for Private Devotion' – 5th Edn. – engraved frontis – browned – cont. English red morocco – gilt – g.e. – 12mo – 1676.
(Sotheby's) $250 £120

WHARNCLIFFE, LORD
'Sketches in Egypt and the Holy Land' – hand col. title and 17 plates – spotted – one loose – orig. morocco backed cloth – rubbed – folio – 1855.
(Sotheby's) $275 £130

WHARTON, EDITH
'Ethan Frome' – 1st English Edn. from American sheets – spine faded and covers a little marked – 1911.
(J. Ash) $8 £4

WHATELY, RICHARD
'Account of an Expedition to the interior of New Holland' – edited by Lady Mary Fox – 1st Edn – without advertisements – contemporary tree calf – gilt – red morocco label – spine gilt in compartments – by Riviere – 8vo. – 1837.
(Christie's) $160 £80

WHATELY, T.
'Observations on Modern Gardening' – 4th Edn. – cont. calf – browned – rubbed – 1777.
(Sotheby's) $90 £45

WHEAT, CARL I.
'Mapping the Transmississippi West' – 5 vols. in 6 – numerous plates – some col. and folding – orig. green morocco backed buckram – uncut – folio – San Francisco 1957-63.
(Sotheby's) $505 £240

WHEATLEY, DENNIS
'The Secret War' – inscribed and signed by author – very good – 1937.
(J. Ash) $25 £12

WHEATLEY, HENRY B.
'London Past and Present' – 3 vols. – cont. red half-levant by Hatchards – joints rubbed – t.e.g. – 1891.
(Christie's S. Kensington) $80 £38

WHEELOCK, REV. ELEAZER
'A Brief Narrative of the Indian Charity School in Lebanon in Connecticut, New England' – 1st Edn. – 48pp – grey paper wrappers – 8vo – J. & W. Oliver, 1766.
(Sotheby's) $105 £50

WHEELWRIGHT, H. W.
'A Spring and Summer in Lapland' – 2nd Edn. – 6 engraved hand col. plates – orig. cloth – 8vo – 1871.
(Sotheby Beresford Adams) $65 £32

WHELER, GEORGE
'A Journey into Greece' – 1st Edn. – 7 engraved plates – illus. in text – 1 folding map repaired – 19th century half calf – rubbed – folio – 1682.
(Sotheby's) $315 £150

WHISTLER, J. M.
'The Gentle Art of Making Enemies' – no. 144 of 250 large paper copies signed by the author, with his butterfly mark – orig. cloth backed boards – slightly soiled – n.d.
(Christie's S. Kensington) $95 £45

"The Virgin and the Child!" it burst,
"The Virgin and the Child!"

"She brings release! she brings us peace,
That the Golden Age may come!
Hurrah, the Brotherhood of Man!
Hurrah, Millenium!"
Then No Man's Land was full of tears,
But she, bewildered by the cheers,
Passed through the midst of them;

And came, at nightfall, to a knoll
On which a gutted chapel stood;
And found some sort of shelter there
Beneath its wind-discovered Rood;

And bared the pure, all-giving fountain
To the pure all-asking thirst;
And watched the soul in those dark eyes
Deep in its book of days engrossed.

L.W.

Fifty copies
Printed for Laurence Whistler
Siegfried Sassoon & Geoffrey Keynes
at the Chiswick Press, May, 1941
No. 7
for Walter de la Mare
from Laurence Whistler.

WHISTLER, LAURENCE
'The Burning Glass' – 1st Edn. – no. 7 of 50 – presentation copy, inscribed by author to De La Mare – orig. wrappers – 8vo – Printed for Whistler, Seigfried Sassoon and Geoffrey Keynes, 1941.
(Sotheby's) $170 £80

For Walter de la Mare
with the love of the author,
L.W. Christmas 1948.

'Rex Whistler' – 1st Edn. – presentation copy, inscribed by author – illus. – orig. cloth – dust jacket – 8vo – 1948.
(Sotheby's) $170 £80

'Audible Silence' – Poems – very good in dust jacket – 1961.
(J. Ash) $8 £4

'Pictures on Glass' – no. 572 of 1,400 copies signed by Whistler – plates – orig. cloth – t.e.g. – slipcase – The Cupid Press, 1972.
(Christie's S. Kensington) $65 £30

'The Engraved Glass of Laurence Whistler' – no. 201 of 550 copies signed by Whistler – plates – orig. cloth – slightly rubbed – t.e.g. – The Cupid Press, 1952.
(Christie's S. Kensington) $90 £42

WHISTLER, LAURENCE AND FULLER, RONALD

'The Work of Rex Whistler' – Presentation copy, signed by Laurence Whistler and with als. from him loosely inserted – plates – some coloured – orig. cloth – dust jacket – 4to – 1960.
(Christie's S. Kensington) $190 £95

WHISTLER, REX

'Whistler (Laurence) The Konigsmark Drawings' – no. 297 of 1,000 copies – 10 mounted col. plates by Whistler – orig. cloth – slipcase – 4to – The Richards Press, 1952.
(Christie's S. Kensington) $115 £55

'The Konigsmark Drawings' – no. 48 of 1,000 copies – 10 mounted illus. by Whistler – orig. cloth – slipcase – 4to – 1952.
(Christie's S. Kensington) $100 £50

WHITAKER, JOHN

'The History of Manchester' – 2 vols. – folding plates – advert leaf at end – half title – cont. calf – 4to – Dodsley, 1771-75.
(Sotheby's) $40 £20

WHITAKER, THOMAS DUNHAM

'The History and Antiquities of the Deanery of Craven in the County of York' – 2nd Edn. – large paper copy – 20 double-page or folding maps and tables and 77 engraved or aquatint plates including 22 aquatint views in Two States – contemporary calf – gilt panelled sides skilfully rebacked – with a fore-edge Painting of Skipton Castle – folio – 1812.
(Christie's) $1,800 £900

'A History of Richmondshire in the North Riding of the County of York' – 2 vols. – 42 plates after Turner and others – 4 hand col., 1 aquatint, 3 plans, 27 genealogical tables, 15 double page – spotting – cont. half russia – worn – folio – 1823.
(Christie's) $200 £95

WHITAKER, THOMAS D. AND THORESBY, RALPH

'Loidis and Elmete; Ducatus Leodiensis' – 2 vols. – engraved portrait and plates – cont. half morocco – rubbed – folio – Leeds and Wakefield, 1816.
(Sotheby's) $145 £70

WHITAKER, WILLIAM

'Disputatio de sacra scriptura, contra . . . Robertum Bellarminum . . . & Thomam Stapletonum' – 1st Edn. – title with reading 'Magistro' – slight browning and soiling – some worming – calf – worn – sm 4to – 1588.
(Sotheby's) $56 £28

WHITTAKER, JOHN

'Ceremonial of the Coronation of his most sacred Bishops, Peers, Knights and principal officers who assisted at that magnificent ceremony' – coloured aquatint frontispiece and 42 plates on thick paper – including title – dedication and folding plate of the Royal Banquet bound at the end – title dedication and text elaborately embossed in gilt within gilt armorial frames – many plates with fine hand coloured aquatint figures – all heightened with gold – folding plate mounted and varnished – contemporary red half morocco – gilt – brass clasps – g.e. – elephant folio – by John Whittaker, 1823.
(Christie's) $11,600 £5,800

WHITE, C.
'Almack's' – 3 vols. – half calf gilt – 1826.
(Phillips) $65 £30

WHITE, CHARLES
'A Treatise on the Management of Pregnant and Lying-in Women' – 3rd Edn. – 2 folding engraved plates – browned – orig. boards – uncut – 8vo – 1785.
(Sotheby's) $170 £80

WHITE, GEORGE FRANCIS
'Views in India, chiefly among the Himalaya Mountains' – 38 engraved plates – slight foxing – cont. diced calf – gilt – hinges and edges slightly worn – 4to – London and Paris, 1838.
(Sotheby's) $150 £75

WHITE, REV. GILBERT
'Naturalist's Calendar' – col frontis – 1st Edn. – cloth – 1795.
(Bonhams) $75 £35

'The Natural History and Antiquities of Selbourne' – 1st Edn. – 3 plates of 9 – cont. calf – lacks cover – soiled – 4to. – 1789.
(Sotheby's) $30 £15

'The Natural History and Antiquities of Selborne' – 1st Edn. – plates, two folding plates rebacked with linen – slight browning – green morocco by Zaehnsdorf – 1901 – spine in plain morocco – t.e.g. – silk endpapers – 4to – 1789.
(Sotheby's) $1,200 £600

'The Natural History and Antiquities of Selborne' – 1st Edn. – plates – cont. calf – worn – joints cracked – bookplate of Peter Sherston – 4to – 1789.
(Sotheby's) $1,600 £800

'The Natural History and Antiquities of Selborne' – 1st Edn. – plates – cont. calf – rubbed – rebacked – 4to – 1789.
(Sotheby's) $680 £340

'The Natural History and Antiquities of Selborne' – 2 vols. – plates – spotted – orig. morocco backed cloth – rubbed – 4to – 1876.
(Sotheby's) $90 £45

'The History and Antiquities of Selborne' – 2 vols. – browned – worn – 1877; a collection of different edns., and a few books on Gilbert White – various bindings – some rubbed; and 3 others.
(Sotheby's) $200 £100

'The Writings' – 2 vols. – Ltd. Edn. – map – slipcase – Nonesuch Press, 1938.
(Sotheby's) $240 £120

of Parsons's new hops. The wort was rich, & the
beer worked well. All ~~~~ well-water.
Jan: 17: 1783. Put half a pound of scalded hops
into the half hogsh: of beer filled up Nov: 5: 1782
Jan: 29: 1783. Drew off the barrel of raisin-wine,
which continued to fret, & would not be fine. Washed
the barrel with scalding water, & cleared it of all
grout, & then I put the wine back, adding a
pint of common brandy. It was made in Feb
1781, & drawn off into the 20 gallon barrel in Oct.
1781. Tho' it has worked so long, is still rich & sweet.
March 6: 1783. Added a ¼ of a pound more of scalded
hops to the strong beer filled up Nov: 5: 1782.

Auto journal – 'An Account of the Brewings of Strong Beer' – kept over a period of 21 years 1772-1793 – 28 pages – morocco by Riviere – 4to.
(Sotheby's) $5,040 £2,400

'The Natural History of Selborne' – New Edn. – 2 vols. – four engraved plates, one hand col. – occasional slight soiling – cont. calf – worn – 1813.
(Christie's S. Kensington) $30 £15

'The Works in Natural History' – 2 vols. in one – 4 engraved plates – two folding – two hand col. – first few leaves slightly spotted – later half calf – worn – 1802.
(Christie's S. Kensington) $25 £12

WHITE, J.
'The First Century of Scandalous, Malignant Priests' – later half cloth – soiled – 1643; 'A Book of the Valuations of Ecclesiasticall Preferments' – cont. calf – dampstains – rubbed – 1680; and 2 others.
(Sotheby's) $40 £20

'A Rich Cabinet, with Variety of Inventions' – frontis – browned – cont. calf – worn – covers detached – 1668.
(Sotheby's) $380 £190

WHITE, T. H.
'The Sword in the Stone' – 1938.
(J. Ash) $40 £18

WHITE, WILLIAM
'History, Gazeteer and Directory of Norfolk 1845'.
(Baitson) $36 £18

WHITE'S DIRECTORY OF HULL
1882.
(Baitson) $50 £23

WHITFIELD, CHRISTOPHER
'Together and Alone' – no. 249 of 500 copies – orig. cloth – t.e.g. – 1945.
(Christie's) $40 £20

WHITMAN, WALT
'Two Rivulets' – 1st Edn. – presentation copy inscribed by author – mounted albumen portrait – spotting – cont. half calf – slightly rubbed – g.e. – Camden New Jersey, 1876.
(Phillips) $145 £70

WHITNEY, GEOFFREY
'A Choice of Emblemes and Other Devises' – 1st Edn. – title in ornamental woodcut border, arms of Earl of Leicester – 248 woodcut emblems in ornamental frames – olive morocco gilt – sm 4to – Leiden, Plantin, 1586.
(Sotheby's) $3,780 £1,800

WHITTOCK, N.
'Art of Drawing and Colouring Flowers, Fruit and Shells' – 48 plates includ. 24 hand col. – some foxing – half calf gilt – 4to – 1829.
(Phillips) $360 £170
'The Youths' New London Self-Instructing Drawing-Book, in Colours' – 1st Edn. – 41 aquatint plates, all but frontispiece in coloured and uncoloured state – cont. half roan – rubbed – oblong 8vo – 1836.
(Sotheby's) $800 £400

WHITWORTH, CHARLES, LORD
'An Account of Russia as it was in the Year 1710' – 1st Edn. – engraved vignette on title – errata leaf – inkspots – modern calf – uncut – 8vo – Strawberry Hill Press, 1758.
(Sotheby's) $105 £50

WHYTT, ROBERT
'The Works' – 1st Edn. – dampstained – cont. calf – rebacked – orig. spine laid down – 4to – Edinburgh, 1768.
(Sotheby's) $315 £150

WICKES, CHARLES
'Illustrations of the Spires and Towers' – 2 vols. – 51 plates – some loose – folio – cloth – 1853-55.
(Phillips) $115 £55

WIDOWSON, HENRY
'Present State of Van Diemen's Land' – 1st Edn. – folding engraved map – spotted – modern green half morocco – uncut – 8vo – 1829.
(Sotheby's) $315 £150

WIERX, HIERONYMUS
'A Collection of 36 engraved plates by Wierx' – slight browning and soiling – cont. limp vellum – rubbed and soiled – bookplate of Holland House – sm 8vo – Antwerp, late 16th century.
(Sotheby's) $505 £240

WIGHT, ISLE OF
'Engraved chart from Le Neptune Francois of the South Coast of England from Sandwich to Thorney Island and includ. Isle of Wight' – compass roses, rust spots etc. – 610 x 875mm – Paris, 1773.
(Sotheby's) $145 £70

WILBERFORCE, R. AND S.
'The Life of William Wilberforce' – 5 vols. – orig. blind stamped cloth expertly rebacked – 1838.
(Baitson) $40 £20

WILBEY, H.
A collection of 17 account and other record books, programmes, letters, press cuttings and other material documenting Wilbey's business of the lending library and his involvement in activities of various organisations for magicians, various sizes.
(Sotheby's) $2 £1

WILD, CHARLES
'English and Foreign Cathedrals' – 2 vols. – 24 hand col. mounted plates – soiled – orig. half calf folders – worn – folio – n.d.
(Sotheby's) $380 £180

WILD, F.
'Shackleton's Last Voyage' – 1st Edn. – plates, 1 col. – illus. orig. decorated cloth – 8vo – 1923.
(Sotheby's) $115 £55

WILDE, O.
'The Ballad of Reading Gaol' – 7th Edn. – 1899; 'The Importance of Being Ernest' – 1st Edn. – 1 of 1,000 copies – 1899 – orig. cloth – rubbed; and 3 others.
(Sotheby's) $110 £55

WILDMAN, THOMAS
'A Treatise on the Management of Bees' – 1st Edn. – 3 folding engraved plates – orig. calf – spine repaired – morocco label – 4to – For the Author . . . by T. Cadell, 1768.
(Sotheby's) $300 £150

WILDRIDGE, T. TINDALL
'The Hull Letters 1625-46' – Hull.
(Baitson) $12 £6

WILENSKI, R. H.
'Flemish Painters' – 2 vols. – includ. one of plates – cloth – t.e.g. – 4to – 1960.
(Phillips) $55 £25

WILHELM, G. T.
'Unterhaltungen aus der Naturgeschichte' – vol. 1 only – 3rd Edn. – 70 hand col. plates – dampstains – old boards – rebacked – Vienna, 1808.
(Christie's) $65 £32

WILKINS, J.
'An Essay towards a Real Character, and a Philosophical Language' – 1st Edn. – plates – lacks final blank – some tears – cont. calf – worn – covers detached – folio – 1668.
(Sotheby's) $100 £50

WILKINS, WILLIAM
'The Antiquities of Magna Graecia' – title with engraved vignette – 73 plates – foxing – cont. calf – gilt – rebacked preserving old spine – worn – large folio – Cambridge, 1807.
(Sotheby's) $800 £400

'The Antiquities of Magna Graecia' – 1st Edn. – large paper copy – engraved title vignette – 73 plans and views, 21 sepia aquatints, 12 engravings in text – cloth backed boards – worn and stained – uncut – large folio – Cambridge, 1807.
(Sotheby's) $360 £170

WILKINSON, G.
'Five Lithographic Views of the Isle of Man' – orig. printed wrappers with vignette of the House of Industry, Douglas – 10.75 x 14.75in. – Day & Haghe – n.d. – oblong folio.
(Lawrence) $180 £90

WILKINSON, J.
'Select Views in Cumberland, Westmoreland and Lancashire' – 1st Edn. – 48 plates – some spotting – cont. half calf – worn – folio – 1810.
(Sotheby's) $540 £270

WILKINSON, J. G.
'Manners and Customs of the Ancient Egyptians, First and Second Series; Modern Egypt and Thebes' – together 8 vol. – plates – a few leaves soiled – cont. calf – rubbed – 1837-43.
(Sotheby Parke Bernet) $200 £100

'Manners and Customs of the Ancient Egyptians' – 1st and 2nd series; 'Modern Egypt and Thebes' – together 8 vols. – plates – a few leaves soiled – cont. calf – rubbed – 1837-43.
(Sotheby's) $200 £100

WILKINSON, REV. JOSEPH
'Collection of 49 Original Watercolour Drawings, All Views of the Lake District' – each circa 10 x 14 inches (250 x 350mm) – mounted on card within grey ink and wash borders – captions in pencil – grey wash pictorial title 'Northern Scenery in a series of drawings by J.W.' signed W. M. Craig, 1796 – bound in levant half morocco – label on upper cover – large folio – 1795-96.
(Christie's) $9,600 £4,800

WILKINSON, LADY
'Weeds and Wild Flowers' 1853 London – John Van Voorst 12 hand coloured plates – Publishers catalogue bound in.
(Baitson) $40 £20

WILKINSON, N. R.
'Wilton House Pictures' – Ltd. Edn. – 2 vols. – signed by author – plates – cloth – gilt – t.e.g. – uncut – folio – 1907.
(Phillips) $85 £40

'Wilton House Pictures' – 2 vols. – one of 300 copies signed by the author – numerous plates – original cloth – gilt – t.e.g. – others uncut – upper cover vol. II stained – large 4to. – 1907.
(Christie's) $150 £75

WILKINSON, R.
'General Atlas of the World' – 48 engraved maps – title stained – cont. half calf – worn – 4to – 1809.
(Sotheby's) $140 £70

WILKINSON, TATE
'Memoirs of His Own Life' – 4 vols. – tree calf – gilt – York, 1790.
(Phillips) $380 £180

WILKINSON, WALTER
'The Peep Show' – 1st Edn. – illus. – orig. cloth – slightly worn – dust jacket – 4to – 1927.
(Sotheby's) $40 £18

WILLIAM IV
Auto annotations on 2 Als by Lord Brownlow, 3 pages, 4to, Belgrave Square, June 1836 to Lord John Russell submitting names for appointment and promotion to Militia, one integral blank removed.
(Phillips) $65 £30

WILLIAMS, CHARLES
'Witchcraft' – 1941.
(J. Ash) $20 £10

WILLIAMS, F. S.
'Our Iron Roads; Their History, Construction and Social Influences' – wood engraved addit. title, plates and illus. – orig. cloth – faded and slightly soiled – 1852.
(Christie's S. Kensington) $45 £22

WILLIAMS, H.
'Travels in Italy, Greece and the Ionian Islands' – 2 vols. – 19 plates – half calf – gilt – 1820.
(Phillips) $250 £120

WILLIAMS, H. M.
'Poems' – 2 vols. – cont. calf – 1786.
(Phillips) $170 £80

WILLIAMS, H. S.
'The Historian's History of the World' – 25 vols. attractively bound in vellum with gilt and col. decorations – The Times, 1907.
(Baitson) $35 £16

WILLIAMS, H. W.
'Select Views in Greece' – 34 plates of 64 – lacks title and prelims. – spotted cont. half morocco – rubbed – 4to – 1829.
(Sotheby's) $80 £40
'Select Views in Greece' – 2 vols. in one – frontis and 64 plates – morocco gilt – g.e. – 4to – 1829.
(Phillips) $275 £130

WILLIAMS, I.
'Early English Watercolours' – plates – orig. cloth.
(Sotheby's) $60 £28

WILLIAMS, LIEUT.-COL. AND STAFFORD, W. C.
'England's Battles by Sea and Land' – 6 vols. – plates – cloth – gilt – g.e. – London Printing – n.d.
(Phillips) $55 £25

WILLIAMS, ROBERT
'Lexicon Cornu-Britannica' – 1st Edn. – orig. cloth binding – 1810.
(Lane) $40 £20

WILLIAMS, T. H.
'Guide to the Picturesque Scenery of Devonshire' – 2 vols. bound as one – orig. boards with uncut edges – 1828-30.
(Lane) $95 £46

WILLIAMS, THOMAS
'The Eddystone Lighthouse' – orig. cloth binding – 1882.
(Lane) $45 £22

WILLIAMS, WILLIAM
'A Dictionary of the New Zealand Language' – 2nd Edn. – some slight soiling – orig. cloth – slightly soiled – 1852.
(Christie's S. Kensington) $45 £22

WILLIAMS-WOOD, C.
'Staffordshire Pot Lids and Their Potters' – plates – orig. cloth – dust jacket – 4to – 1972.
(Sotheby's) $25 £12

WILLIAMSON, A.
'Military Memoirs and Maxims of Marshall Turenne' – 2nd Edn. – calf – 1744.
(Bennett Book Auction) $8 £4

WILLIAMSON, G. C.
'The Book of the Famille Rose' – 1 of 12 copies signed by author – plates, 19 in col. – orig. linen backed boards – some wear – 4to – 1927.
(Phillips) $125 £60
'The History of Portrait Miniatures' – 2 vols. – one of 520 copies – plates – orig. cloth – gilt – soiled – t.e.g. – folio – 1904.
(Sotheby's) $170 £80
'English Conversation Pictures' – Ltd. Edn. – damp marks – 1931.
(Lane) $4 £2

WILLIAMSON

'Life and Works of Ozias Humphry' – Ltd. to 400 copies – plates – orig. vellum backed boards – soiled – t.e.g. – 4to – 1918.
(Christie's) $75 £35

'Andrew and Nathaniel Plimer' – Ltd. Edn. of 365 copies – plates – cloth – 4to – 1903.
(Phillips) $85 £40

'Bryan's Dictionary of Painters and Engravers' – 5 vols. – orig. cloth – Port Washington, 1964.
(Christie's S. Kensington) $105 £50

WILLIAMSON, G. C. AND ENGLEHEART, H. L. D.
'George Engleheart 1750-1829' – no. 15 of 53 copies – plates, 10 hand col. – 4to – slight soiling – orig. cloth soiled – t.e.g. – with the bookplates of Alfred and Geoffrey Harmsworth – Privately printed, 1902.
(Christie's S. Kensington) $115 £55

'I am a creature of habit, and to change station upsets my mind,' he had written from that small fort in Waziristan. His ~~evil genius~~ had nearly driven him homeless again; the evil ~~genius being the news-direction of Lord Beaverbrook's~~ newspapers. The *Daily Express* had, years before, 'splashed' the 'sensational' fact one morning that Colonel T. E. Lawrence was hiding in the Royal Air Force as an aircraftman. One of his ~~officers~~, recognizing him, had sold the 'story' to the ~~*Express*~~ for fifty pounds. So Shaw had been turned out of the R.A.F. He re-enlisted in the Tank Corps. After two years he had been permitted to return to the Air Force, but on condition that his term of service would be terminated instantly 'should that sort of thing happen again'. (Certain senior R.A.F. officers should have educated themselves more fittingly to understand the world, and in particular the world based upon the manufactured lies of newspapers, all produced to make money; they should have realized that T. E. Shaw was not responsible for the great bites that the rapacious vultures of the lower middle-class press took out of the remnants of the private life of this noble Englishman.) And then 'that sort of thing' had happened again, while Shaw was in India, ~~sent there~~ to be out of the way of publicity. ~~The Sunday Express~~, on the flimsiest hearsay—a mere whiff to the vulture—had splashed a story, the sort of sensa-
23

WILLIAMSON, HENRY
'Genius of Friendship T. E. Lawrence' – Proof copy of 1st Edn. – number of auto revisions by author including rewritten passages and note about corrections – signed with initials – orig. wrappers – 8vo – 1941.
(Sotheby's) $460 £220

'Salar the Salmon' – First issue with red top edge – covers rubbed – otherwise nice – 1935.
(J. Ash) $17 £8

'The Village Book' – 1st Edn. – frontispiece portrait – no. 152 of 504 copies signed by the author – vellum backed cloth – t.e.g. – rest uncut – 8vo.
(Lawrence) $60 £30

WILLIAMSON, CAPT. THOMAS
'Agricultural Mechanism or a Display of the Vehicles, Implements and Machinery connected with Husbandry' – 20 plates – may lack half title – half calf – rebacked – 8vo – Black, Parry and Kingsbury, 1810.
(Sotheby's) $180 £85

WILLIAMSON, T. AND BLAGDON, F. W.
'The European in India' – col. plates – marginal worming – morocco – 4to – 1813.
(Sotheby's) $210 £100

WILLIAMSON, T. AND HOWETT, S.
'Oriental Field Sports' – vol. 1 of 2 – 21 plates – some browned – half calf – worn – 1808; and 2 others.
(Sotheby's) $50 £25

WILLIAN, ROBERT
'On Vaccine Inoculation' – 1st Edn. – 2 col. plates – foxing – cont. calf – upper cover detached – 4to – 1806.
(Sotheby's) $210 £100

WILLIS, NATHANIEL PARKER AND BARTLETT, W. H.
'American Scenery' – 2 vols. in one – engraved porttait – 2 additional engraved titles with vignette views – map and 117 engraved plates – portrait title vignettes and all views coloured by hand – contemporary red morocco – sides elaborately gilt rebacked – 4to. – 1840.
(Christie's) £760 £380

WILLIS, R.
'Architectural History of the University of Cambridge' – 4 vols. includ. one of plans – half morocco – gilt – g.e. – 1886.
(Phillips) $125 £60

WILLIS, THOMAS
'Opera Omnia' – 6 parts in one vol. – 36 engraved plates – some folding – lacks frontis – soiling and worming – modern half calf – 4to – Amsterdam, 1682.
(Sotheby's) $55 £25

WILLMANN, CARL
'Apparate fur Handschatten-Spiele' – 49 bits of apparatus almost all in original wrappings with seals intact – cloth box – pictorial lid – 248 x 188mm – Hamburg, n.d.
(Sotheby's) $230 £110

WILLMOT, ELLEN ANN
'The Genus Rosa' – 2 vols. – uncoloured illustrations and 132 chromolithographed plates after drawings by Alfred Parsons – contemporary cloth – t.e.g. – other edges uncut – wrappers to original parts bound at the end of each vol. – folio – 1914.
(Christie's) $800 £400

WILLOUGHBY, FRANCIS
'The Ornithology' – edited by J. Ray – 76 pages of 80 – 4 plates with parts missing – 40 in good condition – calf covers detached – folio – 1679.
(Phillips) $135 £65

WILLYAMS, COOPER
'A Selection of Views in Egypt, Palestine, Rhodes, Italy, Minorca and Gibraltar' – 1st Edn. – 36 hand col. aquatint plates – dust soiling – modern calf morocco – folio – 1822.
(Sotheby's) $840 £400

'A Voyage up the Mediterranean in his Majesty's ship the Swiftsure' – 1st Edn. – engraved hand coloured leaf of dedication and 42 hand coloured aquatint plates – including folding map of the Mediterranean – modern half morocco 4to. – 1802.
(Christie's) $520 £260

WILSON, A. AND BONAPARTE, PRINCE C. L.
'American Ornithology' – 3 vols. – col. plates – lacks 3 in vol. 3 – orig. morocco backed cloth – rubbed – 8vo – n.d.
(Sotheby's) $95 £45

WILSON, SIR CHARLES
'Picturesque Palestine' – 5 vols. – including Supplement by Stanley Lane-Poole – many plates and illustrations – original cloth – g.e. – 4to. – 1880-84.
(Christie's) $220 £110

WILSON, GEORGE
'A Compleat Course of Chymistry' – 3rd Edn. with Appendix – 8 engraved plates – portrait in photographic facsimile – title in red and black – new half calf – 8vo – John Bailey, 1709.
(Sotheby's) $10 £5

WILSON, H.
'Aiana Antiqua. A Descriptive Account of the Coins and Antiquities of Afghanistan' – 36 plates – folding map – subscribers' list – cont. calf – rebacked – 4to – 1841.
(Sotheby's) $190 £90

WILSON, J.
'Illustrations of Zoology' – 36 hand coloured plates – half leather – worn – the North Devon Athenaeum copy, with the Sharland bequest stamp – folio 1831.
(Sotheby's) $1,600 £800

WILSON, J.
'General View of the Agriculture of Renfrewshire' – frontis – hand coloured map – torn – plan – calf – rebacked – Paisley, 1812; and another.
(Sotheby's) $70 £35

WILSON, J. M.
'Rural Cyclopaedia' – 4 vols. – bound in tree calf – 1849.
(Lane) $65 £30

WILSON, JAMES WILLIAM
'Sketches of Louth' – mounted litho addit. title – 11 plates on india paper – soiling – orig. cloth – rubbed – spine torn – folio – Louth, 1840.
(Christie's) $170 £80

WILSON, SIR JOHN
'The Royal Philatelic Collection' – plates – cloth – Dropmore Press, 1952.
(Phillips) $55 £25

WILSON, O. S.
'Larvae of the British Lepidoptera' – 40 col. plates – morocco gilt – sm 4to – 1880.
(Phillips) $85 £40

WILSON, PATTEN
Large ink drawing of girl at spinning wheel – signed and dated '96 – framed and glazed – 310 x 222mm.
(Sotheby's) $180 £85

WILSON, RICHARD
'Studies and Designs done in Rome in the Year 1752' – 1st Edn. – 47 litho plates – india paper – cont. half calf – 4to – 1811.
(Christie Manson & Woods) $75 £35

WILSON, T. L. RODNEY
'Petrus Van Der Velden' – Ltd. Edn. – 2 vols. – plates – some col. and mounted – orig. cloth – slipcase – sm folio – Sydney, 1979.
(Sotheby's) $40 £20

WILSON, THOMAS
'The Works'; 'Bath Folio' – 2 vols. in one – 1782.
(Baitson) $55 £26
'The Rule of Reason' – mostly black letter – title soiled – staining – 19th century quarter calf – sm 4to – I. Kingston, 1567.
(Sotheby's) $145 £70

WIMPFFEN
'Notes d'un Voyageur' – 2 vols. – 1788.
(Moore Allen & Innocent) $250 £120

WINANS, WALTER
'Deer Breeding for Fine Heads' – plates – calf – gilt – sm 4to – 1913.
(Phillips) $85 £40

WINDUS, J.
'A Journey to Mequinez' – 1st Edn. – 6 engraved plates – cont. calf – rebacked – large paper copy – 1725.
(Sotheby's) $80 £40

WINGATE, EDMUND
'Arithmetick' – 8th Edn. – much enlarged – some diagrams – cont. calf – rubbed – upper cover nearly detached – 8vo. – 1683.
(Sotheby's) $10 £5

WINGATE, J.
'Illustrations of the Coinage of Scotland' – one of 150 copies – plates – half title – cont. morocco – gilt – rubbed – 4to – Glasgow, 1868.
(Sotheby's) $90 £45

WINKLER, F.
'Die Zeichnungen Hans Suss von Kulmbachs und Hans Leonhard Schaufeleins' – plates – orig. cloth backed boards – 4to – Berlin, 1942.
(Sotheby's) $95 £45

WINSTANLEY, WILLIAM
'The Lives of the Most Famous English Poets' – frontis – old calf – 1687.
(Phillips) $85 £40

WIRSUNG, CHRISTOPH
'The General Practice of Physick' – 2nd Edn. in English – black letter, device on title – dampstains – defective leaves – cont. calf – worn – folio – 1605.
(Sotheby's) $145 £70

WISDEN CRICKETERS' ALMANACK
for 1941-56, 16 vols. – orig. cloth – with 8 other vols. on cricket – 8vo.
(Sotheby's) $275 £130

WISDEN, JOHN
'Cricketers' Almanack, 48th-47th ed.' – 70 vols. only – plates – orig. bindings – worn – 1911-80.
(Sotheby's) $1,300 £650

'Cricketers' Almanack' – vols. 1-116, lacking vol. 19 and 8 duplicates, together in 122 vols. – nos. 1-15 facsimile edns., most with photographic plates – some orig. wrappers and cloth – 15 rebound – many worn – 8vo – 1879-1979.
(Sotheby's) $2,310 £1,100

WISE, FRANCIS
'A Letter to Dr. Mead concerning the White Horse'; 'Further Observation upon the White Horse' – 2 vols. in one – 5 engraved plates, 3 folding – spotted – cont. half calf – rubbed – 4to – Oxford, 1738-42.
(Sotheby's) $105 £50

WISE, T. J.
'Two Lake Poets . . . Wordsworth and Coleridge' – orig. cloth – Dawsons, 1965.
(Christie's) $30 £15

WISEMAN, RICHARD
'Several Chirurgical Treatises' – 2nd Edn. – lacks half title – soiled – browning – cont. calf – covers detached – folio – 1686.
(Sotheby's) $135 £65

WIT, F. DE
'Atlas' – hand col. engraved frontis, printed title in Latin, French, Dutch and English – 23 engraved maps, hand col. in outline – some stained – cont. paper boards – later cloth spine – folio – Amsterdam, after 1688.
(Sotheby's) $1,050 £500

'Ducatus Pomeraniae Tabula Generalis' – engraved map – hand coloured in outline – principal areas fully coloured – title cartouche in the form of a banner supported by cherubs – 488 x 563mm – Amsterdam, R. & J. Ottens, circa 1740.
(Sotheby's) $50 £25

WITAKER, JOHN
'The Ancient Cathedral of Cornwall' – 2 vols. bound as one in orig. boards with ancient leaf edges – 1804.
(Lane) $65 £30

WITCHCRAFT
9 tracts including Bragge, F. 'The Witch of Walkerne' – half calf – 1712.
(Phillips) $610 £290

WITHER, G.
'Abuses Stript and Whipt' – lacking some leaves – dampstained – cont. calf – rubbed – joints split – 1613.
(Sotheby's) $16 £8

'The Hymnes and Songs of the Church' – later calf – dampstained – rubbed – 8vo – 1623.
(Sotheby's) $96 £48

WITHERBY, H. F. – TUCKER, B. W.
'British Birds' – vols. 1-57 – lacking vols. 35 and 49 – many plates – buckram – 8vo – 1907-64.
(Christie's) $600 £300

WITHERBY, H. F. – JOURDAIN, F. C. R. AND OTHERS
'The Handbook of British Birds' – 1st Edn. – 5 vols. – numerous plates – some coloured – text illustrations and maps – original cloth – 8vo. – 1838-41.
(Christie's) $150 £75

WITHERING, WILLIAM
'Arrangement of British Plants' – 4 vols. – plates – half calf – 1796.
(Phillips) $20 £10

'A Botanical Arrangement of all the Vegetables Naturally Growing in Great Britain' – 1st Edn. – 2 vols. – 12 engraved plates, 2 folding – cont. sprinkled calf – slightly worn – 8vo – 1776.
(Sotheby's) $160 £80

WIZARD, THE
'The Modern Magic Monthly' edited by George Armstrong – No. 1-95, 88 issues only and 5 duplicates – illus. – orig. wrappers – some loose – 8vo – 1947-56.
(Sotheby's) $15 £7

WODEHOUSE, P. G.
'The Code of the Woosters' – 1st English Edn. – half title – inscribed by author – margins browned – orig. cloth – faded – 1938.
(Christie's) $105 £50

WOLCOT, J.
'The Works of Peter Pindar' – 5 vols. – portrait – cont. calf – gilt spines – 1794-1801.
(Sotheby's) $120 £60

WOLF, JOSEPH AND ELIOT, DANIEL
'The Life and Habits of Wild Animals' – 20 plates – half morocco – worn – folio – 1874.
(Christie's) $30 £15

WOLFIUS, J.
'Lectionum Memorabilium et Reconditarum centenarii XVI'– part 1 of 2 – woodcut illus. – browned – cont. pigskin – rubbed – folio – 1600.
(Sotheby's) $76 £38

WOLLEY, HANNAH
'The Queen Like Closet or Rich Cabinet' – 3 parts in one vol. – browning and soiling – cont. calf – very worn – 12mo – 1681-84.
(Sotheby's) $840 £400

WOLLSTONECRAFT, MARY
'Original Stories from Real Life with Conversations calculated to regulate the affections and Form the Mind to Truth and Goodness' – 2nd Edn. – 3 pages adverts at end – some browning and soiling – cont. sheep worn – cover detached – 12mo – 1791.
(Sotheby's) $65 £32

WONG, K. CHIMIN AND TEH, WU LIEN
'History of Chinese Medicine' – 1st Edn. – plates – orig. cloth – slightly soiled – large 8vo – 1932.
(Sotheby's) $125 £60

WOOD, ANTHONY
'Athenae Oxoniensis' – 2nd Edn. – 2 vols. in one – title in red and black – slight browning – cont. calf – worn – Syon Park bookplate – large folio – 1721.
(Sotheby's) $65 £32

'The History and Antiquities of the University of Oxford' – 2 vols. in 3, trans. by John Gutch – 3 engraved plates – offsetting – cont. calf – gilt – worn – 4to –Oxford, 1794.
(Sotheby's) $85 £40

WOOD, A.
'Historia et Antiquitates Universitatis Oxoniensis' – 2 vols. in 1 – 2 copies – one with map torn – other lacking – cont. calf – Oxford, 1685; and 2 others – folio.
(Sotheby's) $84 £42

WOOD, HUGH
'Views in France, Switzerland, The Tyrol and Italy' – cont. half red morocco gilt – larged shaped octagonal morocco label on front cover – some staining – Dickinson & Co. – n.d. – lithographed title and 12 protected hand coloured lithograph plates – 18.25 x 23.5in. – oblong folio.
(Lawrence) $640 £320

WOOD, JAMES
'The Elements of Optics' – 3rd Edn. – orig. boards – worn – Cambridge, 1811.
(Christie's S. Kensington) $45 £22

WOOD, JOHN
Plans of Scottish Towns – no title or text – 48 double-page plans engraved by T. Clerk, W. Murphy, N. Douglas and others – including large folding plan of Stirling on 2 sheets – a few with inset maps – 14 partly hand coloured in outand 3 lithographed – contemporary half roan slightly rubbed – folio 545 x 360mm. – Edinburgh, 1818-28.
(Christie's) $3,800 £1,900

WOOD, JOHN GEORGE
'The Principles and Practice of Sketching Landscape Scenery from Nature' – 3rd Edn. – 4 parts in one – 64 litho plates – cont. half russia – worn – oblong 4to – 1820.
(Sotheby's) $170 £80

WOOD, ROBERT
'The Ruins of Balbec' – 1st Edn. – 47 engraved plates – 11 double page or double page folding – spotted and dampstained – cont. calf – worn – covers detached – folio – 1757.
(Sotheby's) $105 £50

'The Ruins of Palmyra' – engraved plates – loose – orig. boards – worn – folio – 1753.
(Sotheby's) $200 £95

WOOD, W.
'Illustrations of the Linnaean Genera of Insects' – 2 vols. – 86 partly col. plates – some spotting – orig. boards – spines worn – 12mo – 1821.
(Sotheby's) $85 £40
'Index Entomologicus' – 59 plates – Supplement by Westwood – half morocco gilt – spine defective – 8vo – 1854.
(Phillips) $75 £35

WOOD, W.
'Zoography' – 3 vols. – 60 plates – small wormholes in vol. III – cont. calf – browned – rubbed – 1807-11.
(Sotheby's) $65 £32

WOODCOCK, MARTIN
'A Field Guide to the Birds of South East Asia' – orig. drawings for this work in watercolour and gouache, on 64 sheets of drawing board – coloured and in monochrome, together with line illus., ink , for the text-figures – latter loose in a folder, the former in three specially made morocco boxes – folio – 1974-75.
(Sotheby's) $2,000 £1,000

WOODCUT, THE
Nos. 1-4 – plates – orig. cloth backed boards – 4to – 1927-30.
(Sotheby's) $265 £125

WOODFORDE, J.
'The Diary of a Country Parson' – edited J. Beresford – 5 vols. – cloth – worn – 1924-31.
(Bonhams) $40 £18

WOODS, FORESTS AND LAND REVENUES
Report of the Commissioners and 6 vol. of Reports from the Select Committee , together 29 vols., folding maps, disbound, soiled – folio – 1923-58.
(Sotheby's) $460 £220

WOODS, JOSEPH
'Letters of an Architect from France, Italy and Greece' – 2 vols. in one – frontis – 19 plates – illus. in text – foxing – cont. half calf – rebacked – covers worn – 4to – 1828.
(Sotheby's) $65 £30

WOODVILLE, W.
'Medical Botany' – 5 vols. in 2 – 3rd Edn. – edited by W. J. Hooker and G. Spratt – 310 hand coloured engraved plates – slight spotting and offsetting – green morocco – gilt – g.e., by J. Clarke – 4to – 1832.
(Sotheby's) $1,400 £700
'Medical Botany' – vol. 1 of 4 – 1st Edn. – 65 hand col. engraved plates – cont. half calf – worn – 4to – 1790.
(Sotheby Parke Bernet) $260 £130

WOODWARD, B. B.
'The History of Wales' – 5 vols. – engraved addit. title and 75 plates – spotting – orig. cloth – dampstained – 4to – n.d.
(Christie's) $90 £42

WOOLEY, C. L. AND LAWRENCE, T. E.
'The Wilderness of Zin' – plates – folding plans – orig. cloth backed boards – 4to – 1915.
(Sotheby's) $230 £110

WOOLF, VIRGINIA
'Mrs. Dalloway' – Hogarth Press, 1925; 'To the Lighthouse' – Hogarth Press, 1927 – together 2 vols. – both 1st Edns. – orig. cloth – one joint split – 8vo.
(Sotheby's) $180 £90

Leaf extracted from her passport bearing her photo and signature, both overstamped by the Foreign Office – 18th April, 1933.
(Sotheby's) $360 £170

WOOLNOTH, W.
'A Graphical Illustration of the Metropolitan Cathedral Church of Canterbury' – large paper copy – additional engraved title – 18 engraved plates and illustrations by W. Woolnoth and 6 additional engraved plates by I. Kip and others – some plates foxed, some offset, small library stamp on lower margins of printed title, and other pages – contemporary purple straight grained morocco – covers with alternate gilt and blind roll tool panels enclosing gilt vignette – spine gilt in compartments – g.e. slightly rubbed – folio 1816; and three others.
(Christie's) $150 £75

WORDSWORTH, C.
'Greece' – vignette title, plates – morocco gilt – g.e. – 1840.
(Phillips) $65 £32

'Greece' – plates – spotted – cont. morocco – rubbed – 1840; and another.
(Sotheby's) $110 £55

WORGAN, G. B.
'The Agriculture of the County of Cornwall' – 1st Edn. with folding map – engravings – 1811.
(Lane) $125 £60

WORLD MAP
Overton, Henry – 'A New Map of the Whole World' – large engraved map of the hemispheres, smaller maps of the celestial hemispheres above, with the constellations represented pictorially, maps of the polar regions below, elaborate allegorical and other scenes in the outer corners – coloured by hand – some small surface-flaws and some minor loss of surface – mounted on linen – very rare and possibly unique – 1005 x 1022mm – 1715.
(Sotheby's) $1,200 £600

WORLD OF FASHION, THE
Vols. VI and XII – hand coloured plates – soiling – disbound – 1829-35.
(Sotheby's) $880 £440

Vols. 12-34 only in 2 vols. – 256 plates only 215 coloured – a few leaves soiled and spotted – cont. half calf – rubbed – small 4to – 1835-51.
(Sotheby's) $485 £230

About 120 hand coloured fashion plates – a few slightly shaved – some spotting and browning – half morocco – a little rubbed – 4to – 1831.
(Christie's S. Kensington) $380 £180

WORLIDGE, T.
'A Select Collection of Drawings from curious Antique Gems' – engraved plates – cont. morocco – rubbed – 4to – 1768.
(Sotheby's) $115 £55

WORSLEY, SIR RICHARD
'The History of the Isle of Wight' – 1st Edn. – folding map, torn, partly repaired and 31 engraved views and other plates, one shaved, light spotting in some including 12 double-page – contemporary half calf rebacked, worn – 4to. – 1781.
(Christie's) $110 £55

WORTH, R. W.
'History of Plymouth' – 1st Edn. – orig. cloth – 1871.
(Lane) $40 £20

WORTH, W.
'Catalogue of the Greek Coins of Crete and the Aegean Islands' – plates – orig. cloth – 8vo – 1886.
(Sotheby's) $250 £120

WOTTON, SIR HENRY
'The State of Christendom' – 1st Edn. – browning and soiling – cont. sheep – rebacked – worn – folio – 1657.
(Sotheby's) $40 £20

WRIGHT, C. T. HAGBERG AND PURNELL, C. J.
'Subject Index of the London Library' – 2 vols. – 1909-23; 'Catalogue of the London Library' – 4 vols. includ. supplement – 1913-29 – orig. cloth – slightly worn – 4to.
(Sotheby's) $90 £42

WRIGHT, E.
'Some Observations made in Travelling through France, Italy . . .' – 2nd Edn. – 2 vols. in one – 39 engraved plates – two folding – cont. calf – upper cover detached – lower joint cracked – 4to – 1764.
(Christie's S. Kensington) $105 £50

'Some Observations made in Travelling through France' – 2nd Edn. – 2 vols. – 41 engraved plates – some double page – woodcut illus. – cont. calf – rubbed – one cover detached – 4to – 1764.
(Sotheby's) $145 £70

WRIGHT, REV. G. N.
'France Illustrated' – 4 vols. – 4 engraved addit. titles and 144 plates, most after T. Allom – some slight spotting – half calf – rubbed – 4to – n.d.
(Christie's S. Kensington) $275 £130

'The Shores and Islands of the Mediterranean' – engraved title – folding map and 63 plates – spotted and soiled – disbound – g.e. – 4to – n.d.
(Sotheby's) $170 £80

WRIGHT, G. N. (Editor)
'The People's Gallery of Engravings' – 2 vols. – engraved plates – cont. half calf – worn – n.d.
(Christie's S. Kensington) $65 £30

'The Gallery of Engravings' – 2 vols. – plates – spotted – cont. half calf – rubbed – 4to – 1845-1846.
(Sotheby's) $60 £30

'Ireland Illustrated' – engraved title and 80 views on 40 plates after W. H. Bartlett and others – some leaves spotted or stained – cont. half calf – worn – 4to – 1831.
(Sotheby's) $180 £90

WRIGHT, J. AND H.
'Vegetable Grower's Guide' – 4 divisions – 30 coloured plates – cloth – 4to – n.d.
(Bennett Book Auction) $34 £16

WRIGHT, JAMES
'The History and Antiquities of the County of Rutland' – 1st Edn. – title in red and black – double page engraved map – 15 engraved illus. – cont. calf – folio – 1684.
(Sotheby's) $100 £48

WRIGHT, JOHN
'The Fruit Grower's Guide' – 3 vols. in 6 – col. plates – rubbed – 4to – 1891-94.
(Sotheby's) $260 £130

'The Flower Grower's Guide' – 3 vols. in 6 – col. plates – rubbed – 4to – 1896-1901.
(Sotheby's) $170 £85

'The Fruit Grower's Guide' – 4 parts only of 6 – 29 col. plates and numerous illus. in text – orig. pictorial cloth – minor defects – g.e. – 4to – 1891-94.
(Sotheby Beresford Adams) $90 £42

WRIGHT, JOSEPH
'The English Dialect Dictionary' – 6 vols. – orig. cloth – rubbed – 4to – 1898-1905.
(Sotheby's) $230 £110

WRIGHT, LEWIS
'The Illustrated Book of Poultry' – 25 chromo litho plates – half morocco – gilt – g.e. – 4to – 1890.
(Phillips) $170 £80

WRIGHT, M. W. AND F.
'Svenska Faglar' – 3 vols. – 360 col. lithos plates – decorated brown pigskin – worn – folio – Stockholm, 1924-29.
(Sctheby's) $460 £220

WRIGHT, T.
'Works of Gilray the Caricaturist' – plates – spotting – cloth – gilt – rubbed – g.e. – 4to – Chatto, n.d.
(Phillips) $65 £32

WRIGHT, T. AND BARTLETT, W.
'The History and Topography of the County of Essex' – 2 vols. – engraved titles and 98 plates of 100 on india paper – map – spotted – cont. morocco backed cloth – worn – 4to – 1831-35.
(Sotheby's) $160 £80

WRIGHT, THOMAS
'The History and Topography of the County of Essex' – 2 vols. – illus. engravings by W. Bartlett – quarter calf – marbled boards – spine and corners rubbed – foxing – George Virtue, 1831.
(May Whetter & Grose) $180 £85

WRIGHT, THOMAS AND JONES, H. LONGUEVILLE
'Memorials of Cambridge' – 2 vols. – steel engraved addit. titles – one folding map and 73 plates by Le Keux – illus. – some spotting – orig. cloth – spines faded and slightly torn – 1847.
(Christie's S. Kensington) $275 £130

WRIGHT, W. H. K. (Editor)
'Journal of the Ex Libris Society' – vols. 1-6 only – plates – illus. – orig. cloth – orig. wrappers – bound in 4to – 1892-6.
(Christie's S. Kensington) $115 £55

WURTTEMBERG
Collection of over 100 letter signed by rulers of Wurttemberg in the 18th and 19th centuries – 1701-1860.
(Sotheby's, New Bond Street) $585 £260

WYATT, CLAUDE
'British Birds' – 2 vols. in one – 67 hand col. plates – some leaves loose – cont. half morocco – gilt spine – rubbed – t.e.g. – 4to – 1894-99.
(Sotheby's) $840 £400

WYATT, J.
'History of the First Battalion Coldstream Guards' – plates – inscribed by author – orig. cloth – 8vo – 1858.
(Sotheby's) $85 £40

WYATT, SIR M. DIGBY
'Specimens of Ornamental Workmanship' – chromolithographed title and plates – spotted – orig. cloth – gilt – folio – 1852.
(Sotheby's) $85 £40
'The Art of Illuminating' – col. title and half title – 100 col. plates – half vellum gilt – 4to – 1860.
(Phillips) $90 £42
'The Industrial Arts of the Nineteenth Century' – 2 vols. – chromolithographed addit. titles and 158 plates – cont. half morocco – spine slightly rubbed – g.e. – folio – 1851-3.
(Christie's S. Kensington) $440 £210
'Metal Work and Its Artistic Design' – presentation copy signed by author to his prospective father-in-law – chromolithed addit. title – 49 plates by Bedford – some leaves torn – soiled and creased – orig. morocco backed cloth – torn – disbound – folio – Day and Son, 1852.
(Christie's S. Kensington) $65 £30
'Specimens of Ornamental Art Workmanship' – litho plates – some coloured – cont. half morocco – rubbed – folio, 1852.
(Sotheby's) $160 £80

'The Industrial Arts of the Nineteenth Century' – 2 vols. – 2 chromolithographed titles – plates – orig. half morocco – gilt – g.e. – a few slightly spotted – folio – 1851-53.
(Sotheby's) $240 £120

WYATT, T.
'A Manual of Conchology' – 36 litho plates – cloth – 8vo – New York, 1838.
(Sotheby's) $55 £25

WYATVILLE, SIR JEFFRY
'Illustrations of Windsor Castle' – 2 vols. in one – engraved titles and 39 plates – folding – 3 extra engravings inserted – spotted – cont. half morocco – rubbed – t.e.g. – folio – 1841.
(Sotheby's) $250 £120

WYCHERLEY, WILLIAM
'Works' – Ltd. Edn. – 4 vols. – uncut – cloth backed boards – 4to – Nonesuch Press, 1924.
(Phillips) $90 £42

WYETH, N. C.
Illustrations – 'The Little Shepherd of Kingdom Come' – no. 196 of 512 copies – signed – in glassine wrapper – boxed – mint – New York, 1931.
(Robert Skinner) $475 £225

WYLD, J. AND HEWITT, N. R.
'A General Atlas' – engraved vignette title – 44 engraved maps, 2 double page, 42 full page – hand coloured in outline – 2 engraved tables, one a frontispiece – cont. quarter russia – joints cracked – worn – sm folio – 357 x 265mm – Edinburgh, J. Thomson & Co., 1825.
(Sotheby's) $200 £100

WYLD, JAMES
'A New General Atlas' – 43 plates; 'A New General Atlas' – 67 plates – together 113 engraved plates – 109 outline coloured maps – 4 plain – most plates double page – slight soiling – orig. bindings – very worn – large folio – n.d.
(Sotheby's) $600 £280

WYLEY, COL. H. C.
'XVth (The King's) Hussars, 1759 to 1913' – one of 250 large paper copies – 12 coloured plates – blue morocco – gilt – 4to. – 1914.
(Christie's) $160 £80

WYLIE, REV. J. A.
'The History of Protestantism' – illus. – 3 vols. – half leather – 4to.
(Baitson) $8 £4

WYNDHAM, G.
'The Ballad of Mr. Rook' – 6 col. plates by the Hon. Mrs. Percy Wyndham – hinges weak – orig. pictorial cloth – worn – folio – 1901.
(Sotheby's) $60 £28

WYNNE, DAVID
'The Sculpture of David Wynne' – 1st Edn. – intro. by Graham Hughes – no. 17 of 525 copies – signed by the artist – numerous photographic illus. in text – orig. calf – slightly rubbed – t.e.g. – 4to – 1974.
(Sotheby's) $120 £60

WYNNE, GIUSTINIA (Countess of Rosenberg)
'Alticchiero' – engraved title with large vignette by Giovanni de Pian – large folding engraved plan and 29 plates – many folding – by G. de Pian and Antonio Sandi – circular ownership stamp on title – contemporary marbled paper wrappers – uncut – worn – in buckram slipcase – 4to. – Padua, 1787.
(Christie's) $360 £180

XENEPHON OF EPHESUS
'The Ephesian Story' – limited to 300 copies, this no. 12 of 75 specially bound and with addit. illus. by Eric Fraser – orig. morocco – t.e.g. – slipcase – 4to – 1957.
(Christie's) $115 £55

'I Sette Libri' – old vellum – Vinegia, 1547.
(Bonhams) $125 £60

'Cryupaedia or the Institution and Life of Cyrus, King of the Persians' – trans. by P. Holland – engraved title – cont. speckled calf – slightly rubbed – 4to – A. Allot, 1632.
(Sotheby's) $335 £160

'Quae Extant Opera' – 2 parts in one vol. – Latin and Greek text – woodcut device – John Evelyn's bookplate – 17th century calf – spine gilt – folio – Geneva, 1581.
(Sotheby's) $180 £85

XIMENEZ, ANDRES
'Descripcion del Real Monasterio de San Lorenzo del Escorial' – 1st Edn. – title in red and black – engraved portrait – 16 plates and plans – cont. Spanish mottled calf – spine gilt – slight wear – folio – Madrid, 1764.
(Sotheby's) $200 £100

YABLONSKY, VIKTOR
'V Sumerkakh' (In the Evenings) – one of 1,500 copies – illus. and orig. wrappers by S. Polyakov – soiled – torn – 8vo – Moscow, 1922.
(Sotheby's) $75 £35

YACHTS AND YACHTSMEN, BRITISH
Profusely illus. – orig. binding – folio – 1907.
(Phillips) $95 £45

YANAGIHARA GENJIRO
'Ehon Yamato Shikyo' – vols. 1, 2 and 3 – illustrations of genre scenes with proverbial sayings – preface by Bazan Shoshin – dated Meiwa 7, 1770; colophon giving as Artist: Naniwa Gako, Yanagihara Genjiro – Engraver, Fujie Bunsuke – Publishers, Kyoto Shoshi, Kosho – dated Tenmei Tora, 1782 – good condition.
(Sotheby's) $520 £260

YANKEE COMIC TALES
'The Fire Hunt'; 'Boss Ankles'; 'The Coon Hunt'; 'The Great Attraction'; 'How Josh Jefferson Got A Start in the World', 2 copies; 'How Sally Hooper Got Snake Bit', 7 copies – col. litho pictorial wrappers – some worn – 8vo – Cameron and Ferguson – n.d.
(Sotheby's) $12 £6

YAROSLAVSKY, A.
'Svoloch Moskva' (Swine Moscow) – orig. wrappers – slightly soiled – 8vo – Moscow, 1922.
(Sotheby's) $180 £85

YARRELL, WILLIAM
'A History of British Birds' – 1st Edn. – 3 vols. – cont. calf – worn – 1843.
(Sotheby's) $30 £15

'A History of British Birds' – 3 vols. – illus. – slight soiling – cont. half morocco – joints very slightly cracked – t.e.g. – 1843.
(Christie's S. Kensington) $30 £15

YASHIRO, Y.
'Sandro Botticelli' – 3 vols. – no. 163 of 600 copies – plates – orig. cloth – soiled – 4to – 1925.
(Sotheby's) $200 £95

YATES, REV. WILLIAM
'An Illustration of the Monastic History and Antiquities of the Town and Abbey of St. Edmunds Bury' – 15 engraved plates – spotted – cont. half calf – rebacked – rubbed – 4to – 1805.
(Sotheby's) $115 £55

YEARS, ART, THE
1880-1900; 1902-1903; 1906-1912; 1917-1925 and 1927 – 40 vols. – cloth.
(Phillips) $210 £100

YEATS, W. B.
Plays for an Irish Theatre: 'Where There is Nothing'; 'The Hour Glass'; 'The King's Threshold' – 3 vols. 1st English Edn. – orig. cloth backed boards – slightly soiled – 1903-04; 'Ideas of Good and Evil' – orig. cloth backed boards – slightly rubbed – 1903; 'The Collected Plays, Early Poems and Stories, 1925'; 'The Collected Plays, 1934' – all but the first 1st Edns. – orig. cloth unless otherwise described – 8vo.
(Sotheby's) $80 £40

'Stories of Red Hanrahan and the Secret Rose' – illus. by Nora McGuiness – 2 col. – slightly spotted – orig. pictorial cloth gilt – 1927; 'Sophocles' King Oedipus'– orig. wrappers – slightly soiled – 1928; 'Dramatis Personae etc.' – 1st English Edn. – orig. cloth backed boards – soiled – dust jacket – 1937; 'Last Poems and Plays' – orig. pictorial cloth by Sturge Moore – dust jacket – 1940 – all but the third 1st Edns. – 8vo.
(Sotheby's) $110 £55

MAID'S HEAD HOTEL, NORWICH.

Auto letter signed – 2 pages octavo – to Miss Radcliffe discussing the words in Greek and Hebrew which appeared in the cross in her drawing – auto envelope – July, 1913.
(Sotheby's) $210 £100

'The Tower' – 1st Edn. – orig. green cloth – upper cover and spine stamped in gilt after a design by T. Sturge Moore – 1928.
(Christie's S. Kensington) $70 £35

'A Full Moon in March' – 1st Edn., green cloth gilt, 1935; 'Wheels and Butterflies' – 1st Edn., green cloth gilt, 1934; 'Secret Rose' – 1st Edn., blue cloth, gilt, 1897.
(Phillips) $90 £40

YELLOW BOOK, THE
vol. 1-13 plates – orig. cloth – a few vol. slightly soiled – sm 4to – 1894-7.
(Christie's S. Kensington) $315 £150

YORICK
A complete set of 8 ink and watercolour drawings for a comic strip story of a cat and a canary with ink and watercolour drawing entitled 'Why the Chicken Crossed the Road' – signed and dated '04.
(Sotheby's) $80 £38

YORKE, J.
'The Union of Honour' – 1st Edn. – errata leaf – title torn and rebacked – browned – cont. calf – rebacked with morocco – worn folio – 1640.
(Sotheby Parke Bernet) $80 £40

YORKE, PHILIP OF ERTHIG
'The Royal Tribes of Wales' – 12 stipple engraved plates – portraits – cont. blue morocco gilt – rubbed – g.e. – 4to – Wrexham, 1799.
(Sotheby's) $160 £75

YORKSHIRE
Indentures – on vellum, relating to land in Swaledale 1606; Lakeland, 1666 and other places also marriage settlements 1651 and 1688 with a conveyance on paper 1842.
(Phillips) $90 £42

YORKSHIRE MARRIAGE REGISTERS
West Riding – vol. 1-4 – Limited Edn. – orig. cloth – slightly rubbed – 8vo and 4to – 1914-15.
(Sotheby's) $55 £25

YORKSHIRE NUMISMATIC SOCIETY
Transactions – vol. 1-3; New Series vol. 1-2, part 2, in 9 vol. – plates first series in cont. cloth – others in orig. wrappers – 8vo – Hull etc, 1915-66.
(Sotheby's) $120 £58

YORKSHIRE PARISH REGISTER SOCIETY PUBLICATION
Vol. 1-142, lacking 132 and 133 – cont. half morocco or cloth – orig. wrappers – slightly rubbed – most t.e.g. – 8vo – 1899-1979.
(Sotheby's) $630 £300

YORKSHIRE – SPEED, JOHN
Engraved map, col. by hand in outline, cartouches, arms, compass rose, sailing ship etc. – col. – stained – framed – 382 x 510mm – J. Sudbury and G. Humble, 1610.
(Sotheby's) $265 £125

YOUNG, A.
'Six Months Tour Through the North of England' – 1st Edn. – 4 vols. – plates – calf – gilt – rebacked – 8vo – 1870.
(Phillips) $200 £95
'Six Weeks Tour Through the Southern Counties of England and Wales' – 1st Edn. – half title – cont. calf – rubbed – 8vo – 1768.
(Sotheby's) $230 £110

YOUNG, ANDREW
'A Prospect of Flowers' – frontis by John Nash – good – 1945.
(J. Ash) $6 £3

YOUNG, ARTHUR
'Political Essays Concerning the Present State of the British Empire' – 1st Edn. – slight browning – cont. sprinkled calf – label rubbed – signed James Grant, 1772 – 4to – 1772.
(Sotheby's) $200 £95
'A Six Months Tour through the North of England' – 1st Edn. – 4 vols. – 28 plates – some folding and browning – cont. calf – rebacked – covers worn – 8vo – 1770.
(Sotheby's) $120 £60

YOUNG, E.
'Night Thoughts' – 13 hand col. plates – only – later half morocco – rubbed – 1793.
(Sotheby Parke Bernet) $64 £32
'The Farmers' Tour Through Eastern England' – 4 vols. – calf – 1771.
(Irelands) $380 £180

YOUNG, JAMES
'Plymouth Memories' – limited to 300 copies – fine – 1951.
(Lane) $20 £10

YOUNG, JOHN
'A Catalogue of the Collection of Pictures of the Late John Julius Angerstein' – text in French and English – 42 etched plates – some margins damp stained – minor defects – cont. half morocco – rubbed – 4to – 1829.
(Sotheby Beresford Adams) $25 £12

YOUNG, WILLIAM (Editor)
'Roman Architecture and Sculpture and Ornament' – 200 plates in facsimile – cont. half calf – large folio – 1900.
(Sotheby Beresford Adams) $85 £40

YOUNGER, J.
'River Angling for Salmon and Trout' – half calf – Kelso, 1860.
(Bennett Book Auction) $20 £10

YOUTH RECLINING, A
Ink drawing with touches of blue, gold and red – slightly creased and stained – laid down on an album leaf – gilt sprinkled blue border – 16.9 x 28.4cm. – Isfahan, c. 1650.
(Christie's) $1,010 £480

YRIARTE, C.
'Florence' – 500 engravings – quarter morocco – 1882.
(Laurence and Martin Taylor) $17 £8

YSTAD
'Charta Ifver Ysta-Stad' made 1698 by Christopher Stobens, copied 1798 – col. mss plan of town, key at side of plan, scale and diagrammatic compass rose – 372 x 488mm – Stockholm, 1797.
(Sotheby's) $105 £50

YURKUN, YU
'Durnaya Kompaniya' (Bad Company) – plates in 2 states, some hand col. – orig. wrappers by Yu, Annenkov – spine torn – 8vo – Petrograd, 1917.
(Sotheby's) $210 £100

ZACUTO, ABRAHAM
'Sepher ha'Yuhasin' – 2nd Edn. with additions – some waterstaining throughout – modern morocco – sm 4to – Cracow, 1580.
(Christie's) $960 £480

ZALOKOSTAS, G. Ch.
'Ta Apanta' – Collected Poems – Greek text – calf backed boards; and 4 others.
(Sotheby's) $200 £100

ZAMBONI, BALDASSARE
'Memorie Intorno alle Pubbliche Fabbriche piu Insigni dells Citta di Brescia' – engraved title with large vignette by P. Beceni – 10 engraved headpieces – including 5 views of Brescia, by Francesco Zucchi after Francesco Battaglioli – 12 folding engraved plates by P. Beceni after Gasparo Turbini – contemporary paper boards – uncut – soiled – folio – Brescia, Pietro Vescovi, 1778.
(Christie's) $640 £320

ZAMYATIN, E.
'Vereshi' – no. 10 of 125 copies – hand col. illus. – orig. wrappers by N. Lyubavina – 8vo – Petrograd, n.d.
(Sotheby's) $160 £75

ZANETTI, A. M.
'Delle antiche statue greche e romane, Parte Prima' (only) – fine engraved allegorical frontispiece by Sartori after Piazzetta – portrait of Christian VI of Denmark after Piazzetta and 50 plates by Faldoni, et al. – 51 leaves of text – printed on one side only – each within engraved classical border – vignette illustrations – contemporary mottled calf – spine gilt – Garter Arms gilt on sides – joints worn – large folio – G. Albrizzi – 1740.
(Christie's) $90 £45

Baldassare Zamboni. (Christie's)

ZANETTI, ANTONIO MARIA, The Younger
'Le Gemme Antiche' . . . illustrated – large paper copy on thick paper – Latin and Italian titles in red and black with engraved vignette – 73 fine arabesque tailpieces – 81 full page engraved plates – contemporary vellum boards – gilt spine – folio – Giambattista Albrizzi, 1750.
(Christie's) $440 £220

'Varie pittura a fresco de'principali maestri Veneziani' – engraved title with vignette – medallion portrait by Giovanni del Pian after Zanetti – 24 full page engraved plates – probably after Zanetti – showing works of Titian, Giorgione, Tintoretto and others – contemporary quarter calf – rebacked, the sides worn – large 4to. – no printer, 1760 (i.e. 1788).
(Christie's) $240 £120

ZANETTI, ANTONIO MARIA, The Elder & Younger
'Delle Antiche Statue Greche E Romane' – 2 vols. – fine engraved allegorical frontipiece by Sartori after Piazzetta in vol. I – portrait of Christian VI of Denmark by Marco Pitteri after Piazzetta and 100 plates by Faldoni et al. after two Zanetti – text printed on one side only – each page within engraved classical border – vignette illustrations – contemporary half calf – edges rubbed and corners scuffed – large folio – G. Albrizzi – 1740.
(Christie's) $800 £400

ZANETTI, ANTONIO MARIA, The Younger AND A. BONGIOVANNI
'Graeca (Latina et Italica) D. Marci Bibliotheca codicum manuscriptorum ... per titilos digesta' – 2 vols. – engraved frontispiece portrait in each vol. of Cardinal Bessarion within elaborate architectural border – by G. B. Moretti after G. Patrini – title vignettes – head and tailpieces – numerous text engravings after Greek manuscripts in vol. 1, – 3 plates after oriental miniatures in vol. II – contemporary speckled calf – gilt spines – folio – Simone Occhi, 1740-41.
(Christie's) $280 £140

ZANGWILL, ISRAEL
'Dreamers of the Ghetto' – orig. cloth – nice – 1898.
(J. Ash) $40 £18

ZANOTTI, GIAMPIETRO
'Le pitture di Pellegrino Tibaldi e di Niccolo Abbati esistenti nell'Instituto di Bologna' – title with device by Bartolomeo Crivellari after Antonio Maria Zanetti – frontispiece by Crivellari after Giovani Ba Battista Moretti – full page portrait of Benedict XIV by Joseph Wagner after Gaetano Gandolfi – 41 full page engraved plates by Giovanni Battista Brustolon and B. Crivellari after Angelo Carboni – 19 fine head and tailpieces and large engraved capitals – most showing views of Bologna – by Brustolon and Crivellari after Carboni and others – minor foxing to some fore-margins – modern buckram – large folio – Giambattista Pasquali, 1756.
(Christie's) $280 £140

ZANOTTI, G.
'Le Pitture di P. Tibaldi e di N. Abbati, esistenti nell' Instituto di Bologna' – plates, large folio, boards, vellum back – From the Signet Library – 1756.
(Bonham's) $495 £220

ZANZIBAR
Papers of Alexander Stuart Rogers, First Minister and Regent during minority of Sultan Sayyid Ali bin Hamid 1901-05 and other papers relating to Rogers' services in British East Africa.
(Phillips) $250 £120

ZAPPATA, GIAMBATTISTA
'Poesie' – portrait frontispiece – contemporary pink wrappers embossed in gilt with a floral design – a little worn – in buckram slipcase – sm. 8vo. – Coleti 1770; and 8 others.
(Christie's) $50 £25

ZARATE, A. DE
'Histoire de la de'Couverte et de la Conqueste du Perou' – 2nd Edn. – 2 vols. – 15 engraved plates – map – cloth backed boards – Amsterdam, 1717; and 3 others.
(Sotheby's) $120 £60

ZATTA, ANTONIO
'Atlante Novissimo' – 4 vols. – engraved titles by G. Zuliani after P. A. Novelli – including double page emblematic title to vol. 1 – 217 double page engraved maps – including 5 cosmographical charts – all maps and charts hand coloured in outline with wash borders and coloured vignettes – index in vol. 1 – mounted on guards throughout – contemporary half calf and marbled boards – spines gilt with morocco labels – contained in modern grey buckram boxes with morocco labels – folio 390 x 265mm – Antonio Zatta, 1779-84.
(Christie's) $7,600 £3,800

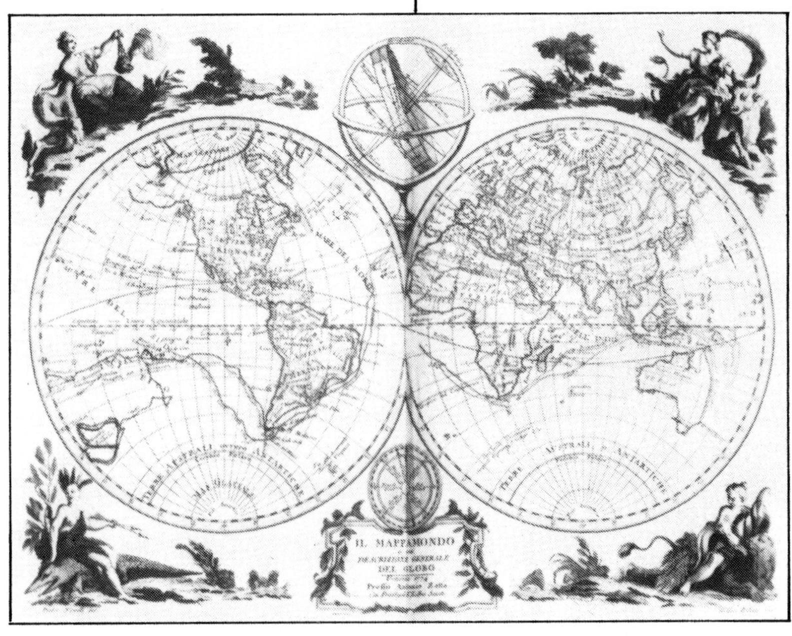

Antonio Zatta – 'Atlante Novissimo'. (Christie's)

'Atlante Novissimo' – vols. 1, 2 and 4 – engraved titles – 135 partly col. double page maps – cont. calf – gilt – folio – Venezia, 1775-85.
(Phillips) $5,460 £2,600

'La Norvegia' – engraved map – hand col. in outline – decorative title cartouche – fully col. – little discoloured – 406 x 313mm – Venice, 1781.
(Sotheby's) $40 £20

'Atlante Novissimo' – vol. 1 only of 4 – engraved title – double page frontis – 71 engraved plates – 66 maps – 5 planispheres and other plates – all maps hand col. in outline – browning – cont. half calf – spine gilt – wormed – folio – Venice, 1779.
(Sotheby's) $2,520 £1,200

'L'Augusta Ducale Basilica Dell'Evangelista San Marco' – engraved frontispiece – title – portrait within fine ornamental border – vignette view of St. Mark's printed in blue and initial in bistre – vignette headpieces and 11 tailpieces – and 8 full page plates, of which three are folding – contemporary half calf rubbed – atlas folio – Antonio Zatta, 1761.
(Christie's) $1,900 £950

ZEILLER, MARTIN
'Itinerarum Hispaniae Oder Raiss Beschreibung Durch . . . Hispanien und Portugal' – 1st Edn. – engraved title with medallion portrait, and view – stains – cont. vellum boards – small 8vo – Nuremberg, 1637.
(Sotheby's) $200 £90

ZEMENKOV, BORIS
'Ot Mamy na Oyat Minut' (From Mama for Five Minutes) – illus. – orig. wrappers – frayed – unopened – 8vo – Moscow, 1920.
(Sotheby's) $250 £120

ZENKEVICH, MIKH
'Pashnya Tankov' (Field of Tanks) – one of 200 copies – orig. wrappers by Zenkevich – 8vo – Moscow, 1921.
(Sotheby's) $65 £30

ZENO, APOSTOLO
'Sammlung' – 3 vol. – plates – orig. wrappers – 8vo – Vienna, 1955-57.
(Sotheby's) $85 £40

'Orazione in Morte di Apostolo Zeno, poeta e storico Cesareo' – printed on large and thick paper – contemporary calf – gilt borders and cornerpieces – g.e. – 8vo. – Simone Occhi, 1750; and 7 others.
(Christie's) $80 £35

ZENO, APOSTOLO, PIER CATERINA ZENO AND SCIPIONE MAFFEI
'Giornale de'Letterati d'Italia' – 38 vols. in 39 – lacking vols. 39-40 of the complete set, and the 3 supplementary vols. – 102 engraved plates of 103 – waterstaining – contemporary vellum boards – most labels lacking – 12mo. – Giovanni Gabriello Hertz, 1710-33.
(Christie's) $140 £70

ZESHIN AND OTHERS
A group of three small prints: A procession of men each wearing a flower-hat for a summer festival, by Zeshin – unsigned; Gesse, by Koson; and Bird on a branch by Gekko – the first in good state, others in indifferent condition.
(Sotheby's) $100 £50

ZHAKAROV-MENSKY, N. N.
'Chernaya Rosa' (Black Rose) – orig. wrappers by E. Buchinsky – 8vo – Moscow, 1917.
(Sotheby's) $210 £100

ZHANG ZHIWAN
'Old Temple in Autumn Mountains' – hanging scroll – ink on paper – signed Ziqing Zhang Zhiwan – with seals – 128 x 56.5cm.
(Sotheby's) $560 £280

ZHEN, WANG (Attributed to)
'Grapes' – hanging scroll – ink and colour on paper – 137 x 34cm. – inscribed and signed Bai long shan ren xie, with two seals, Yiting and Wang Zhen da li.
(Sotheby's) $700 £350

ZHU CHAN (Attributed to)
'Bamboos growing by rock' – hanging scroll – ink and slight colour on paper – signed Zhu Chan and dated Guang Xu period – late 19th century – 127.7 x 62.5cm.
(Sotheby's) $200 £100

ZHU, MENG
'Crane with Peach Flowers' – hanging scroll – ink and colour on paper – 121 x 33.5cm.; and 'A Pheasant with Wisterias' – ink and colour on paper – 121 x 33.5cm. – inscribed and signed Meng lu yi shi Zhu.
(Sotheby's) $300 £150

ZHUPEL
(Bugbear edited by Z. I. Grzhebin) – no. 1-3 – folio – 1905-06.
(Sotheby's) $400 £190

ZIEGLER, J.
'Quae intus continentur, Syria, Palestine, Arabia etc.' – 1st Edn. – 8 maps – title and 2 maps in facsimile – dampstained – later vellum – soiled – sm folio – Strassburg, P. Opilio, 1532.
(Sotheby's) $1,040 £520

ZIMMERMAN, JOHANN GEORG
'Solitude considered with respect to its dangerous influence upon the mind and heart selected and translated from the original German being a sequel to the former English translation' – orig. boards – uncut – new paper label – 8vo – C. Filly, 1798.
(Sotheby's) $80 £40

ZINANNI, G.
'Delle Uova E Dei Nidi Degli Uccelli' – 34 engraved plates – cont. vellum – bookplates of Luigi Pieri and R. W. Oates – 4to – Venice, 1737.
(Sotheby's) $500 £250

ZINN, JOHANN GOTTFRIED
'Dissertatio Inaguralis Medica Sistens Experimenta Quaedam circa Corpus Callosum, Cerebellum, Duram, Meningem, in vivis animalibus instituta' – 56 pp – folding plates – disbound – from the library of Carl Gustav Carus with booklabel – sm 4to – Gottingen, A. Vandenhoeck, 1749.
(Sotheby's) $120 £60

ZOLA, EMILE
Auto mss of a preface to 'Les Soirees Theatricales' – a volume published annually with articles on the theatre – 16 pages octavo auto revisions and corrections – stains – modern blue morocco – 4to.
(Sotheby's) $1,510 £720

Le public des premières

I

M. Arnold Mortier, qui réunit tous les douze mois en un volume les « Soirées théâtrales » si intéressantes et si spirituelles qu'il donne au Figaro, veut bien me demander quelques pages pour servir de préface au volume de cette année. Et j'avoue que je suis un peu embarrassé, car je

Emile Zola. (Sotheby's)

Baron B. F. A. De Zurlauben and J. B. De Laborde. (Christie's)

ZOOLOGICAL RECORD, THE
'Arachnida', a complete set of this section from 1864 to 1970, compiled by Ernest Browning from 1941 to 1969 – 1864-1953 bound in 6 vols. – cloth – rest in orig. wrappers, Zoo. Soc., 1865-1974 – and other parts of the same, includ. a set of the whole work 1952-67 – cloth – and a second set of 'Arachnida' – 1932-62 – one or two parts missing – 8vo and 4to.
(Sotheby's) $160 £80

ZOOLOGICAL SOCIETY
'Proceedings of the Committee of Science and Correspondence of the Zoological Society of London' – 13 vols. 1832-1910, together with 14 vols., original cloth, 8vo.
(Christie's St. James) $65 £30

ZORES, CH.-FERDINAND
Album – 16 col. plates – double page and mounted on guards – occasional slight spotting – orig. cloth – worn inner hinges – split – folio – Paris, 1863.
(Christie's S. Kensington) $60 £28

ZOUCH, T.
'Memoirs of Sir Philip Sidney' – portrait – calf – gilt spine – bit worn – York, 1808; and another.
(Sotheby's) $30 £15

ZURLAUBEN, B. F. A. BARON DE AND LABORDE, J. B. DE
'Tableaux Topographiques Pittoresques, Physiques, Historiques, Moraux, Politiques, Litteraires de la Suisse' – 2 vols. in 4 – engraved frontis – 328 engraved views on 220 plates – 8 engraved maps and plans – 11 plates of portraits – 8 of medals etc. – soiling and discolouration – half morocco, half calf and cont. russia – not uniform – all worn – folio – Clousier and Lamy, 1780-86.
(Christie's) $22,050 £10,500

ZUSTO, GIOVANNI
'Descrizione Istorica dell'Estrazione della Pubblica nave La Fenice Dal Canale Spignon in cui giacque cica tre anni totalmente sommersa' – large paper copy – engraved frontispiece and 7 double page folding plates on guards depicting the construction of the boat and rigging – by G. Daniotto after G. Cason – plates slightly waterstained – modern cloth – 8vo. – Figlioli Ant. Pinelli 1789.
(Christie's) $400 £200

ZWEIG, STEFAN
'Balzac' – translated by William and Dorothy Rose – illus. – very good in dust wrappers – 1947.
(J. Ash) $8 £4